The IDG Books Bible Advantage

The *Photoshop 3 for Windows 95 Bible* is part of the Bible series brought to you by IDG Books Worldwide. We designed Bibles to meet your growing need for quick access to the most complete and accurate computer information available.

Bibles work the way you do: They focus on accomplishing specific tasks — not learning random functions. These books are not long-winded manuals or dry reference tomes. In Bibles, expert authors tell you exactly what you can do with your software and how to do it. Easy to follow, step-by-step sections; comprehensive coverage; and convenient access in language and design — it's all here.

The authors of Bibles are uniquely qualified to give you expert advice as well as insightful tips and techniques not found anywhere else. Our authors maintain close contact with end users through feedback from articles, training sessions, e-mail exchanges, user group participation, and consulting work. Because our authors know the realities of daily computer use and are directly tied to the reader, our Bibles have a strategic advantage.

Bible authors have the experience to approach a topic in the most efficient manner, and we know that you, the reader, will benefit from a "one-on-one" relationship with the author. Our research shows that readers make computer book purchases because they want expert advice on a product. Readers want to benefit from the author's experience, so the author's voice is always present in a Bible series book.

In addition, the author is free to include or recommend useful software in a Bible. The software that accompanies a Bible is not intended to be casual filler but is linked to the content, theme, or procedures of the book. We know that you will benefit from the included software.

You will find what you need in this book whether you read it from cover to cover, section by section, or simply one topic at a time. As a computer user, you deserve a comprehensive resource of answers. We at IDG Books Worldwide are proud to deliver that resource with the *Photoshop 3 for Windows 95 Bible*.

Brenda McLaughlin
Senior Vice President and Group Publisher
Internet: YouTellUs@idgbooks.com

PHOTOSHOP™ 3
FOR WINDOWS® 95
Bible

PHOTOSHOP™ 3
FOR WINDOWS® 95
Bible

by Deke McClelland
& Robert Phillips

IDG Books Worldwide, Inc.
An International Data Group Company

Foster City, CA ◆ Chicago, IL ◆ Indianapolis, IN ◆ Braintree, MA ◆ Southlake, TX

Photoshop™ 3 for Windows® 95 Bible

Published by
IDG Books Worldwide, Inc.
An International Data Group Company
919 E. Hillsdale Blvd.
Suite 400
Foster City, CA 94404

Library of Congress Catalog Card No.: 96-75757

ISBN: 1-56884-882-X

Printed in the United States of America

10 9 8 7 6 5 4 3 2 1

1B/RZ/QU/ZW/IN

Distributed in the United States by IDG Books Worldwide, Inc.

Distributed by Macmillan Canada for Canada; by Computer and Technical Books for the Caribbean Basin; by Contemporanea de Ediciones for Venezuela; by Distribuidora Cuspide for Argentina; by CITEC for Brazil; by Ediciones ZETA S.C.R. Ltda. for Peru; by Editorial Limusa SA for Mexico; by Transworld Publishers Limited in the United Kingdom and Europe; by Al-Maiman Publishers & Distributors for Saudi Arabia; by Simron Pty. Ltd. for South Africa; by IDG Communications (HK) Ltd. for Hong Kong; by Toppan Company Ltd. for Japan; by Addison Wesley Publishing Company for Korea; by Longman Singapore Publishers Ltd. for Singapore, Malaysia, Thailand, and Indonesia; by Unalis Corporation for Taiwan; by WS Computer Publishing Company, Inc. for the Philippines; by WoodsLane Pty. Ltd. for Australia; by WoodsLane Enterprises Ltd. for New Zealand.

For general information on IDG Books Worldwide's books in the U.S., please call our Consumer Customer Service department at 800-762-2974. For reseller information, including discounts and premium sales, please call our Reseller Customer Service department at 800-434-3422.

For information on where to purchase IDG Books Worldwide's books outside the U.S., contact IDG Books Worldwide at 415-655-3021 or fax 415-655-3295.

For information on translations, contact Marc Jeffrey Mikulich, Director, Foreign & Subsidiary Rights, at IDG Books Worldwide, 415-655-3018 or fax 415-655-3295.

For sales inquiries and special prices for bulk quantities, write to the address above or call IDG Books Worldwide at 415-655-3200.

For information on using IDG Books Worldwide's books in the classroom, or ordering examination copies, contact the Education Office at 800-434-2086 or fax 817-251-8174.

For authorization to photocopy items for corporate, personal, or educational use, please contact Copyright Clearance Center, 222 Rosewood Drive, Danvers, MA 01923, or fax 508-750-4470.

 is a trademark under exclusive license to IDG Books Worldwide, Inc., from International Date Group, Inc.

About the Authors

Deke McClelland

A contributing editor to *Macworld,* Deke McClelland also writes for *PC World* and *Publish*. He has authored more than 30 books on desktop publishing and the Macintosh computer. He started his career as artistic director at the first service bureau in the U.S.

McClelland received the Ben Franklin Award for the Best Computer Book in 1989 and won the prestigious Computer Press Award in 1990 and again in 1992. He is the author of *Macworld Photoshop 3 Bible, CorelDRAW! 5 For Dummies, Macworld FreeHand 4 Bible,* and *Pagemaker 5 For Windows For Dummies.*

Robert Phillips

Robert Phillips is a sysop on the CompuServe ADOBEAPPS forum; he supports the Windows versions of Adobe Photoshop and Adobe Illustrator. He has beta tested the Windows version of most Adobe products, and a large number of other industry standards, including Windows 95. Phillips does freelance graphic design as principal of Classical Typography.

In his salaried life, Phillips is Professor of Classics & Ancient History at Lehigh University, Bethlehem, PA. He has published widely on Roman literature and Greco-Roman religion; he is currently finishing a book on Roman religion.

Welcome to the world of IDG Books Worldwide.

IDG Books Worldwide, Inc., is a subsidiary of International Data Group, the world's largest publisher of computer-related information and the leading global provider of information services on information technology. IDG was founded more than 25 years ago and now employs more than 7,700 people worldwide. IDG publishes more than 250 computer publications in 67 countries (see listing below). More than 70 million people read one or more IDG publications each month.

Launched in 1990, IDG Books Worldwide is today the #1 publisher of best-selling computer books in the United States. We are proud to have received 8 awards from the Computer Press Association in recognition of editorial excellence and three from Computer Currents' First Annual Readers' Choice Awards, and our best-selling ...*For Dummies*® series has more than 19 million copies in print with translations in 28 languages. IDG Books Worldwide, through a joint venture with IDG's Hi-Tech Beijing, became the first U.S. publisher to publish a computer book in the People's Republic of China. In record time, IDG Books Worldwide has become the first choice for millions of readers around the world who want to learn how to better manage their businesses.

Our mission is simple: Every one of our books is designed to bring extra value and skill-building instructions to the reader. Our books are written by experts who understand and care about our readers. The knowledge base of our editorial staff comes from years of experience in publishing, education, and journalism — experience which we use to produce books for the '90s. In short, we care about books, so we attract the best people. We devote special attention to details such as audience, interior design, use of icons, and illustrations. And because we use an efficient process of authoring, editing, and desktop publishing our books electronically, we can spend more time ensuring superior content and spend less time on the technicalities of making books.

You can count on our commitment to deliver high-quality books at competitive prices on topics you want to read about. At IDG Books Worldwide, we continue in the IDG tradition of delivering quality for more than 25 years. You'll find no better book on a subject than one from IDG Books Worldwide.

John J. Kilcullen

John Kilcullen
President and CEO
IDG Books Worldwide, Inc.

IDG Books Worldwide, Inc., is a subsidiary of International Data Group, the world's largest publisher of computer-related information and the leading global provider of information services on information technology. International Data Group publishes over 250 computer publications in 67 countries. Seventy million people read one or more International Data Group publications each month. International Data Group's publications include: **ARGENTINA:** Computerworld Argentina, GamePro, Infoworld, PC World Argentina; **AUSTRALIA:** Australian Macworld, Client/Server Journal, Computer Living, Computerworld, Digital News, Network World, PC World, Publishing Essentials, Reseller; **AUSTRIA:** Computerwelt, PC TEST; **BELARUS:** PC World Belarus; **BELGIUM:** Data News; **BRAZIL:** Annuário de Informática, Computerworld Brazil, Connections, Super Game Power, Macworld, PC World Brazil, Publish, SUPERGAME; **BULGARIA:** Computerworld Bulgaria, Networkworld/Bulgaria, PC & MacWorld Bulgaria; **CANADA:** CIO Canada, ComputerWorld Canada, InfoCanada, Network World Canada, Reseller World; **CHILE:** Computerworld Chile, GamePro, PC World Chile; **COLUMBIA:** Computerworld Colombia, GamePro, PC World Colombia; **COSTA RICA:** PC World Costa Rica/Nicaragua; **THE CZECH AND SLOVAK REPUBLICS:** Computerworld Czechoslovakia, Elektronika Czechoslovakia, PC World Czechoslovakia; **DENMARK:** Communications World, Computerworld Danmark, Macworld Danmark, PC World Danmark, PC World Danmark Supplements, TECH World; **DOMINICAN REPUBLIC:** PC World Republica Dominicana; **ECUADOR:** PC World Ecuador, GamePro; **EGYPT:** Computerworld Middle East, PC World Middle East; **EL SALVADOR:** PC World Centro America; **FINLAND:** MikroPC, Tietoverkko, Tietoviikko; **FRANCE:** Distributique, Golden, Info PC, Le Guide du Monde Informatique, Le Monde Informatique, Reseaux & Telecoms; **GERMANY:** Computer Business, Computerwoche, Computerwoche Extra, Computerwoche Focus, Electronic Entertainment, GamePro, I/M Information Management, Macwelt, PC Welt; **GREECE:** GamePro, Macworld & Publish; **GUATEMALA:** PC World Centro America; **HONDURAS:** PC World Centro America; **HONG KONG:** Computerworld Hong Kong, PCWorld Hong Kong, Publish in Asia; **HUNGARY:** ABCD CD-ROM, Computerworld Szamitastechnika, PC & Mac World Hungary, PC-X Magazine; **INDIA:** Computerworld India, PC World India, Publish in Asia; **INDONESIA:** InfoKomputer PC World, Komputek Computerworld, Publish in Asia; **IRELAND:** ComputerScope, PC Live!; **ISRAEL:** PC World 32 BIT, People & Computers; **ITALY:** Computerworld Italia, Computerworld Italia Special Editions, Lotus Italia, Macworld Italia, Networking Italia, PC Shopping, PC World Italia, PC World/Walt Disney; **JAPAN:** Macworld Japan, Nikkei Personal Computing, SunWorld Japan, Windows World Japan; **KENYA:** East African Computer News; **KOREA:** Hi-Tech Information/Computerworld, Macworld Korea, PC World Korea; **MACEDONIA:** PC World Macedonia; **MALAYSIA:** Computerworld Malaysia, PC World Malaysia, Publish in Asia; **MEXICO:** Computerworld Mexico, GamePro, Macworld, PC World Mexico; **MYANMAR:** PC World Myanmar; **NETHERLANDS:** Computable, Computer! Totaal, LAN Magazine, Macworld, Net Magazine; **NEW ZEALAND:** Computer Buyer, Computerworld New Zealand, MTB, Network World, PC World New Zealand; **NICARAGUA:** PC World Costa Rica/Nicaragua; **NIGERIA:** PC World Africa; **NORWAY:** Computerworld Norge, Computerworld Privat, CW Rapport Klient/Tjener, CW Rapport Nettverk & Telecom, CW Rapport Offentlig Sektor, IDG's KURSGUIDE, Macworld Norge, Multimedia World, PC World Ekspress, PC World Nettverk, PC World Norge, PC World's Produktguide, Windows Spesial; **PAKISTAN:** Computerworld Pakistan, PC World Pakistan; **PANAMA:** GamePro, PC World Panama; **PARAGUAY:** PC World Paraguay; **P. R. OF CHINA:** China Computerworld, China Infoworld, Computer & Communication, Electronic Product World, Electronics Today, Game Camp, PC World China, Popular Computer Week, Software World, Telecom Product World; **PERU:** Computerworld Peru, GamePro, PC World Profesional Peru, PC World Peru; **POLAND:** Computerworld Poland, Computerworld Special Report, Macworld, Networld, PC World Komputer; **PHILIPPINES:** Computerworld Philippines, PC Digest, Publish in Asia; **PORTUGAL:** Cerebro/PC World, Correio Informático/Computerworld, Mac•In/PC•In Portugal; **PUERTO RICO:** PC World Puerto Rico; **ROMANIA:** Computerworld Romania, PC World Romania, Telecom Romania; **RUSSIA:** Computerworld Rossiya, Network World Russia, PC World Russia; **SINGAPORE:** Computerworld Singapore, PC World Singapore, Publish in Asia; **SLOVENIA:** MONITOR; **SOUTH AFRICA:** Computing S.A., Network World S.A., Software World; **SPAIN:** Computerworld España, COMUNICACIONES WORLD, Dealer World, Macworld España, PC World España; **SWEDEN:** CAP&Design, Computer Sweden, Corporate Computing, MacWorld, Maxi Data, MikroDatorn, Nätverk & Kommunikation, PC/Aktiv, PC World, Windows World; **SWITZERLAND:** Computerworld Schweiz, Macworld Schweiz, PCtip; **TAIWAN:** Computerworld Taiwan, Macworld Taiwan, PC World Taiwan, Publish Taiwan, Windows World; **THAILAND:** Thai Computerworld, Publish in Asia; **TURKEY:** Computerworld Monitör, MACWORLD Turkiye, PC WORLD Turkiye; **UKRAINE:** Computerworld Kiev, Computers & Software Magazine, PC World Ukraine; **UNITED KINGDOM:** Acorn User, Amiga Action, Amiga Computing, Amiga, Appletalk, CD Powerplay, CD-ROM Now, Computing, Connexion, GamePro, Lotus Magazine, Macaction, Macworld, Open Computing, Parents and Computers, PC Home, PC Works, The WEB; **UNITED STATES:** Cable in the Classroom, CD Review, CIO Magazine, Computerworld, Computerworld Client/Server Journal, Digital Video Magazine, DOS World, Electronic, InfoWorld, I-Way, Macworld, Maximize, MULTIMEDIA WORLD, Network World, PC World, PUBLISH, SWATPro Magazine, Video Event, WebMaster; **URUGUAY:** PC World Uruguay; **VENEZUELA:** Computerworld Venezuela, GamePro, PC World Venezuela; and **VIETNAM:** PC World Vietnam.   10/17/95b

Dedication

To Elizabeth, the best companion on this and many other planets.

Acknowledgments

(The Publisher would like to give special thanks to Patrick J. McGovern, without whom this book would not have been possible.)

Credits

Senior Vice President and Group Publisher
Brenda McLaughlin

Acquisitions Manager
Gregory Croy

Acquisitions Editor
Ellen L. Camm

Brand Manager
Melisa M. Duffy

Managing Editor
Andy Cummings

Executive Assistant
Laura Moss

Editorial Assistant
Tim Borek

Production Director
Beth Jenkins

Production Assistant
Jacalyn L. Pennywell

Supervisor of Project Coordination
Cindy L. Phipps

Supervisor of Page Layout
Kathie S. Schnorr

Reprint/Blueline Coordination
Tony Augsburger
Patricia R. Reynolds
Todd Klemme
Theresa Sánchez-Baker

Media/Archive Coordination
Leslie Popplewell
Melissa Stauffer
Jason Marcuson

Development Editor
Pat O'Brien

Copy Editor
Felicity O'Meara

Technical Reviewer
Eric Thomas, Adobe Systems, Inc.

Associate Project Coordinator
Debbie Sharpe

Project Coordination Assistant
Regina Snyder

Graphics Coordination
Gina Scott
Angela F. Hunckler

Production Page Layout
Brett Black
Cameron Booker
Linda M. Boyer
Dominique DeFelice
Maridee V. Ennis
Drew R. Moore
Anna Rohrer
Kate Snell
Michael Sullivan

Proofreaders
Melissa Buddendeck
Joel Draper
Kathy McGuinnes
Christine Meloy Beck
Dwight Ramsey
Carl Saff
Robert Springer

Indexer
Sherry Massey

Book Design
Drew R. Moore

Cover Design
Three 8 Creative Group

Contents at a Glance

Table of Contents

Introduction

When Deke wrote the *Macworld Photoshop 2.5 Bible* more than a year ago, he was concerned that he had bitten off more than he could chew. So much had already been written about Photoshop that he honestly wondered if he could add anything to the subject. When he called vendors for support and told them the name of the book, they'd generally say something to the effect of, "You're trying to write a *Bible* on Photoshop?" Then, with muffled laughter and a bit too much sympathy, they'd add, "That's an awfully big topic." In other words, "Little man, you ain't got a chance."

But despite his anxieties, he dug in his heels and ingested and purged as much information as he could possibly locate. What Deke discovered, much to his amazement and undeniable pleasure, was that although coverage of Photoshop techniques abounded, in-depth analysis of the inner workings of the program were almost nonexistent. Furthermore, many of the techniques described elsewhere were inefficient, based on a limited understanding of Photoshop's higher functions. Deke was determined to fill in the holes and make *Photoshop Bible* the foremost tool for mastering this vast program.

Three is The Great Mystical Number, and this edition for Windows 95 is Number Three. A few things have changed. When Photoshop 2.5 and the *Macworld Photoshop 2.5 Bible* came out, Windows people had their first chance to get in on the Photoshop action (unless they had, gasp, previously "gotten a Mac"). It wasn't that hard to translate the Mac-speak into PC-lingo, so legions of new Photoshoppers on the Windows side got their start from a *Macworld Photoshop Bible*. It was the same with the *Macworld Photoshop 3 Bible,* although Deke added a Windows icon and tried to address at least a few specific Windows issues. Times change. In the years since Photoshop 2.5 appeared for Windows, Windows people have now invaded the hitherto enchanted forest of Mac digital imaging — more high-end graphics programs have appeared for Windows, and Windows 95 has made the PC into a truly viable platform for computer graphics. Some have regretted the appearance of those whom they consider poachers in this hitherto Mac-only woods and set themselves up as game wardens — Deke, he welcomes his new colleagues. The more Photoshoppers the better, especially because he gets to write more books!

To this end, Deke has brought Robert Phillips into the mix to contribute his perspective on Windows and Photoshop. Robert's a sysop for Photoshop on the ADOBESYS forum on CompuServe, and he's got the Windows deal down cold.

Before the authors brag some more about the book, there's always the chance that you're not even sure what Photoshop is, much less why you'd need a book on the subject. Just so that we're all clear, let's take a little peek behind Curtain Number One.

What is Photoshop?

Photoshop is software for Macintosh and Windows-based computers that enables you to edit photos and artwork scanned to disk and print out your results. Here's an example: Your job is to take a picture of a high-and-mighty CEO, give The Big One all the physical perfection of an Olympian god, and then publish the now-perfect smiling face on the cover of the annual report. No problem. Just shoot the photo, have it digitized to a Photo CD or some other high-tech gizmo, and open it inside Photoshop. Dab on the digital wrinkle cream for those crow's feet, fix her bad hair day or his toupee, and there you go. If you're feeling funky (Photoshop can do that to you), you can even have Aunt Hilda or Rambo (or both) looking on benevolently, for all the world as if they were in the original photo. Come to think of it, don't do that — you'd like the company to hire you again. In any event, the CEO now looks presentable no matter how badly the company is doing.

Photoshop, then, is about changing reality. And it goes beyond just reducing the distance between two Giza pyramids on the cover of *National Geographic* or plopping a leaning Tom Cruise, photographed in Hawaii, onto the supportive shoulder of Dustin Hoffman, photographed in New York, for a *Newsweek* spread (both duller-than-fiction applications of photo-editing software). Photoshop brings you full-tilt creativity. Picture a diver leaping from the summit of Mount Everest, or a bright violet zebra galloping toward a hazel-green sunset, or an architectural rendering with wallpaper that looks exactly like the surface of the moon. Photoshop lets you paint snapshots from your dreams. Or, as the phrase in the Adobe advertisements put it, *if you can dream it, you can do it.*

About This Book

If you're familiar with a *Macworld Photoshop Bible,* you'll find quite a few differences in this edition. The Macintosh editions have 18 chapters, 2 appendixes, and 3 introductory chapters on the CD-ROM. We've changed things here. The original 18 chapters are still here (in case you're doing a section-by-section comparison with the Mac edition — after all, Photoshop *is* cross-platform), all lovingly Windowized and commented upon by Robert Phillips (see his words on this elsewhere in this Introduction). He's written a new Chapter 19 for this Windows 95 edition. Finally, the appendixes have been rearranged. The introductory material is back, but in new clothing: Appendixes cover hardware, software, and installation considerations for Windows 95.

Speaking of color . . .

Compared to the first *Macworld Photoshop 2.5 Bible*, the color insert in this book has been bumped up from 16 pages to 32 pages. Each color plate is numbered according to the chapter that discusses the image; in this way, the color plates serve as a sort of visual index to topics covered in the book.

If you're wondering why the book isn't printed in full color throughout, the answer's simple: It just wouldn't be economically feasible. A full-color book of this size would cost nearly $150. With volume discounts, we could probably pull it off at something in the $85 to $90 range. But even so, that's a little steep for a book that's going to sit on your desk and get coffee stains and pen marks all over it, don't you think? We did, too, and so we opted to forgo full color throughout the book and concentrate on giving you what you really need: tons of useful information at an affordable price.

That silver Frisbee in the back of the book

In the back of this book, you'll find a CD-ROM containing hundreds of pieces of original artwork and stock photography, most in full color. The CD-ROM holds 560MB of data, including over 500MB of royalty-free images and bonus chapters on Windows 3.1 and Windows NT. Appendix E tells the whole story.

The Guts of the Book

Insofar as the actual pages in this massive tome are concerned, well, there are lots of them. But keep in mind that we don't cover every command or option available in Photoshop. That is the job of the Photoshop manual. Our job is to explain the features that really count and explore capabilities that you won't easily glean on your own. We also look at Photoshop's place in the larger electronic design scheme and examine how to best approach Photoshop in ways that will yield the most efficient and accurate results.

This is a big, fat book, so exercise caution. Those of you who like to read in-flight, remember to stow the book under the seat in front of you after you board the plane. It'll just go and damage lesser luggage if you try to stick it in the overhead compartment. If you plan on using the book for self-defense, be sure to spar with a partner armed with a volume of equal size. And please, take out the CD-ROM before using the book to prop up a youngster at the dinner table. That way, you can use the CD-ROM as a coaster in case of spills.

The images inside the book

Before proceeding so much as one step further, a moment to credit the folks who contributed the photos that appear throughout this book. For the most part, the artistic embellishments are Deke's own, but the original images derive from a variety of sources, including PhotoDisc, ColorBytes, Reuters, and the Bettmann Archive, as well as independents Russell McDougal, Mark Collen, and Denise McClelland. (In case you're wondering whether there's some kind of nepotism going on here, the answer is *Bingo*. Denise is Deke's sister.) Every one of these folks generously provided images. But rather than clutter every single figure with credits and copyright statements, this information appears in Appendix D.

How this book is organized

To enhance your enjoyment of Photoshop's mouth-watering capabilities, we've sliced the task into five tasty parts and then diced those parts into a total of 19 digestible chapters. *Bon appétit* and (this is Robert speaking) *de gustibus non disputandum!*

Part I Photoshop Fundamentals

Here's all the basic stuff you need to know about Photoshop. We explain the Photoshop interface, show how to edit colors, explain how channels work, and describe how to print full-color artwork. Whether you're new to Photoshop or an old hand, you'll find a lot you didn't know in these first six chapters.

Part II Retouching with a Purpose

Every month or so, some fraudulent photo sparks a new flame of public scorn and scrutiny. Now you can get in on the action. These chapters show you how to exchange fact with a modicum of fantasy.

Part III Special Effects

Making manual artistic enhancements is all very well and good, but it's easier to let your computer do the work. These chapters show ways to produce highly entertaining and effective results using fully automated operations.

Part IV Corrections and Composites

Here's where you learn what you can do with Photoshop's most powerful color correction commands, how to composite images using overlay modes and channel operations, and what role layers play in all this.

Part V Appendixes

Five appendixes follow Chapter 19. The first looks at some hardware-specific issues for Windows 95 and Photoshop, while the second does the same for software. Neither is intended to be a tutorial for getting up and running with Windows 95, but both address Windows 95 issues that affect your daily use of Photoshop. The third explains how to install Photoshop and looks at the differences between Versions 3/3.01, 3.04, and the currently shipping 3.05. The fourth provides complete information on the photographers, image collections, and news services that contributed images to this book. And the fifth contains details about the attached CD-ROM.

Last but not least is an astonishingly comprehensive index. It'll knock your socks off from the inside, should you happen to be wearing any.

Conventions

Every computer book seems to conform to a logic all its own, and this one's no exception. We hope our logic is justified and that a famous Vulcan Science Officer would approve. Still, there are a couple of conventions that you may not immediately recognize.

Vocabulary

Call it computerese, call it technobabble, call it the synthetic jargon of propeller heads, call it cyber-speak. A rose by any other name . . . the fact is, we can't explain Windows 95 or Photoshop in graphic and gruesome detail without sometimes reverting to the specialized language of the trade. Although we try to avoid gratuitous cyber-speak acronyms, there are times when we need them, if only to alert you to their use when you're communicating with other digital imagers. We've given both the acronym and its expansion the first time we use it. If you come across a strange word, look it up in the index to find the first reference to the word in the book.

Commands and options

To distinguish the literal names of commands, dialog boxes, buttons, and so on, we capitalize the first letter in each word (for example, *click on the Cancel button*). The only exceptions are option names, which can be six or seven words long and filled with prepositions such as *to* and *of*. Traditionally, prepositions and articles (*a, an, the*) don't appear in initial caps, and this book follows that time-honored rule, too.

When discussing menus and commands, we use an arrow symbol to indicate hierarchy. For example, *Choose File⇨Open* means to choose the Open command from the File menu. If you have to display a submenu to reach a command, we list the command used to display the submenu between the menu name and the final command. *Choose*

Image⇨Map⇨Invert means to choose the Map command from the Image menu and then choose the Invert command from the Map submenu. (If this doesn't quite make sense to you now, don't worry. Future chapters will make it abundantly clear.) For an introduction to Photoshop's tools, see "The Photoshop desktop" in Chapter 2.

Version numbers

A new piece of software comes out every 15 minutes. That's not a real statistic, mind you, but we bet it's close. As we write this, Photoshop has advanced to Version 3.05. But by the time you read this, the version number may be seven hundredths of a percentage point higher. So know that when we write *Photoshop 3,* or Photoshop, we mean 3.05 (information specific to the two earlier versions, still in wide circulation, is qualified as the need arises).

Similarly, when we write *Photoshop 2.5,* we mean both Version 2.5 and the more recent 2.5.1. Finally, there are occasional references to the Mac-only earlier versions of Photoshop: *Photoshop 2* means 2 and 2.01, and *Photoshop 1* means anything up to Version 1.0.7. *Illustrator 4/4.1* indicates the Windows editions 4–4.03 and 4.1 — the 4.1 version is the one you should be using with Windows 95 (chances are it's the only one you can run on Windows 95).

The term Windows 95 refers to the shipping version of August 24, 1995. There was a time when it was code named Chicago, in case any troglodytes are reading this. Further, everything about Windows 95 here is based on the shipping version. That's not a gratuitous statement. Microsoft utilized a *pay 30-something bucks, bang on a beta* late in the development cycle, and there may well be a number of those rattling around still, even though they are time-bombed. Obviously, if the Windows 95 material doesn't work for you and you're still using one of those betas, we can't be responsible.

Here's my first icon! Read about it soon. I want to be extra clear about the Windows 95 beta matters, because the 30-something bucks beta was something of an industry first. That beta was sometimes referred to as the Preview Program. It was not the same thing as the regular beta (which I got onto back when this here operating system was still code named Chicago); regular betazoids were in constant touch with Microsoft, saw many interim builds; if I say anything more I'll be violating my nondisclosure agreement and have to kill you. Point is, if you hear someone claiming Windows 95 smarts as a result of being on the beta, find out whether your guru-in-waiting paid Microsoft. That's not to say that there aren't very knowledgeable Windows 95 users whose first exposure to the operating system was the Preview Program, or even the shipping version. There are. But one of the less-savory sides of The Industry is self-promotional hype, and this may help you — obviously, the true measure of the Windows 95 Guru is Windows 95 Smarts, however they were acquired.

Icons

Like just about every computer book currently available on your greengrocer's shelves, this one includes alluring icons that focus your eyeballs smack dab on important information. The icons make it easy for folks who just like to skim books to figure out what the heck's going on. Icons serve as little insurance policies against the notoriously short attention spans of the literacy-challenged. On the whole, the icons are self-explanatory, but we'll explain them anyway.

Caution Caution icon warns you that a step you're about to take may produce disastrous results. Well, perhaps *disastrous* is an exaggeration. Inconvenient, then. Uncomfortable. Use caution — if you ignore our warning, we can't help you.

Note Note icon highlights some little tidbit of information we've decided to share with you that seemed at the time to be remotely related to the topic at hand. Then again, even if it's not remotely related, it's still good info.

Background Background icon is like the Note icon, except that it includes a modicum of history. We tell you how an option came into existence, why a feature is implemented the way it is, or how things used to be better back in the old days. It's a perfect opportunity either to explain or gripe.

Tip This book is bursting with tips and techniques. If we were to highlight every one of them, whole pages would be gray with light bulbs popping out all over the place. Tip icon calls attention to shortcuts that are specifically applicable to the Photoshop application. For the bigger, more useful power tips, we're afraid you'll have to actually read the text.

Robert The Robert icon is new for the Windows 95 edition. It's to make clear when he's speaking in places where it might not otherwise be clear. He doesn't use it all the time — sometimes a section or paragraph flags his none-too-subtle participation; also see his section later.

Cross Ref Cross-Reference icon tells you where to go for information related to the current topic.

On the CD-ROM If we're talking about something that is backed up by something on the CD-ROM, we'll let you know with this catchy little icon.

We thought of including more icons. One that alerted you to every new bit of Windows 95 information, another that specifically flagged Photoshop information for versions earlier than 3.04. But we decided against it, because there would have been so many icons as a result that this book would probably have to have been composed in Photoshop! Besides, that would have robbed you of the fun of discovery.

Words from The Windowizer . . .

Just what is Robert doing here, and what's he done? Although Deke has introduced me, I'm going to jump into the first person and tell you how I came to this project, what I've done, my possible bias, and make some special acknowledgements to the many good people who have, as Yogi Berra put it, *made this all necessary*.

Background

I will never forget that hot August day when I found *Macworld Photoshop 2.5 Bible*. Talk about manna from heaven! Stayed up until sunrise that night reading, too. Photoshop 2.5 for Windows had only recently shipped, and as a newly appointed sysop on CompuServe's Adobe forum I was fielding more questions on more things than I'd ever dreamed possible. Although I'd been on the program's beta test cycle, I felt like the little Dutch boy, even with the very generous help of Adobe's documentation and the many longtime users of the Mac versions of Photoshop. But Deke's magnum opus gave me, for the first time, a real in-depth grasp of Photoshop. Deke started turning up on the forum shortly thereafter, and the amount all of us learned continued to grow exponentially. It was the same when *Macworld Photoshop 3 Bible* shipped.

Thus I was thrilled that there was to be a Windows 95 version of this book, and that I was to be the Windowizer. *Moi?* The chance to go through the book in even more detail, and learn from Deke while doing it, was just irresistible. It also appealed to the evangelist in me — although I'm strongly cross-platform (see Chapter 1), I've often felt that for many reasons (principally inertia), Windows users of Photoshop didn't get the respect and attention they deserved. Here was a chance to do good and make good. And to learn some more.

And so it has been, although there were times when I felt this project was Deke's horrible revenge on me for doing a typo in a forum message that turned DEKE into EKE, to the considerable merriment of all concerned (except possibly Eke — whoops, Deke — himself). And although initially I would dread raising some idea with Deke and hearing him plaintively intone "don't do that," I came very rapidly to covet the extra bits of information he'd impart from his vast and growing accumulation of knowledge. Deke — I'm not acknowledging you down below because I'm acknowledging you here — with more than just gratitude.

What I've done

This is more than just a search-and-replace of Mac-speak commands — as I'd say in these parts, I could train the drunk on Fourth Street to do that. Of course I have done that searching and replacement. But I've scrutinized each and every line. Removed references to Mac-specific information (for example, the Apple Color Picker) and Mac-specific programs, in this latter case putting in PC equivalents. In Part I, this has meant a major reorganization and rewriting — for example, Deke had, understandably, relatively little to say about the BMP and GIF file formats — over here in PC land,

I've had a lot to say. Later on, in the less platform-specific areas, I've worked more in the background, but omnipresently.

You'll know in these ways where I've been at work. Anything that is Windows 95 and PC specific is me talking. Sometimes I've talked with Deke in print, or added a whole section. In these cases, the Robert icon makes it clear, except where I've added an entire section, where a textual allusion shows that it's me talking. Of course, Chapter 19 and Appendixes A, B, C are all my original writing. Finally, there are places where I've done a bit of editorial work — fixed a mixed metaphor, unsplit an infinitive, that sort of thing — that's background, all-in-a-day's-work doings, and I've not called attention to it.

What does this make me? As my editor, Pat O'Brien, so felicitously put it, *second among equals*. As I put it to Pat, *as if Deke had magically become a Windows 95 guru*. That is, I've strived to keep all of the original genius of Deke's work while making it totally usable for Windows 95 people and adding some of myself in the process. Because Deke and I agree on so many issues and even have the same prose style, it has become a marriage made in . . . Photoshop.

I also happen to share Deke's general philosophy. This book is about using Photoshop, and we both want to make you as savvy a user as possible. To this end, I've held nothing back (well, almost nothing — I refuse to tell you how to hack the Registry in Windows 95 — see Appendix B). I'm personally revolted at the all-too-common circumstance in computer publishing where an alleged guru teases you with some information but then requires you to purchase yet another publication by said guru to learn the full details. I can understand the money-making potential of tips and techniques, but it would be a poor guru who had a finite store of them. Put differently — Deke and I can afford to be totally generous. Because it will make you want to read further from us. And because we're constantly coming up with so many new tips and techniques that there's no danger of the well running dry. In short, we're generous because it's the right thing to do, and because we can afford to be generous.

About partiality and impartiality

No one is without bias — that's a given. But there is bias, and there is bias. I want to be straight with you on which is which.

Long before I became a sysop for Adobe on CompuServe, I had started using Adobe products. Was convinced of their value — and my developing relationship with Adobe didn't change that. So let me be clear. The folks in Mountain View (and Seattle) don't pay me one penny. I do what I do for Adobe because I think it matters, and because I like doing it. Adobe certainly does know how to show gratitude, but not in ways that would enable me to purchase an island in the Seychelles. Although Adobe has been very helpful to me in the course of writing this book (see the following), there has not been even a hint of editorial control. I calls 'em as I sees 'em — even if this has led me to question certain things (not many) about Photoshop.

Aaah, you say. *Must be great to do a book and get all those free goodies. Do you really like them that much?* This is precisely the question that dogs the computer press generally. I can't answer for other publications or other authors, but I can tell you this: Software vendors often show appreciation for the beta tester's work by way of special considerations, which may include a gratis copy of the shipping product. That's hardly pay, as any betazoid can tell you — besides, the family income of Henry and Phillips means Robert can, if the need arises, put his money where his mouth is. But because I've been a beta tester for virtually all the Adobe products I discuss here, it's reasonable to infer that I know Adobe has appreciated my work. Likewise if I mention I've beta tested for other vendors (such as Windows 95, Fractal Design Painter, and Kai's Power Tools). But if there's no such indication when I mention a program, I've paid for it myself. Same thing applies to hardware, although I've very seldom mentioned specific products.

I'm sorry to be so vague. But I am totally scrupulous about my NDAs (nondisclosure agreements).

And now the envelope . . .

The IDG Books Worldwide style is to have an acknowledgements section elsewhere, a short and terse production. I've bulldozed them into letting me have this section, for several reasons. I come from academia and academic publishing, where more-detailed acknowledgements are the norm. Again, so many people have helped me get to this stage that I want to give them special emphasis here. But I'm being judicious — I've heard my share of Lethean Oscar acceptance speeches.

The IDG Books crowd — Ellen Camm for getting me into this; Pat O'Brien, my ever-patient editor who eased my move from academic writing to Photoshop writing; and Felicity O'Meara for expert copyediting. On a related note, Matt Wagner, of Waterside Productions, for expert handling of the contractual side of all this.

Adobe Systems, Inc. — and not just for producing Photoshop. Eric Thomas and Web Pearce, of Quality Assurance, and Doug Lemaire, formerly of Adobe, have always stood ready to answer my most obscure queries. At a very busy time for him, Web generously answered several vital last-minute technical questions. Several generations of product managers and beta coordinators for giving me the chance to learn Photoshop as it was being coded.

Also to Adobe Systems under the aegis of its ADOBEAPPS forum on CompuServe. In particular, the two Wizard Sysops, John Cornicello and J.B. Whitwell. John, as Adobe Online Manager, has been my link to others in the Adobe zone and has unfailingly helped me out of more than one trouble spot — and given me some vital down-to-the-wire support. J.B. as volunteer WizOp for many kindnesses that directly affected production matters. Both John and J.B. for making the forum pleasant and happy place to be a sysop. And of course, my sysop colleagues, especially Mark Alger and

Jeff Karasik (Photoshop/PC) and Sherry London (Photoshop/Mac) — along with a very talented and able group of regulars. Bertel Schmitt, sysop for Premiere, generously helped me with points on the filmstrip (FLM) format for Chapter 3. I have learned, and continued to learn, much from all involved.

My e-mail friends have exceeded the call of friendship. Artist Michael Davis generously discussed problems of traditional media and more than once gave me cyber vitamin pills when my courage began to flag. Thomas Lindstrom shared his enthusiasm for Photoshop, Fractal Design Painter, and Kai's Power Tools — and taught me an enormous amount about using those programs together. Finally, John Dowdell (Macromedia tech support) generously discussed issues of cross-platform color palettes and Apple's QuickTime.

Other vendors deserve acknowledgment too. Microsoft and all associated with the regular beta of what started as Chicago and later became Windows 95. In my year-plus of banging on the beta of that operating system, I gained the knowledge and confidence to write about a program that depended on it. Michael Cinque and Kim Hinrichsen of Fractal Design for many chances to learn about Painter, and other Fractal Design programs, at the beta level. Kristin Keyes of MetaTools (formerly HSC Software) for heroic and successful efforts to keep my production coordinated with that of Kai's Power Tools 3.

My family, for all the obvious reasons. Vipsania, Octavia, Marcellus, and Fortunata — your feline antics around the computer and over the piles of CD-ROMs have helped keep me sane. Linda Henry, Esq. — you've been a loving and supportive Spousal Unit, and a skilled reader of my webs of words besides. Alert readers will find some photographic family references in some of the book's illustrations.

Finally, there are two people without whom I quite literally would *not* be writing this. Michael Shahamatdoust, formerly Adobe Online Manager. I will never forget later e-mail that began, "how would you like to be a sysop?" Michael — wherever you are — you got me into this, and I'll always be grateful. Rob Howard, superb illustrator and virtuoso Photoshopper. Although we're unfortunately no longer in contact, during the time we were in touch I learned more than words can say about art. Rob first conned me into learning about color theory and then bulldozed me into learning to draw. He removed multiple layers of concrete from my eyes. That I have attempted to do similarly for others here, especially in Chapter 19, is a direct result. If that chapter could have a dedication, it would surely go to Rob.

How to Bug Us

Even though, counting the versions for Photoshop 2.5, this book is in its fourth edition and has been scanned by thousands of readers' eyes and scanned about sixty times by the eyes of our editors, we'll bet that someone, somewhere, will still manage to locate errors and oversights. If you notice those kinds of things and you have a few spare moments, please let us know what you think. We always appreciate readers' comments. Because there are two of us (double trouble and all that), each with a slightly different online persona, we're each taking a paragraph.

Robert says this. By now you know my role in this book. I'm just as willing as Deke to receive your comments and queries. You'll probably do best not to hold Deke responsible for any platform-specific information here. You can e-mail me on CompuServe at 76711,1337 (or from the Internet at 76711.1337@compuserve.com). I would encourage you, though, to consider posting a message for me in section 12 of CompuServe's ADOBEAPPS forum. That's the Photoshop/PC section. Because I'm a sysop there, I'll obviously get your posting. And you'll have the benefit of feedback from my very able fellow sysops and a host of very able regulars as well. And they from you.

Deke says this. If you want to share your insights, comments, or corrections, please contact me on America Online at DekeMc. You can also reach me via CompuServe at 70640,670. And if you're on Internet, you know to add @aol.com for the first, @compuserve.com for the second (remembering to change the comma to a period in the numerical portion of the CompuServe address). Don't fret if you don't hear from me for a few days, or months, or ever. I read every letter and try to implement nearly every idea anyone bothers to send me.

And remember this. Time moves at an accelerated rate in the Computing Industry — someone once remarked that a week on the Internet is the equivalent of a month (or was it a year?) of traditional time. Or, as the ancient Greek philosopher Heraclitus put it, *you can't step twice in the same river.* That is, Deke and Robert are going to be around. But you never can tell what is going to shake out with online services, so IDG Books will forward all messages that you send to YouTellUs@IDGBooks.com.

Also, remember that you can always reach us by hard copy addressed to either of us c/o IDG Books at the address in the front of the book.

Now, without further ado, we urge you to turn the page and let us help you start getting the most out of Photoshop. If you've previously thought *it's a jungle out there,* we hope to show you it's more like an Enchanted Forest. Think of us not as game wardens trying to ward off poachers, but rather as your guides, determined to keep you out of morasses and away from clouds of Agent Orange. But don't try to traverse the whole forest at once — Robert's ancient Romans had a wonderful phrase: *festina lente* (make haste, slowly). We hope you'll be as happy in the Enchanted Forest as we have been.

Photoshop Fundamentals

Chapters 1 through 6 are among the most important chapters in this book for developing a thorough understanding of Photoshop and the image-editing environment. By the time you finish reading these six chapters, you'll be prepared not only to begin using Photoshop in earnest, but also to engage in witty repartee with friends, neighbors, and business associates who claim to know everything about the product.

In addition to exploring Photoshop itself, this part of the book examines the core image-editing process, taking you from composition and construction to color theory and output. You learn how to change the size and resolution of an image, how to define color and navigate among color channels, and how to print images. We also discuss more than 20 file formats that permit you to compress images on disk, trade images with other pieces of software, and export images for use on other computer platforms, such as Macintosh and high-end imaging systems.

Getting to Know Photoshop

What Is Photoshop?

Adobe Photoshop is the most popular image-editing application available for use on Macintosh and Windows-based computers. Despite hefty competition from programs such as the late, lamented PhotoStyler, Picture Publisher, and xRes, industry analysts report that Adobe sells upwards of four times as many copies of Photoshop as any competing image editor. Some estimates say that Photoshop sales exceed those of all its competitors combined. Software companies regularly announce *Photoshop killers* and reviewers regularly mutter *competes with Photoshop*. But when the virtual dust settles, while pretenders knock on the throne room door, the queen (or king) still reigns.

Note The term *application* — as in *image-editing application* — is just another word for *computer program*. Photoshop satisfies a specific purpose, so programmers abuse the language by calling it an application. We also use the word in the conventional sense throughout the book (for example, *Photoshop has many applications*). We hope you won't become hopelessly confused.

The result of Photoshop's amazingly lopsided sales advantage is that Adobe has the capital to reinvest in Photoshop and regularly enhance its capabilities. Meanwhile, other vendors spin their wheel or let their products die on the vine. Photoshop continues — any reports of its death are always greatly exaggerated — and remains the industry standard. That's an important consideration. You will simply find more of everything for it, whether service bureaus who understand it, online discussion groups, or books about it (including, obviously, this one). Therefore, the legacy of this program reads like a self-perpetuating fantasy. Photoshop hasn't always been the best image editor, but it's long been perceived as such. So now — thanks to substantial capital injections and highly creative programming on the part of Adobe's staff and Photoshop originators Thomas and John Knoll — it has evolved into the most popular program of its kind.

Background Image editing really began on the Mac in the late 1980s. The first image editor for the Mac was ImageStudio, a grayscale program from Fractal Design, creators of ColorStudio and Painter. The first Macintosh image editor to feature color was an Avalon Development Group entry called PhotoMac, which is now all but forgotten. But rumor had it that the *best* photo editor during this time was Lumena from Time Arts, a DOS-based program that ran on IBM PCs and compatibles. Meanwhile, Photoshop was a custom program used within the hallowed walls of George Lucas's Industrial Light and Magic that converted file formats and combined images from different sources. We were almost into a new decade before Adobe purchased the product and set it on its current path.

Note You may have noticed that Fractal Design Painter (now in Version 4) is absent from the list of Photoshop competition. Although some of its capabilities obviously overlap Photoshop's, Painter is a natural media program, enabling you to create digitally the effects of, say, acrylic or watercolor or pastel. And you don't even get your fingers smudged! Thus it doesn't really compete with Photoshop, but complements it. (Obviously, the Fractal Design people would say Photoshop complements Painter!) Certainly Adobe views it this way, the clearest proof of which is the company's recent investment in Fractal Design. If you're serious about doing art in Photoshop — and you should be — consider adding Painter to your software arsenal. It's an absolute must-have, the only software I would so characterize — apart from, obviously, Photoshop and Windows 95! For more on Painter, see the new-for-this-edition Chapter 19.

Image-Editing Theory

Having used mirrors, dry ice, and some rather titillating industry analysis to convince you of Photoshop's prowess, we now should answer that burning question: What the heck does Photoshop *do*?

Like any *image editor,* Photoshop enables you to alter photographs and other scanned artwork. You can retouch an image, apply special effects, swap details between photos, introduce text and logos, adjust color balance, and even add color to a grayscale scan. Photoshop also provides the tools you need to create images from scratch. These tools are fully compatible with pressure-sensitive tablets, so you can create naturalistic images that look for all the world like watercolors and oils.

Bitmaps versus objects

Image editors fall into the larger software category of *painting programs.* In a painting program, you draw a line, and the application converts it to tiny square dots called *pixels.* The painting itself is called a *bitmapped image,* but *bitmap* and *image* are equally acceptable terms. Every program we've discussed so far is a painting program.

Note Photoshop uses the term *bitmap* exclusively to mean a black-and-white image, the logic being that each pixel conforms to one *bit* of data, 0 or 1 (off or on). In order to avoid ad hoc syllabic mergers like *pix-map* — and because forcing a distinction between a painting with exactly 2 colors and one with anywhere from 4 to 16 million colors is entirely arbitrary — we use the term bitmap more broadly to mean any image composed of a fixed number of pixels, regardless of the number of colors involved.

What about other graphics applications, such as Adobe Illustrator, CorelDRAW, and Macromedia FreeHand? These fall into a different category of software called *drawing programs.* Drawings comprise *objects,* which are independent, mathematically defined lines and shapes. For this reason, drawing programs are sometimes said to be *object-oriented.* Some folks prefer the term *vector-based,* but we really hate that one because *vector* implies the physical components direction and magnitude, which generally are associated with straight lines. Besides, our preference suggests an air of romance, as in *Honey, I'm bound now for the Object Orient.*

Note Illustrator and FreeHand are sometimes called *illustration programs,* though this is more a marketing gimmick — you know, like Father's Day — than a legitimate software category. The idea is that Illustrator and FreeHand provide a unique variety of features unto themselves. In reality, their uniqueness extends little beyond more reliable printing capabilities and higher prices.

The ups and downs of painting

Painting programs and drawing programs each have their strengths and weaknesses. The strength of a painting program is that it offers an extremely straightforward approach to creating images. For example, although many of Photoshop's features are complex — *exceedingly* complex on occasion — its core painting tools are as easy to use as a pencil. You alternately draw and erase until you reach a desired effect, just as you've been doing since grade school. (Of course, for all we know, you've been using computers since grade school. If you're pushing 20, you probably managed to log in many happy hours on paint programs in your formative years. Then again, if you're under 20, you're still in your formative years. Shucks, we're *all* in our formative years. Wrinkles, expanding tummies, receding hairlines . . . if that's not a new form, we don't know what is.)

In addition to being simple to use, each of Photoshop's core painting tools is fully customizable. It's as if you have access to an infinite variety of crayons, colored pencils, pastels, airbrushes, watercolors, and so on, all of which are entirely erasable. Doodling on the phone book was never so much fun.

The downside of a painting program is that it limits your *resolution* options. Because bitmaps contain a fixed number of pixels, the resolution of an image — the number of pixels per inch — is dependent upon the size at which the image is printed, as demonstrated in Figure 1-1. Print the image small, and the pixels become tiny, which increases resolution; print the image large, and the pixels grow, which decreases resolution. An image that fills up a standard 14-inch screen (640 × 480 pixels) prints with smooth color transitions when reduced to, say, half the size of a postcard. But if you print that same image without reducing it, you may be able to distinguish individual pixels, which means that you can see jagged edges and blocky transitions. The only way to remedy this problem is to increase the number of pixels in the image, which dramatically increases the size of the file on disk.

 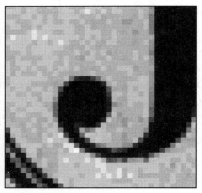

Figure 1-1: When printed small, a painting appears smooth (left). But when printed large, it appears jagged (right).

Cross Ref Bear in mind that this is a very simplified explanation of how images work. For a more complete description that includes techniques for maximizing image performance, refer to "How Images Work" in Chapter 3.

The downs and ups of drawing

Painting programs provide tools reminiscent of traditional art tools. A drawing program, on the other hand, features tools that have no real-world counterparts. The process of drawing might more aptly be termed *constructing,* because you actually build lines and shapes point by point and stack them on top of each other to create a finished image. Each object is independently editable — one of the few structural advantages of an object-oriented approach — but you're still faced with the task of building your artwork one chunk at a time.

Nevertheless, because a drawing program defines lines, shapes, and text as mathematical equations, these objects automatically conform to the full resolution of the *output device,* whether it's a laser printer, imagesetter, or film recorder. The drawing program sends the math to the printer and the printer *renders* the math to paper or film. In other words, the printer converts the drawing program's equations to printer pixels. Your printer offers far more pixels than your screen — a 300-dots-per-inch (dpi) laser printer, for example, offers 300 pixels per inch (dots equal pixels), whereas most screens offer 72 pixels per inch. So the printed drawing appears smooth and sharply focused regardless of the size at which you print it, as shown in Figure 1-2.

 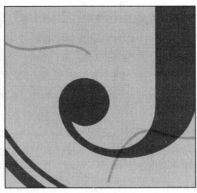

Figure 1-2: Small or large, a drawing prints smooth, but it's a pain to create. This one took more than an hour out of our day, and we didn't even bother with all the letters found in the version created in a painting program, shown in Figure 1-1.

Another advantage of drawings is that they take up relatively little room on disk. The file size of a drawing depends on the quantity and complexity of the objects the drawing contains. Thus, the file size has almost nothing to do with the size of the printed image, which is just the opposite of the way bitmapped images work. A thumbnail drawing of a garden that contains hundreds of leaves and petals consumes several times more disk space than a poster-sized drawing that contains three rectangles.

When to use Photoshop

Thanks to their specialized methods, painting programs and drawing programs fulfill distinct and divergent purposes. Photoshop and other painting programs are best suited to creating and editing the following kinds of artwork:

✦ Scanned photos, including photographic collages and embellishments that originate from scans

✦ Realistic artwork that relies on the play between naturalistic highlights, midranges, and shadows

✦ Impressionistic-type artwork and other images created for purely personal or aesthetic purposes

✦ Logos and other display type featuring soft edges, reflections, or tapering shadows

✦ Special effects that require the use of filters and color enhancements you simply can't achieve in a drawing program

When to use a drawing program

You're probably better off using Illustrator, CorelDRAW, FreeHand, or some other drawing program if you're interested in creating more stylized artwork, such as the following:

✦ Poster art and other high-contrast graphics that heighten the appearance of reality

✦ Architectural plans, product designs, or other precise line drawings

✦ Business graphics, such as charts and other *infographics* that reflect data or show how things work

✦ Traditional logos and text effects that require crisp, ultrasmooth edges. (Drawing programs are unique in that they enable you to edit character outlines to create custom letters and symbols.)

✦ Brochures, flyers, and other single-page documents that mingle artwork, logos, and standard-sized text (such as the text you're reading now)

If you're serious about computer graphics, you should own at least one painting program and one drawing program. If Deke and Robert had to rely exclusively on two graphics applications, they would probably choose Photoshop and Illustrator. Both are Adobe products, and the two function together almost without a hitch. Much to its credit, however, FreeHand also works remarkably well in combination with Photoshop.

The Computer Design Scheme

If your aspirations go beyond image editing into the larger world of computer-assisted design, you'll soon learn that Photoshop is just one cog in a mighty wheel of programs used to create artwork, printed documents, and presentations. Dedicated scanning software, such as Light Source's Ofoto, can match colors in a photograph to their closest on-screen equivalents and remove moiré patterns that occur when scanning published photos. Third-party color-correction software can exceed Photoshop and dramatically improve your ability to match colors between original and printed photographs without losing any image data. Such products go a long way toward turning Photoshop into a professional-quality image production studio.

The natural-media paint program Fractal Design Painter emulates real-world tools such as charcoal, chalk, felt-tip markers, calligraphic pen nibs, and camel's-hair brushes as deftly as a synthesizer mimics a thunderstorm. Three-dimensional drawing applications such as Caligari trueSpace and Ray Dream Designer enable you to create hyper-realistic objects with depth, lighting, shadows, surface textures, reflections, refractions — you name it.

Page-layout programs, such as Adobe PageMaker and QuarkXPress, let you integrate images into newsletters, reports, books (such as this one), and just about any other kind of document you can imagine. If you prefer to transfer your message to slides, you can use Adobe Persuasion or Microsoft PowerPoint to add impact to your images through the use of charts and diagrams. With Adobe Premiere, you can merge images with video sequences recorded in the QuickTime format. You even can edit individual frames in Premiere movies with Photoshop.

Photoshop Scenarios

All the programs just described run on the PC with Windows. Some already exist in Windows 95 versions, and others will shortly. But the number of programs you decide to purchase and how you use them is up to you. The following list outlines a few specific ways to use Photoshop alone and in tandem with other products:

✦ Scan a photograph into Ofoto or another scanning utility or directly into Photoshop. Retouch and adjust the image as desired and then print the final image as a black-and-white composite (like the images in this book) or as color separations using Photoshop or Cachet.

✦ After scanning and adjusting an image inside Photoshop, use a page-layout program (such as PageMaker or QuarkXPress) to place the image into your monthly newsletter and then print the document from the page-layout program.

✦ After putting the finishing touches on a lovely tropical vista inside Photoshop, import the image for use as an eye-catching background inside PowerPoint or Persuasion. Then save the document as a self-running screen presentation or print it to overhead transparencies or slides from the presentation program.

✦ Capture an on-screen image (Print Screen key or Alt-Print Screen for a client area). Then open the screen shot and edit it in Photoshop. Place the corrected image into Illustrator or FreeHand, annotate the screen shot using arrows and labels, and print it from the drawing program.

✦ Paint an original image inside Photoshop using a Wacom pressure-sensitive tablet. Use the image as artwork in a document created in a page-layout program or print it directly from Photoshop.

✦ Scan a surface texture such as wood or marble into Photoshop and edit it to create a fluid repeating pattern (as explained in Chapter 11). Import the image for use as a texture map in a three-dimensional drawing program. Render the 3-D graphic to an image file, open the image inside Photoshop, and retouch as needed.

✦ Create a repeating pattern, save as a .BMP format file, and use it as Windows wallpaper.

✦ Take a problematic Illustrator .EPS file that keeps generating errors when you try to print it, open it inside Photoshop, and render it as a high-resolution bitmap. Then place the image in a document created in a page-layout program or print it directly from Photoshop. Many top drawing programs, including FreeHand and CorelDRAW, support the Illustrator format.

✦ Start an illustration in a drawing program and save it as an Illustrator EPS file. Open the file in Photoshop and use the program's unique tools to add textures and tones that are difficult or impossible to create in a vector-based drawing program.

✦ Do a sketch in traditional media as preparation for a painting. Scan the sketch into Photoshop and test your color schemes without using rolls of canvas and gallons of paint. Or go one step further and do the entire work in Photoshop and Fractal Design Painter, output it to an Iris ink-jet printer, and frame your masterpiece. Or go still another step further and apply some traditional media touches in acrylic or gouache to the output.

Obviously, few folks have the money to buy all these products and even fewer have the energy or inclination to implement every one of these ideas. But quite honestly, these are just a handful of the projects we could list. There must be hundreds of uses for Photoshop that involve no outside applications whatsoever. In fact, so far as we've been able to figure, there's no end to the number of design jobs you can handle in whole or in part using Photoshop.

Simply put, Photoshop is a versatile and essential product for any designer or artist who currently uses or plans to purchase a Macintosh or Windows-based computer. Deke, for one, wouldn't remove Photoshop from his hard drive for a thousand bucks. (Of course, that's not to say he's not willing to consider higher offers. For $1,500 he'd gladly swap it to an optical disk.)

About Versions

Time speeds up in the computer world. You no sooner get one version of a program than news of the next version appears. Incremental upgrades keep appearing, and major ones after that. While the incrementals are often free, or nearly so, the major ones aren't. You may be feeling resentful as the edges of your Visa card start melting, and it is true that upgrades do represent a major source of revenue.

But, contrary to the Jesuits' position, you can serve God and Mammon at the same time. Particularly in the case of Photoshop. Each and every upgrade has good reason for existing — they're not just revenue-producers to keep John Warnock in tweeds. In addition, they have been priced very reasonably, or free. So here's a quick walk-through of the incremental number game.

✦ **3/3.01:** This was the major upgrade from 2.5/2.5.1. Why the two 3-numbers? Adobe keeps the Macintosh and PC versions in tandem, although Macintosh 3 shipped first in this case. In the lag time, some small issues appeared in the Macintosh version; they were fixed in the first PC version. So that's why, although the splash screen (or Help/About Photoshop) says 3.0, Photoshop 3 for Windows is technically 3.01 and is sometimes referred to as that. Be assured that Photoshop 3 equals 3.01 on the PC side.

✦ **3.04:** Initially, new challenges (*problems* is an ugly, pejorative word) appeared while running 3/3.01 on Windows 95. In some cases there were work-arounds; in others, such as using third-party filters, there weren't. 3.04 addressed both categories of issues and was Windows 95-aware. See Appendix C for details.

✦ **3.05:** The latest and greatest. Although 3.04 addressed Windows 95 issues, it did not have everything needed to earn the *Designed for Windows 95* logo from Microsoft. Photoshop 3.05 for Windows does. It also adds some nice extras, such as the ability to create interlaced GIF 89A files with transparent backgrounds — commonly wanted for publishing on the World Wide Web. Implementation of the TWAIN_32 *universal thunker* should clear up the remaining problems with using 16-bit scanner software in the 32-bit environment of Windows 95 and Photoshop. See Appendix C for details.

In this book, when we say *Photoshop* or *Photoshop 3*, what we mean is 3.05. When there is a crucial 3/3.01 or 3.04 issue, we shall identify it by its incremental version number.

But you may be new to Photoshop, or trying to decide whether to buy it. Here, at a glance, is a selection of what we think are its claims to fame:

✦ **Palettes:** Photoshop offers five floating palettes, many of which contain multiple panels. See Chapter 2 to find out how to move and remove panels.

✦ **Image annotation:** You can attach a caption, copyright statement, credits, keywords, categories, and a whole lot more textual information to a file.

✦ **Brush size cursor:** Photoshop shows the actual size of your cursor when you use a brush up to 300 pixels in diameter. Chapter 2.

✦ **Drag and drop:** Want to take a selection from Image A and put it in Image B? Without using the Clipboard or some arcane channel operation? No sweat. Just drag the selection from Image A and drop it into Image B, as explained in Chapter 8.

✦ **Layers:** The newest rage in image editing is layering. Photoshop 3 lets you assign images to separate layers, each of which you can edit independently. When you view a single layer by itself (via the Layers palette), a checkerboard pattern indicates areas that are transparent or translucent. Layers figure considerably into Chapters 8, 9, and 17. (Hey, it's a big topic.)

✦ **The move tool:** When you first see this tool (just below the lasso in the toolbox), you might wonder why Adobe devised it. After all, you can already move selections with the selection tools themselves. The move tool, however, lets you move selections by dragging outside them. You can also move entire layers. For complete information, read Chapter 8.

✦ **Tool modifiers:** You can access all modifiers inside the Brushes/Options palette. Among the snazziest options at your disposal are a shape-changing eraser (discussed in Chapter 11), the sponge tool (Chapter 7), and a combined rectangular and elliptical marquee tool (Chapter 8).

✦ **Toolbox shortcuts:** Access all tools and controls in the toolbox by pressing keys. For example, press M to select the marquee tool, press L to select the lasso. It's so convenient, you'll swear that you died and went to heaven. You can even get to the quick mask mode by pressing Q. Chapter 2 tells all.

✦ **Automated masking:** You can create a mask based on a sample color lifted with the eyedropper. The interface may be a little daunting at first, but with practice you'll find it much more useful than the magic wand (to which it bears a strong functional resemblance). For the big picture, see Chapter 9.

✦ **Out-of-gamut corrections:** You can identify regions of color in an RGB image that lack CMYK equivalents and will therefore print inaccurately. In the past, many users simply converted their work to CMYK and let Photoshop resolve the color conflicts. Chapter 16 shows you how.

✦ **Filter previews:** That's right, no guessing what the Unsharp Mask filter will do; you can preview the filter before you apply it. Photoshop 3 provides a small preview inside most dialog boxes. Lucky Chapter 13 tells it all.

✦ **The Filter Factory:** If you get a thrill out of designing your own effects using the Custom filter or displacement maps, you'll absolutely love Filter Factory, explained in the last portion of Chapter 15. Even if you can't stand math, you can try out some of the predefined filters on the CD included with this book. And keep an eye out for online offerings from fellow artists who manage to make the most out of this powerful new tool.

✦ **More convenient channel operations:** A series of commands, such as Duplicate, Apply Image, and Calculations, take much of the pain out of Channel Operations (CHOPS). For the comprehensive analysis, check out Chapter 17.

About Platforms

(Deke, gimme that keyboard. No, don't — it's a Mac keyboard, and I'm no user of ⌘ and *Option* keys)… Robert here. As the expert at using Photoshop in Windows, I'll finish this chapter by discussing the details of choosing and using Photoshop for Windows.

You may already have decided that Photoshop and Windows 95 are a marriage made in Mountain View and Redmond (heaven can wait!). You've made a great choice (says

Robert, modestly). But you may be trying to decide whether you want to invest in a PC or a Macintosh. You may even be leaning toward the latter, because there's a very good chance any digital artists you know are working on Macs. How to decide?

Effective digital manipulation and, indeed, desktop publishing (DTP) arose on the Macintosh platform through the combination of Apple, John Warnock's invention of Adobe Postscript, and Paul Brainerd's invention of PageMaker (originally an Aldus product). Photoshop arose in this Mac universe, and it was only with the release of Version 2.5 that PC people got in on the action. Digital manipulation virtually demands a GUI (Graphical User Interface) — it was hardwired into the Mac from the beginning, but only achieved viability for PCs with the release of Microsoft Windows 3/3.1 (yes, Verginius, there was a Windows 1.*x* and 2.*x*, but they're best forgotten) and reached near-fulfillment with Windows 95. It means PC people are still playing some catchup.

Not much catchup. You can work as effectively on the PC as the Macintosh. Each platform is different, and each has its advocates who snipe at the other. Nevertheless, there are some good reasons why you might favor a Macintosh:

✦ You've used one for years. Stay with it — you're comfortable there, and there's no point in learning a whole new platform.

✦ The only service bureaus in your area are Mac shops, or they greet you with crucifixes and garlic when you mention the PC. That's changing fast, and I'd suggest you find a new service bureau. Still, there may be some antediluvians around.

✦ There's some *way-cool-dude* filter or complementary program or hardware accelerator that only exists for Macs. This could be persuasive. Because digital manipulation grew up on the Mac side, there has been time for developers to produce more goodies for it. But even the most diehard Mac developers have heard the siren song of revenue from the PC side and have ported, or are planning to port, their applications. Reality check: They're not doing this because they now love PCs so much; rather, they love the possibility of your software dollars. No matter as to their reasons — they're doing it! As I write this, there are relatively few holdouts, and the list keeps shrinking. (This is for commercialware, of course. Shareware is a different matter, and a labor of love. Probably very few, if any, of the authors of Mac shareware plug-in filters for Photoshop will port their filters to the PC.)

✦ And here's the most important reason of all, and probably the only really good one — and it applies equally if you favor the PC. You like the feel of the platform. Why is this important? Because you're going to be spending many hours with your hunk of rust and sand. You'll develop a relationship with it. Its way-of-being will monumentally affect that relationship, how you feel about your work, and how productive you are. And like all relationships, this is a highly personal matter.

In short, if someone says "Get a Mac" to you, remove that person from your Rolodex. Real Photoshoppers don't do platform wars. Real Photoshoppers will respect you and your work, regardless of platform.

About Operating Systems

First, I must regretfully dismiss one excellent operating system: OS/2 (or WARP as it's known in its current incarnation). Photoshop 2.5 and 2.5.1 run beautifully on it — better, in my experience, than on Windows 3.1 or Windows for Workgroups. But, hey, this is a book about Photoshop 3! And the sad fact is that Photoshop 3 will not (absolutely, positively, 100 percent *not*) run on OS/2. The reason? For Windows 3.1 — the version of Windows that OS/2 supports — Photoshop requires the Win32s subsystem (a Microsoft device that allows full-blown 32-bit applications to run on 16-bit operating systems). WARP offers Win32s support, but for a much earlier version than Photoshop needs. Incidentally, don't read Microsoft conspiracy here — they've far bigger fish to fry. No one has succeeded in running Photoshop 3 on OS/2. No one can tell what the future holds — IBM is aware of the problem and allegedly has been working on a fix for the past year.

What about the other versions of Windows (such as 3.1 and NT)? First off, this is a Windows 95 book, and not just because IDG Books wants it that way. I'm genuinely convinced that you can work more effectively on Windows 95 than on any other operating system, and I became convinced while beta testing Windows 95 (then called *Chicago* — this was a long cybertime ago). Some have said it's *Windows 3.1 on steroids* — that may be true, and I like the steroids just fine. Some mutter that it's not a true 32-bit operating system. True enough — it has chunks of 16-bit code for backward compatibility so you can use all your pre-Windows 95 applications and hardware. That's not a bad tradeoff. Besides, if you're worried about 16-bit code versus 32-bit code, you're probably a programmer, Operating System Warrior, or both, and shouldn't be reading this book. Windows 95 is simply a more productive, and more fun, operating system to use. So there!

Note Nevertheless, I've not neglected the other versions of Windows. You'll find Windows 3.1-specific information scattered throughout, and on the included CD-ROM. Windows 3.1 did just fine for me. So I'm not blaming you or locking you out if you're slow to switch. I've not personally used NT, but have any number of friends who do and swear by it. It's relentlessly stable (although I always found even Windows 3.1 to be quite stable). It has built-in security (if that matters to you). It supports all manner of doodads, such as POSIX (an obscure form of Unix). But Windows NT makes wicked resource demands (although Microsoft is addressing this), it can't use your 16-bit drivers for existing hardware (unlike Windows 95), and its support for 16-bit Windows and DOS applications is less than stellar. And although Microsoft is bringing the Windows 95 shell/desktop to NT, certain other Windows 95 features, such as *Plug and Play*, won't be there for quite some time. Yup, you guessed it — the technically most advanced Microsoft operating system still looks like Windows 3.1 — Program Manager, File Manager, and like dat. Still, you may want NT's stability and its ability to utilize multiple CPUs.

Let's be specific now. Whenever I say Windows 3.1, I mean Windows 3.1 *and* Windows for Workgroups 3.11; Windows NT or NT means just one thing. I've tried to scatter some helpful information around, but remember that this is a Windows 95 book! And there are two files on the CD-ROM that address these platforms. 31TECH.TXT (by Mark Alger, a fellow sysop on CompuServe's ADOBEAPPS forum) addresses various Windows 3.1 issues. NTTECH.TXT is an introduction to NT for Photoshop users; it's written by a very knowledgeable NT user, Stefan Steib, a valued regular member of the ADOBEAPPS forum.

Choosing an operating system is very much like choosing a platform (above). It's a means to an end. Choose the one that's most comfortable. That way, you'll work your best. And *in your face* to anyone who argues with you (even to us!).

"We want information . . . "

No matter how skilled a computer user, or artist, or photographer you are, remember that no one is born knowing how to use Photoshop. You've got to learn, and keep learning, how to use it — no one, not even your expert authors, would claim total mastery of Photoshop. If anyone says they've mastered it, think *testosterone poisoning*.

But you need information to that end. And not just any information. Per the introductory quote from "The Prisoner" for this section, recall that the rulers of the village never said what kind of information they wanted. You've got to do better. Remember, too, that they wanted it *by hook or by crook*. So here is a hook and here is a crook!

About literacy

There's an acronym floating around. It seems to have originated with programmers, but support people picked up on it fast: *RTFM*. (It means, er, *Read The Fine Manual*.)

Many people, including some highly visible computer columnists, think there's something wrong with being literate. They'll brag that they don't read the documentation or the help file; they lamely justify it with *If a Windows application is properly designed, you shouldn't need documentation*. Baloney. That may be true for a simple application; for such a functional behemoth as Photoshop, it's just implausible.

Now it's true that not all documentation is as helpful as it could be; some is almost as illiterate as those who decry documentation. Still, even there you can learn something. And if it's well written, as Adobe's is, you can learn a lot. You can solve many problems just by reading, and this includes the README file on the install disks. And if you go online for support (see below), you'll get far better results if you've already done this minimal spadework.

There's another reason to read. No one set of documentation, or no one book (not even this one) can cover everything about such a complex program as Photoshop. There will inevitably be different takes, and different emphases. So *read, Read, READ!*

The most important section of the entire book

One word says it: *Online.*

The computing world constantly changes. Something in this book may become obsolete while you carry it home. Things are changing even faster now than ever before; Windows 95 shipped on August 24, 1995 — since then, there's been a flurry of updates, new hardware, and new drivers that shows no signs of abating. In many cases, rather than present information which would almost certainly be obsolete by the time you read it, I urge you to *check online* for the latest information.

As far as I'm concerned, there's just one place online to get the most and best information for Photoshop, Windows 95, and all of the related hardware and software matters. It's CompuServe (CIS). Obviously, it's not the only major online service; Adobe maintains sections on America Online and Microsoft Network. So do many other vendors. I don't push CIS just because I'm a sysop there for Adobe; on occasion, I also do those chores on the other two services. My recommendation is based on experience. The most Photoshop people hang out on CIS, and so do the most hardware and software vendors. News, patches, and new drivers all come to CIS first. This may change in the future; for the moment, that's the way it is. You should join the ADOBEAPPS forum on CompuServe and then religiously and relentlessly follow the messages in Photoshop Sections 10 (Techniques), 11 (Macintosh) and 12 (PC).

What about the Internet? There is a Photoshop discussion group on Usenet: `Comp.Graphics.Apps.Photoshop`. It's unmoderated. You don't have Adobe employees, let alone sysops, to speak with authority. It's the Information Superhighway, fer shure, but there's wheat and chaff. I can winnow it, but I find a high chaff percentage — why should you bother? It's also less civil — I've seen inexperienced people get flamed, badly flamed (and if they're women, flamed in crude sexist terms), for asking beginners' questions. You don't need that grief — too much pain, not enough gain. I think you're much better off with a system that has knowledgeable people operating under Adobe's aegis to provide you with accurate information (that is, more wheat and less chaff) — and who also ensure that everyone talks nice.

Occasionally, I find something worthwhile on the Internet; on recollection, it's hardly worth the surf. Here's how Jeff Karasik puts it (he's one of my sysop colleagues on the ADOBEAPPS Forum): "It's like you're at a party . . . and everyone is shouting at the top of their lungs . . . and you're not really having a very good time."

Inside Photoshop

CHAPTER 2

A First Look at Photoshop

Photoshop is like the proverbial iron hand in the soft velvet glove. Plenty comfy on the outside, and as hard as nails on the inside. You don't have to drink Liquid Wrench to get up and running with the program — most folks even have a certain amount of fun experimenting with its straightforward image-editing tools — but it takes lots of experience and careful examination to make the program do Two Thumbs Up.

This chapter deals with the soft velvet; future chapters look at the iron hand.

Why bother with the velvet? Certainly, if you're familiar with other Windows applications, you'll have little problem adapting your skills and knowledge to Photoshop. But a few items just a tad (or several tads) off the beaten path bear mentioning. If you're a new user, we recommend that you read this chapter from start to finish so that you don't inadvertently leave any part of the velvet without a good feel. Photoshop offers tons of fundamental capabilities; you don't want to end up discovering some of them a year from now and lamenting how much time they might have saved you. To this end, we've tried to cover the basic functions that you're most likely to miss or that will prove the most valuable.

If you're an experienced Photoshop pro, you should still be here. It's a big, powerful program, and there may well be some doodads that have escaped you. Of course, you should read this book in conjunction with the Photoshop documentation — see Chapter 1 for why.

As Deke's old pappy used to say, *A program that's worth learning is worth learning right.* Well, actually, Deke's pappy didn't say anything much like that (neither did Robert's, but that's a different story), but you get the drift. Read this chapter and you won't be sorry. Or words to that effect.

The Photoshop desktop

Shortly after you launch Photoshop, the Photoshop *splash screen* appears. Shown in Figure 2-1, the splash screen explains the launching process by telling you which plug-in modules are loading. Anytime while running Photoshop, you can reaccess the splash screen by choosing the Help⇨About Photoshop command from the menu bar. If you need help installing the program, read Appendix C, "How to Install Photoshop." We know no one, with the possible exception of the programmers, who cares about the splash screen. But here it is, in all its glory, in Figure 2-1. And therein lies a tale or two.

R
%%
Robert
The Mac version of Photoshop has several other doodads you can view off the main splash screen, although I hardly think this justifies *Get a Mac*. But splash screens, and their hidden features (usually called *Easter eggs*), arouse the ire of PC folks for some reason. Some complain that the programmers should be concentrating on bug-free code rather than writing such doodads. Others complain about how such features bloat the code. Unfounded complaints all! The amount of extra code required to implement those goodies is inconsequentially small, especially in a large program like Photoshop. It's a long-standing programming tradition to finish off one's work with an Easter egg. Programming demands such intense activity that the code pounders need some relaxation — surely you've heard about the water balloon fights in the halls of Microsoft. It takes a relaxed programmer to write good code, and you want your programmers relaxed.

R
%%
Robert
If you're still using the original release (3.0/3.01; see Chapter 1 for the story on this numbering oddity), there *is* something extra. On this, and only this version, you'll get a Tiger Mountain splash screen on April 1 of each year instead of the regular screen. This was by design, although the programmer who designed it is no longer with Adobe (coincidence? Only The Shadow knows, and he's not talking!). I tell you this for a very particular reason. The first April 1 after Photoshop came out, my section in the ADOBEAPPS forum on CompuServe was deluged with messages. Some users thought they had found a bug. Some thought they'd acquired a virus. The answer to both was: NOT. No bug or virus can do something like that. I don't blame the people for wondering, but I do blame those who have created the mass hysteria about bugs and viruses for setting the stage for such rampant paranoia. If you do have 3.0/3.01 and can't wait for April 1, just reset the date on your system clock — but please don't scream!

After you choose the About Photoshop command and wait a moment, the list of programmers and the copyright statement at the bottom of the splash screen begin to scroll. The final line of the scrolling message thanks *you*, of all people, for being *one of our favorite customers*. Just the thing for the megalomaniac who doesn't get out enough. (Hey, both Deke and Robert fell for it.)

Figure 2-1: The Photoshop 3.0 splash screen.

After the launch process is complete, the Photoshop desktop consumes the foreground. Figure 2-2 shows the Photoshop 3.0 desktop as it appears when an image is open and all palettes are visible.

Many of the elements that make up the Photoshop desktop are well known to folks familiar with the Windows environment. For example, the menu bar provides access to menus and commands, the title bar lets you move the window around, and the scroll bars let you view the hidden portions of the image inside the window. Other elements of the Photoshop desktop work as follows:

✦ **Image window:** You can open as many images in Photoshop as RAM and virtual memory allow. Each open image resides inside its own window. The lower left corner of the window features the preview box, which tells the size of the foreground image on disk.

✦ **Toolbox:** The toolbox offers 20 *tool icons*, each of which represents a selection, navigation, painting, or editing *tool*. To select a tool, click on its icon. Then use the tool by clicking or dragging with it inside the image window. The lower third of the toolbox features three sets of controls. The *color* controls let you change the colors you use; the *mask* controls let you enter and exit the quick mask mode; and the *image window controls* enable you to change the state of the foreground window on the desktop.

Toolbox   Menu bar   Title bar   Image window   Layers palette

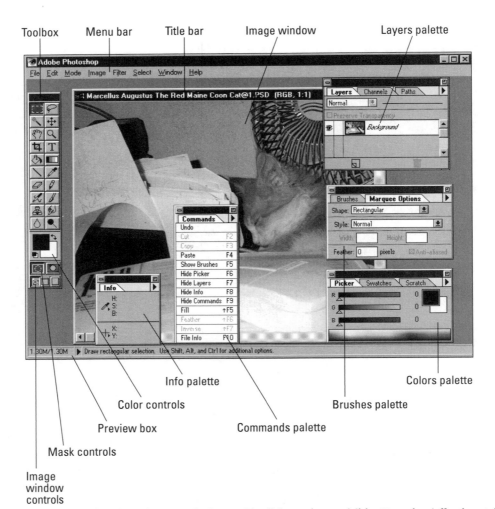

Info palette

Color controls   Brushes palette

Preview box   Commands palette

Mask controls

Colors palette

Image
window
controls

Figure 2-2: The Photoshop 3.0 desktop with all five palettes visible. Note the (affectionate) use of the Windows 95 long filename (LFN) capability.

✦ **Floating palettes:** Photoshop 3 offers five *floating palettes:* Layers, Brushes, Colors, Info, and Commands. The term *floating* refers to the fact that each palette is independent of the image window and of other palettes. Three palettes contain multiple *panels,* which offer related but independent options. For example, the Layers palette contains the Layers, Channels, and Paths panels. Later in this chapter, "The floating palettes" provides a brief explanation of each of these palettes.

Preview box

The preview box in the lower left corner of the image window was expanded in Version 3. It now contains two numbers divided by a slash. The first number is the size of the base image in memory. Photoshop calculates this value by multiplying the height and width of the image (both in pixels) by the *bit depth* of the image, expressed in bytes. A 24-bit RGB image takes up 3 bytes per pixel; an 8-bit grayscale image takes up 1 byte; a 1-bit black-and-white image consumes $1/8$ bit. So a 640 × 480-pixel RGB image takes up 640 × 480 × 3 = 921,600 bytes, which is exactly 900K. (There are 1,024 bytes in 1 kilobyte.)

The number after the slash takes into account any additional layers in your image. Photoshop measures only the visible portion of each layer, which can take up considerably less space than the base layer. If you transfer a 160 × 320-pixel selection of an RGB image to a new layer, for example, that layer consumes only 160 × 320 × 3 = 153,600 bytes = 150K, even when the base image is much larger. When the image contains one layer only, the numbers before and after the slash are the same.

Press and hold on the preview box to display a pop-up window that shows the placement of the image on the printed page. The preview even shows the approximate placement of crop marks, captions, and other elements requested in the Page Setup dialog box (File⇨Page Setup). Press Alt and mouse down on the preview box to view the size and resolution of the image.

The right-pointing arrowhead next to the preview box offers access to a pop-up menu that contains two options: Document Sizes and Scratch Sizes. The first of the two is selected by default and displays the image size values described a moment ago. When you select Scratch Sizes, however, Photoshop changes the values in the preview box to represent memory consumption and availability. The first value is the amount of room required to hold all open images in RAM. This value is generally equal to about $3\,1/2$ times the sum total of all images, including layers. However, the value constantly updates depending on the operations that you perform, growing as large as five times the image size when floating images and complex operations are involved.

The second value indicates the amount of RAM space available to images after the Photoshop application is loaded. This value does not change unless you change the amount of memory Photoshop can gobble up (File Preferences⇨Memory). When the value before the slash in the preview box is larger than the value after the slash, Photoshop has to turn to the scratch disk to do some of its work. This *virtual memory* makes the program run more slowly because it has to do reads and writes from and to your hard drive — this is always far slower than doing the same thing in RAM. To speed things up, close any images you aren't using until the first value is smaller than the second value.

The Getting Started brochure that comes with the documentation has a number of suggestions for improving performance here. You should regularly run ScanDisk (if you're in the pre-Windows 95 world, Chkdsk) to search for, and remove, stray bits and pieces in your scratch disk partition. You should search for .TMP files, especially after Photoshop has crashed. Even when it hasn't crashed you should still search for them. Under normal circumstances Photoshop should clean up after itself; if you're finding .TMP files and haven't been crashing, your system needs some tweaking.

You can also improve efficiency by increasing the amount of free space available for the scratch disk. You can't restrict Photoshop — set its scratch disk to a partition, and it will gobble up what it finds. Note that this has to be free contiguous space — when you've got a lot of fragmentation, Photoshop will only *see* the largest free contiguous block for its scratch disk. Hence the value of dedicating one entire partition to the scratch disk and religiously checking it. When you've got to have the scatch disk in a partition where there are other files, regularly defragment and optimize/pack the free space. What you want is drive space at least five times the size of the image you plan to work on. This is an ideal — you can work with it being only three times the size, or even less.

Photoshop defaults to your startup partition (typically C:) for its scratch disk. We urge you to change it ASAP. Windows 95 uses that partition for its own virtual memory management. We can't prove you will have problems if you let Photoshop in there too, but we sleep much better with Photoshop doing its scratching elsewhere. (Robert sleeps much better with his Maine Coon cats scratching elsewhere, too.)

Note that the various Distort filters perform their operations entirely in physical memory. The scratch disk may hold terabytes, but it won't do you any good. One workaround is performing those filter operations a channel at a time. If you're running under Windows 3.1 or Windows for Workgroups, 16MB is the largest block of memory that can be allocated — this is a limitation of the Win32s subsystem and hence a Microsoft issue. There is no such limitation under Windows 95 or Windows NT.

A final piece of information, *Efficiency,* appears as well. It tells — what the word implies.

R **%%** **Robert** You may wish to set your scratch disk to removable media such as a Bernoulli or Syquest drive. I don't really recommend this, since those drives are substantially slower than your hard drive, meaning that scratch disk operations will inevitably be substantially slower. Still, enough people have asked so it's worth telling you how. In your PHOTOSO30.INI file, add a line that reads `AllowRemovableScratch=1` (the default is 0 for off). When this switch is enabled, removable drives (including floppy drives) will now appear as possible scratch disk choices. Obviously, this may cause problems for Photoshop if media is removed at startup.

Background You may well be wondering why Photoshop uses a scratch disk and doesn't, like other Windows applications, use the main Windows virtual memory scheme. Here's why. Photoshop originated on the Macintosh, with its very slow virtual memory scheme. So built into the program from the start was a private, improved virtual memory scheme (the scratch disk). It would have meant an enormous code overhaul to change this for its move to the Windows environment. Further, having a private scratch disk even under Windows allows Photoshop to operate faster because it doesn't have to share with anybody else. Consider the memorable *Top Gun* expression: *I feel the need for speed.*

R **%%** **Robert** Nevertheless, Photoshop is aware of the Windows virtual memory scheme. Under earlier versions, you had to have a Permanent Swapfile equal to the amount of physical RAM on your system or Photoshop wouldn't open. This changed with 3.04. When the available physical RAM plus the Swapfile equals 21MB or greater, the program will open without complaint. The reason? It was obviously bizarre (to say the least) for a machine with 64MB of RAM to have to have 64MB of swapfile on the hard drive. But the physical RAM isn't quite what you think it is. On, say, a 16MB machine, Photoshop will report about 8MB of RAM available. The reason is that after loading, the program reserves a certain amount of RAM for various other processes. This algorithm is hardwired, and you cannot change it. So, to continue the 16MB example, if you have Windows 3.1/Windows for Workgroups and set the Permanent Swapfile to 13MB, you won't have a memory warning message. In Windows 95 you probably won't have to do this, if you accepted the default (Control Panel⇨System⇨Performance⇨ Virtual Memory) to let Windows 95 manage your virtual memory. If you're running pre-Windows 95 and find that Windows complains when you try to set your Permanent Swapfile to a larger size, ignore that complaint. It's an acknowledged bug. You can set it to the larger size — just look in SYSTEM.INI afterwards, and you'll see that Windows has accepted your setting.

Tools

The following paragraphs explain how to use each tool inside the image window — see Figure 2-3. For example, when an item says *drag,* you click on the tool's icon to select the tool and then drag within the image window, not on the tool icon itself. Keep in mind that these are merely the briefest of all possible introductions to Photoshop's tools. Future chapters reveal the details — in particular, see Chapter 7 for toggles to certain editing tools: Blur toggles to Sharpen, Dodge toggles to Burn and Sponge.

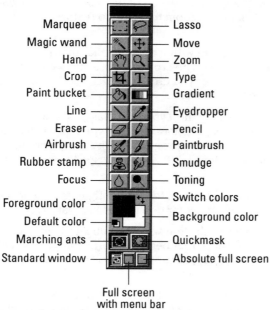

Figure 2-3: The Photoshop 3 toolbox.

Rectangular marquee: Drag with this tool to enclose a portion of the image in a rectangular *marquee,* which is a pattern of moving dash marks indicating the boundary of a selection. The dash marks are sometimes fondly called marching ants (hoorah, hoorah).

Elliptical marquee: Alt-click on the marquee tool to change from the rectangular marquee to the elliptical marquee. Then drag with the elliptical marquee tool to enclose a portion of the window in an oval marquee.

Lasso: Drag with the lasso tool to select a free-form portion of the image.

Magic wand: Click with this tool to select a contiguous area of similarly colored pixels. To select discontiguous areas, click in one area and then Shift-click in another.

Move: Drag with this new tool to move the selected area of the image, whether you're dragging inside the selection or not. When no portion of the image is selected, dragging with the move tool moves the entire layer.

Hand: Drag an image with the hand tool to scroll the window so that you can see a different portion of the image. The hand tool differs from the move tool in that it doesn't actually move pixels or in any way alter the image, it simply shifts the on-screen view to another part of the image. Double-click on the hand tool icon to magnify or reduce the image so that it fits on-screen in its entirety (as when you first open the image).

Zoom: Click with the zoom tool to magnify the image so that you can see individual pixels more clearly. Alt-click to step back from the image and take in a broader view. Drag to enclose the specific portion of the image that you want to magnify. And finally, double-click on the zoom tool icon to restore the image to 100 percent view size.

Crop: Drag with the crop tool to enclose within a rectangular marquee the portion of the image you want to retain. The crop marquee offers corner handles so that you can resize the marquee after you create it. Click inside the marquee to crop away the portions of the image that lie outside it.

Type: Click with the type tool to display the Type Tool dialog box, where you can enter and format text. Note that you cannot use the type tool to edit existing text as you can in page-layout and drawing programs. (Like any other image, bitmapped type is just a bunch of colored dots. If you misspell a word, you must erase it and try again.)

Paint bucket: Click with the paint bucket tool to fill a contiguous area of similarly colored pixels with the foreground color or a predefined pattern.

Gradient: Drag with this tool to fill a selection with a gradual transition of colors (called a gradient or gradation or ramp) that begins with the foreground color and ends with the background color. A gradation can also fade from the foreground color to transparent.

Line: Drag with the line tool to create a straight line. Click on the Start or End option in the Line Tool Options panel of the Brushes palette to add arrowheads.

Eyedropper: Click with the eyedropper tool on a color in the image window to make that color the foreground color. Alt-click on a color in the image to make that color the background color.

Eraser: Drag with the eraser tool to paint in the background color — in effect, erasing portions of the image. Alt-drag to access the *magic eraser,* which changes portions of the image back to the way they appeared when last saved. Photoshop 3 offers four kinds of erasers, which paint like the paintbrush, airbrush, pencil, and old eraser (now called the *block eraser*), respectively. You can cycle through these erasers by Alt-clicking on the eraser tool icon in the toolbox.

Pencil: Drag with the pencil tool to paint hard-edge lines.

Airbrush: Drag with the airbrush tool to paint feathered lines that blend into the image — ideal for creating shadows and highlights.

Paintbrush: Drag with the paintbrush tool to paint soft lines that are not as hard-edged as those created with the pencil, but not as soft as those created with the airbrush.

Rubber stamp: Alt-click with this tool on an element of your image and then drag to create a clone of that element in another portion of the image. Then drag to clone that area to another portion of the image. This method enables you to hide defects in one portion of an image by duplicating another portion. You also can use the rubber stamp tool to paint with a pattern or to change portions of an image to the way they looked when last saved (as with the magic eraser) or when last shot using Edit⇨Take Snapshot.

Smudge: Drag with this tool to smear colors inside the image.

Blur: Drag with the blur tool to decrease the contrast between neighboring pixels, which blurs the focus of the image.

Sharpen: Alt-click on the blur tool icon in the toolbox to access the sharpen tool. Then drag to increase the contrast between pixels, which sharpens the focus.

Dodge: Drag with the dodge tool to lighten pixels in the image.

Burn: Alt-click on the dodge tool icon in the toolbox to access the burn tool, which darkens pixels.

Sponge: Alt-click on the dodge tool icon again to get the new sponge tool. Drag with this tool to decrease the amount of saturation in an image, which eventually removes the color from the image and leaves only grayscale values. You can also increase saturation by changing the setting in the Toning Tool Options palette.

If you used Photoshop 2.5, you should know something else about tools in Version 3: You no longer adjust the performance via a specialized dialog box. You'll now find these same options (and a few more) in the Options panel of the Brushes palette. (To display this panel, choose Window⇨Palettes⇨Show Options and then select the desired tool. Or just double-click on the tool icon like you used to do in the old days.) Only the move tool and type tool lack palette options.

Cursors

Photoshop 3 uses more than 50 cursors. Most cursors correspond to the tool you're using, but a few have nothing to do with the tool. Nonetheless, all cursors have unique meanings.

You may think that learning the meaning of each and every one of these cursors is a big waste of time, and certainly my descriptions don't qualify as a literary treat. But as with the rest of the information in this chapter, taking the time to become familiar with the various cursors leads to a greater understanding of the program. At least, that's the idea. Tell you what: Read the following descriptions if you want to; skip them if you don't. You won't find a better deal than that.

- **Arrow:** The left-pointing arrow appears anytime the cursor is outside of the image window. You can select a tool, set palette options, or choose a command when this cursor is visible.

- **Marquee:** The cross appears when the rectangular or elliptical marquee tool is selected and the cursor is outside of a selected area. You can access the marquee cursor inside a selected area if you press Shift or Control. (Shift adds to the selection; Control subtracts.)

- **Lasso:** The lasso cursor works the same way as the marquee cursor, except that it indicates that the lasso tool is selected.

- **Wand:** Again, this cursor works the same as the lasso and marquee cursors, but it appears when you select the magic wand tool.

- **Right arrow:** The right-pointing arrow appears when the cursor is inside a selected area and the rectangular marquee, elliptical marquee, lasso, magic wand, or type tool is selected. Drag the selected area to move it; Alt-drag to clone it.

- **Move:** The omnidirection move icon appears any time the new move tool is selected. Drag to move a selection. When nothing is selected, drag to move the entire image or layer.

- **Gavel:** After you select an area and rotate it, stretch it, or apply some other transformation, you can accept the effect by clicking inside the selection with the gavel cursor. Until you click inside the selection, Photoshop remains in transformation mode, thus allowing you to test out multiple rotation angles, stretching percentages, and so on, without diminishing the integrity of the selected image.

- **Cancel:** You can click outside a selection during a rotation or a stretch to cancel the transformation and return the selection to its original size and orientation. The cancel cursor warns you that if you click now, you lose your changes.

- **Crop:** This cursor appears when the crop tool is selected and remains on-screen until you marquee the portion of the image that you want to retain.

✂ **Scissors:** Click with the scissors cursor inside the crop marquee to cut away the portions of the image that lie outside the marquee. (When you move outside the marquee, the cancel cursor appears.)

T **Type:** The common I-beam cursor indicates that the type tool is selected and ready to use. Click with this cursor to display the Type Tool dialog box. Remember, you can't use the type tool to edit text. After you've hit OK, the text isn't text any more, but pixels on the screen.

✎ **Pen:** This cursor appears when the pen tool is selected from the Paths panel in the Layers palette, enabling you to add points to the path at hand.

✎₊ **Insert point:** When a small plus sign accompanies the pen cursor, you can insert points into the current path.

✎₋ **Remove point:** When this cursor is active, you can delete points from a path. A new segment joins the remaining points to prevent the path from breaking.

✎ₒ **Close path:** When you position your cursor over the first point in an open path — that is, a path that has a break in it — this symbol appears. Click with the cursor to close the path.

⌐ **Convert point:** Use this cursor to convert a corner to an arc or an arc to a corner. Just click on a point to change it to a corner; drag from a point to change it to an arc.

⌐ **Edit path:** Press the Control key when using the path tool to access the edit path cursor, which lets you move a point or adjust a control handle.

▶ **Drag path:** When you're dragging a point, control handle, or whole path, this cursor replaces the edit path cursor.

▶ **Clone path:** This cursor appears when you Control-Alt-drag on a point or whole path. This technique enables you to make a duplicate of the path and store it separately or with the original path.

✋ **Hand:** The hand cursor appears when you select the hand tool or when you press the spacebar with some other tool selected.

🔍 **Zoom in:** This cursor appears when you select the zoom tool or press Ctrl-spacebar when some other tool is selected. Click or drag to magnify the image on-screen.

🔍 **Zoom out:** The zoom out cursor appears when you press Alt with the zoom tool selected or press Alt-spacebar with some other tool selected. Click to reduce your view of the image.

🔍 **Zoom limit:** This cursor appears when you're at the end of your zoom rope. You can't zoom in beyond 1,600 percent or out beyond 6 percent ($^1/_{16}$).

🖌 **Paint bucket:** This cursor appears when the paint bucket tool is selected.

✛ **Line/gradient:** This cursor appears when you select either the line or gradient tool. Drag with the cursor to determine the angle and length of a prospective straight line or gradient fill.

Eyedropper: This cursor appears when you select the eyedropper tool or when you press Alt while using the type tool, paint bucket tool, gradient tool, or any painting tool other than the eraser. Click to lift a color from the image window.

Crosshair pickup: When the eyedropper cursor gets in the way, preventing you from seeing what you're doing, press the Caps Lock key to display a crosshair cursor, which zeroes in on an exact pixel. This specific crosshair appears when you use the eyedropper tool or press the Alt key with the rubber stamp tool while Caps Lock is down.

Eraser: This cursor appears when you select the eraser tool and the old-style Block option is selected in the Eraser Options panel.

Magic eraser: The magic eraser cursor appears when you press the Alt key while using the eraser tool set to the Block mode. You then drag to change portions of the image back to the way they looked when last saved to disk.

Soft eraser: When you select some option other than Block — such as Paint-brush, Airbrush, or Pencil — in the Eraser Options panel, this cursor appears.

Soft magic eraser: When you Alt-drag with the soft eraser cursor, Photoshop displays this cursor to show you that any dragging will change the image back to the way it looked when last saved.

Pencil: This cursor appears when you select the pencil tool.

Crosshair: You see this cursor when you press the Caps Lock key while using any painting or editing tool. It's a particular blessing while using the rubber stamp, smudge, and other editing tools that can sometimes prevent you from seeing what you're doing.

Brush size: This cursor varies in size to show you the exact diameter of the brush that you're using when dragging with the soft eraser, pencil, airbrush, or paintbrush. You can request this special cursor by choosing File⇨Prefer-ences⇨General and selecting the Brush Size radio button.

Airbrush: You see this cursor by default when you paint with the airbrush.

Paintbrush: When you select the paintbrush, this cursor appears (again, by default).

Stamp: This cursor denotes the selection of the rubber stamp tool.

Stamp pickup: When you press the Alt key while using the rubber stamp tool — and the Caps Lock key is up — you see this cursor. You then can specify which portion of an image you want to clone.

Smudge: This cursor appears when the smudge tool is selected.

Blur: When you use the blur tool, you see this cursor.

Sharpen: This cursor appears when you press the Alt key in combination with the blur tool or when you switch to the sharpen tool by Alt-clicking on the blur tool icon.

Dodge: This cursor appears when you select the dodge tool in order to lighten an image.

Burn: When you prefer to darken portions of an image, press the Alt key while using the dodge tool or Alt-click on the dodge tool icon to switch to the burn tool. Either way, you get this cursor.

Sponge: Alt-click on the burn tool icon in the toolbox to get the sponge tool cursor, which lets you decrease or increase the saturation of colors in an image.

Black eyedropper: This cursor and the two that follow are available only when you work in the Levels and Curves dialog boxes. Click with the black eyedropper to select the color in an image that will change to black.

Gray eyedropper: Click with this cursor to select the color that will change to medium gray (called the *gamma value*).

White eyedropper: Use this cursor to specify the color that will change to white.

Eyedropper plus: New to Version 3, this cursor and the next one are available only via the Color Range and Replace Color dialog boxes. Click with this cursor to add colors to the temporary mask generated by these dialog boxes. For complete information on these commands, read Chapters 9 and 16.

Eyedropper minus: Click with this cursor to remove colors from the temporary mask.

Palette hand: This cursor displays inside all panels of the Layers palette. Drag with the cursor to move a layer, channel, or path above or below other layers, channels, or paths listed in the palette.

Move palette item: When you drag a layer, channel, or path, the palette hand changes to the move palette item cursor.

Group layer: Press the Alt key and position the cursor over the horizontal line between two layers in the Layers panel to get this cursor. Alt-click on the line to group the layers divided by that line.

Ungroup layer: When two layers are grouped, the horizontal line between them becomes dotted. Alt-click on the dotted line to ungroup the two layers.

Hourglass: The hourglass cursor is the universal Windows symbol *for hurry up and wait*. When you see the cursor inside Photoshop 3, you can either sit on your idle hands (waiting for the devil to start playing with them) or you can be industrious (switch to another application, and try to get some work done). Windows 95 lets you change the hourglass to something less lethal (or *more lethal*) in appearance, even with animation. I've not illustrated an hourglass cursor, for two reasons. First, you probably have seen it quite often enough on your screen. Second, you may have changed it, in Windows 95, to something else.

Toolbox controls

You have to love lists. They're fun to write and they're a joy to read. All right, so we're lying. Making your way through lists of information is a monstrous chore, whether you're on the giving or receiving end. But these particular lists happen to contain essential reference information. So on we go with our newest and most astonishing list yet: the one that explains (gasp) the controls at the bottom of the toolbox. (By the way, in that last sentence, you're not supposed to read *gasp,* you're supposed to actually gasp. Try again and see if it works better for you the second time.)

Foreground color: Click on the foreground color icon to bring up the Color Picker dialog box. Select a color from Photoshop's immense palette and press Return to change the foreground color, which is used by all painting tools except the eraser. (I'm not sure why, but many users make the mistake of double-clicking on the foreground or background color icons when they first start using Photoshop. A single click is all that's needed.)

Background color: Click on the background color icon to display the Color Picker and change the background color, which is used by the eraser and gradient tools. Photoshop also uses the background color to fill a selected area when you press the Delete key.

Switch colors: Click on the switch colors icon to exchange the foreground and background colors. When you want a quick way to make the foreground color white, click on the default colors icon and then click on the switch colors icon.

Default colors: Click on this icon to automatically change the foreground color to black and the background color to white.

Marching ants: Click on this icon to exit the quick mask mode, which enables you to edit selection boundaries using painting tools. In the marching ants mode, Photoshop represents selection outlines as animated dotted lines that look like marching ants, hence the name. (Adobe calls this mode the *standard mode,* but we think *marching ants mode* better describes the function.)

Quick mask: Click here to enter the quick mask mode. The marching ants vanish and the image appears half covered by a translucent layer of red, like a rubylith in traditional paste-up. The rubylith covers the deselected — or masked — portions of the image. Paint with black to extend the areas covered by the rubylith, thereby subtracting from the selection. Paint with white to subtract from the rubylith, thereby adding to the selection.

Cross Ref The quick mask mode is too complex a topic to sum up in a few sentences. If you can't wait to find out what it's all about, check out Chapter 9.

Tip You can change the color and translucency of the rubylith by double-clicking on the marching ants or quick mask icon. You also can change which portion of the image is covered by the color — that is, you can cover the selected area or the masked area.

Standard window: Click on this icon to display the foreground image in a standard window, as shown earlier in Figure 2-2. By default, every image opens in the *standard window mode*.

Full screen with menu bar: When you can't see enough of your image inside a standard window, click on this icon. The title bar and scroll bars disappear, as do all background windows, but you still can access the menu bar. A black-and-white dotted background fills any empty area around the image. Figure 2-4 shows this option applied to the image from Figure 2-2.

Absolute full screen: Aesthetically speaking, the black-and-white dotted background that accompanies the full screen with menu bar mode looks awful behind *any* image. We don't know why Adobe didn't just make the background solid gray, or better yet, paisley. But enough griping. To see your image set against a neutral black background — a thoroughly preferable alternative — click on the rightmost of the image window icons. The menu bar disappears, limiting your access to commands (you still can access commands via keyboard equivalents), but you can see as much of your image as can physically fit on-screen. Only the toolbox and palettes remain visible, as shown in Figure 2-5. Adobe calls this mode *Full screen without menu bar;* we call it the *absolute full screen mode,* which seems a bit more descriptive and less cumbersome.

Tip   When the toolbox gets in your way when you're viewing an image in full screen mode, you can hide it and all other open palettes by pressing the Tab key. To bring the toolbox back into view, press Tab again.

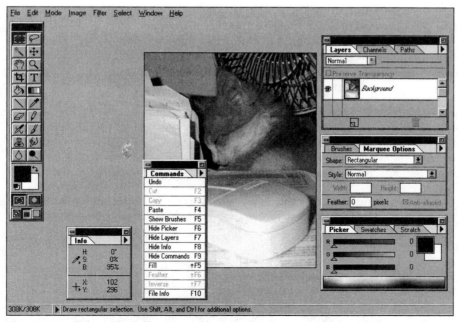

Figure 2-4: Click on the full screen with menu bar icon to hide the title bar, scroll bars, and preview box.

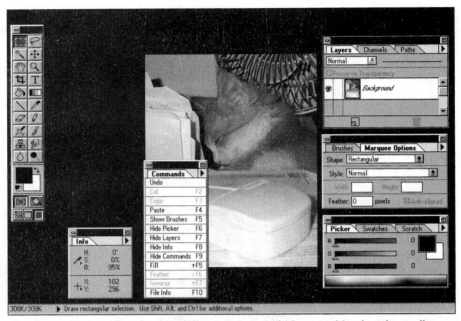

Figure 2-5: Click on the absolute full screen icon to hide everything but the toolbox, floating palettes, and image.

The floating palettes

Although palettes have been revised fairly dramatically in Photoshop 3, they still share many of the same elements they did in Photoshop 2.5. All palettes, for example, offer most of the standard elements labeled in Figure 2-6. (Some panels lack scroll bars and size boxes.) Many of these elements are shrunken versions of the ones that accompany any window. For example, the close box and title bar work identically to their image-window counterparts. The title bar lacks a title, but you can still drag it to move the palette to another location on-screen. Shift-drag the title bar to align the dragged palette with other palettes or with the edge of the screen.

Four elements are unique to floating palettes:

✦ **Palette options:** Each floating palette offers its own collection of options. These options may include tools, icons, pop-up menus, slider bars — you name it.

✦ **Palette menu:** Drag from the right-pointing arrowhead icon to display a menu of commands specific to the palette. These commands enable you to manipulate the palette options and adjust preference settings.

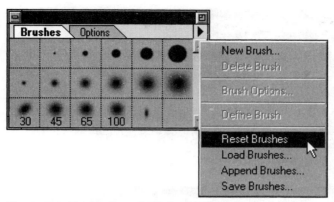

Figure 2-6: Most palettes include the same basic elements as the Brushes palette, shown here.

✦ **Collapse box:** Click on the collapse box to decrease the on-screen space consumed by the palette. If you previously enlarged the palette by dragging the size box, your first click reduces the palette back to its default size. After that, clicking on the collapse box hides all but the most essential palette options.

Tip

In most cases, collapsing a palette hides all options and leaves only the panel tabs visible. But in the case of the Options, Layers, Paths, and Picker panels, clicking on the collapse box leaves a sliver of palette options intact. To eliminate all options for these panels, Alt-click on the collapse box or double-click on one of the panel tabs. Either technique works even if you enlarged the palette by dragging the size box. Figure 2-7 shows how the different palettes appear when partially and fully collapsed.

✦ **Panel tabs:** Click on a *panel tab* to switch from one panel to another inside a palette. (You can also switch panels by selecting commands from the Win-dow⇨Palettes submenu, but it's more convenient to click.)

Tip Photoshop 3 lets you separate and group panels in palettes as you see fit. To separate a panel into its own palette, just drag the panel tab away from the palette, as demonstrated in Figure 2-8. To combine a panel with a different palette, drag the panel tab onto the palette so that the palette becomes highlighted, and then release. The middle and right examples in the figure show off this technique.

The text in this book always assumes the default setup, which may or may not match your configuration. For example, though we may say *check out the Channels panel in the Layers palette,* your Channels panel may be separated into its own palette, or combined with the Info palette.

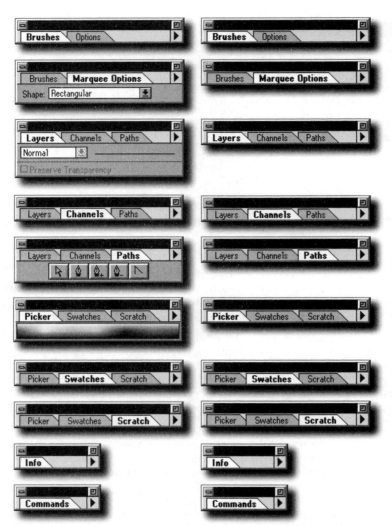

Figure 2-7: The ten palette panels when partially collapsed (left) and fully collapsed (right).

How to get around

All graphics and desktop publishing programs provide a variety of navigational tools and functions that enable you to scoot around the screen, visit the heartlands and nether regions, examine the fine details, and take in the big picture. Photoshop is no exception. In fact, it provides more navigational tricks per square pixel than just about any other graphics program.

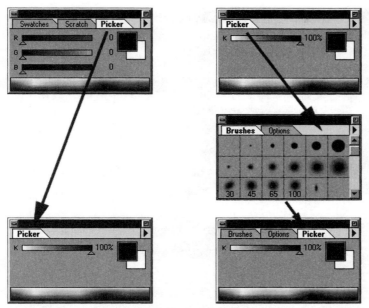

Figure 2-8: Dragging a panel off a palette (left) results in a separate new panel. Dragging a separate panel (right) onto another palette adds that panel to the palette.

Zoom ratio

In Photoshop, you can change the *view size* — the size at which an image appears on-screen — so that you can either see more of an image or concentrate on individual pixels. Each change in view size is expressed as a *zoom ratio,* which is the ratio between screen pixels and image pixels. A 1:1 zoom ratio means 1 screen pixel per each image pixel and is therefore equivalent to a 100 percent view size. A 1:2 zoom ratio equates to a 50 percent view size, as shown in Figure 2-9. A 2:1 zoom ratio is equivalent to a 200 percent view size, as shown in Figure 2-10. All told, Photoshop 3 provides 31 zoom ratios, ranging from 1:16 to 16:1 in single-digit increments (1:15, 1:14, 1:13, and so on).

When you first open an image, Photoshop displays it at the largest zoom ratio (up to and including 1:1) that permits the entire image to fit on-screen in the standard window mode. Assuming that you don't change the size of the image, you can return to this view size — sometimes called the *fit-in-window view* — at any time during the editing cycle by double-clicking on the hand tool icon in the toolbox.

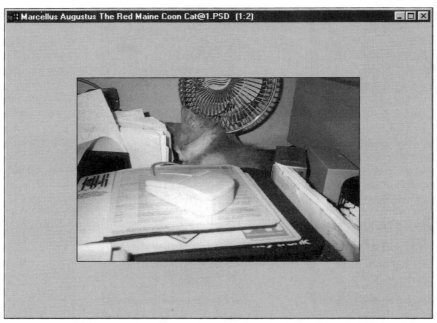

Figure 2-9: When viewing an image at the 1:2 zoom ratio, you see only a quarter of the total pixels in the image (half of the pixels vertically and half horizontally).

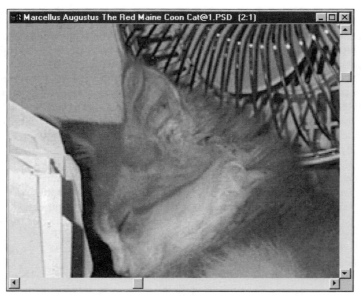

Figure 2-10: At the 2:1 zoom ratio, each pixel in the image measures 2 screen pixels tall and 2 screen pixels wide.

The zoom tool

The zoom tool enables you to change view sizes as follows:

✦ Click in the image window with the zoom tool to magnify the image to twice the previous zoom ratio.

✦ Alt-click with the zoom tool to reduce the image to half its previous zoom ratio.

✦ Drag with the zoom tool to draw a rectangular marquee around the portion of the image you want to magnify. Photoshop magnifies the image so that the marqueed area fits just inside the image window. When the horizontal and vertical proportions of the marquee do not match those of the image window — for example, when you draw a tall thin marquee or a short wide one — Photoshop favors the smaller of the two possible zoom ratios to avoid hiding any detail inside the marquee.

✦ Double-click on the zoom tool icon in the toolbox to restore the foreground image to a 1:1 zoom ratio.

Tip To temporarily access the zoom tool when some other tool is selected, press and hold the Control and spacebar keys. Release both keys to return control of the cursor to the selected tool. To access the zoom out cursor, press both Alt and the spacebar. These keyboard equivalents work from inside many dialog boxes, most notably those that provide preview options (such as the Hue/Saturation, Levels, and Curves dialog boxes discussed in Chapter 16).

When you use the zoom tool, you magnify and reduce the image within the confines of a static image window. To change the dimensions of the window to fit those of the image, click on the zoom box in the upper right corner of the title bar.

Tip To automatically resize the window along with the image, use the Zoom In (Ctrl-plus) and Zoom Out (Ctrl-minus) commands under the Window menu. Frequently, it's more convenient to use these commands than the zoom tool. And if that's not enough, you can zoom in to the highest level of magnification, 16:1, by pressing Ctrl-Alt-plus. Ctrl-Alt-minus zooms out to the smallest view size, 1:16.

Photoshop 3 offers one additional zooming command under the Window menu. Called Zoom Factor, it enables you to set the exact zoom ratio numerically. Choose Window⇨Zoom Factor, select the Magnification or Reduction radio button, enter the desired zoom value (from 1 to 16) in the Factor option box, and press Return. For example, when you select Magnification and enter 3, Photoshop magnifies to a 3:1 zoom ratio. Selecting Reduction with the same Factor value results in a 1:3 zoom ratio.

Creating a reference window

In the old days, paint programs used to provide a cropped view of your image at the 1:1 zoom ratio to serve as a reference when you worked in a magnified view size. Because it's so doggone modern, Photoshop does not, but you can easily create a second view of your image by choosing Window⇨New Window. Use the new window to maintain a 100 percent view of your image while you zoom and edit inside the original window. Both windows track the changes to the image, as shown in Figure 2-11. The paintbrush strokes appear in both windows.

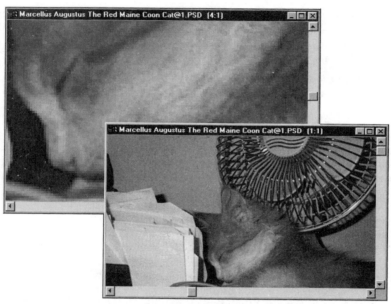

Figure 2-11: You can create multiple windows to track the changes made to a single image by choosing the New Window command from the Window menu.

Scrolling inside the window

In the standard window mode, you have access to scroll bars, just as you do in the vast majority of Windows applications. But as you become more proficient with Photoshop, you'll use the scroll bars less and less. One way to bypass the scroll bars is to use the keyboard equivalents listed in Table 2-1.

Table 2-1	
Scrolling from the Keyboard	
Scrolling Action	*Keyboard*
Up one screen	Page Up
Up slightly	Shift-Page Up
Down one screen	Page Down
Down slightly	Shift-Page Down
To upper left corner	Home
To lower right corner	End

Unfortunately, you can't scroll exclusively left or right from the keyboard. But who cares? You won't be scrolling from the keyboard that often anyway. Most of the time, you'll use the hand tool.

Tip   To temporarily access the hand tool when some other tool is selected, press and hold the spacebar. Releasing the spacebar returns the cursor to its original appearance. This keyboard equivalent even works from inside many dialog boxes.

Moving with the mouse

With all this talk about mousing and menus and keyboard equivalents, you could very easily lose sight of an extremely useful new feature. It doesn't totally belong here, but more here than anywhere else in the book. You can mouse your selections around!

It's very simple, and wildly addictive. Open a new window. When you've got something on the Clipboard, remember that it will be sized to fit that selection. You may want this, or you may not — tinker with the size settings in the New dialog box if necessary. Then just click on the original image and drag it into the new window. When you want to move just a selection from the original window, make the selection, then Ctrl-Alt-click, and then drag to the new window.

Shortcuts

Shortcuts enable you to access commands and other functions without resorting to the laborious task of choosing commands from menus or clicking on some fool icon until your arm falls off. Many shortcuts are fairly obvious. For example, Photoshop lists keyboard equivalents for its commands next to the command in the menu. You can choose File⇨New by pressing Ctrl-N, choose Edit⇨Undo by pressing Ctrl-Z, choose Select⇨All by pressing Ctrl-A, and so on. But a few of Photoshop's shortcuts are either hidden or can be overlooked easily.

Table 2-2 lists my favorite Photoshop shortcuts. We've already mentioned some of these, but they bear repeating. Italicized table entries indicate shortcuts that are new or revised in Version 3.0.

Table 2-2
The Best Photoshop Shortcuts You'll Ever Learn

Operation	Shortcut
Navigation tricks	
Scroll image with hand tool selected	Press the spacebar and drag with any tool
Zoom in without changing window size	Ctrl-spacebar-click
Magnify to custom zoom ratio	Ctrl-spacebar-drag
Zoom in and change window size to fit	Ctrl-plus
Zoom out without changing window size	Alt-spacebar-click
Zoom out and change window size to fit	Ctrl-minus
Zoom to 100%	Double-click on the zoom tool icon
Fit image in window	Double-click on the hand tool icon
Paint and edit tool tricks	
Display crosshair cursor	Caps Lock
Lift foreground color with eyedropper (when any paint tool is selected)	Alt-click
Lift background color with the eyedropper tool	Alt-click
Revert image with magic eraser with the eraser tool	Alt-drag
Select different kind of eraser on eraser tool icon in toolbox	Alt-click
Specify an area to clone with the rubber stamp tool	Alt-click
Dip into the foreground color when smearing with the smudge tool	Alt-drag
Change sharpen tool to blur tool or blur tool to sharpen tool	Alt-click on focus tool icon in toolbox
Sharpen with the blur tool or blur with the sharpen tool	Alt-drag
Change dodge tool to burn tool, burn tool to sponge tool, or sponge tool to dodge tool	Alt-click on toning tool icon in toolbox

Operation	Shortcut
Darken with the dodge tool or lighten with the burn tool	Alt-drag
Paint or edit in a straight line	Click and then Shift-click with the painting or editing tool
Change opacity, pressure, or exposure of paint tools in 10% increments	Press 0 through 9 (1 is 10%, 9 is 90%, 0 is100%)
Cycle through brush shapes	Left or right bracket
Switch to first or last shape in Brushes palette	Shift-left bracket or Shift-right bracket
Selection and layering tricks	
Select area of contiguous color	Ctrl-click when marquee or lasso tool is selected
Add to a selection	Shift-drag with selection tool (Shift-click with magic wand)
Subtract from a selection or delete part of a floating selection	Ctrl-drag with selection tool (Ctrl-click with magic wand)
Drop part of a floating selection	Ctrl-drag with type tool
Subtract all but intersected portion of a selection	Ctrl-Shift-drag with selection tool (Ctrl-Shift-click with magic wand)
Move selection	Drag inside selection with selection tool or drag anywhere with move tool
Constrain movement vertically or horizontally	Shift after you begin to drag inside selection with selection tool
Move selection in 1-pixel increments	Any arrow key
Move selection in 10-pixel increments	Shift-any arrow key
Clone selection	Alt-drag inside selection with selection tool
Clone selection in 1-pixel increments	Alt-any arrow key
Clone selection in 10-pixel increments	Shift-Alt-any arrow key
Clone a selection to a different window	Drag the selection from one window and drop it into another
Move selection boundary independently of contents	Ctrl-Alt-drag inside selection with selection tool
Move selection boundary independently	Ctrl-Alt-any arrow key in 1-pixel increments

(continued)

Table 2-2 *(continued)*

Operation	Shortcut
Move selection boundary independently in 10-pixel increments	Ctrl-Shift-Alt-any arrow key
Fill selection with background color	Delete or Clear (or Ctrl-H) when no path is selected
Fill selection with foreground color	Alt-Del (or Ctrl-Alt-H)
Display Fill dialog box	Shift-Del (or Ctrl-Shift-H)
Float selection (separate it from the rest of the image)	Ctrl-J
Change opacity of floating selection in 10% increments	Press 0 through 9 when a selection tool is active (1 is 10%, 9 is 90%, 0 is 100%)
Send a floating selection to a new layer in the Layers panel	Double-click on the Floating Selection layer name
Change overlay options for layer	Double-click on layer name in Layers panel
Convert mask channel to selection outline	Alt-click on mask channel name in Channels palette or Ctrl-Alt-0 through Ctrl-Alt-9
Select contents of active layer	Ctrl-Alt-T
Toggle quick mask color over masked	Alt-click on quick mask icon in toolbox or selected area
Hide/show marching ants	Ctrl-H
Deselect everything	Ctrl-D

Pen tool and path tricks
(when any tool but a selection tool is active, unless otherwise noted)

Move selected points	Ctrl-drag on point
Select multiple points in path	Ctrl-Shift-click on point
Select entire path	Ctrl-Alt-click on point or segment
Insert point in path	Ctrl-Alt-click on segment when arrow tool in Paths panel is selected
Remove point from path	Ctrl-Alt-click on point when arrow tool is selected
Convert path to selection outline	Press Enter when selection tool is active
Add path to current selection	Shift-Enter when selection tool is active
Subtract path from current selection or delete path from floating selection	Ctrl-Enter when selection tool is active
Subtract all of current selection that isn't intersected by path	Ctrl-Shift-Enter when selection tool is active

Operation	Shortcut
Apply brushstroke, eraser, rubber stamp, or edit around perimeter of path	Enter when appropriate tool is active
Save the current path for future use Paths panel	Double-click on the Work Path name in the

Image and color adjustments

Resize cropping boundary	Drag corner handle
Rotate cropping boundary	Alt-drag corner handle
Move cropping boundary	Ctrl-drag corner handle
Reapply last filter used	Ctrl-F
Display dialog box for last filter used	Ctrl-Alt-F
Replace color in Swatches panel of Picker palette with foreground color	Shift-click on color swatch
Delete color from Swatches panel	Ctrl-click on color swatch
Compare unaltered image from inside color correction dialog box	Mouse down on dialog box title bar when Preview check box is not selected
Reset options inside any color correction dialog box	Alt-click on Cancel button

General

Switch between channels	Ctrl-0 through Ctrl-9 (0 is composite of color channels)
Switch to next layer down	Ctrl-left bracket
Switch to next layer up	Ctrl-right bracket
Switch to layer that contains image	Ctrl-click on image with move tool
Move a panel out of a palette	Drag the panel tab
Display Options panel of Brushes palette	Double-click on tool icon in toolbox
Fully collapse palette	Alt-click on collapse box or double-click on panel tab
Preview how image will sit on printed page	Mouse down on preview box
View size and resolution of image	Alt-mouse down on preview box
Hide or show toolbox and other floating palettes	Tab
Change a command in the Commands palette	Shift-click on command name

(continued)

Table 2-2 *(continued)*	
Operation	**Shortcut**
Delete a command from the Commands palette	Ctrl-click on command name
Change the preference settings	Ctrl-K
Activate Don't Save button	Ctrl-D
Cancel the current operation	Ctrl-period

Toolbox shortcuts

Robert

All right, if this next bit of information doesn't make you squeal with delight, nothing will. With Photoshop 3, you now can select tools and activate controls from the keyboard. Is that the greatest thing since sliced bread or what?

The moment I stumbled on it, I had to get up and do a little dance around my office. (Isn't it nice to know I still take pleasure in life's little pleasures?)

In any case, Figure 2-12 tells the whole wonderful story. Just press the appropriate key, as shown in the figure — no Control, Alt, or other modifiers required. Many of the shortcuts make sense. *M* selects the marquee tool, *L* is for lasso tool. But then there are the weird ones, like *Y* for tYpe, *K* for paint bucKet, *U* for smUdge, *O* for dOdge, and my favorite, *I* for I-dropper. As far as we can tell, the only alphabetical key that doesn't do anything is *J.*

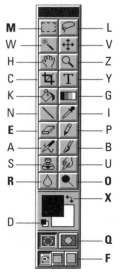 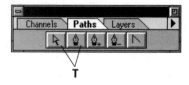

Figure 2-12: Press these keys to select tools and toggle controls in Photoshop 3.

The keys that appear in bold type in Figure 2-12 act as toggles. For example, when you press M once, you get the last marquee tool used (rectangular by default). Press M again to select the other marquee tool. Other toggles work as follows:

✦ **E** takes you from one kind of eraser to the next. (The only way to monitor which eraser is active is to display the Eraser Options panel.)

✦ **R** switches between the blur and sharpen tools.

✦ **O** toggles between the dodge, burn, and sponge tools.

✦ **X** swaps the foreground and background colors and then swaps them back again.

✦ **Q** enters the quick mask mode and then exits it.

✦ **F** takes you from one window mode to another.

✦ **T** switches between the pen tool and the arrow tool in the Paths panel. It even displays the palette if the palette is hidden.

Establishing function key shortcuts

Although it's pretty extensive, Table 2-2 doesn't include *every* shortcut, just the best ones. (We left out most of the keyboard equivalents you can see in the menus.)

If you own an extended keyboard, you can specify additional keyboard equivalents by choosing Window⇨Palettes⇨Show Commands. Shown in Figure 2-13, the Commands palette enables you to assign any command to a function key or Shift-function key combination. You can even assign colors to the commands to logically group them, as shown in the second example in the figure. And if you prefer clicking on-screen to pressing function keys, you can simply click on the command name in the palette to initiate the corresponding command.

Using the Commands palette is a little more involved than using the old Function Key Preferences dialog box. The best way to assign function-key equivalents en masse is to select the Edit Commands option from the Commands palette pop-up menu, which displays the first dialog box shown in Figure 2-14. From here, you can either edit or delete the commands that have already been assigned, or add new commands. To add a command, click on the New button, which displays the second dialog box in the figure. Then choose the desired command from the menu bar along the top of the screen or from any available palette menu. The chosen command appears in the Name option box. Alternatively, you can enter the first few letters of a command name and click on the Find button. When Photoshop finds a match, it automatically displays it in the Name option box.

To assign a key equivalent, select an option from the Function Key pop-up menu. Dimmed options indicate keys that have already been assigned. Select the Shift check box if you want to press Shift with the function key to access the command. Select an option from the Color pop-up menu if you want to assign a color to the button in the Commands palette.

Figure 2-13: The Commands palette as it appears by default, with its pop-up menu.

Note You don't have to assign any key to a command. When you just want to create a button for the command without any means to access it from the keyboard, leave the Function Key option set to None. This way, you can access the command by clicking on its name in the Commands palette, even in the absolute full screen mode when the menu bar is hidden.

To edit a command in the Edit Commands dialog box, double-click on the command name in the scrolling list. To delete a command, select it and click on the Delete button.

Tip You can also delete a command from the scrolling list by Ctrl-clicking on it. When you press the Control key, the scissors cursor appears to show you that your next click will clip away a command. In addition, you can edit and delete commands from outside the Edit Commands dialog box. Ctrl-click on a button in the Commands palette to delete it; Shift-click (or Ctrl-click) to edit the command.

The Columns option box at the bottom of the Edit Commands dialog box controls the number of columns in the Commands palette. Like colors, columns are simply an organizational issue. When you want a long list of commands going down the side of your monitor, leave the option set to one column. When you prefer a shorter and wider Commands palette, go with two or three columns. You can specify as many as nine columns.

Caution When you're finished adding commands and function-key equivalents, be sure to save your settings to disk by selecting the Save Commands option from the palette pop-up menu. If your preferences file ever becomes corrupted or if someone goes and throws it away, you can retrieve the function keys using the Load Commands option in the pop-up menu.

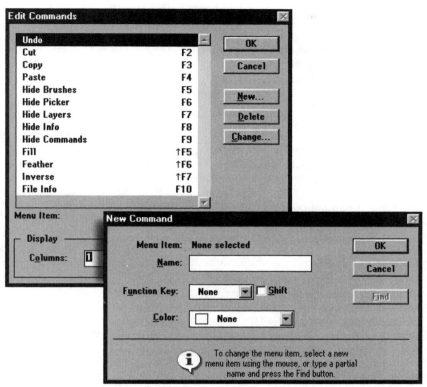

Figure 2-14: Click on the New button in the Edit Commands dialog box (top) to display the New Command dialog box (bottom).

All of this involves using the Commands palette, which is the best our Mac friends have to work with. But for Windows 95 users, *Microsoft has a better idea.* You can access all these customized commands with a click of the right mouse button. This is so important, and new, that I'm not going to let it get buried here. Head to the end of this chapter for more info.

Using a macro utility (Hah!)

Here's an area where Mac folks have an advantage. Programs such as Apple's ResEdit or CE Software's QuickKeys let you roll your own macros and improve your productivity — if you have a Mac. Even at their best, things weren't so good for Windows people. The Windows 3.1 Recorder was anemic at best, although it could be jacked around to actually be useful. But it's gone with the wind; Microsoft did not carry it over to Windows 95. There are various Windows batch languages, such as the 32-bit version of WinBatch, but it's simply too soon to know what can be done.

Interface

In addition to adding your own keyboard equivalents, you can customize the Photoshop interface by changing the *preference settings*. Photoshop ships with certain preference settings already in force (these are called *factory default settings*), but you can change the settings to reflect your personal preferences.

You can change preference settings in two ways. You can make environmental adjustments using commands from the File⬥Preferences submenu, or you can change the operation of specific tools by adjusting settings in the Options panel of the Brushes palette. Photoshop 3 remembers environmental preferences, tool settings, and even the file format under which you saved the last image by saving this information to a file called PHOTOS30.PSP, which lives in \WINDOWS. In versions 3.01 and 3.04, it lives in the Photoshop directory (whatever you may have named it), while in version 3.05 it's in a Photoshop subdirectory named PREFS.

Tip   To restore Photoshop's factory default settings, delete that .PSP file when the application is *not* running. The next time you launch Photoshop, it creates a new preferences file automatically.

Robert   Here's a note on a note! I said *delete* in the previous note. Now Mac people do the same thing, but invariably they use the word *trash* instead. When I first heard them use that verb — well, it conjured up images of doom, as in *Program x trashed my drive*. until I realized that it probably derived from the Macintosh Trash Can. One wonders about the possibilities of the Windows 95 Recycle Bin.

Robert   Deleting the file is also a great thing to do when Photoshop starts acting funny. For reason that QA (*quality assurance,* geek-speak for bug swatters) is still examining, the .PSP file is often subject to corruption — same thing on the Mac side, where it's called the Preferences file. Back it up first just to be safe — because if the file isn't corrupt, there's no sense in losing your customizations. That's the kicker — deleting the .PSP file may make Photoshop healthy again, but at the price of restoring the, er, factory defaults. If you're like me, most of those factory defaults are long gone — I've got my own ideas of how Photoshop should behave. All in all, though, it's not a bad trade-off. After you have things just so, you might want to save your .PSP file just in case of a future disaster. Do not change its file attribute to Read only, because Photoshop has to be able to write to it.

The File Preferences commands

These commands have an enormous amount to do with the feel and usability of your Photoshop environment — and one (Memory) has to do with whether you can open Photoshop at all. Read carefully and think carefully before changing, but don't be paranoid!

✦ **General (Ctrl-K):** This command provides access to the preference settings you'll need to adjust most often. The next section of this chapter examines the General Preferences dialog box.

✦ **Gamut Warning:** This command controls the color that Photoshop uses to highlight screen colors that will not print correctly. You request this feature by choosing Mode⇨Gamut Warning.

✦ **Plug-ins:** This command lets you change the directory in which Photoshop searches for the plug-in modules it loads during the launch cycle. This setting doesn't take effect until you relaunch the program. We don't advise changing this, because if you point it elsewhere from its own plug-ins subdirectory, you'll lose far more than you gain.

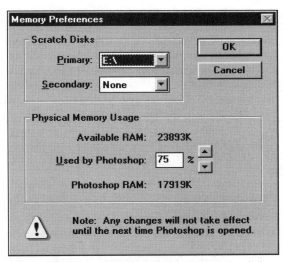

Figure 2-15: The File⇨Preferences⇨Memory dialog box. Your best friend for optimizing and troubleshooting Photoshop.

✦ **Memory:** Discussed above in detail, this command lets you specify the hard drive or removable media device where Photoshop stores its temporary virtual memory files. It also lets you determine how much RAM to feed Photoshop. It's invaluable for optimizing and troubleshooting, particularly when you're running pre-Windows 95. Again, this setting doesn't take effect until you relaunch the program.

✦ **Transparency:** You may have noticed that Photoshop 3 momentarily displays a checkerboard pattern after you open an image or switch application. This checkerboard represents *transparency,* which is the utter absence of data. As explained in Chapter 8, transparency is required to mix one layer with the layer in back of it. You can change the checkerboard pattern by using File⇨Preferences⇨Transparency. The command has no effect on the way transparency or layers work; it's purely a visual thing, as is so often the case with preferences.

✦ **Units:** This command enables you to change the units of measure that appear in the Info palette, as well as in every dialog box in which you can specify the size of something. If you prefer picas to inches, for example, choose this command.

The lower portion of the File⇨Preferences submenu lets you adjust how colors appear on-screen (*monitor calibration*) and when printed (*color separation*). These options are explained in greater depth in Chapter 6, but here's a quick rundown:

✦ **Monitor Setup:** You can change the way Photoshop displays colors on your monitor. You can specify the brand of monitor you use and the ambient lighting conditions of the room in which you work. You also can adjust the *gamma,* which affects the brightness of the medium-range colors (or *midtones*) displayed on your monitor.

✦ **Printing Inks Setup:** This controls the output of color proofs and CMYK (cyan, magenta, yellow, and black) separations for four-color offset reproduction. Together with the preceding command, Printing Inks Setup determines the way Photoshop converts colors between the RGB and CMYK modes.

✦ **Separation Setup:** This controls the generation of four-color separations. You can adjust the black separation both independently and in tandem with the cyan, magenta, and yellow separations.

✦ **Separation Tables:** This command enables you to save the settings you selected in the Printing Inks Setup and Separation Setup dialog box to a special file for later use. Even though both of those dialog boxes provide save options of their own, only the Separation Tables dialog box lets you save both together.

General environmental preferences

Of all the Preferences commands, the General command is the most important. We touch on the other valuable commands throughout the remainder of this book, but the General command deserves your immediate attention because it affects the widest range of Photoshop functions. Why else do you think they call it *General* (as opposed to *Corporal* or *Potato Peeler, 3rd Class*)? Figure 2-16 shows the General Preferences dialog box in all its splendor.

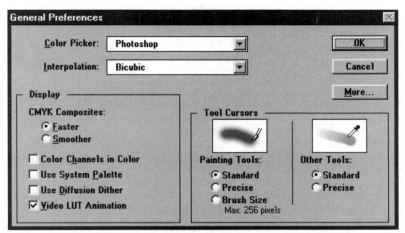

Figure 2-16: The General Preferences dialog box contains the options for the most important environmental settings.

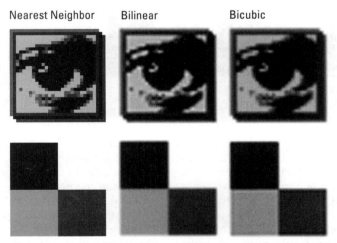

Figure 2-17: The Photoshop application icon and a simple box pattern shown as they appear when enlarged to 400 percent and subjected to the three different types of interpolation.

In brief, the options inside this dialog box work as follows:

✦ **Color Picker:** When you click on the foreground or background color control icon in the toolbox, Photoshop displays one of two *color pickers,* its own or the one provided by Windows 95. You may be tempted to use this latter one because it's familiar. Don't. Photoshop color pickers possibilities are staggering; bite the bullet and learn it.

✦ **Interpolation:** When you resample an image using Image⊃Image Size or transform it using one of the commands in the Image⊃Rotation or Image⊃Effects
submenu, Photoshop has to make up — or *interpolate* — pixels to fill in the gaps.
You can change how Photoshop calculates the interpolation by choosing one of
the three options demonstrated in Figure 2-17.

When you choose Nearest Neighbor, Photoshop simply copies the next-door
pixel after creating a new one. This is the fastest but least helpful setting. The
Bilinear option smoothes the transitions between pixels by creating intermedi-
ary shades. It takes more time, but typically, the softened effect is worth it. Still
more time-intensive is the default setting, Bicubic, which boosts the amount of
contrast between pixels in order to offset the blurring effect that generally
accompanies interpolation.

Nearest Neighbor   Bilinear   Bicubic

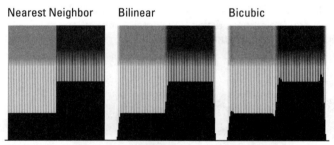

Figure 2-18: A cross-section of the gray boxes from the
previous figure mapped onto a graph.

Figure 2-18 shows how the Bicubic setting adds special dips and peaks in color
transitions that the Bilinear setting leaves out. (The names *bilinear* and *bicubic*
refer to the complexity of the polynomial used to calculate the interpolations.
Better names might be *softened* and *softened with enhanced contrast*.) Figure 2-18
shows the gray boxes from the previous figure mapped onto bar graphs. Taller
vertical graph lines indicate darker values. You can see that whereas bilinear
interpolation simply rounds off the transition between neighboring colors,
bicubic interpolation creates dips and peaks in color transitions that accentuate
contrast and prevent overblurring.

✦ **CMYK Composites:** RGB is the color mode used to display images on a monitor;
CMYK is the color mode used to print colors on paper. In effect, when you edit a
CMYK image, you're trying to display images on-screen in the wrong color
mode. Photoshop 3 provides two solutions: When you select the Smoother
option, Photoshop preserves the actual CMYK color values in an image and
converts them on the fly to your RGB display — a precise but excruciatingly
slow process. When you specify the Faster option, Photoshop cheats by converting the colors in an image to their nearest RGB equivalents according to a
color lookup table (CLUT), which speeds up the screen display dramatically but
sacrifices image quality.

✦ **Color Channels in Color:** Individual color channels contain only 8 bits of information per pixel; they display grayscale images. Photoshop can colorize the channel according to the primary color it represents. For example, when this option is turned on, the red color channel looks like a grayscale image viewed through red acetate. The effect isn't very helpful and does more to obscure your image than to make it easier for you to see what's going on.

✦ **Use System Palette:** This option is irrelevant when you're using HiColor or True Color (16-bit and 24-bit, respectively) video drivers. And you really ought to be, if you're serious about Photoshop. Still, you may have just finished playing a game that only runs in 256-color mode (we all play computer games; I've got one minimized even as I type this, but I'll never tell), the Muse has bitten you, and you want to get some work done in Photoshop. Then you may want this option. You're telling Photoshop to ignore its custom color tables and use your hardware color support. That means better representation of the image you're working on, because Photoshop can optimize for those colors and fob off the colors of inactive windows on the system colors. Make sure you use Diffusion Dither (next note). Don't believe us? Try it without and your eyes should tell you.

✦ **Use Diffusion Dither:** When you're in less than 24-bit color mode, this lets you tell Photoshop how to deal with the resultant color mismatches. When you leave this unchecked, you'll get the default patterned dither, which is only good for eyestrain. Diffusion dither under these circumstances imitates colors slightly more accurately. But, because it follows no specific pattern, you sometimes see distinct edges between selected and deselected portions of your image after applying a filter or some other effect.

Tip

To eliminate any visual disharmony that may occur after using the Use Diffusion Dither option, you can force Photoshop to redraw the entire image by double-clicking on the zoom tool icon or performing some other zoom function.

✦ **Video LUT Animation:** This speeds up screen redraws as you doctor your image. Photoshop uses a color lookup table (old *CLUT* again, or in Photoshop lingo, *LUT*). If you've ever worked inside one of Photoshop's color correction dialog boxes — such as Levels or Curves — with the Preview option turned off, you've seen *LUT animation* in progress. Photoshop changes the LUT on the fly according to your specifications and, in doing so, more or less previews the color change over the entire image. It's not a real preview, but it's the next best thing. When LUT animation causes a problem with your video board, you can turn it off using this option. Otherwise, leave it on.

Caution This animation is also important in other areas. For example, if you look at the Adobe documentation at page 202 (and compare with Chapter 16 of the book you're now reading) you'll see a way to identify highlights and shadows in the Levels command — this method relies on LUT animation. But here's the kicker. If you're running with more video colors than 256, it won't seem to work. That's right. Same thing happened under Photoshop 2.5, but the workaround was that some of the video board manufacturers worked with Adobe to produce .8BX plug-ins for their cards — these allowed LUT to work with the higher color number drivers. In Photoshop 2.5 for Windows, those plug-ins were installed below the plug-ins directory in a video subdirectory. Alas, not so (for the moment) with Photoshop 3.

✦ **Painting Tools:** When you use paint or edit tools in an image, Photoshop can display one of three cursors. The default Standard cursor looks like a paint-brush, airbrush, finger, or whatever. These cursors are only helpful when you have problems keeping track of what tool you selected. The Precise and Brush Size options are more functional. Precise displays crosshairs, the same ones that appear when you press the Caps Lock key. Brush Size shows the actual size of the brush up to 300 screen pixels in diameter. This means that when the zoom ratio is 1:2 and the brush size is 500 pixels wide, the brush only looks 250 pixels wide on-screen and displays fine. But when you zoom in to actual size, the brush size is too large to display, and the standard cursor appears instead.

When Standard or Brush Size is selected, pressing the Caps Lock key displays the precise crosshair cursors. But when Precise is selected, pressing Caps Lock displays the actual brush size.

✦ **Other tools:** Again, you can select Standard to get the regular cursors, or Precise to get crosshairs. We like to leave this option set to Standard, because you can easily access the crosshairs by pressing Caps Lock. The Precise option locks you into crosshairs whether you like it or not.

The number of General Preference options has grown so much that a second dialog box has been created to accommodate them. Click on the More button to display this overflow dialog box, shown in Figure 2-19. Its options work as follows:

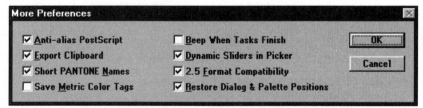

Figure 2-19: The More Preferences dialog box contains a bunch of ragtag options that don't fit in the General Preferences dialog box.

✦ **Image Previews:** The Windows version of Photoshop doesn't offer image previews, unlike the Macintosh version. It is one of the most requested features by Windows users; alas, all I can tell you is that Adobe has heard you. For the moment, when you want previews of your .PSD files, you have to go elsewhere.

✦ **Anti-alias PostScript:** Photoshop can swap graphics with Adobe Illustrator 4 and 4.1 via the Clipboard. The Anti-alias PostScript option smoothes out the edges of PostScript paths pasted into Photoshop from the Clipboard. When you don't want anti-aliased (softened) edges, turn this option off.

✦ **Export Clipboard:** When selected, this option ensures that Photoshop transfers a copied image from its internal Clipboard to the system's Clipboard when you switch applications. This enables you to paste the image into another running application. Turn this option off when you plan to use copied images only within Photoshop and you want to reduce the lag time that occurs when you switch from Photoshop to another program. Even with this option off, you can paste images copied from other programs into Photoshop.

✦ **Short Pantone Names:** Photoshop uses updated Pantone naming conventions. When you plan to import a Photoshop image that contains Pantone colors into an aging desktop publishing or drawing package, you may need to select this option to ensure that the receiving application recognizes the color names. More recent upgrades, such as QuarkXPress 3.3 and PageMaker 5, support the updated names and thus do not require you to select this option. (Incidentally, you only have to worry about this option when you're creating duotones.)

✦ **Save Metric Color Tags:** When you use EFI's EfiColor for Photoshop to help with screen and printer calibration, and you import and print images inside QuarkXPress, turn this option on. Photoshop then references the active EfiColor separation table when saving an image in the TIFF or EPS file format, making the table available to XPress and thus maintaining consistent color between the two applications. If you don't use EfiColor, leave the option off.

✦ **Beep When Tasks Finish:** You can instruct Photoshop to beep at you whenever it finishes an operation that displays a Progress window. But we believe that computers should be seen and not heard.

R%%
Robert Like Deke, I also think that silence is golden when using a computer. Besides, having a sound card introduces yet another potential source of conflicts, especially when you're trying to run a CD-ROM off it — see Appendix A for further fulminations. You want Brahms or Yanni drifting through the background? Then get a stereo. Let your computer do what it does best.

✦ **Dynamic Sliders in Picker:** When selected, this option instructs Photoshop to preview color effects within the slider bars of the Picker palette. After the option is turned off, the slider bars show the same colors regardless of your changes. Unless you're working on a slow machine, leave this option on.

✦ **2.5 Format Compatibility:** This option allows Photoshop 2.5 to open files saved in the Photoshop 3 format. But this backwards compatibility comes at a price. It works like this: the only file format that retains layers is the Photoshop 3 format. Even though Photoshop 2.5 does not support layers, it can open a flattened version of the image in which all the layers are fused together, as long as the 2.5 Format Compatibility option is selected. *So,* you say, *I should leave this option on.* Ah, not so fast. When the option is on, Photoshop has to insert an additional flattened version of the image into the file, which takes up a huge amount of disk space. You reduce the file size by as much as 50 percent by deselecting 2.5 Format Compatibility. Photoshop 2.5 won't be able to open it — nor will other programs that support the 2.5 format — but unless you're working with folks that are behind the times, who cares?

✦ **Restore Palette & Dialog Box Positions:** When this option is selected, Photoshop remembers the location of the toolbox and floating palettes from one session to the next. After you deselect this checkbox, Photoshop displays the toolbox in the upper left corner of the screen and the Brushes, Layers, and Picker palettes in formation at the bottom of the screen each time you run the program.

Out of context like this, Photoshop's preference settings can be a bit confusing. In future chapters, I'll try to shed some additional light on the settings you're likely to find most useful.

Image

If you work for a stock agency or you distribute your work by some other means, you'll definitely be interested in this feature. You can now attach captions, credits, bylines, photo location and date, and other information, as prescribed by the IPTC (International Press Telecommunications Council). We're talking official worldwide guidelines here. Who'd have thought Photoshop would ever become so mainstream?

Choose File⇨File Info to display the five-paneled File Info dialog box. You switch from one panel to another by pressing Control with a number key (1, 2, 3, 4, or 5). The first and third panels appear in Figure 2-20.

R%%
Robert

When I first read this section I thought *Much ado about nothing.* I was wrong! This is a remarkably useful feature. All of the image information is right there in your file; no more Post-its to wade through. As Pericles might have said, *The spring has returned to the year.* Incidentally, you may be wondering why we've only shown two of the five panels, and wondering even more if you've seen Deke's *Macworld Photoshop 3 Bible*, which displays all five. The Windows panels are larger than the Mac ones; to get all five in — well, you'd need a trip to the ophthalmologist!

Although it's loaded with options, the Caption dialog box is straightforward. When you want to create a caption, enter it into the Caption option box. The Keywords panel holds descriptive words to help folks find the image in a large electronic library. Enter the desired word and press Return (or click on the Add button) to add it to the list. Alternatively, you can replace a word in the list by selecting it and pressing Return (or clicking on Replace). Browser utilities let you search images by keyword, as do some dedicated image servers.

The Categories panel may seem foreign to anyone who hasn't worked with a news service. Many news services use a system of 3-character categories to organize stories and photographs. If you're familiar with this system, you can enter the 3-character code into the Category option box and even throw in a few supplemental categories up to 32 characters long. Finally, use the Urgency pop-up menu to specify the editorial timeliness of the photo. The High option tells editors to hold the presses and yell *Copyboy!* Low is for celebrity mug shots that can be tossed in the morgue so they're handy when the subject leads police on a nail-biting tour of Los Angeles.

Although these options are obviously geared toward news photographers, any Joe off the street can take advantage of them. It's an excellent way to keep image information right there with the file. No lost slips of paper, no jungle of yellow Post-it notes to wade through. You can view the captions on-screen by choosing File⇨File Info, or you can print them with the image by choosing File⇨Page Setup and selecting the Caption checkbox.

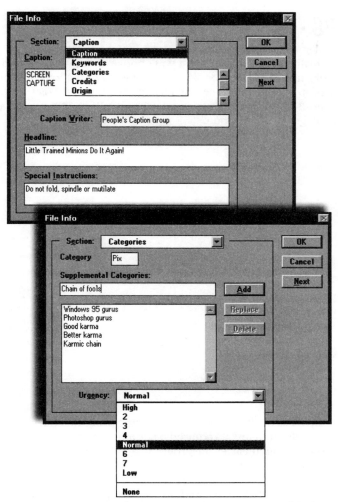

Figure 2-20: You can document your image as compulsively as you like with the panels of the File Info dialog box (panels one and three shown here)

File information is saved with an image regardless of the format you use. Photoshop merely tacks the text onto the image as a resource. Because you cannot format the text in the File Info dialog box, it consumes very little space on disk (1 byte per character), which means that all the text in Figure 2-20 doesn't even take up 1K.

And also starring . . .

 I've lapsed into television-speak for good reason. Think of your favorite show — *Melrose Place* is a big favorite in these parts, but if you choose another, I do not mind. (this is a Photoshop book, not a Premiere book!). The prime star positions are the first and the last. Photoshop and its splash screen have gotten the first position. So we've chosen the right mouse button for this second prime position. It may appear out of sequence, but it will get your attention.

Undo
Cut
Copy
Paste
Hide Brushes
Hide Picker
Hide Layers
Hide Info
Hide Commands
Fill
Feather
Inverse
File Info

Figure 2-21:
Access your Commands
palette via your right
mouse button.

Until Windows 95, we've lived in a left-button universe. Some programs did implement right-button functionality, but not many; it required a fair amount of special coding. Not so with Windows 95 — it's much easier for programmers to implement, and Microsoft has pushed its functionality vigorously.

You're probably not in the right-button habit. So for Photoshop and Windows 95, steal a line from Bill Clinton's presidential campaign: *It's the right button, stupid.* I put this on a yellow Post-it when I first started beta testing Windows 95 — I am not making this up. It's slick, Slick.

Right-click on your Photoshop desktop. You'll see a series of commands probably identical to those that appear in Figure 2-21; these are identical to the ones that appear on the Commands palette. This means you can customize ad infinitum (let us hope not ad nauseam) per the section above. As you tinker with the Commands palette, your tinkerings will appear in the right-button pop-up. Some will be grayed out — make a selection in an image and see how those grays spring to life.

We find this possibly the most useful feature of Photoshop 3.04 and higher under Windows 95. Even if you're a diehard keyboarder, give this here right-button doodad a try. You may be converted!

Image Fundamentals

How Images Work

Think of a bitmapped image as a mosaic made out of square tiles of various colors. When you view the mosaic up close, it looks like something you might use to decorate your bathroom. You see the individual tiles, not the image itself. But if you back a few feet away from the mosaic, the tiles lose their definition and merge together to create a recognizable work of art, presumably Medusa getting her head whacked off or some equally appetizing thematic classic.

Similarly, images are colored pixels pretending to be artwork. If you enlarge the pixels, they look like an unrelated collection of colored squares. Reduce the size of the pixels, and they blend together to form an image that looks for all the world like a standard photograph. Photoshop deceives the eye by borrowing from an artistic technique older than Mycenae or Pompeii.

Of course, there are differences between pixels and ancient mosaic tiles. Pixels come in 16 million distinct colors. Mosaic tiles of antiquity came in your basic granite and sandstone varieties, with an occasional chunk of lapis lazuli thrown in for good measure. Also, you can resample, color separate, and crop electronic images. We know from the time-worn scribblings of Dionysius of Halicarnassus that these processes were beyond the means of classical artisans.

But we're getting ahead of ourselves. We won't be discussing resampling, cropping, or Halicarnassus for several pages. In the meantime, we'll address the inverse relationship between image size and resolution.

Because my day job is Professor of Classics and Ancient History, I applaud Deke's bow to the classical tradition. But doing this book is a labor of love — that's not to say I don't love my ancients, but everything in its place. So don't get me started! If you must, read my articles.

Size and resolution

If you haven't already guessed, the term *image size* describes the physical dimensions of an image. *Resolution* is the number of pixels per linear inch. We say *linear* because you measure pixels in a straight line. If the resolution of an image is 72 *ppi* — that is, pixels per inch — you get 5,184 pixels per square inch (72 pixels wide × 72 pixels tall = 5,184).

Assuming that the number of pixels in an image is fixed, increasing the size of an image decreases its resolution and vice versa. Therefore, an image that looks good when printed on a postage stamp will probably look jagged if it's printed as an 11 × 17-inch poster.

Figure 3-1 shows a single image printed at three different sizes and resolutions. The smallest image is printed at twice the resolution of the medium-size image, and the medium-size image is printed at twice the resolution of the largest image. One inch in the smallest image includes twice as many pixels vertically and twice as many pixels horizontally as an inch in the medium-size image, for a total of four times as many pixels per square inch. The result is an image that covers one-fourth of the area of the medium-size image.

The same relationships exist between the medium-size image and the largest image. An inch in the medium-size image comprises four times as many pixels as an inch in the largest image. Consequently, the medium-size image consumes one-fourth of the area of the largest image.

Cross Ref The number of pixels in an image doesn't grow or shrink automatically when you save the image or print it, but you can add or subtract pixels using one of the techniques discussed in the "Resampling and Cropping Methods" section later in this chapter. However, doing so may lead to a short-term sacrifice in the appearance of the image.

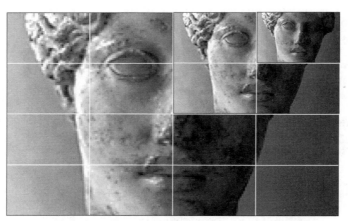

Figure 3-1: These three images contain the same number of pixels but are printed at different resolutions. Doubling the resolution of an image reduces it to 25 percent of its original size.

Printing versus screen display

You should select the resolution for an image based on what you want to do with the image. When printing an image, a higher resolution translates to a sharper image with greater clarity. If you plan to use the image in an on-screen presentation, the resolution of the image should correspond to the resolution of your monitor.

Printed resolution

When figuring the resolution of a printed image, Photoshop considers two factors:

✦ You can specify the working resolution of an image by choosing Image⇨Image Size and entering a value into the Resolution option box, either in pixels per inch or pixels per centimeter. The default resolution for a Photoshop screen image is 72 ppi. To avoid changing the number of pixels in the image, be sure that the File Size check box is selected.

✦ You can instruct Photoshop to scale an image during the print cycle by choosing File⇨Page Setup and entering a percentage value into the Reduce or Enlarge option box.

To determine the printed resolution, Photoshop divides the Resolution value by the Reduce or Enlarge percentage. For example, if the image resolution is set to 72 ppi and you reduce the image during the print cycle to 48 percent, the printed image has a resolution of 150 ppi (72 divided by .48).

Note At the risk of boring some folks, I'll briefly remind the math haters in the audience that whenever you use a percentage in an equation, you first convert it to a decimal. For example, 100 percent is 1.0, 64 percent is .64, 5 percent is .05, and so on.

Both the Resolution and Reduce or Enlarge values are saved with an image. The Resolution setting determines the size and resolution at which an image imports into object-oriented applications, most notably desktop publishing programs such as PageMaker and QuarkXPress.

Moiré patterns

For best results, the resolution of the image should jibe with the resolution of your printer, which is measured in *dots per inch* (*dpi*). For example, suppose that you are printing a 72-ppi image to a 300-dpi laser printer. Assuming that the Reduce or Enlarge option is set to 100 percent, each image pixel wants to take up $4\,^1/_6$ printer dots ($300 \div 72 = 4\,^1/_6$). By definition, a printer dot can't be divvied up into pieces, so there is no such thing as a $^1/_6$ printer dot. Each image pixel must be represented by a whole number of printer dots. But your laser printer can't simply round down every pixel in the image to four printer dots, or it would shrink the image. To maintain the size of the image, the printer assigns four dots to each of the first five pixels and five dots to the sixth. These occasionally larger pixels result in a throbbing appearance, called a *moiré pattern*. (In case you're wondering where this weird term came from, *moiré* — pronounced *moray* — is a French technique for pressing wavy patterns into fabric.)

To eliminate moiré patterns, set the resolution of the image so that it divides evenly into the printer resolution. To avoid moiré patterns in the preceding example, you could set the Resolution value to 100 ppi, which divides evenly into 300 dpi (300 ÷ 100 = 3). Alternatively, you could set the Reduce or Enlarge value to 72 percent, which would effectively change the resolution of the printed image to 100 ppi (72 ÷ .72 = 100).

Tip   Use the Resolution option to account for the final output device resolution; use the Reduce or Enlarge option to account for the proof printer resolution. For example, suppose that you want to print your final image to a 2540-dpi Linotronic 330 imagesetter and proof it to a 300-dpi Postscript laser printer. You can account for the imagesetter by setting the Resolution option to 127 ppi. However, although 127 divides evenly into 2,540 dpi, it doesn't divide evenly into 300 dpi. To fudge the difference, set the Reduce or Enlarge option to 127 percent, which changes the image resolution to 100 ppi (127 ÷ 1.27 = 100).

If you use this technique, be sure to change the Reduce or Enlarge option back to 100 percent before printing the final image to the imagesetter.

Screen resolution

Regardless of the Resolution and Reduce or Enlarge values, Photoshop displays each pixel on-screen according to the zoom ratio. (The zoom ratio, displayed in the title bar, is discussed in Chapter 2.) If the zoom ratio is 1:1, for example, each image pixel takes up a single screen pixel. Zoom ratio and printer output are unrelated.

When creating an image for a screen presentation or display, you want the image size to fill every inch of the prospective monitor at a 1:1 zoom ratio. We say *prospective* monitor because although you may use a 15-inch monitor when you create the image, you may want to display the final image on a 21-inch monitor. And herein lies a tale. Several tales in fact. So conjure up a Robert icon over the remainder of this section, gather, and surmise.

Robert   An image of, say, 640 × 480 pixels is absolute in size, regardless of where you display it. Take that as our starting point. The amount of screen real estate it consumes is a function of what your video driver is doing. That is, if your driver is set to 640 × 480, that image will take up the entire screen, regardless of monitor size. Of course, it will look bigger on the 21-inch monitor than on the 15-inch monitor, but that's because 21 inches is bigger than 15 inches. But suppose your driver is set to 1024 × 768. The 640 × 480 image will take up a much smaller portion of the screen, regardless of monitor size. In this case, it will still look pretty big on the 21-inch monitor, but will start looking rather small on the 14-inch monitor. If you want to compare total number of pixels, you may get a better feel for it: 640 × 480 has 307,200 pixels, and 1024 × 768 has 786,432 pixels. A higher-resolution video driver will display smaller images in their entirety, but a lower-resolution video driver will only display part of a larger image. Put differently and practically, you now see why graphics people use at least a 17-inch monitor with 1024 × 768 video drivers. You can see all of those pixels easily. You can run a 1024 × 768 driver on a 14-inch monitor, but you'll probably be ready for a trip to the ophthalmologist.

But a picture is worth a thousand words — actually, the preceding paragraph has 255 words, but you get the point of that bromide. So I've made it all graphical for you in Figure 3-2. It shows a full screen capture of my Windows 95 screen running 1024 × 768 video drivers. Notice how each smaller resolution (800 × 600, 640 × 480) fills less of the screen. And you can imaginatively reverse this. If you're using a 640 × 480 video driver, imagine the lighter central rectangle filling your entire screen (it will!). And thus you can see how much of the larger sizes will run off the screen (or, in Photoshop, give you scroll bars if you're viewing in 1:1 mode). By the way, don't try to read the various icon titles and other doodads on my screen — this figure is to illustrate image sizes. Remember the ophthalmological warning of the last paragraph!

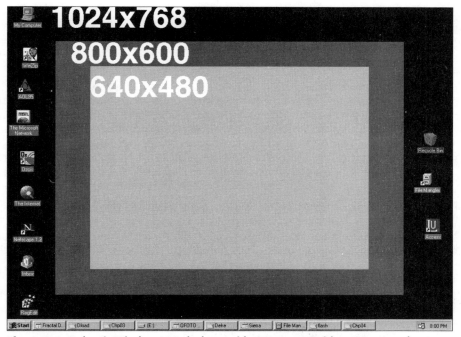

Figure 3-2: Robert's Windows 95 desktop with 1024 × 768 video. Compare the screen real estate of the other sizes — this remains constant regardless of monitor size.

Obviously all this has significant effect on your working conditions too. The very best information on how to fine-tune the size of what appears on your screen, along with many helpful down-and-dirty details, appears in another IDG Books Worldwide offering (surprise!): Brian Livingston and Davis Straub, *Windows 95 SECRETS*, on pp. 536–545. But you should have acquired a copy by now. In fact, you should have done so even before buying this here wonderful Photoshop book — and that's our highest praise.

How to Open, Duplicate, and Save Images

Before you can work on an image in Photoshop — whether you're creating a brand new document or opening an image from disk — you must first load the image into an image window. Here are the four basic ways to create an image window:

✦ **File⇨New:** Create a new window by choosing FileÍNew (Ctrl-N). After you fill out the desired size and resolution specifications in the New dialog box, Photoshop confronts you with a stark, white, empty canvas. You then face the ultimate test of your artistic capabilities — painting from scratch. Feel free to go nuts and cut off your ear.

✦ **File⇨Open:** Open an image saved to disk or CD-ROM by choosing File⇨Open (Ctrl-O). Of the four ways to create an image window, you most likely will use this method most frequently. You can open images scanned in other applications, images purchased from stock photo agencies, slides and transparencies digitized to a Kodak Photo CD, or images you previously edited in Photoshop.

✦ **Edit⇨Paste:** Photoshop automatically adapts a new image window to the contents of the Clipboard (provided those contents are bitmapped). So if you copy an image inside a different application or in Photoshop and then choose File⇨New, Photoshop enters the dimensions and resolution of the image into the New dialog box. All you have to do is accept the settings and choose Edit⇨Paste (Ctrl-V) to introduce the image into a new window. This technique is useful for editing screen shots captured to the Clipboard and for testing out filtering effects on a sample of an image without harming the original.

Robert For PC users, doing screen captures is just a tad trickier. You do an Alt-Print Screen. Fire up Photoshop and paste it in. No problem. Then you switch to where you're taking screen captures and do another. Back to Photoshop — but you don't get this new capture. You get the old one — even though the Clipboard Viewer confirms that you've got the new one. Is it hair-pulling time? Nah. There are three workarounds. The first is to minimize Photoshop each time you leave it to grab another screen. Then restore and paste. The second involves adding a line to `PHOTOS30.INI`: `ALWAYSIMPORTCLIP=1` (the default is 0). The third is to utilize an add-on that lets you capture multiple Clipboard images — remember, natively the Clipboard will replace whatever is on it with your latest capture.

I heartily recommend the shareware program Clipmate, widely available online and on the CD-ROM that comes with IDG's *Windows 95 Secrets*. This "feature" appears to be unique to Photoshop; other programs can bring in multiple screen captures without a tweak. But you wouldn't want to use other programs, would you?

✦ **Scanning:** If you own a scanner, chances are it's a TWAIN-compliant model. Install the TWAIN module in accordance with the manufacturer's instructions. This will let you scan directly into Photoshop — or, for that matter, into any TWAIN-enabled application (most are). To initiate a scan, choose the scanner driver from the File⇨Acquire⇨Select TWAIN Source and select for your scanner from the resultant dialog box. If you have one scanner and one scanner driver, you won't have to do this again. Even so, you may have to choose between TWAIN, TWAIN32, or TWAIN_32. If you're using a real mode (16-bit) scanner driver, the first option applies to you. But if you're using a protected mode driver, whether 16 or 32 bit, it gets tricky. In Photoshop 3.04 you'll have the first two choices, while 3.05 gives you the first and third (the plug-in for the second choice is on Adobe's CD-ROM, but you'll have to install it manually — only do this if you have a specific need to). Or you will have all three choices, a veritable Trinity Of TWAIN, if you've downloaded the TWAIN_32.8ba module from Adobe and stuck it into 3.04. At any event, once you've selected your source, Photo-shop will remember your selection. You then do File⇨Acquire⇨Scan, using the same TWAIN name you just used when selecting. See the note that follows and Appendix A for more on this apparent profusion of confusion, which Figure 3-3 illustrates. Your TWAIN module will appear, you scan, and then the image appears in a new image window.

Figure 3-3: A double Trinity of TWAIN! Note the three choices each for source and scanning.

Of course, there are snakes in this scanning Garden of Eden. Until Windows 95, most TWAIN modules have been 16 bit, which means they won't work in a 32-bit application like Photoshop. With 3.04, Adobe introduced a thunking layer to work around this, while 3.05 introduces the still-more-improved work-around of a *universal thunker*. Ultimately, the scanner makers will need to produce true 32-bit TWAIN modules, but this may take time. In the interim, check online and read the further details (not always gory) in the Appendixes here.

— Robert

Useful as the TWAIN standard is, I think there's a better way to scan. Get Ofoto 2 from Lightsource. It's a stand-alone program that gives you an extraordinary amount of control over your scans — far more, in fact, than even the best TWAIN modules. It has automatic moiré removal and any number of high-end features. True, you have to either Clipboard your image or else save and open in Photoshop. True, it's a 16-bit application. True, it doesn't support every scanner on the market, because it's not TWAIN. But any number of professional illustrators use it exclusively — and I found that the quality of my scans improved by a quantum factor over the most relentless tweaking of my TWAIN module. See Appendix A and give it your serious consideration.

— Robert

Creating a new image

Whether you are creating an image from scratch or transferring the contents of the Clipboard to a new image window, choose File⇨New or press Ctrl-N to bring up the New dialog box shown in Figure 3-4. If the Clipboard contains an image, the Width, Height, and Resolution option boxes show the size and resolution of that image. Otherwise, you can enter your own values in one of five units of measurement: pixels, inches, centimeters, picas, or points. (A pica, incidentally, is equal to roughly ¹/₆ inch, and a *point* is ¹/₁₂ pica, or roughly ¹/₇₂ inch.) If you're not sure exactly what size image you want to create, enter a rough approximation. You can always change your settings later.

Background By default, Photoshop assigns *exactly* 72 points per inch and 6 picas per inch (which works out to be 1 point per screen pixel). Before the advent of computers, however, picas and points represented their own distinct measurement system. Although there are exactly 12 points in a pica, 1 inch really equals about 72.27 points, or 6.02 picas. If you prefer to use the traditional system — as when pasting up a page with an X-Acto knife and hot wax — choose File⇨Preferences⇨Units and select the Traditional (72.27 points/inch) radio button.

Tip You can change the default unit of measure that appears in the Width and Height pop-up menus by choosing File⇨Preferences⇨Units and selecting a different option from the Ruler Units pop-up menu. You can also change the unit of measure by selecting Palette Options from the Info palette pop-up menu.

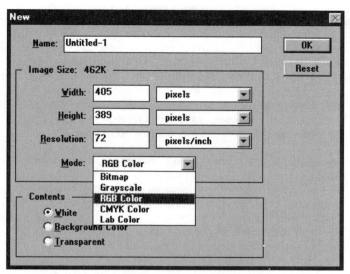

Figure 3-4: Use the New dialog box to specify the size, resolution, and color mode of your new image.

Column width

A sixth unit of measure, Column, is available from the Width pop-up menu. If you want to create an image that fits exactly within a certain number of columns when it's imported into a desktop publishing program, select the Column option. You can specify the width of a column and the gutter between columns by choosing File➪Preferences➪Units and entering values into the Column Size option boxes.

The Gutter value affects multiple-column images. Suppose that you accept the default setting of a 15-pica column width and a 1-pica gutter. If you specify a one-column image in the New dialog box, Photoshop makes it 15 picas wide. If you ask for a two-column image, Photoshop adds the width of the gutter to the width of the two columns and creates an image 31 picas wide.

The Height pop-up menu in the New dialog box doesn't include a Column option because vertical columns have nothing to do with an image's height.

On-screen image size

In most cases, the on-screen dimensions of an image depend on your entries in the Width, Height, and Resolution option boxes. If you set both the Width and Height values to 10 inches and the Resolution to 72 ppi, the new image will measure 720 × 720 pixels. The exception occurs if you choose pixels as your unit of measurement, as in Figure 3-4. In that case, the on-screen dimensions depend solely on the Width and Height options, and the Resolution value determines the size at which the image prints.

Color mode and background

Use the Mode pop-up menu to specify the number of colors that can appear in your image. Choose Bitmap to create a black-and-white image and choose Grayscale to access only gray values. RGB Color, CMYK Color, and Lab Color all provide access to the full range of 16 million colors, although their methods of doing so differ.

Cross Ref — RGB stands for red-green-blue; CMYK for cyan-magenta-yellow-black; and Lab for luminosity and two abstract color variables, a and b. To learn how each of these color modes works, read the "Working in Different Color Modes" section of Chapter 4.

In Photoshop 3, the New dialog box provides three Contents radio buttons that let you change the color of the background for the new image. You can fill the new image with white, with the current background color (assuming, of course, that the background color is something other than white), or with no color at all. This last setting, Transparent, results in a floating layer with no background image whatsoever, which can be useful when editing one layer independently of the rest of an image or when preparing a layer to be composited with an image. (For an in-depth examination of the more nitty-gritty aspects of layering, see Chapter 17.) White is the default setting.

If you do select a transparent background, you won't be able to save the image in any format other than Photoshop 3, because only the Photoshop 3 format is capable of saving layers. If you want to save the image in some other format, you'll have to make the image opaque by choosing the Flatten Image option from the Layers palette pop-up menu. (To display the Layers palette, choose Window⇨Palettes⇨Show Layers.) Or choose File⇨Save a Copy to save a flattened copy of the image to disk.

Just in case you're thinking, *Cool, Photoshop supports transparent backgrounds. Now I can import images into QuarkXPress and see text and other page elements behind them,* the answer is, *Sorry, Contestant Number Four, but that conclusion is false.* You can only make a color transparent if the image is black and white — or, more correctly, black and transparent — and you save the image in the EPS format (as we'll discuss in the section "Saving an EPS document" later in this chapter). Otherwise, you have to create a stencil for the image using Photoshop's clipping path function, as explained in the "Retaining transparent areas in an image" section of Chapter 8.

Naming the new image

The New dialog box now provides a Name option. If you know what you want to call your new image, enter the name now. Or don't. It doesn't matter. Either way, when you choose File⇨Save, Photoshop asks you to specify the location of the file and confirm the file's name. So don't feel compelled to name your image anything initially.

R %%% Robert — You may be tempted to go hog-wild with LFNs (long file names), which Windows 95 and Photoshop now allow — after all, *the Mac has had this for years.* Be careful! While it is more descriptive to name something My Dinner with Robert rather than ROBFEED.PSD, there's a gotcha. If you're sending your file to a service bureau that doesn't have Windows 95, it won't have any problem reading the resultant 8+3 file name; in the example just given, My Dinner with Robert becomes MYDINN~1.PSD. But supposing you make some changes to your file and so does your service bureau. If your service bureau changes the file name, it will come back in as, say MYDINN~2.PSD and that's what you'll see. But if it didn't rename the short file name, even though it worked on MYDINN~1.PSD and you sent it My Dinner with Robert — what it sends back to you (the former) will overwrite what you originally sent (the latter).

Robert

Maybe you don't like the way the title got truncated when it went to 8+3. There's a way to change Windows 95 to use "user-friendly" 8+3 file names. I'm not going to tell you how to do it, or where to find it, for a benevolent (that is, nonauthoritarian) reason: It's dangerous. It can play havoc with installing various Windows 95 applications; some won't install, or some will install with, er, regrettable results. For safety's sake, just let Windows 95 do its thing when creating 8+3 file names — of course, you're allowed to groan and wonder what the Kids in Redmond were up to.

Cross Ref

Editing the Registry is not something you should do lightly, or even at all. There are many "tips" circulating on how to do it. Some seem to work. But no one knows enough about the possible side effects — at least yet. See Appendix B for further cautions.

Opening an existing image

If you want to open an image stored on disk, choose File┃Open or press Ctrl-O to display the Open dialog. The scrolling list contains the names of documents Photoshop recognizes that it can open. If you cannot find a desired document, try typing *.* followed by an Enter. If you're lucky, you'll see something that makes sense, along with a file extension that probably makes no sense — or there may not be an extension at all. The lack of an extension typically arises in either of two ways. Sometimes files transmitted electronically (via CompuServe, for example) lose their extensions en route. This can be compounded if the person sending you the file uses a Mac. The Macintosh doesn't use file extensions; the file type information is saved internally. That is, your Mac friend may have produced a PSD file and named it Deke's Unmentionable File. On the Mac side, there's no problem with Photoshop opening it. But just try it on the PC — even though you and your friend swear it's a PSD file, Photoshop won't touch it with a ten-foot pole (Note: Most Eastern Europeans are not that tall). Solution? Rename it Deke's Unmentionable File.PSD and all will be well.

But, you say, *I don't see file extensions when I go trolling in the Windows 95 Explorer.* The reason you don't see them is because you've probably got the option selected that hides the extensions of registered file types. Uncheck the option and there your extensions will be. Even with LFNs. Need more convincing? Save a file with an LFN in Photoshop. Then go into Explorer, or try opening it again in Photoshop. Yup, you guessed it — there's the extension.

But what if you don't know the type of file you're getting? There are two solutions. You can try opening it in a viewer that does a text/binary dump (such as QuickView, which comes with Windows 95, or Windows Write, which came with Windows 3.1 and which Robert keeps around for precisely these purposes). In some instances, at the top of the file you'll be able to see the magic letters like BMP or JPEG — you're set. If you don't see that, or don't have the option of viewing that way, it's a matter of renaming, cycling through the various file extensions, and praying you hit one right.

Duplicating an image

Have you ever wanted to try out an effect without permanently damaging an image? Certainly, you can undo the last action performed in Photoshop (by choosing Edit⇨Undo), but what if the technique involves multiple steps? And what if you want to apply two or more effects to an image independently and compare them side by side? And later maybe even merge them? This is a job for image duplication.

Lots of new users think that Window⇨New Window will satisfy this need. But as we discussed in Chapter 2, the New Window command simply creates another view of the same image. It's great for monitoring an effect in two different zoom ratios or two different color modes or whatever, but the two images you see on-screen are not independent.

To create a new window with an independent version of the foreground image, choose Image⇨Duplicate. A dialog box appears requesting a name for the new image. Just like the Name option in the New dialog box, the option is purely an organizational tool that you can use or ignore. If your image contains multiple layers, Photoshop will, by default, retain all layers in the duplicate document. Alternatively, you can merge all visible layers into a single layer by selecting the Merged Layers Only check box. (Hidden layers remain independent.) Press Return to create your new, independent image. (This image is unsaved; you need to choose File⇨Save to save any changes to disk.)

If you're happy to let Photoshop automatically name your image and you don't care what it does with the layers, press the Alt key while choosing Image⇨Duplicate to bypass the Duplicate Image dialog box and immediately create a new window.

Saving an image to disk

The first rule of storing an image on disk is to save it frequently. If the foreground image is untitled, as it is when you work on a new image, choosing File⇨Save displays the Save dialog box, enabling you to name the image, specify its location on disk, and select a file format. After you save the image once, choosing the Save command updates the file on disk without bringing up the Save dialog box.

Choose File➪Save As to change the name, location, or format of the image stored on disk. By the way, if your only reason for choosing the Save As command is to change the file format, it's perfectly acceptable to overwrite (save over) the original document, assuming that you no longer need that copy of the image. Granted, your computer could crash during the Save As operation, in which case you would lose both the new document and the original. But crashing during the Save As operation is extremely unlikely and no more likely than crashing during any other save operation.

Robert

This gets us right to the edge of plunging into the file formats. So it's the right time for Robert's Most Important Tip For Chapter 3. Unfortunately, IDG Books will only allow me one type of Robert Icon, and if it gave me two, Deke might get cranky (not that he needs additional reasons). So think screaming red (RGB 255, 0, 0) for what I'm about to tell you.

First, even if you're absolutely positive that you'll be needing your image in, say, JPEG or GIF format, don't save to that other format initially. Always save your working image to the native Photoshop format (discussion coming up Real Soon Now); when you're done, it's time enough to take it out to the other format. This is for your safety (and sanity). JPEG is a compressed image format, and even with Excellent for image quality (see the discussion of the format further below) you lose some data. Data losses can add up. GIF is a 256-color (Indexed color) format (also later in the chapter). Suppose you need to do a major reworking of your image. You'll have been saving with a limited 256-color palette and various palette options, and things may go crazy when you try to work on it. To repeat: Finish your work and save in native PSD format; then, and only then, take it out to your format of choice.

Second, what if you find that when you try to produce your image as a JPEG or GIF, Photoshop won't let you — you only get PSD as the possible format? Essentially, this means that your PSD file has more native Photoshop features than either of those formats can support. See below under those formats for details (this note is getting way too long anyhow).

Image File Formats

Photoshop 3 supports an impressive variety of file formats from inside its Open and Save dialog boxes. It can support even more through the addition of plug-in modules, which attach commands to the File➪Acquire and File➪Export submenus. Typically this capacity has been more utilized on the Mac side, but Adobe released its GIF 89a export plug-in even before Photoshop 3.05 began to ship.

File formats represent different ways to save a file to disk. Some formats provide unique *image compression schemes,* which save an image in a manner that consumes less space on disk. Other formats enable Photoshop to trade images with different applications both on the PC and on other platforms.

Native formats

Photoshop 3.0 supports two *native formats* (that is, formats that are optimized for Photoshop's particular capabilities and functions), one for Version 2.5 and one for Version 3. But you'll only see one .PSD choice when you save. This format is compatible with Photoshop 2.5 *if* the 2.5 Format Compatibility check box is selected inside the More Preferences dialog box (which you reach by pressing Ctrl-K and then clicking on the More button). If this check box is turned off, Photoshop 2.5 will *not* be able to open an image saved in Photoshop 3 format.

Robert   Which to do? It's a judgment call. You save space with 2.5 Format Compatibility turned off. But in these early days of Windows 95, it's worth keeping it on (besides, hard drives are dirt cheap right now). Obviously, you'll keep it on if you're sending files to someone who has Photoshop 2.5 — such people do exist, because not everyone buys into the *latest is greatest* upgrade mantra (although with Adobe Photoshop upgrades, it's a mantra worth chanting). Second, not all of the kinks have been worked out of scanning and third-party filters; in a pinch, I find it comforting to know I can go into 2.5 and do those operations.

Adobe has specifically optimized the Photoshop 3 format to retain every smidgen of data, including additional masking channels and a few other elements that may be lost when saving to other formats. It's also worth noting that Photoshop can open and save in its native format more quickly than in any other format. The Photoshop 3 format offers a compression option missing from the earlier format. The compression does *not* result in any loss of data.

Robert   Furthermore, the Photoshop 3 format moves easily between the PC and the Mac. I do it all the time.

Your workhorse formats

These are the formats in widest use with the most applications. You may, of course, be busily exchanging images with someone operating on a Unix workstation, in which case the RAW format, described further below, is *your* workhorse format. So the characterization is a judgment call — what most Photoshop users will be using most of the time. A judgment call, but not judgmental.

Windows BMP

BMP (*Windows Bitmap*) arose as the native format for Microsoft Windows system graphics and for Microsoft Paint (Windows 1.*x*, 2.*x*), its successor, Paintbrush (Windows 3.*x*), and its Windows 95 successor, Paint. There is also an OS/2 flavor; Photoshop supports both with up to 16 million colors. Typically, you'll only want the OS/2 variety for very specialized programming uses (obviously!). A variety of Windows system resources use BMP files, and enough people compile their own help files, so we've added a tip at the end of this section. But if you're not of the programming persuasion, your most common use of BMP will be for wallpaper.

In fact, rolling your own wallpaper is an excellent way to get to know Photoshop — it's what I did. Just remember that if you're trading wallpaper with friends, you may want to save in indexed color format; a high-color wallpaper displayed in 256-color video looks, well, excruciating. See Chapter 4 for further details on Photoshop's several indexed color schemes and Figure 3-5.

There is also the option of RLE (*Run-Length Encoding*), a lossless compression scheme specifically applicable to the BMP format. Windows can use RLE for wallpaper, but you have to direct it to a specific file (unlike with BMP files, which it automatically recognizes) unless you're using a third-party wallpaper management utility (if you're a wallpaper fanatic, you probably do that already).

The term *lossless* refers to compression schemes such as BMP's RLE and TIFF's LZW (*Lempel-Ziv-Welch*) that enable you to save space on disk without sacrificing any data in the image. The only reasons *not* to use lossless compression are that it slows down the open and save operations and it may prevent less-sophisticated applications from opening an image. *Lossy* compression routines, such as JPEG, sacrifice a user-defined amount of data to conserve even more disk space.

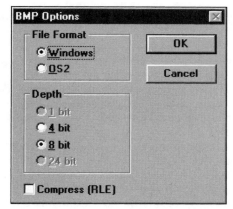

Figure 3-5: When saving a file as a BMP, you have several format and color depth options.

Because BMP is also the native Windows resource format, you may run into a problem if you're trying to take a 16-color BMP file into a Help file. Typically the compiler will complain and, sometimes, crash. This is a problem with Photoshop and BMP (and also PCX). Photoshop seems able to do the required 4-bit (16-color) index color. But looks are deceiving! If you look at the color table you will see that in reality, it's a 256-color table. The 16 colors are there, and all the rest are black. Photoshop has fibbed to you just a bit. There's no work-around other than to take the file into a program, such as MS Paint, that can save a true 4-bit index color file.

CompuServe's GIF

Originally, CompuServe designed GIF (Graphics Interchange Format) as a means of compressing 8-bit images so that users could transfer photographs via modem to and from the company's commercial bulletin board service more quickly. There has been much brouhaha recently involving the algorithm (which CompuServe obtained elsewhere), attendant licensing fees, and even talk about replacing the GIF standard altogether, much as ZIP replaced ARC for compressed files. But as things stand right now, GIF is around and thriving; license fees don't involve you as the end user.

Like TIFF, GIF uses LZW compression, but unlike TIFF, GIF can't handle more than 256 colors. Remember that fact when you're working in Photoshop to produce what will ultimately become a GIF. Do all of your work in RGB mode, and save in the native PSD format, for all the reasons I've enumerated above. When you're ready to go GIF, set Mode to Indexed Color. Then you can either save as a regular GIF (87a) or as a transparent, interlaced GIF for Web uses (89a). If you don't change to Indexed Color at the end, you'll never be able to produce a GIF.

You can use either GIF 87a or GIF 89a. Use the former for doing a picture that doesn't have a colored background you want transparent, or when you don't need interlacing — that is, for non-Web uses. Of course you can use the GIF 87a format on the Web, but you may care about interlacing and transparency, for which you'll want the GIF 89a format.

Interlacing means the GIF will start displaying as soon as the host computer begins sending it to your Web browser. First you'll see some fuzzies, then more detail and finally the entire picture. Thus your browser isn't tied up waiting for the entire GIF to transmit before it lets you look at the text on the page — you can start reading (assuming, of course, that everyone on the Internet reads — we have our doubts) while the interlaced GIF is coming in. For big GIF files this can make a substantial difference. Of course, many people, your authors included, don't think you should force a big graphics file on someone initially — after all, not everyone has an ISDN line, or even a 28.8 modem. Still, there are some souls out there who feel they must show you a 560K GIF of Aunt Hilda's birthday party as soon as you hit their home page, and nuts to you if you don't have a speedy connection. An interlaced GIF can take a lot of the sting out of this. Of course, you can simply turn off the graphics display in your browser. Thoughtful Web content providers use small (under 50K) GIFs, where interlacing makes less of a speed difference.

Transparent means that, say, if you've got a logo on a white background, it will display on any Web browser as if the logo is seamlessly integrated into the default Web background gray (RGB 192, 192, 192, incidentally). No white showing! The same should hold true if you've changed the default background color of your Web browser, or if the content provider has hardwired a background color into the page at his or her end. We say *should* advisedly; for reasons that are still being debated, the Netscape browser will sometimes do some ghostly dithering where the transparency ought to be. It doesn't happen on the other browsers, and there are times when it doesn't happen with Netscape. The latest information is that it's an interaction of video drivers and Netscape's dithering scheme. So don't let this make you crazy if you're testing your own Web pages in Netscape. Figure 3-6 shows you the difference between a nontransparent GIF 87 (left) and a transparent GIF 89 (right).

You'll notice I've stuck Deke with the lack of transparency — think of it as my Ultimate Revenge (There could be a movie here: *The Revenge of the Windowizer*. I wonder if Ward Bond is available?) for those nasty things he once wrote about GIFs.

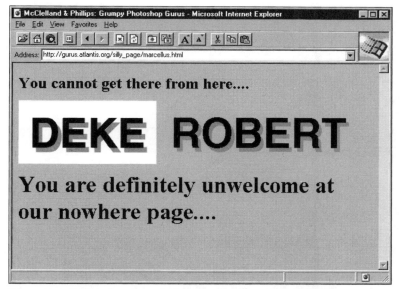

Figure 3-6: Which do you prefer? Nontransparent Deke (left) or transparent Robert (right)?

Of course, you might think to avoid all that by just setting your GIF background to the aforementioned Web gray. That's fine as long as your audience keeps their browsers set to gray. If they change to a colored background, your gray shows up. Or if you change your background color, your gray shows up. In short, do transparency if you have logos and doodads (balls and lines seem to be current favorites) that you want to have just sit on the background seamlessly.

Putting this into practical terms. If you're just showing a regular picture, save as a regular GIF 87a. If you're thoughtful, should this GIF be of any size, you'll put it on another page and link to it so people aren't forced to see Aunt Hilda. If you're really thoughtful, you'll interlace it (GIF 89a coming right up). And if you're infesting your page with balls and lines, you'll want both to interlace them and to make them transparent (GIF 89a).

Inside Photoshop 3.05, under File⇨Export, you'll find the module for GIF 89a; if you're using 3.04, you can download the module from Adobe and place it in your plug-ins directory. Invoking that module provides the dialogue box shown in Figure 3-7. Adobe's documentation is excellent and dense, so there are no particular additions to make — except for one. The module gives you a remarkable range of options, more than any other program I've seen. The price is the time and the learning curve. For just balls and lines, it's overkill. Get a shareware program like LViewPro or PaintShop Pro — you can whiz-bang things in one minute, tops. Save the Adobe module for when you want to take advantage of some of its subtle special capabilities.

Figure 3-7: New for Photoshop 3.05: the GIF 89a export module.

Robert

In *Macworld Photoshop 3 Bible*, Deke observed that "…the lion's share of the world's GIF images are pornographic. (In fact, I often wonder how many folks never venture beyond using Photoshop and other image editors to view naked women.)" In the couple of years since Deke penned that, times have changed; in particular, the explosive growth of the World Wide Web on the Internet has produced a boom for the format, because GIFs remain the most versatile and easily displayed graphics formats on Web pages. I've talked with Deke about this and he's recanted his views.

Still, with the straw man set up, it would be a pity not to pummel him a bit. We actually have trolled around on the Internet in places where those, er, *art* images reside — the places from which our duly elected members of Congress would like to protect us all. We did not inhale, but we did notice the file formats being used. There are GIFs, but even the prurience pushers have seen the virtues of JPEG images, which seemed a clear majority in my mercifully brief visits. But let's not talk prurience — the night belongs to Photoshop (with a "Robert" icon hanging heavily over this entire section).

JPEG

Photoshop supports the JPEG format, named after the folks who designed it, the Joint Photographic Experts Group. JPEG is the most efficient and essential compression format currently available and is likely to be the compression standard for years to come. It is a *lossy* compression scheme, which means that it sacrifices image quality to conserve space on disk. However, you can control how much data is lost during the save operation.

When you save an image in the JPEG format, Photoshop displays the dialog box in Figure 3-8, which offers a scant four compression settings. Just select a radio button to specify the quality setting. The Low option takes up the least space on disk but distorts the image rather severely; Maximum retains the highest amount of image quality but consumes more disk space.

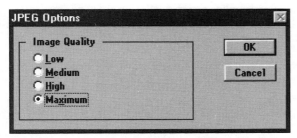

Figure 3-8: The new JPEG Options dialog box provides four compression settings, ranging from Low image quality (excellent compression) to Maximum image quality (fair compression).

JPEG evaluates an image in 8×8-pixel blocks, using a technique called Adaptive Discrete Cosine Transform (or ADCT, as in *Yes, I'm an acronym ADCT*). It averages the 24-bit value of every pixel in the block (or 8-bit value of every pixel in the case of a grayscale image). It then stores the average color in the upper left pixel in the block and assigns the remaining 63 pixels smaller values relative to the average.

Next, JPEG divides the block by an 8×8 block of its own called the *quantization matrix,* which homogenizes the pixels' values by changing as many as possible to zero. It's this process that saves the majority of disk space and loses data. When Photoshop opens a JPEG image, it can't recover the original distinction between the zero pixels, so the pixels become the same or similar colors. Finally, JPEG applies lossless Huffman encoding to translate repeating values to a single symbol.

In most instances, we recommend that you use JPEG only at the Maximum quality setting, at least until you gain some experience with it. The smallest amount of JPEG compression saves more space on disk than any non-JPEG compression format and still retains nearly every bit of detail from the original image. Figure 3-9 shows a grayscale image saved at each of the four compression settings.

The samples are arranged in rows from highest image quality (upper left) to lowest quality (lower right). Below each sample is the size of the compressed document on disk. Saved in the only moderately compressed Photoshop 3 format, the image consumes 116K on disk. From 116K to 28K — the result of the lowest-quality JPEG setting — is a remarkable savings, but it comes at a price.

We've taken the liberty of sharpening the focus of strips in each image so that you can see more easily how JPEG averages neighboring pixels to achieve smaller file sizes. The first strip in each image appears in normal focus, the second strip is sharpened once by choosing Filter⇨Sharpen⇨Sharpen More, and the third strip is sharpened twice. We've also adjusted the gray levels to make the differences even more pronounced. You can see that although the lower image quality setting leads to a dramatic saving in file size, it also gums up the image excessively. The effect, incidentally, is more obvious on-screen. After you familiarize yourself with JPEG compression, you'll be able to spot other people's overly compressed JPEG images a mile away. It's not something that you want to exaggerate in your images.

To see the impact of JPEG compression on a full-color image, check out Color Plate 3-1. The original image consumes 693K in the Photoshop 3 format, but 116K when compressed at the JPEG module's Maximum setting. To better demonstrate the differences between different settings, we enlarged one portion of the image and oversharpened another.

Maximum   66K   High   50K

Medium   33K   Low   28K

Figure 3-9: The four JPEG settings from the preceding figure applied to a single image, with the highest image quality setting illustrated at the upper left and the lowest at bottom right.

JPEG is a *cumulative compression scheme,* meaning that Photoshop recompresses an image every time you save it in the JPEG format. There's no disadvantage to repeatedly saving an image to disk during a single session, because JPEG always works from the on-screen version. But if you close an image, reopen it, and save it in the JPEG format, you inflict a small amount of damage. Therefore, use JPEG sparingly. In the best of all possible worlds, you should only save to the JPEG format after you finish *all* work on an image. Even in a pinch, you should apply all filtering effects before saving to JPEG, because these have a habit of exacerbating imperfections in image quality.

JPEG is best used when compressing *continuous-tone* images (images in which the distinction between immediately neighboring pixels is slight). Any image that includes gradual color transitions, as in a photograph, qualifies for JPEG compression. JPEG is not the best choice for saving screen shots, line drawings (especially those converted from Illustrator EPS graphics), and other high-contrast images. Those are better served by a lossless compression scheme such as TIFF with LZW. The JPEG format is available when you are saving grayscale, RGB, and CMYK images.

Robert

Let me put that another way. If you've been working on an Indexed Color image, you can't even try to save it as JPEG — the option simply won't appear in the File⇨ Save list box. Same thing if you've got layers. In either case, save to native .PSD format. Then, as needed, change to one of the supported color modes and/or use the menu on the Layers palette to flatten the layers.

Still can't save (or open)? Did you install Photoshop 3 into the same directory as Photoshop 2.5? That's a bad move in general unless the vendor has specifically told you to. Look in the plug-ins subdirectory. Get rid of anything there with a JPEG in the file name (as many as two, in fact). That may get you going. But if this is the case, we strongly urge you to delete the entire directory and install Photoshop 3 from scratch at the EOM (Earliest Opportune Moment).

If you're using Photoshop 2.5 under Windows 3.1, your Windows permanent swapfile must be set to at least 8MB. Any less and JPEG isn't an option. This may seem a bit of gratuitous arcana in this latest-and-greatest digital world. But not everyone rushes to upgrade — and if these couple of lines can help someone, they're worth it.

PCX

PCX doesn't stand for anything. Rather, it's the extension that Windows Paint assigns to images saved in its native file format. By all accounts, PCX is one of the most popular image file formats in use today, largely due to the fact that PC Paintbrush is the oldest painting program for DOS. Photoshop supports PCX images with up to 16 million colors. Z-Soft, inventor of the DOS-based Publisher's Paintbrush program, invented the format, and Microsoft licensed part of the program for inclusion in Windows. This means that there's an enormous amount of art, usually clip art, around in this format. But there's no good reason to save files to this format unless a client specifically demands PCX files. Other formats are better.

Photo CD PCD images

Photoshop can open Eastman Kodak's Photo CD and Pro Photo CD formats directly. A Photo CD contains compressed versions of every image in each of the five scan sizes provided on Photo CDs — from 128 × 192 pixels (72K) to 2,048 × 3,072 pixels (18MB). The Photo CD format uses the YCC color model, a variation on the CIE (Commission Internationale de l'Eclairage) color space discussed in the next chapter. YCC provides a broader range of color — theoretically, every color your eye can see.

The Pro Photo CD format can accommodate each of the five sizes included in the regular Photo CD format, plus one additional size — 4,096 × 6,144 pixels (72MB) — that's four times the size of the largest image on a regular Photo CD. As a result, Pro

Photo CDs hold only 25 scans; standard Photo CDs hold 100. Like their standard Photo CD counterparts, Pro Photo CD scanners can accommodate 35mm film and slides. But they can also handle 70mm film and 4×5-inch negatives and transparencies. The cost might knock you out, though. While scanning an image to a standard Photo CD costs about $1, scanning it to a Pro Photo CD costs about $9. It just goes to show you; once you gravitate beyond consumerland, everybody expects you to start coughing up the big bucks.

By opening Photo CD files directly, you can translate the YCC images directly to Photoshop's Lab color mode, another variation on CIE color space that ensures no color loss. The Photo CD files are found inside the Images directory on the Photo CD, as shown in Figure 3-10.

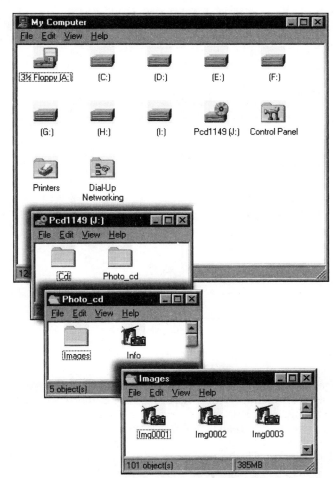

Figure 3-10: Navigating the folders from the CD-ROM (top) to where the PCD images live (bottom).

Photoshop 3.0 includes the new Kodak Color Management Software (CMS), which tweaks colors in Photo CD images based on the kind of film they were scanned from. When you open a Photo CD image, Photoshop displays the dialog box shown in Figure 3-11. Here you can specify the image size you want to open by selecting an option from the Resolution pop-up menu. The dialog box even shows you a preview of the image. But the options that make a difference are the Source and Destination buttons:

✦ **Source:** Click on this button to specify the kind of film from which the original photographs were scanned. You can select from two specific Kodak brands — Ektachrome and Kodachrome — or settle for the generic Color Negative Film option. Your selection determines the method by which Photoshop transforms the colors in the image.

✦ **Destination:** After clicking on this button, select an option from the Device pop-up menu to specify the color model you want to use. Select Adobe Photoshop RGB to open the image in the RGB mode; select Adobe Photoshop CIELAB to open the image in the Lab mode. (A CMYK profile can be purchased separately from Kodak.)

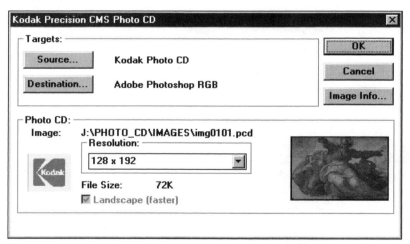

Figure 3-11: Use these options to select a resolution and calibrate the colors in the Photo CD image.

To access Photo CD images, you need a single-session or multisession CD-ROM device and drivers that support it; see Appendix A for further details. For more information on the relationship between YCC, Lab, RGB, and every other color mode you ever thought you might want to learn about, read Chapter 4, "Defining Colors."

Photoshop cannot save to the Photo CD format. So far, Kodak hasn't licensed other vendors to write images using its proprietary code.

Robert

If you've got Photoshop 3.05, you may be wondering. The *Getting Started* booklet at page 9 refers to a YCC Export Plug-in. That's right. And wrong. There were plans to do one, but the project didn't come to completion. In short, the printed reference is now a typo.

TIFF

Developed by Aldus back in the early days of the Mac to standardize an ever-growing population of scanned images, TIFF (*Tagged Image File Format*) is the most widely supported bitmapped format across both the Macintosh and PC platforms. It can't handle object-oriented artwork and doesn't support JPEG compression, but it is otherwise unrestricted. In fact, TIFF offers a few tricks of its own that are worth mentioning. When you save an image in the TIFF format, Photoshop displays the TIFF Options dialog box (see Figure 3-12), which offers these options:

✦ **Byte Order:** Leave it to Photoshop to name a straightforward option in the most confusing way possible. Byte Order? No, this option doesn't have anything to do with how you eat your food. Rather, because Macintosh TIFF and PC TIFF are two slightly different formats, this option permits you to specify whether you want to use the image on the Mac or on an IBM PC-compatible machine. We're sure it has something to do with the arrangement of 8-bit chunks of data, but who cares? You want Mac or you want PC? It's that simple.

✦ **LZW Compression:** Like Huffman encoding (described earlier in the "Saving an EPS document" section), the LZW (Lempel-Ziv-Welch) compression scheme digs into the computer code that describes an image and substitutes frequently used codes with shorter equivalents. But instead of substituting characters, as Huffman does, LZW substitutes strings of data. Because LZW doesn't so much as touch a pixel in your image, it's entirely lossless. Most image editors and desktop publishing applications — including FreeHand, PageMaker, and QuarkXPress — import LZW-compressed TIFF images, but a few have yet to catch on.

Robert

This could as easily be a Caution icon. I think LZW is dangerous. Yes, I know people use it all the time. But I've seen too many cases of file corruption, or TIFF files that nobody could open, which had LZW Compression as the apparent cause. Others have shown mysterious color shifts. For all these reasons I never use it. Use a ZIP file if you need compression; don't tinker with the file format options.

Longtime Photoshop users may have noticed the disappearance of an option, Save Alpha Channels. In Photoshop 3, the TIFF format now supports up to 24 channels, which is the maximum number permitted in a document. In fact, TIFF is the only format other than raw and the native Photoshop format that can save more than four channels. To save a TIFF file without extra mask channels, choose File⇨Save a Copy and select the Don't Include Alpha Channels check box. For complete information on channels, read Chapter 5.

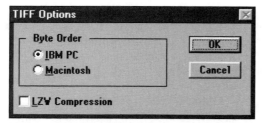

Figure 3-12: Photoshop lets you save TIFF files in either the Mac or PC format and compress the image using LZW.

Cross-platform formats

These are the formats you could go for years without using — but when you need them, you really need them. They allow Photoshop images to go beyond the Mac-PC loop. You can exchange images with an Amiga fanatic, for example. Or if you're outputting images to an Iris inkjet printer, you may find your service bureau request the Scitex format. The Photoshop programmers have been very comprehensive here. Robert recalls a sign in a pharmacy near campus in his undergraduate college days: *If you want it, and we don't have it — you don't need it.*

Amiga's IFF and HAM

Popular among video enthusiasts, the now discontinued Commodore Amiga is a variety of personal computer that offers an operating system similar to the Mac's.

Deke owned the first-model Amiga 1000, a machine that Commodore almost immediately abandoned. You'd think he would have learned his lesson after having previously owned a Commodore Plus/4, possibly the worst computer ever made.

Nowadays, the only reason to use an Amiga — particularly because the company recently bit the dust — is because it supports NewTek's much-celebrated Video Toaster. If you know someone who uses an Amiga, maybe you can talk the poor soul into hawking it at a yard sale and using the money to make a down payment on a PC. Until then, you can trade images using the IFF (Interchange File Format) format, which is the Amiga's all-around graphics format. Photoshop includes a plug-in module that lets you export an image to a compressed variation of IFF called HAM (Hold and Modify) by choosing File⇨Export⇨Amiga HAM. Unfortunately, HAM is generally useless for images that don't conform to one of two standard image sizes — 320 × 200 pixels or 320 × 400 pixels. Most Amiga applications treat nonstandard images as having rectangular as opposed to square pixels, thus stretching the image out of proportion.

Photoshop can open HAM images with up to 256 colors and IFF images with up to 16 million colors.

PIXAR workstations

PIXAR has created some of the most memorable computer-animated shorts and commercials in recent memory. (That "recent memory" bit is just a saying, of course. *All* computer animation has occurred in recent memory.) The most famous examples are *Terminator 2* and *Toy Story*, the latter of which has done wonders for Pixar stock.

PIXAR develops a few 3-D graphics applications for the nonworkstation crowd, including MacRenderMan, ShowPlace, and Typestry (PC and Mac). But the company works its 3-D magic using mondo-expensive PIXAR workstations. Photoshop enables you to open a still image created on a PIXAR machine or save an image to the PIXAR format so you can integrate it into a 3-D rendering. The PIXAR format supports grayscale and RGB images. (Note that Pixar announced in 1994 it would cease developing for PC and Mac.)

Scitex image processors

High-end commercial printers use Scitex computers to generate color separations of images and other documents. Photoshop can open images digitized with Scitex scanners and save the edited images to the Scitex CT (Continuous Tone) format. because you need special hardware to transfer images from the Mac to a Scitex drive, you'll probably want to consult with your local Scitex service bureau technician before saving to the CT format. It's very possible that the technician will prefer that you submit images in the native Photoshop, TIFF, or JPEG format. The Scitex CT format supports grayscale and CMYK images.

TGA

TrueVision's Targa and NuVista video boards let you overlay Macintosh graphics and animation onto live video. The effect is called *chroma keying* because typically, a key color is set aside to let the live video show through. TrueVision designed the TGA (Targa) format to support 32-bit images that include 8-bit *alpha channels* capable of displaying the live video. Though support for TGA is scarce among Macintosh applications, it is widely implemented among professional-level color and video applications on the PC.

Quirky but important formats: EPS and DCS and FLM

The Q-word may sound judgmental, but it's not. These are very specific formats for the Mac and PC. They're probably more useful than the Cross-Platform formats described above. But, as you'll see from the following information, they have very specific uses and requirements and can be very unforgiving if you ignore those requirements. Also, as with the cross-platform formats, you may not ever need them — but when you do, you need them a lot.

Illustrator file

Photoshop supports Adobe Illustrator files saved in the EPS format. EPS (Encapsulated PostScript) is specifically designed for saving object-oriented graphics that you intend to print to a PostScript output device. All drawing programs and most page-layout programs let you save EPS documents. However, many versions of EPS exist, and Photoshop supports Illustrator's version only. To make life a little more straightforward, Illustrator uses a small subset of PostScript commands in its EPS files. This way, Illustrator and Photoshop can swap files back and forth with relative ease; if Photoshop tried to support the full gamut of EPS, the size of each program would easily double.

You may have noticed that Photoshop offers separate EPS and Adobe Illustrator options. This may have led you to believe that Photoshop 3 now at least makes an attempt to open a vanilla EPS illustration exported from FreeHand, Canvas, or CorelDRAW. *Eeeh. Ouch, I'm afraid this is not your day, Contestant Number Four. And you did so well in the rehearsals.* The fact is, the EPS format refers to EPS *images* — not objects — such as those created in Photoshop itself. So if you create a drawing in FreeHand, Canvas, or CorelDRAW, you still need to export it to the Illustrator format (with the .AI extension if you work on Windows) before opening it in Photoshop.

When you open an Illustrator EPS graphic, Photoshop *renders* (or *rasterizes*) the artwork — that is, it converts it from a collection of objects to a bitmapped image. During the open operation, Photoshop presents the EPS Rasterizer dialog box (see Figure 3-13), which enables you to specify the size and resolution of the image, just as you do in the New dialog box. Because the graphic is object-oriented, you can render it as large or as small as you want without any loss of image quality.

R %% Robert   There may be something multiligate lurking in the rasterizing process. Any number of people have reported that the rasterizer simply stops working, typically with an error message for either KERNEL32.DLL or AIPARSER.8BY. I've been there myself. At least one person further reported that the bug just seemed to go away. As I write this, Photoshop QA and I have had many exchanges about the issue, and only time will tell if the bug appears in 3.05. For the moment, though, here is some guidance. Reinstalling Photoshop does not cure it. Neither does deleting the Photoshop PSP file. Neither does putting Photoshop in the default installation directory (some people have claimed this works, but I think it's coincidental). Feeling gloomy? Here are two things you can do. First, there's some evidence that the problem is related to either number or quality of TrueType fonts on your system. Some have reported success by removing all the fonts except the basic ones Windows installs (and never, ever remove Marlett, unless you want a hosed system — MARLETT.TTF is a hidden file, but Windows users are inveterate snoopers. . .); others have selectively deinstalled and reinstalled fonts and discovered corrupted fonts.

R %% Robert   I personally think that if the solution lies with fonts, it's a font corruption issue. I had far fewer TrueType fonts than the number of fonts some users reduced their swollen number to. It worked for them, it didn't work for me.

What I did was the Brute Force approach. I did a totally clean reinstall of Windows 95. I'd installed over Windows 3.1, and about two dozen beta builds had gone on over that. So it couldn't hurt to clear out the gunk — and I was amazed at how much faster my system became. My theory was that a DLL had gotten tromped on, and I'm carefully monitoring things to determine further. My brutal approach worked, but I'd urge you to try the font approach just mentioned.

You should always select the Anti-aliased check box unless you're rendering a very large image — say, 300 ppi or higher. *Anti-aliasing* blurs pixels to soften the edges of the objects so that they don't appear jagged. When you're rendering a very large image, the difference between image and printer resolution is less noticeable, so anti-aliasing is unwarranted.

Photoshop 3 renders illustrations against a transparent background. Before you can save the rasterized image to a format other than Photoshop 3, you have to eliminate the transparency by choosing Flatten Image from the Layers palette pop-up menu. Or save a flattened version of the image to a separate file by choosing File⇨Save a Copy.

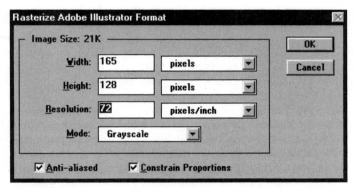

Figure 3-13: You can specify the size and resolution at which Photoshop renders an EPS illustration.

If you want to introduce an EPS graphic into the foreground image rather than rendering it into a new image window of its own, choose File⇨Place. Unlike other File menu commands, Place supports only the Illustrator variety of the EPS format. After you import the EPS graphic, it appears selected with a great X across it, allowing you to move it into position. (You have to drag it; you can't use the arrow keys.) When the graphic is properly situated, click with the gavel cursor to render the illustration against the bitmapped background. In this way, Photoshop 3 lets you combine illustrations that have transparent backgrounds with existing images. (To keep the imported graphic independent from the rest of the image, send the graphic to a separate layer *after* clicking with the gavel cursor. Chapter 8 explains how.)

Rendering an EPS illustration is an extremely useful technique for resolving printing problems. If you work in Illustrator often, you no doubt have encountered limitcheck errors, which occur when an illustration is too complex for an imagesetter or other high-end output device to print. If you're frustrated with the printer and you're tired of wasting your evening trying to figure out what's wrong (sound familiar?), use Photoshop to render the illustration at 300 ppi and print it. Nine out of ten times, this technique works flawlessly.

If Photoshop can't *parse* the EPS file — which is a techy way of saying that Photoshop can't break down the individual objects (or that Photoshop doesn't know this EPS file from Shinola) — it attempts to open the TIFF preview header. Most of the time, this exercise is totally useless, but you may occasionally want to take a quick look at an illustration in order to, say, match the placement of elements in an image to those in the drawing.

Saving an EPS document

To use a Photoshop image inside Illustrator, you must save it in the EPS format. This may be Illustrator's most prominent drawback. Photoshop can open 19 formats, acquire several more, and swap Sanskrit parchments among Buddhist monks. Meanwhile, Illustrator only supports EPS, which wouldn't be so bad if EPS weren't such a remarkably inefficient format for saving images. An EPS image may be three to four times larger than the same image saved to the TIFF format with LZW compression. Granted, EPS is more reliable for PostScript printing, but that's an internal translation issue that Illustrator should be able to handle, as do FreeHand, PageMaker, QuarkXPress, and many other programs.

Deke's right to be cranky about this. So am I, for yet another reason (so let's pile Ossa on Pelion, as the Titans storm the Olympus of EPS). Photoshop can certainly read its own EPS files, so if you're willing to sacrifice the disk space, I suppose you can save this way. But the kicker is that there are a bewildering variety of flavors of EPS. In particular, some TWAIN modules let you save as EPS, and I've seen all too many people who have saved "the perfect scan" in EPS and then find they can't open it anywhere. Not even in Photoshop. Thinking EPS for bitmap work is bad news, unless you're doing clipping paths.

Now that we're both done complaining (for the moment — don't lose hope — we're never truly done complaining), here's how the process works. When you save an image in the EPS format, Photoshop 3 displays the dialog box shown in Figure 3-14. The options in this dialog box are:

✦ **Preview:** Technically, an EPS document comprises two parts: a pure PostScript-language description of the graphic for the printer; and a bitmapped preview that enables you to see the graphic on-screen. Typically you'll want to use the 8-bit format. The 1-bit options provide black-and-white previews only, which are useful if you want to save a little room on disk. Select the None option to include no preview and save even more disk space.

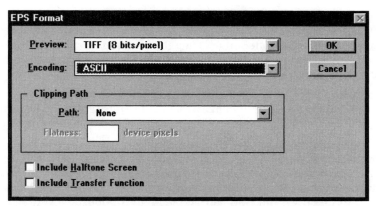

Figure 3-14: When saving an image in the EPS format, you can specify the type of preview and tack on some printing attributes.

✦ **Encoding:** If you're exporting an image for use with Illustrator, select the Binary encoding option (also known as Huffman encoding), which compresses an EPS document by substituting shorter codes for frequently used characters. The letter *A,* for example, receives the 3-bit code *010* rather than its standard 8-bit ASCII code, *01100001* (the binary equivalent of what we humans call *97*). Some programs — namely FreeHand and PageMaker — don't recognize Huffman encoding, in which case you must select the ASCII option. (ASCII stands for American Standard Code for Information Interchange, which is fancy jargon for text-only.) In other words, you can open and edit an ASCII EPS document in a word processor, provided you know how to read and write PostScript.

R %% **Robert** This can be a very useful technique if you've gotten a file from a Mac source that won't open, especially if it's been sent electronically. Chances are there's a Mac-ish header that got into the works. Open the file in a word processor and look at the very beginning. The very start should have these four characters: %!PS. Delete any garbage that comes before (that is, the Mac-ish header), save in text format, and chances are your file will now open.

The new option is JPEG, which builds JPEG compression into the EPS image. This saves a lot of room on disk, but it also sacrifices data, as described in the upcoming "JPEG" section. Only select this option if you'll be taking your artwork into a program that supports it, and outputting to a PostScript Level 2 printer.

✦ **Clipping Path:** These options let you select a path that you created using the path tool and saved in the Paths panel of the Layers palette. You can then use that path to mask the contents of the EPS image. For complete information about clipping paths, see the "Retaining transparent areas in an image" section of Chapter 8.

✦ **Include Halftone Screen:** I've been badmouthing EPS pretty steadily, but it does have one advantage over other image formats: It can retain printing attributes. If you specified a custom halftone screen using the Screen button inside the Page Setup dialog box, you can save this setting with the EPS document by selecting the Include Halftone Screen check box.

✦ **Include Transfer Function:** As described in Chapter 6, you can change the brightness and contrast of a printed image using the Transfer button inside the Page Setup dialog box. To save these settings with the EPS document, select the Include Transfer Function check box.

✦ **Transparent Whites:** When saving black-and-white EPS images in Photoshop, select this option to make all white pixels in the image transparent. (The option doesn't appear in Figure 3-5 because the image being saved is in color.) Incidentally, the EPS format is the only format that offers this option. So if you want to create transparent images, black-and-white and EPS are the ways to go.

R
%%
Robert

Your most common use of the EPS format will be to take clipping path images out into other programs. But there's a gotcha in taking them into Adobe Illustrator 4 and 4.1.2. When Photoshop creates an EPS file, it also creates either an 8-bit preview (color), 1-bit preview (B&W), or no preview. This preview is a TIFF file of Version 6. Illustrator cannot read it, which means at best you'll get a very garbled screen image. But even though you can't see the clipping path, it will print correctly to a PostScript printer because the information on the clipping path is stored in the EPS file, not in the preview.

There is also an anomaly with PageMaker 5. While the image may superficially look fine, you may notice that for grayscale images with a clipping path, you get a white background from the path to the edge of the bounding box. For a color image, you get a black background from the path to the bounding box. Photoshop is doing everything correctly; here, as in the Illustrator case, it's an issue of the receiving application reading the TIFF preview absolutely correctly.

QuarkXPress DCS

Quark developed a variation on the EPS format called DCS (Desktop Color Separation). When you work in QuarkXPress, this format lets you print color separations of imported artwork. If you save a CMYK image in the EPS format, Photoshop displays the additional Desktop Color Separation options shown in Figure 3-15. When you save to the DCS format, Photoshop creates five files on disk: one master document plus one file each for the cyan, magenta, yellow, and black color channels. Select Off (Single File) to save the image as a single standard EPS document. Select one of the three On options to save the separations as five independent DCS files.

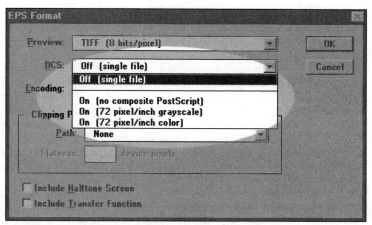

Figure 3-15: Photoshop offers four DCS options when you save a CMYK image in the EPS format.

Photoshop also gives you the option of saving a 72-ppi PostScript-language version of the image inside the DCS master document. Independent from the bitmapped preview — which you specify as usual by selecting a Preview option — the 72-ppi *composite* image enables you to print a low-resolution version of a DCS image imported into QuarkXPress to a consumer-quality printer such as a LaserWriter. If you're using a black-and-white printer, select the 72 pixel/inch grayscale option; if you're using a color printer, select the final option. Note that the composite image significantly increases the size of the master document on disk.

Caution You convert an image to the CMYK mode by choosing Mode➪CMYK Color. Do not choose this command casually. Converting back and forth between RGB and CMYK results in a loss of color information. Only use the CMYK Color command if you want to convert an image to CMYK color forever. For more information, read Chapter 4, "Defining Colors."

FLM Filmstrip

Adobe Premiere is the foremost movie-editing application for both Mac and PC. The program is a wonder when it comes to fades, frame merges, and special effects, but it offers no frame-by-frame editing capabilities. For example, you can't draw a mustache on a person in the movie, nor can you make brightly colored brush strokes swirl about in the background — at least not inside Premiere.

However, you can export the movie to the Filmstrip format, which is a file-swapping option exclusive to Photoshop and Premiere. A Filmstrip document organizes frames in a long vertical strip. A gray bar separates each frame. The number of each frame appears on the right; the SMPTE (Society of Motion Picture and Television Engineers) time code appears on the left. The structure of the three-number time code is minutes:seconds:frames, with 30 frames per second.

If you change the size of a Filmstrip document inside Photoshop in any way, you cannot save the image back to the Filmstrip format. Feel free to paint and apply effects, but stay the heck away from the Image Size and Canvas Size commands.

I don't really delve into the Filmstrip format anywhere else in this book, so I want to pass along a couple of quick Filmstrip tips right here and now. First, you can scroll up and down exactly one frame at a time by pressing Shift-Page Up or Shift-Page Down, respectively. Second, you can move a selection exactly one frame up or down by pressing Shift-up arrow or Shift-down arrow. If you want to clone the selection as you move it, press Shift-Option-up arrow or Shift-Option-down arrow. And finally — here's the great one — you can select several sequential frames and edit them all at once by following these steps:

Steps: Selecting sequential frames in a movie

1. Select the rectangular marquee tool by pressing the M key. Then drag with the tool to select the first frame that you want to edit in the movie. (This is the only step that takes any degree of care or coordination whatsoever.)

2. Switch to the quick mask mode by pressing the Q key. The areas around the selected frame are overlaid with pink.

3. Double-click on the magic wand tool icon in the toolbox to display the Magic Wand Options panel in the Brushes palette. Enter 0 for the Tolerance value and deselect the Anti-aliased check box.

4. Click inside the selected frame (the one that's not pink) with the magic wand tool. This selects the unmasked area inside the frame.

5. Press Shift-Alt-down arrow to clone the unmasked area to the next frame in the movie. When you exit the quick mask mode, both this frame and the one above it will be selected.

6. Keep Shift-Alt-down arrowing until you've gotten rid of the pink stuff on all the frames that you want to select.

7. Exit the quick mask mode by pressing the Q key again. All frames appear selected.

8. Edit the frames to your heart's content.

If you're new to Photoshop, half of those steps, if not all of them, probably went sailing over your head like so many extraterrestrial spaceships. If you want to learn more about selections and cloning, read Chapter 8. In Chapter 9, we explore the quick mask mode and other masking techniques in depth. After you finish reading those chapters, come back to this section and see if it makes a little more sense.

The process of editing individual frames, as just described, is sometimes called *rotoscoping,* named after the traditional technique of combining live-action film with animated sequences. You also can try out some *scratch-and-doodle* techniques, which is where an artist scratches and draws directly on frames of film. If that's not enough, you can emulate *xerography,* in which an animator makes Xerox copies of photographs, enhances the copies using markers or whatever else is convenient, and shoots the finished artwork, frame by frame, on film. In a nutshell, Photoshop extends Premiere's functionality by adding animation to its video-editing capabilities.

You can save an image in the Filmstrip format only if you opened the image as a Filmstrip document and did not change the size, resolution, or color mode of the image. Just press Control-S.

A quirky format: raw

A *raw document* is a plain binary file stripped of all extraneous information. It contains no compression scheme, it specifies no bit depth or image size, and it offers no color mode. Each byte of data indicates a brightness value on a single color channel, and that's it. Photoshop offers this function specifically so that you can open images created in undocumented formats, such as those sometimes created on mainframe computers and workstations. Think of it as the Cross-Platform format of last resort — never choose it if you've got any other option. Adobe has provided a PDF file on its Photoshop CD-ROM, 4214.PDF, which describes the basics. Still, some elaboration is in order.

Opening a raw document

To open an image of unknown origin, choose File⇨Open As and select Raw from the File Format pop-up menu. Then select the desired image and click on the Open button or press Return. The dialog box shown in Figure 3-16 appears and features these options:

✦ **Width, Height:** If you know the dimensions of the image in pixels, enter the values in these option boxes.

✦ **Swap:** Click on this button to swap the Width value with the Height value.

✦ **Channels:** Enter the number of color channels in this option box. If the document is an RGB image, enter 3; if it is a CMYK image, enter 4.

✦ **Header:** This value tells Photoshop how many bytes of data at the beginning of the file comprise header information that it can ignore.

✦ **Interleaved:** If you choose this, the color values are stored sequentially.

✦ **Depth:** The choices are 8 or 16 bits. This allows you to import 24 or 48 bit RGB images from, typically, mainframe computers. In the former case you have three color channels of 8 bits each, while for the latter three color channels of 16 bits each. Note that you must set the Channels (above) to three.

✦ **Byte Order:** If you've set 16 bits in the previous radio button, you get a choice of Mac or IBM PC. This is to deal with whether the upper and lower bytes are reversed. You may have to experiment. If you've set the button to 8 bits, this will be grayed out; byte reversal isn't an issue.

✦ **Retain When Saving:** If the Header value is greater than 0, you can instruct Photoshop to retain this data when you save the image in a different format.

✦ **Guess:** If you know the Width and Height values but you don't know the number of bytes in the header — or vice versa — you can ask Photoshop for help. Fill in either the size or header information and then click on the Guess button to ask Photoshop to take a stab at the unknown value. Photoshop estimates all this information when the Raw Options dialog box first appears. Generally speaking, if it doesn't estimate correctly the first time around, you're on your own. But hey, the Guess button is worth a shot.

Note

There's not a lot you can do with a 48-bit image at this time: Levels (and Auto Levels), Curves, Duplicate, and convert to 24 bit.

Tip

If a raw document is a CMYK image, it opens as an RGB image with an extra masking channel. To correctly display the image, choose Mode⇨Multichannel to free the four channels from their incorrect relationship. Then recombine them by choosing Mode⇨CMYK Color.

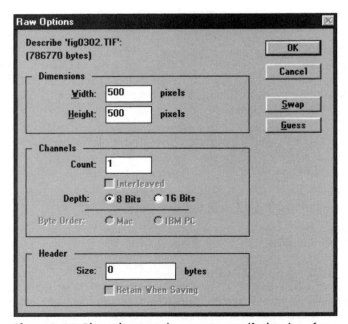

Figure 3-16: Photoshop requires you to specify the size of an image and the number of color channels when you open an image that does not conform to a standardized file format.

Saving a raw document

Photoshop also allows you to save to the raw document format. This capability is useful when you create files that you want to transfer to mainframe systems or output to devices that don't support other formats, such as the Kodak XL7700.

Caution Do not save 256-color indexed images to the raw format, or you will lose the color lookup table and therefore lose all color information. Be sure to first convert such images to RGB or one of the other full-color modes before saving.

When you save an image in the raw document format, Photoshop presents the dialog box shown in Figure 3-17. The dialog box options work as follows:

✦ **File Type:** This is a carry-over from the Macintosh, because only Macs use this code. It's grayed out in the Windows version of Photoshop.

✦ **File Creator:** This too is grayed out, giving you the default code 8BIM.

✦ **Header:** Enter the size of the header in bytes. If you enter any value but 0, you must fill in the header using a data editor such as Norton DiskEdit.

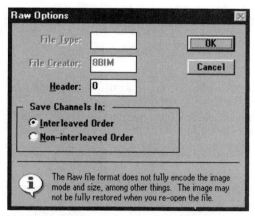

Figure 3-17: When saving a raw document, at most you'll only need to enter header size.

Native Macintosh formats

Deke's *Macworld Photoshop 3 Bible* discusses two of these formats in not-so-loving detail. For MacPaint, "Last updated in 1987, MacPaint 2.0 is severely lacking by today's standards. . . . If you dig, you can find truckloads of old clip art in the MacPaint format, which is the only reason Photoshop bothers to support it at all." PixelPaint doesn't fare much better: "In fact, PixelPaint's demise started about the same time that Photoshop arrived on the scene. Some coincidence, huh?"

More from *Macworld Photoshop 3 Bible*: "PICT (*Macintosh Picture*) is the Macintosh system software's native graphics format. Based on the QuickDraw display language that the system software uses to convey images on-screen, PICT is one of the few file formats that handles object-oriented artwork and bitmapped images with equal aplomb. It supports images in any bit depth, size, or resolution. It even supports 32-bit images, so you can save a fourth masking channel when working in the RGB mode."

In short, the formats are for backwards-compatibility and cross-platform ecumenicism. Few images in these formats are worth the bother. PICT images sometimes are. But getting any of them into Photoshop is problematic to terrifying. Failure is often more frequent than success. Thoroughly contemporary illustrators on either platform will have images in more mainstream formats, and we strongly suggest you use them.

For more about Mac formats, talk to your Mac-based friends and check out *Macworld Photoshop 3 Bible*. It is purely coincidental that this section comes after a "quirky format" section.

Back and forth

If you have problems opening or saving the formats described in this chapter, you may be asking more of the format than it can handle; see the preceding comments on GIF, JPEG, TIFF, and EPS files. Experience on CompuServe's ADOBEAPPS suggests that advice should cover most issues. It's the remainder that can drive you crazy.

File format specs evolve. That can break things on both ends. Adobe Illustrator 4 and 4.1 can't handle the TIFF 6 spec, but PageMaker 5 can. At the other end, there are some very early TIFF files that neither can handle. JPEG is notorious (there were several private implementations). Some JPEGs can only be read by the originating application. And even the most evolved spec can be implemented differently across various programs. Sometimes it's not a problem; other times, a program can't read a TIFF 6 every other program can.

There's another dodge. Chances are you've got a program that can read and write the problem format. Our hard drive happens to have the excellent shareware LViewPro and PaintShop Pro, and the alleged Photoshop competition (look at the start of Chapter 1 for why we say "alleged") of the Windows 95 versions of Corel PhotoPaint and Micrografx Picture Publisher. It's worth trying the problem file in every program you have — and every program your friends have. After all, what are friends for?

Robert

What if you're still out of it? HiJaak is a very popular program. But I have seen any number of system problems that were solved by removing HiJaak, under both Windows 3.1 and Windows 95. Further, there is evidence that its Windows 95 version is not entirely stable — and this goes beyond the usual multiligate critters that every Windows application has. Still, its popularity and dizzying range of features compel attention — I've given you my totally personal opinion. TransverterPro is less well known; I've found it invaluable. It's stronger on the vector formats than the bitmap ones, but I've never had the least problem with it living on my system. So you could invest in either.

Still out of it? Go online. Chapter 1 made clear why I push ADOBEAPPS on CompuServe — over and above my presence on it. We get regular postings about file format issues. If it can't be solved online, typically a sysop will ask you to e-mail the file — it's a rare week that I'm not tinkering with one.

Resampling and Cropping Methods

Image size and resolution aren't set in stone. Photoshop provides two methods for changing the number of pixels in an image: resampling and cropping.

Resizing versus resampling

Typically, when folks talk about *resizing* an image, they mean enlarging or reducing it without changing the number of pixels in the image, as demonstrated back in Figure 3-1. To *resample* an image is to scale it so that it contains more or fewer pixels. With resizing, there is an inverse relationship between size and resolution; size goes up when resolution goes down. Resampling affects either size or resolution alone. Figure 3-18 shows an image resized and resampled to 50 percent of its original dimensions. The resampled and original images have identical resolutions, but the resized image has twice the resolution of its companions.

Resizing an image

To resize an image, use the techniques from the "Printed resolution" section near the beginning of this chapter. Either choose File⇨Page Setup and enter a percentage value into the Reduce or Enlarge option box, or choose Image⇨Image Size and enter a value into the Resolution option box (assuming that the File Size check box is selected). Neither technique affects the on-screen appearance of the image, only the way it prints.

Resampling an image

Image⇨Image Size also resamples an image. The difference is that you turn off the File Size check box, as shown in Figure 3-19. In fact, the File Size option is the key.

When selected, File Size ensures that the number of pixels in the image remains fixed. Any change to the Resolution inversely affects the Width and Height values if they are set to any measurement unit but pixels (see the following note).

When File Size is deselected, the Resolution value is independent of the Width and Height values. You then can increase or decrease the number of pixels in an image by increasing or decreasing any of the three values. Photoshop resizes the image

Figure 3-18: An image (top) resized (bottom left) and resampled (bottom right) down to 50 percent.

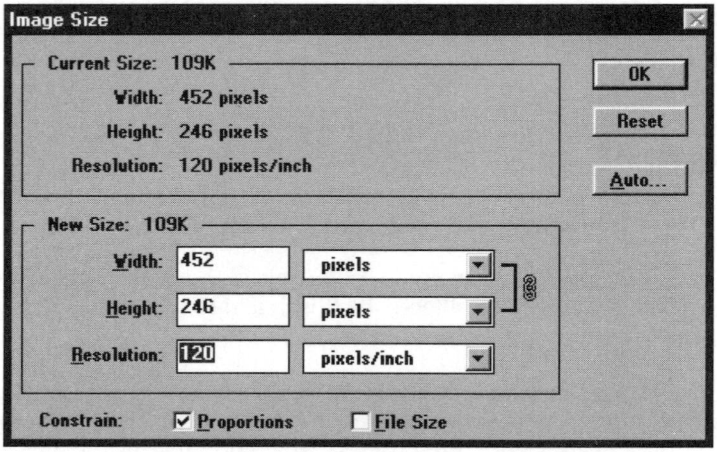

Image Size	⊠

Current Size: 109K

Width: 452 pixels

Height: 246 pixels

Resolution: 120 pixels/inch

[OK]
[Reset]
[Auto...]

New Size: 109K

Width: `452` | pixels ▼

Height: `246` | pixels ▼

Resolution: `120` | pixels/inch ▼

Constrain: ☑ Proportions ☐ File Size

Figure 3-19: The setting of the File Size option determines whether you resize or resample an image.

according to the new specifications. To do so, it must interpolate the image's pixels, as explained in the "General environmental preferences" section of Chapter 2 (see Figure 2-17).

Note If the unit of measurement is pixels, the Resolution option does not affect the Width or Height values whether File Size is on or off. In fact, the rules change. To resize, change the Resolution value. To resample an image, change the Width and Height values.

Cropping

You also can change the number of pixels in an image by *cropping* it, which means to clip away pixels around the edges of an image without changing any remaining pixels. (When you rotate a cropped image, pixels in the image change color because Photoshop has to interpolate pixels to account for the rotation.)

Cropping enables you to focus in on an element in your image. For example, Figure 3-20 shows an image Deke's sister photographed. It has good color balance, but the image is crooked and we're too far from the central character. No problem. All we do is crop around the lion's head to delete all the extraneous image elements, as shown in Figure 3-21.

Figure 3-20: This image has too much extraneous information in it.

Figure 3-21: Cropping lets you focus in on the essential image elements.

Changing the canvas size

One way to crop an image is to choose Image⇨Canvas Size, which displays the Canvas Size dialog box shown in Figure 3-22. The options in this dialog box let you scale the imaginary canvas on which the image rests separately from the image itself.

If you enlarge the canvas, Photoshop surrounds the image with a white background (if the background color is white). If you reduce the canvas, you crop the image. Click inside the Placement grid to specify the image placement on the new canvas. To add space to the bottom of an image, enlarge the canvas size and then click inside the upper middle square. To crop away the upper left corner of an image, create a smaller canvas size and then click on the lower right square.

Crop tool

Canvas Size is most useful for enlarging the canvas or shaving a few pixels off the edge of an image. To crop a large portion of an image, the crop tool is a better choice.

To crop the image, drag with the crop tool to create a rectangular marquee that surrounds what you want to retain. If you don't get it right the first time, change the horizontal and vertical dimensions by dragging any one of the four *corner handles,* as shown in Figure 3-23. When the marquee surrounds the exact portion of the image you want to keep, click inside it with the scissors cursor. This action clips away all pixels except those that lie inside and along the border of the crop marquee.

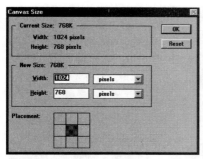

Figure 3-22: Choose Image⇨Canvas Size to crop an image or add empty space around the perimeter of an image

Crop marquee   Crop handle

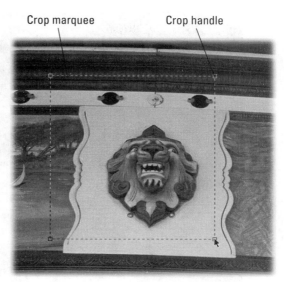

Figure 3-23: Drag a corner handle to resize the crop marquee.

Rotating and moving a crop marquee

You can rotate a crop marquee by Option-dragging a corner handle prior to clicking inside the marquee with the scissors cursor. Straightening an image by Option-dragging the corner handle of a crop marquee can be a little tricky. It happens all the time: you think you have the marquee rotated properly, then find that the image is still crooked after you've clicked inside it with the scissors cursor. In such a case, choose Edit⇨Undo and try again. Do *not* use the crop tool again to rotate the already rotated image. If you do, Photoshop interpolates between already interpolated pixels, resulting in more lost data.

Tip A better solution is to do it right the first time. Locate a line in your image that should be straight up and down. Alt-drag the crop marquee so that it aligns *exactly* with that line, as shown in Figure 3-24. Don't worry that this isn't how you want to crop the image — you're just using the line as a reference. After you arrive at the correct angle, release the Option key and drag the handles to specify the crop boundary.

Tip You can also move the entire crop marquee by Control-dragging on any one of the handles. This is a great way to reposition a cropping boundary without having to fiddle around with moving each handle separately.

Figure 3-24: Option-drag exactly over a long line in your image to determine the proper angle of rotation.

Selection

Another way to crop an image is to drag with the rectangular marquee tool around the portion of the image you want to keep and then choose Edit⇨Crop. One advantage is that it lets you crop the canvas to the boundaries of an image pasted from the Clipboard (or dragged and dropped from another image). As long as the boundaries of the pasted image are rectangular, as in the case of an image copied from a different application, you can choose Edit⇨Paste followed by Edit⇨Crop to both replace the former image and to crop the window to fit the new image.

Another reason for this technique is its speed. Deke and Robert, on, respectively, a Power Mac and Pentium 133, are frustrated with how slowly the cropping marquee updates. Though you can't resize a selection marquee so easily, it sure responds quickly.

Defining Colors

Colors

Every once in a while, the development of computer graphics technology reminds us of the development of television. First it was black and white for everyone. Then color appeared, but at such a price that only the upper echelon could afford to work in it. Now, just as there's a color TV available for almost everyone, so it is for Photoshop users. Powerful graphics cards are affordable, and excellent, inexpensive color printers have made the wonderful world of color accessible to every user.

Still, you shouldn't forget black and white, or grayscale. Just as black and white are a subset of gray, gray is a subset of color. Many folks have problems accepting this premise. But gray values are just variations on what Noah Webster called "The sensation resulting from stimulation of the retina of the eye by light waves of certain lengths." And grayscale has its uses, over and above screen captures. Just consider that some of the world's great artists, cinema directors, and photographers often choose to work in monochrome.

Specifying colors

Four color controls are in the toolbox (Figure 4-1).

✦ **Foreground color:** Indicates the color you apply when you use the type, paint bucket, line, pencil, airbrush, or paintbrush tool or if you Alt-drag with the smudge tool. It also begins any gradation created with the gradient tool. Apply the foreground color to a selection by choosing Edit⇨Fill or Edit⇨Stroke or by pressing Alt-Del. To change the foreground color, click on the foreground color icon to display the Color Picker dialog box or click in an open image window with the eyedropper tool.

✦ **Background color:** Indicates the color you apply with the eraser tool. It also ends any gradation created with the gradient tool. You can apply the background color to a selection by pressing the Delete key. To change the background color, click on the background color icon to display the Color Picker dialog box or Alt-click in any open image window with the eyedropper tool.

✦ **Switch colors:** Click on this icon (or press the X key) to exchange the foreground and background colors.

✦ **Default colors:** Click on this icon (or press the D key) to make the foreground color black and the background color white.

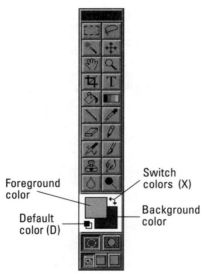

Figure 4-1: The color controls provided with Photoshop 3.0 (along with keyboard shortcuts in parentheses, where applicable).

Using the Color Picker

When you click on the foreground or background color icon, Photoshop displays the Color Picker dialog box. (This assumes that you have chosen to use the Photoshop Color Picker in the General Preferences dialog box. If you select the Windows option there, the generic Windows Color Picker appears; see Chapter 2 on why we discourage this.) Figure 4-2 labels the wealth of elements and options in the Color Picker dialog box, which works as follows:

✦ **Color slider:** Homes in on the color you want to select. Drag up or down on either of the slider triangles to select a color from a particular 8-bit range. The colors represented inside the slider correspond to the selected radio button. For example, if you select the H (hue) radio button, the default setting, the slider colors represent the full 8-bit range of hues. If you select S (saturation), the slider shows the current hue at full saturation at the top of the slider, down to no saturation — or gray — at the bottom of the slider. If you select B (brightness), the slider shows the 8-bit range of brightness values, from solid color at the top of the slider to absolute black at the bottom. You also can select R (red), G (green), or B (blue); the top of the slider shows you what the current color looks like when subjected to full-intensity red, green, or blue (respectively), and the bottom of the slider shows every bit of red, green, or blue subtracted.

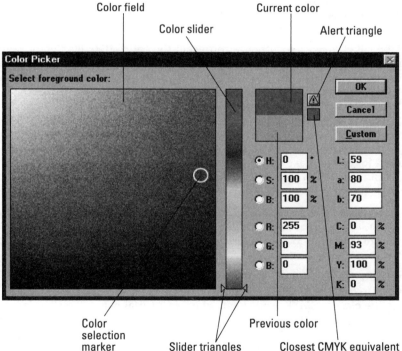

Figure 4-2: Use the elements and options in the Color Picker dialog box to specify a new foreground or background color from the 16-million-color range.

Cross Ref For a proper introduction to the HSB and RGB color models, including definitions of specific terms such as *hue, saturation,* and *brightness,* read the "Working in Different Color Modes" section later in this chapter.

✦ **Color field:** A 16-bit range of variations on the current slider color. Click inside it to move the color selection marker and select a new color. The field graphs colors against the two remaining attributes not represented by the color slider. For example, if you select the H (hue) button, the field graphs colors by brightness vertically and saturation horizontally, as demonstrated in the first example of Figure 4-3. The other examples show what happens to the color field when you select the S (saturation) and B (brightness) buttons.

Likewise, Figure 4-4 shows how the field graphs colors when you select the R (red), G (green), and B (blue) radio buttons. We recommend experimenting with the Color Picker inside your version of Photoshop or refer to Color Plate 4-1 to see how the dialog box looks when the H (hue), S (saturation), and B (brightness) options are selected.

Background Slider and field always work together to represent the entire 16-million-color range. The slider displays 256 colors, and the field displays 65,000 variations on the slider color; 256 times 65,000 is 16 million. Therefore, no matter which radio button you select, you have access to the same colors. It's just that your means of accessing them changes.

✦ **Current color:** The color currently selected from the color field appears in the top rectangle immediately to the right of the color slider. Click on the OK button or press Return to make this the current foreground or background color (depending on which color control icon in the toolbox you clicked to display the Color Picker dialog box in the first place).

✦ **Previous color:** The bottom rectangle just to the right of the color slider shows how the foreground or background color — whichever one you are in the process of editing — looked before you displayed the Color Picker dialog box. Click on the Cancel button or press Ctrl-period to leave this color intact.

✦ **Alert triangle:** The alert triangle appears when you select a bright color that Photoshop can't print using standard process colors. The box below the triangle shows the closest CMYK equivalent, which is invariably a duller version of the color. Click either on the triangle or box to bring the color into the printable range.

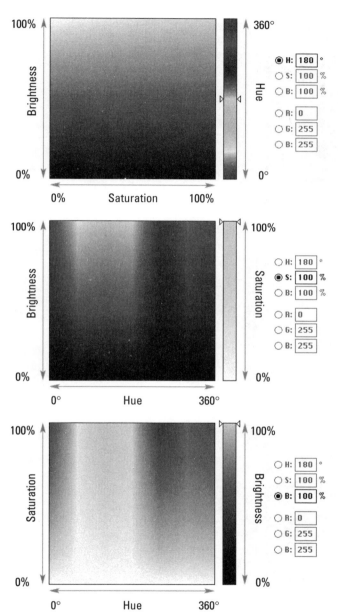

Figure 4-3: The color field graphs colors against the two attributes that are not represented in the slider. Here you can see how color is laid out when you select (top to bottom) the H (hue), S (saturation), and B (brightness) radio buttons.

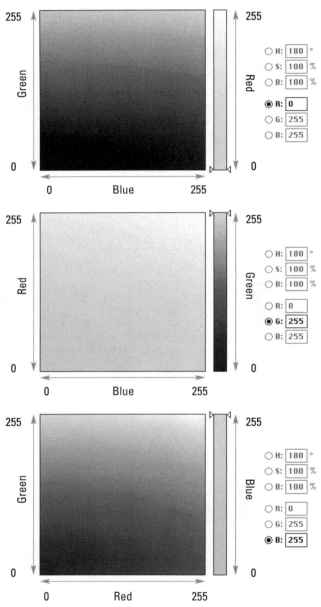

Figure 4-4: The results of selecting (top to bottom) the R (red), G (green), and B (blue) radio buttons.

Entering numeric color values

In addition to selecting colors using the slider and color field, you can enter specific color values in the option boxes in the lower right region of the Color Picker dialog box. Photoshop novices and intermediate users may find these options less satisfying than the slider and field. However, the options enable artists and print professionals to specify exact color values for controlled adjustments to a color already in use or matching a color used in another document. These options fall into one of four camps:

✦ **HSB:** These options stand for hue, saturation, and brightness. Hue is measured on a 360-degree circle. Saturation and brightness are measured from 0 to 100 percent. These options permit access to more than 3 million color variations.

✦ **RGB:** You can change the amount of the primary colors red, green, and blue by specifying the brightness value of each color from 0 to 255. These options permit access to more than 16 million color variations.

✦ **Lab:** This acronym stands for *luminosity,* measured from 0 to 100 percent, and two arbitrary color axes, *a* and *b,* whose brightness values range from –128 to 127. These options permit access to more than 6 million color variations.

✦ **CMYK:** These options display the amount of cyan, magenta, yellow, and black ink required to print the current color. In fact, when you click on the alert triangle, these are the only values that don't change because these are the values that make up the closest CMYK equivalent.

In my opinion, the numerical range of these options is extremely bewildering. Numerically speaking, the CMYK options enable you to create 100 million unique colors, whereas the RGB options permit the standard 16 million variations, and the Lab options permits a scant 6 million. Yet in point of fact, Lab is the largest color space, theoretically encompassing all colors from both CMYK and RGB. The printing standard CMYK provides by far the fewest colors, just the opposite of what you may expect. What gives? Misleading numerical ranges. How do these weird color models work? Keep reading and you'll find out.

Working in Different Color Modes

The four sets of option boxes inside the Color Picker dialog box represent *color models* — or, if you prefer, *color modes* (one less letter, no less meaning). Color models are ways to define colors both on-screen and on the printed page. Of course, all this talk about color models may make you queasy, and you may be using the Windows 95 color picker anyway (shown in Figure 4-5). That's fair enough, but think of the Windows 95 color picker as training wheels — after you read this chapter, we hope you'll want to graduate to the Photoshop picker.

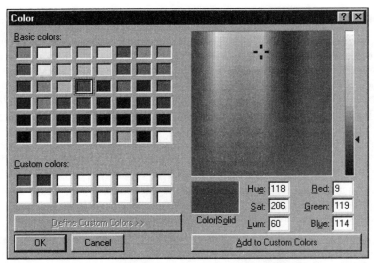

Figure 4-5: The Windows 95 color picker — great for getting started, but strive to graduate.

Outside the Color Picker dialog box, you can work inside any one of these color models by choosing a command from the Modes menu. In doing so, you generally change the colors in your image by dumping a few hundred or even thousand colors that have no equivalents in the new color model. The only exception is Lab, which in theory encompasses every unique color your eyes can detect.

Note Rather than discuss the color models in the order in which they occur in the Modes menu, we cover them in logical order, starting with the most common and widely accepted color model, RGB. Also note that we don't discuss the duotone or multichannel modes at this time. Mode⇨Duotone represents an alternative method for printing grayscale images, and is therefore discussed in Chapter 6. The multichannel mode, meanwhile, is not even a color model. Rather, Mode⇨Multichannel lets you separate an image into entirely independent channels, which you then can swap around and splice back together to create special effects. For more information, see the "Using multichannel techniques" section of Chapter 5.

RGB

RGB is a theoretical color model for of light which enables light's colors to be described by scientists, or practically re-created on a computer monitor. It comprises three primary colors — red, green, and blue — each of which can vary between 256 levels of intensity (called brightness values, as discussed in previous chapters). The RGB model is also called the *additive primary model,* because a color becomes lighter as you add higher levels of red, green, and blue light. All monitors, projection devices, and other items that transmit or filter light, including televisions, movie projectors, colored stage lights, and even stained glass, rely on the additive primary model.

Red, green, and blue light mix as follows:

✦ **Red and green:** Full-intensity red and green make yellow. Subtract some red to make chartreuse; subtract some green to make orange. All these colors assume a complete lack of blue.

✦ **Green and blue:** Without red, full-intensity green and blue form cyan. If you try hard enough, you can come up with 65,000 colors in the turquoise/jade/sky blue/sea green range.

✦ **Blue and red:** Full-intensity blue and red make magenta. Subtract some blue to make rose; subtract some red to make purple. All these colors assume a complete lack of green.

✦ **Red, green, and blue:** Full-intensity red, green, and blue mix to create white, the absolute brightest color in the visible spectrum.

✦ **No light:** Low intensities of red, green, and blue plunge a color into blackness.

Insofar as image editing is concerned, the RGB color model is ideal for editing images on the screen because the RGB model provides access to the entire range of 24-bit screen colors. Furthermore, you can save an RGB image in any file format supported by Photoshop. As shown in Table 4-1, the only other color mode that is compatible with such a wide range of file formats is grayscale. (It should be noted, however, that GIF is an 8-bit format. So if you save an RGB image in GIF, the image will be reduced to 256 colors.)

Table 4-1
File-Format Support for Photoshop 3.0's Color Models

	Bitmap	Grayscale	Duotone	Indexed	RGB	Lab	CMYK
EPS	yes	yes	yes	yes	yes	yes	yes
GIF	yes	yes	no	yes	yes	no	no
JPEG	no	yes	no	no	yes	no	yes
PCX	yes	yes	no	yes	yes	no	no
Scitex	no	yes	no	no	yes	no	yes
TIFF	yes	yes	no	yes	yes	yes	yes

Note Table 4-1 lists color models in the order they appear in the Modes menu. Again, we left out the multichannel mode because it is not a color model. (Also, the multichannel mode can only be saved in the Photoshop and raw formats.) The native Photoshop format, not listed in the table, supports all color models.

On the downside, the RGB color model provides access to a wider range of colors than you can print. Therefore, if you are designing an image for full-color printing, you can expect to lose many of the brightest and most vivid colors in your image. The only way to entirely avoid such color loss is to scan your image and edit it in the CMYK mode, which can be an exceptionally slow proposition. The better solution is scanning your images to Photo CDs and then opening and editing those images in the Lab mode, as explained in the upcoming "CIE's Lab" section.

HSB

Back when Photoshop was Mac-only in version 2, the Modes menu provided access to the HSB — hue, saturation, brightness — color model, now relegated to the Color Picker dialog box and the Picker palette (discussed later in this chapter). *Hue* is pure color, the stuff rainbows are made of, measured on a 360-degree circle. Red is located at 0 degrees, yellow at 60 degrees, green at 120 degrees, cyan at 180 degrees (midway around the circle), blue at 240 degrees, and magenta at 300 degrees. It's basically a pie-shaped version of the RGB model at full intensity.

Saturation represents the purity of the color. A 0 percent saturation value equals gray. White, black, and any other colors you can express in a grayscale image have no saturation. Full saturation (100 percent) produces the purest version of a hue.

Brightness is the lightness or darkness of a color. A 0 percent brightness value equals black. Full brightness (100 percent) combined with full saturation (100 percent) results in the most vivid version of any hue.

Robert on the HSB color model

Deke wasn't particularly effusive about HSB in the Mac edition. I feel differently. The RGB or CMYK models aren't particularly intuitive. In fact, if you're honest (c'mon now — fess up) you'll admit that defining a color in those models is often hit or miss for you. That's not surprising, because they're not based on what you see. RGB is based on computer values, and CMYK on printer's ink percentages. But you can easily intuit from the three dimensions of HSB — it just feels like you see.

Even better hue, saturation, and brightness become hue, chroma, and value in the Munsell color model. Wait a minute, you say. I don't see any HCV color model in Photoshop. That's right, you don't — and in my more saturnine moods I think that's Photoshop's biggest failing. The Munsell color model was developed as a system of color notation in 1915 by that eminent Bostonian, Albert Henry Munsell. Color theorists in the know and traditional artists with a whit of common sense couldn't live without it — it's the only accurate way to measure how colors interact and to describe their fundamental characteristics. If you've got to match a computer color with, say, an acrylic, several vendors give Munsell values on their tubes. It's not exact, but you've got better odds than trying to match one of the other models. Since Photoshop's programmers were neither theorists nor traditional artists, it's not surprising that they didn't use it. More's the pity. See further at the end of this chapter and throughout Chapter 19.

Moreover, if you're new to this whole color business, you'll find HSB much easier to use because of its very intuitiveness. In fact, most of the time I have my color picker set to HSB mode, and I fancy I know my way around RGB percentages and Pantone numberings. Give it a whirl, whether you're novice or old hand. You may find it easier to use, and if you heed Chapter 19, you may be convinced it's the only model to use.

CMYK

In nature, our eyes perceive pigments according to the *subtractive color model*. Sunlight contains every visible color found on earth. When sunlight is projected on an object, the object absorbs (subtracts) some of the light and reflects the rest. The reflected light is the color that you see. For example, a fire engine is bright red because it absorbs all non red light — meaning all blue and green — from the white-light spectrum.

Pigments on a sheet of paper work the same way. You can even mix pigments to create other colors. Suppose you paint a red brush stroke, which absorbs green and blue light, over a blue brush stroke, which absorbs green and red light. You get a blackish mess that has only a modicum of blue and red light left, along with a smidgen of green because the colors weren't absolutely pure.

But wait — every child knows that red and blue mix to form purple. So what gives? What gives is that what you learned in elementary school is only a rude approximation of the truth. Did you ever try mixing a vivid red with a canary yellow only to produce an ugly orange-brown gloop? The reason you didn't achieve the bright orange you wanted is obvious if you stop and think about it. The fact that red starts out darker than bright orange means that you have to add a great deal of yellow before you arrive at orange. And even then, it had better be an incredibly bright lemon yellow, not some deep canary yellow that already has a lot of red in it.

Commercial subtractive primaries

The subtractive primary colors used by commercial printers — cyan, magenta, and yellow — are for the most part very light. Cyan absorbs only red light, magenta absorbs only green light, and yellow absorbs only blue light. On their own, these colors don't do a very good job of producing dark colors. In fact, at full intensities, cyan, magenta, and yellow all mixed together don't get much beyond a muddy brown. That's where black comes in. Black accentuates shadows, deepens dark colors, and (of course) prints real blacks.

In case you're wondering how colors mix in the CMYK model, it's basically the opposite of the RGB model. However, because pigments are not as pure as primary colors in the additive model, there are some differences:

✦ **Cyan and magenta:** Full-intensity cyan and magenta mix to form a deep blue with a little violet in it. Subtract some cyan to make purple; subtract some magenta to make a dull medium blue. All these colors assume a complete lack of yellow.

✦ **Magenta and yellow:** Full-intensity magenta and yellow mix to form a brilliant red. Subtract some magenta to make vivid orange; subtract some yellow to make rose. All these colors assume a complete lack of cyan.

✦ **Yellow and cyan:** Full-intensity yellow and cyan mix to form a bright green with a hint of blue in it. Subtract some yellow to make a deep teal; subtract some cyan to make chartreuse. All these colors assume a complete lack of magenta.

✦ **Cyan, magenta, and yellow:** Full-intensity cyan, magenta, and yellow mix to form a muddy brown.

✦ **Black:** Darkens any other color.

✦ **No pigment:** Produces white (assuming that white is the color of the paper).

Editing in CMYK

If you're used to editing RGB images, editing in the CMYK mode requires some new approaches, especially when editing individual color channels. When you view a single color channel in the RGB mode (as discussed in the following chapter), white indicates high-intensity color, and black indicates low-intensity color. It's just the opposite in CMYK. When you view an individual color channel, black means high-intensity color, and white means low-intensity color.

This doesn't mean that RGB and CMYK color channels look like inverted versions of each other. In fact, because the color theory is inverted, they look pretty much the same. But if you're trying to achieve the full-intensity colors mentioned in the preceding section, you should apply black to the individual color channels, not white as you would in the RGB mode.

Should I edit in CMYK?

Boy, this is a thorny issue, but we're going to attack it anyway. Here's the deal: RGB doesn't accurately represent the colors you get when you print an image, because RGB lets you represent many colors — particularly very bright colors — that CMYK can't touch. That's why colors appear duller when you switch from RGB to CMYK.

Consequently, lots of folks advocate working in the CMYK mode. We, however, do not. While working in CMYK eliminates color disappointments, it is also much slower because Photoshop has to convert CMYK values to your RGB screen on the fly.

Furthermore, your scanner and monitor are RGB devices. No matter how you work, a translation from RGB to CMYK color space must occur at some point in time. If you pay the extra bucks to purchase a Scitex CMYK scan, for example, you simply make the translation at the beginning of the process — Scitex has no option except using RGB sensors internally — rather than at the end. In fact, every color device on earth is RGB except printers.

Ergo — it makes us sound like really smart guys in lab coats if we say ergo — you should wait to convert to the CMYK mode until right before you print. After your artwork is final, choose Mode⇨CMYK and make whatever edits you deem necessary. For example, you may want to introduce a few color corrections, apply some sharpening, and even retouch a few details by hand. Photoshop applies your changes more slowly in the CMYK mode, but at least you're slowed only at the end of the job, not throughout the entire process.

Tip This is not to say that you can't edit in the RGB mode and still get a picture of what the image will look like in CMYK. If you choose Mode⇨CMYK Preview, Photoshop displays colors in the CMYK color space on-screen while allowing you to continue to work in the larger world of RGB. Colors that occur in the RGB color space but are missing from CMYK are said to be *out of gamut*. Chapter 16 explains how to use Photoshop's capabilities to correct out-of-gamut colors before you switch to the CMYK mode. If you switch modes without first addressing these out-of-gamut colors, Photoshop adjusts the colors automatically. This may result in flat areas in your image because several out-of-gamut colors may automatically gravitate toward a single CMYK value. If you can spare the time, we strongly advise you to check out Chapter 16 before choosing Mode⇨CMYK.

RGB isn't the only mode that responds quickly and provides a bountiful range of colors. Photoshop's Lab color space comprises all the colors from RGB and CMYK and is every bit as fast as RGB. Many high-end users prefer to work in this mode, and we certainly advocate it if you're brave enough to take it on. Read the next section for the full story.

Lab

Whereas the RGB mode is the color model of your luminescent computer screen, and the CMYK mode is the color model of the reflective page, Lab is independent of light or pigment. Perhaps you already know that, in 1931, an international color organization called the *Commission Internationale d'Eclairage* (CIE) developed a color model that in theory contains every single color the human eye can see. (Gnats, iguanas, fruit bats, go find your own color models. Mutants and aliens — maybe CIE, maybe not, too early to tell.) Then, in 1976, the significant birthday of our nation, the CIE celebrated by coming up with two additional color systems. One of those systems was Lab, and the other was shrouded in secrecy. Well, at least we don't know what the other one was. Probably something that measures how it is that the entire visible spectrum of color can bounce off your retina when using flash photography and come out looking the exact shade of red one normally associates with lab (not Lab) rabbits. But that's just a guess.

The beauty of the Lab color model is that it fills gaps in both the RGB and CMYK models. RGB, for example, provides an overabundance of colors in the blue-to-green range, but is stingy on yellows, oranges, and other colors in the green-to-red range. Meanwhile, the colors missing from CMYK are enough to fill the Royal Albert Hall. Lab gets everything just right.

Understanding Lab anatomy

The Lab mode features three color channels, one for luminosity and two others for color ranges known simply by the initials a and b. (The Greeks would have called them alpha and beta, if that's any help.) Upon hearing *luminosity,* you may think *Ah, just like HSL.* Well, just to make things confusing, Lab's luminosity is like HSB's brightness. White indicates full-intensity color.

Meanwhile, the a channel contains colors ranging from deep green (low brightness values) to gray (medium brightness values) to vivid pink (high brightness values). The b channel ranges from bright blue (low brightness values) to gray to burnt yellow (high brightness values). As in the RGB model, these colors mix together to produce lighter colors. Only the brightness values in the luminosity channel darken the colors. Therefore, you can think of Lab as a two-channel RGB with brightness thrown on top.

To get a glimpse of how it works, try the following simple experiment.

Steps: Testing out the Lab mode

1. Create a new image in the Lab mode — say, 300 × 300 pixels.

2. Press the D key to return the default colors — black and white — to the toolbox. Then press Ctrl-2 to go to the a channel.

3. Double-click on the gradient tool in the toolbox. Make sure that you see the words Normal, Foreground to Background, and Linear in the Gradient Tool Options panel of the Brushes palette. If those words aren't visible, select them from the first, second, and third pop-up menus, respectively.

4. Shift-drag with the gradient tool from the top to the bottom of the window.

5. Press Ctrl-3 to go to the b channel. Shift-drag from left to right with the gradient tool to create a horizontal gradation.

6. Press Ctrl-0 to return to the composite display, which lets you view all channels at once. If you're using a 24-bit monitor, you should be looking at a window filled with an incredible array of super-bright colors. In theory, these are the brightest shades of all the colors you can see. In practice, however, the colors are limited by the display capabilities of your RGB monitor.

7. If you really want a sobering sight, choose Mode⇨CMYK and watch those bright colors disappear. Aagh! Isn't it pitiful? Luckily, CMYK is capable of doing a slightly better job than this. Choose Image⇨Adjust⇨Levels (or press Ctrl-L). Then click on the Auto button and press Return. That's better — much better, in fact — but it's still much more muted its Lab counterpart.

Using Lab

Being device independent, the Lab mode can be used to edit any image. Editing in the Lab mode is as fast as editing in the RGB mode and several times faster than editing in the CMYK mode. If you plan on printing your image to color separations, you may want to experiment with using the Lab mode instead of RGB, because Lab ensures that no colors are altered when you convert the image to CMYK, except to change colors that fall outside the CMYK range. In fact, any time you convert an image from RGB to CMYK, Photoshop automatically converts the image to the Lab mode as an intermediate step.

Tip   If you work with Photo CDs often, open the scans directly from the Photo CD as Lab images. Kodak's proprietary YCC color model is nearly identical to Lab, so you can expect an absolute minimum of data loss; some people claim there is no loss whatsoever.

Indexed colors

In Chapter 2, we mentioned that Photoshop automatically dithers your images to the bit depth of your monitor. Therefore, you can create 24-bit images regardless of the screen you use. However, if you specifically want to create an 8-bit or less-colorful image, you can choose Mode⇨Indexed Color to round off all the colors to a finite palette, known as a *color lookup table* (CLUT).

Using the Indexed Color command

To index the colors in an image, choose Mode⇨Indexed Color. (It's called indexing, incidentally, because you're reining in colors that used to roam free about the spectrum into a rigid, inflexible, maniacally oppressive CLUT. Will you ever be able to look another color in the face?) Photoshop displays the Indexed Color dialog box shown in Figure 4-6, which offers these tempting options:

✦ **Resolution:** Select one of these radio buttons to specify the number of colors you want to retain in your image. If the image already contains fewer than 256 colors, Photoshop computes this number and automatically enters it into the Other option box. If the Other option box is empty, you'll probably want to select the 8 Bits/Pixel option. This is the default setting.

✦ **Palette:** These options determine how Photoshop computes the colors in the CLUT. If the image already contains fewer than 256 colors, select Exact to transfer every color found in the image to the CLUT. The next option is labeled *System* if the 8 Bits/Pixel option is selected; otherwise, it is labeled *Uniform*. Either way, Photoshop computes a CLUT based on a uniform sampling of colors from the RGB spectrum. (We discuss this option in more detail later in this chapter.) The Adaptive option selects the most frequently used colors in the image, which typically delivers the best possible result. Finally, you can select Custom to load a CLUT palette from disk, or Previous to use the last CLUT created by the Indexed Color command. This last option is dimmed unless you have previously employed the command during the current session.

Robert   That System option can cause you some grief — it sounds like if you choose it, you're getting the Windows 95 system colors. Not so — there are at most 20 Windows static "system" colors — in terms of how things are laid out, the top 10 and bottom 10 (black and white are fixed). If you want to see which ones they are, either bring up Display from the Control Panel, or right-click on the Windows 95 desktop. Select the Appearance tab and drop down the color box next to the Item entry.

Tip   You can influence the performance of the Adaptive option by selecting an area of your image before choosing Mode⇨Index. Photoshop will then favor the selected area when creating the palette. For example, when indexing an image of a person wearing a brightly colored costume, you may want to make sure that the flesh colors are not underrepresented in the new palette. To do this, you would select a portion of exposed skin and then choose the Index command.

Robert   Although the Adaptive option represents a good default choice, you have to use your head. Imagine a photograph of me in a blue suit in a blue room, waving an artist's palette of oil paints (great illustration idea for the end of this chapter). If you chose Adaptive, Photoshop would weight towards the blues, and the artist's palette may well get lost in the resultant color shuffle. You'd be far better off using the Uniform palette in this case.

✦ **Dither:** Use the Dither options to specify how Photoshop distributes CLUT colors throughout the indexed image. If you select None, Photoshop maps each color in the image to its closest equivalent in the CLUT, pixel for pixel. This option is useful only if you selected Exact from the Palette options or if you want to perform further editing on an image that requires uninterrupted expanses of color. The Pattern option is available only if you selected System from the Palette options — but even then, avoid it like the plague, because it dithers colors in a geometric pattern, as shown in the lower right example of both Figure 4-7 and Color Plate 4-2. The final option, Diffusion, dithers colors randomly to create a naturalistic effect, as shown in the lower left example of Figure 4-7 and Color Plate 4-2. Nine out of ten times, Diffusion is the option you'll want to use.

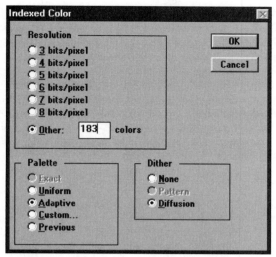

Figure 4-6: The Indexed Color options let you specify how many colors you want to retain in your image, how Photoshop computes the color lookup table, and the way in which colors are distributed throughout the image.

Note For some reason, Photoshop doesn't let you index Lab or CMYK images. If the Indexed Color command is dimmed, choose Mode⇨RGB to convert the image to the RGB mode and then choose Mode⇨Indexed Color.

Tip Some of Photoshop's functions, including the gradient tool, all the edit tools, and the commands under the Filter menu, refuse to work in the indexed color mode. Others, like feathering and the paintbrush and airbrush tools, don't work the way they ought to. If you plan on doing much editing on an 8-bit image in Photoshop, convert it to the RGB mode, edit it as desired, and then switch back to the indexed color mode when you're finished.

Creating images for the screen

Many people make the mistake of using the Indexed Color command to make an image smaller on disk. Certainly, an 8-bit indexed image is smaller than its 24-bit counterpart in RAM. However, this savings doesn't necessarily translate to disk. For example, the JPEG format almost always compresses a 24-bit image to a smaller size on disk than the same image indexed to 8-bit and saved in some other format. (As shown back in Table 4-1, JPEG doesn't support indexed images.) Furthermore, JPEG sacrifices considerably less information than does the Indexed Color command.

Therefore, the only reason to index an image is to prepare it for display with a video card running with 256-color (8-bit) drivers. Suppose you created a repeating pattern that you want to apply to your Windows desktop. Even if you did your work while running High-Color or True Color video drivers, you may well want to save the resultant BMP file as Indexed Color. Here's why. Supposing you want bragging rights — you post your file online, or send it to your friends. If they don't have the higher color capabilities, they'll howl at how your wallpaper appears on their 256-color screens. Choose the Indexed Color command, select 8 Bits/Pixel from the Resolution options, and select System from the Palette options to use the system software's CLUT palette. Finally, select Diffusion from the Dither options to achieve the most satisfying effect. After indexing the image, you can pump it out and start bragging.

Editing indexed colors

If you're creating images to be displayed in 256-color mode by an application, you may be better off selecting Adaptive from the Palette radio buttons in the Indexed Color dialog box. This setup lets Photoshop pick the most popular colors from the 24-bit version of the image instead of constraining it to the system palette. But even the Adaptive option doesn't get things 100 percent right. On occasion, Photoshop selects some colors that look noticeably off base.

To replace all occurrences of one color in an indexed image with a different color, choose Mode➪Color Table. The ensuing Color Table dialog box, shown in Figure 4-8, enables you to selectively edit the contents of the CLUT. To edit any color, click on it to display the Color Picker dialog box, select a different color, and click on the OK button to return to the Color Table dialog box. Then click on the OK button to close the Color Table dialog box and change every pixel colored in the old color to the new color.

The Color Table dialog box also lets you open and save CLUTs and select predefined CLUTs from the Table pop-up menu. What the Color Table dialog box doesn't let you do is identify a color from the image. For example, if you're trying to fix a color in your image, you can't display the Color Table dialog box, click on the color in the image, and have the dialog box show you the corresponding color in the CLUT. The only way to be sure you're editing the correct color — and be forewarned, this is a royal pain in the behind — is to slog through the following steps, which begin before you choose Mode➪Color Table.

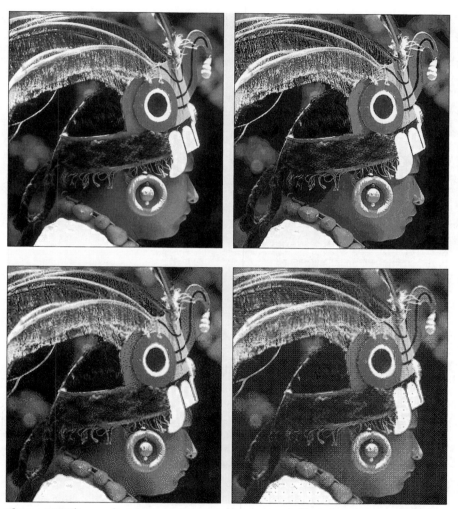

Figure 4-7: The results of converting an image (upper left) to the System CLUT palette subject to each of the three Dither options: (clockwise from upper right) None, Pattern, and Diffusion.

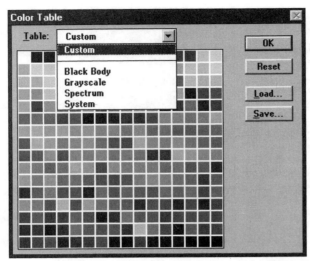

Figure 4-8: Use the Color Table command to edit colors in the color lookup table.

Steps: Editing a specific CLUT color

1. Use the eyedropper tool to click on the offending color in the image, making it the foreground color.

2. Click on the foreground color icon to display the specs for the color in the Color Picker dialog box. Write down the RGB values on a handy piece of paper, the palm of your hand, a bald friend's scalp, or whatever. (Don't edit the color inside the Color Picker dialog box at this time. If you do, you just change the color without changing any pixel in the image associated with that color.) Press Ctrl-period to escape the dialog box.

3. Choose Mode➪Color Table. Now here's the fun part: Click on a color that looks as if it may be the right one. After the Color Picker appears, compare the color's RGB numbers to those you wrote down. If they match, boy, did you ever luck out. Go ahead and edit the color as desired. If the RGB values don't match, press Ctrl-period to return to the Color Table dialog box and try again. And again. And again.

Tip To create a *color ramp* — that is, a gradual color progression — in the CLUT, drag rather than click on the colors in the palette to select multiple colors at a time. Photoshop then displays the Color Picker dialog box, letting you edit the first color in the ramp. After you select the desired color and press Return, the Color Picker reappears, this time asking you to edit the last color in the ramp. After you specify this color, Photoshop automatically creates the colors between the first and last colors in the ramp in even RGB increments.

Grayscale

Grayscale is possibly our favorite color mode. It frees you from all the hassles and expense of working with color and provides access to every bit of Photoshop's power and functionality. Anyone who says you can't do just as much with grayscale as you can with color missed out on *Citizen Kane, L'Avventura, To Kill a Mockingbird,* and *Raging Bull.* You can print grayscale images to any laser printer, reproduce them in any publication, and edit them on nearly any machine. Besides, they look great, they remind you of old movies, and they make a hefty book like this one affordable. What could be better?

Other than extolling its virtues, however, there isn't a whole lot to say about grayscale. You can convert an image to the grayscale mode regardless of its current mode, and you can convert from grayscale to any other mode just as easily. In fact, choosing Mode⇨Grayscale is a necessary step in converting a color image to a duotone or black-and-white bitmap.

Search your channels before converting

When you convert an image from one of the color modes to the grayscale mode, Photoshop normally weights the values of each color channel in a way that retains the apparent brightness of the overall image. For example, when you convert an image from RGB, Photoshop weights red more heavily than blue when computing dark values because red is a darker-looking color than blue (much as that may seem contrary to popular belief).

 Tip

But if you choose Mode⇨Grayscale while viewing a single color channel, Photoshop retains all brightness values in that channel only and abandons the data in the other channels. This can be an especially useful technique for rescuing a grayscale image from a bad RGB scan.

Therefore, before switching to the grayscale mode, be sure to take a look at the individual color channels — particularly the red and green channels (the blue channel frequently contains substandard detail) — to see how each channel may look on its own. To browse the channels, press Ctrl-1 for red, Ctrl-2 for green, and Ctrl-3 for blue. Or Ctrl-1 for cyan, Ctrl-2 for magenta, Ctrl-3 for yellow, and Ctrl-4 for black. Or even Ctrl-1 for luminosity, Ctrl-2 for *a,* and Ctrl-3 for *b*. The next chapter describes color channels in more detail.

Dot gain interference

You should be aware of a little item that may throw off your gray value calculations. If the Use Dot Gain for Grayscale Images check box in the Printer Inks Setup dialog box (File⇨Preferences⇨Printer Inks Setup) is selected, Photoshop figures in dot gain when calculating the lightness and darkness of grayscale images.

Cross Ref Dot gain is more thoroughly discussed in the "Printer calibration" section of Chapter 6, but the basic concept is this: Printed images are made up of tiny dots of ink called *halftone cells*. During the printing process, the halftone cells expand — it's sort of like what happens to drops of water plopped onto a paper towel. The Use Dot Gain for Grayscale Images feature lightens the gray values in an image, which reduces the size of the halftone cells, thereby giving the dots some room to bleed.

Suppose that you click on the foreground color icon and change the B (Brightness) value in the Color Picker dialog box to 50 percent. Later, after applying the 50 percent gray to the current image, you move your cursor over some of the medium gray pixels while the Info palette is displayed. You notice that the Info palette interprets the pixels to be 56 percent gray, 6 percentage points darker than the color you specified. This happens because Photoshop automatically darkens the colors in your image to reflect how they will print subject to the dot gain specified in the Printing Inks setup dialog box.

Background At this point, we need to insert two bits of information to avoid (or perhaps enhance) confusion. First, as long as the S (saturation) value is 0, the B (brightness) value is the only Color Picker option you need to worry about when editing grayscale images. Second, although the B (brightness) value measures luminosity, ranging from 0 percent for black to 100 percent for white, the K value in the Info dialog box measures ink coverage, thus reversing the figures to 100 percent for black and 0 percent for white. Ignoring dot gain for a moment, this means that a 50 percent brightness translates to 50 percent ink coverage, a 40 percent brightness translates to 60 percent ink coverage, a 30 percent brightness translates to 70 percent ink coverage, and so on.

In theory, automatic dot gain compensation is a good idea, but in practice, it frequently gets in the way. For example, in creating the displacement map gradations in the preceding chapter, we had a heck of a time trying to achieve a medium gray that didn't slightly move pixels in the affected image. The culprit was dot gain. Luckily, the Use Dot Gain for Grayscale Images check box is no longer selected by default in Version 3, but it's still something to keep an eye on.

Black and white (bitmap)

Choose Mode⇨Bitmap to convert a grayscale image to exclusively black and white pixels. This may sound like a pretty boring option, but it can prove useful for gaining complete control over the printing of grayscale images. After all, output devices such as laser printers and imagesetters render grayscale images as series of tiny dots. Using the Bitmap command, you can specify the size, shape, and angle of those dots.

When you choose Mode⇨Bitmap, Photoshop displays the Bitmap dialog box, shown in Figure 4-9. Here you specify the resolution of the black-and-white image and select a conversion process. The options work as follows:

✦ **Output:** Specify the resolution of the black-and-white file. If you want control over every single pixel available to your printer, raise this value to match your printer's resolution. As a rule of thumb, try setting the Output value somewhere between 200 and 250 percent of the Input value.

✦ **50% Threshold:** Select this option to make every pixel that is darker than 50 percent gray black and every pixel that is 50 percent gray, or lighter, white. Unless you are working toward some special effect — for example, overlaying a black-and-white version of an image over the original grayscale image — this option most likely isn't for you. (And if you're working toward a special effect, Image⇨Map⇨Threshold is the better alternative.)

✦ **Pattern Dither:** This option dithers an image using that worthless geometric pattern we discussed in the "Indexed colors" section. Not only are the images produced by this option ugly, as demonstrated in the left example in Figure 4-10, but the space between dots has a tendency to fill in, especially when you output to a laser printer.

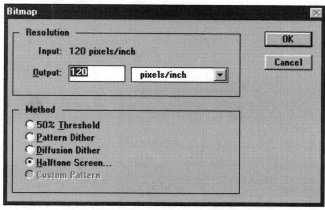

Figure 4-9: The Bitmap dialog box converts images from grayscale to black and white.

✦ **Diffusion Dither:** Select this option to create a mezzotint-like effect, as demonstrated in the second example in Figure 4-10. Again, because this option converts an image into thousands of stray pixels, you can expect your image to darken dramatically when output to a low-resolution laser printer and when reproduced. Be sure to lighten the image with something like the Levels command, as described in the "Making Custom Brightness Adjustments" section of Chapter 16, before selecting this option.

✦ **Halftone Screen:** When you select this option and press Return, Photoshop displays the Halftone Screen dialog box shown in Figure 4-11, which is nearly an exact duplicate of the one you access by clicking on the Screen button in the Page Setup dialog box. Enter the number of halftone cells per inch in the Frequency option box and the angle of the cells in the Angle option box. Then select a cell shape from the Shape pop-up menu. Figure 4-12 shows examples of four cell shapes, each with a frequency of 20 lpi (lines per inch). (The image appears reduced in the figure; therefore, the halftone frequency appears higher.)

Figure 4-10: The results of selecting the Pattern Dither option (left) and the Diffusion Dither option (right).

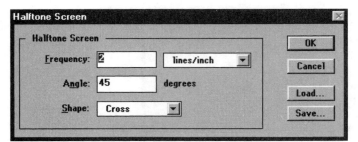

Figure 4-11: This dialog box appears when you select the Halftone Screen option in the Bitmap dialog box.

✦ **Custom Pattern:** If you specified a repeating pattern by choosing Edit⇨Define Pattern, you can use it as a custom halftoning pattern. Figure 4-13 shows two custom examples. The first pattern was created using the Add Noise, Emboss, and Ripple filters (as discussed in the "Creating texture effects" section of Chapter 15. The second is the Twirl Pattern file, which you'll find in \PLUG-INS\DISPMAPS under your main Photoshop directory. (In fact, the Displacement Maps directory contains several images you can use as custom halftoning patterns. Check them out.)

The wackiest image appears in Figure 4-14. It may be hard to tell what's going on in this example because it contains an image inside an image. But if you look closely, you can see a bunch of tiny Lenins. (You know, the guy in the mausoleum.)

We describe how to create this seamless repeating pattern in an exercise in the "How to create patterns" section of Chapter 11. Granted, the Lenin pattern competes with the original image to the extent that you can barely distinguish any of the cherub's features. But what the hey, it's worth a chuckle or two.

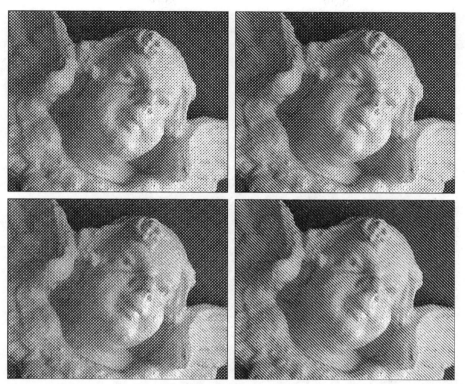

Figure 4-12: Four examples of halftone cell shapes, including (clockwise from upper left) Round, Diamond, Line, and Cross.

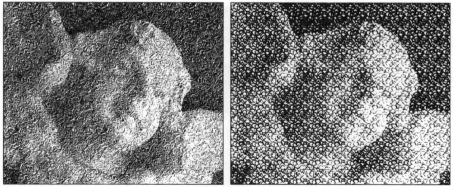

Figure 4-13: Two examples of employing repeating patterns as custom halftoning patterns. The patterns include the Ripple filter texture from the previous chapter (left) and the Twirl pattern image in the Displacement Maps folder (right).

Caution Photoshop lets you edit individual pixels in the so-called bitmap mode, but that's about the extent of it. After you go to black-and-white, you can't perform any serious editing, and worse, you can't expect to return to the grayscale mode. So be sure to finish your image editing before choosing Mode⇨Bitmap. More important, be sure to save your image before converting it to black-and-white. Frankly, saving is a good idea when performing any color conversion.

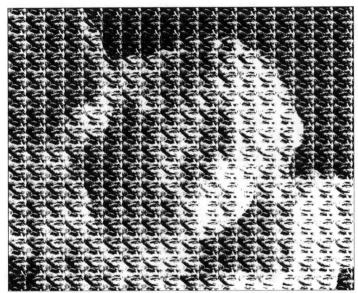

Figure 4-14: A black-and-white cherub composed entirely of itsy-bitsy Lenin faces. Ten years ago, we could have been deported for this.

Using Photoshop's Other Color Selection Methods

Besides the Color Picker dialog box, Photoshop provides a handful of additional techniques for selecting colors. The sections that finish out this chapter explain how to use the Custom Colors dialog box, the Colors palette, and the eyedropper tool.

Predefined colors

If you click on the Custom button inside the Color Picker dialog box, Photoshop displays the Custom Colors dialog box shown in Figure 4-15. In this dialog box you can select from a variety of predefined colors by choosing the color family from the Book pop-up menu, moving the slider triangles up and down to specify a general range of colors, and then select a color from the color list on the left. If you own the swatchbook for a color family, you can locate a color by entering its number on the keyboard.

The color families represented in the Book pop-up menu fall into seven brands: ANPA (now NAA), DIC, Focoltone, Pantone, Toyo, and TruMatch. You're likely to find certain brands more useful than others. The following sections briefly introduce the brands in order of their impact on the American market from smallest impact to greatest.

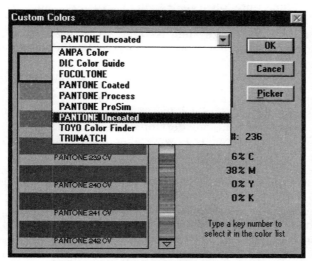

Figure 4-15: The Custom Colors dialog box lets you select predefined colors from brand-name libraries.

Background The number one use for predefined colors in Photoshop is in the creation of duotones, tritones, and quadtones (described in Chapter 6). You can also use predefined colors to match the colors of an image to a commercial standard.

Focoltone, DIC, and Toyo

Focoltone, Dianippon Ink and Chemical (DIC), and Toyo have negligible impact. All are color standards with followings abroad. Focoltone is an English company. DIC and Toyo are popular in the Japanese market, but have next to no subscribers outside Japan.

Newspaper Association of America

ANPA — *American Newspaper Publishers Association* — recently changed its name to NAA, which stands for *Newspaper Association of America,* and updated its color catalog. NAA provides a small sampling of 33 process colors (mixes of cyan, magenta, yellow, and black ink) plus 5 *spot colors* (colors produced by printing a single ink). The NAA colors isolate the color combinations that reproduce most successfully on inexpensive newsprint and provide advertisers with a solid range of colors to choose. You can purchase a Pocket Tint Chart from NAA for $175. Members pay only $100.

TruMatch

TruMatch remains our personal favorite process-color standard. Designed entirely using a desktop system and created especially with desktop publishers in mind, the TruMatch Colorfinder swatchbook features more than 2,000 process colors, organized by hue, saturation, and brightness. Each hue is broken down into 40 tints and shades. Tints are created by reducing the saturation in 15 percent increments; shades are created by adding black ink in 6 percent increments. The result shows you exactly which colors you can attain using a desktop system. If you're wondering what a CMYK blend will look like when printed, you need not look past the TruMatch Colorfinder.

Pantone

Deke's been hard on Pantone over the years, and for good reason. Prior to TruMatch, Pantone dominated the desktop market, and acted like it. It was unresponsive to criticism, condescending to service bureaus and desktop designers, and slow to improve its product. Since TruMatch came along, however, Pantone has acted like a different company.

On the heels of TruMatch, Pantone released a 3,006-color Process Color System Guide (labeled *Pantone Process* in the Book pop-up menu). Pantone also produces the foremost spot color swatchbook, the Color Formula Guide 1000, and the Process Color Imaging Guide, which enables you to quickly figure out whether you can closely match a Pantone spot color using a process-color blend. Pantone spot colors are ideal for creating duotones, as in Chapter 6. Furthermore, Pantone is supported by every computer application for the color prepress market. Expect Pantone to remain the primary color printing standard for years to come.

The Picker palette

Another means of selecting colors in Photoshop is to use the Picker palette, shown in Figure 4-16. If you're willing to sacrifice on-screen real estate to define colors without calling up the Color Picker dialog box, the Picker palette is a useful tool indeed. To display the palette, choose Window➪Palettes➪Show Picker. You then can use the elements and options inside the palette as follows:

✦ **Foreground color/background color:** Click on the foreground or background color icon in the Picker palette to specify the color that you want to edit. If you click on the foreground or background color icon that's already highlighted (as indicated by a double-line frame), the Color Picker dialog box is displayed.

✦ **Slider bars:** The triangles edit the highlighted color. By default, the sliders represent the red, green, and blue primary colors. You can change the slider bars by choosing a different color model from the palette menu.

✦ **Alert triangle:** Photoshop displays the alert triangle when a color falls outside the CMYK color gamut. The color swatch to the right of the triangle shows the closest CMYK equivalent. Click on the triangle or the color swatch to replace the current color with the CMYK equivalent.

✦ **Color bar:** The bar along the bottom of the Picker palette displays all colors contained in the CMYK spectrum. Click or drag inside the color bar to lift a color and make it the current foreground or background color (depending on whether the foreground or background icon is selected above). The sliders update as you drag. Alt-click or drag to lift the background color if the foreground icon is selected, or the foreground color if the background color is selected.

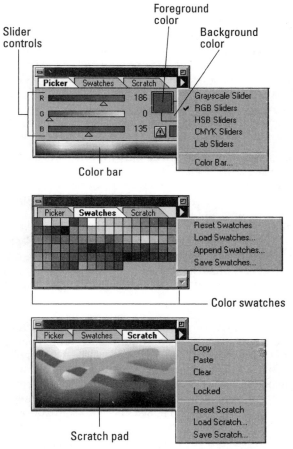

Figure 4-16: The three-paneled Picker palette enables you to edit colors without having to display the Color Picker dialog box.

✦ **Color Bar option:** You don't have to accept the CMYK spectrum in the color bar. To change to a different spectrum, select the Color Bar command from the palette pop-up menu (or Ctrl-click on the color bar itself). The resulting dialog box lets you change to the RGB spectrum or select a black-to-white gradation (Grayscale Ramp). If you select Foreground to Background, the color bar is filled with a gradation from the current foreground color to the current background color. Unless you select the Lock to Current Colors check box, the color bar continuously represents the newest foreground and background colors.

Swatches panel

As shown in Figure 4-16, the Picker palette offers two additional panels. The Swatches panel lets you collect colors for future use, like a favorite-colors reservoir. To select a color, click on it. To add the current foreground color to the panel, Alt-click on an existing color swatch to replace the old color, or click in an empty swatch to append the new color. In either case, your cursor temporarily changes to a paint bucket. To delete a color from the panel, Ctrl-click on a color swatch. Your cursor changes to a pair of scissors.

You can also save and load color palettes. Load Swatches replaces the panel colors with the file colors; Append Swatches tacks the colors onto the end of the palette. The Color Palettes folder, inside the same folder as the Photoshop application, contains palettes for the major color libraries. When a palette is loaded, positioning your cursor over a color swatch makes the name of that color appear in the panel tab.

Scratch panel

The Scratch panel lets you mix colors outside of the image window. You can paint and edit inside the scratch pad using any of the tools in the toolbox. To sample a color from the pad, click on it with the eyedropper tool. To erase the scratch pad, drag inside it with the eraser tool or select the Clear option from the palette pop-up menu.

You can also copy and paste the contents of the scratch pad. Just select what you want to copy and select the Copy option in the pop-up menu. Or select the Paste option to paste the contents of the Clipboard into the pad. The pasted image always appears in the scratch pad at actual size. You have the option of moving it around right after you select Paste. To deselect the image, click in the scratch pad with a selection tool.

Tip   You can't access the Copy and Paste options from the keyboard, but there's an easier way to transfer images back and forth between image window and scratch pad. Select an area inside the image window, drag it over the scratch pad, and drop it in place. You can likewise drag a selection from the scratch pad into the image window. In both cases, Photoshop clones the selection rather than moving it. (For more information about selecting, cloning, and dragging and dropping, see Chapter 8.) If you only want to lift colors from the scratch pad and not paint on it, select the Locked option. As long as this option is checked, your cursor will change to an eyedropper inside the Scratch panel. You will not be allowed to erase the contents of the scratch pad or paste an image inside it.

The eyedropper tool

The eyedropper tool — which you can select by pressing the I key — is the most convenient means of selecting colors in Photoshop. Very quickly, here's how it works:

 ✦ **Selecting a foreground color:** To select a new foreground color, click on the desired color inside any open image window with the eyedropper tool. (This assumes that the foreground icon in the Picker palette is selected. If the background icon is selected, Alt-click with the eyedropper tool to lift the foreground color.) You can even click inside a background window to lift a color without bringing that window to the foreground.

✦ **Selecting a background color:** To select a new background color, Alt-click on the desired color with the eyedropper tool. (Again, this assumes that the foreground icon is selected in the Picker palette. If the background icon is selected, click with the eyedropper to lift the background color.)

✦ **Skating over the color spectrum:** Animate the foreground color control box by dragging with the eyedropper tool in the image window. When you achieve the desired color, release your mouse button. To animate the background color icon, Alt-drag with the eyedropper tool. The icon color changes as you drag.

✦ **Sampling multiple pixels:** To average the colors of several neighboring pixels, double-click on the eyedropper icon in the toolbox and select a different option from the Sample Size pop-up menu in the Eyedropper Option panel of the Brushes palette.

Tip To temporarily access the eyedropper tool when using the type, paint bucket, gradient, line, pencil, airbrush, or paintbrush tool, press the Alt key. The eyedropper cursor remains in force while the Alt key is down. You can select only a foreground color while Alt-clicking with any of these tools, even if the background color icon is selected in the Picker palette. To select a background color, select the eyedropper (press the I key) and then Alt-click (or click) in an image window.

What's Wrong with RGB, CMYK, and Associates

If a section could have an icon, this one would have my Robert icon. I'm taking issue with Deke, and with what you may think you know about color. Thus I've saved this section for last. Now that you've studied these color models, you may think that you're ready to become a color maven. Think again. Color models don't always behave like traditional media. Let's start with an experiment. If you don't want to do this experiment, open CARROT.JPG from the Chapter 19 directory of the CD-ROM and follow along.

Steps: You can't trust models

1. Set up a new image at screen resolution (72 dpi) about 400 pixels square in RGB mode.

2. Using the Paintbrush with a big brush selection and 100 percent opacity, paint a big solid area carrot orange. You can use RGB 247, 108, 13 or HSB 24, 95, 97.

3. Now add a layer. Set the opacity to 100%. Cover half of the orange area with a sky blue color: RGB 4, 137, 42 or HSB 206, 98, 95.

4. Now start moving the opacity slider for Layer 1 downward. As you move it, watch the area of orange overlaid with blue. The color will change to a purplish-brownish-yuckish neutral color. Now sit down — you definitely want to be sitting when you read what follows.

If you've studied color theory, you may expect to get the neutralized color you're now looking at. But what you're seeing on-screen is not what you get if you mix those two colors in traditional media. In watercolor, oils, or pastels, you'd get a striking yellowish green. (If you twiddle the Layer 1 opacity slider a bit, you may see just a tinge of green at one point. But it's nowhere close to the yellowish green you'd get in traditional media.)

Need more convincing? Buy a pastel pencil for each color. Draw a series of closely parallel lines with one pencil; on top of that, draw parallel lines at a 90 degree angle with the other pencil. Now use a tissue or a rolled scrap of paper and rub the colors. If an art supply store seems like enemy territory, look at CARROT.JPG in the Chapter 19 directory of the CD-ROM; all the results are there, including a scan of the traditional media experiment.

Note   If you try the preceding demonstration with Fractal Design Painter, you'll notice that Painter comes a lot closer. This is precisely why I advocate using Painter for mixing colors — head to Chapter 19 for all the details.

Here's why Photoshop gives bogus results: In the CMYK section, Deke hinted at discrepancies. Unfortunately, (this is probably the only place I've ever thought Deke was wrong) that color interaction works the same way using lights and pigments. The lights approach is a technical one from the physical sciences. That, and its direct link to color film, is the problem. Color film has less color capability than traditional artists' colors or human eyes. You don't need me to tell you this. You've probably seen transparencies or art books of paintings by the Old Masters that just don't capture the originals. In fact, an artist can whip up a painting that brings the best color system to its knees.

Robert   This is one of the two things wrong with Bill Gates buying the digital reproduction rights to Old Master paintings. These paintings have more color subtlety than any process can capture. I've spent countless hours with Microsoft Art Gallery and its rendition of Titian's *Bacchus and Ariadne,* a painting I know very well. Even with endless Photoshop tweaks, there is no way that the digital version matches the original. (What's the second thing wrong? It's not clear that museums can sell the rights — after all, Titian didn't sign a contract with London's National Gallery. But that's another matter.)

The programmers who design digital color models rely on film, reproduction, and color physics to represent how colors interact. But painters deal with perception. For example, a shadow on a green background is not a darker green, green with black added to it, or (worst) black. (This is why shadows in computer art look so dull and muddy.) Look carefully at the shadow a tree casts on a lawn — the shadow is affected by the light reflecting off the entire surrounding area and isn't true black at all. Remember that the Impressionists used to scream *there is no black in nature.* Smart cookies, those Impressionists.

It would be unfair to expect computer programmers to be colorists as well. What they have done, they have done superbly — but you, the Photoshop user, should be wary. Use the tools they have given you, but watch how colors interact in the real world.

Navigating Channels

Color Channels

Have you ever seen a set of separated CMYK transparencies?
Print professionals see these things all the time; even if you're an
absolute beginner, you may have come in contact with them —
perhaps on a grade school field trip to the print shop. Some
nebulous adult — life was a stream of nebulous adults back
then — held up four sheets of acetate. One sheet showed a cyan
picture, another showed the same picture in magenta, a third
showed it in yellow, and the last depicted the scene in a rather
washed-out black. By themselves, the pictures appeared exceedingly light and rather sparse in the detail department. But when
they were put together — one layered in front of another — you
saw a full-color picture. *Whoa. Neato. Cool.*

Sound familiar? Those sheets of acetate have a functional
equivalent inside Photoshop: *channels.* In a CMYK image, for
example, there is one cyan channel, one magenta channel, one
yellow channel, and one black channel. They mix on-screen to
form a full-color image. The RGB mode features a red channel, a
green channel, and a blue channel. Because RGB is the color
model of light, the three images mix together like three different-
color slides in different projectors aimed at the same screen. In
other words, regardless of color mode, channels are distinct
planes of primary color.

Background Channels frequently correspond to the structure of an input or
output device. Each channel in a CMYK image, for example,
corresponds to a different printer's plate when the document
goes to press. The cyan plate is inked with cyan, the magenta
plate is inked with magenta, and so on. Each channel in an RGB
image corresponds to a pass of the red, green, or blue scanner
sensor over the original photograph or artwork. Only the Lab
mode is device independent, so its channels don't correspond to
any piece of hardware.

Why you should care

Even if you don't like to rebuild car engines or poke preserved frog entrails with sharp knives, you'll get a charge out of editing channels. The fact is, channels provide you with yet another degree of selective control over an image.

Consider this example: Your client scanned an image that he wants integrated into some goofy ad campaign for his car dealership. Unfortunately, the scan is downright rotten. The image is a picture of his favorite daughter, after all, so you praise him on his fine scan and say something like *No problem, boss.*

Suddenly, it occurs to you to look at the channels. With very little effort, you discover that the red and green channels look okay, but the blue channel looks like it's melting.

You've located the cancer, Doctor. You merely have to fix this one channel. A wave of the Gaussian Blur filter here, an application of the Levels command there, and some selective rebuilding of missing detail borrowed from the other channels result in an image that resembles a living, breathing human being. It may not be absolute perfection, but it's solid enough to pass muster.

How channels work

Photoshop devotes 8 bits of data to each pixel in each channel, thus permitting 256 brightness values, from 0 (black) to 255 (white). Therefore, each channel is actually an independent grayscale image. At first, you may be thrown off by this. If an RGB image is made up of red, green, and blue channels, why do all the channels look gray? Photoshop provides an option in the General Preferences dialog box (Ctrl-K) called Color Channels in Color that, when selected, displays each channel in its corresponding primary color. But although this feature can be reassuring — particularly to novices — it's equally counterproductive. When you view an 8-bit image composed exclusively of shades of red, for example, it's easy to miss subtle variations in detail that may appear obvious when you print the image. You may have problems accurately gauging the impact of filters and tonal adjustments. Let's face it, red isn't a friendly shade to stare at for a half hour of intense editing. So leave the Color Channels in Color option off and temporarily suspend your biological urge for on-screen color. With a little experience, you'll be able to better monitor your adjustments and predict the outcome of your edits in plain old grayscale.

Tip Editing a single channel doesn't mean that you have to work with blinders on. At any time, you can see how your changes affect the full-color image. Simply create a new view of your image by choosing Window⇨New Window. Leave this window set to the standard composite view (presumably RGB, but it could be CMYK, Lab, or any other color mode) and edit away on the individual channel in the first image. (Don't worry, we explain how to switch channels in the very next section.)

Images that include 256 colors or fewer can be expressed in a single channel and therefore do not include multiple channels that you can edit independently. A grayscale image, for example, includes a single channel. A black-and-white image permits only 1 bit of data per pixel, so a single channel is more than enough to express it. Indexed images represent the only case where a single channel can express different hues, because each of the 256 colors is customized according to a CLUT (as described in the previous chapter). Duotones are the really weird ones. Though they may contain two, three, or four plates of color, Photoshop treats them as a single channel of 8-bit color. We explain duotones in detail in Chapter 6.

Cross Ref You can add channels above and beyond those required to represent a color or grayscale image for the purpose of storing masks, as described in the "Creating an Independent Mask Channel" section of Chapter 9. Even then, each channel is limited to 8 bits of data per pixel — meaning that it's just another grayscale image. Mask channels don't affect the appearance of the image on-screen or when it is printed. Instead, they save selection outlines, as Chapter 9 explains.

How to switch and view channels

To access channels in Photoshop, display the Channels panel of the Layers palette by choosing Window➪Palettes➪Show Channels. Every channel in the image will appear — including any mask channels — as shown in Figure 5-1. Photoshop even shows little thumbnail views of each channel so you can see what it looks like.

To switch to a different channel, click on a channel name in the Channels palette. The channel name becomes gray — like the Mask channel in Figure 5-1 — so you can now edit it independently of other channels in the image.

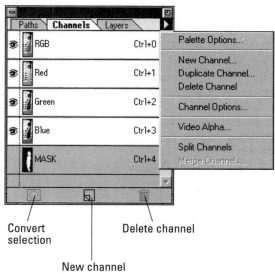

Figure 5-1: The Channels palette provided by Photoshop 3.

Tip   To edit more than one channel at a time, click on one channel name and then Shift-click on another. You can also Shift-click on an active channel to deactivate it independently of any others.

When you select a channel, Photoshop normally displays the channel that you want to edit. However, you can view additional channels beyond those that you want to edit. To specify which channels appear, click in the far left column of the Channels palette. Click on an eyeball icon to make it disappear and hence hide that channel. To display the channel, click where there is no eyeball.

When only one channel is visible, that channel appears gray or in color (depending on the setting of the Color Channels in Color check box in the General Preferences dialog box). However, when more than one channel is visible, you always see color. If both the blue and green channels are visible, for example, the image appears blue-green. If the red and green channels are visible, the image has a yellow cast, and so on. If a mask channel and another channel are visible, the mask appears by default as a pink overlay. (The color of the mask can be changed.) For more information on viewing two or more individual channels simultaneously — and why in the world you'd want to do so — read the "Viewing mask and image" section of Chapter 9.

In addition to the individual channels, Photoshop provides access to a *composite view* that displays all colors in an RGB, CMYK, or Lab image at once. (The composite view does not show mask channels; you have to specify their display separately.) The composite view is listed first in the Channels palette and is displayed by default. Notice that when you select the composite view, the names of the individual color channels in the Channels palette turn gray along with the composite channel. This shows that all the channels are active. The composite view is the one in which you will perform the majority of your image editing.

Tip   Press Control plus a number key to switch between color channels. Ctrl-1 always takes you to the red (RGB), cyan (CMYK), or luminosity (Lab) channel; Ctrl-2 takes you to the green, magenta, or *a* channel; and Ctrl-3 takes you to the blue, yellow, or *b* channel. In the CMYK mode, Ctrl-4 displays the black channel. Other Ctrl-key equivalents — up to Ctrl-9 — take you to mask channels. Ctrl-0 takes you to the composite view.

The shortcuts are slightly different when you're working on a grayscale image. You access the image itself by pressing Ctrl-1. Ctrl-2 and higher take you to the mask channels.

Note   Don't freak or in any way feel inadequate if your images don't contain mask channels. As we mentioned earlier, we won't be talking about masks until Chapter 9.

Trying Channels On for Size

Color Plate 5-1 shows the yellow-orange dome of the United States Capitol building set against a deep blue evening sky. Those colors — yellow-orange and deep blue — are very nearly opposites. Therefore, you can expect to see a lot of variation between the images in the independent color channels.

RGB channels

Suppose that the Capitol is an RGB image. Figure 5-2 compares a grayscale composite of this same image (created by choosing Mode⇨Grayscale) with the contents of the red, green, and blue color channels from the original color image. The green channel is more or less in keeping with the grayscale composite because it is the neutral channel in this image (that is, no element in Color Plate 5-1 is predominantly green). But the red and blue channels differ significantly. The pixels in the red channel are lightest on the Capitol dome because the dome contains a high concentration of red. The pixels in the blue channel are lightest in the sky because — you guessed it — the sky is blue.

Grayscale composite   Red

Green   Blue

Figure 5-2: A grayscale composite of the image from Color Plate 5-1 followed by the contents of the red, green, and blue color channels.

Notice how the channels in Figure 5-2 make interesting grayscale images in and of themselves? The blue channel, for example, looks like a photo of the Capitol on a cloudy day, although the picture actually was shot at night.

We mentioned this point as a tip in the previous chapter, but it bears a bit of casual drumming into the old noggin. When converting a color image to grayscale, you have the option of calculating a grayscale composite or simply retaining the image exactly as it appears in one of the channels. To create a grayscale composite, choose Mode⇨ Grayscale when viewing all colors in the image in the composite view, as usual. To retain a single channel only, switch to that channel and then choose Mode⇨Grayscale. Instead of the usual *Discard color information?* message, Photoshop displays the message *Discard other channels?* If you click on the OK button, Photoshop chucks the other channels into the electronic abyss.

CMYK channels

In the name of fair and unbiased coverage, Figures 5-3 and 5-4 show the channels from the image after it was converted to other color modes. In Figure 5-3, we converted the image to the CMYK mode and examined its channels. Here, the predominant colors

Cyan

Magenta

Yellow

Black

Figure 5-3: The contents of the cyan, magenta, yellow, and black channels from the image shown in Color Plate 5-1.

Grayscale composite

Luminosity

a (black is green, white is magenta)

b (black is blue, white is yellow)

Figure 5-4: The grayscale composite followed by the contents of the luminosity channel and the *a* and *b* color channels after converting the image shown in Color Plate 5-1 to the Lab mode.

are cyan (the sky) and yellow (the dome). Because this color mode relies on pigments rather than light, as explained in the "CMYK" section of Chapter 4, dark areas in the channels represent high color intensity. For that reason, the sky in the cyan channel is dark, whereas it is light in the blue channel shown in Figure 5-2.

Lab channels

To create Figure 5-4, we converted the image in Color Plate 5-1 to the Lab mode. The image in the luminosity channel looks a lot like the grayscale composite because it contains the lightness and darkness values for the image. Because the *b* channel maps the yellows and blues in the image, it contains the highest degree of contrast. Meanwhile, the *a* channel, which maps colors from green to magenta, is almost uniformly gray. The only remarkable greens occur in the statue at the top of the dome and in the bright area inside the rotunda.

You can achieve some entertaining effects by applying commands from the Image⬧ Map and Image⬧Adjust submenus to the *a* and *b* color channels. For example, if we reverse the brightness values in the *b* channel in Figure 5-4 by choosing

Image⇨Map⇨Invert (Ctrl-I), the building turns bright blue, and the sky changes to a moody orange-brown. If we apply Image⇨Map⇨Equalize to the *a* channel, the sky lights up with brilliant blue and purple sparks, and the Capitol becomes deep emerald.

Other Channel Functions

In addition to viewing and editing channels using any of the techniques discussed in future chapters of this book, you can choose commands from the pop-up menu in the Channels palette and select icons along the bottom of the palette (both shown back in Figure 5-1).

Robert   About those three useful little icons at the bottom of the palette: Look at the one on the right for Delete. It's a Trash Can. That's right — a tiny little holdover from Photoshop's Mac heritage. Perhaps the next version will have the Windows 95 Recycle Bin (are you listening, Adobe?).

These commands and icons work as follows:

✦ **Palette Options:** Here's an exciting one. When you choose this command, Photoshop displays four Thumbnail Size radio buttons, enabling you to change the size of the thumbnail previews that appear along the left side of the Channels palette. Figure 5-5 shows the four thumbnail settings — nonexistent, small, medium, and large.

✦ **New Channel:** Choose this command to add a mask channel to the current image. The Channel Options dialog box appears, letting you name the channel. You also can specify the color and translucency that Photoshop applies to the channel when you view it with other channels. We explain how these options work in the "Changing the red coating" section of Chapter 9. An image can contain no more than 24 total channels, regardless of color mode. You can also create a new channel by clicking on the new channel icon at the bottom of the Channels palette.

✦ **Duplicate Channel:** Choose this command to create a duplicate of the selected channel, either inside the same document or as part of a new document. (If the composite view is active, the Duplicate Channel command is dimmed, because you can only duplicate one channel at a time.) The most common reason to use this command is to convert a channel into a mask. Again, you can find real-life applications in Chapter 9.

Tip   You can also duplicate a channel by dragging the channel name onto the new channel icon. No dialog box appears; Photoshop merely names the channel automatically. To copy a channel to a different document, drag the channel name and drop it into an open image window. Photoshop automatically creates a new channel for the duplicate.

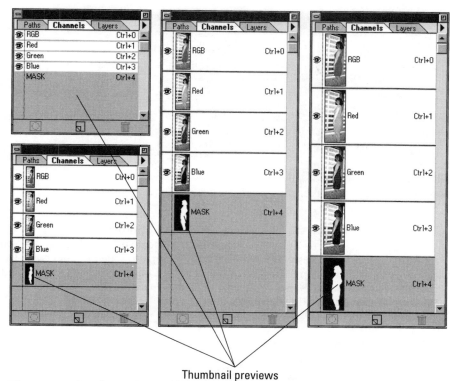

Thumbnail previews

Figure 5-5: The Channels Palette Options dialog box lets you select between four thumbnail preview options.

✦ **Delete Channel:** To delete a channel from an image, click on the channel name in the palette and choose this command. You can delete only one channel at a time. The Delete Channel command is dimmed when the composite view or any single essential color channel is active or when more than one channel is selected. If choosing a command is too much effort, just drag the channel onto the delete channel icon (the little trash icon in the lower right corner of the Channels palette).

✦ **Channel Options:** Choose this command or double-click on the channel name in the palette's scrolling list to change the name, color, and translucency settings of a mask channel, as described in the "Viewing mask and image" section of Chapter 9. The Channel Options command is dimmed when the composite view or any of the color channels is active. It is applicable to mask channels only.

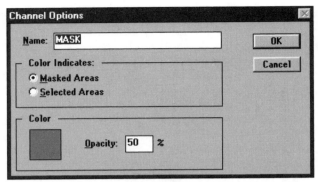

Figure 5-6: You have several options when adding a channel.

✦ **Split Channels:** When you choose this command, Photoshop splits off each channel in an image to its own independent grayscale image window. As demonstrated in Figure 5-7, Photoshop automatically appends the channel color to the end of the window name. The Split Channels command is useful as a first step in redistributing channels in an image prior to choosing Merge Channels (as demonstrated later in this chapter).

Figure 5-7: When you choose the Split Channels command, Photoshop relocates each channel to an independent image window.

✦ **Merge Channels:** Choose this command to merge several images into a single multichannel image. The images you want to merge must be open, they must be grayscale, and they must be of absolutely equal size — the same number of pixels horizontally and vertically. When you choose Merge Channels, Photoshop displays the Merge Channels dialog box, shown in Figure 5-8. It then assigns a color mode for the new image based on the number of open grayscale images that contain the same number of pixels as the foreground image.

You can override Photoshop's choice by selecting a different option from the Mode pop-up menu. (Generally, you won't want to change the value in the Channels option box; it causes Photoshop to automatically select Multichannel from the Mode pop-up menu. We explain multichannel images in the upcoming "Multichannel techniques" section.) After you press Return or click on the OK button, Photoshop displays a second dialog box. In this dialog box, you can specify which grayscale image goes with which channel by choosing options from pop-up menus, as demonstrated in the second example in Figure 5-8. When working from an image split with the Split Channels command, Photoshop automatically organizes each window into a pop-up menu according to the color appended to the window's name. For example, Photoshop associates the window *Capitol Dome.Red* with the Red pop-up menu.

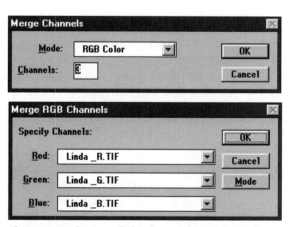

Figure 5-8: The two dialog boxes that appear after you choose Merge Channels enable you to select a color mode for the merged image (top) and to associate images with color channels (bottom).

✦ **Convert selection:** Click on the convert selection outline icon — the one in the bottom left corner of the Channels palette — to convert a selection outline to a new mask channel. Drag a channel name onto the convert selection icon to convert the mask into a selection outline. You can also convert a mask to a selection by Alt-clicking on the mask channel name.

Color Channel Effects

Now that you know how to navigate channels and apply commands, allow us to suggest a few reasons. The most pragmatic applications for channel effects involve bad color scans. Incidentally, if you're new to Photoshop (or even if you aren't), you should also work through Chapter 2 ("Retouching a Scanned Image") of the Tutorial that comes with Photoshop.

Improving the appearance of color scans

The following techniques can improve poorly scanned full-color images. They don't work miracles, but they can make an image tolerable.

(Don't forget that it's a good idea to first choose Window⇨New Window to maintain a composite view. Be sure to drag the composite view to an empty portion of your screen so you can see how applying a change to a channel affects the full-color image.)

✦ **Aligning channels:** Sometimes a scan still looks out of focus even after you use Photoshop's sharpening commands. If you can see slight shadows or halos around colored areas, a color channel probably is out of alignment. To remedy the problem, switch to the color channel that corresponds to the halo color. Then choose Select⇨All (Ctrl-A) and use the arrow keys to nudge the channel into alignment. Use the separate composite view (created by choosing Window⇨New Window) to monitor your changes.

✦ **Channel focusing:** If all channels seem aligned (or, as aligned as they're going to get), one may be poorly focused. Use the Ctrl-key equivalents to search for the responsible channel. If you find it, use the Unsharp Mask filter to sharpen it. You may also find it helpful to blur a channel, as when trying to eliminate moiré patterns in a scanned halftone. (For more, see the "Cleaning Up Scanned Halftones" section in Chapter 13.)

✦ **Bad channels:** If you discover that a channel is simply rotten to the core, you may be able to improve its appearance by overlaying the other channels on top of it. Suppose that the blue channel is awful, but the red and green channels are decent. First, save your image. Then switch to the red channel (Ctrl-1), select the entire image (Ctrl-A), and copy it (Ctrl-C). Switch back to the blue channel (Ctrl-3), paste the contents of the Clipboard (Ctrl-V), and change the opacity of the pasted red channel to between 30 and 50 percent. Next, switch to the green channel (Ctrl-2) and repeat the process.

Note As discussed in Chapter 17, the Calculations command from the Image menu is an alternate method for blending channels. The dialog box may give you a mild twinge of panic. Give it a chance. It's faster than the Clipboard.

When you choose Image⇨Calculations, a dialog box asks you to select two source channels, a method for blending them, and a destination channel. For example, to mix the red and blue channels in a 30 percent/70 percent blend, select the red channel as Source 1 and the blue channel as Source 2, then enter 30 into the Opacity option box, select the same document name from the Result pop-up menu, and choose Blue from the final Channel pop-up menu. Look to Chapter 17 for a full explanation.

Multichannel techniques

When you choose Mode⇨Multichannel, channels no longer have a specific relationship to one another. They don't create a full-color image; instead, they exist independently within the confines of a single image. The multichannel mode is generally a step for converting between color modes without recalculating the contents of the channels.

For example, normally when you convert between the RGB and CMYK modes, Photoshop maps RGB colors to the CMYK color model, changing the contents of each channel as in Figures 5-2 and 5-3. The following steps convert from RGB to the multichannel mode and then from multichannel to CMYK.

Steps: Using the Multichannel Mode as an intermediary step

1. Open an RGB image. If the image is already open, make sure that it is saved to disk.

2. Choose Mode⇨Multichannel to eliminate any relationship between the formerly red, green, and blue color channels.

3. Choose the New Channel command from the Channels palette pop-up menu to add a mask channel to the image. When the Channel Options dialog box appears, press Return to accept the default settings. This empty channel will serve as the black channel in the CMYK image. (Photoshop won't let you convert from the multichannel mode to CMYK with less than four channels.)

4. Unfortunately, the new channel comes up black, which would make the entire image black. So make the channel white by choosing Select⇨All (or Ctrl-A) and pressing the Delete key. (This assumes that the background color is white. If it isn't, press the D key.)

5. Choose Mode⇨CMYK. The image looks washed out and a tad dark compared to its original RGB counterpart, but the overall color scheme of the image remains more or less intact. This is because the red, green, and blue color channels each have a respective opposite in the cyan, magenta, and yellow channels.

6. The one problem with the image is that it lacks any information in the black channel. So although it may look OK on-screen, it will lose much of its definition when printed. To fill in the black channel, convert the image to the RGB mode and then convert it back to the CMYK mode. Photoshop automatically adds an image to the black channel in keeping with your specifications in the Separation Setup dialog box (as described in the "CMYK conversions" section of Chapter 6).

These steps aren't recommended procedure for converting RGB images to a CMYK images. Rather, they are intended to suggest how channel conversions can create a halfway-decent image. You can likewise experiment with converting among the Lab, multichannel, and RGB modes; or Lab, multichannel, and CMYK.

Color channels

To abuse the colors in an RGB or CMYK image, there's nothing like replacing one color channel with another. Color Plate 5-2 shows examples applied to an RGB image. In the upper left example, we copied the blue channel image (Ctrl-3, Ctrl-A, Ctrl-C) and pasted it into the red channel (Ctrl-1, Ctrl-V). The result was a green Capitol against a purple sky. For the upper right example (starting again from the original RGB image), we copied the green channel and pasted it into the blue channel. The result this time was a pink building against a deep jade sky. To create a lemon yellow Capitol against a backdrop of bright blue, shown in the lower left corner of Color Plate 5-2, we copied the red channel and pasted it into the green channel.

Cross Ref Again, instead of copying and pasting, you can transfer images between channels without upsetting the contents of the Clipboard by choosing Image⇨Calculations. We discuss this and other applications for this command in Chapter 17.

You can also swap the contents of color channels. In the lower right example of Color Plate 5-2, we swapped the contents of the red and blue channels to create a blue Capitol against an orange-brown sky (like inverting the *b* channel in the Lab mode, as we suggested in the "Lab channels" section of this chapter). We chose the Split Channels command from the Channels palette menu. We then chose the Merge Channels command and accepted the default settings in the Merge Channels dialog box. When the Merge RGB Channels dialog box appeared, we selected the blue channel from the Red pop-up menu and the red channel from the Blue pop-up menu.

 Tip When experimenting, save the original contents of each color channel. Use the Duplicate Channel command to save each color channel to a separate mask channel. You then can replace channels with impunity, knowing that you have backups if you need them.

Printing Images

Welcome to Printing

On the one hand, printing can be a very straightforward topic. You choose the Print command, press the Enter key, wait for something to come out of your printer, and admire yet another piece of forestry that you've gone and destroyed. On the other hand, printing can be a ridiculously complicated subject, involving dot gain compensation, hardware calibration, under color removal, toxic processor chemicals, separation table generation, and so many infinitesimal color parameters that you're liable to spend half your life trying to figure out what's going on.

This chapter is about finding a middle ground. Although it is in no way intended to cover every possible facet of printing digitized images, it walks you through the process of preparing and printing the three major categories of output: composites, color separations, and duotones. By the end of this chapter, you'll be familiar with all of Photoshop's printing options. You'll also be prepared to communicate with professionals at your service bureau or commercial printer, if need be, and to learn from their expertise.

Robert Printing is a ridiculously complicated subject. But in addition to our words of wisdom here, there's now a superb book by David Blatner and Bruce Fraser, *Real World Photoshop 3* (Peachpit Press). Deke and I have agreed that this book deserves a plug here and that we're not in competition for your book-buying dollars. Although it's Mac-oriented, the techniques are totally usable by us Windows 95 types. Think of this chapter as the foundation, and then go get that book. You won't regret it.

Note The Mac and Windows 95 implement printing somewhat differently; Macs have some options that Windows 95 doesn't, and vice versa. Documentation on the Windows 95 side is, as this is written, seriously lacking for printing. Most third-party books just tell you about selecting a printer, and then tell you to go print. We're going past that point. There's much more involved than that — read on, and realize that we're moving into uncharted territory.

Understanding Printing Terminology

We're not big believers in glossaries. Generally, they contain glib, jargony, out-of-context definitions that add as much understanding of a concept as a seminar in which all the presenters read "The Ratcatcher's Daughter" in double Dutch (as Jude the Obscure so eloquently put it in the Thomas Hardy novel).

Robert

(Don't blame Deke for that tortured turn of phrase — I'm exercising my prerogative to fix one of his metaphors with vintage Robert. After all, today was a very good year.)

Nonetheless, before delving into the inner recesses of printing, here's a smattering of the printing terms you'll encounter, presented in a semilogical, semirandom order. Ood-gay uck-lay.

✦ **Service bureau:** A service bureau is a shop filled with earnest young graphic artists (at least they were young and earnest when *Deke* worked there), printer operators, and about a billion dollars worth of hardware. A small service bureau is usually outfitted with a few laser printers, photocopiers, and self-service computers. Big service bureaus offer scanners, imagesetters, film recorders, and other varieties of professional-quality input and output equipment.

Robert

Remember what I said about platform matters in Chapter 1. There was a time when the only way to do this sort of work was on the Macintosh. That has now changed, but it means there's a substantial legacy of Mac-based service bureaus. Some have seen the viability of the PC and are equally ready to help Photoshoppers on both platforms. But there are still some who, at best, will take your Photoshop file and run it out through a Mac. There's nothing inherently wrong with that, unless a problem arises. All other things being equal, we would urge you to talk with your service bureau and ensure that it outputs from Photoshop for Windows and has the requisite technical skills to do so.

✦ **Commercial printer:** Generally speaking, a commercial printer takes up where the service bureau leaves off. Commercial printers reproduce black-and-white and color pages using offset presses, web presses, and a whole bunch of other age-old technology that isn't covered in this miniglossary (or anywhere else in this book, for that matter). Suffice it to say, the process is less expensive than photocopying when you're dealing with large quantities — say, more than 100 copies — and it delivers professional-quality reproductions.

✦ **Output device:** This is just another way to say printer. Rather than writing *Print your image from the printer,* which sounds repetitive and a trifle obvious, we write *Print your image from the output device.* Output devices also include laser printers, imagesetters, film recorders, and a whole bunch of other machines.

✦ **Laser printer:** A laser printer works much like a photocopier. First, it applies an electric charge to a cylinder, called a *drum,* inside the printer. The charged areas, which correspond to the black portions of the image being printed, attract fine, petroleum-based dust particles called *toner.* The drum transfers the toner to the page, and a heating mechanism fixes the toner in place. Most laser printers have resolutions of 300 dots (or printer pixels) per inch. A few offer higher resolutions, such as 600 and 1,200 dots per inch (dpi).

✦ **Color printers:** Color printers fall into three categories: ink-jet and thermal-wax printers at the low end and dye-sublimation printers at the high end. Ink-jet printers deliver colored dots out of disposable ink cartridges. Thermal-wax printers apply wax-based pigments to a page in multiple passes. Both kinds of printers mix cyan, magenta, yellow, and (on some printers) black dots to produce full-color output. Generally speaking, these printers produce mediocre detail and acceptable, though not necessarily accurate, color. If you want photographic-quality prints, the kind you'd be proud to hang on your wall, you must migrate up the price ladder to dye-sublimation printers. Dye-sub inks permeate the surface of the paper, literally dying it different colors. Furthermore, the cyan, magenta, yellow, and black pigments mix in varying opacities from one dot to the next, resulting in a continuous-tone image that appears nearly as smooth on the page as it does on the screen.

✦ **Imagesetter:** A typesetter that is equipped with a graphics page-description language, such as PostScript, is called an imagesetter. Unlike a laser printer, an imagesetter prints photosensitive paper or film by exposing the portions of the paper or film that correspond to the black areas of the image. The process is a lot like exposing film with a camera, but an imagesetter only knows two colors, black and white. The exposed paper or film collects in a lightproof canister. In a separate step, the printer operator develops the film in a processor that contains two chemical baths (developer and fixer), a water bath to wash away the chemicals, and a heat dryer to dry off the water. Developed paper looks like a typical glossy black-and-white page. Developed film is black where the image is white and transparent where the image is black. Imagesetters typically offer resolutions between 1,200 and 2,600 dpi. But the real beauty of imageset pages is that blacks are absolutely black (or transparent), as opposed to the deep, sometimes irregular gray you get with laser-printed pages.

✦ **Film recorder:** This device transfers images to full-color 35mm slides that are perfect for professional presentations. Slides also can be useful as a means for providing images to publications and commercial printers. Many publications can scan from slides, and commercial printers can use slides to create color separations. So if you're nervous that a color separation printed from Photoshop won't turn out well, ask your service bureau to output the image to a 35mm slide. Then have your commercial printer reproduce the image from the slide.

✦ **PostScript:** The PostScript page-description language was the first project developed by Adobe, the same folks who sell Photoshop, and is now a staple of hundreds of brands of laser printers, imagesetters, and film recorders. A *page-description language* (PDL) is a programming language for defining text and graphics on a page. PostScript specifies the locations of points, draws line segments between them, and fills in areas with solid blacks or *halftone cells* (dot patterns that simulate grays). PostScript Level 2, an updated version of the original PostScript, speeds up output time and provides improved halftoning options, better color separations, automated anti-aliasing of jagged images, and direct support for Lab images (discussed in the "CIE's Lab" section of Chapter 4).

✦ **Spooling:** Printer spooling lets you work on an image while another image prints. Rather than communicating directly with the output device, Photoshop describes the image to the system software. Under Windows 3.1, Print Manager controls this. Under Windows 95, you set spooling options via Control Panel⇨Printers⇨Properties (right-click on the icon for your specific printer), and then select the Details tab and click on the Spool Settings button. When Photoshop finishes describing the image — a relatively quick process — you are free to resume working while the system software prints the image in the background.

Robert

Under Windows 95, this is a serious lifesaver — while this is being typed, any number of screen shots are cranking out in the background.

✦ **Calibration:** Traditionally, *calibrating* a system means synchronizing the machinery. However, in the context of Photoshop, it means to adjust or compensate for the color displays of the scanner, monitor, and printer so that what you scan is what you see on-screen, which in turn is what you get from the printer. Colors match from one device to the next. Empirically speaking, this is impossible; a yellow image in a photograph won't look exactly like the on-screen yellow or the yellow printed from a set of color separations. But calibrating is designed to make them look as much alike as possible while accounting for the fundamental differences in hardware technology. Expensive hardware calibration solutions seek to change the configuration of scanner, monitor, and printer. Less-expensive software solutions, including those provided by Photoshop, manipulate the image to account for the differences between devices.

✦ **Brightness values/shades:** As described at length in Chapter 4, there is a fundamental difference between the way your screen and printer create gray values and colors. Your monitor shows colors by lightening an otherwise black screen; the printed page shows colors by darkening an otherwise white piece of paper. Therefore, on-screen colors are measured in terms of brightness values. High values equate to light colors; low values equate to dark colors. On the printed page, colors are measured in percentage values called shades, or if you prefer, tints. High percentage values result in dark colors, and low percentage values result in light colors.

✦ **Composite:** A *composite* is a page that shows an image in its entirety. A black-and-white composite printed from a standard laser printer or imagesetter translates all colors in an image to gray values. A color composite printed from a color printer or film recorder shows the colors as they actually appear. Composites, or comps (as they're often affectionately called), are useful anytime you want to proof an image or print a final grayscale image from an imagesetter, an overhead projection from a color printer, or a full-color image from a film recorder.

✦ **Proofing:** To *proof* an image is to see how it looks on paper in advance of the final printing. In professional circles, laser printers are considered proofing devices because they lack sufficient quality or resolution to output final images. Color printers are necessarily proofing devices because commercial printers can't reproduce from any color composite output except slides. (Well, they *can* reproduce from other kinds of color composites, but you don't get the same quality results.)

✦ **Bleeds:** Simply put, a *bleed* is an area outside the perimeter of a page that can be printed. You use a bleed to reproduce an image all the way to the edge of a page, as in a slick magazine ad. By way of example, this book includes bleeds. Most of the pages — like the page you're reading — are encircled by a uniform 2-pica margin of white space. This margin keeps the text and figures from spilling off into oblivion. However, a few pages — including the parts pages and the color plates in the middle of the book — print all the way to the edges. In fact, the original artwork goes two picas beyond the edges of the paper. This ensures that if the paper shifts when printing, as it invariably does, you don't see any thin white edges around the artwork. The two picas of extra artwork are the bleed. In Photoshop, you create a bleed by clicking on the Bleed button in the Page Setup dialog box.

✦ **Color separations:** To output color reproductions, commercial printers require *color separations* (or slides, which they can convert to color separations for a fee). A color-separated image comprises four printouts, one each for the cyan, magenta, yellow, and black primary printing colors. The commercial printer transfers each printout to a *plate* that is used in the actual reproduction process.

✦ **Duotone:** A grayscale image in Photoshop can contain as many as 256 brightness values, from white to black. A printer can convey significantly fewer shades. A typical laser printer, for example, provides 26 shades at most. An imagesetter typically provides from 150 to 200 shades, depending on resolution and screen frequency. And that's assuming perfect printing conditions. You can count on at least 30 percent of those shades getting lost in the reproduction process. A *duotone* helps to retain the depth and clarity of detail in a grayscale image by printing with two inks. Suddenly, the number of shades available to you jumps from 150 to 22,000 (150^2). Photoshop also permits you to create *tritones* (three inks) and *quadtones* (four inks). Note, however, that using more inks translates to higher printing costs. Color Plate 6-1 shows a quadtone.

Welcome to Printing and Windows 95

Overall, this chapter is probably about the most technical you're likely to get in the entire book, and possibly the most important, unless you're working entirely for screen output (such circumstances do exist!). That's why the following five paragraphs come directly from Robert's pen.

I want to warn you about the profusion of confusion you may encounter — not here, hopefully, but Out There, as you start installing printers and looking at the ways to set them up.

The Windows platform is in flux right now, and this has printing implications beyond Deke's worst nightmare (not that Mac people stay up nights worrying about Windows 95 people; still, Deke is very cross-platform and ecumenical — if he weren't, we wouldn't be here). Some people are using Windows 3.1 to run Photoshop via the Win32s subsystem. That subsystem is constantly evolving — as this is written, it's up to version 1.30something. As Win32s evolves, newer versions break the latest printer drivers for a particular model. Not a pretty sight. Users had to either return to an earlier printer driver (assuming they hadn't hosed it — after all, isn't *latest* the same as *greatest?* Hah!) or else return to an earlier version of Win32s.

On Windows 95, matters can be equally convoluted. It's still a relatively new operating system, so printer manufacturers are struggling to bring out Windows 95 drivers. In some cases, those drivers are in quasi-beta form. In other cases, the manufacturer will tell you to use its Windows 3.1 drivers. Sometimes you need to get seriously down and dirty by using an older printer DLL (dynamic link library — one of the basic components of Windows-anything) with a later printer driver. These nightmares are definitely not what the people in Adobe's Press Relations department had in mind when they coined the advertising phrase *If you can dream it, you can do it.*

The following is my prescription for banishing a number of headaches (in my salaried professional life I have the title *Dr.*, but it's a Ph.D. — not an M.D.). Checking online, both on CompuServe's ADOBEAPPS forum and on your printer manufacturer's forum on that system (if the company has one; if not, it surely has a BBS) will keep you absolutely au courant.

And don't borrow trouble. It may be that you're working at a service bureau and regularly have to output from Photoshop to, say, an Iris. That's why you need to stay in close touch via the ways we've mentioned. But suppose you're proofing on a laser or ink-jet printer, and doing final output via a service bureau — that is, you're a small operation (much like us). In this case, you let *them* worry — at least part of the time. No matter how good your service bureau people, one of the marks of a Photoshop guru is remaining ever compulsive and ever vigilant. But accept your service bureau's guidance about image resolution and file format (you may need to use TGA or Scitex — see Chapter 3 for details). All you have to do is follow its instructions and get the file to it. If you're aiming for final output on a high-end device (such as Iris), have the service bureau produce a cheaper laser proof in color for you — it will cost a little extra, but it's worth it to avoid unpleasant surprises under deadline (hey, aren't we all always working under deadline?).

Composites

It's time to get ready for output, now that you can speak service bureau-speak. This section explores the labyrinth of options available for printing composite images. Later in this chapter, we cover color separations and duotones.

Like any Windows 95 application, Photoshop can print composite images to any supported output device you hook up to your PC. Assuming that your printer is turned on, properly attached, and in working order, printing a composite image from Photoshop is a five-step process, more or less, as outlined below.

Steps: Printing a composite image

1. Use Control Panel⇨Printers to select the output device you want to print to. Unless your computer is part of a network that includes multiple printers, you probably rely on a single output device, in which case you can skip this step. See Figure 6-1.

2. Right-click on the printer icon and select Properties. Click on the Paper tab to specify the page size and the size and orientation of the image on the page. Or you can go inside Photoshop to access this tab using File⇨Page Setup. (You can also use Photoshop's Image⇨Image Size to control the size of the image by changing its resolution, as explained in the "Printed resolution" section of Chapter 3.)

3. Inside Photoshop's File⇨Page Setup, click on the Screens button to change the size, angle, and shape of the halftone screen dots. This step is purely optional, useful mostly for creating special effects.

4. Click on the Transfer button to map brightness values in an image to different shades when printed. This step is also optional, though frequently very useful.

5. Exit the Page Setup dialog box and choose File⇨Print (Ctrl-P) to print the image according to your specifications.

The following sections describe each of the preceding steps in detail.

Caution If you've already got your printer set up to your satisfaction, you may be thinking about drag-and-drop printing (drag the file from Explorer and drop it onto the printer icon). The file will print, using the application for which the file type is registered. If you're using a native Photoshop file (PSD) that's one thing. But if you want to print, say, a TIFF out of Photoshop, you may be in for a surprise; Windows 95 will print out of the application for which TIFF is a registered file format. Unless you've changed things in the Registry, this will not be Photoshop because, thoughtfully, it only registers its native file format (see Appendix B for further particulars). This may not be what you want. It's best to do all your Photoshop printing directly from Photoshop.

R %% Robert This is too important to bury elsewhere, even though it may seem a bit out of sequence here. In My Humble Opinion (IMHO, as I'd say online), what follows can do more than practically anything else I have to say to keep you out of trouble. (Drums roll, bugles blare.) Pay attention to the overlap between the tabs you get using Windows 95's Control Panel Printers Properties and the ones you get inside Photoshop with File⇨Page Setup.

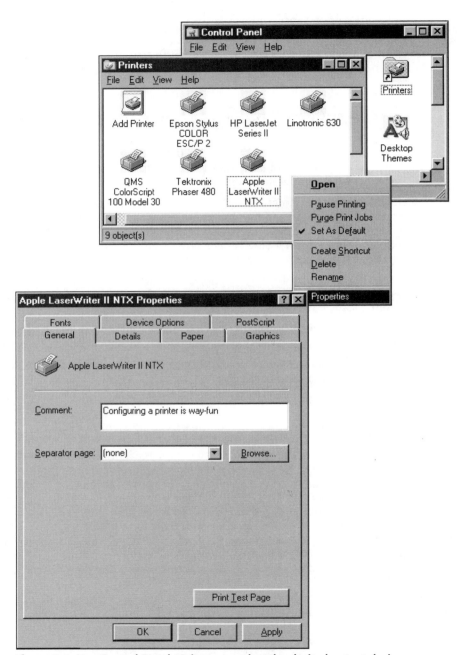

Figure 6-1: Use Control Panel⇨Printers to select the desired output device.

In Windows 95, there are seven tabs for the LaserWriter: General, Details, Paper, Graphics, Fonts, Device Options, and PostScript. Inside Photoshop there are three: Paper, Graphics, and PostScript.

Those three are, obviously, the overlap — see Figure 6-2. You should use the classic Roman military strategy: Divide and conquer. Use the Windows 95 tabs that *don't* overlap for setting global default options — you're unlikely to want to change those often. But the three common tabs (Paper, Graphics, and Postscript) — only set them inside Photoshop.

Here's why. Suppose you want to do a four-up (called 4 Up in Photoshop) print job. You can set it up in Photoshop, and it will be specific for that print job. When you exit Photoshop, no more four-up. But you can also configure a four-up print job on that very same Paper tab out in Windows 95. Of course, you'll get your four-up in Photoshop. Now suppose some minor distractions arise — the cats have decided to have a game on your monitor, the shingles blow off your roof. Time passes. You decide to print an Excel spreadsheet. Surprise — it comes out four-up. Because you'd set that as the default out in Windows 95, Excel picked up on it.

Adobe actually made it all rather idiotproof. The options that, if set globally, can mess you up the most are precisely the three tabs that are available inside Photoshop. Use them only in Photoshop. If you don't — well, far be it from us to say *We told you so* — but we told you so.

Choosing a printer

To select a printer, bring up Control Panel from the Start menu and select Printers, or select Printers directly from Start⇨Settings⇨Printers — see Figure 6-1. Right-click on your printer of choice and, on the resultant pop-up menu, select Set As Default. If you want to add a printer, double-click on the Add Printer icon, and be sure to have either your Windows 95 CD-ROM (or floppies) handy, or a drivers disk from your printer manufacturer.

Printer drivers help the PC hardware, Windows 95, and Photoshop translate the contents of an image to the printer hardware and the page-description language it uses. If you intend to use a PostScript-compatible printer, you'll generally want to select the LaserWriter driver (although some PostScript printers include drivers of their own). You even can prepare an image for output to a PostScript printer when no such printer is currently hooked up to your computer. For example, you can use this technique prior to submitting a document to be output on an imagesetter at a service bureau.

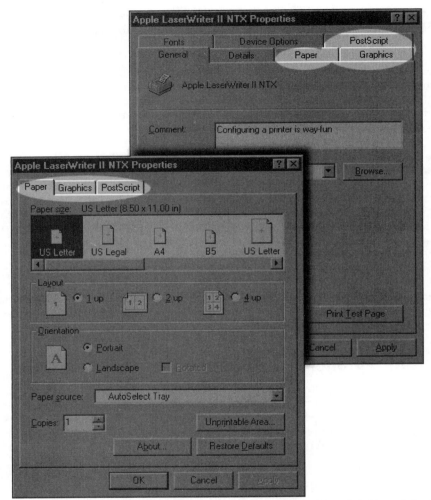

Figure 6-2: The printer setup tabs in Windows 95's Control Panel (left), and the subset of those tabs in Photoshop's Page Setup. The tabs common to both are highlighted.

R
%%
Robert
At this point in *Macworld Photoshop 3 Bible,* Deke warns, "Spooling can interrupt foreground tasks and increase the likelihood of printing errors." That's fair enough for the Mac side, where Deke's an acknowledged guru. But, hey, this is a Windows 95 book, and *I'm* the guru. And one of the things that gets lost in all the mutterings about *The Mac's had that for years* is the matter of multitasking and background printing. The Mac hasn't had that for years at all. Still doesn't. Background printing, yes. But preemptive multitasking — no. Maybe it will when its new operating system (let's see — what *is* it called? I think it begins with a *C*) comes out. I don't want to say background printing is bulletproof on Windows 95 — nothing on any computer is bulletproof, not

even on those ultimate user-friendly computers on *Star Trek*. But I've never heard of anyone having a problem. If you think I'm descending into Platform Wars, think again — reread what I wrote in Chapter 1. I calls 'em like I sees 'em — and for background printing, it's no contest. Windows 95 wins.

Starting with Windows 3.1, certain applications (such as PageMaker) could take advantage of *PostScript printer description (PPD)* files. A single driver can't account for the myriad differences between different models of PostScript printers, so each PPD serves as a little guidance file, customizing the driver to accommodate a specific printer model. Basically, each printer manufacturer writes its PPD file and sends it to Adobe for *blessing* (that's not a throwaway term — that's what they call the process). Windows 95 now lets you attach a PPD file globally to your PostScript printer, for which you need both the PPD file and the INF file to tell Windows 95 what to install. (That's as we write this; Adobe has made both sets of files, along with detailed installation instructions, available on its BBS and will have them available online elsewhere very shortly — most probably even as you read this.)

What about the Adobe PostScript driver? Currently in version 3.0.1, it supports PostScript Level 2 and PPD files. The joker is that Windows 95 treats it as a GDI printer driver rather than as a PostScript printer. You may want to consider using it, but we would advise reading its documentation very carefully and asking for the latest news online. A new version, which Windows 95 *will* see as a PostScript driver, is promised for 1996.

Using the common tabs: Paper, Graphics, PostScript

Here you'll be using the three common tabs we've been stressing. Although you can do this out of the Properties pop-up menu in the Control Panel, reread the preceding warning. Do it all inside Photoshop's File⇨Page Setup.

The Paper tab

Here you define the relationship between the current image and the page on which it prints. Figure 6-3 displays the LaserWriter Paper tab.

Assuming that you're using the Apple LaserWriter IINTX driver that ships with Windows 95 (and we've chosen this because it's about as close to a generic printer driver as you can get), this dialog box provides the following options:

✦ **Paper size:** Select the option from the Paper pop-up menu that corresponds to the size of the paper loaded into your printer's paper tray. The paper size you select determines the *imageable area* of a page — that is, the amount of the page that Photoshop can use to print the current image. For example, the US Letter option calls for a page that measures 8.5 × 11 inches, but only 7.7 × 10.2 inches is imageable.

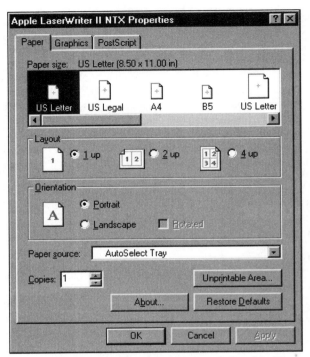

Figure 6-3: Use this tab to specify the relationship between the printed image and the page on which it appears.

✦ **Layout:** This option lets you print more than one page per sheet of paper. For example, if you wanted to proof the layout of a 16-page QuarkXPress document, you could select the 4 up option to print four quarter-sized versions of each page on each piece of paper. You save paper, kill fewer trees, and even waste a little less time. However, because there is no such thing as a multipage document in Photoshop, this option serves no purpose. If you select the 4 up option, for example, you simply get one image reduced to 25 percent its normal size in the upper left corner of the printed page. So always leave this option set to 1 up when printing from Photoshop.

✦ **Orientation:** You can specify whether an image prints upright on a page (called the *portrait setting*) or on its side (called the *landscape setting*) by selecting the corresponding Orientation icon. The landscape setting is useful when an image is wider than it is tall.

(In the Photoshop manual, Adobe recommends that you rotate the image 90 degrees by choosing Image➪Rotate➪90° CCW and print it at the Portrait setting in order to save on printing time. We don't recommend this technique because rotating the image takes time and you have to rerotate it if you want to edit it again. But it's an option.)

✦ **Scaling:** Enter a percentage value into this option box to enlarge or reduce the size of the image when printed. For more information on this option, read the "Printing versus screen display" section of Chapter 3. If you enter too large a value you'll get an error message: *One or more of your settings is invalid.* After specifying the Reduce or Enlarge percentage and Orientation icon, you can check to see how the image fits on the page. To do so, press Enter to exit the LaserWriter Page Setup dialog box and click and hold on the preview box in the lower left corner of the image window. The rectangle with the inset X that appears inside the pop-up window represents the image on the page.

What about the other two common tabs?

The Graphics tab

✦ **Resolution:** In most cases, you don't want to tinker with this. After all, we're all trying to get more resolution, not less. But there are exceptions. For example, some ink-jet printers use different resolution in different printing modes. See the experiment at the end of this section if you'd like to learn more.

✦ **Halftoning:** Don't touch this. Set your halftoning inside Photoshop (discussed later).

✦ **Special:** This offers you negative image and mirror image. You might find this of some use, but you can do the same thing in Photoshop. So why bother here?

The PostScript tab

✦ **PostScript output format:** This can be useful. Typically, you'll want to optimize for speed if you're printing directly to a printer. You may want to consider optimizing for portability using the Adobe Document Structuring Convention (ADSC) if you'll be printing to file and taking that file elsewhere. But don't do this for prophylaxis — only if the need arises, or if your service bureau requests it. Click on the little question mark icon at the top of the dialog box, and then click on the PostScript output format to see what Microsoft has to say — it's a pretty good summary.

You will only want to consider the other options in very special cases, typically when output problems arise.

R
%%
Robert

Of course, we've been limited so far to the LaserWriter. Other printers offer other choices. For example, most non-PostScript printers have a Device options tab but no PostScript tab. A few PostScript printers have both. Color printers can have very different Graphics tabs. I'm tempted to do a screen shot to illustrate this. But there are so many choices that things could get out of hand rapidly, as they often do with screen shots. Why not investigate for yourself? Install some printers out of the Printers icon in Windows 95's Control Panel — try the ones I've used in Figure 6-1. Then play around with the various tabs. Don't worry — you're not messing up your system — when you're done having a good look 'round, just delete those extra printers. Unless you want to leave them there to gain caste with a visiting panjandrum (as I've done).

On to the special Photoshop printing options

So far I've described the situation for the three tabs you'll see in Photoshop if you're using the LaserWriter driver. But it's a different story when you descend to the options at the bottom of the LaserWriter Page Setup dialog box. See Figure 6-4.

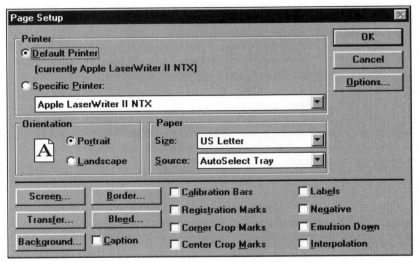

Figure 6-4: The LaserWriter Page Setup dialog box inside Photoshop.

These options are specific to Photoshop. First we'll describe how to use the buttons on the left, and then we'll explain the check boxes on the right.

✦ **Screen:** Click on this button to enter a dialog box that lets you change the size, angle, and shape of the printed halftone cells, as described in the upcoming "Changing the halftone screen" section.

✦ **Transfer:** The dialog box that appears when you click on this button lets you redistribute shades in the printed image, as explained in the upcoming "Transfer function" section.

✦ **Background:** To assign a color to the area around the printed image, click on this button and select a color from the Color Picker dialog box, which is described in the "Using the Color Picker" section of Chapter 4. This button and the one that follows (Border) are designed specifically for use when printing slides from a film recorder.

✦ **Border:** To print a border around the current image, click on this button and enter the thickness of the border into the Width option box. The border automatically appears in black.

✦ **Bleed:** This button lets you print outside the imageable area of the page when outputting to an imagesetter. (Imagesetters print to huge rolls of paper or film, so you can print far outside the confines of standard page size. Most other printers use regular old sheets of paper; any bleed — were the printer to even acknowledge it — would print off the edge of the page.) Click on the Bleed button and enter the thickness of the bleed into the Width option box. Two picas (24 points) is generally a good bet. (Bleeds are defined in the "Understanding Printing Terminology" glossary at the beginning of this chapter.)

As for the check boxes in the lower middle- and right-hand sections of the dialog box, most of these options — all except Negative, Emulsion Down, and Interpolation — append special labels and printer marks to the printed version of the image. These labels and marks are demonstrated in Figure 6-5.

Tip By the way, Figure 6-5 shows the actual labels and marks exactly as they print. This may not sound like much, but in the past, such printer's marks have been very difficult to capture because there was no way to save them in a reliable file format. Book writers like us either had the option of printing the file to disk as an EPS file (which might or might not print accurately when placed into a page-layout program) or simply printing the page independently and manually pasting it into the book. But thanks to the fact that Illustrator 5.5 opens Adobe Acrobat PDF (portable document format) files, Deke was able to create an editable version of the printed image. (Why Deke and not Robert? Read on!)

In the name of full disclosure (our job is to pass along information, not store up trade secrets), here's how we accomplished this smallish feat: We first printed the Photoshop image to disk as an EPS file (as described in the "Printing pages" section later in this chapter) — labels, printer's marks, and all. We then converted the EPS file to the PDF format using Acrobat Distiller (included with Illustrator 5.5). Finally, we used Illustrator to convert the PDF file to the more reliable Illustrator EPS format and to assign the callouts — those little labels like *Calibration bars* and *Modern youngster.*

Caution The previous instructions rely on capabilities of Adobe Illustrator that are present in the Mac version but not yet in the Windows version (Illustrator 4.1). Adobe has promised a major upgrade for Windows users in 1996. So heed the following description — the time will come when you'll be able to use it in Windows 95.

Here's how the check box options work:

✦ **Caption:** To print a caption beneath the image, select this option. Then press the Enter key to exit this dialog box, choose File⇨File Info, and enter a caption into the File Info dialog box. The caption prints in 9-point Helvetica. It's strictly an image-annotation feature, something to help you 17 years down the road when your brain starts to deteriorate and you can't remember why you printed the darn thing. (You might also use the caption to keep images straight in a busy office where hundreds of folks have access to the same images, but we don't like this alternative as much because we can't make fun of it.)

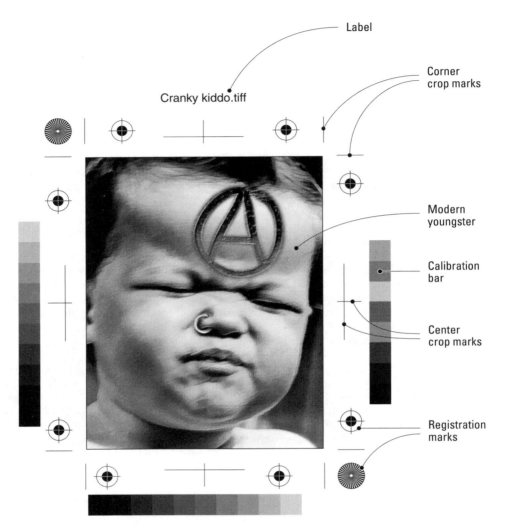

Label

Cranky kiddo.tiff

Corner
crop marks

Modern
youngster

Calibration
bar

Center
crop marks

Registration
marks

Hey, don't mess with me, man. I'm grumpy 'cause ●───────── Caption
I can't change the font for this caption. Aargh!

Figure 6-5: An image printed with nearly all of the Page Setup check boxes turned on.

✦ **Calibration Bars:** A calibration bar is a 10-step grayscale gradation that starts at 10 percent black and ends at 100 percent black. The function of the calibration bar is to ensure that all shades are distinct and on target. If not, the output device isn't properly calibrated, which is a fancy way of saying that the printer's colors are out of whack and need realignment by a trained professional armed with a hammer and hacksaw. When you print color separations, the Calibration Bars check box instructs Photoshop to print a gradient tint bar and a progressive color bar, which are also useful to printing professionals.

✦ **Registration Marks:** Select this option to print eight crosshairs and two star targets near the four corners of the image. Registration marks are absolutely imperative when you print color separations because they provide the only reliable means for ensuring exact registration of the cyan, magenta, yellow, and black printing plates. When printing a composite image, however, you can ignore this option.

✦ **Corner Crop Marks:** Select this option to print eight hairline crop marks (two in each of the image's four corners), which indicate how to trim the image in case you anticipate engaging in a little traditional paste-up work.

✦ **Center Crop Marks:** Select this option to print four pairs of hairlines that mark the center of the image. Each pair forms a cross. Two pairs are located on the sides of the image, one is above the image, and the fourth is below.

✦ **Labels:** When you select this check box, Photoshop prints the name of the image and the name of the printed color channel in 9-point Helvetica. If you process lots of images, you'll find this option extremely useful for associating printouts with documents on disk.

✦ **Negative:** When you select this option, Photoshop prints all blacks as white and all whites as black. In-between colors switch accordingly. For example, 20 percent black becomes 80 percent black. Imagesetter operators use this option to print composites and color separations to film negatives.

✦ **Emulsion Down:** The *emulsion* is the side of a piece of film on which an image is printed. When the Emulsion Down check box is turned off, film prints from an imagesetter emulsion side up; when the check box is turned on, Photoshop flips the image so that the emulsion side is down. Like the Negative option, this option is useful only when you print film from an imagesetter and should be set in accordance with the preferences of your commercial printer.

✦ **Interpolation:** If you own an output device equipped with PostScript Level 2, you can instruct Photoshop to anti-alias the printed appearance of a low-resolution image by selecting this option. The output device resamples the image up to 200 percent and then reduces it to its original size using bicubic interpolation (as described in the "General environmental preferences" section of Chapter 2), thereby creating a less jagged image. This option has no effect on older-model PostScript devices.

Changing the halftone screen

Before we go any further, we need to explain a bit more about how printing works. To keep costs down, commercial printers use as few inks as possible to create the appearance of a wide variety of colors. Suppose that you want to print an image of a pink flamingo wearing a red bow tie. Your commercial printer could print the flamingo in one pass using pink ink, let that color dry, and then load the red ink and print the bow tie. But why go to all that trouble? After all, pink is just a lighter shade of red. Why not imitate the pink by lightening the red ink?

Unfortunately, with the exception of dye-sublimation printers, output devices can't print lighter shades of colors. They recognize only solid ink and the absence of ink. So how do you print the lighter shade of red necessary to represent pink?

The answer is *halftoning*. The output device organizes printer pixels into spots called halftone cells. Because the cells are so small, your eyes cannot quite focus on them. Instead, the cells appear to blend with the white background of the page to create a lighter shade. Figure 6-6 shows a detail of an image enlarged to display the individual halftone cells.

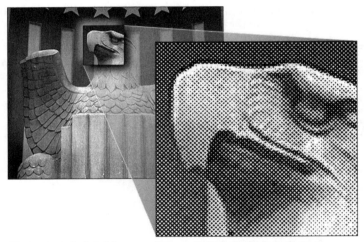

Figure 6-6: A detail from an image (left) enlarged so that you can see the individual halftone cells (right).

The cells grow and shrink to emulate different shades of color. Large cells result in dark shades; small cells result in light shades. Cell size is measured in printer pixels. The maximum size of any cell is a function of the number of cells in an inch, called the screen frequency.

For example, the default frequency of the Apple LaserWriter is 60 halftone cells per linear inch. Because the resolution of the LaserWriter is 300 printer pixels per linear inch, each halftone cell must measure 5 pixels wide by 5 pixels tall ($300 \div 60 = 5$), for a total of 25 pixels per cell (5^2). When all pixels in a cell are turned off, the cell appears white; when all pixels are turned on, you get solid ink. By turning on different numbers of pixels — from 0 up to 25 — the printer can create a total of 26 shades, as demonstrated in Figure 6-7.

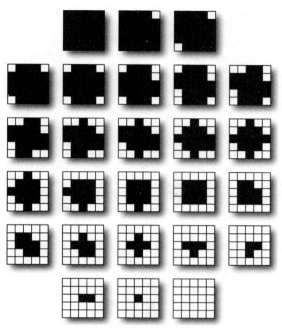

Figure 6-7: 5 × 5-pixel halftone cells with different numbers of pixels activated, ranging from 25 (top left) to 0 (bottom right). Each cell represents a unique shade from 100 to 0 percent black.

Photoshop lets you change the size, angle, and shape of the individual halftone cells used to represent an image on the printed page. To do so, click on the Screen button in the LaserWriter Page Setup dialog box. The Halftone Screens dialog box shown in Figure 6-8 appears.

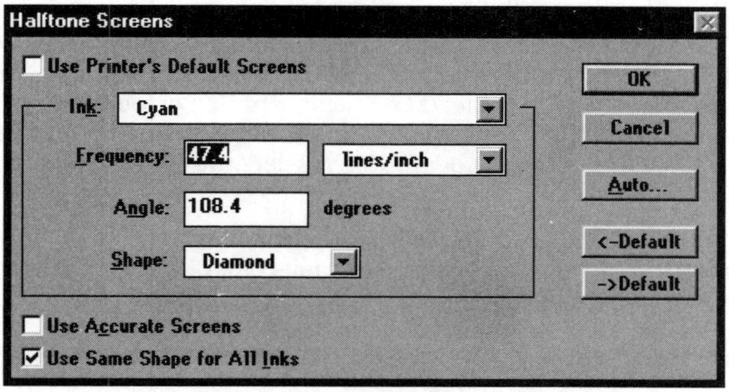

Figure 6-8: Use the Halftone Screens dialog box to edit the size, angle, and shape of the halftone cells for any one ink.

In the dialog box, you can manipulate the following options:

✦ **Use Printer's Default Screens:** Select this check box to accept the default size, angle, and shape settings built into your printer's ROM. All other options in the Halftone Screens dialog box automatically become dimmed to show they are no longer in force.

✦ **Ink:** If the current image is in color, you can select the specific ink that you want to adjust from the Ink pop-up menu. When you work with a grayscale image, no pop-up menu is available.

✦ **Frequency:** Enter a new value into this option box to change the number of halftone cells that print per linear inch. A higher value translates to a larger quantity of smaller cells; a smaller value creates fewer, larger cells. Frequency is traditionally measured in lines per inch, or lpi (as in lines of halftone cells), but you can change the measurement to lines per centimeter by selecting Lines/cm from the pop-up menu to the right of the option box.

 Higher screen frequencies result in smoother-looking printouts. However, raising the Frequency value also decreases the number of shades an output device can print because it decreases the size of each halftone cell and likewise decreases the number of printer pixels per cell. Fewer printer pixels means fewer shades. You can calculate the precise number of printable shades using the following formula:

$$\text{Number of shades} = (\text{printer resolution} \div \text{frequency})^2 + 1$$

✦ **Angle:** To change the orientation of the lines of halftone cells, enter a new value into the Angle option box. In the name of accuracy, Photoshop accepts any value between negative and positive 180.0000 degrees.

When printing color composites to ink-jet and thermal-wax printers and when printing color separations, Photoshop calculates the optimum Frequency and Angle values required to print seamless colors. In such a case, you should change these values only if you know exactly what you're doing. Otherwise, your printout may exhibit moiré patterns, as described in the "Moiré patterns" section of Chapter 3. When printing grayscale images, however, you can edit these values to your heart's content.

✦ **Shape:** By default, most PostScript printers rely on roundish halftone cells. You can change the appearance of all cells for an ink by selecting one of six alternate shapes from the Shape pop-up menu. (For a demonstration of four of these shapes, see Figure 4-12 in the "Black and white (bitmap)" section of Chapter 4.) If you know how to write PostScript code, you can select the Custom option to display a text-entry dialog box, and code away.

✦ **Use Accurate Screens:** If your output device is equipped with PostScript Level 2, select this option for updated screen angles for full-color output. Otherwise, don't worry about this option.

✦ **Use Same Shape for All Inks:** Select this option if you want to apply a single set of size, angle, and shape options to the halftone cells for all inks used to represent the current image. Unless you want to create some sort of special effect, leave this check box deselected. The option is not available when you are printing a grayscale image.

✦ **Auto:** Click on this button to display the Auto Screens dialog box shown in Figure 6-9, which automates the halftone-editing process. Enter the resolution of your output device in the Printer option box. Then enter the screen frequency you would like to use in the Screen option box. After you press the Enter key to confirm your change, Photoshop automatically calculates the optimum screen frequencies for all inks. This technique is especially useful when you print full-color images; Photoshop does the work for you, so you can't make a mess of things.

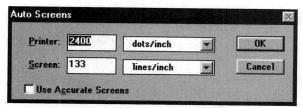

Figure 6-9: To automate the halftone-editing process, enter the resolution of the output device and the screen frequency you want to use into the Auto Screens dialog box.

✦ **Load/Save:** You can load and save settings to disk in case you want to reapply the options to other images. These buttons are especially useful if you find a magic combination of halftone settings that results in a really spectacular printout.

Tip You can change the default size, angle, and shape settings that Photoshop applies to all future images. Press Alt, and don't panic as you see the button captions change — click on Default. To restore the original defaults, press Alt and this time click on →Default←.

Transfer function

A *transfer function* enables you to change the way on-screen brightness values translate — or *map* — to printed shades. By default, brightness values print to their nearest shade percentages. A 30 percent gray on-screen pixel (which equates to a brightness value of roughly 180) prints as a 30 percent gray value.

Problems arise, however, when your output device prints lighter or darker than it should. For example, in the course of using a LaserWriter NTX over the last three years or so, Deke has discovered that all gray values print overly dark. Dark values fill in and become black; light values appear a dismal gray, muddying up any highlights. The problem increases if the image is reproduced on a photocopier.

To compensate for this over-darkening effect, click on the Transfer button in the LaserWriter Page Setup dialog box and enter the values shown in Figure 6-10. Notice that the 30 percent on-screen grays are lightened to 10 percent printer grays; 90 percent on-screen grays are lightened to 80 percent printer grays. The result is a smooth, continuous curve that maps each gray value of an image to a lighter value on paper.

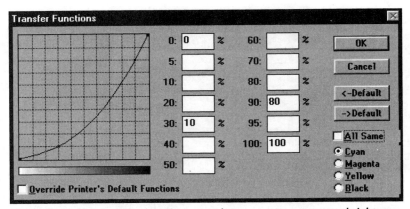

Figure 6-10: The transfer function curve lets you map on-screen brightness values to specific shades on paper.

The options in the Transfer Functions dialog box work as follows:

✦ **Transfer graph:** The *transfer graph* is where you map on-screen brightness values to their printed equivalents. The horizontal axis of the graph represents on-screen brightness values; the vertical axis represents printed shades. The *transfer curve* charts the relationship between on-screen and printed colors. The lower left corner is the origin of the graph — the point at which both the on-screen brightness value and the printed shade are white. Move to the right in the graph for darker on-screen values; move up for darker printed shades. Click in the graph to add points to the line. Drag up on a point to darken the output; drag down to lighten the output.

Cross Ref

For a more comprehensive explanation of how to graph colors on a curve, read about the incredibly powerful Curves command, covered in Chapter 16.

✦ **Percentage option boxes:** The option boxes are labeled according to the on-screen brightness values. To lighten or darken the printed brightness values, enter higher or lower percentage values in the option boxes. Note that there is a direct correlation between changes made to the transfer graph and the option boxes. For example, if you enter a value in the 50 percent option box, a new point appears along the middle line of the graph.

✦ **Override Printer's Default Functions:** As an effect of printer calibration, some printers have custom transfer functions built into their ROM. If you have problems making your settings take effect, select this check box to instruct Photoshop to apply the transfer function you specify regardless of the output device's built-in transfer function.

✦ **Load/Save:** Use these buttons to load and save settings to disk. Alt-click on the buttons to retrieve and save default settings.

✦ **Ink controls:** When you print a full-color image, five options appear in the lower right corner of the Transfer Functions dialog box. These options enable you to apply different transfer functions to different inks. Select the All Same check box to apply a single transfer function to all inks. To apply a different function to each ink, select one of the radio buttons and edit the points in the transfer graph as desired.

Printing pages

When you finish slogging your way through the mind-numbingly extensive Page Setup options, you can initiate the printing process by choosing File⇨Print (Ctrl-P). The Print dialog box or its equivalent appears, as shown in Figure 6-11.

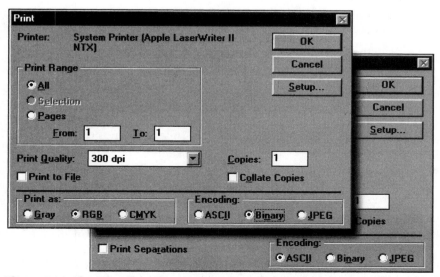

Figure 6-11: The Print dialog box as it appears when printing an RGB (top) and a CMYK (bottom) image.

Most of the options of this dialog box are a function of Windows 95, but a few at the bottom of the dialog box are exclusive to Photoshop. The options work as follows:

✦ **Copies:** Enter the number of copies you want to print in this option box. You can print up to 999 copies of a single image, although why you would want to do so is beyond us.

✦ **Print Range:** There is no such thing as a multipage document in Photoshop. Need we say more?

✦ **Paper Source:** If you want to print your illustration on a letterhead or other special piece of paper, select Options, then the Paper tab, and in the Paper Source drop-down menu, choose Manual Feed.

✦ **Print to File:** This option allows you to generate a PostScript-language definition of the file on disk rather than printing it directly to your printer. Select the Printer option to print the image to an output device as usual. Select File to write a PostScript-language version of the image to disk. Because Photoshop offers its own EPS option via the Save dialog box, you'll probably want to ignore this option. In fact, the only reason to select File is to capture printer's marks, as we did back in Figure 6-5. If you select File, a second dialog box appears, asking you where you want to save the EPS file. You can navigate just as in the Open and Save dialog boxes. For the best results, select the Binary radio button.

✦ **Print Quality:** Really only useful if your printer gives you a choice of resolutions for various kinds of output. Otherwise, ignore.

✦ **Collate Copies:** See "Print Range" above.

✦ **Print as:** Select one of these radio buttons to specify the type of composite image Photoshop prints. Select the first radio button to print the image as a grayscale composite. Select the second radio button to let the printer translate the colors from the current color mode to CMYK. Select the third radio button to instruct Photoshop to convert the image to CMYK colors during the print process. These options are not available when you print a grayscale image. (When printing a CMYK image, the Print In options change to a single Print Separations check box, which is described in the next section.)

Relying on the output device to translate colors can result in printing errors, thanks to the low memory capabilities of most printers. If an image refuses to print, try selecting either the Gray or CMYK radio button. Use the first option when you print to black-and-white devices such as laser printers and imagesetters; use the last option when printing to color printers and film recorders.

✦ **Encoding:** If you're printing over a network that doesn't support binary encoding, select the ASCII option to transfer data in the text-only format. The printing process takes much longer to complete, but at least it's possible.

The Setup button takes you to the Page Setup dialog box, which we've discussed earlier. Here's a chance for a last-minute reality check. Press Enter inside the Print dialog box to start the printing process on its merry way. To cancel a print in progress your best move is to bring up the Control Panel, then double-click on the Printers icon, and right-click on the printer you're using. Select Open, and you'll be able to see the job(s) in progress.

Creating Color Separations

If printing a composite image is moderately complicated, printing color separations is a terrific pain in the behind. Printer manufacturers and software developers are working to simplify this process, but for the present, Photoshop requires you to stagger through a maze of variables and obtuse options.

We wish that we could offer some conciliatory advice like *Hang in there and you'll make it,* but every day that we work with Photoshop's color separation capabilities adds to our conviction that this is an unnecessarily complicated process, designed by people who are nearly as confused as we are.

On that cheery note, the upcoming steps explain how to muddle your way through the color-separation process. You'll recognize many of the steps from the process described for printing a grayscale or color composite.

Note
If you're a prepress professional or computer artist looking for a means to enhance the printing process, you owe it to yourself to check out Light Source's Ofoto 2. Ofoto provides automatic calibration capabilities that match scanner, monitor, and printer at any stage in the image-editing process.

Steps: Printing CMYK color separations

1. If your computer is part of a network that includes many printers, use the Control Panel's Printers selection to select the printer to which you want to print, as described previously in the "Choosing a printer" section.

2. Calibrate your system to the specific requirements of your monitor and the selected printer using File⇨Preferences⇨Monitor Setup and File⇨Preferences⇨ Printing Inks Setup. You only need to complete this step once for each time you switch hardware. If you always use the same monitor and printer combination, you need to repeat this step very rarely, say once every six months, to account for screen and printer degradation.

3. Use File⇨Preferences⇨Separation Setup to control how Photoshop converts RGB and Lab colors to CMYK color space. Again, you need to perform this step only when you want to compensate for a difference in the output device or if you simply want to fine-tune Photoshop to create better separations.

4. Choose Mode⇨CMYK Color to convert the image from its present color mode to CMYK. The CMYK mode is explained in the "CMYK" section of Chapter 4.

5. Switching color modes can dramatically affect the colors in an image. To compensate for color and focus loss, you can edit the individual color channels as described in the "Color Channel Effects" section of Chapter 5.

6. If your image features many high-contrast elements and you're concerned that your printer might not do the best job of registering the cyan, magenta, yellow, and black color plates, you can apply Image⇨Trap to prevent your final printout from looking like the color funnies.

7. Choose File⇨Page Setup to specify the size of the pages and the size and orientation of the image on the pages, as described earlier in this chapter. Also be sure to select — at the very least — the Calibration Bars, Registration Marks, and Labels check boxes.

8. Click on the Screen button to change the size, angle, and shape of the halftone screen dots for the individual color plates, as described earlier in the "Changing the halftone screen" section. This step and Step 9 are optional.

9. Click on the Transfer button to map brightness values in each of the CMYK color channels to different shades on the printed plates, as described in the "Transfer function" section earlier in this chapter.

10. Choose File⇨Print (Ctrl-P) and select the Print Separations check box in the lower left corner of the dialog box (see Figure 6-11). Photoshop then prints the color separations according to your specifications.

Steps 1, 7, 8, 9, and 10 repeat concepts explained in earlier sections of this chapter. To fully understand steps 4 and 5, read the larger color theory discussions in Chapter 4. That leaves steps 2, 3, and 6, which are explained in the following sections.

Cross Ref You also can create color separations by importing an image into a desktop publishing program, such as QuarkXPress. To do so, export the image in the DCS format, as described in the "QuarkXPress DCS" section of Chapter 3. Then print the separations directly from the desktop publishing program. Because DCS is a subset of the EPS format, it enables you to save halftone screen and transfer function settings. QuarkXPress doesn't require that you export the image in the CMYK mode, but we recommend using the CMYK mode because it gives you greater control over the separation process.

Monitor calibration

Choose File⇨Preferences⇨Monitor to display the Monitor Setup dialog box shown in Figure 6-12. Along with the Gamma control panel, which offers the added capability of adjusting specific red, green, and blue color intensities, this dialog box represents the extent of Photoshop's monitor-calibration capabilities. However, unlike Gamma, the Monitor Setup dialog box provides options that directly affect the conversion of scanned colors to their CMYK equivalents. These options advise Photoshop that certain on-screen color distortions are in effect, and instruct the program to make accommodations when converting between the RGB and CMYK color modes.

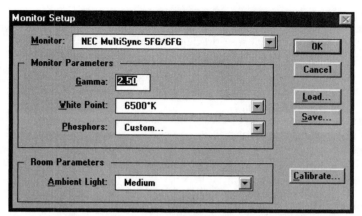

Figure 6-12: The options in the Monitor Setup dialog box tell Photoshop how to compensate for on-screen colors when preparing color separations.

The options in the Monitor Setup dialog box work as follows:

✦ **Monitor:** In the best of all possible worlds, you can select your exact model of monitor from this pop-up menu. Photoshop automatically changes the settings in the Monitor Parameters box (Gamma, White Point, and Phosphors) in accordance with the recommendations of the monitor's manufacturer. If you can't find your exact model, look for a model that is made by the same manufacturer and whose only difference from your model is screen size. If you can't find a suitable model, select the Other option.

Do not assume that all monitors from the same vendor are basically alike. Most vendors sell screens manufactured by different companies. Refresh rates can differ, screen technology can differ. Do not select a monitor other than the one you use unless the only difference in the name is screen size — and even there, be careful.

✦ **Gamma:** This value represents the brightness of medium colors on-screen. Low values down to 0.75 darken the image to compensate for an overly light screen; high values up to 3.00 lighten the image to compensate for an overly dark screen. Generally speaking, 1.8 is the ideal value.

✦ **White Point:** This value represents the temperature of the lightest color your screen can produce. Measured on the Kelvin temperature scale, it refers to the heat at which a so-called black body would turn to white. So theoretically, if you took the Maltese Falcon and heated it to 6,500 degrees Kelvin, it would turn white (if it didn't catch on fire first). The only way to achieve the correct value for this option is to consult the technical support department for your make of monitor or use a hardware testing device such as Minolta's $10,000 Minolta CRT Color Analyzer CA-100.

✦ **Phosphors:** This pop-up menu lets you select the kind of screen used in your monitor. Select the NTSC option if you're using a television monitor. Otherwise, consult your vendor's technical support department.

✦ **Ambient Light:** Select the amount of light in your office or studio from this pop-up menu. In a dark room, Photoshop slightly darkens the image. In a light room, Photoshop lightens it so that you can see it clearly despite the ambient light.

When you finish setting the options, press Enter to close the dialog box. Photoshop takes a few moments to adjust the display of the on-screen image.

This sounds as if it has the potential to be a nightmare. It does, but don't get paranoid. Still, the various calibration options and settings and results have occasioned an enormous amount of discussion in the Photoshop/PC section of CompuServe's ADOBEAPPS forum. You might want to check, on the CD-ROM, YXYMAS.EXE, a calibration package written by Stefan Steib, forum regular and NT guru (see his tech file on the same CD-ROM).

Printer calibration

To prepare an image that is to be reproduced on a commercial offset or web press, choose File➪Preferences➪Printing Inks Setup to display the Printing Inks Setup dialog box shown in Figure 6-13.

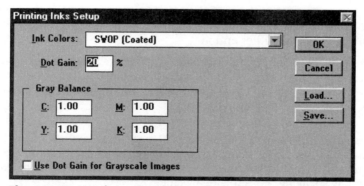

Figure 6-13: Use the options in the Printing Inks Setup dialog box to prepare an image for printing on a commercial offset or web press.

Like the Monitor Setup options, these settings are very technical and can be properly set only with the assistance of your commercial printer. But just so you have an inkling about inks, here's how the options work:

✦ **Ink Colors:** Select the specific variety of inks and paper stock that will be used to reproduce the current image. (Consult your commercial printer for this information.) Photoshop automatically changes the settings of the Dot Gain and Gray Balance options to the most suitable values.

✦ **Dot Gain:** Enter any value from –10 to 40 percent to specify the amount by which you can expect halftone cells to shrink or expand during the printing process, a variable known as *dot gain*. When printing to newsprint, for example, you can expect halftone cells to bleed into the page and expand by about 30 percent. When you convert to the CMYK color mode, Photoshop automatically adjusts the brightness of colors to compensate for the dot gain.

✦ **Gray Balance:** Assuming that the inks are up to snuff, equal amounts of cyan, magenta, yellow, and black ink should produce gray. But inks can fade and become impure over time. To compensate for this, you can vary the amount of ink that mixes to produce medium gray by entering values from 0.50 to 2.00 in the Gray Balance option boxes. Think of it as a recipe — 0.75 parts cyan mixed with 1.50 parts magenta, and so on. Again, consult with your commercial printer before changing these values.

✦ **Use Dot Gain for Grayscale Images:** When this option is turned off, the Dot Gain value only affects the creation and editing of CMYK images. If you select this check box, however, you also can apply the value to grayscale images. Then, any time you select a gray value, Photoshop automatically treats it as if it were lighter or darker, depending on whether the Dot Gain value is negative or positive, respectively.

Caution Rather than getting 50 percent gray when you select 50 percent gray, for example, you might get 58 percent gray. This can cause problems when you want to create displacement maps, create precise gradations, or simply achieve exact brightness values. We strongly recommend that you turn this check box off unless you have some specific reason for turning it on, such as suddenly taking leave of your senses.

CMYK conversions

Now that you've told Photoshop how to compensate for the foibles of your screen and commercial printer, you need to explain what kind of separation process you intend to use. To do this, choose File⇨Preferences⇨Separation Setup to display the Separation Setup dialog box, shown in Figure 6-14. Unlike the options in the Printing Inks Setup dialog box, which describe the specific press belonging to your commercial printer, these options describe a general printing process. Even so, you'll probably find it helpful to consult with your commercial printer before changing the settings.

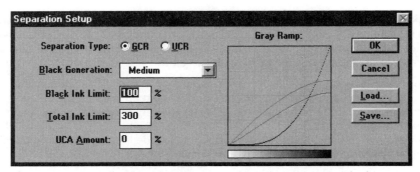

Figure 6-14: Describe the printing process using the options inside the Separation Setup dialog box.

The options in the Separation Setup dialog box work as follows:

✦ **Separation Type:** When the densities of cyan, magenta, and yellow inks reach a certain level, they mix to form a muddy brown. The GCR (gray component replacement) option avoids this unpleasant effect by overprinting these colors with black to the extent specified with the Black Generation option. If you select the UCR (under color removal) option, Photoshop removes cyan, magenta, and yellow inks where they overlap black ink. Generally speaking, GCR is the setting of choice except when you're printing on newsprint.

✦ **Black Generation:** Available only when the GCR option is active, the Black Generation pop-up menu lets you specify how dark the cyan, magenta, and yellow concentrations have to be before Photoshop adds black ink. Select Light to use black ink sparingly and Heavy to apply it liberally. The None option prints no black ink whatsoever, while the Maximum option prints black ink over everything. You may want to use the UCA Amount option to restore cyan, magenta, and yellow ink if you select the Heavy or Maximum option.

✦ **Black Ink Limit:** Enter the maximum amount of black ink that can be applied to the page. By default this value is 100 percent, which is solid ink coverage. If you raise the UCA Amount value, you'll probably want to lower this value by a similar percentage to prevent the image from over-darkening.

✦ **Total Ink Limit:** This value represents the maximum amount of all four inks permitted on the page. For example, assuming that you use the default Black Ink Limit and Total Ink Limit values shown in Figure 6-14, the darkest printable color contains 100 percent black ink. Therefore, the sum total of cyan, magenta, and yellow inks is 200 percent. (You subtract the Black Ink Limit value from the Total Ink Limit value to get the sum total of the three other inks.)

✦ **UCA Amount:** The opposite of UCR, UCA stands for under color addition, which lets you add cyan, magenta, and yellow inks to areas where the concentration of black ink is highest. For example, a value of 20 percent raises the amount of cyan, magenta, and yellow inks applied with black concentrations between 80 and 100 percent. This option is dimmed when the UCR radio button is active.

The Gray Ramp graph demonstrates the effects of your changes to any option in the Separation Setup dialog box. Four lines, one in each color, represent the four inks. Though you can't edit the lines in this graph by clicking and dragging on them, as you can in the Transfer Functions dialog box, you can observe the lines to gauge the results of your settings.

Color trapping

If color separations misalign slightly during the reproduction process (a problem called *misregistration*), the final image can exhibit slight gaps between colors. Suppose that an image features a 100 percent cyan chicken against a 100 percent magenta background. (Pretty attractive image idea, huh? Go ahead, you can use it if you like.) If the cyan and magenta plates don't line up exactly, you're left with a chicken with a white halo around it. Yuck.

A *trap* is a little extra bit of color that fills in the gap. For example, if you choose Image⇨Trap and enter 4 into the Width option box, Photoshop outlines the chicken with an extra 4 pixels of cyan and the background with an extra 4 pixels of magenta. Now the registration can be off a full 8 pixels without any halo occurring.

Caution Continuous-tone images, such as photographs and natural-media painting, don't need trapping because there are no harsh color transitions. In fact, trapping will actually harm such images by thickening up the borders and edges, smudging detail, and generally dulling the focus.

Therefore, the only reason to use the Trap command is to trap rasterized Illustrator drawings. Some state-of-the-art prepress systems trap documents by first rasterizing them to pixels and then modifying the pixels. Together, Photoshop and Illustrator constitute a more rudimentary but nonetheless functional trapping system. When you open an Illustrator document in Photoshop, the latter converts the illustration into an image according to your size and resolution specifications, as described in Chapter 3. Once the illustration is rasterized, you can apply Image⇨Trap to the image as a whole. Despite the command's simplicity, it handles nearly all trapping scenarios, even going so far as to incrementally reduce the width of the trap as the colors of neighboring areas grow more similar.

Duotones

It's been a few pages since the "Understanding Printing Terminology" section, so here's a quick recap: A duotone is a grayscale image printed with two inks. This technique expands the depth of the image by allowing additional shades for high-lights, shadows, and midtones. If you've seen one of those glossy Calvin Klein magazine ads, you've seen a duotone. Words like rich, luxurious, and palpable come to mind.

Photoshop also allows you to add a third ink to create a tritone and a fourth ink to create a quadtone. Color Plate 6-1 shows an example of an image printed as a quadtone. Figure 6-15 shows a detail from the image printed in its original grayscale form. See the difference?

Figure 6-15: This salute to all-around athlete Jim Thorpe by artist Mark Collen looks pretty good, but if you want to see great, check out the quadtone in Color Plate 6-1.

Creating a duotone

To convert a grayscale image to a duotone, tritone, or quadtone, choose Mode⇨Duotone. Photoshop displays the Duotone Options dialog box shown in Figure 6-16. By default, Duotone is the active Type option, and the Ink 3 and Ink 4 options are dimmed. To access the Ink 3 option, select Tritone from the Type pop-up menu; to access both Ink 3 and Ink 4, select Quadtone from the pop-up menu.

You specify the color of each ink you want to use by clicking on the color box associated with the desired ink option. Select a color from the Custom Colors dialog box as described in the "Predefined colors" section of Chapter 4. (In some cases, Photoshop displays the Color Picker dialog box, described in the "Using the Color Picker" section of that same chapter.)

Tip When creating duotones, tritones, and quadtones, prioritize your inks in order from darkest at the top to lightest at the bottom when you specify them in the Duotone Options dialog box. Because Photoshop prints inks in the order in which they appear in the dialog box, the inks will print from darkest to lightest. This ensures rich highlights and shadows and a uniform color range.

After selecting a color, you can use either of two methods to specify how the different-color inks blend. The first and more dependable way is to click on the transfer function box associated with the desired ink option. Photoshop then displays the Transfer Functions dialog box, described back in the "Transfer function" section of this chapter. This enables you to emphasize specific inks in different portions of the image according to brightness values.

For example, Figure 6-16 shows the inks and transfer functions assigned to the quadtone in Color Plate 6-1. The Navy Blue color is associated only with the darkest brightness values in the image; Rose peaks at about 80 percent gray and then descends; Teal covers the midtones in the image; and Dull Orange is strongest in the light values. The four colors mix to form an image whose brightness values progress from light orange to olive green to brick red to black.

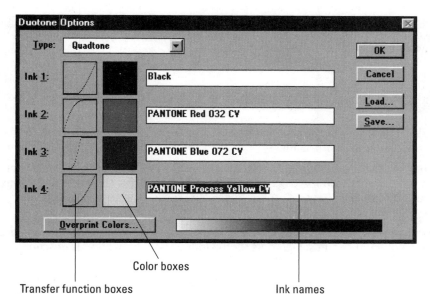

Color boxes

Transfer function boxes   Ink names

Figure 6-16: The Duotone Options dialog box lets you apply multiple inks to a grayscale image.

The second method for controlling the blending of colors is to click on the Overprint Colors button. An Overprint Colors dialog box appears, showing how each pair of colors will mix when printed. Other color swatches show how three and four colors mix, if applicable. To change the color swatch, click on it to display the Color Picker dialog box.

The problem with this second method is that it complicates the editing process. Photoshop doesn't actually change the ink colors or transfer functions in keeping with your new specifications; it just applies the new overprint colors without any logical basis. What's more, you lose all changes made with the Overprint Colors dialog box when you adjust any of the ink colors or any of the transfer functions.

Note   To go back and change the colors or transfer functions, choose Mode⇨Duotone again. Instead of reconverting the image, the command now lets you edit the existing duotone, tritone, or quadtone.

Reproducing a duotone

If you want a commercial printer to reproduce a duotone, tritone, or quadtone, you must print the image to color separations, just like a CMYK image. However, because you already specified which inks to use and how much of each ink to apply, you don't have to mess around with all those commands in the File⇨Preferences submenu. Just take the following familiar steps:

Steps: Printing a duotone, tritone, or quadtone

1. Select a printer with the Chooser desk accessory, as described previously in the "Choosing a printer" section.

2. Choose File⇨Page Setup to specify the size of the pages and the size and orientation of the image on the pages, as described earlier in this chapter in the "Using the common tabs: Paper, Graphic, PostScript" section. Be sure to select the Registration Marks option.

3. If you're feeling inventive, click on the Screen button to change the size, angle, and shape of the halftone screen dots for the individual color plates, as described previously in the "Changing the halftone screen" section.

4. Choose File⇨Print (Ctrl-P). Select the Print Separations check box in the lower left corner of the dialog box to print each ink to a separate sheet of paper or film.

To prepare a duotone to be imported into QuarkXPress, Illustrator, or some other application, save the image in the EPS or DCS format, as described in Chapter 3. As listed back in Table 4-1 of Chapter 4, EPS (and its DCS variation) is the only file format other than the native Photoshop format that supports duotones, tritones, and quadtones.

Tip   If you'll be printing your duotone using CMYK colors, and you can't quite get the effect you want inside the Duotone Options dialog box, you can convert the duotone to the CMYK mode (by choosing Mode⇨CMYK). Not only will all the duotone shades remain intact, but you'll have the added advantage of being able to tweak colors and even add color using Photoshop's standard color correction commands and editing tools. You can even edit individual color channels, as described in the previous chapter.

Spot-Color Separations

Photoshop 3 offers no new capability that accommodates spot-color printing. Photoshop is, after all, designed for creating and editing continuous-tone images; although spot colors work well for printing duotones, they more often lend themselves to high-contrast artwork created in drawing and page-layout programs.

But what if you want to add a spot-color highlight to an image? For example, suppose that you have a full-color image of a jet ski. The logo along the side of the boat is fully visible, just as the client wants it to be, but the color is off. Normally, the logo appears in Pantone 265 purple. But the CMYK equivalent for this color looks about three shades darker, four shades redder, and several times muddier. The only solution is to assign the proper spot color — Pantone 265 — to the logo. But how do you do it? Here are your options:

✦ Paint over the logo in the actual image. Then import the image into Illustrator or FreeHand and recreate the logo as object-oriented text. Then assign the text Pantone 265 and export the document in the EPS format or print it directly from the drawing program. The logo will appear on its own separation.

✦ Select the logo using the magic wand tool (or some more exacting method, as described in Chapters 8 and 9) and remove it using Edit⇨Cut (Ctrl-X). Then create a new channel by choosing the New Channel command from the Channels palette pop-up menu. After the Channel Options dialog box appears, click on the Color swatch and change it to a color that matches Pantone 265 as closely as possible. Press Enter twice to create the new channel and then press Ctrl-I to invert the channel and make it white. Paste in the logo art (Edit⇨Paste or Ctrl-V). As long as your selection outline is still intact, the logo is pasted in the exact same position as in the original image. To see the logo and image together, click on the eyeball icon in front of the CMYK composite view to show all channels at once. The logo will automatically appear in the purple color that you selected in the Channel Options dialog box. Edit the CMYK image and logo as desired.

If you opt for the second option, you can print the image directly from Photoshop in two passes. First, you switch to the CMYK composite view (Ctrl-0) and print the traditional four-color separation. Then you switch to the logo channel (Ctrl-5) and print this channel independently.

However, you cannot import the image into page layout programs such as Adobe Pagemaker or QuarkXPress. Photoshop doesn't offer any file formats that support more than four color channels, except the native Photoshop format (which most other programs don't support, and certainly not for the purpose of printing quality separations). If you were to save the image to the EPS or DCS format, for example, Photoshop would simply jettison the logo channel.

Windows 95 and Color

Given all the convolutions of color models and color spaces and calibrations, what's a poor Photoshopper to do? Microsoft is attempting to offer a solution in Windows 95 through ICM (Image Color Matching). ICM is designed to utilize a color profile from the manufacturer of a given device. That profile should allow ICM to map colors from Windows' logical color space to the color capabilities of the given output device — thus the device's drivers work in conjunction with the system to perform color matching. Finally, ICM is implemented as a DLL (Dynamic Link Library), and more than one can be loaded at a time for maximum flexibility.

Sounds pretty good, doesn't it? It may well be. But just try to find a color profile in the ICC (International Color Consortium) format — or an application that utilizes it. It's going to mean that device drivers not only need to be redone as 32 bit for Windows 95, they also have to support ICC profiles. Of course, things change rapidly in computing, and it may well be that the situation is changing by the time you read this. Definitely something to keep your eye on for the future.

Retouching with a Purpose

etouching is perhaps the most controversial of image-editing functions because an adept artist can dramatically alter the contents of a photo without the viewer being the least bit aware. The idea is particularly worrisome to news and action photographers because any alteration to such a photo represents a departure from reality. After all, what's the point of risking personal injury to shoot a photo of an underwater shark encounter if some fool in the graphics department is going to enhance the photo by adding a few Great Whites?

In the following chapters, we explain how to edit photos as realistically as possible. However, I recommend that you temper the applications of your skills with a smidgen of responsibility. Some retouching is perfectly acceptable. A photographer friend of Deke's, for example, runs an image-editing service on the side so that he can edit his own photos according to a client's needs. Seems okay. Certainly, retouching is so rampant and blatant in advertising that most consumers have grown savvy enough not to mistake advertising for reality. Not ideal, but again, okay. Where the merit of retouching is most tenuous is in the depiction of real events. In this case, it's not enough to edit the photo with the approval of the photographer; you also need to bring the edit to the attention of the viewer. There has been talk of adopting a symbol to indicate manipulated news photos, such as an *M* in a circle. Even better is an addition to the credit line: *Photo by X. Photo manipulation by Y.*

Ultimately, the whens and whys of image editing are up to you. We're here to show you how to retouch images. So without further ado, the following chapters show you how to edit an image so its own mother wouldn't recognize it.

Painting and Editing

Paint and Edit Tool Basics

You may still be wondering why we seem to be back where we were with Chapter 2. What is our problem? Can't we get to the point any faster?

No. And you know why? Because the introductory material is very important. From this point on, we want to share a verbal and theoretical vocabulary with you. We want you to understand not only how to perform a certain task, but also why we're approaching it in a particular way. If we just sit here and fire off a bunch of techniques, you'll probably be able to repeat those techniques with relatively little effort. But if you take the time to understand the larger issues of how image editing works and how Photoshop's specific capabilities relate to the real world, you'll be better prepared to branch out beyond the specific techniques to develop your own. This is when a real mastery of Photoshop begins: when you understand the principles so you can put them to work.

Painting primer

This chapter, in case you're still curious, is about painting and editing images using a bunch of tools in Photoshop's toolbox. Now, you may be thinking that these tools require you to possess a modicum of artistic talent. Actually, each tool provides options for just about any level of proficiency or experience. Photoshop offers get-by measures for novices who just want to make a quick edit and put the tool down before they make a mess of things. If you have a few hours of experience with other painting programs, you'll find that Photoshop's tools provide at least as much functionality and, in many cases, more. And if you're a graphics professional, you'll have no problem making Photoshop obey you. Suffice it to say that no matter who you are, you'll find electronic painting and editing tools to be more flexible, less messy, and more forgiving than their traditional counterparts.

But electronic painting and editing tools aren't the same as their traditional counter-parts. I've muttered about this before, and will mutter again (you have been warned!), especially in Chapter 19.

Robert

Cross Ref If you screw something up in the course of painting your image, stop and choose Edit⇨Undo. If that doesn't work, try one of the reversion techniques described in the "Selectively Undoing Changes" section of Chapter 11. As long as a previous version of the image is saved on disk, you have a way out.

Meet your tools

Photoshop provides three paint tools: *pencil, paintbrush,* and *airbrush.* You also get six edit tools: *smudge, blur, sharpen, burn, dodge,* and *sponge.* Figure 7-1 shows all of these tools. The keyboard equivalent for each tool appears in parentheses.

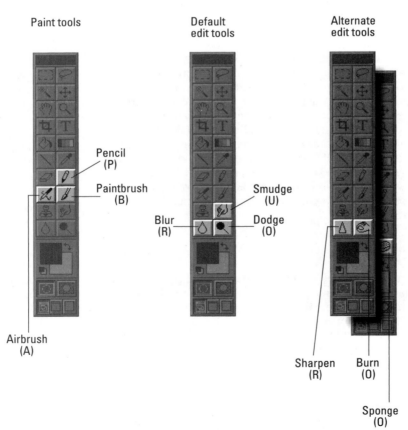

Figure 7-1: The three paint tools, the three edit tools that appear in the toolbox by default, and the three alternative edit tools.

Cross Ref In case you're wondering about all the other tools, Figure 7-2 segregates tools by category and lists the chapter in which you can find more information.

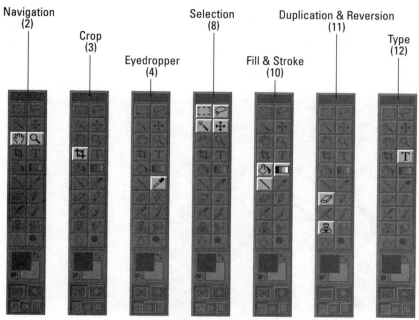

Figure 7-2: The rest of Photoshop's tools fall into the categories listed above each toolbox. The number of the chapter in which we discuss each category appears in parentheses.

The paint tools

The paint tools apply paint in the foreground color. In this and other respects, they work like their counterparts in other painting programs, but there are a few exceptions:

✦ **Pencil:** Unlike pencil tools found in most other painting programs, which paint lines 1 pixel thick, Photoshop's pencil paints a hard-edged line of any thickness. Figure 7-3 compares the default single-pixel pencil line with a fatter pencil line, a paintbrush line, and an airbrush line.

✦ **Paintbrush:** The paintbrush works just like the pencil tool, except that it paints an anti-aliased line that blends in with its background. The paintbrush also offers a Wet Edges option. (Double-click on the paintbrush tool icon in the toolbox and you'll see the Wet Edges check box in the bottom left corner of the Paintbrush Options panel of the Brushes palette.) When this option is turned on, the paintbrush creates a translucent line with darkened edges, much like painting with watercolors. Soft brush shapes produce more naturalistic effects. An example of this effect is shown in Figure 7-3.

✦ **Airbrush:** It's tempting to describe Photoshop's airbrush tool as a softer version of the paintbrush, because it uses a softer brush shape by default. Photoshop's default settings also call for a lighter pressure, so the airbrush paints a semitranslucent line. But if you set the airbrush to the same brush shape and pressure as the paintbrush, you will notice only one distinction: The paintbrush stops applying paint when you stop dragging, but the airbrush continues to apply paint as long as you press the mouse button or stylus. Figure 7-3 shows the dark glob of paint that results from pressing the mouse button while holding the mouse motionless at the end of the drag.

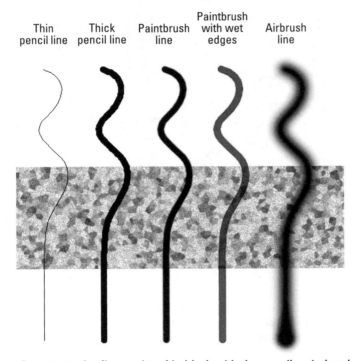

Figure 7-3: Five lines painted in black with the pencil, paintbrush, and airbrush tools. The Wet Edges option (second from right) causes the line to appear translucent. The airbrush tool was held in place for a few moments at the end of the rightmost line.

Edit tools

The edit tools don't apply color; rather, they influence existing colors in an image. Figure 7-4 shows each of the five edit tools applied to a randomized background.

Smudge   Blur   Sharpen   Dodge   Burn   Sponge

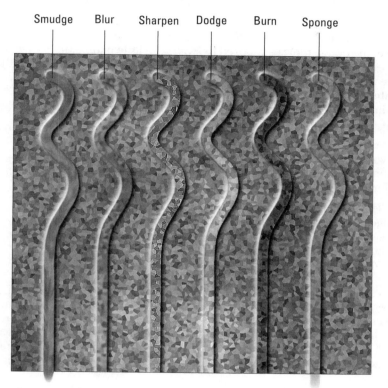

Figure 7-4: The effects of dragging with each of Photoshop's edit tools. The boundaries of each line are highlighted so that you can clearly see the distinctions between line and background.

The tools work as follows:

✦ **Smudge:** The smudge tool smears colors in an image. The effect is much like dragging your finger across wet paint.

✦ **Blur:** The first of the two focus tools (as they are now known in Photoshop 3), the blur tool blurs an image by lessening the amount of color contrast between neighboring pixels.

✦ **Sharpen:** The second focus tool selectively sharpens by increasing the contrast between neighboring pixels. Generally speaking, we find both the blur and sharpen tools to be less useful than their command counterparts in the Filters menu. They provide less control and usually require scrubbing at an image. (Your wrist may ache while using these tools. If you like the basic principle behind the tools but you want to avoid carpal tunnel syndrome, you can achieve consistent, predictable results without scrubbing by using the tools in combination with the Shift key, as described in the next section.)

✦ **Dodge:** The first of three toning tools, the dodge tool lets you lighten a portion of an image by dragging across it. Named after a traditional film exposure technique, the dodge tool is supposed to look like a little paddle thingie (you know, like one of those spoons you put over your eye at the optometrist's) that you wave over an image to diffuse the amount of light that gets to the film and thus lighten the print. Thank golly we no longer have to wave little paddle thingies in our modern age.

✦ **Burn:** The second toning tool, the burn tool, enables you to darken a portion of an image by dragging over it. The effect is similar to burning a film negative by holding your hand in an O shape to focus the light. It's kind of like frying a worker ant by using a magnifying glass (except not quite so smelly). At least, that's what they tell us.

✦ **Sponge:** The last toning tool (and one of only two tools added to Photoshop 3), the sponge tool robs an image of both saturation and contrast. Alternatively, you can set the tool so that it boosts saturation and adds contrast. For information about the newest of Photoshop's editing tools, stay tuned for the upcoming section "Mopping up with the sponge tool."

Temporarily to access (and not to split infinitives) the sharpen tool when the blur tool is selected, press and hold the Alt key while using the tool. The sharpen tool remains available only as long as you press the Alt key. You also can press Alt to access the blur tool when the sharpen tool is selected; to access the burn tool when the dodge tool is selected; and to access the dodge tool when the burn tool is selected. (If the sponge tool is active, pressing the Alt key has no effect, except maybe to give your finger a cramp.)

Tip   In Photoshop, you can replace the blur tool with the sharpen tool in the toolbox by Alt-clicking on the tool's icon. To toggle (switch) back to the blur tool, Alt-click on the sharpen icon. Likewise, you can Alt-click on the dodge tool icon to toggle among the dodge, burn, and sponge tools.

As explained in Chapter 2, the keyboard equivalents also toggle between the tools. When the blur tool is selected, press R to toggle to the sharpen tool. Another tap of the R key takes you back to blur. When the dodge tool is selected, press O to toggle to the burn tool, and then press O again to get the sponge. Press O one more time to take the trail herd back to Dodge. (What dodge tool discussion would be complete without at least one *Gunsmoke* joke?)

Tip   To modify the performance of a tool, double-click on its icon in the toolbox to display the customized Options panel in the Brushes palette. Alternatively, you can simply press the Enter key while the tool is selected. All the options inside the various Options panels are discussed throughout the remainder of this chapter.

Basic techniques

We know several people who claim that they can't paint, and yet they create beautiful work in Photoshop. Even though they don't have sufficient hand-eye coordination to write their names on the screen, they have unique and powerful artistic sensibilities, and they know lots of tricks that enable them to make judicious use of the paint and edit tools. We can't help you in the sensibilities department, but we can show you a few tricks that will boost your ability and inclination to use the paint and edit tools.

Straight line

You're probably already aware that you can draw a straight line with the line tool. If not, try it out. The line tool is that diagonal line on the left side of the toolbox. After selecting the tool, drag with it inside the image window to create a line. Pretty hot stuff, huh? Well, no, it's actually pretty dull. (Attention, dull guy: Check it out.) In fact, the only reason we ever use this tool is to draw arrows like those shown in the upcoming Figure 7-6. If you don't want to draw an arrow, you're better off using Photoshop's other means for drawing straight lines: the Shift key.

Cross Ref To access options that let you add an arrowhead to a line drawn with the line tool, double-click on the line tool icon in the toolbox to display the Line Tool Options panel in the Brushes palette. These options are explained in the "Applying Strokes and Arrowheads" section of Chapter 10.

To draw a straight line with any of the paint or edit tools, click on one point in the image and then press Shift and click on another point. Using the currently selected tool, Photoshop draws a straight line between the two points.

To create free-form polygons, continue to Shift-click with the tool. The left image in Figure 7-5 was created by Shift-clicking with the airbrush tool. Just to firm things up a bit, we applied the Unsharp Mask filter with a radius of 8 pixels (as described in great detail in the "Using the Unsharp Mask Filter" section of Chapter 13). The result is shown in the right example. We think it's supposed to be a cross between George Washington and Popeye. But it's hard to say; we only created the thing.

Tip The Shift key makes the blur and sharpen tools halfway useful. Suppose that you want to edit the perimeter of the car shown in Figure 7-6. The arrows in the figure illustrate the path your Shift-clicks should follow. Figure 7-7 shows the effect of Shift-clicking with the blur tool; Figure 7-8 demonstrates the effect of Shift-clicking with the sharpen tool.

Figure 7-5: This image was traced over a lightened scan of Mount Rushmore by clicking and Shift-clicking with the airbrush tool (left). We then sharpened the image using Filter➪Sharpen➪Unsharp Mask.

Figure 7-6: It takes one click and 24 Shift-clicks to soften or accentuate the edges around this car using the blur or sharpen tool.

Figure 7-7: The results of blurring the car's perimeter with the pressure set to 50 percent (top) and 100 percent (bottom). You set the pressure using the slider bar in the Focus Tools Options panel of the Brushes palette.

Figure 7-8: The results of sharpening the car with the pressure set to 50 percent (top) and 100 percent (bottom).

Perpendicular line

To draw a perpendicular line — that is, one that is either vertical or horizontal — with any of the paint or edit tools, press and hold the mouse button, press the Shift key, and begin dragging in a vertical or horizontal direction. Don't release the Shift key until you finish dragging or until you want to change the direction of the line, as demonstrated in Figure 7-9. Notice that pressing the Shift key in mid-drag snaps the line back into perpendicular alignment.

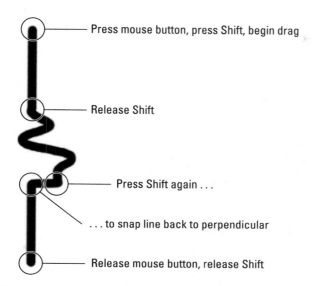

Press mouse button, press Shift, begin drag

Release Shift

Press Shift again . . .

. . . to snap line back to perpendicular

Release mouse button, release Shift

Figure 7-9: Pressing the Shift key after you start to drag with a paint or edit tool results in a perpendicular line for as long as the key is pressed.

One way to exploit the Shift key's penchant to snap to the perpendicular is to draw ribbed structures. Both of the central outlines around the skeleton that appears at the top of Figure 7-10 were created by dragging the paintbrush from right to left. Each rib was painted by pressing and releasing the Shift key while dragging with the paintbrush tool. Pressing Shift snapped the line to the horizontal axis, whose location was established by the beginning of the drag.

In the figure, we represented the axis for each line in gray. After establishing the basic skeletal form, some free-form details were added with the paintbrush and pencil tools, as shown in the middle image in Figure 7-10. We then applied the Emboss filter to create the finished fossil image. Nobody's going to confuse our work with a bona fide fossil (*Hey Marge, look what I done tripped over in the back forty!*) but it's not half bad for a cartoon.

Tip It's no accident that Figure 7-10 features a swordfish instead of your everyday round-nosed carp. In order to snap to the horizontal axis, the direction of the drag had to be established as being more horizontal than vertical. Photoshop would have interpreted a fish-faced convex arc drag as vertical and snapped to the vertical axis.

Figure 7-10: The basic structure for our bony pal was created by periodically pressing and releasing the Shift key while dragging with the paintbrush tool (top). We added embellishments to the fish by using the paintbrush and pencil tools (middle). Finally, a general area was selected around the image; choosing Filter⇨Stylize⇨Emboss transformed fish into fossil (bottom).

Painting with the smudge tool

Lots of first-time Photoshop artists misuse the smudge tool to soften color transitions. In fact, softening is the purpose of the blur tool. The smudge tool *smears* colors by shoving them into each other. The process bears more resemblance to the finger painting you did in grade school than to any traditional photographic editing technique.

In Photoshop, the performance of the smudge tool depends in part on the settings of the Pressure and Finger Painting options. Both reside in the Smudge Tool Options panel of the Brushes palette (see Figure 7-11), which you access by double-clicking on the smudge tool icon in the toolbox. These two options work as follows:

> ✦ **Pressure:** Measured as a percentage of the brush shape, this option determines the distance that the smudge tool drags a color. Higher percentages and larger brush shapes drag colors farthest. A Pressure setting of 100 percent equates to infinity, meaning that the smudge tool drags a color from the beginning of your drag until the end of your drag, regardless of how far you drag. Cosmic, Daddy-O.

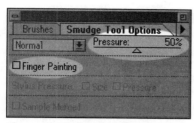

Figure 7-11: Combined with brush shape, the Pressure and Finger Painting options are the most important considerations when using the smudge tool.

✦ **Finger Painting:** The folks at Adobe used to call this effect *dipping,* which we think more accurately expressed how the effect works. When you select this option, the smudge tool begins by applying a smidgen of foreground color, which it eventually blends in with the colors in the image. It's as if you dipped your finger in a color and then dragged it through an oil painting. Use the Pressure setting to specify the amount of foreground color applied. If you turn on Finger Painting and set the Pressure to 100 percent, the smudge tool behaves exactly like the paintbrush tool.

For some examples of the smudge tool in action, take a look at Figure 7-12. The figure shows the effects of using the smudge tool set to four different Pressure percentages and with the Finger Painting option both off and on. In each instance, the brush shape is 13 pixels in diameter and the foreground color is set to black.

The third option highlighted in Figure 7-11 is Sample Merged. (You'll also find this option inside the Focus Tools Options panel, which controls the operation of the blur and sharpen tools.) This option lets the smudge tool grab colors from the background layers and smudge them into the current layer. Whether the option is on or off, only the current layer is affected; the background layers remain intact. For example, suppose that the inverted eyes of the woman at the top of Figure 7-13 are on a different layer from the rest of the face. If we use the smudge tools on the eyes layer with Sample Merged turned off, Photoshop ignores the face layer when smudging the eyes. As a result, details like the nose and teeth remain unsmudged, as you can see in the lower left example. If we turn Sample Merged on, Photoshop lifts colors from the face layer and mixes them in with the eyes layer, as shown in the lower right example.

Note that all of this activity occurs exclusively on the eyes layer. Just to give you a better look, the two lower examples on the eyes layer are shown independently of those on the face layer in Figure 7-14. You can now clearly see the proliferation of face details mixed into the eyes in the right example. Meanwhile, the face layer remains absolutely unaffected.

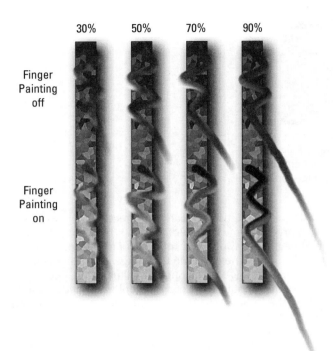

Figure 7-12: Eight drags with the smudge tool subject to different Pressure and Finger Painting settings.

Incidentally, in case you're wondering where the heck the option name Sample Merged comes from, Photoshop is saying that it will *sample* — that is, lift colors — as if all layers were merged into one. For more information about setting up and merging layers, read Chapter 17.

Mopping up with the sponge tool

The sponge tool is actually a pretty darn straightforward tool, hardly worth expending valuable space on in a book as tiny as this one. In fact, if it weren't so brand-spankin' new, we'd probably breeze right past it. But here's the deal: Double-click on the sponge tool icon in the toolbox to gain access to the Toning Tool Options panel. In the upper left corner of the panel is a pop-up menu that offers two options, Desaturate and Saturate. When set to the former, as by default, the tool reduces the saturation of the colors over which you drag. When you're editing a grayscale image, the tool reduces the contrast. If you select the Saturate option, the sponge tool increases the saturation of the colors over which you drag or increases contrast in a grayscale image. Higher Pressure settings produce more dramatic results.

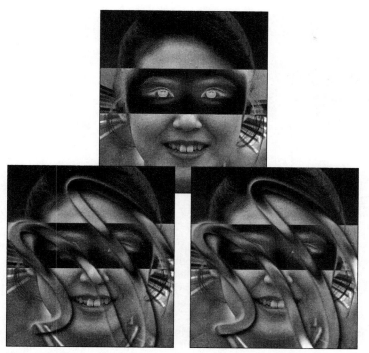

Figure 7-13: The original image (top) features inverted eyes on a layer above the rest of the face. We first smudged the eyes with Sample Merged turned off (lower left) and then with the option turned on (lower right).

Consider Color Plate 7-1. The upper left example shows the original PhotoDisc image. The upper right example shows the result of applying the sponge tool set to Desaturate. We dragged with the tool inside the pepper and around in the corner area. The Pressure was set to 100 percent. Notice that the affected colors are on the wane, sliding toward gray. In the lower right example, the effect is even more pronounced. Here we applied the sponge tools with great vim and vigor two additional times. There's hardly any hint of color left in these areas now.

To create the lower left example in Color Plate 7-1, we applied the sponge tool set to Saturate. This is where things get a little tricky. If you boost saturation levels with the sponge tool in the RGB or Lab color modes, you can achieve colors of absolutely neon intensity. However, these high-saturation colors don't stand a snowball's chance in a microwave of printing in CMYK. Therefore, we recommend that you choose Mode⇨CMYK Preview before boosting saturation levels with the sponge tool. This way, you can accurately view the results of your edits. After you're finished, choose Mode⇨CMYK Preview to turn off the CMYK preview and return to the RGB view.

Figure 7-14: The eyes layer from the previous figure shown by itself.

Figure 7-15 shows the yellow channel from Color Plate 7-1. Because yellow is the most prevalent primary color in the image, it is the most sensitive to saturation adjustments. When we boosted the saturation in the lower left example, the yellow brightness values deepened, adding yellow ink to the CMYK image. When we lessened the saturation in the two right-hand examples, the amount of ink diminished.

One of Adobe's recommended purposes of the sponge tool is to reduce the saturation levels of out-of-gamut RGB colors before converting an image to the CMYK mode. We're not too crazy about this use of the tool, for the simple reason that it requires a lot of scrubbing. It's generally easier to select the out-of-gamut area and reduce the colors using more-automated controls (as discussed in Chapter 16). Instead, you might prefer to use the sponge tool when a more selective, personal touch is required, as when curbing a distracting color that seems to be leaping a little too vigorously off the screen or boosting the saturation of a detail in the CMYK mode.

Brush Shape and Opacity

So far, we've mentioned the words *brush shape* seven times, and we have yet to explain what the Sam Hill we're talking about. Luckily, it's very simple. The brush shape is the size and shape of the tip of your cursor when you use a paint or edit tool. A big, round brush shape paints or edits in broad strokes. A small, elliptical brush shape is useful for performing hairline adjustments.

Photoshop gives brush size the respect it deserves. You have the option of displaying a cursor whose outline reflects the selected brush shape. To access this incredibly useful cursor, press Ctrl-K to bring up the General Preferences dialog box and then select Brush Size from the Tool Cursors radio buttons. Photoshop then displays the actual size of the brush you're using, up to 300 pixels in diameter. If the brush is bigger — no doubt there's someone out there with some reason for wielding a gigantic 600-pixel brush, though we can't imagine what that reason might be — the standard tool cursor appears instead.

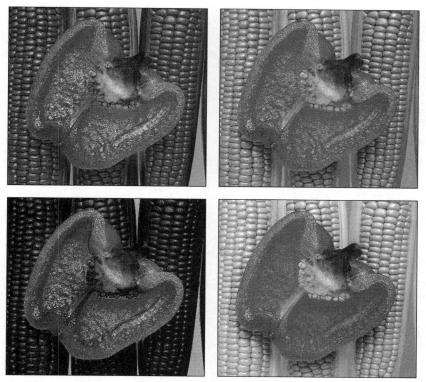

Figure 7-15: The yellow channel from Color Plate 7-1 shows the greatest amount of variation when the saturation is reduced or boosted with the sponge tool.

When you're using very small brushes, as when you're using the single-pixel pencil to do very precise retouching, the cursor includes four dots around its perimeter, making the cursor easier to locate. If you need a little more help, press the Caps Lock key to access the more obvious crosshair cursor.

Brushes palette

You access brush shapes by choosing Window⇨Palettes⇨Show Brushes to display the Brushes palette. (Alternatively, you can double-click on one of the painting or editing tools to display the Options panel of the Brushes palette and then click on the Brushes tab to display the brush shapes themselves. We know this doesn't sound any easier, but you don't have to negotiate submenus.) Figure 7-16 shows the Brushes palette with the pop-up menu wide open for your viewing pleasure.

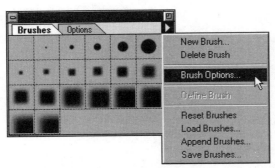

Figure 7-16: Photoshop 3's Brushes palette is much like the Brushes palette of its predecessor.

Tip You can switch brush shapes from the keyboard without displaying the Brushes palette. Press the left-bracket key to select the previous brush shape in the palette; press the right-bracket key to select the next brush shape. You can also press Shift-left bracket to select the first brush shape in the palette and Shift-right bracket to select the last shape.

Editing a brush shape

To edit a brush shape in the Brushes palette, select the brush you want to change and choose Brush Options from the palette menu (as in Figure 7-16). To create a new brush shape, choose New Brush. Either way, the dialog box shown in Figure 7-17 appears. (If you choose the New Brush command, the title bar is different but the options are the same.)

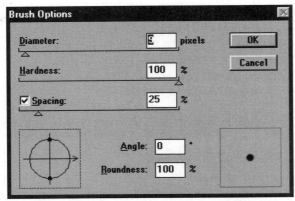

Figure 7-17: The Brush Options dialog box lets you change the size, shape, and hardness of the brush shape.

Tip If you hate menus — and who doesn't? — you can more conveniently edit a brush shape by simply double-clicking on it. To create a new brush shape, click once on an empty brush slot, as shown in the first example in Figure 7-18. (Incidentally, you can also delete a brush from the palette. To do so, press the Control key to display the scissors cursor, as in the second example in Figure 7-18, and then click. It's a great little housekeeping tip.)

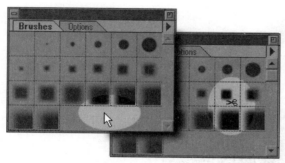

Figure 7-18: Clicking on an empty brush slot (left) brings up the New Brush dialog box so that you can create a new brush shape. Ctrl-clicking on a brush shape (right) deletes it from the palette.

Whether you're editing an existing brush or creating a new one, you have the following options at your disposal:

✦ **Diameter:** This option determines the width of the brush shape. If the brush shape is elliptical instead of circular, the Diameter value determines the longest dimension. You can enter any value from 1 to 999 pixels. Brush shapes with diameters of 30 pixels or higher are too large to display accurately in the Brushes palette and instead appear as circles with inset Diameter values.

✦ **Hardness:** Except when you use the pencil tool, brush shapes are always anti-aliased. However, you can further soften the edges of a brush by dragging the Hardness slider bar away from 100 percent. The softest setting, 0 percent, gradually tapers the brush from a single solid color pixel at its center to a ring of transparent pixels around the brush's perimeter. Figure 7-19 demonstrates how low Hardness percentages expand the size of a 100-pixel brush beyond the Diameter value (as demonstrated by the examples set against black). Even a 100 percent hard brush shape expands slightly because it is anti-aliased. The Hardness setting is ignored when you use the pencil tool.

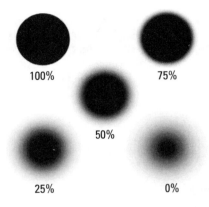

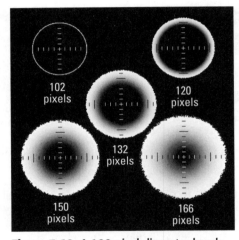

Figure 7-19: A 100-pixel diameter brush shown as it appears when set to a variety of Hardness percentages. Below, we changed the background pixels from white to black so that you can see the actual diameter of each brush shape. The tick marks indicate 10-pixel increments.

✦ **Spacing:** The Spacing option controls how frequently a tool affects an image as you drag, measured as a percentage of the brush shape. Suppose that the Diameter of a brush shape is 12 pixels and the Spacing is set to 25 percent (the setting for all default brush shapes). For every 3 pixels (25 percent of 12 pixels) you drag with the paintbrush tool, Photoshop lays down a 12-pixel-wide spot of color. A Spacing of 1 percent provides the most coverage, but may also slow down the performance of the tool. If you deselect the Spacing check box, the effect of the tool is wholly dependent on the speed at which you drag, which can be useful for creating nonuniform or splotchy lines. Figure 7-20 shows examples.

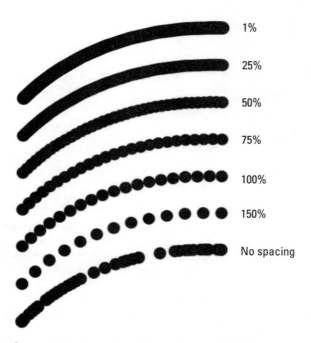

1%

25%

50%

75%

100%

150%

No spacing

Figure 7-20: Examples of lines drawn with different Spacing values in the Brush Options dialog box. Gaps or ridges generally begin to appear when the Spacing value exceeds 30 percent. The final line was created by turning off the Spacing option.

✦ **Angle:** This option enables you to pivot a brush shape on its axes. However, it won't make a difference in the appearance of the brush shape unless the brush is elliptical.

✦ **Roundness:** Enter a value of less than 100 percent into the Roundness option to create an elliptical brush shape. The value measures the width of the brush as a percentage of its height, so a Roundness value of 5 percent results in a long, skinny brush shape.

Tip You can adjust the angle of the brush dynamically by dragging the gray arrow inside the box to the left of the Angle and Roundness options. Drag the handles on either side of the black circle to make the brush shape elliptical, as demonstrated in Figure 7-21.

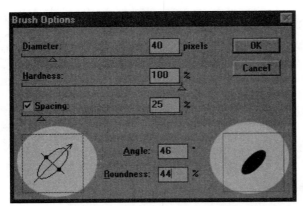

Figure 7-21: Drag the gray arrow or the black handles to change the angle or roundness of a brush, respectively. The Angle and Roundness values update automatically, as does the preview of the brush in the lower right corner of the dialog box.

We heartily recommend that you take a few moments one of these days to experiment at length with the Brush Options dialog box. By combining paint and edit tools with one or more specialized brush shapes, you can achieve artistic effects unlike anything permitted via traditional techniques. Starting with a PhotoDisc image lightened and filtered to serve as a template, Figure 7-22 was painted by using the flat, 45-pixel brush shape shown in the dialog box. (For a color version of the effect, take a look at Color Plate 7-2.) No other brush shape or special effect was applied. Think of what you can accomplish if you don't limit yourself as ridiculously as we did.

Creating and using custom brushes

You can define a custom brush shape by selecting a portion of your image that you want to change to a brush and choosing the Define Brush command from the Brushes palette pop-up menu. You can even draw your brush in the Scratch panel of the Picker palette, select the brush, and choose Define Brush to capture it.

In addition to giving you the flexibility to create a brush from an element in your image, Photoshop ships with a file called Assorted Brushes that contains all kinds of little symbols and doodads you can assign as custom brush shapes. You can load the contents of the Assorted Brushes file into the Brushes palette by choosing the Load Brushes command from the palette menu (or Append Brushes, if you don't want to lose the brush shapes that currently occupy the palette). You'll find Assorted Brushes inside the Brushes and Patterns folder, which resides in the same folder as the Photoshop application. Figure 7-23 shows an inspirational image created using Photoshop's predefined custom brushes.

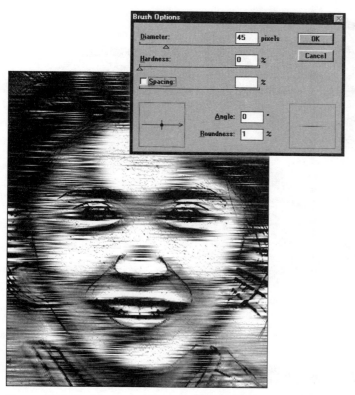

Figure 7-22: Just to show off, we painted over a scanned image with the paintbrush tool, using the brush shape shown in the dialog box at top.

You can adjust the performance of a custom brush in the following ways:

✦ **Brush options:** Choose the Brush Options command from the palette menu or double-click on the custom brush in the Brushes palette to bring up the dialog box shown in Figure 7-24. Here you can adjust the spacing of the brush shape and specify whether Photoshop anti-aliases (softens) the edges or leaves them as is. If the brush is sufficiently large, the Anti-aliased check box appears dimmed. All custom brushes are hard-edged when you use the pencil tool.

Figure 7-23: Yes, it's Boris, the sleeping custom-brush guy. If you suspect that this image is meant to suggest that custom brushes are more amusing than utilitarian, you're right. The brushes from the Assorted Brushes file appear on the right.

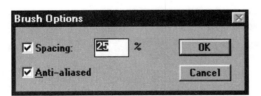

Figure 7-24: The dialog box that appears when you double-click on a custom brush.

✦ **Brush color:** The foreground color affects a custom brush just as it does a standard brush shape. To erase with the brush, select white as the foreground color. To paint in color, select a color.

✦ **Opacity and brush modes:** The setting of the Opacity slider bar and the brush modes pop-up menu also affect the application of custom brushes. For more information on these options, keep reading this chapter.

Tip You can achieve some unusual and sometimes interesting effects by activating the smudge tool's Finger Painting option and painting in the image window with a custom brush. At high Pressure settings, say 80 to 90 percent, the effect is rather like applying oil paint with a hairy paintbrush, as illustrated in Figure 7-25.

Figure 7-25: We created this organic, expressive image by combining the smudge tool's dipping capability with four custom brushes. We don't know what those finger-like growths are, but they'd probably feel right at home in an aquarium.

 Tip To restore the factory-default brush shapes, choose Reset Brushes from the Brushes palette menu. It's a lot easier than searching around for the Default Brushes file, as you had to do in the old days.

Opacity, pressure, and exposure

The brush shapes in the Brushes palette affect two tools other than the paint and edit tools, these being the eraser and the rubber stamp, both discussed in Chapter 11, "Duplicating and Reverting." But the slider bar in the upper right corner of the Options panel of the Brushes palette additionally affects the paint bucket, gradient, and line tools. Photoshop assigns one of three labels to this slider bar, illustrated in Figure 7-26.

✦ **Opacity:** The Opacity slider bar determines the translucency of colors applied with the paint bucket, gradient, line, pencil, paintbrush, eraser, or rubber stamp tool. At 100 percent, the applied colors appear opaque, completely covering the image behind them. (The one exception is the paintbrush with Wet Edges active, which is always translucent.) At lower settings, the applied colors mix with the existing colors in the image.

✦ **Pressure:** The Pressure slider bar affects different tools in different ways. When you use the airbrush tool, the slider bar controls the opacity of each spot of color the tool delivers. (In this case, the slider bar really ought to be labeled *Opacity,* because your settings produce the same results as the Opacity settings for the pencil or paintbrush tools. The effect appears unique because the airbrush spews out more color than the pencil or paintbrush. Apparently the folks at Adobe don't agree, however, because they've left the option labeled *Pressure* in Version 3.)

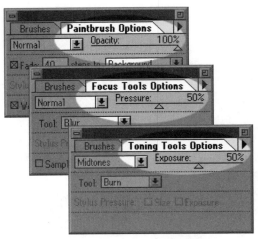

Figure 7-26: The slider bar in the upper right corner of the Brushes palette assumes one of these functions, depending on the selected tool. The slider disappears altogether when you select one of the navigation tools, one of the selection tools, the crop tool, or the eyedropper.

When you use the smudge tool, the slider bar controls the distance that the tool drags colors in the image. And in the case of the blur, sharpen, or sponge tool, the slider bar determines the degree to which the tool changes the focus or saturation of the image, 1 percent being the minimum and 100 percent being the maximum.

✦ **Exposure:** If you select the dodge or burn tool, the slider bar title changes to *Exposure.* A setting of 100 percent applies the maximum amount of lightening or darkening to an image, which is still far short of either absolute white or black.

The factory default setting for all Exposure and Pressure slider bars is 50 percent; the default setting for all Opacity sliders is 100 percent.

Tip   As long as one of the tools listed in this section is selected, you can change the Opacity, Pressure, or Exposure setting in 10 percent increments by pressing a number key on the keyboard or keypad. Press 1 to change the setting to 10 percent, press 2 for 20 percent, and so on, all the way up to 0 for 100 percent. This tip works whether or not the Options panel of the Brushes palette is visible. This is one of the best and most easily overlooked Photoshop tips ever. Get in the habit of using the number keys and you'll thank yourself later.

Tapered Lines

Photoshop provides two ways to create tapering lines that are reminiscent of brush strokes created using traditional techniques. You can specify the length over which a line fades by entering a value into the Fade option box, as described in the next section. Or, if you own a pressure-sensitive drawing tablet, you can draw brush strokes that fade in and out automatically according to the amount of pressure you apply to the stylus. Both techniques enable you to introduce an element of spontaneity into what otherwise seems at times like an absolute world of computer graphics.

Fading the paint

All three paint tools offer Fade check boxes in their respective Options panels that let you create lines that gradually fade away as you drag. Figure 7-27 shows the Fade option as it appears in the Paintbrush Options panel, along with some examples of the effect.

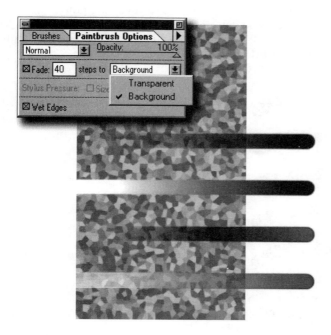

Figure 7-27: The Fade check box as it appears in the Paintbrush Options panel, along with four examples.

After selecting the Fade check box, enter a value into the option box to specify the distance over which the color fading should occur. The fading begins at the start of your drag and is measured in brush shapes.

For example, assume that the foreground color is black. If you enter 40 into the Fade option box, as in Figure 7-27, Photoshop paints 40 brush shapes, the first in black and the remaining 39 in increasingly lighter shades of gray.

Cross Ref   You can paint gradient lines by selecting the To Background radio button. Photoshop fades the line from the foreground color to the background color, in much the same way that the gradient tool fades the interior of a selection. For more information on the gradient tool, see the "Applying Gradient Fills" section of Chapter 10.

Fading and spacing

The physical length of a fading line is dependent both on the Fade value and on the value entered into the Spacing option box in the Brush Options dialog box, discussed back in the "Editing a brush shape" section earlier in this chapter.

To recap, the Spacing value determines the frequency with which Photoshop lays down brush shapes, and the Fade value determines the number of brush shapes laid down. Therefore, as demonstrated in Figure 7-28, a high Fade value combined with a high Spacing value creates the longest line.

1%

12%

25%

37%

50%

Figure 7-28: Five fading lines drawn with the paintbrush tool. In each case, the Fade option is set to 36 brush shapes. The Spacing value was changed incrementally from 1 to 50 percent, as labeled.

Sparkles and comets

Fading lines may strike you as pretty ho-hum, but they enable you to create some no-brainer, cool-mandoo effects, especially when combined with the Shift key techniques discussed earlier, in the "Drawing a straight line" section.

Figures 7-29 and 7-30 demonstrate two of the most obvious uses for fading straight lines: creating sparkles and comets. The top image in Figure 7-29 features two sets of sparkles, each made up of 16 straight lines emanating from the sparkle's center. To create the smaller sparkle on the right, the Fade value was set to 60 and each of the four perpendicular lines was drawn with the paintbrush tool. The Fade value was changed to 36 before drawing the four 45-degree diagonal lines. The eight very short lines that occur between the perpendicular and diagonal lines were drawn with a Fade value of 20. Likewise, the larger sparkle on the left was created by periodically adjusting the Fade value, this time from 90 to 60 to 42.

For comparison's sake, we used different techniques to add a few more sparkles to the bottom image in Figure 7-29. To achieve the reflection in the upper left corner of the image, Filter⇨Stylize⇨Lens Flare was chosen and 50–300mm Zoom was selected from the Lens Type options. The two tiny sparkles on the right edge of the bumper were created by using a custom brush shape; select the custom brush, set the foreground color to white, and click once with the paintbrush tool in each location. So many sparkles make for a tremendously shiny image.

In Figure 7-30, the car is copied and pasted on top of a NASA photograph of Jupiter. Clicking and Shift-clicking with the paintbrush tool created the comets — well, if you must know, they're actually cosmic rays — that you see shooting through and around the car.

After masking portions of the image (a process described at length in Chapter 9), rays were drawn behind the car (one ray even shoots up through the car and out the spare tire). The three bright lights in the image — above the left fin, above the roof, and next to the right turn signal — are more products of the Lens Flare filter.

Note All of the fading lines in Figures 7-29 and 7-30 were added with the paintbrush tool, using a variety of default brush shapes. Because we didn't edit any brush shape, the Spacing value for all lines was a constant 25 percent.

Lines created with pressure-sensitive tablets

The pressure-sensitive tablet has to be the single most useful piece of optional hardware available to computer artists. Not only can you draw with a penlike stylus instead of a clunky mouse, you also can dynamically adjust the thickness of lines and the opacity of colors by changing the amount of pressure you apply to the stylus. Some of the most recent tablets offer an eraser as well. At this writing, three vendors — Wacom, CalComp, and Kurta — manufacture pressure-sensitive tablets.

Figure 7-29: Sparkles were drawn in the top image by using the paintbrush tool. The second image features a reflection applied with the Lens Flare filter (upper left corner) and two dabs of a custom brush shape (right edge of the bumper).

Of these, our favorite is Wacom's ArtZ, a 6 × 8-inch tablet that plugs into a serial port. If you have two serial ports and a mouse port, you're ready to go — you won't have to give up (or shuffle) mouse and modem. But if your mouse is running off a serial port — well, things can get a tad problematic. See Appendix A for further details. The ArtZ offers 120 levels of pressure and a transparent overlay to hold pages you want to trace. It also has a cordless stylus that weighs less than an ounce and features both a pressure-sensitive nib and a side switch.

Figure 7-30: Remember when gas was cheap and you all piled in the car to go for a drive in space? Unfortunately, you always had to worry about those cosmic rays. Luckily, they're a cinch to draw: Set the Fade option to 110 and then click and Shift-click on opposite sides of the image with the paintbrush tool.

If you haven't seen the surface of your desk for several solar years — we've busily blighted *our* desks with an urban sprawl of 3-foot-high piles of papers, disks, CDs, manuals, and sodas (Robert prefers Canada Dry Diet Lemon Ginger Ale) — consider the new Wacom ArtPad. Measuring a diminutive 4×5 inches, this thing is smaller than a standard mouse pad. Its price is a mere $200 (or less) retail.

If you're an artist and you've never experimented with these or any other pressure-sensitive tablets, we recommend that you do so at your earliest convenience. You'll be amazed at how much it increases your range of artistic options. Minutes after installing his first tablet, Deke drew the cartoon shown in Figure 7-31 (and in Color Plate 7-3) from scratch on a 13-inch monitor in about 30 minutes. Whether you like the image or not — there is a certain troglodyte quality to the cut of his forehead, and that jaw could bust a coconut — it shows off the tablet's ability to paint tapering lines and accommodate artistic expression.

R%% **Robert** I share Deke's enthusiasm, even though he may pity me for using a "legacy" (that is, slightly older, in cyber-speak euphemism) Wacom SD-510. But a little Op-Ed is appropriate if you have experience in traditional media. For all the ease of drawing, you won't get the sort of tactile feedback between medium and paper that you're used to. It may take some mental adjustment on your part. This is especially true in the natural media program Fractal Design Painter. It can mimic the look of pastels (regular pastels, that is; I've never used its oil pastels — no greasy kid stuff here!) with un-canny accuracy. But you haven't got the feeling of that stick in your hand, and the sheet of Canson underneath. Of course, you haven't got pastel dust flying around either. I would only add that virtuoso illustrator Rob Howard (some of his gems appear on the CD-ROM that accompanies this book) has worked regularly with a mouse, even though he once remarked that it was like drawing with a bar of soap.

Figure 7-31: Although Deke painted this caricature years ago, it embodies the range of artistic freedom provided by a Wacom tablet.

How to undo pressure-sensitive lines

Pressure-sensitive lines can be hard to undo. Because a Wacom or other stylus is so sensitive to gradual pressure, you can unwittingly let up and re-press the stylus during what you think is a single drag. If, after doing so, you decide you don't like the line and choose Edit⇨Undo, Photoshop deletes only the last portion of the line, because it detected a release midway through. As a result, you're stuck with half a line that you don't want or, worse, that visually mars your image.

Problems are even more likely to occur if you use a stylus with a side switch, such as the one included with Wacom's ArtZ or CalComp's DrawingPad. It's very easy to accidentally press your thumb or forefinger against the switch as you drag. If you have the switch set to some separate operation, such as double-clicking, you interrupt your line. This not only creates an obvious break but also makes the error impossible to undo.

To prepare for this eventuality — and believe us, it *will* happen — make sure to save your image at key points when you're content with its appearance. Then, if you find yourself stuck with half a line, you can remove the line by Alt-dragging with the eraser tool, as discussed in the "Selectively Undoing Changes" section of Chapter 11.

Pressure-sensitive options

We're happy to report that Photoshop 3 has gotten its act back together in the pressure-sensitivity department. Like its predecessor, it offers three options for interpreting pressure-sensitive input. But unlike Version 2.5, which was unable to properly taper lines, Version 3 varies the thickness of a line every bit as well as Photoshop 2. Thanks, Adobe, for setting this one straight.

All paint and edit tools, as well as the eraser and rubber stamp, provide three check boxes for controlling Photoshop's reaction to stylus pressure (see Figure 7-32). Available from the Options panel only when a pressure-sensitive tablet is hooked up to your computer, these options include the following:

✦ **Size:** If you select the Size check box, Photoshop varies the thickness of the line. The more pressure you apply, the thicker the line. The Size check box is selected by default. Figure 7-33 shows three paintbrush lines drawn with the Size option selected. We created the first line using a hard brush, the second with a soft brush, and the third with a hard brush and with the Wet Edges check box selected.

✦ **Color:** Select this option to create custom gradient lines. Full pressure paints in the foreground color; very slight pressure paints in the background color; medium pressure paints a mix of the two.

✦ **Opacity:** This option paints an opaque coat of foreground color at full pressure that dwindles to transparency at very slight pressure.

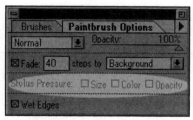

Figure 7-32: Photoshop provides three check boxes for interpreting the signals from a pressure-sensitive tablet.

Because Photoshop presents its pressure options as check boxes, you can select more than one option at a time. For example, you can select both Size and Color to instruct Photoshop to change both the thickness and color of a line as you bear down or lift up on the stylus.

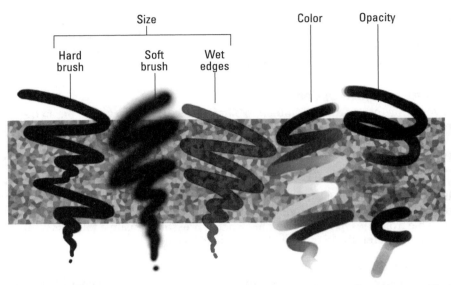

Figure 7-33: The effects of the Size, Color, and Opacity options on lines drawn with the paintbrush tool and a pressure-sensitive tablet.

Brush Modes

The pop-up menu in the Options panel provides access to Photoshop's *brush modes,* which control how paint and edit tools affect existing colors in the image. Brush modes are not available when you use a navigation tool, the crop tool, the eyedropper, a selection tool, or the type tool. Figure 7-34 shows which brush modes are available when you select various tools.

Cross Ref With the exception of the specialized brush modes provided for the dodge, burn, and sponge tools, brush modes and the overlay modes described in Chapter 17 are varieties of the same animal. Read this section to get a brief glimpse of brush modes; read Chapter 17 for a more detailed account that should appeal to brush-mode aficionados.

Paint tool brush modes

Photoshop provides a whopping 15 brush modes when you're using the pencil, paintbrush, airbrush, or any of the other tools shown on the left side of Figure 7-34. Just so that you can get an idea of what these various brush modes look like when applied to an image, Color Plate 7-4 shows each and every one of them. In each case, a red stroke is painted with the paintbrush tool. For maximum effect, we divided the underlying images into two halves. The colors are simply washed out in the right half; in the left half, the colors are shifted toward blue-green, thus providing the maximum contrast to the red paint applied with the brush.

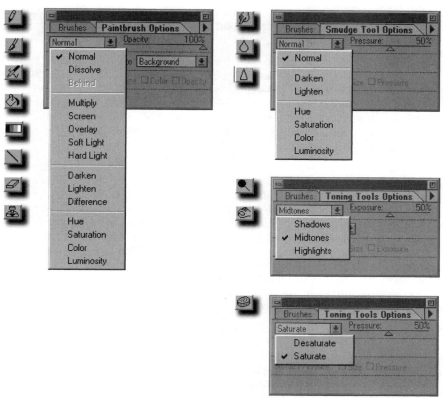

Figure 7-34: The number of options in the brush modes pop-up menu varies depending on whether you select a paint tool (left), an edit tool (top right), the dodge or burn tool (middle right), or the sponge tool (bottom right).

The 15 standard brush modes work as follows:

✦ **Normal:** Choose this mode to paint or edit an image normally. A paint tool coats the image with the foreground color and an edit tool manipulates the existing colors in an image according to the setting of the Opacity or Pressure slider bar.

✦ **Dissolve:** This mode and the six that follow are not applicable to the edit tools (though we wonder why — the Dissolve mode would be especially useful with the smudge tool). Dissolve scatters colors applied with a paint tool randomly throughout the course of your drag. The Dissolve mode produces the most pronounced effects when used with soft brushes and the airbrush tool.

✦ **Behind:** This one is applicable exclusively to layers with transparent back-grounds. When Behind is selected, the paint tool applies color behind the image on the layer, showing through only in the transparent and translucent areas. In

Color Plate 7-4, for example, the brush stroke appears behind the image, but not in front of it. When you're working on an image without layers or on the background layer of a multilayered image, the Behind mode is dimmed.

✦ **Multiply:** The Multiply mode combines the foreground color with an existing color in an image to create a third color that is darker than the other two. Red times white is red, red times yellow is orange, red times green is brown, red times blue is violet, and so on. The effect is almost exactly like drawing with felt-tipped markers, except that the colors don't bleed. (This mode has no effect on the paintbrush when it's set to Wet Edges; the Wet Edges brush already multiplies.)

✦ **Screen:** The inverse of the Multiply mode, Screen combines the foreground color with an existing color in an image to create a third color that is lighter than the other two. Red times white is white, red times yellow is off-white, red times green is yellow, red times blue is pink, and so on. The effect is unlike any traditional painting technique; not even chalk lightens an image in this way. It's like some impossibly bright, radioactive Uranium-238 highlighter hitherto used only by G-Men to mark the pants cuffs of Communist sympathizers. (If the Wet Edges option always multiplies, combining it with the Screen mode must — you guessed it — render the brush invisible. If the paintbrush tool doesn't seem to be working, this could be your problem.)

Tip

Overlay, Soft Light, and Hard Light are new to Photoshop 3. Because they are liable to give even seasoned Photoshop experts pause, we've created a separate full-color figure for these three modes (Color Plate 7-5). All three modes work by multiplying dark colors and screening light colors as you lay them down with a paint tool. The darkness and lightness of the existing colors in the image also enter the equation, but the ways in which these basic operations are applied and the manners in which the colors mix are unique. (In other words, you can't emulate the Soft Light mode by simply applying the Hard Light mode at 70 percent or some similar Opacity.)

✦ **Overlay:** Okay, here goes: Overlay is the kindest of the three new modes. It always enhances contrast and it always boosts the saturation of colors in an image. In fact, it works rather like a colored version of the sponge tool set to Saturate. But although it generously infuses an image with the foreground color, it is not the same as the Color brush mode (described shortly). Rather, it mixes the colors in the image with the foreground color to come up with a vivid blend that is almost always visually pleasing. This may be the most interesting and downright useful brush mode available in Photoshop 3.

✦ **Soft Light:** According to the Photoshop documentation, Soft Light casts a diffused spotlight on the image. It strikes us as more of a glazing. In fact, Soft Light is remarkably similar to applying a diluted wash of paint to a canvas. It never completely covers up the underlying detail — even black or white applied at 100 percent Opacity does no more than darken or lighten the image — but it does slightly diminish contrast.

✦ **Hard Light:** This mode might better be named *Obfuscate*. It's as if you were applying a thicker, more opaque wash to the image. Light colors screen the holy heck out of the image; dark colors multiply the image into obscurity. You might think of Hard Light as Normal with a whisper of underlying detail mixed in.

You want one more analogy? If Soft Light is like shining colored light onto the subject of the photograph, Hard Light is like shining the light directly onto the camera lens. (Of course, this analogy fails to account for dark colors — you can hardly make an image darker by casting light on it — but you get the idea.)

✦ **Darken:** Ah, back to the old familiars. If you choose the Darken mode, Photoshop applies a new color to a pixel only if that color is darker than the present color of the pixel. Otherwise, the pixel is left unchanged.

✦ **Lighten:** The opposite of the previous mode, Lighten ensures that Photoshop applies a new color to a pixel only if the color is lighter than the present color of the pixel. Otherwise, the pixel is left unchanged.

✦ **Difference:** Although this operation is new to the brush modes, Photoshop has offered a Difference command since Version 1.0. When a paint tool is set to the Difference mode, Photoshop subtracts the brightness value of the foreground color from the brightness value of each affected pixel in the image — if the result is a negative number, Photoshop simply makes it positive — to create an inverted effect. Black has no effect on an image; white completely inverts it. Colors in between create psychedelic effects.

Tip

Because the Difference mode inverts an image, it results in an outline around the brush stroke. You can make this outline thicker by using a softer brush shape. For a really trippy effect, try combining the Difference mode with a soft brush shape and the paintbrush tool with Wet Edges turned on.

✦ **Hue:** Understanding the next few modes requires a color theory recap. Remember how the HSL color model calls for three color channels? One is for *hue,* the value that explains the colors in an image; the second is for *saturation,* which represents the intensity of the colors; and the third is for *luminosity,* which explains the lightness and darkness of colors. Therefore, if you choose the Hue brush mode, Photoshop applies the hue from the foreground color without changing any saturation or luminosity values in the existing image. This option has no effect when you work on a grayscale image.

✦ **Saturation:** If you choose this mode, Photoshop changes the intensity of the colors in an image without changing the colors themselves or the lightness and darkness of individual pixels. This option has no effect on a grayscale image.

✦ **Color:** This mode might be more appropriately titled *Hue and Saturation.* It lets you change the colors in an image and the intensity of those colors without changing the lightness and darkness of individual pixels. This option has no effect on a grayscale image.

✦ **Luminosity:** The opposite of the Color mode, Luminosity changes the lightness and darkness of pixels but leaves the hue and saturation values unaffected. When you work on a grayscale image, this mode operates identically to the Normal mode.

The three dodge and burn modes

Phew, that takes care of the brush modes available to the paint tools, the smudge tool, and the two focus tools. We already explained the Desaturate and Saturate modes available to the sponge tool (back in the "Mopping up with the sponge tool" section of this chapter). That leaves us with the three brush modes available to the dodge and burn tools:

✦ **Shadows:** Along with the Midtones and Highlights modes (described next), Shadows is unique to the dodge and burn tools. When you select this mode, the dodge and burn tools affect dark pixels in an image more dramatically than they affect light pixels and shades in between.

✦ **Midtones:** Select this mode to apply the dodge or burn tools equally to all but the very lightest or darkest pixels in an image.

✦ **Highlights:** When you select this option, the dodge and burn tools affect light pixels in an image more dramatically than they affect dark pixels and shades in between.

Selecting Shadows when using the dodge tool or selecting Highlights when using the burn tool has an equalizing effect on an image. Figure 7-35 shows how using either of these functions and setting the Exposure slider bar to 100 percent lightens or darkens pixels in an image to very nearly identical brightness values.

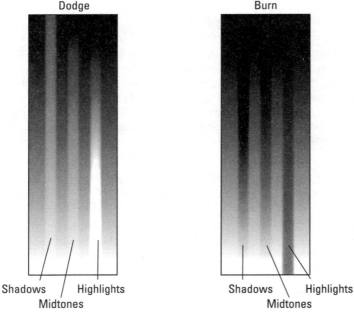

Figure 7-35: The dodge and burn tools applied at 100 percent Exposure settings subject to each of the three applicable brush modes.

Drawing Selection Outlines

Selection Fundamentals

Selections provide protection and automation. If it weren't for
Photoshop's selection capabilities, we'd all be flinging paint on
the canvas for all we were worth, like so many Jackson Pollock
and Wassily Kandinsky wannabes, without any means to constrain, discriminate, or otherwise regulate the effects of our
actions. Without selections, there'd be no filters, no color
correction, no special effects. In fact, we'd all be dangerously
close to real life, that dreaded environment we've spent so much
time and money to avoid.

That's why this chapter and the one that follows are the most
important chapters in this book.

Pretty cool, huh? You put a provocative sentence like that on a
line by itself and everyone reads it. Granted, it's a little over-
stated, but can you blame us? The thing is, you can't have a
sentence like *If you want our opinion, we think that these are some
pretty doggone important chapters — at least, that's the way it
seems to us; certainly, you might have a different opinion* on a line
by itself. The other paragraphs would laugh at it.

At any rate, it's vital that you pay close attention to the selection
concepts discussed in this chapter, because they're key to using
Photoshop successfully. It's equally essential to understand how
to apply masks in Photoshop, which is the subject of Chapter 9.

How selections work

Before you can edit a portion of an image, you must first *select*
it — which is computerese, in this context, for marking the
boundaries of the area that you want to edit. To *select* part of an

image in a painting program, you must surround it with a *selection outline* or *marquee,* which tells Photoshop where to apply your editing instructions. The selection outline appears as a moving pattern of dash marks, lovingly termed *marching ants* by doughheads who've been using Photoshop too long. (See Figure 8-1 for the inside story.)

Figure 8-1: A magnified view of a dash mark in a selection outline reveals a startling discovery.

Photoshop provides five tools for drawing selection outlines, which are described in the following list. You can access the tools from the keyboard, as noted in the parentheses.

✦ **Rectangular marquee (M):** The rectangular marquee tool has long been a staple of painting programs. It lets you select rectangular or square portions of an image.

✦ **Elliptical marquee (M):** Now relegated to being an alternative tool in the upper left corner of the toolbox, the elliptical marquee tool works just like the rectangular marquee except that it selects elliptical or circular portions of an image.

✦ **Lasso (L):** The lasso tool lets you select a free-form portion of an image. You simply drag with the lasso tool around the area you want to edit. However, unlike some lasso tools, particularly those in most Macintosh painting programs, which shrink selection outlines to disqualify pixels in the background color, Photoshop's lasso tool selects the exact portion of the image you enclose in your drag.

Cross Ref If this seems like a limitation, see the tips later in this chapter under "Manually adding and subtracting" and "Modifying the contents of a layer."

✦ **Magic wand (W):** Originally introduced by Photoshop, this tool enables you to select a contiguous region of similarly colored pixels by clicking inside it. For example, you might click inside the boundaries of a face to isolate it from the hair and background elements. Novices tend to gravitate toward the magic wand because it seems like such a miracle tool, but in fact, it's the least predictable and ultimately least useful of the bunch.

✦ **Pen (T):** Available from the Paths panel in the Layers palette (which you can display by choosing Window➪Palettes➪Show Paths), the pen tool is both the most difficult to master and the most accurate and versatile of the selection tools. You use the pen tool to create a *path,* a special breed of selection outline. You click and drag to create individual points in the path. You can edit the path after the fact by moving, adding, and deleting points. You can even transfer a path via the Clipboard to or from Adobe Illustrator. For a discussion of the pen tool, read the "How to Draw and Edit Paths" section later in this chapter.

Note Technically, the type tool also is a selection tool, because Photoshop converts each character of type into its own floating selection boundary. However, the type tool automatically fills these boundaries with the foreground color and is otherwise sufficiently different from other selection tools to warrant its own chapter later in the book (Chapter 12, "Text Effects").

If that's all there were to using the selection tools in Photoshop, the application would be on a par with the average paint program. Part of what makes Photoshop exceptional, however, is that it provides literally hundreds of little tricks to increase the functionality of each and every selection tool.

Furthermore, all of Photoshop's selection tools work together in perfect harmony. You can exploit the specialized capabilities of all five tools to create a single selection boundary. After you come to understand which tool best serves which purpose, you'll be able to isolate any element in an image, no matter how complex or how delicate its outline.

Geometric selection outlines

The default tool in the upper left corner of the toolbox is the rectangular marquee tool. You can access the elliptical marquee tool by Alt-clicking on the marquee tool icon or by pressing the M key when the rectangular marquee tool is already selected. Alt-clicking or pressing M again takes you back to the rectangular marquee tool.

Both marquee tools are more versatile than they may appear at first glance. You can adjust the performance of each tool as follows:

✦ **Constraining to a square or circle:** Press and hold Shift *after* beginning your drag to draw a perfect square with the rectangular marquee tool or a perfect circle with the elliptical marquee tool. (Pressing Shift *before* dragging adds to a selection, as explained in the "Ways to Change Existing Selection Outlines" section later in this chapter.)

Tip In a popular online forum, someone once asked how to create a perfect circular marquee; despite more than a month of helpful suggestions, no one managed to come up with the easiest one of them all. So remember to press Shift after you begin to drag and you'll be one step ahead of the game.

✦ **Drawing out from the center:** Alt-drag to draw the marquee from the center outward instead of from corner to corner. This technique is especially useful when you draw an elliptical marquee. Frequently, it is easier to locate the center of the area you want to select than one of its corners — particularly because ellipses don't have corners.

✦ **Selecting a single-pixel line:** You can constrain the rectangular marquee tool so that it selects a single row or column of pixels. To do so, double-click on the tool's icon in the toolbox to display the Marquee Options panel of the Brushes palette, shown in Figure 8-2. Then choose the Single Row or Single Column option from the Shape pop-up menu. This option can be used to fix screw-ups such as a missing line of pixels in a screen shot, to delete random pixels around the perimeter of an image, or to create perpendicular lines within a fixed space.

✦ **Constraining the aspect ratio:** If you know that you want to create an image that conforms to a certain height/width ratio — called the *aspect ratio* — you can constrain either marquee tool so that no matter how large or small a marquee you create, the ratio between height and width remains fixed. To accomplish this, double-click on the appropriate marquee tool icon in the toolbox and select Constrained Aspect Ratio from the Style pop-up menu. Then enter the desired ratio values into the Width and Height option boxes. For example, if you want to crop an image to the ratio of a 4×5-inch photograph, you double-click on the rectangular marquee tool icon, enter 4 and 5 respectively into the Width and Height option boxes, and press Enter to confirm your changes. Then select the area of the image that you want to retain and choose Edit⇨Crop.

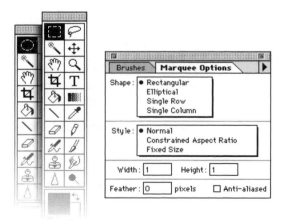

Figure 8-2: Both marquee tools now occupy the same slot in the toolbox. On the right is the Marquee Options panel as it appears with the contents of the Shape and Style pop-up menus in full view.

✦ **Sizing the marquee numerically:** If you're editing a screen shot or some other form of regular or schematic image, you may find it helpful to specify the size of a marquee numerically. To do so, select the Fixed Size option from the Style pop-up menu and enter size values into the Width and Height option boxes. Suppose that you want to select a bunch of option boxes in a screen shot, like the three that appear in Figure 8-2. You select one of them and note its size, 36×16 pixels, which is displayed in the last item of the Info palette. You enter 36 and 16 respectively into the Width and Height option boxes. You then Shift-click in the upper left corner of each remaining option box to add it to the selection and perform the desired color manipulations.

Robert

We used this technique a lot for doing screen shots. But we have to warn you about something very obvious. Once you're done selecting, be sure to set the marquee back to its default, undoctored form. Otherwise, you'll be very unnerved the next time you try to select an area and that fixed-size doodad appears on-screen (of course, Ctrl-D will fix you up).

Cross Ref

The Info palette can be extremely useful for making precise selections and image adjustments. For more information on this feature, read the "Making precision movements" section later in this chapter.

✦ **Drawing feathered selections:** A Feather option box is available when you use either of the marquee tools. To *feather* a selection is to soften its edges beyond the automatic anti-aliasing afforded to most tools. For more information on feathering, refer to the "Softening selection outlines" section later in this chapter.

✦ **Creating jagged ellipses:** By default, elliptical selection outlines are anti-aliased. If you don't want anti-aliasing (you might prefer harsh edges when editing screen shots or designing screen interfaces), deselect the Anti-aliased check box. (This option is dimmed when you use the rectangular marquee because anti-aliasing is always off for this tool. Perpendicular lines are smooth without the help of anti-aliasing.)

Tip

Frequently, Photoshop's lack of geometric shape tools throws novices for a loop. In fact, such tools do exist — you just don't recognize them. To draw a rectangle or ellipse in Photoshop, draw the shape as desired using the rectangular or elliptical marquee tool. Then choose Edit⇨Fill or Edit⇨Stroke, respectively, to color the interior or outline of the selection. It's that easy.

Free-form outlines

In comparison with the rectangular and elliptical marquee tools, the lasso tool provides a rather limited range of options. Generally speaking, you just drag in a free-form path around the image you want to select. The few special considerations are as follows:

✦ **Feathering and anti-aliasing:** To adjust the performance of the lasso tool, double-click on its icon in the toolbox (or press Enter while the lasso tool is selected) to display the Lasso Options panel shown in Figure 8-3. Just as you can feather rectangular and elliptical marquees, you can feather selections drawn with the lasso tool. You can also soften the edges of a lasso outline by selecting the Anti-aliased check box (which is now the factory default setting).

You should be aware that although you can adjust the feathering of any selection after you draw it by choosing Select⇨Feather, you must specify anti-aliasing before you draw a selection. So unless you have a specific reason for doing otherwise, leave the Anti-aliased check box selected.

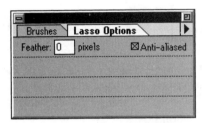

Figure 8-3: Double-click on the lasso tool icon to access the veritable truckload of options shown here.

✦ **Drawing polygons:** If you press and hold the Alt key, the lasso tool works like a standard polygon tool. (*Polygon,* incidentally, just means a shape with multiple straight sides.) With the Alt key down, you click to specify corners in a free-form polygon, as shown in Figure 8-4. If you want to add curves to the selection outline, just drag with the tool while still pressing the Alt key. Photoshop closes the selection outline the moment you release both the Alt key and the mouse button.

You can extend a polygon selection outline to the absolute top, right, or bottom edges of an image. To do so, Alt-click with the lasso tool on the scroll bar or title bar of the image window, as illustrated by the gray lines and squares in Figure 8-4.

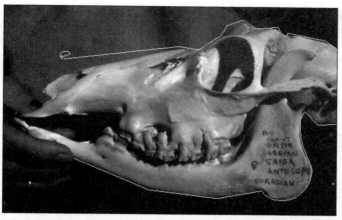

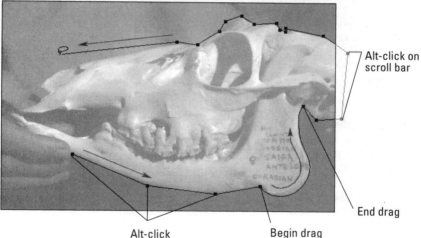

Figure 8-4: Alt-click with the lasso tool to create corners in a selection outline, shown as black squares in the bottom image. Drag to create free-form curves. Surprisingly, you can Alt-click on the scroll bar to add corners outside the boundaries of the image window.

The world of the wand

Using the magic wand tool is a no-brainer, right? You just click with the tool and it selects all the neighboring colors that fall within a selected range. The problem, however, is getting the wand to recognize the same range of colors you recognize. For example, if you're editing a photo of a red plate against a pink tablecloth, how do you tell the magic wand to select the plate and leave the tablecloth alone?

Sadly, adjusting the performance of the wand is not that easy. If you double-click on the magic wand icon in the toolbox, you'll see three options inside the Magic Wand Options panel of the Brushes palette, as shown in Figure 8-5. The Anti-aliased option softens the selection, just as it does for the lasso tool described in the preceding section. The Tolerance value determines the range of colors the tool selects when you click with it in the image window. And the Sample Merged check box allows you to take all visible layers into account when defining a selection.

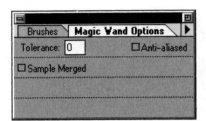

Figure 8-5: Double-click on the magic wand icon to specify the range of colors you want to select the next time you use the tool.

Adjusting the tolerance

By now you already understand what's up with the Anti-aliased option, so we'll start with Tolerance. You may have heard the standard explanation for adjusting the Tolerance value: You can enter any number from 0 to 255 in the Tolerance option box. Enter a low number to select a small range of colors; increase the value to select a wider range of colors.

There's nothing wrong with that explanation — it's accurate in its own small way — but it doesn't provide one iota of information you couldn't glean on your own. The fact is, if you really want to understand this option, you must dig a little deeper.

When you click on a pixel with the magic wand tool, Photoshop first reads the brightness value assigned to that pixel by each of the color channels. If you're working with a grayscale image, Photoshop reads a single brightness value from the one channel only; if you're working with an RGB image, it reads three brightness values, one each from the red, green, and blue channels; and so on. Because each color channel permits 8 bits of data, brightness values range from 0 to 255.

Next, Photoshop applies the Tolerance value, or simply *tolerance,* to the pixel. The tolerance describes a range that extends in both directions (lighter and darker) from each brightness value.

Suppose that you're editing a standard RGB image. The tolerance is set to 32 (as it is by default), and you click with the magic wand on a turquoise pixel whose brightness values are 40 red, 210 green, and 170 blue. Photoshop adds and subtracts 32 from each brightness value to calculate the magic wand range, which in this case is 8 to 72 red, 178 to 242 green, and 138 to 202 blue. Photoshop selects any pixel that both falls inside this range *and* can be traced back to the original pixel via an uninterrupted line of other pixels that also fall within the range.

From this information, you can draw the following basic conclusions about the magic wand tool:

✦ **Creating a contiguous selection:** The magic wand selects a contiguous region of pixels emanating from the pixel on which you click. If you're trying to select land masses on a globe, for example, clicking on Saint Louis selects everything from Juneau to Mexico City, but it doesn't select London because the cities are separated by an ocean of water that doesn't fall within the tolerance range.

✦ **Clicking midtones maintains a higher range:** Because the tolerance range extends in two directions, you cut off the range when you click on a light or dark pixel. If the tolerance is 40 and you click on a grayscale pixel with a brightness value of 20, Photoshop calculates a range from 0 to 60. If you instead click on a pixel with a brightness value of 40, you increase your range to 0 to 80. Therefore, clicking on a medium-brightness pixel permits the most generous range.

✦ **Selecting brightness ranges:** Many people have the impression that the magic wand selects color ranges. In fact, it selects brightness ranges within color channels. So if you want to select a flesh-color region — regardless of shade — set against an orange or red background that is roughly equivalent in terms of brightness values, you probably should use a different tool.

✦ **Selecting from a single channel:** If the magic wand repeatedly fails to select a region of color that appears to be unique from its background, try isolating that region on a single color channel. You probably will have the most luck isolating a color on the channel that least resembles it. For example, to select a yellow flower petal that's set against an azure sky filled with similar brightness values, go to the blue channel (by clicking on the Blue option in the Channels palette). Because yellow contains no blue and azure contains lots of blue, the magic wand can distinguish the two relatively easily. Experiment with this technique and it will prove more and more useful over time.

Making the wand see beyond a single layer

The final option, Sample Merged, is much like the identically named option available to the smudge and focus tools (see "Painting with the smudge tool" in Chapter 7). This option lets you take into account colors from different layers. In this particular case, Sample Merged allows the wand to draw selection outlines around similarly colored areas on different layers.

For example, returning to our earlier land mass example, suppose that you set Europe on one layer and North America on the layer behind it. (We explain how to establish layers in the "Sending a floating selection to its own layer" section later in this chapter.) The two continents overlap. Now normally, if you clicked inside Europe with the magic wand tool, the wand would select an area inside Europe without extending out into the area occupied by North America. This is because the wand doesn't even see the contents of other layers; anything outside of Europe is just an empty void of space. We're talking pre-Columbus Europe here.

But if you select the Sample Merged option, things change. Suddenly, the wand can see all the layers that you can see. If you click on Europe, and North America and Europe contain similar colors, the wand selects across both shapes.

Mind you, the Sample Merged option does *not* permit the wand to select images on two separate layers. In fact, strange as it may sound, no selection tool can pull off this feat. You can only select, paint, and edit inside one layer at a time. (The one exception is the move tool, which lets you move multiple layers in their entirety, as explained in the upcoming "Sending a floating selection to its own layer" section.) Sample Merged merely allows the wand to draw selection outlines that appear to encompass colors on many layers. What good is that? Well, suppose that you want to apply an effect to both Europe and North America. With the help of Sample Merged, you can draw a selection outline that encompasses both continents. After you apply the effect to Europe, you can switch to the North America layer — the selection outline remains intact — and then reapply the effect.

Ways to Change Existing Selection Outlines

If you don't draw a selection outline correctly the first time, you have two options. You either can draw it again from scratch, which is a real bore, or change your botched selection outline, which is likely to prove the more gratifying solution. You can deselect a selection, add to a selection, subtract from a selection, and even select the stuff that's not selected and deselect the selected stuff. (If that sounds like a load of nonsense, keep reading.)

Quick changes

Some methods of adjusting a selection outline are automatic: You just choose a command and you're done. The following list explains how a few commands — all members of the Select menu — work:

✦ **Hide Edges (Ctrl-H):** Get those marching ants out of here! We're all grown-ups, right? Do we really need these constant streams of marching ants to tell us what we've selected? We were there, we remember. The point is that although visible selection outlines can be helpful sometimes, they just as readily can impede your view of an image. When they annoy, press Ctrl-H.

R
%%%
Robert
To coin a phrase, "There you go again." This is the second time we see that Deke and the formicacious aren't the best of friends! I'm not nearly as exercised, but *de gustibus non disputandum*. Besides, Deke, what kind of insects would you prefer? These, or the multiligate creatures that inhabit programs and make them crash?

✦ **Deselect (Ctrl-D):** You can deselect the selected portion of an image in three ways. You can select a different portion of the image; click anywhere in the image window with the rectangular marquee tool, the elliptical marquee tool, or the lasso tool; or choose Select⇨None. Remember, however, that when no part of an image is selected, the entire image is susceptible to your changes. If you apply a filter, choose a color-correction command, or use a paint tool, you affect every pixel of the foreground image.

✦ **Inverse:** Choose Select⇨Inverse to reverse the selection. Photoshop deselects the portion of the image that was previously selected and selects the portion of the image that was not selected. This way, you can start out a selection by outlining the portion of the image that you want to protect rather than the portion you want to affect.

Manually adding and subtracting

Ready for some riddles? When editing a portrait, how do you select both eyes without affecting any other portion of the face? Answer: By drawing one selection and then tacking on a second. How do you a select a doughnut and leave the hole behind? Answer: Encircle the doughnut with the elliptical marquee tool and then use that same tool to subtract the center.

Photoshop enables you to whittle away at a selection, add pieces back on, whittle away some more, ad infinitum, until you get it exactly right. Short of sheer laziness or frustration, there's no reason you can't eventually create the selection outline of your dreams.

✦ **Adding to a selection outline:** To increase the area enclosed in an existing selection outline, Shift-drag with the rectangular marquee, elliptical marquee, or lasso tool. You also can Shift-click with the magic wand tool or Shift-click with one of the marquee tools when the Fixed Size option is active (as described back in the "Geometric selection outlines" section earlier in this chapter).

✦ **Subtracting from a selection outline:** To take a bite out of an existing selection outline, press the Control key while using one of the selection tools.

Tip

Here's a way to change the lasso tool behavior. First, drag with the lasso around the portion of the image that you want to select. Then double-click on the magic wand tool icon in the toolbox, change the Tolerance value to zero, and deselect the Anti-aliased check box. Press Enter to tell Photoshop to accept your changes and then Ctrl-click with the magic wand tool on a portion of the selection that appears in the background color. Photoshop deselects this portion. Very Mac-ish.

✦ **Intersecting one selection outline with another:** Another way to subtract from an existing selection outline is to Ctrl-Shift-drag around the selection with the rectangular marquee, elliptical marquee, or lasso tool. You also can Ctrl-Shift-click with the magic wand tool. Ctrl-Shift-dragging instructs Photoshop to retain only that portion of an existing selection that also falls inside the new selection outline. (We frequently use this technique to confine a selection within a rectangular or elliptical border.)

Adding and subtracting by command

Photoshop provides several commands under the Select menu that automatically increase or decrease the number of selected pixels in an image according to numerical specifications. The commands in the Select⟹Modify submenu work as follows:

✦ **Border:** This command selects an area of a specified thickness around the perimeter of the current selection outline and deselects the rest of the selection. For example, to select a 6-point-thick border around the current selection, choose Select⟹Modify⟹Border, enter 6 into the Width option box, and press Enter. But what's the point? After all, if you want to create an outline around a selection, you can accomplish this in fewer steps by choosing Edit⟹Stroke. The Border command, however, broadens your range of options. You can apply a special effect to the border, move the border to a new location, or even create a double outline effect by first applying Select⟹Modify⟹Border and then Edit⟹Stroke.

✦ **Smooth:** This command rounds off the sharp corners and weird anomalies in the outline of a selection. When you choose Select⟹Modify⟹Smooth, the program asks you to enter a Sample Radius value. The first in about 6,000 Radius options available in Photoshop, this one represents the maximum distance that the Smooth command can move any point on the selection outline. So if you enter a value of 6 pixels, the smoothed selection outline can roam a maximum of 6 points in any direction from its current course, but no further. Go ahead, give it a try. It won't bite.

Deke, have you forgotten the (*mumble, mumble*) ants?

✦ **Expand and Contract:** With this command, Select⟹Modify⟹Expand and Select⟹Modify⟹Contract perform much-needed services that were previously available only via a few rather challenging masking operations. Both commands do exactly what they say, either expanding or contracting the selected area by 1 to 16 pixels. For example, if you want an elliptical selection to grow by 8 pixels, choose Select⟹Modify⟹Expand, enter 8, and call it a day.

Tip

Keep an eye out for the fact that both commands have a flattening effect on a selection. To round things off, apply the Smooth command with a Sample Radius value equal to the number you just entered into the Expand Selection or Contract Selection dialog box. You'll end up with a pretty vague selection outline, but what do you expect from automated commands?

In addition to the Expand command, Photoshop provides two older commands — Grow and Similar — that increase the area covered by a selection outline. Both commands resemble the magic wand tool in that they measure the range of eligible pixels by way of a Tolerance value. In fact, the commands rely on the very same Tolerance value found inside the Magic Wand Options panel. Therefore, if you want to adjust the impact of either command, you must first select the magic wand icon in the toolbox.

✦ **Grow (Ctrl-G):** Choose Select⇨Grow to select all pixels that both neighbor an existing selection and resemble the colors included in the selection, in accordance with the Tolerance value. In other words, Select⇨Grow is the command equivalent of the magic wand tool. If you feel constrained by the fact you can click on only one pixel at a time with the wand tool, you may prefer to select a small group of representative pixels with a marquee tool and then choose Select⇨Grow to initiate the wand's magic.

✦ **Similar:** Another member of the Select menu, the Similar command works just like the Grow command except that the pixels don't have to be adjacent to one another. When you choose Select⇨Similar, Photoshop selects any pixel that falls within the tolerance range, regardless of its location in the foreground image.

One of the best applications for the Similar command is to isolate a complicated image that's set against a consistent background whose colors are significantly lighter or darker than the image. Consider Figure 8-6, which features a dark and ridiculously complex foreground image set against a continuous background of medium to light brightness values. Though the image features sufficient contrast to make it a candidate for the magic wand tool, we'd never in a million years recommend that you use that tool, because so many of the colors in the foreground image are discontiguous. The following steps explain how to separate this image using the Similar command in combination with a few other techniques we've described thus far.

Steps: Isolating a complex image set against a plain background

1. Use the rectangular marquee tool to select some representative portions of the background. In Figure 8-6, the lightest and darkest portions of the background were selected along with some representative shades in between. Remember, you make multiple selections by Shift-dragging with the tool.

2. Double-click on the magic wand tool icon to display the Tolerance option box. For our image, a Tolerance value of 16 was entered, a relatively low value, in keeping with the consistency of the background. If your background is less homogenous, you may want to enter a higher value. Make sure that the Anti-aliased check box is turned on. Then press Enter to exit the dialog box.

3. Choose Select⇨Similar. Photoshop should select the entire background. If it fails to select all of the background, choose Edit⇨Undo (Ctrl-Z) and use the rectangular marquee tool to select more portions of the background. You may also want to increase the Tolerance value in the Magic Wand Options dialog box. If Photoshop's selection bleeds into the foreground image, try reducing the Tolerance value.

4. Choose Select⇨Inverse. Photoshop selects the foreground image and deselects the background.

Figure 8-6: Before choosing Select⇨Similar, select a few sample portions of the background so that Photoshop has something on which to base its selection range.

5. If the detail you want to select represents only a fraction of the entire image, Ctrl-Shift-drag around the portion of the image that you want to retain using the lasso tool. In Figure 8-7, a polygon was drawn with the lasso by Ctrl-Shift-Alt-dragging.

If the technique in Step 5 sounds tempting but you have problems keeping three fingers planted on the keyboard as you draw, here's a little hint. You only have to press Ctrl-Shift at the beginning of the drag or until after you complete the first click. After the selection process is established, you can release the Control and Shift keys. The Alt key, however, must remain pressed if you want to draw a polygon.

6. Congratulations, you've isolated your complex image. Now you can filter it, colorize it, or perform whatever operation inspired you to select this image in the first place. We wanted to superimpose the image onto a different background. To do so, the image was copied to the Clipboard (Edit⇨Copy), the desired background image was opened, and then the first image was pasted into place (Edit⇨Paste). The result, shown in Figure 8-8, still needs some touching up with the paint and edit tools, but it's not half bad for an automated selection process.

Figure 8-7: Ctrl-Shift-Alt-drag with the lasso tool to intersect the area that you want to select with a free-form polygon.

Figure 8-8: The completed selection superimposed onto a new background.

Caution Although all the commands discussed in this section are applicable to any kind of selection outline, you should at least hesitate before modifying selections right after you paste or move them. Such selections are termed *floating,* because they hover independently in front of the rest of the image. If you apply Border, Smooth, Expand, Contract, Grow, or Similar to a floating selection, Photoshop adheres the selection to the image and then applies the automated changes. (The same goes for the Inverse command, described earlier, and the Feather command, described next.) Therefore, if you try to move the selection after choosing one of these commands, you'll take part of the image with you. For more information on floating and how it impacts your day-to-day life, see the upcoming section "Floating a selection."

Softening selection outlines

You can soften a selection in two ways. The first method is anti-aliasing, introduced in Chapter 3. Anti-aliasing is an intelligent and automatic softening algorithm that mimics the appearance of edges you'd expect to see in a sharply focused photograph. Where does the term *anti-alias* come from? Well, to *alias* an electronic signal is to dump essential data, thus degrading the quality of a sound or image. Anti-aliasing boosts the signal and smoothes out the rough spots in a way that preserves the overall quality.

When you draw an anti-aliased selection outline in Photoshop, the program calculates the hard-edged selection at twice its actual size. It then shrinks the selection in half using bicubic interpolation, as described in the "General environmental preferences" section of Chapter 2. The result is a crisp image with no visible jagged edges.

The second softening method, *feathering,* is less scientific. Feathering gradually dissipates the opacity of the pixels around the edge of a selection. You can specify the number of pixels affected, either before or after drawing a selection, by entering a value into the Feather Radius option box. To feather a selection before you draw it, double-click on the rectangular marquee, elliptical marquee, or lasso tool icon. To feather a selection after drawing it, choose Select⇨Feather.

The Feather Radius value determines the distance over which Photoshop fades a selection, measured in pixels in both directions from the original selection outline. Therefore, if you enter a radius of 4 pixels, Photoshop fades the selection over an 8-pixel stretch. Figure 8-9 shows three selections lifted from the image at the bottom of the figure. The first selection is anti-aliased only. The second and third selections were feathered, assigning Feather Radius values of 4 and 12, respectively. As you can see, a small feather radius makes a selection appear fuzzy; a larger radius makes it fade into view.

Figure 8-9: Three clones selected with the elliptical marquee tool. The top image is anti-aliased and not feathered; the next is feathered with a radius of 4 pixels; and the third is feathered with a radius of 12 pixels.

You can use feathering to remove an element from an image while leaving the background intact, a process described in the following steps. The image described in the following steps, shown in Figure 8-10, is a NASA photo of a satellite with the earth in the background. We wanted to use this background with another image, but to do so we first had to get rid of that satellite. By Ctrl-Alt-dragging, feathering, and cloning, we covered the satellite with a patch so seamless you'd swear that the satellite was never there.

Figure 8-10: The mission was to remove the satellite by covering it up with selections cloned from the background; the procedure is described in "Steps: Removing an element from an image."

Steps: Removing an element from an image

1. Draw a selection around the element using the lasso tool. The selection doesn't have to be an exact fit; in fact, you want it to be rather loose, allowing a buffer zone of at least 6 pixels between the edges of the image and the selection outline.

2. Now that you've specified the element you want to remove, you have to find some portion of the image that will cover the element in a manner that matches the surrounding background. In Figure 8-11, the best match seemed to be an area just below and to the right of the satellite. To select this area, move the selection outline independently of the image by Ctrl-Alt-dragging. Be sure to allow some space between the selection outline and the element you're trying to cover.

3. Choose Select⇨Feather. Enter a small value (8 or less) in the Feather Radius option box — just enough to make the edges fuzzy. (In this case, 3 was entered.) Then press Enter to initiate the operation.

4. Alt-drag the feathered selection to clone and position the patch over the element you want to cover, as shown in Figure 8-12. To correctly align the patch, choose Select⇨Hide Edges (Ctrl-H) to hide the marching ants and then nudge the patch into position with the arrow keys.

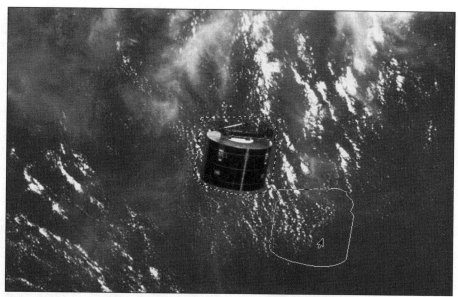

Figure 8-11: After drawing a loose outline around the satellite with the lasso tool, the outline was Ctrl-Alt-dragged to select a portion of the background.

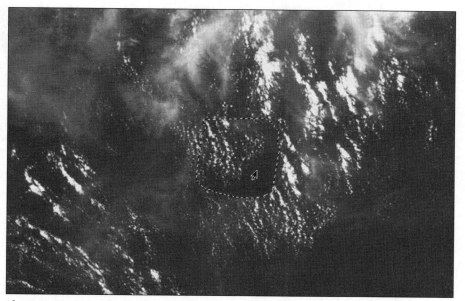

Figure 8-12: Next, the feathered selection was Alt-dragged over the satellite. The patch was imperfect and required further adjustments.

5. The patch was only partially successful. The upper left corner of the selection matches clouds in the background, but the lower right corner is dark and cloudless, an obvious rift in the visual continuity of the image. The solution: Try again. With the lasso tool still active, we drew a loose outline around the dark portion of the image and then Ctrl-Alt-dragged it up and to the left as shown in Figure 8-13.

6. It's all déjà vu from here on out. We chose Select⇨Feather and entered 6 into the Feather radius option box — thus allowing the clouds a sufficient range to taper off — and pressed Enter. Then we Alt-dragged the feathered patch over the dark, cloudless rift; nudged, nudged, nudged; and voilà! No more satellite. Figure 8-14 shows $200 million worth of hardware vaporized in less than five minutes.

Figure 8-13: We drew a new outline around the dark, cloudless portion of the patch and then Ctrl-Alt-dragged it to a different spot in the background.

Figure 8-14: A new bit of cloudy sky was selected and placed over the formerly cloudless portion of the patch. Satellite? What satellite?

Moving, Duplicating, and Layering Selections

After you select a portion of an image, you can move either the selection or selection outline to a new location. To move a selection, just drag it while any one of the selection tools is active, regardless of which tool you used to select the image in the first place. For example, after selecting part of an image with the rectangular marquee tool, you can drag it to a new location using the elliptical marquee, lasso, or magic wand tool. You can even move a selection with the arrow tool found in the Paths panel of the Layers palette.

As if you don't already have enough options, there's a dedicated move tool just below the lasso in the toolbox. You can select it at any time by pressing the V key. This tool lets you drag a selected area, whether or not you begin your drag on the selection. For example, if the lower right corner of an image is selected, you can drag in the upper left corner with the move tool and still grab the selection. This is especially useful when you're trying to move a very small or highly feathered selection that keeps becoming deselected when you try to move it. If you've ever found yourself hunting down the perfect place to drag a selection, waiting for that moment when the cursor becomes an arrow to show that you're finally over the selection and ready to drag it, the move tool is your saving grace. There's no chance of deselecting an image or messing up a path with this tool.

Normally, Photoshop displays the outline of the selected area during a move, as shown in the top image in Figure 8-15. But you can also preview the selected area in all its splendor as you move it, as shown in the bottom image in the figure. As you might expect, this significantly slows down the screen refresh speed. It also prevents you from viewing the portion of the image behind the selection. But there are times when this capability comes in extremely handy.

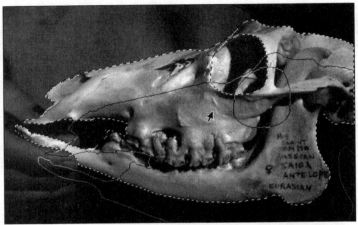

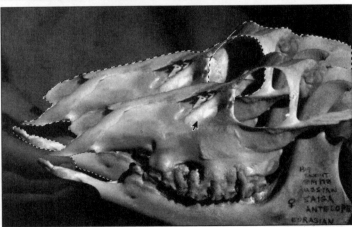

Figure 8-15: You can drag a selection right off the bat to see only its outline (top), or you can press and hold the mouse button for a moment before beginning your drag to preview the selection (bottom).

Tip   To preview a selection as you move it, click and hold on the selection for a few moments before moving the mouse. The watch cursor appears. The moment the cursor changes back to the standard move cursor — which may happen very fast on some high-end computers — you can start dragging.

Making precision movements

Photoshop provides three methods for moving selections in prescribed increments. First, you can nudge a selection in 1-pixel increments by pressing an arrow key on the keyboard, or in 10-pixel increments by pressing Shift with an arrow key. This technique is useful for making precise adjustments to the position of an image. Second, you can press Shift during a drag to constrain a move to some 45-degree direction — that is, horizontally, vertically, or diagonally. And third, you can use the Info palette to track your movements and help locate a precise position in the image.

To display the Info palette, choose Window⇨Palettes⇨Show Info. Figure 8-16 shows the Info palette as it appears in Photoshop 3. The last four items in the palette monitor movement, as follows:

✦ **X, Y:** These values show the coordinate position of your cursor. The distance is measured from the upper left corner of the image in the current unit of measure. The unit of measure in Figure 8-16 is pixels.

✦ **ΔX, ΔY:** These values indicate the distance of your move as measured horizontally and vertically.

✦ **A, D:** The A and D values reflect the angle and direct distance of your drag.

✦ **W, H:** These values reflect the width and height of your selection.

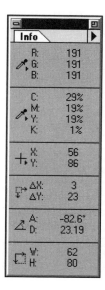

Figure 8-16: The Info palette provides a world of numerical feedback when you move a selection.

Cloning a selection

When you move a selection, you leave a hole in your image in the background color, as shown in the top half of Figure 8-17. If you prefer instead to leave the original in place during a move, you have to *clone* the selection — that is, create a copy of the selection without upsetting the contents of the Clipboard. Photoshop provides four different means for cloning a selection:

✦ **Alt-dragging:** Press the Alt key and drag a selection to clone it. The bottom half of Figure 8-17 shows a selection that was Alt-dragged three times. (Between clonings, we changed the gray level of each selection to make the selections more identifiable.)

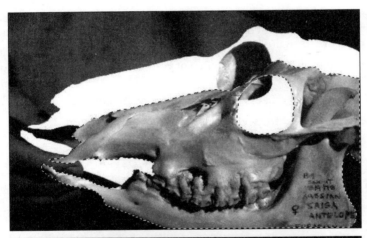

Figure 8-17: When you move a selection, you leave a gaping hole in the selection's wake (top). When you clone an image, you leave a copy of the selection behind. (The selection in the bottom image was cloned several times.)

✦ **Alt-arrowing:** Press Alt in combination with one of the arrow keys to both clone the selection and nudge it 1 pixel away from the original. If you want to move the image multiple pixels, Alt-arrow the first time only. Then just nudge the clone using the arrow key alone. Otherwise, you create a bunch of clones that you can't undo.

✦ **Floating:** Choose Select⇨Float (Ctrl-J) to clone the selection in place. You then can move the clone to a new location as desired. (For more information about floating, read the upcoming "Floating a selection" section.)

✦ **Drag and drop:** Like just about every other program on the planet, Photoshop lets you clone a selection between documents by dragging it from one open window to another, as demonstrated in Figure 8-18. As long as you manage to drop into the second window, the original image remains intact and selected in the first window. Our advice: Don't worry about exact positioning during a drag and drop; first get it into the second window and then worry about placement.

Moving a selection outline independently of its contents

If a selection outline surrounds the wrong portion of an image, you can move it independently of the image by Ctrl-Alt-dragging. This technique serves as yet another means for manipulating inaccurate selection outlines. It also enables you to mimic one portion of an image in another portion of the image.

In the top image in Figure 8-19, we Ctrl-Alt-dragged the skull outline down and to the right so that it still overlapped the skull. Note that the image itself remains unaltered. We then lightened the new selection, applied a couple of strokes to set it off from its background, and gave it stripes. (For all we know, this is exactly what a female Russian Saiga antelope looks like.)

Tip You can nudge a selection outline independently of its contents by pressing Ctrl-Alt-arrow key. Ctrl-Shift-Alt-arrow key moves the outline in 10-pixel increments.

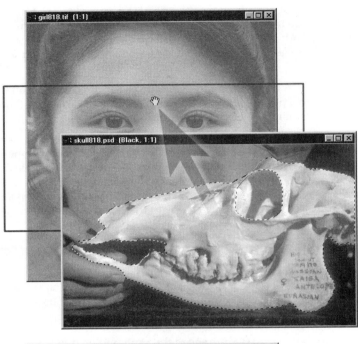

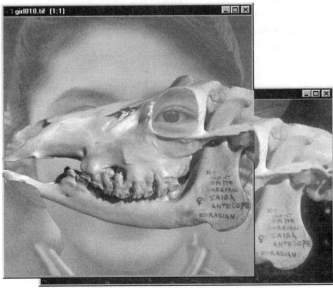

Figure 8-18: Drag a selection from one open window and drop it into another (top) to create a clone of the selection in the receiving window (bottom).

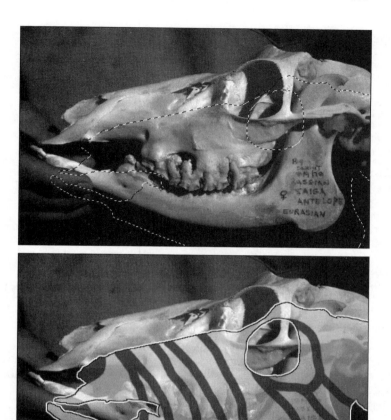

Figure 8-19: Ctrl-Alt-drag to move a selection outline independently of its image (top). The area to which you drag the selection outline becomes the new selection (bottom).

Floating a selection

A *floating selection* is a selection that hovers above the surface of the image. The beauty of a floating selection is that you can manipulate it by painting inside it, applying filters, coloring the image, and so on, all without affecting the underlying image itself. Then you can mix the floating selection with the underlying image by adjusting the Opacity slider bar in the Layers palette or by selecting an overlay mode from the pop-up menu in the upper left corner of the Layers palette.

You can float a selection in any of the following ways:

✦ **Paste:** When you paste an image from the Clipboard into the image window, the pasted image floats inside a selection outline, waiting for your next instructions.

✦ **Move:** When you move a selection by dragging it or pressing an arrow key, Photoshop floats the selection at its new location.

✦ **Clone:** Whether you clone a selection by Alt-dragging it or pressing Alt in combination with an arrow key, Photoshop floats the cloned selection.

✦ **Select⇨Float:** As we mentioned a moment ago in the "Cloning a selection" discussion, you can clone a selection in place, which has the added effect of floating it, by choosing Select⇨Float (Ctrl-J).

Conversely, any of the following techniques *defloat* a selection — that is, drop it in place — again making the image itself susceptible to changes:

✦ **Deselect:** Because a floating selection must remain selected to remain floating, choosing Select⇨None (Ctrl-D) defloats a selection. Likewise, any operation that has the added effect of deselecting an image, such as selecting a different portion of the image, changing the canvas size, or choosing File⇨Revert, defloats the selection.

✦ **Add to the selection:** If you add to a selection outline by pressing Shift while using any of the selection tools (or adding a path to a selection outline from the Make Selection dialog box, as we'll describe shortly), Photoshop defloats the image. However, you can subtract from a selection outline and intersect it without defloating it.

✦ **Automatically adjusting the selection outline:** All the commands in the Select menu that affect the shape of a selection outline — including Inverse, Feather, Grow, Similar, and the commands in the Select⇨Modify submenu — set down the selection. Like Shift-dragging with a selection tool, these commands add pixels to the selection outline, which invariably require a defloat.

✦ **Stroke the selection:** Photoshop automatically defloats a selection when you apply Edit⇨Stroke.

✦ **Editing a mask:** Photoshop retains selection outlines when you switch to a different color or mask channel. However, if you edit the selection in a different channel, you immediately defloat it. Furthermore, Photoshop automatically defloats a selection when you switch to the quick mask mode, whether you edit the mask or not. For more information on masks, read Chapter 9.

✦ **Select⇨Defloat:** You can drop a selection by choosing Select⇨Defloat (Ctrl-J).

Setting down portions of a floating selection

While a selection is floating, you can chip away portions of it by Ctrl-dragging with a marquee tool or the lasso tool or by Ctrl-clicking with the magic wand. The area around which you Ctrl-drag (or on which you Ctrl-click) disappears. Similarly, you can

Ctrl-Shift-drag with a marquee or lasso tool or Ctrl-Shift-click with the magic wand tool to specify the portion of the selection you want to retain. Anything not included inside the Ctrl-Shift-drag or Ctrl-Shift-click disappears.

Tip But what if, rather than deleting a portion of a floating selection, you simply want to set it down? For example, perhaps you have pasted two eyes against a new background and you want to set one of them down and move the other one to a new position. The solution is to Ctrl-drag or Ctrl-Shift-drag with the type tool. (When you press the Control key, the I-beam cursor changes to a lasso cursor, but the tool doesn't work like the lasso tool.) Either Ctrl-drag around the eye that you want to set down or Ctrl-Shift-drag around the eye that you want to leave floating. Either way, you'll still have both eyes, which is a must for decent depth perception.

Removing halos

When you move or clone an anti-aliased selection, you sometimes take with you a few pixels from the selection's previous background. These pixels can create a haloing effect if they clash with the selection's new background, as demonstrated in the top image in Figure 8-20.

You can instruct Photoshop to replace the fringe pixels with colors from neighboring pixels by choosing Select⇨Matting⇨Defringe. Enter the thickness of the perceived halo in the Width option box to tell Photoshop which pixels you want to replace. To create the image shown in the bottom half of Figure 8-20, we entered a Width value of 2. If you have to use a higher value than 2, you're probably better off redrawing your selection.

Photoshop provides two additional commands under the Select⇨Matting submenu: Remove Black Matte and Remove White Matte. If you're familiar with Photoshop 2.5, these commands are identical to the Black Matte and White Matte overlay modes that used to be available from the Brushes palette pop-up menu. Just in case you never came to grips with how those options worked — frankly, it's unlikely that you'd have much call to use them — here's the scoop:

✦ **Remove Black Matte:** This command removes the residue around the perimeter of a floating selection that was copied from a black background. For example, consider the first example in Figure 8-21, which shows a feathered selection set down against a black background. When we floated the selection again and set it against a stucco background, we got a black ring around the image, as demonstrated in the top half of the second example in the figure. To eliminate the black ring, we chose Select⇨Matting⇨Remove Black Matte.

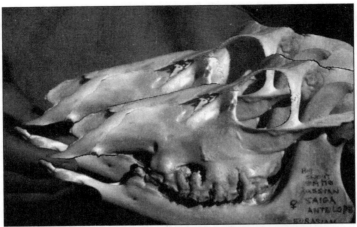

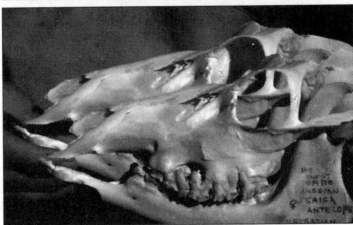

Figure 8-20: To remove the halo around the cloned skull (top), we used the Defringe command to replace the pixels around the perimeter of the selection with colors borrowed from neighboring pixels (bottom).

Figure 8-21: If you drop a feathered selection onto a black background (top) and try to reuse it, you get a black ring (upper half, bottom example). Luckily, you can eliminate this ring with the Remove Black Matte command (lower half, bottom example).

✦ **Remove White Matte:** In the first example of Figure 8-22, the feathered selection is set onto a white background. When we later tried to apply the selection to the stucco texture, we got a white ring, as you can see in the top half of the bottom example. To eliminate the ring, we chose Select⭢Matting⭢Remove White Matte.

Figure 8-22: Conversely, if you drop a feathered selection onto a white background (top) and try to reuse it, you get a white ring (upper half, bottom example), which you can just as easily eliminate by choosing Remove White Matte (lower half, bottom example).

Sending a floating selection to its own layer

Layers are easily the most powerful and amazing new feature added to Photoshop 3. Their impact is also wide ranging, which is why we'll be discussing them in bits and pieces. For a thorough overview of the subject, check out Chapter 17. In the meantime, however, here's a preview of how layers work.

Do this: Select an area of an image, float it (Ctrl-J), and then display the Layers palette (Window➪Palettes➪Show Layers). You'll see two items in the palette's scrolling list, Floating Selection and Background. The first item represents the floating selection. (Big surprise there.) The second is the underlying image. All standard images — that is, anything that hasn't been specially set up in Photoshop — contain a single Background layer. Throughout any layering you do, the Background represents the opaque base image; it is forever the rearmost layer in the image.

To send a floating selection to its own independent layer, choose the Make Layer command from the Layers palette pop-up menu, as in Figure 8-23. The Make Layer dialog box (also shown in the figure) appears, asking you to name the layer. You can also change the opacity and overlay mode or group the layer with the one in back of it. (That stuff is all discussed in Chapter 17; there's no need to worry about it now.) You can easily change any of these settings after the fact — at which time you can actually view the results of your changes — so it generally makes more sense to simply name the layer and press Enter.

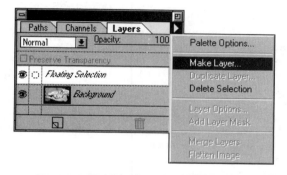

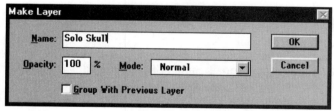

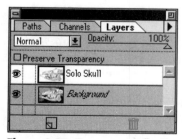

Figure 8-23: To convert a floating selection to an independent layer, choose the Make Layer command from the Layers palette menu (top) and enter a name for the layer into the Make Layer dialog box (middle). The new layer name appears in the palette above the layer you were previously editing (bottom).

Tip   Rather than choosing Make Layer, you can simply drag the Floating Selection item onto the new layer icon at the bottom of the Layers palette (labeled in Figure 8-23). Or, better yet, you can double-click on the Floating Selection item to bring up the Make Layer dialog box. To bypass the dialog box and let Photoshop name the new layer automatically — again, you can change the name later if you don't like it — Alt-double-click on the Floating Selection item.

Although the contents of the image window change only slightly — the image suddenly appears deselected (which, incidentally, is no cause for alarm) — Photoshop shows you that the floating selection has been converted to a layer by the way it displays the item in the Layers palette (as in the bottom example in Figure 8-23). Instead of *Floating Selection* appearing in italic letters, your specified layer name now appears in upright type. This shows that the layer is independent and can be swapped with other layers later on down the line. A small preview of the layer appears to the left of the layer name. And that meaningless dotted circle icon in the column just to the right of the eyeball icon disappears.

Note   You don't have to float a selection to convert it to a new layer. That's simply the most convenient alternative. If you feel like working up a sweat, you can copy the selection, choose Edit⇨Paste Layers, name the layer, and press Enter. But that technique replaces the contents of the Clipboard and can be slow when you're working on very large images.

Caution   Only one file format, the native Photoshop 3 format, saves images with layers. If you want to save a flattened version of your image — that is, with all layers fused together into a single image — in some other file format, choose File⇨Save a Copy and select the format you want from the Format pop-up menu. (If you select any format other than Photoshop 3, a Flatten Image check box appears in the lower left corner of the dialog box. The check box is automatically selected and dimmed so that you can't deselect it.)

Understanding transparency

Probably the most frightening thing about creating a new layer is watching the selection outline disappear. Deke's first reaction was, *Hey, do you mind? I might want to do something with that!* But the truth is, it doesn't matter. Everything that was selected is now independent and ready for you to edit. Every little nuance of the selection outline — whether it's a jagged border, a little bit of anti-aliasing, or a feathered edge — is still 100 percent intact. Anything that wasn't selected is now transparent.

To see this transparency in action, click on the eyeball icon in front of the Background item in the Layers palette. This hides the Background layer and lets you view the new layer by itself. As shown in Figure 8-24, the transparent areas are covered in a checkerboard pattern. Opaque areas look like the standard image, and translucent areas appear as a mix of image and checkerboard.

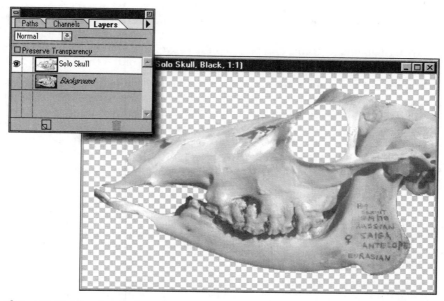

Figure 8-24: The checkerboard pattern represents the transparent portions of the layer.

Tip If the checkerboard pattern is hard to distinguish from the image, you can change the appearance of the pattern. Choose File⇨Preferences⇨Transparency to display the Transparency Options dialog box. Then edit away.

If you apply an effect to the layer while no portion of the layer is selected, Photoshop changes the opaque and translucent portions of the image but leaves the transparent background intact. For example, try choosing Image⇨Map⇨Invert (Ctrl-I), which inverts the colors to create a photographic negative effect. The image inverts, and the checkerboard remains unchanged. If you click in the left column in front of the Background item to bring back the eyeball icon, you may notice a slight halo around the inverted image, but the edge pixels blend with the background image just as well as they ever did. In fact, it's exactly as if you applied the effect to a floating selection. The only difference is that this selection is permanently floating. You can do anything you want to it without running the risk of harming the underlying background.

Modifying the contents of a layer

Generally, editing a layer is just like editing a floating selection, except far more versatile. The following items document some of your new options and provide additional insights into the fantastic world of layers:

✦ **Activating layers:** When working with a floating selection, you can edit only the floating selection; you can't access the image behind the selection. With layers, you can edit any layer you want, whether it's the frontmost layer, the rearmost layer, or any layer in between. To select the layer you want to edit — called the active layer — simply click on that layer name in the Layers palette. The layer name becomes white, showing that it is now active. Any edits now apply to this layer. (If an image from a different layer is preventing you from seeing all your edits, just hide it by clicking on the eyeball icon in front of the intrusive layer.)

✦ **Tightening selection outlines:** You may find it frustrating that Photoshop's selection tools — particularly the lasso tool — don't create selection outlines that automatically tighten around an image. Well, they do on layers. Try selecting an area of your image with the marquee or lasso tool. Make sure to select opaque and transparent areas alike. Now press Ctrl-J to float the selection. The moment you float the image, the selection outline tightens to fit the exact contours of the image. The same holds true if you move the selection, clone it, or copy and paste it.

✦ **Selecting everything and tightening:** If you want to select everything on a layer as well as tighten the selection all at once, just press Ctrl-Alt-T. The contents of the layer are selected based on their degree of opacity. Opaque pixels are fully selected, transparent pixels are fully deselected, and translucent pixels are partially selected.

✦ **Transferring a selection outline:** As soon as you introduce multiple layers to an image, the selection outline becomes an independent creature. For example, take your tightened selection outline from the previous paragraph. You can use that same outline to select part of the Background layer. Simply click on the Background item in the Layers palette to make it active and then move the selection outline or apply some effect. You are now editing the Background layer using another layer's selection outline.

✦ **Importing a selection outline from the Clipboard:** One upshot of all this is that you can retain only the selection outline from an image copied to the Clipboard. Huh? Well, suppose that you copy part of a different image. You paste it into your new image but find that it's not exactly what you want. Eventually, you arrive at the conclusion that you'd like to use the selection outline from the floating pasted image, but you want to jettison the contents. In the old days, you had to turn the Opacity down to 1 percent and then defloat the selection to grab the underlying image. But this leaves a slight residue. (You might have to look hard to see it, but it's there.)

Tip

With layers, you have a more satisfactory solution: Send the floating selection to its own layer. Unfortunately, that deselects the image. To get the selection outline back, press Ctrl-Alt-T and drag the new layer name to the delete layer icon (the one that looks like a little trash can) at the bottom of the Layers palette. This deletes the contents of the selection but leaves the selection outline intact.

✦ **Using the move tool with layers:** When no portion of the image is selected, you can move an entire layer by dragging it with the move tool. If part of the layer disappears beyond the edge of the window, no problem. Photoshop still saves every bit of the hidden image (as long as you save the document in the native Photoshop 3 format).

✦ **Dragging multiple layers:** You can even move multiple layers, in their entirety, at one time. Just click in the second column on the left side of the Layers palette in front of any inactive layer that you want to move. Two little move icons appear in the column, one in front of the inactive layer and the other in front of the active layer, as in Figure 8-25. This shows that both layers will move in unison. Click in front of other layers to display and hide other move icons. Then drag with the move tool to move all layers together. (Note that this only works when nothing is selected. If a portion of the image is selected, the move tool moves only the selection on the active layer.)

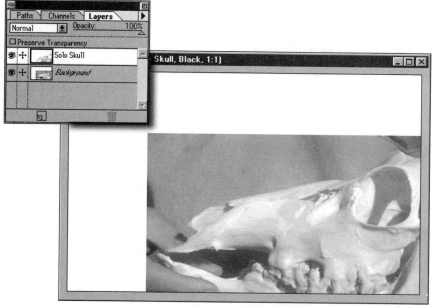

Figure 8-25: Click in the second column in the Layers palette to display or hide move icons (upper left). All layers with move icons move in unison when you drag with the move tool.

✦ **Mixing a layer with the layer behind it:** To blend between layers with the smudge, blur, or sharpen tool, double-click on the tool icon in the toolbox and select the Sample Merged check box in the Options panel of the Brushes palette. You can also apply any of the commands in the Select⇨Matting submenu to a layer, whether selected or not.

✦ **Turning a layer back into a floating selection:** If you decide that you'd rather have a floating selection than a layer — you won't gain any options, but you may simply feel more comfortable working with a floating selection for a certain operation — press Ctrl-A to select the entire layer and Ctrl-C to copy it. Now delete the layer by dragging its name to the little trash can icon at the bottom of the Layers palette. Press Ctrl-V to paste the image. The selection outline tightens around the floating image.

Cross Ref   That's enough layers for now. If you haven't quite gotten your fix, you'll find more information about layers in Chapters 9 and 17. Chapter 9 shows how to mask layers, and Chapter 17 explains how to mix them with the background image.

How to Draw and Edit Paths

Photoshop's path tools provide the most flexible and precise ways to define a selection short of masking. But though a godsend to the experienced user, the path tools represent something of a chore to novices and intermediates. It takes most people quite a while to become comfortable with the path tools because you have to draw a selection outline one point at a time.

Note   If you're familiar with Illustrator's pen tool and other path-editing functions, you'll find that Photoshop's tools are nearly identical. Photoshop doesn't provide the breadth of options available in Illustrator — you can't transform paths in Photoshop, for example — but the basic techniques are the same.

The following pages are designed to get you up and running with paths. We'll explain how you approach drawing a path, how you edit it, how you convert it to a selection outline, and how you stroke it with a paint or edit tool. All in all, you'll learn more about paths than you ever wanted to know.

Paths overview

To access Photoshop's path tools, choose Window⇨Palettes⇨Show Paths to display the Paths panel of the Layers palette (which we'll simply call the Paths palette). Here you'll find five path tools, lots of commands, and an extensive panel of editing options, as shown in Figure 8-26. On the whole, this palette represents a fully functioning path-drawing environment that rivals similar features provided by Illustrator or FreeHand.

How paths work

Paths differ from normal selections in that they exist on the equivalent of a distinct, object-oriented layer that sits in front of the bitmapped image. This setup enables you to edit a path with point-by-point precision after you draw it, to make sure that it meets the exact requirements of your artwork. It also prevents you from accidentally messing up the image, as you can when you edit ordinary selection outlines. After creating the path, you convert it into a standard selection outline before using it to edit the contents of the image, as explained in the section "Converting and saving paths," later in this chapter.

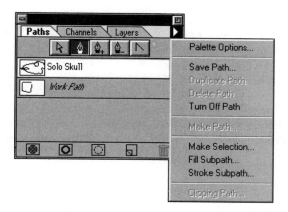

Figure 8-26: The Paths palette provides access to every one of Photoshop's path-drawing and editing functions.

The following steps explain the basic process of drawing a selection outline with the path tools.

Steps: Drawing a selection with the path tools

1. Use the pen tool to draw the outline of your prospective selection.

2. If the outline of the path requires some adjustment, reshape it using the other path tools.

3. When you get the path exactly the way you want it, save the path in Photoshop by choosing the Save Path command from the Paths palette menu. (Alternatively, you can double-click on the Work Path item in the scrolling list.)

4. Convert the path to a selection by choosing the Make Selection command or pressing the Enter key when a path or selection tool is active.

That's all there is to it. After you convert the path to a selection, it works just like any of the selection outlines described earlier. You can feather a selection, move it, copy it, clone it, or apply one of the special effects described in future chapters.

Using the Paths palette tools

Before we get into our long-winded description of how you draw and edit paths, here's a quick introduction to the tools available from the Paths palette:

Arrow: This tool lets you drag points and handles to reshape a path. You can access the arrow tool at any time by pressing and holding the Control key when a path, paint, or edit tool is selected.

Pen: Use the pen tool to draw paths in Photoshop one point at a time. We explain this tool in detail in the following section. Press the T key to select the tool.

Insert point: Click on an existing path to add a point to it. You can access this function when the arrow tool is selected by Ctrl-Alt-clicking on a segment in the path. When the pen tool is active, click.

Remove point: Click on an existing point in a path to delete the point without creating a break in the path's outline. To accomplish this when the arrow tool is selected, Ctrl-Alt-click on a point in a path.

Convert point: Click or drag on a point to convert it to a corner or smooth point. You also can drag on a handle to convert the point.

Note The terms *point, smooth point,* and others associated with drawing paths are explained in the upcoming section.

Drawing with the pen tool

When drawing with the pen tool, you build a path by creating individual points. Photoshop automatically connects the points with *segments,* which are simply straight or curved lines.

All paths in Photoshop are *Bézier* (pronounced *bay-zee-ay*) *paths,* meaning that they rely on the same mathematical curve definitions that make up the core of the PostScript printer language. The Bézier curve model allows for zero, one, or two levers to be associated with each point in a path. These levers, labeled in Figure 8-27, are called *Bézier control handles* or simply *handles.* You can move each handle in relation to a point, enabling you to bend and tug at a curved segment like a piece of soft wire.

The following list summarizes how you can use the pen tool to build paths in Photoshop:

✦ **Adding segments:** To build a path, create one point after another until the path is the desired length and shape. Photoshop automatically draws a segment between each new point and its predecessor.

✦ **Closing the path:** If you plan on eventually converting the path to a selection outline, you need to complete the outline by clicking again on the first point in the path. Every point will then have one segment coming into it and another segment exiting it. Such a path is called a *closed path* because it forms one continuous outline.

✦ **Leaving the path open:** If you plan on applying the Stroke Path command (explained later), you may not want to close a path. To leave it open, so that it has a specific beginning and ending, deactivate the path by saving it (choose the Save Paths command from the Paths palette menu). After you complete the save operation, you can click in the image window to begin a new path.

✦ **Extending an open path:** To reactivate an open path, click or drag on one of its endpoints. Photoshop draws a segment between the endpoint and the next point you create.

✦ **Joining two open paths:** To join one open path with another open path, click or drag on an endpoint in the first path and then click or drag on an endpoint in the second.

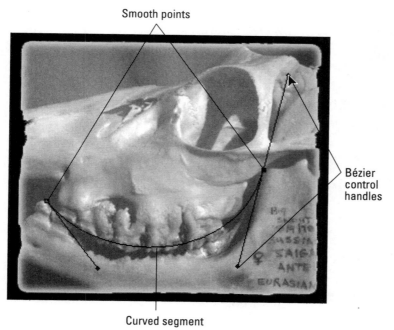

Smooth points

Bézier control handles

Curved segment

Figure 8-27: Drag with the pen tool to create a smooth point flanked by two Bézier control handles.

Points in a Bézier path act as little road signs. Each point steers the path by specifying how a segment enters it and how another segment exits it. You specify the identity of each little road sign by clicking, dragging, or Alt-dragging with the pen tool. The following items explain the specific kinds of points and segments you can create in Photoshop. See Figure 8-28 for examples.

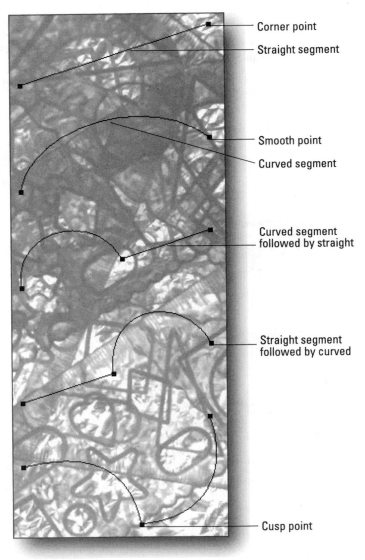

Corner point

Straight segment

Smooth point

Curved segment

Curved segment
followed by straight

Straight segment
followed by curved

Cusp point

Figure 8-28: The different kinds of points and segments you can draw with the pen tool.

✦ **Corner point:** Click with the pen tool to create a *corner point,* which represents the corner between two straight segments in a path.

✦ **Straight segment:** Click at two different locations to create a straight segment between two corner points. Shift-click to draw a 45-degree-angle segment between the new corner point and its predecessor.

✦ **Smooth point:** Drag to create a *smooth point* with two symmetrical Bézier control handles. A smooth point ensures that one segment meets with another in a continuous arc.

✦ **Curved segment:** Drag at two different locations to create a curved segment between two smooth points.

✦ **Curved segment followed by straight:** After drawing a curved segment, Alt-click on the smooth point you just created to delete the forward Bézier control handle. This converts the smooth point to a corner point with one handle. Then click at a different location to append a straight segment to the end of the curved segment.

✦ **Straight segment followed by curved:** After drawing a straight segment, drag from the corner point you just created to add a Bézier control handle. Then drag again at a different location to append a curved segment to the end of the straight segment.

✦ **Cusp point:** After drawing a curved segment, Alt-drag from the smooth point you just created to redirect the forward Bézier control handle, converting the smooth point to a corner point with two independent handles, sometimes known as a *cusp point.* Then drag again at a new location to append a curved segment that proceeds in a different direction than the previous curved segment.

Reshaping existing paths

As you become more familiar with the pen tool, you'll draw paths correctly on your first try more and more frequently. But you'll never get it right 100 percent of the time or even 50 percent of the time. From your first timid steps until you develop into a seasoned pro, you'll rely heavily on Photoshop's ability to reshape paths by moving points and handles, adding and deleting points, and converting points to change the curvature of segments. So don't worry if you don't draw a path correctly the first time. The paths tools provide all the second chances you'll ever need.

The arrow tool

The arrow tool represents the foremost path-reshaping function in Photoshop. After selecting this tool, you can perform any of the following functions:

✦ **Selecting points:** Click on a point to select it independently of other points in a path. Shift-click to select an additional point, even if the point belongs to a different path than other selected points. Alt-click on a path to select all its points in one fell swoop. You can even marquee points by dragging in a rectangle around them. You cannot, however, apply commands from the Select menu, such as All or None, to the selection of paths.

✦ **Drag selected points:** To move one or more points in a path, select the points you want to move and then drag one of the selected points. All selected points move the same distance and direction. When you move a point while a neighboring point remains stationary, the segment between the two points shrinks, stretches, and bends to accommodate the change in distance. Segments located between two selected or deselected points remain unchanged during a move.

Tip You can move selected points in 1-pixel increments by pressing arrow keys. If both a portion of the image and points in a path are selected, the arrow keys move the point only. Because paths reside on a higher layer, they take precedence in all functions that might concern them.

✦ **Drag a segment directly:** You also can reshape a path by dragging its segments. When you drag a straight segment, the two corner points on either side of the segment move as well. As illustrated in Figure 8-29, the neighboring segments stretch, shrink, or bend to accommodate the drag. When you drag a curved segment, however, you stretch, shrink, or bend that segment only, as demonstrated in Figure 8-30.

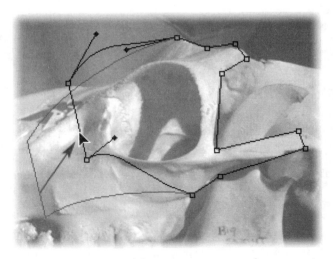

Figure 8-29: Drag a straight segment to move the segment and change the length, direction, and curvature of the neighboring segments.

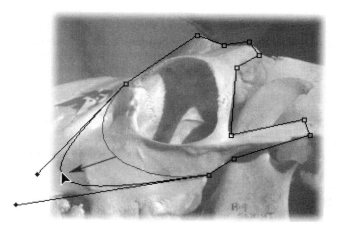

Figure 8-30: Drag a curved segment to change the curvature of that segment only and leave the neighboring segments unchanged.

Tip   When you drag a curved segment, drag from the middle of the segment, approximately equidistant from both its points. This method provides the best leverage and ensures that the segment doesn't go flying off in some weird direction you hadn't anticipated.

✦ **Drag a Bézier control handle:** Select a point and drag either of its Bézier control handles to change the curvature of the corresponding segment without moving any of the points in the path. If the point is a smooth point, moving one handle moves both handles in the path. If you want to be able to move a smooth handle independently of its partner, you must use the convert point tool, as discussed in the "Converting points" section later in this chapter.

✦ **Clone a path:** To make a duplicate of a selected path, Alt-drag it to a new location in the image window. Photoshop automatically stores the new path under the same name as the original.

Tip   Press and hold the Control key to temporarily access the arrow tool when the pen tool or any of the path or edit tools are selected. When you release the Control key, the cursor returns to the selected tool.

Adding and deleting points

The quantity of points and segments in a path is forever subject to change. Whether a path is closed or open, you can reshape it by adding and deleting points, which in turn forces the addition or deletion of a segment.

✦ **Appending a point to the end of an open path:** If an existing path is open, you can activate one of its endpoints by either clicking or dragging on it with the pen tool, depending on the identity of the endpoint and whether you want the next segment to be straight or curved. Photoshop is then prepared to draw a segment between the endpoint and the next point you create.

✦ **Closing an open path:** You also can use the technique just described to close an open path. Just select one endpoint, click or drag on it with the pen tool to activate it, and then click or drag on the opposite endpoint. Photoshop draws a segment between the two endpoints, closing the path and eliminating both endpoints by converting them to *interior points,* which simply means that the points are bound on both sides by segments.

✦ **Joining two open paths:** You can join two open paths to create one longer open path. To do so, activate an endpoint of the first path and then click or drag with the pen tool on an endpoint of the second path.

✦ **Inserting a point in a segment:** Select the insert point tool and click anywhere along an open or closed path to insert a point and divide the segment on which you click into two segments. Photoshop automatically inserts a corner or smooth point, depending on its reading of the path. If the point does not exactly meet your needs, use the convert point tool to change it.

Tip

To access the insert or remove point tool, press Control and Alt when using the arrow tool. Ctrl-Alt-click on an existing segment to insert a point; Ctrl-Alt-click on a point to remove it.

✦ **Deleting a point and breaking the path:** The simplest way to delete a point is to select it with the arrow tool and press either the Delete or Clear key. (You also can choose Edit⇨Clear, though why you would want to expend so much effort is beyond me.) When you delete an interior point, you delete both segments associated with that point, resulting in a break in the path. If you delete an endpoint from an open path, you delete the single segment associated with the point.

✦ **Removing a point without breaking the path:** Select the remove point tool and click on a point in an open or closed path to delete the point and draw a new segment between the two points that neighbor it. The removed point tool ensures that no break occurs in a path.

✦ **Deleting a segment:** You can delete a single interior segment from a path without affecting any point. To do so, first click outside the path with the arrow tool to deselect the path. Then click on the segment you want to delete and press the Delete or Clear key. When you delete an interior segment, you create a break in your path.

✦ **Deleting a whole path:** To delete an entire path, select any portion of it and press the Delete or Clear key twice. The first time you press Delete, Photoshop deletes the selected point or segment and automatically selects all other points in the path. The second time you press Delete, Photoshop gets rid of everything it missed the first time around.

Converting points

Photoshop lets you change the identity of an interior point. You can convert a corner point to a smooth point and vice versa. You perform all point conversions using the convert point tool as follows:

✦ **Smooth to corner:** Click on an existing smooth point to convert it to a corner point with no Bézier control handle.

✦ **Smooth to cusp:** Drag one of the handles of a smooth point to move it independently of the other handle, thus converting the smooth point to a cusp.

✦ **Corner to smooth:** Drag from a corner point to convert it to a smooth point with two symmetrical Bézier control handles.

✦ **Cusp to smooth:** Drag one of the handles of a cusp point to lock both handles back into alignment, thus converting the cusp to a smooth point.

Painting along a path

After you finish drawing a path and getting it exactly the way you want it, you can convert it to a selection outline, as described in the next section, or you can paint it. You can either paint the interior of the path by choosing the Fill Path command from the Paths palette menu, or you can paint the outline of the path by choosing Stroke Path. The Fill Path command works very much like Edit⇨Fill. However, the Stroke Path command is altogether different from Edit⇨Stroke. Whereas Edit⇨Stroke creates outlines and arrowheads, the Stroke Path command lets you paint a brush stroke along the contours of a path. It may not sound like a big deal at first, but this feature enables you to combine the spontaneity of the paint and edit tools with the structure and precision of a path.

Cross Ref Because the Fill Path command is very nearly identical to the standard fill options available to any selection — in fact, you can use selections and paths in tandem to specify a filled area — we discuss it in the "Filling paths" section of Chapter 10.

To paint a path, choose the Stroke Path command from the Paths palette menu to display the Stroke Path dialog box shown in Figure 8-31. In this dialog box, you can choose the paint or edit tool with which you want to *stroke* the path (which just means to paint a brush stroke along a path). Photoshop drags the chosen tool along the exact route of the path, retaining any tool or brush shape settings that were in force when you chose the tool.

Tip You can also display the Stroke Path dialog box by Option-clicking on the stroke path icon at the bottom of the Paths palette (labeled back in Figure 8-26). If you prefer to bypass the dialog box, select a paint or edit tool and either click on the stroke path icon or simply press the Enter key on the numeric keypad. Instead of displaying the dialog box, Photoshop assumes that you want to use the selected tool and strokes away.

Note If the path is selected, the Stroke Path command becomes a Stroke Subpath command. Photoshop then only strokes the selected path, rather than all paths saved under the current name.

The following steps walk you through a little project that was created by stroking paths with the paintbrush and smudge tools. Figures 8-32 through 8-34 show the progression and eventual outcome of the image.

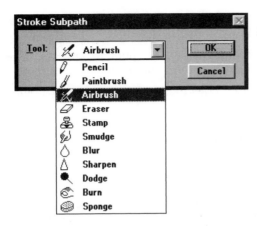

Figure 8-31: Photoshop displays this dialog box when you choose the Stroke Path command while a tool other than a paint or edit tool is selected.

Steps: Stroking paths with the Paintbrush and Smudge tools

1. After opening a low-resolution version of a hurricane image, we drew the zigzag path shown in Figure 8-32. As you can see, the path emits from the eye of the hurricane. We drew the path by starting at the eye and working upward, which is very important because Photoshop strokes a path in the same direction in which you draw it.

2. We saved the path by double-clicking on the Work Path name in the Paths palette, entering a name, and pressing Enter.

3. We used the Brushes palette to specify three brush shapes, each with a Roundness value of 40. The largest brush had a diameter of 16, the next largest had a diameter of 10, and the smallest had a diameter of 4.

4. After double-clicking on the paintbrush tool, we set the Fade-out value to 400. Then we selected the To Background radio button so that Photoshop would draw gradient strokes between the foreground and background colors.

5. We stroked the path with the paintbrush three times using the Stroke Path command, changing the foreground and background colors for each stroke. The first time, we used the largest brush shape to stroke the path from gray to white; the second time, we used the middle brush shape to stroke the path from black to white; and the final time, we used the smallest brush shape to stroke the path from white to black. The result of all this stroking is shown in Figure 8-33.

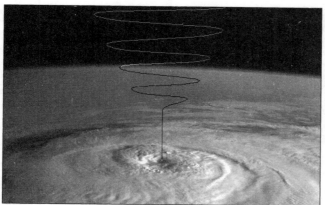

Figure 8-32: This path was drawn by starting at the eye of the hurricane and working upward.

6. Next, two clones of the zigzag path were created by Option-dragging the path with the arrow tool. We pressed the Shift key while dragging to ensure that the paths aligned horizontally. Clicking in an empty portion of the image window deselected all paths so that they appeared as shown in Figure 8-33. This allowed all to be stroked simultaneously in Step 9.

Figure 8-33: After stroking the path three times with the paintbrush tool, we cloned the path twice.

7. We created a 60-pixel version of the brush shape and reduced its Hardness value to 0 percent. We then painted a single white spot at the bottom of each of the new paths. We painted a black spot at the bottom of the original path.

8. We selected the smudge tool, moved the Pressure slider bar in the Brushes palette to 98 percent, and selected a brush shape with a radius of 16 pixels. At this setting, the tool has a tremendous range but eventually fades out.

9. We chose the Stroke Path command to apply the smudge tool to all three paths at once. The finished image appears in Figure 8-34.

Figure 8-34: All three paths were stroked with the smudge tool set to 98 percent pressure to achieve this effect.

Tip   If you're feeling precise, you can specify the location of every blob of paint laid down in an image. When the Spacing option in the Brush Options dialog box is deselected, Photoshop applies a single blob of paint for each point in a path.

Converting and saving paths

Two commands switch between paths and selections; both are located in the Paths palette menu. Make Selection converts paths to selection outlines; Make Path converts selections to a path. However you create a path, you can save it with the current image, which enables you to reuse the path, hide it, and display it at will.

Tip   After you choose Make Selection and establish the default settings, you can reapply the command by pressing the Enter key on the numeric keypad. While a path or selection tool is active, Enter converts the path to a selection. If another tool is selected, you can click on the convert-to-selection/path icon at the bottom of the Paths palette (see Figure 8-26). To call the Make Selection dialog box, Alt-click on the convert-to-selection/path icon.

Converting paths to selections

Choosing the Make Selection command or clicking on the convert-to-selection/path icon when an area of your image is selected displays the dialog box shown in Figure 8-35. You can specify whether to anti-alias or feather the selection, and to what degree. Photoshop can also combine the selection outline with any existing selection in the image. The Operation options correspond to the keyboard functions discussed in the "Manually adding and subtracting" section earlier in this chapter.

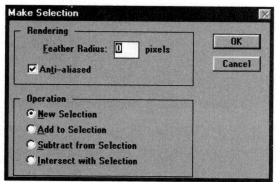

Figure 8-35: When you choose the Make Selection command, you have the option of combining the path with an existing selection.

Note   If you haven't saved a path before you convert it, Photoshop leaves the path on-screen in front of the converted selection. If you try to copy, cut, delete, or nudge the selection, you perform the operation on the path instead. If you save the path before converting it, Photoshop hides the path and provides full access to the selection.

Converting selections to paths

When you choose the Make Paths command, Photoshop produces a single Tolerance option. Unlike the Tolerance options you've encountered so far, this one is accurate to $1/10$ pixel and has nothing to do with colors or brightness values. It specifies Photoshop's sensitivity to twists and turns in a selection outline. The value you enter determines how far the path can vary from the original selection. The lowest possible value, 0.5, retains every nuance of the selection, but it can also result in overly complicated paths. If you enter the highest value, 10, Photoshop uses very few points. If you plan on editing the path, you probably won't want to venture any lower than 2.0, the default setting.

Saving paths with an image

We mentioned at the beginning of the paths discussion that saving a path is an integral step in the path-creation process. You can store every path you draw in case you decide later to select an area again. Photoshop defines paths as compact mathematical equations, so they take virtually no room on disk.

You save paths by choosing the Save Path command from the Paths palette menu or double-clicking on the Work Path item in the scrolling list. After the save operation, the path name appears in upright characters. Path names can include any number of separate paths. If you save a path and then start drawing another one, Photoshop adds that path in with the saved path. To start a new path under a new name, you first have to hide the existing path. You can hide and display a saved path by clicking on its name.

Tip   To hide all paths, click in the empty portion of the scrolling list below the last saved path name. You can even hide unsaved paths in this way. However, if you hide an unsaved path and then begin drawing a new one, the unsaved path is deleted.

Paths with Illustrator

Photoshop can swap paths with Illustrator. Just copy a path to the Clipboard and paste it into the other program. This cross-application compatibility expands and simplifies a variety of path-editing functions. For example, to scale, rotate, or flip a path — operations you can't perform inside Photoshop — you can copy a path, paste it into Illustrator, transform it, copy it again, and paste it back into Photoshop.

When you copy a path in Illustrator and paste it into Photoshop, a dialog box offers you the option of rendering the path to pixels (just as you can render an Illustrator EPS document using File⇨Open) or keeping the path information intact. In other words, you can turn the path into an image or bring it in as a path, which you can then use as a selection outline. If you want to save the path in the Paths palette, be sure to select the Paste As Paths option.

Tip   Things can get muddled in the Clipboard, especially when you're switching applications. If you copy from Illustrator, but the Paste command is dimmed inside Photoshop, you may be able to force the issue. Inside Photoshop, bring up the Windows 95 Clipboard Viewer. Don't worry if you see a message about an unsupported format. Just minimize it again — and try to paste. (Computers are slow sometimes. Every once in a while, you have to give them a kick in the pants.)

Exporting to Illustrator

If you don't have enough memory to run Illustrator and Photoshop at the same time, export Photoshop paths to disk and then open them in Illustrator. To export all paths in the current image, choose File⇨Export⇨Paths to Illustrator. Photoshop saves the paths as editable Illustrator documents. This scheme enables you to trace images with paths in Photoshop and then combine those paths as objects with the exported EPS version of the image inside Illustrator. Tracing an image in Illustrator can be a little tricky because of resolution differences and other previewing limitations, but you can trace images in Photoshop as accurately as you like.

Note   Illustrator provides no equivalent function to export paths for use in Photoshop, nor can Photoshop open Illustrator documents from disk and interpret them as paths. The Clipboard is the only way to use an Illustrator path in Photoshop.

Retaining transparent areas in an image

Photoshop 3's transparency feature does not translate to other programs, not even Illustrator. (The PostScript language doesn't permit the kind of transparency that Photoshop uses.) However, Illustrator, QuarkXPress, and other object-oriented applications let you mask image areas that you want to appear transparent by using *clipping paths.* Elements inside the clipping path are opaque; elements outside the clipping path are transparent. Photoshop lets you export an image in the EPS format with an object-oriented clipping path intact. When you import the image into the object-oriented program, it appears premasked with a perfectly smooth perimeter, as illustrated in Figure 8-36.

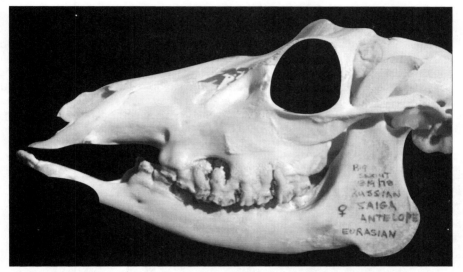

Figure 8-36: One path was drawn around the perimeter of the skull and another around the eye socket. After defining the paths as clipping paths, we exported the image in the EPS format, imported it into Illustrator, and set it against a black background for contrast.

The following steps explain how to assign a set of saved paths as clipping paths.

Steps: Saving an image with Clipping Paths

1. Draw paths around the areas that you want opaque. Areas outside the paths will be transparent.

2. Save the paths by double-clicking on the Work Path name in the Paths palette, entering a name, and pressing Enter. (Try to use a name that will make sense.) The name appears in outline type in the Paths palette.

3. Choose the Clipping Path command from the Paths palette menu. A dialog box enables you to select the saved paths that you want to assign as the clipping path. (This step is optional. You can override your choice in the next step.)

   You enter a value into the Flatness option box. This simplifies the clipping paths by printing fluid curves as polygons. The Flatness value represents the distance (from 0.2 to 100) in printer pixels that the polygon may vary from the true mathematical curve. Higher values lead to polygons with fewer sides. Unless you experience a *limitcheck* error when printing from Illustrator, don't enter a value for this option. Even then, try simplifying your illustration first.

4. Choose File⇨Save and select EPS from the Format menu. The EPS Format dialog box (shown in Figure 3-5) now has a Clipping Path pop-up menu. If the proper path name appears in the menu — it will if you followed the previous step — press Enter. An EPS image with masked transparencies is saved to disk.

Figure 8-37 is an enhanced version of the skull from Figure 8-36. In addition to exporting the image with clipping paths in the EPS format, we saved the paths to disk by choosing File⇨Export⇨Paths to Illustrator. Inside Illustrator, we used the exported paths to outline the clipped image and create the shadow behind the image. The white of the eyeball is a reduced version of the eye socket, as are the iris and pupil. The background features flipped and reduced versions of the paths. The only drawing was to create the two initial Photoshop paths.

Figure 8-37: It's amazing what you can accomplish by combining scans edited in a painting program with smooth lines created in a drawing program.

Note   Be prepared for your images to grow by leaps and bounds when they're imported into Illustrator. The EPS illustration shown in Figure 8-36 takes 600K on disk. The Photoshop image alone consumes only 100K as an LZW-compressed TIFF file.

R%%%
Robert
There are some small gotchas on the PC side of things; these are detailed in Chapter 3 in the EPS format section.

Creating Masks

Selecting via Masks

Most Photoshop users don't use masks. If our experience is any
indication, it's not just that masks seem complicated, it's also
that they don't strike most folks as particularly useful. Like
nearly everyone, when Deke first started using Photoshop, he
couldn't even imagine any possible application for a mask. *I've
got my lasso tool, my magic wand, my pen tool — what more could
I possibly want?*

But in truth, masks are absolutely essential. They are, in fact, the
most accurate method for defining selection outlines in Photoshop. Quite simply, masks enable you to devote every one of
Photoshop's powerful capabilities to the task of creating a
selection outline.

Background For those folks who aren't clear on what a Photoshop mask is —
which is nearly everyone — let us take a moment to fill you in. A
mask is an 8-bit representation of a selection outline that you can
save to a separate channel. *Huh?* you might ask, all quizzical and
curious-like. Well, here's another way to put it: A mask is a
selection outline expressed as a grayscale image. Selected areas
appear white, deselected areas appear black. Anti-aliased edges
become gray pixels. Feathered edges are also expressed in
shades of gray, from light gray near the selected area to dark
gray near the deselected area.

Figure 9-1 shows two selection outlines and their equivalent
masks. The top left example shows a rectangular selection that
has been inverted (using Image➪Map➪Invert). Below it is the
same selection expressed as a mask. Because the selection is
hard-edged with no anti-aliasing or feathering, the mask appears
hard-edged. The selected area is white and is said to be *unmasked;* the deselected area is black, or *masked.* The top right
example shows a feathered selection outline. Again, we've
inverted the selection so that you can better see the extent of
the selection. (Marching ants can't accurately express softened
edges, so the inversion helps show things off a little better.) The
bottom right image is the equivalent mask. Here, the feathering
effect is completely visible.

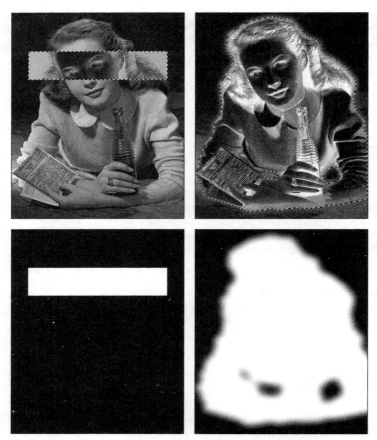

Figure 9-1: Two selection outlines with inverted interiors (top) and their equivalent masks (bottom).

When you look at the masks in Figure 9-1, you may wonder where the heck the image went. One of the wonderful things about masks is that they can be viewed independently of an image, as in Figure 9-1, or with an image, as in Figure 9-2. Here, the mask is expressed as a color overlay. By default, the color of the overlay is a translucent red, like a conventional rubylith. (To see the overlay in its full, natural color, see Color Plate 9-1.) Areas covered with the rubylith are masked (deselected); areas that appear normal — without any red tint — are unmasked (selected). When you return to the marching ants mode, any changes you make to your image will not affect masked areas, only the unmasked portions.

Figure 9-2: The masks from Figure 9-1, shown as they appear when viewed along with an image.

Now that you know roughly what masks are (it will become progressively clearer throughout this chapter), the question remains, What good are they? Because a mask is essentially an independent grayscale image, you can edit the mask using any of the paint and edit tools discussed in Chapter 7, any of the filters discussed in Chapters 13 through 15, any of the color correction options discussed in Chapter 16, or just about any other function described in any other chapter. You can even use the selection tools, as discussed in the previous chapter. With all these features at your disposal, you can't help but create a more accurate selection outline, and in a shorter period of time. All your changes affect the mask — and thus the shape and softness of the selection outline — only. The image itself remains inactive as you edit the mask.

Cross Ref For an example of using filters and color correction options to edit a mask, see the "Softening a selection outline" section of Chapter 13.

Painting and Editing inside Selections

Before we immerse ourselves in 8-bit masking techniques, let's start with a warm-up topic: *selection masking*. When you were in grade school, perhaps you had a teacher who nagged you to color within the lines. (We didn't. Our teachers were more concerned about preventing us from doing things like writing on the walls and coloring on the other kids.) At any rate, if you don't trust yourself to paint inside an image because you're afraid you'll screw it up, selection masking is the answer. Regardless of which tool you use to select an image — marquee, lasso, magic wand, or pen — you can paint or edit only the selected area. The paint can't enter the deselected (or *protected*) portions of the image, so you can't help but paint inside the lines. As a result, all selection outlines act as masks, hence the term *selection masking*.

Figures 9-3 through 9-6 show the familiar skull image subjected to some pretty free-and-easy use of the paint and edit tools. (You think Deke ought to lay off the heavy metal or what?) The following steps describe how these images were created by using a selection mask.

Steps: Painting and editing inside a selection mask

1. Sometime while we were working on Chapter 8, we selected the slightly rotting skull of the enchanting Russian Saiga antelope. You can see the selection outline in such golden oldies as Figures 8-15 and 8-17. If those figures are too remote, just look at the top example in Figure 9-3. For the record, we drew this selection outline by using the pen tool.

2. To edit the area surrounding the skull, we chose Select⇨Inverse to reverse which areas were selected and which were not. Pressing the Delete key filled the selected area with the background color — in this case, white — as shown in the bottom half of Figure 9-3.

3. The next step was to paint inside the selection mask. Before beginning, we chose Select⇨Hide Edges (Ctrl-H). This allows painting without being distracted by those infernal marching ants. (In fact, this is one of the most essential uses for the Hide Edges command.)

4. We selected the paintbrush tool and the 21-pixel soft brush shape in the Brushes palette. The foreground color was black. Dragging with the paintbrush around the perimeter of the skull set it apart from its white background, as shown in Figure 9-4. However sloppily painted, the skull remained unscathed.

5. We selected the smudge tool and set the Pressure slider bar inside the Smudge Tool Options panel to 80 percent by pressing the 8 key. We dragged from inside the skull outward 20 or so times to create a series of curlicues. Dragging from outside the skull inward created white gaps between the curlicues. As shown in Figure 9-5, the smudge tool can smear colors from inside the protected area, but it does not apply these colors until you go inside the selection. This is an important point to keep in mind, because it demonstrates that although the protected area is safe from all changes, the selected area may be influenced by colors from protected pixels.

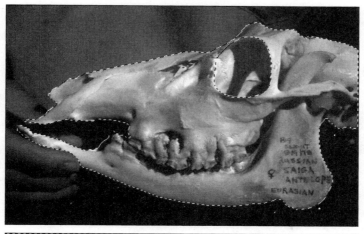

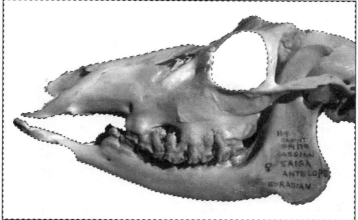

Figure 9-3: After drawing a selection outline around the antelope skull (top), we inversed the selection and deleted the background (bottom).

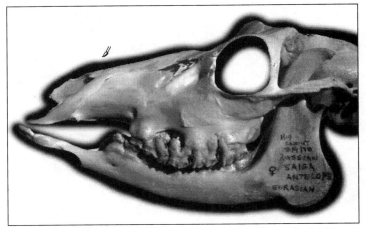

Figure 9-4: A 21-pixel soft brush shape was used to paint inside the selection mask.

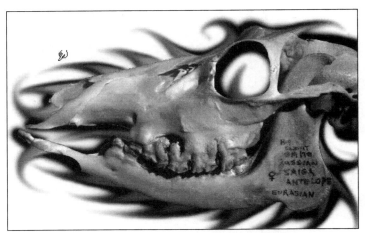

Figure 9-5: Dragging with the smudge tool smeared colors from pixels outside the selection mask without changing the appearance of those pixels.

6. Double-clicking on the airbrush tool icon in the toolbox displayed the Airbrush Options panel. We selected the Fade check box and set the Fade value to 20, leaving the Transparent option selected in the pop-up menu. We selected a 60-pixel soft brush shape and again dragged outward from various points along the perimeter of the skull. As demonstrated in Figure 9-6, combining airbrush and mask is as useful in Photoshop as it is in the real world.

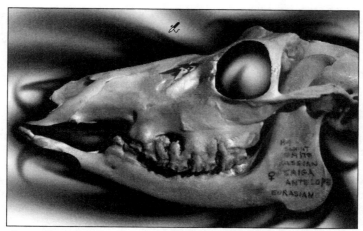

Figure 9-6: Dragging around the skull with the airbrush further distinguishes it from its background. Pretty cool effect, huh? Well, if it's not your cup of tea, maybe you can track down a teenager who'll appreciate it.

Temporary Masking Functions

Selection masks give you an idea of what masks are all about, but they only scrape the surface. The rest of the discussions in this chapter revolve around using masks to define complex selection outlines (which you can later use as selection masks or simply to select one image and move it, copy and paste it into another document, filter it, or whatever).

The most straightforward environment for creating a mask is the *quick mask mode*. To experience it for yourself, select some portion of an image and click on the quick mask mode icon in the toolbox, which is the right-hand icon directly under the color controls. Or just press the Q key. All the deselected areas in your image appear covered in a translucent coat of red, and the selected areas appear without red coating, just as shown in Color Plate 9-1.

Another convenient method for creating a mask is the Color Range command under the Select menu. When you select this command, you use the eyedropper to specify areas of like color that you want to select, and other areas that you don't want to select. It's kind of like a magic wand tool on steroids, in that it lets you change the tolerance of the selection on the fly.

Both options fall under the category of temporary masking functions because neither option allows you to retain the mask for later use. You have to use the selection outline immediately, just as if you had drawn it with the marquee, lasso, or magic wand. I'll describe a more permanent solution (saving masks to a separate mask channel) later in this chapter.

Using the quick mask mode

Upon pressing the Q key to enter the quick mask mode after wreaking our most recent havoc on the extinct antelope's skull, we saw the image shown in Figure 9-7. The skull receives the mask because it was not selected. (In Figure 9-7, the mask appears as a light gray coating; on your color screen, the mask appears in red.) The area outside the skull looks just the same as it always did because it was selected and therefore not masked.

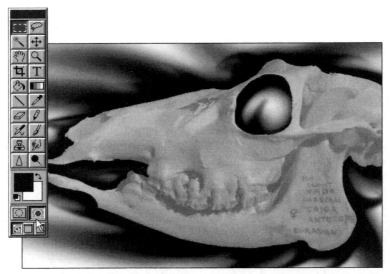

Figure 9-7: Click on the quick mask mode icon (left) to instruct Photoshop to temporarily express the selection as a grayscale image.

Background Notice that the selection outline disappears when you enter the quick mask mode. That's because it temporarily ceases to exist. Any operations that you apply affect the mask itself and leave the underlying image untouched. When you click on the marching ants mode icon (to the left of the quick mask mode icon) or again press the Q key, Photoshop converts the mask back into a selection outline and again allows you to edit the image.

Note Have you ever clicked on the quick mask mode icon without seeing anything change on-screen? Don't worry, your computer isn't broken. It just means that you didn't have anything selected before you entered the mode. When nothing is selected, Photoshop allows you to edit the entire image; in other words, everything's selected. (Only a few commands under the Edit menu, Image⇨Effects submenu, and Select menu require something to be selected before they work.) If everything is selected, the mask is white. Therefore, the quick mask overlay is transparent and you don't see any difference on-screen. Rest assured, however, that you are in the quick mask mode and you can apply any of the edits listed in this section.

Once in the quick mask mode, you can edit the mask in the following ways:

✦ **Subtracting from a selection:** Paint with black to add red coating and thus deselect areas of the image, as demonstrated in the top half of Figure 9-8. This means that you can selectively protect portions of your image by merely painting over them.

✦ **Adding to a selection:** Paint with white to remove red coating and thus add to the selection outline. You can use the eraser tool to whittle away at the masked area (assuming that the background color is set to white). Or you can swap the foreground and background colors so that you can paint in white with one of the painting tools.

✦ **Adding feathered selections:** If you paint with a shade of gray, you add feathered selections. You also can feather an outline by painting with black or white with a very soft brush shape, as shown in the bottom image in Figure 9-8.

✦ **Cloning selection outlines:** You can clone a selection outline by selecting it with one of the standard selection tools and Alt-dragging it to a new location in the image, as shown in Figure 9-9. Although the lasso tool was used in the figure, the magic wand tool also works well for this purpose. To select an anti-aliased selection outline with the wand tool, set the tolerance to about 10 and be sure that the Anti-aliased check box is active. Then click inside the selection. It's that easy.

✦ **Transform selection outlines:** That's right, the quick mask mode provides a method for transforming a selection outline independently of its contents. Just enter the quick mask mode, select the mask using one of the standard selection tools, and transform it by choosing the desired command from the Image⇨Flip, Image⇨Rotate, or Image⇨Effects submenu.

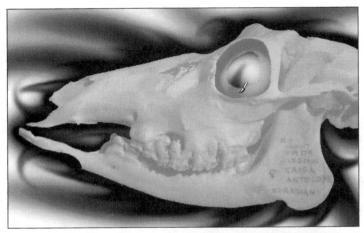

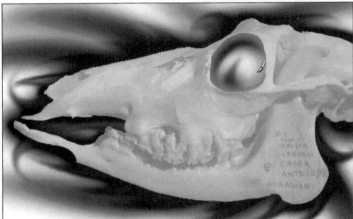

Figure 9-8: After subtracting some of the selected area inside the eye socket by painting in black with the paintbrush tool (top), the outline was feathered by painting with white, using a soft 45-pixel brush shape (bottom).

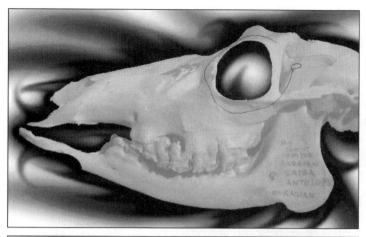

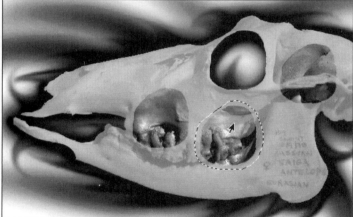

Figure 9-9: The eye socket selection was cloned by lassoing around it (top) and Alt-dragging (bottom).

These are just a few of the unique effects you can achieve by editing a selection in the quick mask mode. Others involve tools and capabilities we haven't yet discussed, so expect to hear more about this feature in future chapters.

When you finish editing your selection outlines, click on the marching ants mode icon (just to the left of the quick mask mode icon) or just press the Q key again to return to the marching ants mode. Your selection outlines again appear flanked by marching ants, and all tools and commands return to their normal image-editing functions. Figure 9-10 shows the results of switching to the marching ants mode and deleting the contents of the selection outlines created in the last examples of the previous two figures.

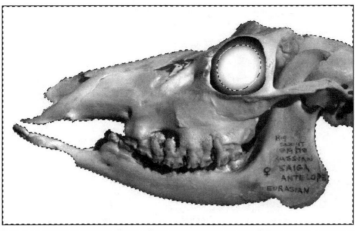

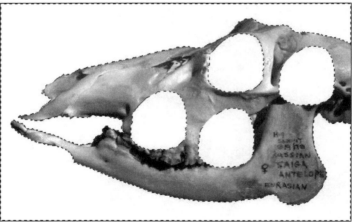

Figure 9-10: The results of deleting the regions selected in the final examples of Figures 9-8 (top) and 9-9 (bottom). Does it remind you of *It's the Great Pumpkin, Charlie Brown?* We mean, who wouldn't give this antelope a rock?

Tip   As demonstrated in the top example of Figure 9-10, the quick mask mode offers a splendid environment for feathering one selection outline while leaving another hard-edged or anti-aliased. Granted, because most selection tools offer built-in feathering options, you can accomplish this task without resorting to the quick mask mode. But the quick mask mode lets you change feathering selectively after drawing selection outlines. It also lets you see exactly what you're doing.

Changing the red coating

By default, the protected region of an image appears in translucent red in the quick mask mode, but you can change it to any color and any degree of opacity that you like. To do so, double-click on the quick mask icon in the toolbox (or double-click on the Quick Mask item in the Channels palette) to display the dialog box shown in Figure 9-11.

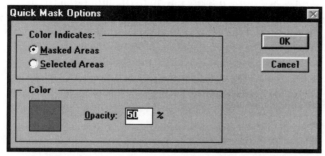

Figure 9-11: Double-click on the quick mask mode icon to access the Quick Mask Options dialog box. You then can change the color and opacity of the protected or selected areas when viewed in the quick mask mode.

✦ **Color Indicates:** Select the Selected Areas option to reverse the color coating — that is, to cover the selected areas in a translucent coat of red and view the deselected areas normally. Select the Masked Areas option (the default setting) to cover the deselected areas in color.

You can reverse the color coating without ever entering the Quick Mask Options dialog box. Simply Alt-click on the quick mask icon in the toolbox to toggle between coating the masked or selected portions of the image. The icon itself changes to reflect your choice.

✦ **Color:** Click on the Color icon to display the Adobe Color Picker dialog box and select a different color coating. For a detailed explanation of this dialog box, see the "Using the Color Picker" section of Chapter 4.

✦ **Opacity:** Enter a value to change the opacity of the translucent color that coats the image. A value of 100 percent is absolutely opaque.

Change the color coating to achieve the most acceptable balance between being able to view and edit your selection and being able to view your image. For example, the red coating shows up badly on grayscale screen shots, so we changed the color coating to light blue and the Opacity value to 65 percent before shooting the screens featured in Figures 9-7 through 9-9.

Generating masks automatically

When you choose Select⇨Color Range, Photoshop displays the Color Range dialog box shown in Figure 9-12. As we mentioned earlier, it's basically an enhanced version of the magic wand tool combined with the Similar command. It selects areas of related color, whether they're contiguous or not. However, instead of clicking with the magic wand to select colors, you click with an eyedropper tool. And instead of adjusting a Tolerance value before you use the tool, you adjust a Fuzziness option any old time you like. So why didn't the folks at Adobe merely enhance the functionality of the magic wand? Probably because the magic wand wouldn't let you load and save mask settings on disk the way the Color Range dialog box does. Also, the dialog box displays a preview of the mask, which is pretty essential for gauging the accuracy of your selection.

Figure 9-12: The Color Range dialog box enables you to generate a mask by dragging with the eyedropper tool and adjusting the Fuzziness option.

Notice that when you move your cursor outside the Color Range dialog box, it changes to an eyedropper. Click with the eyedropper to specify the color on which you want to base the selection — which we call the *base color* — just as if you were using the magic wand. Alternatively, you can click inside the preview area, labeled in Figure 9-12. In either case, the preview area updates to show the resulting mask. You can also do the following:

✦ **Add colors to the selection:** To add base colors to the selection, select the add color tool inside the Color Range dialog box and click inside the image window or preview area. You can also access the tool while the standard eyedropper is selected by Shift-clicking (just as you Shift-click with the magic wand to add colors to a selection). You can Shift-drag with the eyedropper to add multiple colors in a single pass, which you can't do with the wand tool.

✦ **Remove colors from the selection:** To remove base colors from the selection, click with the remove color tool or Ctrl-click with the eyedropper. You can also drag or Ctrl-drag to remove many colors at a time.

✦ **Adjust the Fuzziness value:** This option resembles the Tolerance value in the Magic Wand Options panel in that it determines the range of colors that will be selected beyond the ones you click on. Raise the Fuzziness value to expand the selected area; lower the value to contract the selection. A value of 0 selects the clicked-on color only. Unlike changes to Tolerance, however, changing the Fuzziness value adjusts the selection on the fly; no reclicking is required, as it is with the wand tool.

Another difference between Fuzziness and the less-capable Tolerance option is the kind of selection outline each generates. Tolerance entirely selects all colors within the specified range and adds anti-aliased edges. If the selection were a mask, most of it would be white with a few gray pixels around the perimeter. By comparison, Fuzziness entirely selects only the colors on which you click and partially selects the other colors in the range (just as if the selection outline were feathered). That's why most of the mask is expressed in shades of gray. The light grays in the mask represent the most similar colors; the dark grays represent the least similar pixels that still fall within the Fuzziness range.

✦ **Toggle the preview area:** Use the two radio buttons below the preview area to control the preview's contents. If you select the first option, Selection, you see the mask that will be generated when you press Enter. If you select the Image option, the preview shows a reduced version of the image.

✦ **Control the contents of the image window:** The Selection Preview pop-up menu at the bottom of the dialog box lets you change what you see in the image window. Select Grayscale to see the mask on its own. Select Quick Mask to see the mask and image together. Select Black Matte or White Matte to see what the selection would look like against a black or white background. Though they may sound weird, the Matte options let you get an accurate picture of how the selected image will mesh with a different background. Use the Fuzziness option in combination with Black Matte or White Matte to come up with a softness setting that will ensure a smooth transition. Leave this option set to None (the default setting) to view the image normally in the image window.

✦ **Select by predefined colors:** Choose an option from the Select pop-up menu at the top of the dialog box to specify the means of selecting a base color. If you choose any option besides Sampled Colors, the Fuzziness option and eyedropper tools become dimmed to show that they're no longer operable.

Instead, Photoshop selects colors based on their relationship to a predefined color. For example, if you select Red, the program entirely selects red and partially selects other colors based on the amount of red they contain. Colors composed exclusively of blue and green are not selected.

The most useful option in this pop-up menu is Out of Gamut, which selects all the colors in an RGB or Lab image that fall outside the CMYK color space. You can use this option to select and modify the out-of-gamut colors before converting an image to CMYK. Chapter 16 examines a use for this option.

✦ **Load and save settings:** Click on the Save button to save the current settings to disk. Click on Load to open a saved settings file.

When you define the mask to your satisfaction, click on the OK button or press Enter to generate the selection outline. Although the Color Range command is more flexible than the magic wand, you can no more expect it to generate perfect selections than any other automated tool. Therefore, after Photoshop draws the selection outline, you'll probably want to switch to the quick mask mode and paint and edit the mask to taste.

If you learn nothing else about the Color Range dialog box, at least learn to use the Fuzziness option and the eyedropper tools. There are basically two ways to approach these options. If you want to create a diffused selection with gradual edges, set the Fuzziness option to a high value — 40 or more — and click and Shift-click only two or three times with the eyedropper. To create a more precise selection, enter a low Fuzziness value and Shift-drag and Ctrl-drag with the eyedropper tool several times until you get the exact colors you want.

Figure 9-13 shows some sample results. To create the left images, the eyedropper tool was clicked once on the bridge of the woman's nose and the Fuzziness was set to 130. To create the right images, the Fuzziness value was lowered to 6; clicking, Shift-clicking, and Ctrl-clicking with the eyedropper then lifted exactly the wanted colors. The top examples show special effects applied to the two images (Filter⇨ Stylize⇨Find Edges). In the bottom example, the selections were copied and pasted against an identical background of Cheerios. (Breakfast food suits this woman well.) In both examples, the higher Fuzziness value yields more generalized and softer results; the lower value results in a more exact but harsher selection.

 Tip   You can limit the portion of an image that Select⇨Color Range affects by selecting part of the image before choosing the command. When a selection exists, the Color Range command masks only those pixels that fall inside it. Even the preview area reflects your selection. Try it and see.

Fuzziness: 130   Fuzziness: 6

Figure 9-13: After creating two selections with the Color Range command — one with a high Fuzziness value (left) and one with a low one (right) — the Find Edges filter was applied (top) and the selections were pasted against a different background (bottom).

Tip   Goodie, another tip. If you get hopelessly lost when creating your selection and you can't figure out what to select and what to deselect, just click with the eyedropper tool to start over. This clears all the colors from the selection except the one you click on. Alternatively, you can press the Alt key to change the Cancel button to a Reset button. Alt-click on the button to return the settings inside the dialog box to those that were in force when you first chose Select⇨Color Range.

Creating an Independent Mask Channel

The problem with masks generated via the quick mask mode and Color Range command is that they're here one day and gone the next. Photoshop is no more prepared to remember them than it is a lasso or wand selection.

Most of the time, that's okay. You'll only use the selection once, so there's no reason to sweat it. But what if the selection takes you a long time to create? What if, after a quarter hour of Shift-clicking here and Ctrl-dragging there, adding a few strokes in the quick mask mode, and getting the selection outline exactly right, a slight twitch pulses through your finger and you inadvertently double-click in the image window with the lasso tool? Good job — not only have you deselected the selection, you've eliminated your only chance to undo the deselection. To coin a euphemism from the world of women's lingerie, you're hosed.

For this reason, you'll probably want to back up your selection if you've spent any amount of time on it. Even if you're in the middle of creating the selection that you've been grinding at for quite a while, stop and take a moment to save it before all heck breaks loose. You wouldn't let a half hour of image editing go by without saving, and the rules don't change just because you're working on a selection.

Saving a selection outline to a mask channel

The following steps describe a wonderful method for backing up a selection to an independent *mask channel*, which is any channel above and beyond those required to represent a grayscale or color image. Mask channels are saved along with the image itself, making it a safe and sturdy solution.

Steps: Transferring a selection to an independent channel

1. Choose Select⇨Save Selection, which lets you save the selection as a mask. The dialog box shown in Figure 9-14 appears, asking you where you want to put the mask. In most cases, you'll want to save the mask to a separate channel inside the current image. To do so, make sure that the name of the current image appears in the Document pop-up menu and then select New from the Channel pop-up menu and press Enter.

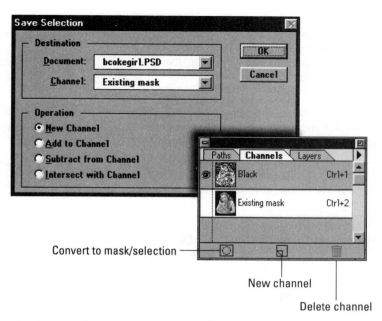

Convert to mask/selection

New channel

Delete channel

Figure 9-14: The Save Selection dialog box lets you convert your selection outline to a mask and save it to a new or existing channel.

If you have an old channel that you want to replace, select the channel's name from the Channel pop-up menu. The radio buttons at the bottom of the dialog box become available, allowing you to add the mask to the channel, subtract it, or intersect it. These radio buttons work just like the equivalent options that appear when you make a path into a selection outline (see "Converting paths to selections" in Chapter 8), but they blend the masks together instead. The result is the same as if you were adding, subtracting, or intersecting selection outlines, except that it's expressed as a mask.

Alternatively, you can save the mask to a new document all its own. To do this, choose New from the Document pop-up menu and press Enter.

Tip

Man, what a lot of options! If you just want to save the selection to a new channel and be done with it, don't bother with Select⇨Save Selection. Just click on the convert to mask/selection icon at the bottom of the Channels palette (labeled in Figure 9-14). Photoshop automatically creates a new channel, converts the selection to a mask, and places the mask in the channel. (Regardless of which of these methods you choose, your selection outline remains intact.)

2. To view the saved selection in its new mask form, display the Channels palette by choosing Window➪Palettes➪Show Channels. Then click on the appropriate channel name in the Channels palette, presumably #2 if you're editing a grayscale image or #4 if you're working in the RGB or Lab mode. In Figure 9-14, we replaced the contents of an existing mask called — what else? — Existing Mask, so this is where the mask now resides.

3. Return to the standard image-editing mode by clicking on the first channel name from the Channels palette. Better yet, press Ctrl-1 if you're editing a grayscale image or Ctrl-0 if the image is in color.

4. Save the image to disk to store the selection permanently. Only the TIFF and native formats can handle more than four channels. But you ought to be saving regularly in native format anyhow.

5. To later retrieve your selection, choose Select➪Load Selection. A dialog box nearly identical to the one shown in Figure 9-14 appears, except for the addition of an Invert check box. Select the document and channel that contains the mask you want to use. You can add it to a current selection, subtract it, or intersect it. Select the Invert option if you want to switch the selected and deselected portions of the mask. (Inverting a mask is the same as applying Select➪Inverse to a selection outline because it makes the white areas black and the black areas white.)

Tip   Want to avoid the Load Selection command? Just Alt-click on the channel name in the Channels palette that contains the mask you want to use. For example, if we Alt-clicked on the Existing Mask item in Figure 9-14, Photoshop would load the equivalent selection outline into the image window. Or press Ctrl-Alt plus the channel number to convert the channel to a selection. For example, Ctrl-Alt-2 would convert the Existing Mask channel. (You can also drag the channel name onto the convert to mask/selection icon at the bottom of the Channels palette, but that takes so much more effort.)

You can also add to and subtract from a selection using keyboard shortcuts. Shift-Alt-click on a channel to add it to the current selection outline; Ctrl-Alt-click to subtract the mask from the selection; Ctrl-Shift-Alt-click to find the intersection. Cool stuff, eh?

Tip   Watch out, it's Tip City around here. Did you know that you can also save a quick mask to its own channel? It's true. When you enter the quick mask mode, the Channels palette displays an item called *Quick Mask*. The italic letters show that the channel is temporary and is not saved with the image. To clone it to a permanent channel, just drag the Quick Mask item onto the new channel icon at the bottom of the Channels palette (labeled in Figure 9-14). Now save the image to the TIFF or Photoshop format, and you're backed up.

Viewing mask and image

Photoshop lets you view any mask channel along with an image, just as you can view mask and image together in the quick mask mode. To do so, click in the first column of the Channels palette to toggle the display of the eyeball icon. An eyeball in front of a channel name indicates that you can see that channel. If you are currently viewing the image, for example, click in front of the mask channel name to view the mask as a translucent color coating, again as in the quick mask mode. Alternatively, if the contents of the mask channel appear by themselves on-screen, click in front of the image name to display it as well.

Using a mask channel is different from using the quick mask mode in that you can edit either the image or mask channel when viewing the two together. You can even edit two or more masks at once. To decide which channel you want to edit, click on the channel name in the palette. To edit two channels at once, click on one and Shift-click on another. All active channel names appear gray.

You can change the color and opacity of each mask independently of other mask channels and the quick mask mode. Click on the mask channel name to select one channel only and then choose the Channel Options command from the Channels palette menu. Or just double-click on the mask channel name. (This is not an option when you're editing a standard color channel.) A dialog box similar to the one shown back in Figure 9-11 appears, the only difference being that this one contains a Name option box so that you can change the name of the mask channel. You can then edit the color overlay as described in the "Changing the red coating" section earlier in this chapter.

Tip If you ever need to edit a selection outline inside the mask channel using paint and edit tools, click on the quick mask mode icon in the toolbox. It may sound like a play within a play, but you can access the quick mask mode even when working in a mask channel. Just make sure that the mask channel color is different from the quick mask color so that you can tell what's going on.

Deriving selections from images

Here's your chance to see the mask channel in action. In the following steps, we start with the unadorned image of the Great Wall shown in Figure 9-15 and add the glow shown in Figure 9-18. Normally, this would be a fairly complex procedure. But when you employ a mask channel, it takes only minutes.

Instead of selecting a portion of the image and saving it to a channel, as described in the previous sections, we created the selection mask in the following steps by copying a portion of an image, pasting it into a mask channel, and editing it.

We have yet to cover a couple of the techniques used in the following steps: filling a selection and applying the Threshold command. For more information, read Chapter 10, "Filling and Stroking," and Chapter 16, "Mapping and Adjusting Colors."

Figure 9-15: A 1940s photograph of the Great Wall from the Bettmann Archive.

Steps: Using a mask channel to enhance an image

1. The process started by duplicating the image of the Great Wall to the mask channel. To do this, we dragged the Black item onto the new channel icon at the bottom of the Channels palette, thus cloning the channel.

Note

This is a grayscale image, so it only contains one channel: Black. If it were an RGB image, we would search through each of the Red, Green, and Blue channels to find the one with the most contrast. You could do the same in the Lab or CMYK modes. Then we would drag the high-contrast channel onto the new channel icon. (You cannot drag the color composite view — the one at the top of the Channels palette — onto the new channel icon, because you can only clone one channel at a time.)

2. Photoshop automatically took us to the new mask channel, which it kindly labeled #2. To convert the image to a mask, we chose Image⇨Map⇨Threshold (Ctrl-T), which changed all pixels in the mask channel to either white or black. This allowed us to isolate gray values in the image and create the reasonable beginnings of a selection outline.

Because we haven't described the Threshold command yet, let us take a moment to do so. Inside the Threshold dialog box, you move a slider bar to specify a brightness value. All pixels lighter than that value turn to white, and all pixels darker than that value change to black. We used the value 233 to arrive at the image shown in Figure 9-16.

3. The black-and-white image from Figure 9-16 was far from perfect, but it was as good as it was going to get using Photoshop's automated color mapping. From here on, we had to rely on our tracing abilities. We used the pencil tool to fill in the gaps in the wall and the eraser tool to erase the black pixels from the sky. Notice that we did not use the paintbrush or airbrush tools; at this stage, we wanted hard edges.

Figure 9-16: After duplicating the Black channel, we changed all pixels to white or black using the Threshold command and set about painting away the imperfections.

4. We softened portions of the boundaries between the black and white pixels by using the blur tool at the default 50 percent pressure and with a small brush shape. (For a better way to accomplish this, read the "Softening a selection outline" section of Chapter 13.)

5. To create the glow, we Alt-dragged the elliptical marquee tool to draw the marquee from the center outward. Before releasing, we pressed and held Shift (as well as Alt) to constrain the marquee to a circle. After drawing the marquee, we Ctrl-Alt-dragged it to position the selection outline exactly where we wanted it, as shown in the top half of Figure 9-17.

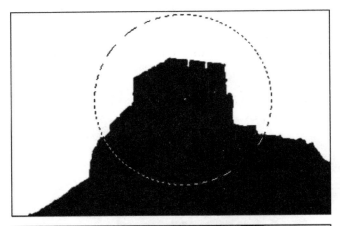

Figure 9-17: We established the selection outline for the glow by Alt-dragging with the elliptical marquee tool (top) and pressing Alt-Del to fill the selection with black. The paintbrush and smudge tools were then used to paint in the rays (bottom).

6. Pressing Alt-Del filled the circular selection with black.

7. After double-clicking on the paintbrush tool icon and selecting the Fade check box in the Paintbrush Options panel, we set the value to 40 pixels and drew several long rays about the perimeter of the circle.

8. Using the smudge tool set to 50 percent pressure, dragging outward from the circle created the tapering edges shown in the bottom half of Figure 9-17.

9. To apply the finished selection to the image, we pressed Ctrl-1 to return to the standard image mode. (This is a grayscale image. If it had been color, we would have pressed Ctrl-0.) We chose Select⇨Load Selection to copy the selection from the mask channel.

10. Because only the upper third of the image was edited in the mask channel, the lower two thirds of the document appeared selected. To deselect this region, we Ctrl-dragged the rectangular marquee tool around it.

11. Because Photoshop selects the portions of the mask channel that are white, only that portion of the sky outside the glow was selected. The rest of the image was masked. Pressing Alt-Del filled the selection with black. Figure 9-18 shows the result.

Figure 9-18: Returning back to the standard image mode, the selection outlines were loaded from the mask layer; pressing Alt-Del filled the selected area with black.

Color Plate 9-2 shows an alternative color scheme applied to Figure 9-18. Instead of filling the background with black, we filled it with a gradation from dark blue to light blue. Also, the interior of the glow was filled with yellow, and a gradation was applied from green to red across the Great Wall and hills. In less than an hour, we converted an old grayscale stock photo into a full-color dazzler. For more information on applying colors to images using Photoshop's fill and gradient features, read the next chapter.

Masking and Layers

Layers offer special masking options unto themselves. You can paint inside the confines of a layer as if it were a selection mask, you can add a special mask for a single layer, or you can group multiple layers together and have the bottom layer in the group serve as the mask. Quite honestly, these are the kinds of thoughtful and useful functions that we've come to expect from Photoshop. Though they're fairly complicated — you really have to be on your toes once you start juggling layers (carnival music, please) — you'll discover a world of opportunity and flexibility once you come to terms with these amazing controls.

Preserving transparency

You may have already noticed a little check box near the top of the Layers palette called Preserve Transparency. If not, the option appears spotlighted in Figure 9-19. When checked, it prevents you from painting inside the transparent portions of the layer.

Consider the image shown in Figure 9-19. It comprises five layers in addition to the background image, each of which contains a modified version of the woman's head. (She's pining for her boyfriend overseas — that's what the letter in her hand is all about — so her head's all over the place. Literally, that is.) Arrows point from each of the layer names in the Layers palette to the contents of that layer in the image. Just to be safe, we've also included numbers — 1 is the lowest layer, 5 is the highest. Figure 9-19 is a masterpiece of overannotation, if we do say so ourselves.

We're happy with the transition between the large face in the lower right corner (numbered 3) and the two faces that border it (1 and 2). What we'd like to do is create a slight shadow around face 3 to distinguish it more clearly. If we just start painting, however, we run the risk of getting paint all over faces 1 and 2, because both faces are behind face 3.

Everything making sense so far? If this were a flat, nonlayered image, you'd have to carefully draw a selection outline between the borders of faces 1, 2, and 3 and then paint inside the resulting selection mask. But there's no need when you're using layers. Because all the faces are on separate layers, an implied selection mask exists between them. All opaque pixels are inside the selection; all transparent pixels are outside of it.

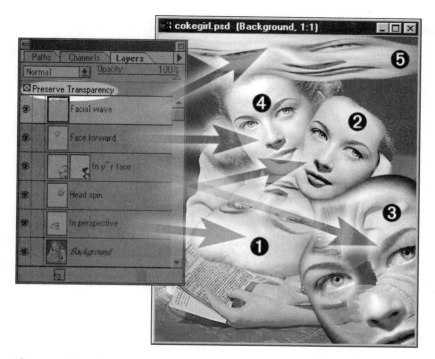

Figure 9-19: An image composed of five layers and a background image. Arrows join the layer names to their contents. The numbers show the layering order of the faces, from 1 at the bottom to 5 at the top.

The first example in Figure 9-20 shows face 3 on its own. (All the other layers have been hidden by Alt-clicking on the eyeball icon in front of the face 3 layer name.) The transparent and therefore implicitly deselected areas appear in the checkerboard pattern. When the Preserve Transparency option is turned off, you can paint anywhere inside the layer that you want. The implied selection mask is off. But with Preserve Transparency on, the selection mask is on and the checkerboard area is off limits.

The right image in Figure 9-20 shows what happens when Preserve Transparency is selected and the airbrush is used to paint inside the face. Notice that no matter how much paint is applied, none of it leaks out onto the neighboring faces. As the old geezers at the Home for Retired Image Editors are always saying, *good masks make good neighbors*. How true it is.

Figure 9-20: The third layer as it appears on its own (left) and when airbrushed with the Preserve Transparency check box turned on (right).

Note   The setting of the Preserve Transparency check box applies to each layer independently. Therefore, if we select the option for the face 3 layer and then switch to face 2, the option turns off because it is not in effect for this layer. If we then switch back to face 3, the check box becomes selected again because the effect is still on for this layer.

Also worth noting: The Preserve Transparency option is dimmed when the Background layer is active, because this layer is entirely opaque. There's no transparency to preserve, eh? (That's Deke's impression of a Canadian explaining layer theory. It needs a little work, but he thinks he's getting close.)

Layer-specific masks

In addition to the implied selection mask that comes with every layer, you can add a mask to a layer to specify which portions of the layer are transparent or translucent and which parts are opaque. Won't simply erasing portions of a layer make those portions transparent? Yes, it will, but when you erase, you permanently delete them. By creating a layer mask, you instead make pixels temporarily transparent. You can come back later and bring those pixels back to life again simply by adjusting the mask. Therefore, layer masks add yet another level of flexibility to a program that's already a veritable image-editing contortionist.

To create a layer mask, select the layer that you want to mask and choose the Add Layer Mask command from the Layers palette pop-up menu. A second thumbnail preview appears to the left of the layer name, as labeled in Figure 9-21. A heavy outline around the preview shows that the layer mask is active.

Figure 9-21: When the layer mask is active (as indicated by the heavy outline around the mask thumbnail in the Layers palette), paint with black to make pixels transparent and paint in white to make them opaque. The mask itself appears in the right window.

To edit the mask, simply paint in the image window. Paint with black to make pixels transparent. (Because black represents deselected pixels in an image, it makes these pixels transparent in a layer.) Paint with white to make pixels opaque. The irony of this setup is that painting with the eraser tool when the background color is white — as is the default setting — actually makes pixels opaque. Strange but true.

The left image in Figure 9-21 finds us painting a soft hole into face 3 with the paintbrush. Notice that while the eyes, nose, mouth, and face outlines remain at least opaque, other areas are translucent or altogether transparent. Make a mistake — like accidentally slicing off the nose? No sweat. Just paint with white to bring it back again.

The right image in Figure 9-21 shows the mask by itself. A layer mask is actually a temporary channel. To view it with the image, go to the Channels panel of this same palette and click in the left column in front of the item that bears the name of the layer — in our case, *In y^r face Mask*. To view the channel by itself, click on the eyeball icon in front of the composite view item.

R
%/%
Robert
That's no typo in the Mask name, either two sentences back or in the screen shots. We started with original files from a Macintosh for these screen shots. The original file, on the Mac, has *your* when viewed either on the computer or in the screen shot. Coming over to Windows, Photoshop certainly reads the file right, but notice how *your* has become *yür*. We've left this deliberately as a warning. We're in a cross-platform world, but there are some little gotchas.

Tip   Actually, you can do all this without ever leaving the Layers panel. To view the mask by itself, Alt-click on the layer mask thumbnail. To see both mask and image together, Shift-click on the left layer thumbnail and then click again on the layer mask thumbnail to keep the mask active (so that you don't end up editing the image itself). You can also turn the mask on and off by Ctrl-clicking on the mask thumbnail. A red X covers the thumbnail when it's inactive, and all masked pixels in the layer appear opaque.

You can also double-click on the layer mask thumbnail to view the Layer Mask Options dialog box. Mostly, these options are the same as those described in the earlier section "Changing the red coating," except the two Position Relative To radio buttons and the Do Not Apply to Layer check box. The latter simply turns off the layer, as when you Ctrl-click on the mask thumbnail. The Position Relative To options specify whether the mask moves with the layer when you use the move tool. If you select Layer, you can move the mask and layer at once. If you select Image, the layer moves independently of the mask. You can always move the mask independently of the layer with the move tool or move the layer independently by selecting it and then moving it, so I recommend selecting the Layer radio button.

When and if you finish using the mask (you don't have to ever finish with it if you don't want to), you can choose Remove Layer Mask from the Layers palette menu. An alert box asks you if you want to discard the mask or permanently apply it to the layer. Click on the button of your choosing.

Masking groups of layers

This is about the point at which we grow a little fatigued with the topic of layering masking. But one more option requires discussion. You can group multiple layers into something called a *clipping group,* in which the lowest layer in the group determines the way all other layers in the group are masked. (Note that a clipping group has no practical similarities to a clipping path — that is, it doesn't allow you to prepare transparent areas for import into Illustrator or QuarkXPress.)

Creating a clipping group is easy. Just Alt-click on the horizontal line between any two layers to group them into a single unit. Your cursor changes to the group layer icon shown in Figure 9-22 when you press Alt; the horizontal line becomes dotted after you click. To break the layers apart again, just Alt-click on the dotted line to make it solid.

All layers in the group remain discrete units. You can't select across layers or paint on two layers at once. (You can paint on one layer and have it flow out in front of other layers, but you can do that without grouping.) The move tool still moves the layers independently unless you specifically instruct it to do otherwise (as explained in the previous chapter).

The only thing that the layers in a clipping group share is a common selection mask. The lowest layer in the clipping group acts as a selection mask for the other layers in the group. Where the lowest layer is transparent, the other layers are hidden; where the lowest layer is opaque, the contents of the other layers are visible. In Figure 9-22,

Figure 9-22: Alt-click on the horizontal line between two layers to group them together. Layers divided by dotted lines are part of the same clipping group.

for example, face 1 (the upside-down face) is the lowest layer in the group. We've added a slight halo under the layer to show it off a little better. As you can see, just the base of the chin from face 2 and a sliver of the large face 3 — the other members of the clipping group — can be seen. It's not an effect you're likely to find much use for.

That's why it's best to throw in a base layer whose only function is to serve as the selection mask. In the first example of Figure 9-23, we've created a new empty layer called Clipper and made it the lowest layer in the clipping group. Because it's completely transparent, all the other layers in the group are invisible. We select a large oval area with the elliptical marquee tool and press Alt-Del to fill it with black. Actually, it doesn't matter which color is used, just as long as it's opaque. The selection mask immediately grows to fill the oval. As a result, all pixels in the other layers in the group that fit inside the opaque area become opaque as well, as shown in the bottom example of the figure. Now faces 1 and 2 are completely visible because they fit entirely inside the oval; face 3 is half obscured.

Note
If you're familiar with Illustrator, you'll recognize this clipping group metaphor as a relative to Illustrator's clipping path. One object in the illustration acts as a mask for a collection of additional objects.

Figure 9-23: Starting with an entirely transparent bottom layer inside the clipping group (top), an oval area is selected and filled with opaque color, making the overlapping portions of the layers above the clipping group visible (bottom).

Filling and Stroking

Filling Portions of an Image

To *fill* a selection is to put color inside it; to *stroke* a selection is to put color around it. Simple stuff, actually. Many of you already knew it and are getting plenty hot under the collar that you had to waste valuable seconds of your day reading such a flat-out obvious sentence. And you're getting even more steamed that you have to read sentences like these that don't add much to your overall understanding of Photoshop.

In fact, Photoshop's fill and stroke functions are so straight-forward that you may have long since dismissed them as wimpy little tools. The truth is, you can do a world of stuff with them. In this chapter, for example, we'll show you how to create an antique framing effect; how to create drop shadows, halos, and spotlights; how to use gradations in masks; and how to create arrowheads that leap off the page — all in addition to the really basic stuff that you may already know. Actually, you may even want to read about the basic stuff on the off chance that you missed some golden nugget of information in your Photoshopic journeys thus far.

Filling an Area with Color

You can fill an area of an image with color in four ways:

✦ **The paint bucket tool:** You can apply the foreground color or a repeating pattern to areas of related color in an image by clicking in the image window with the paint bucket tool (known in some circles as the fill tool). For example, if you want to turn all midnight blue pixels in an image into red pixels, you just set the foreground color to red and then click on one of the blue pixels.

✦ **The Fill command:** Select the portion of the image that you want to color and fill the entire selection with the foreground color or a repeating pattern by choosing Edit⇨Fill or pressing Shift-Del.

✦ **Delete-key techniques:** Select part of an image and fill the selection with the background color by pressing the Delete key. To fill the selection with the foreground color, press Alt-Del.

✦ **The gradient tool:** Select an area and drag across it with the gradient tool to fill it with a multicolor gradation. Although it does not match the power of gradient tools in some other programs, Photoshop's gradient tool is still so special and wide-ranging in its capabilities that we devote several pages to it in "Applying Gradient Fills" later in this chapter.

The following sections discuss each of these options in depth.

The paint bucket tool

Unlike remedial paint bucket tools in other painting programs, which apply paint exclusively within outlined areas or areas of solid color, thereby exhibiting all the subtlety of dumping paint out of a bucket, the Photoshop paint bucket tool offers several useful adjustment options. To explore them, double-click on the paint bucket icon in the toolbox to display the Paint Bucket Options panel of the Brushes palette, shown in Figure 10-1. (Alternatively, you can press the K key to select the paint bucket tool and then press Enter to display the options panel.)

Three of the options, Tolerance, Anti-aliased, and Sample Merged, work exactly like their counterparts in the Magic Wand Options panel, which we explained in the "The world of the wand" section of Chapter 8. The brush modes pop-up menu and the Opacity slider bar work just like those in the Paintbrush Options panel, which we covered at extreme length in Chapter 7. But in case you need a refresher, here's how these and the other options work, in the order in which they appear in the panel:

✦ **Brush modes:** Select an option from the brush modes pop-up menu to specify how and when color is applied. If you select Darken, the paint bucket tool affects a pixel only if the foreground color is darker than that pixel. If you select Color, the paint bucket colorizes the image without changing the brightness value of any pixel. See "The 15 paint tool brush modes" section in Chapter 7.

✦ **Opacity:** Drag the Opacity slider or press a number key to change the translucency of a color applied with the paint bucket.

✦ **Tolerance:** Applying color with the paint bucket tool is a three-step process. After you click on a pixel with the tool, Photoshop reads the brightness value of that pixel from each color channel. Next, it calculates a tolerance range according to the value you enter in the Tolerance option box (you can enter any value from 0 to 255). It adds the Tolerance value to the brightness value of the pixel on which you click with the paint bucket tool to determine the top of the range; it subtracts the Tolerance value from the brightness value of the pixel

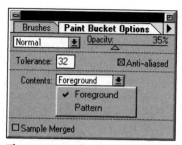

Figure 10-1: The Paint Bucket Options panel governs the performance of the paint bucket tool.

to determine the bottom of the range. For example, if the pixel's brightness value is 100 and the Tolerance value is 32, the top of the range is 132 and the bottom is 68. After establishing a tolerance range, Photoshop applies the foreground color to any pixel that both falls inside the tolerance range and is contiguous to the pixel on which you clicked. A large Tolerance value causes the paint bucket to affect a greater number of pixels than a small Tolerance value. See Figure 10-2.

✦ **Anti-aliased:** Select this option to soften the effect of the paint bucket tool. As demonstrated in the top example of Figure 10-3, Photoshop creates a border of translucent color between the filled pixels and their unaffected neighbors. If you don't want to soften the transition, deselect the Anti-aliased check box. Photoshop then fills only those pixels that fall inside the tolerance range, as demonstrated in the bottom example of the figure.

✦ **Contents:** You can apply the foreground color or a pattern created using Edit⇨Define Pattern. See the "Applying Repeating Patterns" section of Chapter 11.

✦ **Sample Merged:** This makes the paint bucket see beyond the current layer. The tool takes all visible layers into account when calculating the area to be filled. Mind you, it only fills the active layer — as we've mentioned before, only the move tool can affect more than one layer at a time — but the way it fills an area is dictated by all layers. For example, suppose that you have an image of a dog on one layer and a fire hydrant on the other. The two images do not overlap. If you were to click on the fire hydrant when the dog layer was active *and* the Sample Merged option was turned off, you'd fill most of the image. The paint bucket can't see the hydrant; all it can see is the transparent area of the dog layer, so it tries to fill that. (This assumes that the Preserve Transparency option in the Layers palette is turned off.) However, if you were to select Sample Merged, the paint bucket would fill the portion of the hydrant on which you click. It would apply the paint to the dog layer, but the paint would follow the contours of the hydrant. In fact, as long as the dog layer was above the hydrant layer, it would look just as if you had filled the hydrant itself (but you would have the option of mixing hydrant fill and hydrant together, as discussed in Chapter 17).

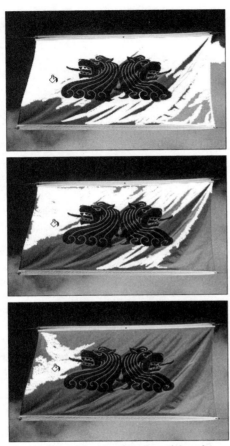

Figure 10-2: The results of applying the paint bucket tool to the exact same pixel after setting the Tolerance value to 32 (top), 16 (middle), and 8 (bottom). In each case, the foreground color is white.

Tip   To limit the area affected by the paint bucket, select a portion of the image before using the tool. As when you use any other tool, the region outside the selection outline is protected from the paint bucket.

Figure 10-3: The results of selecting (left) and deselecting (right) the Anti-aliased check box prior to using the paint bucket tool. The inset rectangles show magnified pixels.

Fill command

The one problem with the paint bucket tool is its lack of precision. Though undeniably convenient, the paint bucket suffers the exact same limitations as the magic wand. The effects of the Tolerance value are so difficult to predict that you typically have to click with the tool, choose Edit⇨Undo when you don't like the result, adjust the Tolerance value, and reclick with the tool several times more before you fill the image as desired. For our part, we've almost given up using the paint bucket for any purpose other than filling same-colored areas. In this case, the Tolerance option is nearly always set to 0 and Anti-alias is always off, which puts the command right back in the all-the-subtlety-of-dumping-paint-out-of-a-bucket camp. (For an exception to this, see the upcoming "Creating Special Fill Effects" section.)

A better option is to select the area that you want to fill and choose Edit⇨Fill or press Shift-Del. In this way, you can define the exact area of the image you want to color using the entire range of Photoshop's selection tools — including the path tools, quick mask mode, Color Range command, and so on — instead of limiting yourself to the equivalent of the magic wand. For example, instead of putting your faith in the paint bucket tool's Anti-aliased option, you can draw a selection outline that features hard edges in one area, anti-aliased edges elsewhere, and feathered edges in between.

When you choose the Fill command, Photoshop displays the Fill dialog box shown in Figure 10-4. In this dialog box, you can apply a translucent color or pattern by entering a value into the Opacity option box and choose a brush mode option from the Mode pop-up menu. In addition to its inherent precision, the Fill command maintains all the functionality of the paint bucket tool — and then some.

If you display the Contents pop-up menu, as shown in the lower example in Figure 10-4, you'll see a collection of things you can use to fill the selected area. Foreground Color and Pattern are in the menu, as with the paint bucket tool. So are Background Color and such monochrome options as Black, White, and 50% Gray. Black and White are useful if the foreground and background colors have been changed from their defaults; 50% Gray lets you access the absolute medium color without having to mess around with the Color Picker dialog box or Picker palette. Saved and Snapshot let you revert the selected area to a previous appearance, as discussed in the "Reverting selected areas" section of Chapter 11.

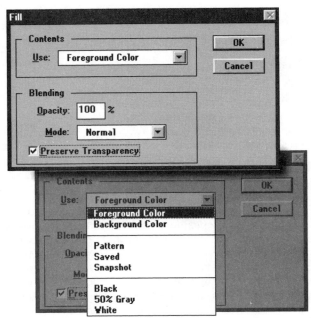

Figure 10-4: The Fill dialog box combines the Opacity and brush mode options from the Paint Bucket Options panel with an expanded collection of Contents options.

The Preserve Transparency check box works like the identically named option in the Layers palette (see Chapter 9). When the option is turned on, you can't fill the transparent pixels in the current layer. Because you're already filling one selection mask, Photoshop gives you the option of considering the implied selection mask of the layer as well. When Preserve Transparency is turned off, you fill the selection outline uniformly. (The option is dimmed when you're working on the background layer or when the Preserve Transparency option in the Layers palette is checked for the current layer.)

Paths

Photoshop provides a variation on Edit⇨Fill that lets you fill paths that were created with the pen tool without first converting them to selections. After drawing a path, choose the Fill Path command from the Path palette pop-up menu or Alt-click on the fill path icon in the lower left corner of the palette. Photoshop displays a slight variation of the Fill dialog box from Figure 10-4, the only difference being the inclusion of two Rendering options. Enter a value into the Feather Radius option box to blur the edges of the fill as if the path were a selection with a feathered outline. Select the Anti-aliased check box to slightly soften the outline of the filled area.

If one path falls inside another, Photoshop leaves the intersection of the two paths unfilled. Suppose that you draw two round paths, one fully inside the other. If you save the paths and then choose the Fill Path command, Photoshop fills only the area between the two paths, resulting in a letter *O*.

Note   If the Fill Path command fills only part or none of the path, it's very likely because the path falls outside the selection outline. Choose Select⇨None (Ctrl-D) to deselect the image and then choose the Fill Path command again.

Note   If you select one or more paths with the arrow tool, the Fill Path command changes to Fill Subpaths, enabling you to fill the selected paths only.

Delete-key techniques

Of all the fill techniques, the Delete key is by far the most convenient and, in most respects, every bit as capable as the others. The key's only failing is that it can't fill a selection with a repeating pattern. But because you'll rarely *want* to fill a selection with a repeating pattern, you can rely on the Delete key for the overwhelming majority of your fill needs.

Here's how to get a ton of functionality out of the Delete key:

✦ **Background color:** To fill a selection with solid background color, press Delete. The selection outline remains intact. Keep in mind that this technique works only when the selection is *not* floating. If you float the selection and then press Delete, you delete the selection entirely.

✦ **Foreground color:** To fill a selection with solid foreground color, press Alt-Del You can fill floating and nonfloating selections alike by pressing Alt-Del.

✦ **Black or white:** To fill an area with black, press D to get the default foreground and background colors and then press Alt-Del. To fill it with white, press D for defaults, X to switch them, and then Alt-Del. This method works on both floating and nonfloating selections.

✦ **Translucent color:** To fill a selection with a translucent coating of foreground color, choose Select⇨Float (Ctrl-J) to float the selection. Then press Alt-Delete, press the M key to make sure that a selection tool is active, and press a number key to change the setting of the Opacity slider bar in the Layers palette.

✦ **Accessing brush modes:** To mix foreground color and original image using brush modes, float the selection, press Alt-Del, and select a mode from the pop-up menu on the left side of the Layers palette.

Creating Special Fill Effects

Even Photoshop has its share of dull moments. Filling selections? Boring! Oh, sure, you were mesmerized by our entertaining text blended cleverly with comprehensive coverage, but in the background, you were probably lamenting your misspent youth. Face it, nowhere in the recipe for image-editing fun is there mention of a paint bucket, a Fill command, or a Delete key.

Ah ha, that's what *you* think. In reality, all three of these functions are capable of delivering some pretty wonderful results. Okay, so the paint bucket is a pitiful creature by anyone's standards, but the Delete key alone is a cosmic and powerful force if you'll only take the time to unleash it correctly. So don't be so quick to dismiss a bunch of capable functions just because they're dull.

A use for the paint bucket discovered

The following steps explain how to create an effect that you can perform only with the paint bucket tool. Doubtless it's the only such example you'll ever discover using Photoshop — after all, the paint bucket *is* mostly useless and you *can* fill anything with the Delete key — but we're men enough to eat our rules just this once.

The steps explain how to create an antique photographic frame effect like the one shown in Figure 10-5.

Steps: Creating an antique photographic frame

1. Use the rectangular marquee tool to select the portion of the image that you want to frame. Make sure that the image extends at least 20 pixels outside the boundaries of the selection outline.

2. Choose Select⬦Feather, and specify a Radius value somewhere in the neighborhood of 6 to 12 pixels. We've found that these values work for just about any resolution of image. (If you enter too high a value, the color you'll add in a moment with the paint bucket will run out into the image.)

3. Choose Select⬦Inverse to exchange the selected and deselected portions of the image.

4. Press the D key to make sure that the background color is white. Then press the Delete key to fill the selected area with the background color.

5. Double-click on the paint bucket tool icon in the toolbox to display the Paint Bucket Options panel. Enter 20 to 30 in the Tolerance option box, and select the Anti-aliased check box. (You can also experiment with turning this option off.)

6. Click inside the feathered selection to fill it with black (or whatever other fore-ground color you prefer). The result is an image fading into white and then into black, like the edges of a worn slide or photograph, as shown in Figure 10-5.

Figure 10-5: This antique frame effect was created by filling a feathered selection with the paint bucket tool.

Figure 10-6 shows a variation on this effect that you can create using the Dissolve brush mode. Rather than setting the Tolerance value to 20, raise it to something in the neighborhood of 60. Then, after selecting the paint bucket tool, select the Dissolve option from the brush modes pop-up menu in the Paint Bucket Options panel. When you click inside the feathered selection with the paint bucket tool, you create a frame of random pixels, as illustrated in the figure.

Creating drop shadows, halos, and spotlights

Okay, so there's one use for the paint bucket tool. Big whoop. In most cases, you don't need it. For example, you can create three of the most useful (and, some might argue, overused) of all image-editing enhancements — drop shadows, halos, and spotlights — using nothing but the selection tools and Alt-Del. Rather than throw a lot of in-depth analysis your way, we'll just jump right in and show you how.

In the first steps, we'll take the dolphin from Figure 10-7 and insert a drop shadow behind it. This might not be the exact subject to which you'll apply drop shadows — sea critters so rarely cast such shadows onto the water's surface — but it accurately demonstrates how the effect works.

Figure 10-6: Select Dissolve from the Brushes palette pop-up menu to achieve a speckled frame effect.

Figure 10-7: A dolphin in dire need of a drop shadow.

Steps: Creating a drop shadow

1. Select the subject that you want to cast the shadow. In this case, the dolphin is selected by painting the mask shown in Figure 10-8 inside a separate mask channel. (It's usually a good idea to use a mask to distinguish the foreground image from its background.) The mask is converted to a selection outline by Alt-clicking on the mask name in the Channels palette and then pressing Ctrl-0 to switch back to the composite view.

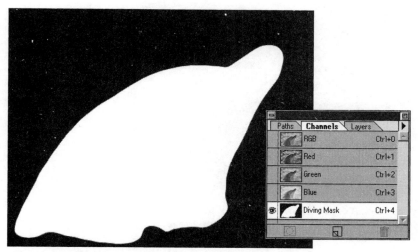

Figure 10-8: This mask separates the dolphin from its watery home.

2. Float the selection with Ctrl-J. Send the selection to its own layer by switching to the Layers panel and Alt-double-clicking on the Floating Selection item in the scrolling list. Now that the selection is elevated, slip the drop shadow underneath it.

3. In order to create the drop shadow, you need to retrieve the selection outline and apply it to the background layer. To do this, press Ctrl-Alt-T to select the layer and tighten the selection outline, and click on the Background item in the Layers palette to apply the selection outline to the original image. (If you saved the mask to a separate channel, as we did, you could alternatively Alt-click on the Mask item in the Channels panel to retrieve the selection.)

4. To create a softened drop shadow, indicative of a diffused light source, choose Select⮞Feather. The Radius value you enter depends on the resolution of your image. We recommend dividing the resolution of your image by 20. When working on a 200-ppi image, for example, enter a Radius value of 10. Our image is a mere 140 ppi, so we entered 7. Then press Enter to soften the image.

5. Press Ctrl-J to float the selection and Ctrl-H to hide the edges. Then fill the selection with black (D, Alt-Del). A slight halo of dark pixels forms around the edges of the image.

6. Use the arrow keys to nudge the shadow to the desired location. In Figure 10-9, the shadow is nudged 12 pixels to the right.

Figure 10-9: A drop shadow nudged 12 pixels due right from the dolphin head, which is situated on the layer above it.

7. If the shadow is too dark — black lacks a little subtlety — press M to make sure that a selection tool is active and then press a number key to change the opacity of the shadow. 7, for 70 percent, is usually a good choice.

Tip   If you don't like a black drop shadow, you can make a colored one with only slightly more effort. Instead of filling the shadow with black in Step 5, select a different foreground color and press Alt-Delete. For the best result, select a color that is the complementary opposite of the color of your background. In Color Plate 10-1, for example, the background is blue, so a reddish orange is used as the foreground color. Next, choose Multiply from the overlay modes pop-up menu on the left side of the Layers palette. This burns the colors in the shadow into those in the image to create a darkened mix. Finally, press a number key to specify the opacity. (70 percent is used again in the color plate.)

Creating a halo is very similar to creating a drop shadow. The only differences are that you have to expand the selection outline and that you fill the halo with white (or some other light color) instead of black. The following steps tell it all.

Steps: Creating a downright angelic halo

1. Follow Steps 1 through 3 of the previous instructions. You'll end up with a version of the selected image on an independent layer and a matching selection outline applied to the Background image. (See, we told you that this was just like creating a drop shadow.)

2. Unlike a drop shadow, which is offset slightly from an image, a halo fringes the perimeter of an image pretty evenly. Therefore, you need to expand the selection outline beyond the edges of the image so that you can see the halo clearly. To do this, choose Select⇨Modify⇨Expand. You'll be greeted by an Expand By option box. Generally speaking, you want the expansion to match the size of your feathering so that the softening occurs outward; in this case, the value 7 was used. (The maximum permissible value is 16; if you want to expand more than 16 pixels, you have to apply the command twice.)

3. Choose Select⇨Feather, and enter the same value you entered in the Expand By option box. Again, you decide this value by dividing the resolution of your image by 20. Or not. Let experimentation be your guiding light.

4. Float the selection. Change the foreground color to white (by pressing D and then X) and then press Alt-Del.

That's all there is to it. Figure 10-10 shows a particularly enlightened-looking dolphin set against a halo effect. We also drew a conventional halo above its head, added some sparklies, and even changed our finned friend's eye using the eyeball brush shape included in the Assorted Brushes document. If this aquatic mammal's not bound for glory, we don't know who is.

Tip Incidentally, you don't have to create a white halo any more than you have to create a black drop shadow. In Step 4, select some foreground color other than white. Then select the Screen option from the overlay modes pop-up menu in the Layers palette, thus mixing the colors and lightening them at the same time. If you don't like the effect, just select a different foreground color and press Alt-Del again. As long as the halo is floating, you can do just about anything you want and run no risk of harming the underlying original.

Now, finally, for the spotlight effect. We use spotlights about a billion times in this book to highlight some special option that we want you to look at in a palette or dialog box. We've gotten so many questions on how to perform this effect that we decided we might as well write it down once in the book and be done with it.

Figure 10-10: Few dolphins reach this level of spiritual awareness, even if you do set them off from their backgrounds using the halo effect. He kind of looks like one of the cast members of *Cocoon,* don't you think?

Steps: Shining a spotlight on something inside an image

1. Using the elliptical marquee tool, draw an oval selection inside your image. This represents the area where the spotlight will shine. If you don't like where the oval is located but you basically like its size and shape, Ctrl-Alt-drag it to a more satisfactory location.

2. Choose Select⇨Feather, and enter whatever Radius value you please. Again, you may want to follow the divide-the-resolution-by-20 rule, but feel free to use whatever value you like. (There's no such thing as a wrong Radius value.) To create Figure 10-11, the Radius value is doubled to 14 pixels to create a very soft effect.

3. You really want to darken the area outside the spotlight, not lighten the spotlight itself. So choose Select⇨Inverse to swap what's selected and what's not.

4. Float the selection, hide the outline, and fill it with black. That's Ctrl-J, Ctrl-H, D, Alt-Del. Then change the Opacity setting by pressing a number key. To get Figure 10-11, we pressed 6 for 60 percent.

Figure 10-11: Create an elliptical selection, feather it, inverse it, float it, fill it with black, and lower the opacity to create a spotlight effect like this one.

Actually, the image in Figure 10-11 isn't all that convincing. Although the steps above are fine for spotlighting flat images such as screen shots, they tend to rob photographs of a little of their depth. After all, in real life, the spotlight wouldn't hit the water in the exact same way it hits the dolphin. But there is a way around this. You can combine the oval selection outline with the mask used to select the foreground image, thereby eliminating the background from the equation entirely.

Assuming that your image has a mask saved in a separate channel, do this: After Step 2, duplicate the mask channel so that you don't harm the original by selecting it in the Channels palette and choosing the Duplicate Channel command from the palette menu. Then choose Select⇨Save Selection. Inside the dialog box, select the duplicate mask channel from the Channel pop-up menu and then select the Intersect with Channel radio button. This creates a mask that retains only those selected areas that were selected in both the selection outline and the mask. Alt-click on the revised mask channel in the Channels palette to convert it to a selection outline and switch to the composite view. Then inverse the selection, float it, fill it with black, and change the opacity as explained in Steps 3 and 4 above. See Figure 10-12.

Cross Ref   Sometimes, the darkness of the area around the spotlight appears sufficiently dark that it starts bringing the spotlighted area down with it. To brighten the spotlight, inverse the selection (Select⇨Inverse) so that the spotlight is selected again. Then apply the Levels command (Image⇨Adjust⇨Levels) to brighten the spotlighted area. The Levels command is explained at length in Chapter 16.

Figure 10-12: You can mix the feathered selection with the contents of a mask channel to limit the spotlighting effect to the foreground character only.

Color Plate 10-2 shows one result of combining the spotlight effect with the halo effect. The area outside the spotlight is filled with a deep blue. (In this case, a similar color looked better than a complementary one.) Then, using the original mask, the dolphin is placed on a separate layer and a yellowish, pinkish halo is created behind it. (Just to be safe, the floating halo goes on its own layer.) Then Edit⇨Fill returns the Background image to its original appearance (by selecting the Saved option from the Use pop-up menu in the Fill dialog box) and inverts the background by pressing Ctrl-I. An interestingly lit dolphin in a radioactive bath is the result.

Gradient Fills

Although an image editor inherently provides a better environment for creating and editing gradations, Photoshop's gradient tool is fast becoming one of the least capable gradation generators available inside a high-end graphics application. Illustrator, FreeHand, and CorelDraw — all object-oriented drawing programs — provide more versatile and more precise gradient tools than Photoshop.

Photoshop still has the upper edge for two simple reasons: You can blur and mix colors in a gradation if they start banding — that is, if you can see a hard edge between one color and the next — and you'll never have problems printing gradations from Photoshop the way you will from Illustrator or its ilk. In a drawing program, each color is expressed as a separate shape, meaning that one gradation can contain hundreds or even thousands of objects. Gradations in Photoshop are just plain old colored pixels, the kind we've been editing for nine and a half chapters.

If you want a more comprehensive gradation generator, use the Gradient Explorer module of Kai's Power Tools (a set of filters sold separately by MetaTools, formerly HSC Software). Otherwise, the next several pages explain how to use Photoshop's gradient tool to create standard gradations and special effects. You can even use the tool to edit selection outlines in the quick mask mode. Even though Photoshop's gradient tool isn't everything it could be, it nonetheless opens up a world of opportunities that you can't attain by pressing Alt-Del.

The gradient tool

A *gradation* (also called a *gradient fill*) is a progression of colors that fade gradually into one another, as in Figure 10-13. The foreground color represents the first color in the gradation; the background color is the final color. Photoshop automatically generates the hundred or so colors in between to create a smooth transition.

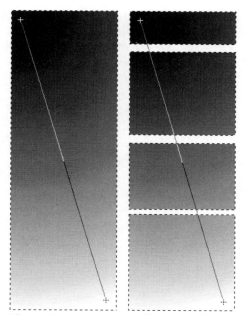

Figure 10-13: Dragging with the gradient tool within a single selection (left) and across multiple selections (right).

You create gradations using the *gradient tool* (just to the right of the paint bucket in the toolbox). Unlike the paint bucket tool, which fills areas of similar color whether or not they are selected, the gradient tool fills the confines of a selection. If you don't select a portion of your image, Photoshop applies the gradation to the entire image.

To select the gradient tool, press the G key. To use the tool, drag inside the selection, as shown in the left example of Figure 10-13. The point at which you begin dragging (upper left corner in the figure) defines the location of the foreground color in the gradation. The point at which you release (lower right corner) defines the location of the background color. (Alternatively, gradations in Photoshop 3 can fade to transparency.) If multiple portions of the image are selected, the gradation fills all selections continuously, as demonstrated by the right example of Figure 10-13.

Gradient tool options

To master the gradient tool, you have to fully understand how to modify its performance. Double-click on the gradient tool icon in the toolbox to display the Gradient Tool Options panel, shown in Figure 10-14. This panel lets you specify the colors in a gradation as well as the arrangement of those colors by using the following options:

✦ **Brush mode and Opacity:** These options work the same as they do in the paint and edit tool Options panels, in the Paint Bucket Options panel, in the Fill dialog box, and everywhere else that they pop up. Select a different brush mode to change the way colors are applied; lower the Opacity value to make a gradation translucent. In both cases, you have to adjust the options before using the gradient tool. They do not affect existing gradations.

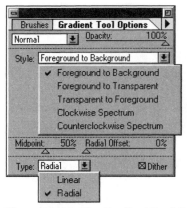

Figure 10-14: The Gradient Tool Options panel as it appears with both the Style and Type pop-up menus open to scrutiny.

✦ **Style:** The five options in the Style pop-up menu determine how Photoshop selects colors in a gradation. The first option enables you to simply create a gradation from the foreground color to the background color. In Photoshop 3, you can also choose to fade the colors from the foreground color to transparency, or from transparency to the foreground color. (In the latter case, where you begin dragging determines the point of transparency, rather than the location of the foreground color.) When either Transparency option is selected, only the foreground color is treated as opaque; all other colors fade through various levels of translucency until they reach absolute transparency.

The two Spectrum options are a little more complicated. Think of the foreground and background colors as points in the HSB color wheel, as illustrated in both Figure 10-15 and Color Plate 10-3. When you select the default Foreground to Background option, Photoshop selects colors in a beeline from the foreground color to the background color within the HSB color wheel. Such gradations typically travel through colors of low saturation (that is, gray) near the middle of the wheel. To maintain a high level of saturation, pick the Clockwise Spectrum option, which selects colors in a clockwise direction around the color wheel, or Counterclockwise Spectrum, which selects colors in a counterclockwise direction. Figure 10-15 illustrates all these options, as does Color Plate 10-3. Color Plate 10-4 shows linear examples of the three gradations created using cyan as the foreground color and red as the background color. The only difference among the gradations is the setting of the Style options.

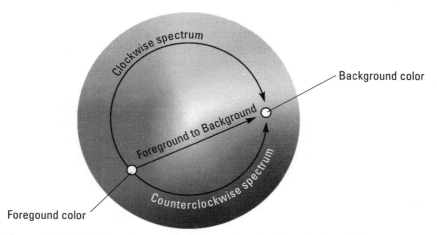

Figure 10-15: The Spectrum options determine the direction in which a gradation progresses with respect to the HSB color wheel.

Note

The two Spectrum options have no effect on grayscale gradations, nor do they influence gradations between any color and black, white, or any other shade of gray. To ensure the fastest gradations under these conditions, select the Foreground to Background option.

The two Transparency options are equally applicable to color or grayscale images; however, you cannot subject them to alternative Spectrum settings for the simple reason that they involve different opacities of one color only, this being the foreground color.

✦ **Type:** Though situated at the bottom of the Options panel, the Type pop-up menu is the next logical option to discuss. Select Linear or Radial to specify the variety of gradation you want to create. A *linear gradation* progresses in linear bands of color in a straight line between the beginning and end of your drag, like the gradation shown back in Figure 10-13. A *radial gradation* progresses outward from a central point in concentric circles, like those in Figures 10-16 and 10-17. The point at which you begin dragging defines the center of the gradation; the point at which you release defines the outermost circle. (Incidentally, the radial gradations in Figures 10-16 and 10-17 were created by using white as the foreground color and black as the background color.)

✦ **Midpoint Skew:** This slider bar determines the location of the halfway point in the gradation. The default value of 50 percent sets the halfway point smack dab in the middle of your drag. If you lower the value, Photoshop arranges most of the colors in the gradation close to the beginning of your drag. This creates a gradation that progresses quickly at first and more slowly toward the end. If you raise the Midpoint Skew value above 50 percent, Photoshop arranges most of the colors toward the end of your drag, resulting in a gradation that progresses slowly at first and more quickly toward the end. Figure 10-16 shows four radial gradations subjected to different Midpoint Skew values, ranging from the minimum to maximum allowed values.

✦ **Radial Offset:** This slider is applicable exclusively to radial gradations. It defines the size of the central circle of foreground color as a percentage of the size of the entire gradation. A value of 0 percent results in a dab of foreground color in the center of the gradation; a value of 99 percent results in a huge circle of foreground color with a thin band of other colors around its perimeter. Figure 10-17 shows four examples of radial gradations subject to different Radial Offset values. Note that the foreground color is white and the background color is black.

✦ **Dither:** Photoshop 3 offers a Dither option that mixes up the pixels a bit, thus helping to eliminate banding. (If selecting the Dither check box doesn't completely take care of the banding, see the next section.) We recommend that you leave this option on unless you want to use the banding to create a special effect.

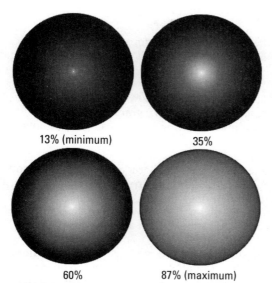

Figure 10-16: Four white-to-black radial gradations subject to different Midpoint Skew values.

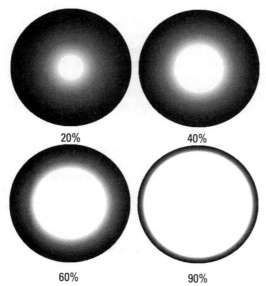

Figure 10-17: Four examples of Radial Offset values. In each case, the Midpoint Skew value was 50 percent.

Eliminating banding

Thanks to the Dither check box in the Gradient Tool Options panel, banding is less of a problem in Photoshop 3 than it was in earlier versions. If you do experience banding, this section describes how to get rid of it.

As explained in Chapter 13, the Add Noise filter randomizes pixels in a selection. Therefore, when you apply Filter⇨Noise⇨Add Noise to a gradation, it randomly mixes the bands of color, very much like a variable dithering function. In fact, it allows you to outdither the Dither check box.

The first column in Figure 10-18 shows linear and radial gradations. In the second column, the Add Noise filter was applied three times in a row to both gradations. To make the effect as subtle as possible, an Amount value of 8 was specified and the Uniform radio button inside the Add Noise dialog box was selected. Repetitions of a subtle noise effect are preferable to a single application of a more radical effect.

If noise isn't enough, or if the noise appears a little too obvious, you can further mix the colors in a gradation by applying a directional blur filter. To blur a linear gradation, apply the Motion Blur filter in the direction of the gradation. In the top right example of Figure 10-18, Filter⇨Blur⇨Motion Blur was applied with an Angle value of 90 degrees (straight up and down) and a Distance value of 3 pixels.

To blur a radial gradation, apply the Radial Blur filter (Filter⇨Blur⇨Radial Blur). To mix the noise around the center of the gradation, select the Spin option in the Radial Blur dialog box. To blend color in the bands, select the Zoom option. The lower right example in Figure 10-18 is divided into halves. To create the top half, the Spin option was applied with an Amount value of 10; to create the bottom half, Zoom was applied with an Amount value of 20. (If you can barely see any difference between the two — that's the idea when it comes to gradations — look closely at the perimeter of the gradients. The top one, created with the Spin option, is smooth; the one created with the Zoom option is rougher.)

To further deemphasize color bands in a horizontal linear gradation, you can apply the Wind filter (Filter⇨Stylize⇨Wind). Color Plate 10-5 shows the three gradation styles from Color Plate 10-4 subject to the Add Noise, Wind, and Motion Blur filters. In each case, the Add Noise filter was applied three times (just as in Figure 10-18), the Blast option in the Wind dialog box twice (once in each direction), and the Motion Blur filter in a horizontal direction at 10 pixels.

Cross Ref You can get a sense of what the Add Noise, Motion Blur, Radial Blur, and Wind filters do just by experimenting with them for a few minutes. If you want to learn even more, we discuss all four in Chapter 13, "Corrective Filtering."

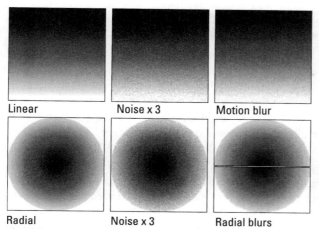

Linear   Noise x 3   Motion blur

Radial   Noise x 3   Radial blurs

Figure 10-18: The results of applying noise (middle column) and directional blur effects (right column) to linear and radial gradations.

Gradations and brush modes

As with any paint, edit, or fill tool, the brush mode and Opacity settings make a tremendous impression on the performance of the gradient tool. The following sections and steps examine a few ways to use brush modes to achieve special effects. These examples only scrape the surface of what's possible, but hopefully they'll inspire you to experiment and discover additional effects.

Randomized gradations

The following steps describe how to use one brush mode option, Dissolve, in combination with a radial gradation to create an effect not unlike a supernova. Figures 10-19 through 10-21 show the nova in progress. In addition to enabling you to experiment with a brush mode setting, the following steps offer some general insight into creating radial gradations.

Steps: Creating a gradient supernova

1. Create a new image window — say, 500 × 500 pixels. A grayscale image is fine for this exercise.

2. Click with the pencil tool at the apparent center of the image. Don't worry if it's not the exact center. This point is merely intended to serve as a guide. If a single point is not large enough for you to easily identify, draw a small cross.

3. Alt-drag from the point with the elliptical marquee tool to draw the marquee outward from the center. Before releasing the mouse button, press and hold the Shift key to constrain the marquee to a circle. Draw a marquee that fills about 3/4 of the window.

4. Image⇨Map⇨Invert (Ctrl-I) fills the marquee with black and makes the center white.

5. Choose Select⇨None (Ctrl-D) to deselect the circle. Then Alt-drag again from the center point with the elliptical marquee tool, again pressing Shift to constrain the shape to a circle, to create a marquee roughly 20 pixels larger than the black circle.

6. Ctrl-drag from the center point with the elliptical marquee tool and press and hold both Shift and Alt midway into the drag to create a marquee roughly 20 pixels smaller than the black circle. The result is a doughnut-shaped selection — a large circle with a smaller circular hole — as shown in Figure 10-19.

7. Choose Select⇨Feather and enter 10 for the Radius value. Then press Enter to feather the section outline.

8. Click on the default colors icon in the toolbox and then click on the switch colors icon to make the foreground color white and the background color black.

9. Double-click on the gradient tool icon. Select the Radial option from the Type pop-up menu, and set the Radial Offset value to 60 percent to increase the size of the central circle of foreground color to roughly the same size as the center marquee.

10. Select Dissolve from the brush modes pop-up menu on the left side of the Gradient Tool Options panel.

11. Drag from the center point in the image window to anywhere along the outer rim of the largest marquee. The result is the fuzzy gradation shown in Figure 10-20.

12. Choose Select⇨None (Ctrl-D) to deselect the image. Then choose Image⇨Map⇨Invert (Ctrl-I) to invert the entire image.

13. Click on the default colors icon to restore black and white as foreground and background colors, respectively. Then use the eraser tool to erase the center point. The finished supernova appears in Figure 10-21.

Amorphous gradient bubbles

Image-editing expert Kai Krause came up with a way to mix radial gradations with the Lighten brush mode option to create soft bubbles like those shown in Figure 10-22. We call this the Larva Effect because the darn thing looks like a goopy larva tail.

If you want to create this effect, press Ctrl-A to select the entire image, press D to switch to the default colors, and then press Alt-Del to fill the image with black. Set the gradient tool to create radial gradations, and select Lighten from the brush modes pop-up menu. Then drag with the tool in the image window to create one radial

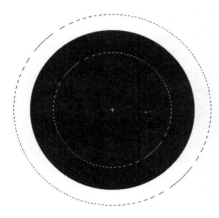

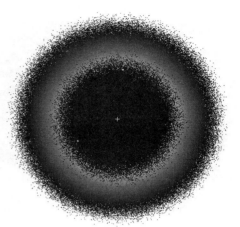

Figure 10-19: The result of creating a black circle and two circular marquees, all centered on a single point.

Figure 10-20: The Dissolve brush mode option randomizes the pixels around the feathered edges of the selection outlines.

gradation after another. The Lighten option instructs Photoshop to apply a color to a pixel only if the color is lighter than the pixel's existing color. As a result, you only paint over part of a neighboring gradation when you create a new one, resulting in adjoining gradient bubbles like those shown in Figure 10-22.

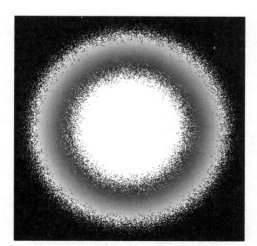

Figure 10-21: By inverting the image from the previous figure and erasing the center point, you create an expanding series of progressively lighter rings dissolving into the black void of space, an effect better known to its friends as a supernova.

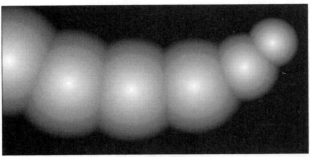

Figure 10-22: We painted this larva tail by filling the image with black, selecting Lighten from the brush modes pop-up menu, and creating six radial gradations from white to black with the gradient tool.

Tip   To make the bubbles of larva flesh appear to emerge from a gradient pool, set the gradient tool to draw linear gradations and then drag upward from somewhere near the bottom of the image. The linear gradation starts out white at the bottom of the window and slowly fades to black, partially submerging the larva in gooey, glowing sludge. In Figure 10-23, the gradient tool was dragged from the top of the image to create a sort of larva cavern. Far out!

Robert   That there larva doodad is certainly a fine example of what algorithms and filters can accomplish in the hands of a master. There's just one problem — lighting. Look at the bubbles' highlights: same relative position, same size. This never happens in nature, at least not in our galaxy. Likewise the shadows. No artist working in traditional media would ever do this, unless he/she was trying to create bubbles existing in another galaxy where all our rules about lighting and shadows become irrelevant. Think I'm being too harsh? Read Chapter 19 and think again.

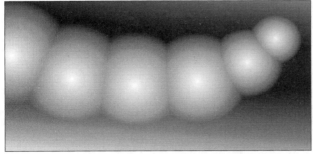

Figure 10-23: The larva cavern created by adding two linear gradations, one beginning in the upper right corner of the image and the other beginning in the lower left corner.

Sharpened amorphous bubbles

The problem with the Larva Effect is that it results in amorphous blobs that look great on-screen but offer too little contrast for most printing situations. Luckily, you can add definition to the blobs using the Unsharp Mask filter with a Radius value of 2.0 or higher.

Cross Ref Like Add Noise and Motion Blur, the strangely named Unsharp Mask filter (which merely sharpens the focus of an image) is covered in greater detail than you probably bargained for in Chapter 13, "Corrective Filtering."

For example, Figure 10-24 shows the results of applying Unsharp Mask with an Amount value of 500 percent, a Radius of 2.0, and a Threshold of 0. The high Radius value helps the filter find the extremely soft edges in the image. (A lower Radius value would just heighten the contrast between individual pixels, creating a grainy effect — if any effect whatsoever.) The filter was applied once to achieve the top example in the figure and then applied a second time to create the bottom example.

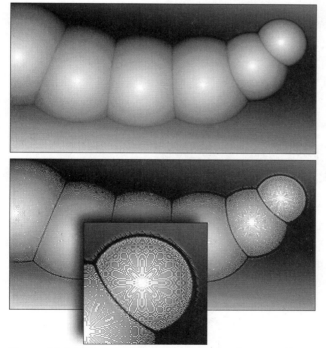

Figure 10-24: The edges of the larva were sharpened by applying the Unsharp Mask filter with a 2.0 Radius value once (top) and twice (bottom). Snowflake patterns begin to emerge with the second application of the filter (magnified inset).

As demonstrated in the magnified inset in Figure 10-24, crystalline snowflake patterns begin to emerge with the second application of Unsharp Mask. However, if you would rather skip the snowflakes and further reinforce the edges, you're better off applying higher Radius values from the get-go. The top example in Figure 10-25 shows the result of applying the Unsharp Mask filter with a Radius value of 10.0; the bottom example shows the result of a 20.0 Radius value applied twice.

Cross Ref
If you're more interested in snowflakes than in sharpening, try applying an edge-detection effect with the Custom filter (Filter⇨Other⇨Custom). This filter requires you to enter numbers into a matrix of option boxes. Figure 10-26 shows some interesting crystals along with the Custom matrix values used to create them. Now, we'll warn you, some folks go nuts over these effects; some folks break into a cold sweat and have nightmares about their algebra teachers for weeks. Whatever your reaction may be, consider Figure 10-26 the smallest of all possible enticements for reading Chapter 15.

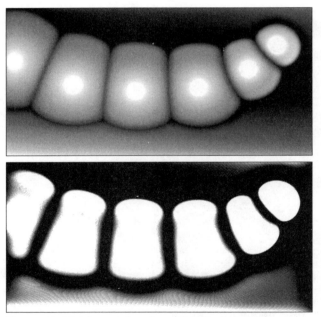

Figure 10-25: The results of applying Unsharp Mask once with a 10.0 radius (top) and twice with a 20.0 radius (bottom).

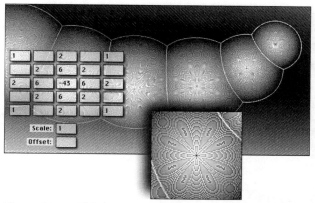

Figure 10-26: This image was filtered by entering some pretty extreme edge-detection values into the Custom dialog box (inset lower left). Edge-detection snowflakes (magnified inset) tend to be more spectacular than their Unsharp Mask equivalents.

Gradations as masks

If you think that the Feather command is a hot tool for creating softened selection outlines, wait until you get a load of gradations in the quick mask mode. There's no better way to create fading effects than selecting an image with the gradient tool.

Fading an image

Consider the Moses set against a white background in Figure 10-27. He's high art, he's got a beard that just won't quit, and he's got muscles bulging out of every corner of his body, including his neck, for heaven's sake. Now suppose that you decide that maybe Moses could be even more impressive if he were to fade into view. You're in luck, because that is one of the easiest effects to pull off in Photoshop.

Switch to the quick mask mode by pressing the Q key. Then use the gradient tool to draw a linear gradation from black to white. The white portion of the gradation represents the portion of the image that you want to select. To select and delete the bottom portion of Moses, draw the gradation from top to bottom, as shown in the first example of Figure 10-28.

Banding is typically even more noticeable when you use a gradation as a selection outline. Therefore, to eliminate the banding effect, apply the Add Noise filter at a low setting several times. To create the right example in Figure 10-28, the Add Noise filter was applied six times using an Amount value of 8 and the Uniform distribution option.

Figure 10-27: Michelangelo's Moses on a white background.

Figure 10-28: After drawing a linear gradation in the quick mask mode from top to bottom (left), the Add Noise filter was applied six times to mix up the colors a bit (right). Both images are shown narrower than their actual size.

To apply the gradation as a selection, return to the marching ants mode by again pressing Q. Press Ctrl-H so that you can see what you're doing. With white as the background color, press Delete to fill the selected portion of the image with white, creating a fading effect. In Figure 10-29, a faded Moses was combined with a traditional gradient background created in the marching ants mode.

Figure 10-29: The result of selecting the bottom portion of the image with a gradation and pressing Delete to fill it with white. A gradient background was also added to make the image more powerful.

Applying special effects gradually

You also can use gradations in the quick mask mode to taper the outcomes of filters and other automated special effects. For example, we applied a filter around the edges of the banner image that appears in Figure 10-30 by switching to the quick mask mode, choosing Select⇨All (Ctrl-A), and pressing Alt-Del to fill the entire mask with black. After double-clicking on the gradient tool icon in the toolbox , we selected Linear from the Type pop-up menu inside the Gradient Tool Options panel and then selected Lighten from the brush modes pop-up menu in the upper left corner. (The default option, Foreground to Background, was selected in the Style pop-up menu.)

We made the foreground color white and the background color black by pressing the X key. Dragging the gradient tool from each of the four edges of the image inward created a series of short gradations that trace the boundaries of the banner, as shown in Figure 10-31. The white areas of the figure represent the portions of the image that were selected.

Figure 10-30: The background around the banner was highlighted by applying a gradual filtering effect.

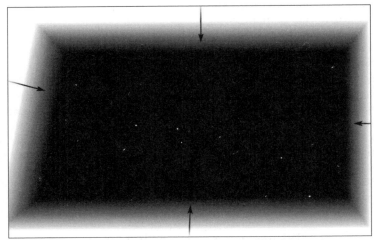

Figure 10-31: Inside the quick mask mode, the gradient tool was dragged from each of the four edges (as indicated by the arrows). The Lighten brush mode was active; white and black were the foreground and background colors, respectively.

After the preceding steps, we selected the marching ants mode and applied the desired effect, which in this case was the Color Halftone filter from the Filter⇨Stylize submenu. The result appears in Figure 10-32.

Tip Notice the harsh corners in the mask in Figure 10-31? They were needed for the effect in Figure 10-32, but you may not always want them. To bevel the corners, either select the Foreground to Transparent option from the Style pop-up menu or select the Screen option from the brush modes pop-up menu. For a really unusual corner treatment, leave the Style option set to Foreground to Background and choose Difference from the brush modes menu.

Figure 10-32: After switching back to the marching ants mode, Filter⇨Stylize⇨Color Halftone was chosen to create the halftoning effect shown here.

Applying Strokes and Arrowheads

The "Painting along a path" section of Chapter 8 discussed how to use one of the paint or edit tools to trace along a path created with the pen tool. The following sections discuss the more mundane aspects of stroking, namely how to apply a border around a selection outline (which isn't particularly interesting) and create arrowheads (which can yield more interesting results than you might think).

Stroking a selection outline

Stroking is useful for creating frames and outlines. Generally speaking, you can stroke an image in Photoshop in three ways:

✦ **Using the Stroke command:** Select the portion of the image that you want to stroke and then choose Edit⇨Stroke to display the Stroke dialog box shown in Figure 10-33. Enter the thickness of the stroke, in pixels, into the Width option box. Select a Location radio button to specify the position of the stroke with respect to the selection outline. The Stroke dialog box also includes Opacity, Mode, and Preserve Transparency options that work just like those in the Fill dialog box.

When in doubt, select Inside from the Location radio buttons. This ensures that the stroke is entirely inside the selection outline in case you decide to move the selection. If you select Center or Outside, Photoshop applies part or all of the stroke to the deselected area around the selection outline.

✦ **Using the Border command:** Don't forget about Select➪Modify➪Border, described back in Chapter 8. Select a portion of the image and choose the Border command to retain only the outline of the selection. Specify the size of the border by entering a value, in pixels, into the Width option box and pressing Enter. To fill the border with the background color, press Delete. To fill the border with the foreground color, press Alt-Del. To apply a repeating pattern to the border, choose Edit➪Fill and select the Pattern option from the Use pop-up menu. You can even apply a command under the Filter menu or some other special effect.

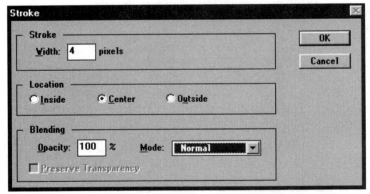

Figure 10-33: Use the options in the Stroke dialog box to specify the thickness of a stroke and its location with respect to the selection outline.

✦ **Framing the image:** Okay, so this is a throwaway, but it's pretty useful just the same. To create an outline around the entire image, change the background color to the color that you want to apply to the outline. Then choose Image➪Canvas Size and add twice the desired border thickness to the Width and Height options, in pixels. For example, to create a 1-pixel border, add 2 pixels to the Width value (1 for the left side and 1 for the right) and 2 pixels to the Height value (1 for the top edge and 1 for the bottom). When you press Enter, Photoshop enlarges the canvas size according to your specifications and fills the new pixels around the perimeter of the image with the background color.

Applying arrowheads

The one function missing from all the operations in the previous list is applying arrowheads. The fact is, in Photoshop, you can only apply arrowheads to straight lines drawn with the line tool. To create an arrowhead, double-click on the line tool icon in the toolbox (or press N to select the line tool and then press Enter) to display the Line Tool Options panel shown in Figure 10-34. Enter a value into the Line Width option box to specify the thickness of the line — better known as the line's *weight* — and then use the Arrowheads options as follows:

✦ **Start:** Select this check box to append an arrowhead to the beginning of a line drawn with the line tool.

✦ **End:** Select this check box to append an arrowhead to the end of a line. (Like you needed us to tell you *that*.)

✦ **Shape:** Click on the Shape button to display the Arrowhead Shape dialog box, which also appears in Figure 10-34.

The Arrowhead Shape dialog box contains three options that let you specify the size and shape of the arrowhead as a function of the line weight:

✦ **Width:** Enter the width of the arrowhead, in pixels, into this option box. The width of the arrowhead is completely independent of line weight.

✦ **Length:** Enter the length of the arrowhead, measured from the base of the arrowhead to its tip, into this option box. Again, length is measured in pixels and is independent of line weight.

✦ **Concavity:** You can specify the shape of the arrowhead by entering a value, between negative and positive 50 percent, into the Concavity option box. Figure 10-35 shows examples of a few Concavity settings applied to an arrowhead 50 pixels wide and 100 pixels long.

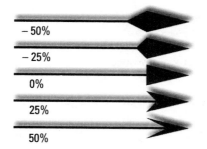

Figure 10-35: Examples of a 50 × 100-pixel arrowhead subject to five different Concavity values.

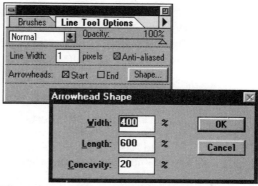

Figure 10-34: Click on the Shape button in the Line Tool Options panel (top) to display the Arrowhead Shape dialog box (bottom). The line tool remains the only way to create arrowheads in Photoshop.

Appending arrowheads onto curved lines

Applying arrowheads to straight lines is a simple matter. Double-click on the line tool icon, select a few choice options, and draw a line with the line tool. Applying an arrowhead to a stroked selection outline is a little trickier, but still possible. The following steps explain the process.

STEPS: Adding an arrowhead to a free-form stroke

1. You revert your image later in these steps, so save your image to disk now by choosing File⇨Save.

2. Draw any selection outline you desire, and stroke it by choosing Edit ⇨Stroke and applying whatever settings strike your fancy. Remember the value you enter into the Width option. In Figure 10-36, we applied a 2-point stroke to a circular marquee.

Figure 10-36: Stroke a selection, deselect it, and Alt-drag with the eraser tool to create gaps in the stroke for the arrowheads.

3. Choose Select⇨None (Ctrl-D) to deselect all portions of the image.

4. As you'll discover in the next chapter, the eraser tool allows you to revert portions of an image to their previous appearance. Select the eraser tool by pressing the E key and Alt-click anywhere in the image window to instruct Photoshop to load the saved image into memory. When the cursor returns to its eraserlike appearance, Alt-drag to revert the portions of the stroke at which you want to add arrowheads. To add arrowheads around the lions' tongues, Alt-drag around each tongue as demonstrated in Figure 10-36.

5. Double-click on the line tool icon. Enter the line weight that you used when stroking the selection outline (Step 2) into the Line Width option box. Select the Start check box and deselect the End check box, if necessary. Then click on the Shape button and specify the width, length, and concavity of the arrowhead as desired.

6. Zoom in on the point in the image at which you want to add the arrowhead. Draw a very short line exactly the length of the arrowhead at the tip of the stroke, as demonstrated in Figure 10-37. This may take some practice to accomplish. Make sure to start the line a few pixels away from the end of the stroke, because the tip of the arrowhead is narrower than the line weight. If you mess up the first time, choose Edit ⇨Undo (Ctrl-Z) and try again.

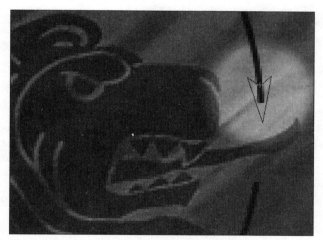

Figure 10-37: Draw a line no longer than the arrowhead with the line tool to append the arrowhead to the end of the stroke. The view size of this image is magnified 400 percent.

That's all there is to it. From there on, you just keep attaching as many arrowheads as you like. Figure 10-38 shows four arrowheads attached to the circular stroke, one above and one below each of the two tongues. Notice that the area of the stroke that overlapped the lions' manes is also reverted. We then created a circular feather marquee inside the circular stroke and drew six large arrowheads inside the selection mask. Finally, we inversed the selection and applied the Tiles and Radial Blur filters.

Figure 10-38: The finished image contains four arrowheads at the end of free-form strokes, as well as six additional arrows inside a feathered selection.

The old translucent-gradient-arrowheads-with-halos trick

The exercise in the following set of steps takes advantage of several things you've learned throughout the chapter. Back in Figure 9-19 in the preceding chapter, a bunch of arrowheads join a bunch of layers to the images that resided on those layers inside the document. Those arrowheads could have been created in a drawing program to get nice sharp points and smooth outlines. They were created in Photoshop to take advantage of two options that drawing programs don't offer: gradient lines and halos.

Now you might be thinking *Gee wizickers, you can't create gradient lines in Photoshop either.* Of course you can. Would the topic be here if you couldn't do it? Just quit interrupting for a moment and you'll find out how.

The following steps explain how to add fading arrows as shown in Figure 10-39.

Stpes: Creating fading arrows with halos

1. Save your image (Ctrl-S), deselect everything (Ctrl-D), and switch to the quick mask mode (Q). The image should appear absolutely normal.

2. Double-click on the line tool icon in the toolbox, and adjust the line weight and arrowhead settings in the Line Tool Option panel to fit your needs. To create our first arrow (the one that comes inward from the corner in Figure 10-39), we set the Line Width value to 20 and the Width, Length, and Concavity values in the Arrowhead Shape dialog box to 400, 600, and 20, respectively.

Figure 10-39: Drag from the point at which you want the arrow to begin fading to the base of the line (left) parallel to the line itself (indicated here by the white arrow) to fade the line out (right).

3. Press D to switch to the default colors. Then draw your line, which will show up in red. (If you don't get it right the first time, as is often the case with this tool, just press Ctrl-Z and try again.) The beauty of drawing a line in the quick mask mode is that you can edit it without damaging the image. (You could also do the same on a separate layer, but the quick mask mode affords you a little more flexibility in this specific exercise.)

4. Double-click on the gradient tool icon in the toolbox, and make sure that the Style option is set to Foreground to Background, the Type option is set to Linear, and the Opacity slider is set to 100 percent. Then choose Lighten from the brush modes pop-up menu.

5. You can now use the gradient tool to fade the base of the line. Drag with the gradient tool from the point at which you want the line to begin to fade down to the base of the line. Try to make the direction of your drag parallel to the line itself, thus ensuring a smooth fade. The first example in Figure 10-39 shows the progress of dragging along one of our arrows with the gradient tool. The small white arrow shows the direction of the drag. (The black line shows the actual cursor that you see on-screen.) The second example shows the result of the drag.

6. Choose Image⇨Map⇨Invert (Ctrl-I) to invert the quick mask, thus making the arrow the selected area.

7. Drag the quick mask item in the Channels palette onto the new channel icon at the bottom of the palette to copy the quick mask to a permanent mask channel. You'll need it again.

8. Time now to create the halo. Press Q to switch back to the marching ants mode. Choose Select➪Modify➪Expand and enter the desired value. As described in the "Creating drop shadows, halos, and spotlights" section earlier in this chapter, base the value on the resolution of your image. We entered 6.

9. Choose Select➪Feather, enter the same value, and press Enter.

10. Make sure that the default colors are in force. (Just because they're in force in the quick mask mode doesn't mean that they are in the marching ants mode, so you may want to press D to be sure.) Then press the Delete key to fill the selected areas with white.

11. Alt-click on the Quick Mask Copy item in the Channels palette to regain your original arrow selection outlines.

12. Choose Select➪Fill to bring up the Fill dialog box. Then select Saved from the Use pop-up menu to revert the portion of the image inside the arrows, and press Enter.

13. Float the selection outlines by pressing Ctrl-J. Change the foreground color to your favorite color, and press Alt-Delete to fill the selection.

14. Press the M key to activate a selection tool. Then choose Multiply from the overlay modes pop-up menu in the upper left corner of the Layers palette, and press a number key to change the Opacity setting. We used 4 for 40 percent.

After that, the process was repeated to keep adding more and more arrows. Every once in a while, the image was saved so more arrows could be created on top of arrows. Most notably, the image was saved before adding the last big arrow that shoots up from the bottom. When the arrow was filled with the saved version, bits and pieces of a couple of the other arrows were brought back. (Without first saving the image, the arrow fragments behind the big arrow would have disappeared.)

Duplicating and Reverting

Introducing the Amalgamated Rubber Stamp

This chapter is primarily about just one tool, the rubber stamp tool. Although the eraser figures into the reversion discussion in this chapter, and there's even a small reference to the pencil tool, the main ingredient is the rubber stamp tool. This tool provides four distinct but loosely related distinct capabilities, every one of which deserves to be split off into a tool of its own.

The name *rubber stamp* is pretty misleading because this particular tool has nothing to do with rubber stamps. First of all, no tree sap is involved — let's get that sticky issue resolved right off the bat. Secondly, you don't use it to stamp an image. When you think of rubber stamps, you may think of those things you see in stationery stores that plunk down laudatory exclamations and smiley faces and Pooh bears. Elementary school teachers and little kids use rubber stamps. You never see a professional image editor walking around with a rubber stamp, do you?

So put rubber stamps entirely out of your mind for the moment. To discover exactly what the stamp tool does, you must double-click on its icon in the toolbox. Photoshop then displays the Rubber Stamp Options panel of the Brushes palette, shown in Figure 11-1. In addition to the standard brush modes pop-up menu, Opacity slider, Stylus Pressure options, and Sample Merged check box provided with half a dozen paint and edit tools (see Chapter 7 if your memory's getting a tad fuzzy), the Rubber Stamp Options panel includes an Option pop-up menu. The real heart of the tool, this pop-up menu includes the following options:

In This Chapter

A complete description of the rubber stamp tool and its many settings

Cloning portions of an image to touch up blemishes and eliminate elements from an image

Using the rubber stamp to paint with a repeating pattern

A step-by-step guide to creating seamless patterns and textures

Descriptions of the Undo and Revert commands

Lots of kudos for the newly enhanced eraser tool

Ways to use the magic eraser and rubber stamp tools to selectively revert portions of an image

An explanation of the Take Snapshot command

✦ **Cloning:** Select one of the two Clone options to duplicate portions of an image by dragging over it. Alt-click with the tool to specify a point of reference and then drag in a different area of the image to begin cloning. (Don't worry, we cover the difference between the two Clone options in the upcoming "Aligned and non-aligned cloning" section.)

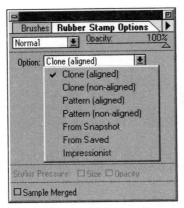

Figure 11-1: Select an option from the Option pop-up menu to define the way the rubber stamp tool works.

✦ **Pattern application:** Select one of the two Pattern options to paint an image with a repeating pattern rather than the standard foreground color. Before using this option, you must establish a pattern by selecting a portion of the image and choosing Edit⇨Define Pattern.

✦ **Reversion:** The From Snapshot option lets you use the rubber stamp tool to revert portions of your image to the way they appeared when you last chose Edit⇨Take Snapshot. From Saved enables you to revert portions of an image to the way they appeared when you last saved the image.

✦ **Impressionist:** The last option, Impressionist, retrieves the last saved version of the image and sort of smears it around to create a gooey, unfocused effect. You can achieve some mildly interesting and halfway useful effects — and we're being generous here — by combining this function with the Overlay, Hard Light, or Soft Light brush modes, but it wouldn't be our first choice for any job. This is our nomination for the least useful of the rubber stamp settings, and this is the last time we'll mention it.

Note If there is a tie that binds the rubber stamp's various capabilities, it is the fact that most of them enable you to paint with images. When you clone with the rubber stamp tool, for example, you paint with a displaced version of the image itself. When you paint a pattern, you paint with an image fragment. When you revert, you paint with the saved version of the image. Even Impressionist paints with the saved image in its own skewed sort of way. (Ah, man, we weren't going to mention that option again.)

As you can see, a better name for the rubber stamp tool might be the *clone/pattern/revert/stupid effects tool* or maybe the *junk-drawer tool*. Then again, *the mother of all mixed-up tools* has a certain ring to it. In any case, the remainder of this chapter explores every one of the rubber stamp's capabilities.

Cloning Image Elements

So far, our take on the rubber stamp tool may sound a bit derogatory. But in truth, most of its capabilities can come in very handy. All except that dumb Impressionist option — which, really, we're going to stop mentioning.

Take cloning, for example. As any dyed-in-the-wool Photoshop user will tell you, the rubber stamp is an invaluable tool for touching up images, whether you want to remove dust fragments, hairs, and other blotches scanned with a photo or eliminate portions of an image (as described in the "Softening selection outlines" section of Chapter 8).

You also can use the rubber stamp to duplicate specific elements in an image, such as flowers and umbrellas, as described in the Photoshop manual. But by all accounts, this is an inefficient use of the tool. If you want to duplicate an element, you'll have better luck if you select it and clone it by Alt-dragging the selection. By taking that approach, you can specify the exact boundaries of the element, the softness of its edges, and the precise location of the clone. Duplicating by cloning an element with the rubber stamp is more of an ordeal, because it's easy to accidentally clone areas around the element and to begin a clone in the wrong location.

The cloning process

To clone part of an image, double-click on the rubber stamp tool icon and select either the Clone (aligned) or Clone (non-aligned) option. (The upcoming section explains the difference between the two.) Alt-click in the image window to specify a point of reference in the portion of the image you want to clone. Then click or drag with the tool in some other region of the image to paint a cloned spot or line.

Figure 11-2, for example, was created by first Alt-clicking just above and to the right of the bird's head, as demonstrated by the appearance of the stamp pickup cursor. We then painted the line shown inside the white rectangle. The rubber stamp cursor shows the end of the drag; the cross-shaped clone reference cursor shows the corresponding point in the original image.

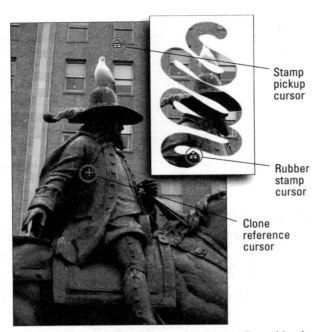

Stamp
pickup
cursor

Rubber
stamp
cursor

Clone
reference
cursor

Figure 11-2: After Alt-clicking at the point indicated by the stamp pickup cursor, we painted the image by dragging with the rubber stamp tool. (The only reason for painting inside the white rectangle is so that you can see the line better.)

Photoshop lets you clone not only from within the image you're working on, but also from an entirely separate image window. This technique enables you to merge two different images together, as demonstrated in Figure 11-3. To achieve this effect, Alt-click in one image, bring a second image to the foreground, and then drag with the rubber stamp tool to clone from the first image.

Aligned and non-aligned cloning

Now that we've explained how to use the tool, we return to the options in the Rubber Stamp Options panel:

✦ **Clone (aligned):** To understand how this option works, think of the locations where you Alt-click and begin dragging with the rubber stamp tool as opposite ends of an imaginary straight line, as illustrated in the top half of Figure 11-4. The length and angle of that imaginary line remains fixed until you Alt-click a second time. As you drag, Photoshop moves the line, cloning pixels from one end of the line and laying them down at the other. Regardless of how many times you start and stop dragging with the stamp tool, all lines match up as seamlessly as pieces in a puzzle.

✦ **Clone (non-aligned):** If you want to repeatedly clone from a single portion of an image, select this option. The second example in Figure 11-4 shows how the length and angle of the imaginary line change every time you paint a new line with the rubber stamp tool.

Figure 11-3: We merged the area around horse and rider with a water image from another open window (see the upcoming Figure 11-6). The translucent effects were created by periodically adjusting the Opacity slider bar to settings ranging from 50 to 80 percent.

Stamp differences

When cloning, the Photoshop 3 rubber stamp tool works just like the Version 2.5 rubber stamp, which is different from the previous Mac-only Version 2 stamp. The Version 2 setup had its merits. In Version 2, the rubber stamp clones the image as it exists before you start using the tool. Even when you drag over an area that contains a clone, the tool references the original appearance of the image to prevent recloning. This keeps you from creating more than one clone during a single drag, as witnessed in the first example of Figure 11-5.

Figure 11-4: Select the Clone (aligned) option to instruct Photoshop to clone an image continuously, no matter how many lines you paint (top). If you select Clone (non-aligned), Photoshop clones each new line from the point at which you Alt-click.

In Photoshop 3, however, any changes you make to the image affect the tool as you use it, which can result in repeating patterns like those shown in the second example of the figure. Although you can create some interesting effects, avoid cloning and recloning areas when retouching, because it can result in obvious patterns that betray your adjustments.

Tip   To avoid recloning areas, clone from a duplicate of the image. Begin by choosing Image⇨Duplicate to create a copy of the current image (as explained back in Chapter 3). Alt-click with the rubber stamp tool somewhere in the duplicate window. Then switch to the original image and drag freely with the tool to clone from the duplicate. Because your changes don't affect the duplicate image, there's no chance of recloning.

Figure 11-5: Photoshop 2's rubber stamp tool clones the image as it exists before you start using the tool (top). That, of course, was when Photoshop was Mac-only (so we have to trust Deke). In Version 3, the tool clones and reclones images during a single drag (bottom).

Touching up blemishes

One of the best uses for the rubber stamp tool is to touch up a scanned photo. Figure 11-6 shows a Photo CD image that desperately needs the stamp tool's attention. Normally, Kodak's Photo CD process delivers some of the best consumer-quality scans money can buy. But this particular medium-resolution image looks like the folks at the lab got together and blew their respective noses on it. It's a little late to go back to the service bureau and demand that it rescan the photo, so the only option is to touch it up in Photoshop.

The best way to fix this image — or any image like it — is to use the rubber stamp over and over again, repeatedly Alt-clicking at one location and then clicking at another. Begin by selecting a brush shape that's a little larger than the largest blotch. Of the default brushes, the hard-edged varieties with diameters of 5 and 9 pixels generally work best. (The soft-edged brush shapes have a tendency to incompletely cover the blemishes.)

Alt-click with the stamp tool at a location that is very close to the blemish and features similarly colored pixels. Then click — do not drag — directly on the blemish. The idea is to change as few pixels as possible.

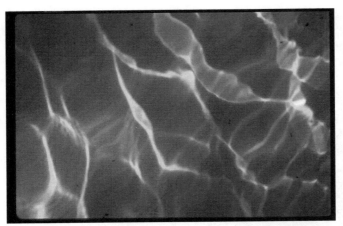

Figure 11-6: This appallingly bad Photo CD image is riddled with blotches and big hurky wads of dust that didn't exist on the original 35mm slide.

If the retouched area doesn't look quite right, choose Edit⇨Undo (Ctrl-Z), Alt-click at a different location, and try again. If your touch-up appears seamless — *absolutely* seamless — move on to the next blemish, repeating the Alt-click and click routine for every dust mark on the photo.

This process isn't necessarily time-consuming, but it does require patience. For example, although it took more than 40 Alt-click and click combinations (not counting 10 or so undos) to arrive at the image shown in Figure 11-7, the process itself took less than 15 minutes. Boring, but fast.

It's a little trickier to retouch hairs than dust and other blobs. That's because a hair, although very thin, can be surprisingly long. However, the retouching process is the same. Rather than dragging over the entire length of the hair, Alt-click and click your way through it, bit by little bit. The one difference is brush shape. Because you'll be clicking so many times in succession and because the hair is so thin, you'll probably achieve the least conspicuous effects if you use a soft brush shape, such as the default 9-pixel model in the second row of the Brushes palette.

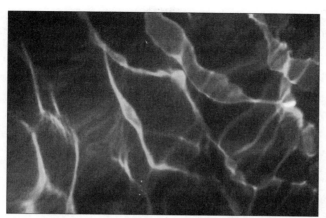

Figure 11-7: The result of Alt-clicking and clicking more than 40 times on the photo shown in Figure 11-6. Notice that the image has been cropped and a border has been added. Now the image can be used as a background, as in Figure 11-3.

Cross Ref

Before going to the effort with the rubber stamp tool, you might want to first check how well the new Dust & Scratches filter (Filter⇨Noise⇨Dust & Scratches) remedies your problems. It performed remarkably poorly where Figure 11-6 was concerned, but if your image isn't quite so bad, it may help a good deal. To find out more information on this and other corrective filters, read Chapter 13.

Tip

The rubber stamp cursor is the most intrusive of all Photoshop's cursors. After all, when you're cloning an element, you need to see exactly what you're doing. You don't need to see a blocky icon that has nothing to do with the current operation. To get rid of this eyesore and view a simple crosshair cursor instead, press the Caps Lock key. You can also go into the General Preferences dialog box (Ctrl-K) and select the Brush Size radio button, but this does not affect the appearance of the stamp cursor when you press the Alt key.

Eliminating distracting background elements

Another way to apply the stamp tool's cloning capabilities is to eliminate background action that competes with the central elements in an image. Figure 11-8, for example, shows a one-in-a-million news photo from the Reuters image library. Although the image is well-photographed and historic in its implications — in case you missed the last decade, that's Comrade V. I. Lenin (Vlad to his mom) — that rear workman doesn't contribute anything to the scene and, in fact, draws your attention away from the foreground drama. (*Hail to the worker* and everything, but the image would be better off without him.) The following steps explain how the offending workman was eradicated from the scene.

Note   Keep in mind as you read the following steps that deleting an image element with the rubber stamp tool is something of an inexact science; it requires some trial and error. So regard the following steps as an example of how to approach the process of editing your image rather than a specific procedure that works for all images. You may need to adapt the process slightly depending upon your image.

Figure 11-8: You have to love that old Soviet state-endorsed art. So bold, so angular, so politically intolerant. But you also have to lose that rear workman.

Steps: Eliminating distracting elements from an image

1. First, we cloned the area around the neck of the statue with a soft brush shape. Abandoning the controlled clicks recommended in the last section, we dragged the tool because relatively large portions of the image needed to be covered. The apartment building (or whatever that structure is) behind the floating head is magnificently out of focus, just the thing for hiding any incongruous transitions that might be created with the rubber stamp. So we retouched this part of the image first. Figure 11-9 shows our progress.

Notice that we covered the workman's body by cloning pixels from both his left and right sides. We added a vertical bar where the workman's right arm used to be to maintain the rhythm of the building. Remember that variety is the key to using the rubber stamp tool; if you consistently clone from one portion of the image, you create an obvious repetition that the viewer can't help but notice.

Figure 11-9: Cloning over the background worker's upper torso was fairly easy because the background building is so regular and out of focus, providing a wealth of material from which to clone.

2. The next step was to eliminate the workman's head. This was a little tricky because it involved rubbing up against the focused perimeter of Lenin's neck. We cloned the more intricate areas using a hard-edged brush; also, we duplicated some of the neck edges to maintain continuity. In addition, we touched up the left side of the neck (your left, not Lenin's) and removed a few of the white spots from his face. You see our progress in Figure 11-10.

Figure 11-10: The workman's head is eliminated and details are touched up around the perimeter of the neck.

3. Now for the hard part, eliminating the worker's legs and lower torso. See that fragment of metal that the foreground worker is holding? What a pain. Its edges were so irregular that there was no way to restore it with the rubber stamp tool if we made a mistake while trying to eradicate the background worker's limbs. So we selected the fragment by lassoing and then chose Select⇨Inverse to protect it. Choosing Select⇨Feather and giving it a Radius value of 1 slightly softens its edges. This prevents changes to the metal, no matter what edits are made to the background worker's remaining body parts.

4. From here on out, it was just more cloning. Unfortunately, there was barely anything to clone from. See that little bit of black edging between the two "legs" of the metal fragment? That's it. That's all we had to draw the strip of edging to the right of the fragment that eventually appears in Figure 11-11. To pull off this feat, we double-clicked on the rubber stamp tool icon in the toolbox and chose the Clone (non-aligned) option. After Alt-clicking on the tiny bit of edging, just click, click, click down the street.

5. Unfortunately, the strip laid down in step 4 appeared noticeably blobular — it looked for all the world like a bunch of clicks. Darn. To fix this problem, we clicked and Shift-clicked with the smudge tool set to about 30 percent pressure. This smeared the blobs into a continuous strip, but again, the effect was noticeable. It looked like a smeared strip. The solution was more cloning, this time with the Opacity slider bar set to 50 percent.

6. To polish off the image, we chose Select⇨None (Ctrl-D) and passed the sharpen tool along the edges of the metal fragment. This helped to hide the retouching around it and further distinguished the fragment from the unfocused background. Also we cropped away 20 or so pixels from the right side of the image to correct the balance of the image.

Figure 11-11: After about 45 minutes worth of monkeying around with the rubber stamp tool — a practice declared illegal during Stalin's reign — the rear workman is gone, leaving an unfettered view of the dubious one himself.

This section demonstrates that cloning with the rubber stamp tool requires that you alternate between patching and whittling away. There are no rights and wrongs, no hard-and-fast rules. Anything you can find to clone is fair game. As long as you avoid mucking up the foreground image, you can't go wrong (so maybe there is *one* hard-and-fast rule). If you're careful and diligent, no one but you is going to notice your alterations.

Caution Any time you edit the contents of a photograph, you tread on very sensitive ground. Though some have convincingly argued that electronically retouching an image is theoretically no different from cropping a photograph, a technique that has been available and in use since the first daguerreotype, photographers have certain rights under copyright law that cannot be ignored. A photographer may have a reason for including an element that you wish to eliminate. So before you edit any photograph, be sure to get permission either from the original photographer or from the copyright holder.

Applying Repeating Patterns

Before you can use the rubber stamp tool to paint with a pattern, you must define a pattern by selecting a portion of the image with the rectangular marquee tool and choosing Edit⇨Define Pattern. For the Define Pattern command to work, you must use the rectangular marquee — no other selection tool will do. In addition, the selection cannot be feathered, smoothed, expanded, or in any other way altered. If it is, the command is dimmed.

Figure 11-12 shows an example of how you can apply repeating patterns. The single apartment window (surrounded by marching ants) was selected and Edit⇨Define Pattern was chosen. The pattern was applied with the rubber stamp tool at 80 percent opacity over the horse and rider statue.

Caution Like the Clipboard, Photoshop can retain only one pattern at a time and remembers the pattern throughout a single session. Any time you choose Edit⇨Define Pattern, you delete the previous pattern as you create a new one. Photoshop also deletes the pattern when you quit the program. Therefore, each time you launch Photoshop, you must define the pattern from scratch.

Pattern options

To paint with a pattern, double-click on the rubber stamp tool icon and select either the Pattern (aligned) or Pattern (non-aligned) option from the Option pop-up menu in the Rubber Stamp Options panel. These options work as follows:

✦ **Pattern (aligned):** Select this option to align all patterns you apply with the stamp tool, regardless of how many times you start and stop dragging. The two left examples in Figure 11-13 show the effects of selecting this option. The elements in the pattern remain exactly aligned throughout all the lines. The top image was painted with the Opacity slider bar set to 50 percent, which is why the lines darken when they meet.

✦ **Pattern (non-aligned):** To allow patterns in different lines to align randomly, select this option. The positioning of the pattern within each line is determined by the point at which you begin dragging. We dragged from right to left to paint the horizontal lines and from top to bottom to paint the vertical lines. The two right examples in Figure 11-13 show how nonaligned patterns overlap.

Figure 11-12: After marqueeing a single window (top) and choosing Edit⇨Define Pattern, we painted a translucent coat of the pattern over the statue with the rubber stamp tool (bottom).

After you select Pattern (aligned) or Pattern (non-aligned), you're free to start dragging with the stamp tool. You don't need to Alt-click or make any other special provisions, as you do when cloning.

Cross Ref   As discussed in Chapter 10, you can also apply a pattern to a selected portion of an image by choosing Edit⇨Fill and selecting the Pattern option from the Use pop-up menu. The problem with this technique is that it involves choosing Edit⇨Define Pattern to establish the pattern in the first place. Photoshop 3 offers a new function that lets you load an image from disk and apply it as a repeating pattern throughout the selection. Choose Filter⇨Render⇨Texture Fill to open any image saved in the native Photoshop format and then repeat it as many times as the selection will permit.

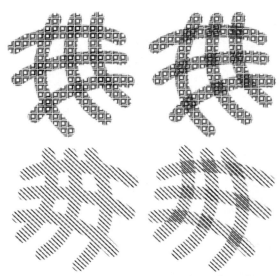

Figure 11-13: Select the Pattern (aligned) option to align the patterns in all brush strokes painted with the stamp tool (left). If you select Pattern (non-aligned), Photoshop aligns each pattern with the beginning of the line (right).

How to create patterns

The biggest difficulty with painting patterns is not figuring out the rubber stamp tool, but creating the patterns in the first place. Ideally, your pattern should repeat continuously, without vertical and horizontal seams. Here are some ways to create repeating, continuous patterns:

✦ **Load a displacement map:** Photoshop offers a Displacement Maps (DISPMAPS by default) directory below the Plug-ins directory. This directory contains several images, each of which represents a different repeating pattern, as illustrated in Figure 11-14. To use one of these patterns, open the image, choose Select⊃All (Ctrl-A), and choose Edit⊃Define Pattern. (For more information on displacement maps, see Chapter 15.)

✦ **Illustrator patterns:** Check out the Patterns subdirectory of your main Photoshop directory. You'll find 20 Adobe Illustrator files that contain repeating object patterns. The patterns, some of which appear in Figure 11-15, are all seamless repeaters. You can open them and rasterize them to any size you like. Then press Ctrl-A, choose Edit⊃Define Pattern, and you have your pattern.

If you have problems opening these patterns — and some do — you've run into an issue that, as I write this, is still uncertain. See "Quirky but important formats: EPS and DCS" in Chapter 3 for further details.

Robert

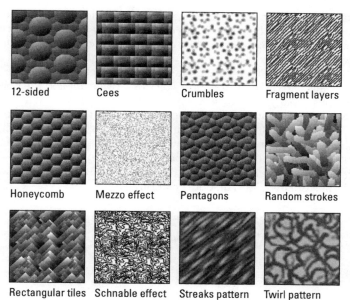

Figure 11-14: The 12 patterns contained in \PLUG-INS\DISPMAPS below the main Photoshop directory.

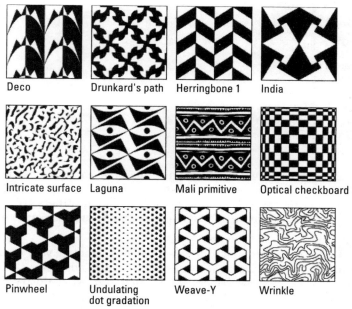

Figure 11-15: A random sampling of the illustrations contained in the Patterns directory below the main Photoshop directory.

✦ **Using filters:** As luck would have it, you can create your own custom textures without painting a single line. In fact, you can create a nearly infinite variety of textures by applying several filters to a blank document. To create the texture shown in the bottom right box in Figure 11-16, for example, a 128 × 128-pixel area was selected. After choosing Filter⇨Noise⇨Add Noise, we entered the value 32, and selected the Gaussian radio button. Pressing Ctrl-F twice applied the noise filter two more times. Finally, we chose Filter⇨Stylize⇨Emboss; we entered 135 into the Angle option box, 1 into the Height option box, and 100 percent into the Amount option box. The result is a bumpy surface that looks like stucco. This is merely one example of the myriad possibilities filters afford. There's no end to what you can do, so experiment away. (For more information on using Add Noise, see Chapter 13, "Corrective Filtering." For info about Emboss and other filter commands, see Chapter 14, "Full-Court Filtering.")

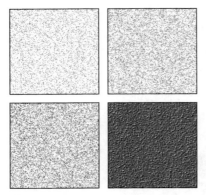

Figure 11-16: To create a stucco texture, apply Filter⇨Noise⇨Add Noise three times in a row (upper left, upper right, lower left). Then choose Filter⇨Stylize⇨Emboss and enter a Height value of 1 (lower right).

✦ **Marquee and clone:** You can use the rectangular marquee and rubber stamp tools to transform a scanned image into a custom pattern. Because this technique is more complicated as well as more rewarding than the others, we explain it in the upcoming section, "Steps: Building a repeating pattern from a scanned image."

✦ **Texture collections:** If you don't have the time or energy to create your own custom patterns but you do have some extra cash lying around, all sorts of texture libraries are available on CD-ROM. It's a veritable growth industry. Figure 11-17 shows some examples.

Robert

There's a bit more to keep in mind about texture collections. Some of the collections are very good, some are very good for specific uses, and some are terrible (we name no names). Check carefully for two things. You may want patterns that tile seamlessly; that is, they don't look as if they're composed of one block repeated several times. If so, check carefully — if the patterns are seamless, the manufacturer will be proud of it and will trumpet it. This can save you endless twiddles of a tile. Second, consider the usage. If you're working for screen resolution, virtually any collection will serve. But you may need higher-resolution images if you're aiming for an output device, especially a high-end one. Check carefully.

Robert

✦ **Roll your own:** Good as the commercial collections can be, you shouldn't be beholden to them. If you've got a scanner (and you surely do, because you've got Photoshop), be bold. Scan things and start tweaking them. Scan even not-so-obvious things — one of Deke's best textures started as a scan of a blue denim shirt. Scan objects too, and everything from sand to dry cat food — just be sure to protect the surface of your scanner.

Robert

There's another little-known source — the RAW image format, described in Chapter 3. Open a file, any file, in RAW format. You will be amazed at the working texture you've got. Another one of Deke's best textures started by opening the main Photoshop executable file in RAW format.

Figure 11-17: A repeating texture from Form and Function's Wraptures collection (top), and a nonrepeating background image from D'pix's Folio collection (bottom).

The following steps describe how to change a scanned image into a seamless, repeating pattern. To illustrate how this process works, Figures 11-18 through 11-21 show various stages in a project. You need only two tools to carry out these steps: the rectangular marquee tool and the rubber stamp tool with the Clone (aligned) option active.

Steps: Building a repeating pattern from a scanned image

1. Begin by marqueeing a portion of your scanned image and copying it to the Clipboard. For best results, specify the exact size of your marquee by double-clicking on the rectangular marquee icon in the toolbox, selecting Fixed Size from the Style pop-up menu (in the Marquee Options panel), and entering specific values into the Width and Height option boxes. This way, you can easily reselect a portion of the pattern in the steps that follow and use the fixed-size marquee to define the pattern when you're finished. To create the patterns shown in the example, the marquee is set to 128 × 128 pixels.

2. Choose File⊅New (Ctrl-N) and triple the values Photoshop offers as the default image dimensions. In this case, Photoshop offered 128 × 128 pixels because that was the size of the image copied to the Clipboard. Therefore, the image size was changed to 384 × 384 pixels.

3. Paste the marqueed image into the new image window. It appears smack dab in the center of the window, which is exactly where you want it. This image will serve as the central tile of your repeating pattern. Clone the selection by Alt-dragging it eight times to create a 3 × 3-tile grid, as shown in Figure 11-18.

Figure 11-18: To build the repeating pattern shown in Figure 11-21, we began by creating a grid of nine image tiles. As you can see, the seams between the tiles in this grid are harsh and unacceptable.

4. Drag the title bar of the new image window to position it so that you can see the portion of the image you copied in the original image window. If necessary, Ctrl-drag the title bar of the original image window to reposition it as well. This way, you can clone from the original image without switching back and forth between windows.

5. Double-click on the rubber stamp tool icon in the toolbox, select the Clone (aligned) option, and press Enter to exit the dialog box.

6. To specify the image you want to clone, Alt-click with the stamp tool in the original image window — no need to switch out of the new window — on an easily identifiable pixel that belongs to the portion of the image you copied. The *exact* pixel you click is very important. If you press the Caps Lock key, you get the crosshair cursor, which allows you to narrow in on a pixel. In this case, we clicked on the center of Lenin's right eye.

7. Now click with the stamp tool on the matching pixel in the central tile of the new window. If you've clicked on the correct pixel, the tile should not change one iota. (If it does, choose Edit⇨Undo and repeat Steps 6 and 7.)

8. Now that you've aligned the cloned image within the new window, use the stamp tool to fill in portions of the central tile. For example, in Figure 11-19, the chin was extended down into the lower row of tiles, the central face was extended to meet the Lenin on the left, and the head was extended upward into the jawline of the top-row Lenin.

9. After you establish one continuous transition between two tiles in any direction — up, down, left, or right — select a portion of the image with the rectangular marquee tool and clone the selection repeatedly to fill out a single row or column. In this case, a smooth transition was created between the central and left-hand tiles. Therefore, a region was selected that includes half of the left tile and half of the central tile. Because the rectangular marquee was fixed to a 128 × 128-pixel square, clicking on an area selected it. (Drag to position the marquee exactly where you want it.) Next, that selection was cloned along the entire length of the middle row.

10. If you started by creating a horizontal transition, use the rubber stamp tool to now create a vertical transition. (Likewise, if you started vertically, now go horizontally.) You may very well need to Alt-click again on that special pixel in the original window. By Alt-clicking, you allow yourself to build onto one of the perimeter tiles. In this case it takes an Alt-click again in the original right eye. Next, click on the matching pixel in the left tile and drag around to build out the left Lenin's chin. To complete the vertical transition, we Alt-clicked a third time and then clicked on the matching pixel in the lower center tile, building a transition between the lower Lenin's head and the central Lenin's neck, as shown in Figure 11-20.

Figure 11-19: We used the rubber stamp's cloning capability to extend the features in the central face toward the left and downward.

Figure 11-20: After completing a smooth transition between the central tile and the tiles below and to the left of it, we selected a portion of the image and chose and Edit➪Define Pattern.

11. After you build up one set of both horizontal and vertical transitions, you can select a portion of the image and choose Edit⇨Define Pattern. Figure 11-20 shows where the 128 × 128-pixel selection boundary was positioned. It included both halves of the chin along with a smooth transition between head, jaw, and left side of the face (Lenin's left, that is). Don't worry that the image doesn't appear centered inside the selection outline. What counts is that the selection repeats seamlessly when placed beside itself.

12. To confirm that the pattern is indeed seamless and every bit as lovely as you had hoped, double-click on the rubber stamp icon in the toolbox and select the Pattern (aligned) option. After closing the Rubber Stamp Options dialog box, drag around inside the current image with the rubber stamp tool and a large brush shape. Figure 11-21 shows the seamless results of dragging.

13. Be sure to save your completed image. You don't want to go to all this trouble for nothing.

Figure 11-21: This Big Brother montage is the result of applying the Lenin pattern. We half expect him to say something about how the Great and Powerful Wizard of Oz has spoken, but we don't think that movie got out much in Russia.

Selectively Undoing Changes

Welcome to the second act of this chapter. It's a short act — more like a scene, really — so you'll have to forgo the intermission.

Now that we've explained the cloning and related patterning attributes of the rubber stamp tool, it's time to turn your attention — come on, turn, turn, just a little more, there you go — to a new topic. The rest of this chapter deals with *reversion,* which is a fancy word for returning your image to the way it looked before you went and made an unholy mess of it.

Using the traditional undo functions

Before we dive into the rubber stamp's reversion capabilities, allow us to introduce the more traditional reversion functions that are found in nearly all paint applications, including Photoshop:

✦ **Undo:** To restore an image to the way it looked before the last operation, choose Edit⇨Undo (Ctrl-Z). You can undo the effect of a paint or edit tool, a change made to a selection outline, or a special-effect or color-correction command. You can't undo disk operations, such as opening or saving. However, Photoshop does let you undo an edit after printing an image. You can test out an effect, print it, and then undo it if you think it looks awful.

✦ **Revert:** Choose File⇨Revert to reload an image from disk. Most folks think of this as the last-resort function, the command you choose after everything else has failed. But really, it's quite useful as a stopgap measure. Suppose that you're about to embark on a series of filtering operations that may or may not result in the desired effect. You're going to perform multiple operations, so you can't undo them if they don't work. Before choosing your first filter, choose File⇨Save. Now you're ready for anything. You can wreak a degree of havoc on your image that no user in his or her right mind would dare. If everything doesn't go exactly as you planned or hoped, you can simply choose File⇨Revert and you're back in business.

✦ **The eraser tool:** Drag with the eraser tool to paint in white or some other background color. This lets you revert portions of your image back to bare canvas.

The eraser is not hard-edged. If you double-click on the eraser — go ahead, it doesn't erase the entire image as it once did — you'll display the Eraser Options panel. As shown in Figure 11-22, the panel offers a pop-up menu of eraser styles. Block is the old 16 × 16-pixel square eraser that's great for hard-edged touch-ups. The other options work exactly like the tools for which they're named. And you don't even have to go to the trouble of selecting the options from the pop-up menu. When the eraser is selected, pressing the E key cycles through the different eraser styles. (Coincidentally, you can also select the eraser tool by pressing E.)

As if that weren't enough, the eraser is also pressure-sensitive, it responds to Opacity settings, and you can create fading eraser strokes. For cryin' in a bucket, you even have access to the Wet Edges check box described back in Chapter 7. The only thing missing is the brush modes menu, which we're afraid you'll just have to live without. (Of course, if you really need to access a brush mode, you can just switch the foreground and background colors and paint with the paintbrush, airbrush, or pencil.)

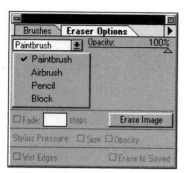

Figure 11-22: The eraser tool can now paint like the paintbrush, the airbrush, the pencil, or the old eraser (Block). The only question is: Why didn't Adobe do this a long time ago?

✦ **Erasing on a layer:** By now, some of you are probably thinking, *You know, why does Photoshop even have an eraser? If all it does is paint in the background color, who needs it? You can do that with any paint tool just by pressing the X key.* You're right. And if you had asked that question about Version 2.5, we would have had no answer for you. What makes Photoshop 3's eraser tool unique is layers. When you're working on a layer with the Preserve Transparency check box turned off, the eraser tool actually removes paint and exposes portions of the underlying image. Suddenly, the eraser tool performs like a *real* eraser. (If the Preserve Transparency option is on, however, Photoshop won't let the eraser bore holes in the layer and instead paints in the background color.)

Tip

Change the Opacity setting in the Eraser Options panel to make portions of the layer translucent in inverse proportion to the Opacity value. For example, if you set the Opacity to 90 percent, you remove 90 percent of the opacity from the layer and therefore leave 10 percent of the opacity behind. The result is a nearly transparent stroke through the layer.

✦ **The eraser compared with layer masks:** As described in the "Layer-specific masks" section of Chapter 9, you can also erase holes in a layer using a layer mask. But although a layer mask doesn't do any permanent damage to an image, erasing actually gets rid of pixels for good. On the other hand, using the eraser tool doesn't increase the size of your image, as a layer mask does. It's a trade-off.

✦ **Erasing everything:** In case you're curious, you now restore the entire image window to the background color by clicking on the Erase Image button in the Eraser Options panel. When you're working on a layer, the button changes to Erase Layer and erases the current layer only. Considering how often most folks need to start over at square one — that is, almost never — this seems a much more sensible way to handle the function.

✦ **Erasing with the pencil:** If you double-click on the pencil icon in the toolbox and select the Auto Erase check box in the Pencil Options panel, the pencil draws in the background color any time you click or drag on a pixel colored in the foreground color. This can be very useful when you're drawing a line against a plain background. Set the foreground color to the color of the line; set the background color to the color of the background. Then use the pencil tool to draw and erase the line until you get it just right. (Unlike the eraser, the pencil always draws either in the foreground or background color, even when used on a layer.)

Reverting to the last saved image

The traditional reversion functions just described are all very well and good. But they don't hold a candle to Photoshop's *selective reversion* functions, which allow you to restore specific portions of an image to the way they looked when you last saved the image to disk.

The most convenient selective reversion function is the magic eraser tool. To access the magic eraser, press the Alt key while using the standard eraser tool. (You can also select the Erase to Saved check box in the Eraser Options panel, in which case dragging with the eraser reverts and Alt-dragging paints in the background color.) A tiny page icon appears behind the eraser cursor. Alt-drag with the magic eraser to paint with the last saved image or, if you prefer to think of it in a different way, to scrape away paint laid down since the last time you saved the image to disk. The process is demonstrated in Figure 11-23.

Tip   Before Photoshop can begin to selectively revert an image, it must load the last saved version of the image into memory. This operation takes a little time — the same amount of time, in fact, that it took Photoshop to open the image in the first place. You probably won't want to hold the mouse button down for the entire time. Therefore, if this is the first time you've selectively reverted inside the current image, Alt-click with the eraser tool and then wait for Photoshop to load the image. Your click won't affect the image in the slightest. After the load operation is completed, Alt-drag with the eraser as described earlier.

Reverting with the rubber stamp tool

Thanks to the improved performance of the eraser tool in Photoshop 3, the rubber stamp tool offers only two advantages over the magic eraser. The first is that you can take advantage of brush modes. By choosing a different brush mode from the pop-up menu in the upper left corner of the Rubber Stamp Options panel, you can mix pixels from the changed and saved images to achieve interesting and sometimes surprising effects.

The other advantage is that you can revert to one of two different images. Either choose From Saved from the Option pop-up menu in the Rubber Stamp Options panel to revert to the last image saved to disk, or choose From Snapshot to revert to the last image stored in memory as a *snapshot.*

Figure 11-23: After making a dreadful mistake (top), we Alt-dragged with the eraser tool to restore the image to the way it looked when we last saved it (bottom).

To keep the current version of an image in memory, choose Edit⇨Take Snapshot. The operation takes no time because the image is already in memory. By choosing the Take Snapshot command, you merely instruct Photoshop not to get rid of this image.

There's no waiting when you use the tool, either. When you drag with the rubber stamp tool set to From Snapshot, you don't have to wait for the image to load into memory as you do when reverting to a saved version, because it's already there.

Caution Photoshop can remember only one snapshot at a time. Therefore, when you choose the Take Snapshot command, you not only capture the current image, you abandon any snapshot previously stored in memory. You cannot undo the Take Snapshot command, so be careful how you use it.

Reverting selected areas

As explained in the preceding section, you can also revert areas of an image. After selecting the portion of the image you want to revert, choose Edit⇨Fill to display the

Fill dialog box. Then select the Saved or Snapshot option from the Use pop-up menu and press the Enter key. The selected area reverts to the saved image or snapshot, according to your choice.

Because you're filling the selected area with the saved image or snapshot, all the operations mentioned in Chapter 8 are equally applicable to reversions. (The Fill dialog box offers its own Mode pop-up menu, but it's easier to apply the overlay modes to a floating selection from the Layers palette because you can preview the results as they occur.) This capability came with Photoshop 2.5.1; Mac people had to kludge it in the Bad Old Days, but Windows people have always had it.

Reversion limitations

Photoshop doesn't allow you to revert from disk if you have in any way changed the number of pixels in the image since it was last saved. The process won't work if you have chosen Image⇨Image Size or Image⇨Canvas Size or if you have used the crop tool or Edit⇨Crop command.

Photoshop also can't revert an image if you haven't yet saved the image or if it can't read the document from disk (as when the image is saved in a format that requires conversion or can only be opened by means of a plug-in module).

You can, however, work around the image size problem by taking the following steps.

Steps: Selectively reverting a resized image

1. Select the entire image and copy it to the Clipboard.

2. Alt-click on the preview box in the lower left corner of the window to view the size of the document in pixels. Write this information down or assign it to memory (the memory in your head, that is).

3. Choose File⇨Revert to load the last-saved version of the image into the image window.

4. Choose Image⇨Canvas Size to resize the image to the dimensions you noted when Alt-clicking the preview box in Step 2.

5. After completing the resize operation, save the image to disk.

6. Paste the copied changes back into the image window and use the rubber stamp or magic eraser to selectively revert the image.

That's all there is to it. In fact, it's so simple that Photoshop should be able to revert from a resized image without your help. Hopefully, the folks at Adobe will remedy this problem in the future as well as they remedied so many other functions covered in this chapter.

Special Effects

Special effects comprise a tremendous variety of automated functions that can change an image slightly or completely alter it beyond recognition. Photoshop's type tool, for example, provides one of the great means for applying special effects to an image. Each character is a predefined graphic that you can edit using any of the techniques described in previous and future chapters. If you're thinking that type effects probably aren't Photoshop's forte — after all, type creating in a painting program is pretty jagged, right? — a quick browse through Chapter 12 should change your mind.

All the special-effects commands discussed in Chapters 13, 14, and 15 reside under the Filter menu, but that doesn't mean that they produce even vaguely similar effects. Chapter 13 deals primarily with Photoshop's most subtle filters, which affect the focus of an image. After you become familiar with commands such as Unsharp Mask and Gaussian Blur, chances are you'll use one or the other at least once every time you edit an image in Photoshop.

Chapter 14 delves into the world of special-effects filters. These commands wreak a variety of havoc on images that Louis Daguerre and Ansel Adams — had they a moment to discuss the matter — would have judged impossible. In addition to covering the usual crowd of destructive filters that cluster images into geometric patterns, trace outlines, and distort an image by poking it, twisting it, and generally putting it through the wringer, Photoshop's new lighting filters that let you diffuse brightness values and add light to a textured surface are explained.

Chapter 15 shows you how to create your own special effects using the Custom and Displace filters; both provide access to all kinds of effects that you simply can't accomplish using any other Photoshop function. And if you're really feeling ambitious, find out how to program your own interactive filter using the new Filter Factory.

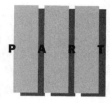

P A R T

◆   ◆   ◆   ◆

◆   ◆   ◆   ◆

Text Effects

Type Basics

What we're about to say is going to shake you to the very core. Warning: This is a biggie. You may want to sit down before you read any further. In fact, after you sit down, you may want to strap yourself in. Maybe go ahead and soundproof the room so that no one's alarmed when you scream *Oh, no, it can't be true!* and *Say it ain't so!*

(Ahem.) Type and graphics are the same thing.

There, there now. We understand. We reacted the same way when we heard the news. Dry your eyes while we explain. You see, your computer treats each character in a word as a little picture. The letter *O*, for example, is a big black oval with a smaller transparent oval set inside it. The only difference between a character of type and a standard graphic is that you don't have to draw type; every letter is already drawn for you. A font, therefore, is like a library of clip art you can access from the keyboard.

Bitmapped type

Now that you understand the realities of type, it should come as no surprise to learn that Photoshop treats type just like any other collection of pixels in an image. Type legibility is dependent upon the size and resolution of your image.

Figure 12-1, for example, shows four lines of type printed at equal sizes but at different resolutions. If these lines were printed at equal resolutions, each line would be twice as large as the line that precedes it. Hence, big type printed at a high resolution yields smooth, legible output, just as a big image printed at a high resolution yields smooth, detailed output. In fact, everything that you can say about an image is true of bitmapped type.

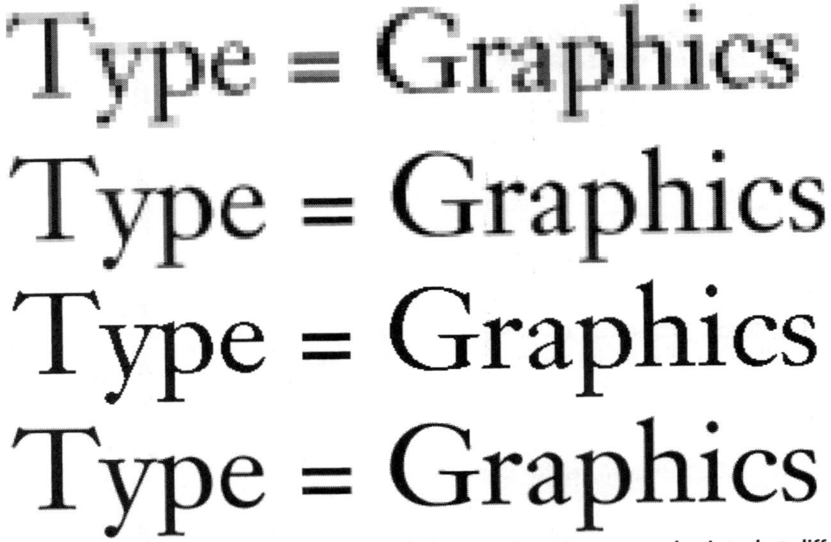

Type = Graphics
Type = Graphics
Type = Graphics
Type = Graphics

Figure 12-1: Four lines of type set in the Type 1 font Janson and printed at different resolutions.

R
%%
Robert
One picture is supposed to be worth a thousand words. Nevertheless, there's something to say about Figure 12-1. In the Macintosh version of this book, Deke used the TrueType font Geneva. I've fixed that here, for several reasons. First, Geneva is a Mac font, and this is a Windows 95 book. Second, because this is a type chapter, it seemed only appropriate to use a really good font — and Janson is one of the great typefaces of all time. Third, finally, last and by no means least — Adobe invented, and produces, PostScript Type 1 fonts. TrueType was Microsoft's attempt to kill the Type 1 industry, and to give Adobe some comeuppance for not licensing Type 1 technology to Microsoft on Microsoft's terms. Fair's fair — this is a book about an Adobe product, so I'm giving Type 1 fonts priority. (There are other reasons for this priority, too — see below.)

R
%%
Robert
Photoshop lets you use both Type 1 (PostScript) fonts and TrueType fonts. To use your TrueType fonts, there's nothing extra to do. To use Type 1 fonts, you must have installed Adobe Type Manager (ATM); see Appendix C for details. If you already have ATM installed, make sure that it's Version 3 or higher — if not, let the Installer put it on. Earlier versions of ATM can function less well, or not at all, both with Photoshop and Windows 95. I do not say this gratuitously — every so often on the ADOBEAPPS forum on CompuServe, I field distress calls from people using ATM 2.02. Let me add that there's no ATM for Windows NT yet and that the ATM available now will not run on it, because NT is a secure operating system and won't let ATM do the behind-the-scenes work it needs to do.

The disadvantages of working with type in a painting program are obvious. First, the resolution of the type is fixed. Rather than matching the resolution of printed text to that of your printer — a function provided by drawing, word processing, and desktop publishing programs, just to name a few — Photoshop prints type at the same resolution at which it prints the rest of the image.

In addition, after you add a line of type to an image, you can't go back and add and delete characters from the keyboard as you can in an object-oriented program. If you misspell a word or just want to rephrase some text, you must erase the offending characters or words and start over again. When it comes to entering type, Photoshop is more likely to remind you of a typewriter and a bottle of correction fluid than a typical computer program.

But although the disadvantages of creating type in a painting program may initially hamper your progress, the advantages are tremendous. You can do all of the following:

✦ **Create translucent type:** Photoshop enables you to change the translucency of type by using the Opacity slider bar in the Layers palette. With this technique, you can merge type and images to create subtle overlay effects, as illustrated in the top example in Figure 12-2.

✦ **Use type as a selection:** As we mentioned in Chapter 8, text is just another variety of selection outline. You can mask portions of an image and even select elements and move, copy, or otherwise manipulate them using character outlines, as demonstrated in the middle example in Figure 12-2. We explore this option in detail in the upcoming "Character Masks" section.

✦ **Customize characters:** You also can customize a character of type by converting it to a path, editing the path using the tools in the Paths palette, and converting it back to a selection outline. Only high-end drawing (that is, object-oriented) programs such as Illustrator and FreeHand match this capability.

✦ **Edit type as part of the image:** You can erase type, paint over type, smear type, fill type with a gradation, draw highlights and shadows, and create a range of special text effects that fall well outside the capabilities of an object-oriented program. The last example in Figure 12-2 is just one of the bazillion possibilities.

✦ **Trade images freely:** If you've ever traded documents over a network or otherwise tried to share a file created in a word processing or desktop publishing program with associates and coworkers, you know what a nightmare fonts can be. If other people's machines aren't equipped with the fonts you used in your document — which seems to be the case more often than not — your document looks awful on their screens. *What's wrong with this file you gave me? Why did you use this font? I liked what you wrote in your report, but it sure is ugly!* — those are only a few of the responses you can expect.

Figure 12-2: Examples of translucent white type (top), type used as a selection (middle), and type enhanced with painting and editing tools (bottom). On the whole, these effects are beyond the means of object-oriented programs.

When you work with images, however, your font worries are over, because type in an image is bitmapped. Other users don't need special screen or printer fonts to view your images exactly as you created them. Mind you, we don't recommend that you use Photoshop as a word processor, but it's great for creating headlines and short missives that you want to fling about the office.

The type tool

In a drawing or desktop publishing program, the type tool typically serves two purposes. You can create text with the tool, or you can edit the characters of existing text by highlighting them and either replacing characters or applying formatting commands. However, Photoshop doesn't allow you to reword or reformat text after you add it to an image.

To create text, click with the type tool in the image window (or just press the Y key). Instead of producing a blinking insertion marker in the window, as other graphics programs do, Photoshop displays the Type Tool dialog box shown in Figure 12-3.

R
%%
Robert Be careful about how many fonts you have installed. Under Windows 3.1, both TrueType and Type 1 entries were stored in WIN.INI — and as that file got close to 64K in size, very strange and unpleasant things could happen. Also, the more the fonts there were, the longer it took Windows to load, and type dialog boxes became slower in any program. Although Windows 95 stores TrueType font entries in the Registry now, I still think you should keep your total number of installed fonts to under 200 — if nothing else, it will make it easier to scroll through font lists. Consider investing in Ares Software's Font Minder 3 — it lets you set up groups of fonts that you can swap in and out with minimum trouble. It works just fine with both Windows 3.1 and Windows 95. See Appendix B for further details on font management issues.

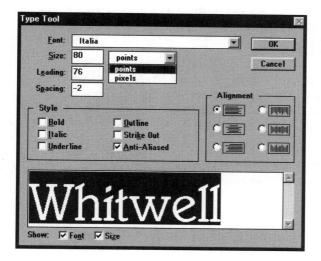

Figure 12-3: To create type in Photoshop, enter it into the Type Tool dialog box, which appears after you click with the type tool. The bottom example shows the type as it appears in the image window.

Selecting type

When it comes down to picking which type to use, you should be aware of two key issues.

Robert

First is the question of TrueType or PostScript. I don't want to get into Font Wars here, so let's just say this: Both formats are sophisticated and very capable. Both have excellent typefaces available. Both can coexist in Photoshop and Windows 95. But there are more high-quality Type 1 fonts to be had than TrueType. When Microsoft introduced TrueType with Windows 3.1 and followed it up with two extra packages of fonts, it priced them at loss-leader levels. The quality was excellent, but the pricing was way below what would compensate for the amount of work involved in producing such excellent versions. One unconfirmed theory is that it represented part of Microsoft's plan to derail the Type 1 font business generally, Adobe's in particular (see previous section). It did have the salutary effect of causing Type 1 foundries (including Adobe) to lower their prices. But it also made people think that all fonts should be priced so low — which just can't be done if the type designers and digitizers are to be fairly compensated for their labors. Think I'm exaggerating? Fire up Fontographer 3.5 (from Macromedia) and try designing a font from scratch; you'll change your mind very fast.

Robert

Second, and related, is the issue of quality. So far, only Type 1 fonts have the typographic refinements of ligatures, old style numerals, and small caps. If you're serious about typography, you need those refinements — they're a considerable part of what makes digital type avoid looking like digital type. Regardless of which format you choose, though, you should learn about typefaces. Even though your type is rasterized in Photoshop, there's still the garbage in/garbage out principle. Use a badly designed face, whether Type 1 or TrueType, and it will look bad in Photoshop. Get to know typefaces and the basics of typography if you want to use type like a pro in Photoshop.

Entering and editing type

At the bottom of the Type Tool dialog box is the text-entry box, where you enter and edit the text you want to add to the current image.

You can edit text up to the moment you add it to the image. To make your edits, first select the characters you want to change by dragging over them with the cursor. Then enter new text from the keyboard. To select a whole word, double-click on it. You can also cut, copy, and paste text by choosing commands from the Edit menu or using keyboard equivalents.

If the text you are typing reaches the right edge of the text-entry box, the word in progress automatically drops down to the next line. However, when you click on the OK button or press Enter on the keypad to exit the dialog box, all text appears on the same line unless you specifically entered carriage returns between lines (by pressing Enter). Each carriage return indicates the end of one line and the beginning of the next, just as it does when you use a typewriter.

Caution When you're actively using the text-entry box, pressing Enter will insert a carriage return — that is, you're still in the Type Tool dialog box. But when you're making entries in the Size, Leading, or Spacing option boxes, pressing Enter will exit you from the Type Tool dialog box. If you don't think, you may get some extra spacing in your text. Robert's solution? Only use Enter when you want a carriage return when you're entering text. Press the OK button to get out of the dialog box.

If your text doesn't look the way you anticipated after you exit the Type Tool dialog box, choose Edit⇨Undo (Ctrl-Z) or simply press Delete. Then start the process over again by clicking with the type tool. When the Type Tool dialog box appears, your previous text is displayed in the text-entry box.

Formatting type

Photoshop formats *all* text entered into the text-entry box identically according to the specifications in the Type Tool dialog box. You can't select a single character or word in the text-entry box and format it differently from its deselected neighbors.

The formatting options in the Type Tool dialog box work as follows:

✦ **Font:** Select the typeface and type style you want to use from the Font pop-up menu. Alternatively, you can just select the plain version of the font, such as Times Roman or Helvetica Regular, and apply styles using the Style options.

✦ **Size:** Type size is measured either in points (1 point equals $1/72$ inch) or pixels. You can select the desired measurement from the pop-up menu to the right of the Size option box, as shown in Figure 12-3. If the resolution of your image is 72 ppi, points and pixels are equal. However, if the resolution is higher, a single point may include many pixels. The resolution of Figure 12-3, for example, is 140 ppi, which is why the final text in the image (shown at bottom) is almost twice as large as the 72-ppi text in the dialog box. The moral? Select the points option when you want to scale text independently of image resolution; select pixels when you want to map text to an exact number of pixels in an image.

Background Type is measured from the top of its *ascenders* — letters like *b, d,* and *h* that rise above the level of most lowercase characters — to the bottom of its *descenders* — letters like *g, p,* and *q* that sink below the baseline. That's the way it's supposed to work, anyway. Characters from fonts in the Adobe Type Library, including those built into all PostScript laser printers and imagesetters, measure only 92 percent as tall as the specified type size.

Robert

Let me put this a different way. Supposing you try to recreate the top two boxes in Figure 12-4 — the TrueType font Arial in the top one, the Type 1 font "equivalent" Helvetica in the one below it. You do a rectangular box 120 pixels high, stroke it for visibility, and then put in some type at 120 pixels high. It apparently doesn't fit. Hey — isn't 120 supposed to equal 120? Well, it does, but appearances are deceiving (not the first time I've said that — look at what I said about colors in Chapter 4). Think of it like this, and let's switch to typographers' points for this discussion. In the days when type was cast in metal, a 72-point size was the total height of the matrix. Inside that, the type designer fitted the letters. Sometimes he (then was a different era — women weren't encouraged to become type designers) would use the entire 72 points of available height when measuring from the top of the highest ascender to the bottom of the lowest descender. That's what Hermann Zapf did with Palatino (see the lower two rows in Figure 12-4). But sometimes a designer wouldn't. The 72-point size, however, was absolute — even if the letters don't get that high, it's still 72-point type because that's the height of the matrix the letters were cast on. And that convention continues to this day, even with digital type.

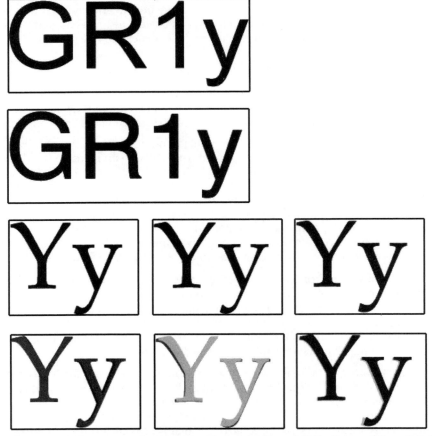

Figure 12-4: From top to bottom, TrueType Arial, Type 1 Helvetica, and Type 1 Palatino and two variations (TrueType Bookman Antiqua, Type 1 Zapf Calligraphic), in various combinations superimposed and color-coded to show design differences (see text for details).

Robert

There's something else you should know about, and Figure 12-4 is doing double duty for this. Not all type is created equal. Look at the Arial and Helvetica boxes. Look carefully at the first three characters (don't look at the fourth, the lower-case *y*, because I put it there to illustrate the previous note). You'll see significant differences between the two typefaces — I could tell you, but you'll get more out of this by doing your own analysis. Moral of the story: Don't be trusting when you hear that a font is *like* or *similar to* another font. The lower two lines show this in a different way. On the third line, from left to right, is the Type 1 font Palatino, designed by the great Hermann Zapf — I've chosen his *Y* because it shows his calligraphic genius so well. Next to it is the TrueType "equivalent" known as Bookman Antiqua. Finally, there's Bitstream's Type 1 font Zapf Calligraphic, a digitized typeface that Zapf himself supervised and that many consider to be the best of the lot (that's no diss on Adobe — Palatino was one of the very earliest Type 1 fonts the company produced). Do they look identical? Nope, but the differences are less obvious. Go down to the fourth and final row, where I've superimposed various combinations. Left to right are Palatino underneath Bookman Antiqua (black underneath medium gray), Bookman Antiqua underneath Zapf Calligraphic (medium gray underneath light gray), and Zapf Calligraphic underneath Palatino (light gray underneath black). Look carefully at what colors are peeping out — your eyes will tell you. Too tedious? Hey, I can do this, and I use bifocals! Deke may not have chosen to make you into a type maven, but *I* have a different agenda.

✦ Leading: Also called line spacing, *leading* is the vertical distance between the baseline of one line of type and the baseline of the next line of type within a single paragraph, as illustrated in Figure 12-5. (Remember, in the text-entry box you must separate lines of type manually by pressing the Enter key.) Leading is measured in the unit you selected from the Size pop-up menu. If you don't specify a leading value, Photoshop automatically inserts leading equal to 125 percent of the type size.

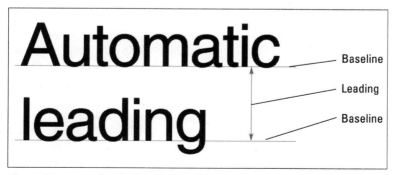

Figure 12-5: Leading is the distance between any two baselines in a single paragraph of text created with the type tool. Here, the type size is 120 pixels and the leading is 150 pixels.

✦ **Spacing:** Each character in a font carries with it a predetermined amount of *side bearing* that separates it from its immediate neighbors. Although you can't change the amount of side bearing, you can insert and delete the overall amount of space between characters by entering a value into the Spacing option box. Enter a positive value to insert space; enter a negative value to delete space. The value is measured in the unit you selected from the Size pop-up menu.

✦ **Style:** Select one or more Style check boxes to specify the type styles you want to apply to your text. If you choose the plain version of a font, the Bold and Italic options call up the bold and italic PostScript or TrueType font definitions. If you apply the Bold option to a font that is already bold, such as Helvetica Bold or Helvetica Black (both shown in Figure 12-6), Photoshop makes the characters slightly heavier. If you apply the Italic option to a font that is already italicized, such as Helvetica Oblique (again, see Figure 12-6), Photoshop slants the characters even more.

Helvetica Regular
Helvetica Regular Bold
Helvetica Bold
Helvetica Bold Bold
Helvetica Black
Helvetica Black Bold
Helvetica Regular Italic
Helvetica Oblique
Helvetica Oblique Italic

Figure 12-6: The Style options affect fonts that are already bold or italic. Bolding a plain font produces the same result as choosing the bold version of the font (second and third lines), just as italicizing the plain style is the same as choosing an italicized font (seventh and eighth lines). But you can achieve unique results by applying styles to already stylized fonts (fourth, sixth, and ninth examples).

Tip   The Outline option produces unspeakably ugly results, as demonstrated by the top two examples in Figure 12-7. You can create a better outline style using Edit⇨Stroke. First, create your text using the Type Tool dialog box as usual. (Don't you dare select the Outline option.) Press Enter to exit the dialog box. With the foreground color set to black, choose Image⇨Map⇨Invert (Ctrl-I) to change the selected text to white. Finally, choose Edit⇨Stroke and enter the outline thickness of your choice. Figure 12-7 shows two stroked examples, one with a 1-pixel outline and the other with a 2-pixel outline.

The Shadow option produces equally unattractive results. To create attractive shadowed type, try out one of the techniques discussed in the "Character Masks" section of this chapter.

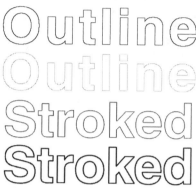

Figure 12-7: Photoshop's automated outline style, shown here when jagged (top) and anti-aliased (second), is nothing short of hideous. You can get better results by stroking the characters with 1-pixel or 2-pixel outlines (third and bottom).

✦ **Anti-Aliased:** This Style option is special enough to mention separately. When you select Anti-Aliased, Photoshop softens characters by slightly blurring pixels around the perimeter, as shown in Figure 12-8. Unless you want to create very small type or intend to match the resolution of your output device — printing a 300-ppi image to a 300-dpi printer, for example — select this check box. Photoshop takes longer to produce anti-aliased type, but it's worth it. Unless otherwise indicated, we created all figures in this chapter with the Anti-Aliased check box selected.

Antialiased
Jagged as
all get out

Figure 12-8: The difference between 120-pixel type when the Anti-Aliased option is selected (top line) versus deselected (bottom). Both examples were printed at 190 ppi.

✦ **Alignment:** Select one of these radio buttons to specify the way lines of type in a single paragraph align to the point at which you originally clicked with the type tool. Photoshop 3 offers three additional options for creating vertically aligned text. In my opinion, every one of them is a waste of time, particularly because you have no control over how the text aligns horizontally within the vertical columns. In Figure 12-9, for example, you can see how the characters in each vertical line are always aligned along their left edges. (Incidentally, we used capital letters to show off the vertical alignment options because vertically aligned lowercase letters always look bad, regardless of the program that creates them.)

Figure 12-9: A single paragraph of type shown as it appears if you select each of the six Alignment radio buttons. The I-beam cursor shows the point at which we clicked to display the Type Tool dialog box.

✦ **Show:** Photoshop's Type Tool dialog box can preview your settings for the Font, Size, and Style options. Select the Font check box at the bottom of the dialog box to preview font and type style; select the Size check box to preview type size. The size preview is always at 72 ppi, so the size is accurate only if you selected Pixels from the Size pop-up menu. That's why the text outside the dialog box back in Figure 12-3 is larger than the text inside the text entry area. Your settings for the Leading, Spacing, and Alignment options as well as the Anti-Aliased check box are not reflected in the preview.

Manipulating type in the image window

After you confirm the contents of the Type Tool dialog box by clicking on the OK button or pressing Enter, the type appears selected in the image window. You can move it, clone it, copy it to the Clipboard, transform it by applying commands from the Image⇔Flip, Image⇔Rotate, or Image⇔vEffects submenus, or perform any other operation that's applicable to a floating selection.

If you want to hide the marching ants that surround selected characters, choose Select⇔Hide Edges (Ctrl-H). To make the selected text transparent, adjust the Opacity slider bar in the Layers palette while the type tool, one of the four selection tools, or one of the tools in the Paths palette is active. You also can select a brush mode from the pop-up menu on the left side of the Layers palette.

Tip   Pressing the Alt key when the type tool is selected brings up the eyedropper cursor. Therefore, to clone selected text, you either have to switch to one of the selection tools (rectangular marquee, elliptical marquee, lasso, or magic wand) and Alt-drag the text or press Alt with an arrow key.

In addition, you can move characters of text independently of one another by Ctrl-dragging with the type tool. When you press and hold the Ctrl key, the standard I-beam cursor changes to a lasso cursor. Ctrl-drag around the portions of the floating selection that you want to deselect and set in place. The rest of the text remains selected and floating.

This technique is ideal for *kerning* — that is, adjusting the amount of space between two neighboring characters. Suppose that you want to adjust the distance between the *P* and *a* in the last line of the novel-turned-top-40-song title shown in Figure 12-10. First, you position the paragraph in your image. You then Ctrl-drag around the portion of the paragraph that you want to set down, as shown in the top example in the figure. To kern the text that remains floating, you Shift-drag it into place, as shown in the bottom half of the figure. Or you can just as easily nudge the selected text with the left and right arrow keys.

Tip Want an even better method of kerning? Create your text directly in the quick mask mode. This way, you can adjust the location of individual characters without deselecting any of them. Just switch to the quick mask mode, create your text, and then select individual characters and adjust their positioning as desired. When you finish, choose Image⇨Map⇨Invert (Ctrl-I) to make the text white so that it will serve as the selection. Then switch back to the marching ants mode. Your text is both kerned and 100 percent selected.

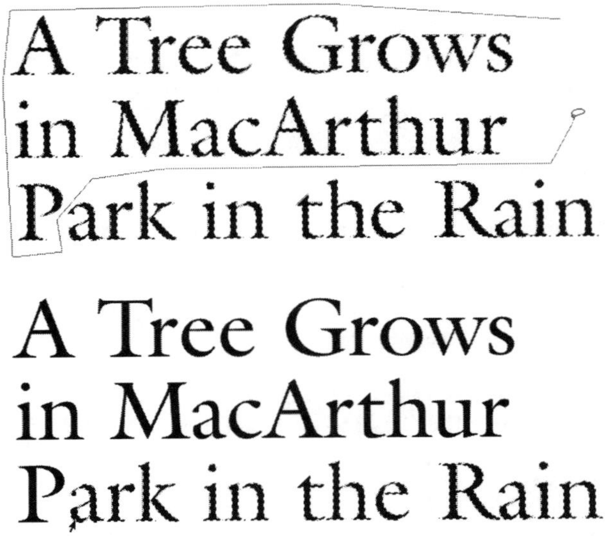

A Tree Grows
in MacArthur
Park in the Rain

A Tree Grows
in MacArthur
Park in the Rain

Figure 12-10: After Ctrl-dragging with the type tool around the text that we wanted to set down (top), we Shift-dragged the text that remained selected to close the gap between the *P* and *a* in Park (bottom).

You also can Ctrl-drag around a portion of a floating selection with the rectangular marquee, elliptical marquee, or lasso tool. However, if you do so, you don't just deselect the portion of the selection around which you drag; you delete it. Try it out and you'll see what we mean. Click with the type tool, enter the word *Park,* and then press Enter. While the text remains floating, select the lasso tool and Ctrl-drag around the *P.* The *P* disappears, leaving you stranded with an *ark.* After choosing Edit⇨Undo (Ctrl-Z) to reinstate the *P,* select the type tool and Ctrl-drag around the *P.* This time you deselect the *P* and make it part of your image, enabling you to nudge the *ark* into a better location.

Tip We mentioned this tip in Chapter 8, but folks always ooh and ah over it when we tell them about it, so we figure that the message isn't getting out there. Repetition might help. You can Ctrl-drag with the type tool to set down portions of any floating selection, not just text. You can also Ctrl-Alt-drag to draw a polygon around an area, as demonstrated in the first example of Figure 12-10, or Ctrl-Shift-drag to intersect the portion of the floating selection that you want to remain selected and set down the portion outside your drag.

Character Masks

Recapping today's news: Type outlines are selections. Except for the fact that they arrive on the scene already filled with the foreground color, they act like any other selection outline. With that in mind, you can create an inexhaustible supply of special type effects.

The following sections demonstrate a few examples. Armed with these ideas, you should be able to invent enough additional type effects to keep you busy into the next millennium. Honestly, you won't believe the number of effects you can invent by screwing around with type outlines.

Good fonts, bad things.

Robert

Filling type with an image

One of the most impressive and straightforward applications for text in Photoshop is to use the character outlines to mask a portion of an image. In fact, the only trick is getting rid of the foreground fill. You can accomplish this in a matter of a few straightforward steps.

Steps: Selecting part of an image using character outlines

1. Begin by opening the image you want to mask. Then create your text by clicking with the type tool, entering the text you want to use as a mask, formatting it as desired, and pressing Enter to display the type in the image window. Large, bold characters work best. In Figure 12-11, we used the PostScript font Eras Ultra — an extremely bold type style — with a Size value of 260 and a Spacing value of negative 10.

Figure 12-11: When you use type to mask an image, bold and blocky characters produce the best results because they enable you to see large chunks of unobstructed image.

   2. Choose Edit⇨Cut (Ctrl-X) to delete the text from the image and transfer it to the Clipboard.

   3. Choose Select⇨All (Ctrl-A) to marquee the entire image. Then press the Alt key and choose Edit⇨Paste Into to paste the text in back of the image. The result is that you can see the character outlines without seeing the foreground fill, as demonstrated in Figure 12-12.

Figure 12-12: By pasting the text behind the image, you can use the selection outlines without worrying about the foreground fill of the characters.

Color Plate 3-1:
This little warlock shows off the differences between the four different JPEG compression settings, from maximum quality, minimum compression (upper left) to minimum quality, maximum compression (lower right). Inspect the enlarged eye and sharpened staff for subtle erosions in detail.

Maximum   116K

High   66K

Medium   50K

Low   46K

Color Plate 3-2:
My personal 1,024 x 768-pixel startup screen features effects created with Kai's Power Tools, Xaos Paint Alchemy, Xaos Terrazzo, Aldus Gallery Effects, and Alien Skin.

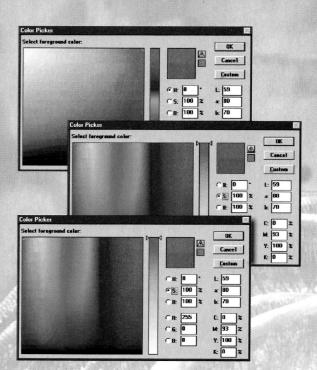

Color Plate 4-1:
The colors inside the field and slider in the Color Picker dialog box change to reflect the selection of the H (Hue), S (Saturation), and B (Brightness) radio buttons.

Color Plate 4-2:
I reduced a 24-bit color image (upper left) to the 8-bit System palette using three different Dither options: None (upper right), Pattern (lower right), and Diffusion (lower left). Of the three, Diffusion is almost always the best choice.

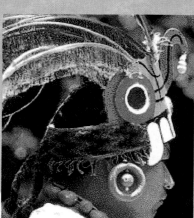

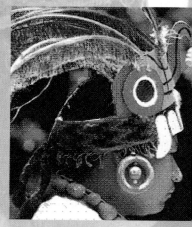

Replace red with blue

Replace blue with green

Replace green with red

Swap red and blue

Color Plate 6-1:
A grayscale image printed as a quadtone using the colors navy blue, rose, teal, and dull orange. All colors were defined and printed using CMYK pigments.

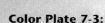

Color Plate 7-1:
Starting with an image of typical saturation (upper left), I applied the sponge tool set to Desaturate to the inside of the pepper and the corn in the background (upper right). I then repeated the effect twice more to make the areas almost gray (lower right). Returning to the original image, I then selected the Saturate icon and again scrubbed inside the pepper and in the corn to boost the colors (lower left).

Color Plate 7-3:
I painted this image for Macworld magazine in 1990 using a Wacom SD-510 pressure-sensitive tablet and Photoshop 1.0.7. A pressure-sensitive tablet transforms Photoshop into a fully functioning artist's studio.

Color Plate 7-2:
To create this image, I traced an image from the PhotoDisc library using the paintbrush tool and a flat brush shape. Although Photoshop offers automated filters that you can use to create similar effects, nothing is so versatile and precise as a simple paintbrush.

Normal

Dissolve

Behind

Multiply

Screen

Overlay

Soft Light

Hard Light

Darken

Lighten

Difference

Hue

Saturation

Color

Luminosity

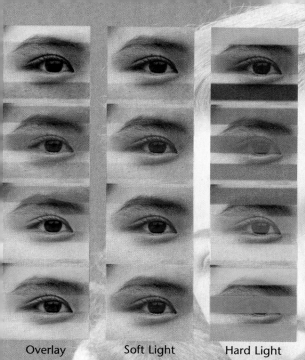

Overlay   Soft Light   Hard Light

Color Plate 7-5:
Using the paintbrush tool, I've painted 12 lines in 12 evenly spaced hues — each exactly 20 degrees apart on the color wheel — in each of the three newest and most difficult to understand brush modes. Although all three brush modes mix the foreground color applied by the brush with the existing colors in the image, subtle but important differences distinguish one mode from the next.

Color Plate 9-1:
Two inverted selections (top) and their equivalent masks (bottom). In this case, you can see both mask and image. Red-tinted areas are masked, representing deselected areas in the image; untinted areas are unmasked and represent selected areas.

Color Plate 9-2:
A colorized version of one of the parapets from the Great Wall created by converting the image itself to a mask. I drew the mask for the stylized sun using the elliptical marquee, paintbrush, and smudge tools.

Color Plate 10-1:
After filling my floating drop shadow with a reddish orange (top), I chose the Multiply option from the overlay modes pop-up menu in the Layers palette to mix the drop shadow with the underlying image (middle). Then I changed the Opacity setting to 70 percent (bottom) to create the finished colored drop shadow.

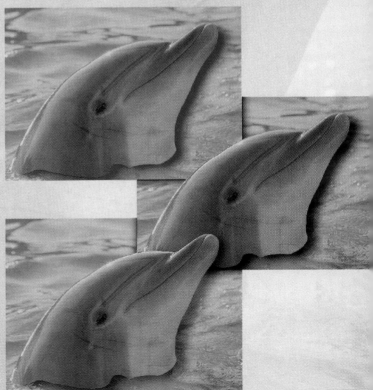

Color Plate 10-2:
The popular cartoon character Neutron Mammal — what, you've never heard of Neutron Mammal? — is the result of applying both the haloing and spotlighting effects described in Chapter 10 and then setting the whole thing against an inverted background.

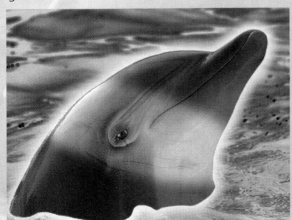

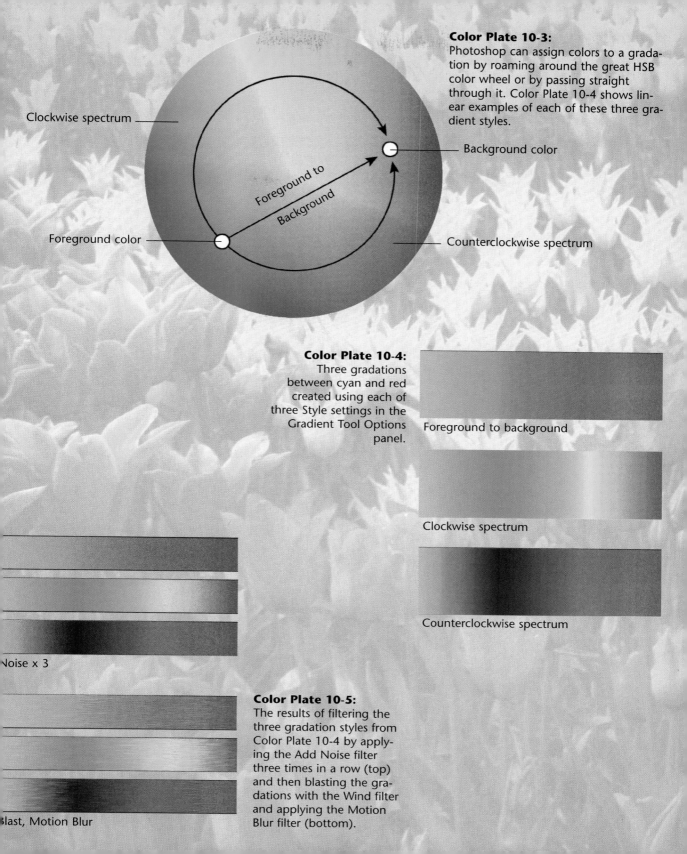

Clockwise spectrum

Foreground color

Foreground to Background

Background color

Counterclockwise spectrum

Color Plate 10-3:
Photoshop can assign colors to a gradation by roaming around the great HSB color wheel or by passing straight through it. Color Plate 10-4 shows linear examples of each of these three gradient styles.

Color Plate 10-4:
Three gradations between cyan and red created using each of three Style settings in the Gradient Tool Options panel.

Foreground to background

Clockwise spectrum

Counterclockwise spectrum

Noise x 3

Blast, Motion Blur

Color Plate 10-5:
The results of filtering the three gradation styles from Color Plate 10-4 by applying the Add Noise filter three times in a row (top) and then blasting the gradations with the Wind filter and applying the Motion Blur filter (bottom).

Color Plate 13-1:
Clockwise from upper left, the effects of the Motion Blur, Sharpen Edges, Median, and High Pass corrective filters. Normally, the High Pass filter takes the saturation out of an image, leaving many areas gray, like an old, sun-bleached slide. To restore the colors, I pasted the original image in front of the filtered one and chose Color from the Brush ⌐Modes pop-up menu in the Brushes palette.

Color Plate 13-2:
Clockwise from upper left, the effects of the destructive filters Crystallize, Lens Flare, Color Halftone, and Twirl. The Lens Flare filter is applicable to color images only. Perhaps surprisingly, you can apply the Color Halftone filter to grayscale and color images alike.

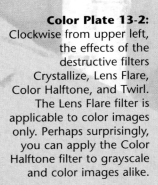

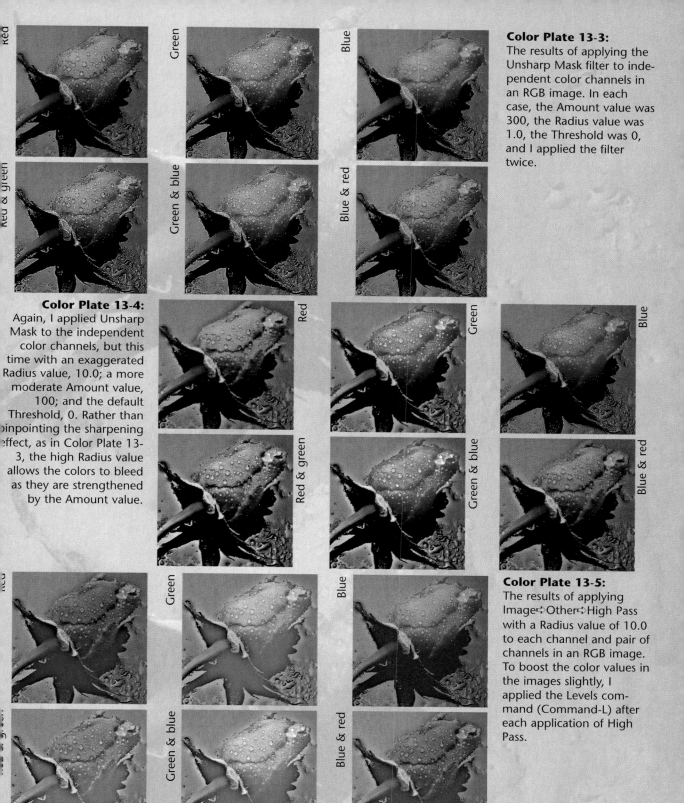

Red | Green | Blue

Color Plate 13-3:
The results of applying the Unsharp Mask filter to independent color channels in an RGB image. In each case, the Amount value was 300, the Radius value was 1.0, the Threshold was 0, and I applied the filter twice.

Red & green | Green & blue | Blue & red

Color Plate 13-4:
Again, I applied Unsharp Mask to the independent color channels, but this time with an exaggerated Radius value, 10.0; a more moderate Amount value, 100; and the default Threshold, 0. Rather than pinpointing the sharpening effect, as in Color Plate 13-3, the high Radius value allows the colors to bleed as they are strengthened by the Amount value.

Red | Green | Blue

Red & green | Green & blue | Blue & red

Green | Blue

Green & blue | Blue & red

Color Plate 13-5:
The results of applying Image⇨Other⇨High Pass with a Radius value of 10.0 to each channel and pair of channels in an RGB image. To boost the color values in the images slightly, I applied the Levels command (Command-L) after each application of High Pass.

Color Plate 13-6:
After floating the image and applying the Gaussian Blur filter, I applied various Opacity and overlay mode settings. Clockwise from upper left, the overlay modes are Normal, Luminosity, Darken, and Lighten. I varied the Opacity value anywhere from 60 to 80 percent, depending on the image.

Color Plate 13-7:
After selecting the background using a very precise mask that I created using the High Pass, Threshold, Gaussian Blur, and Levels commands, I applied two variations on directional blurring effects. I applied the Wind and Motion Blur filters to make the background appear as if it were spinning around the woman (top). Starting over with the base image, I applied the Radial Blur filter set to Zoom to make the background appear to rush toward the viewer (bottom).

Noise, red

Noise, green

Noise, blue

Median, red

Median, green

Median, blue

Color Plate 13-8:
The top row shows the results of applying the Add Noise filter to each of the red, green, and blue channels with an Amount value of 75 and Gaussian selected. The bottom row shows the effects of the Median filter when applied to individual color channels when set to a Radius of 10.

Color Plate 13-9:
An image scanned from an old issue of *Macworld* magazine shown as it appears in the normal RGB mode (top right) and when each channel is viewed separately (top left). The middle images show the effects of the Dust & Scratches filter set to a Radius of 2 and a Threshold of 20. The bottom images show how the channels look after suppressing the moiré patterns with the Gaussian Blur, Median, and Unsharp Mask filters.

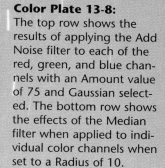

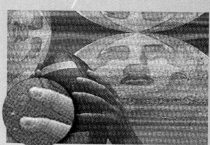

Color Plate 14-1:
The result of applying the Extrude filter to the lower left rose image from Color Plate 13-4. If you select the Blocks and Solid Front Faces options, the filter transforms the image into mosaic tiles and shoves the tiles out at you in 3-D space.

RGB   Lab   CMYK

Color Plate 14-2:
After floating the image, I applied the Mezzotint filter set to the Long Strokes effect in each of the RGB, Lab, and CMYK color modes (top row). I then mixed the filtered image with the underlying original using the Overlay mode and an Opacity setting of 40 percent (bottom row).

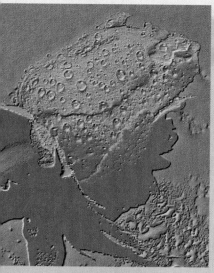

Color Plate 14-3:
Here I've taken a floating selection and applied the Emboss filter armed with an Angle of 135 degrees, a Height value of 2, and an Amount of 300 percent. To create the left image, I mixed the floater with the underlying original using the Luminosity overlay mode and an Opacity setting of 80 percent. To get the psychedelic effect on the right, I chose the Difference overlay mode and reduced the Opacity value to 40 percent.

Color Plate 14-4:
After selecting an image from the PhotoDisc library (left), I floated the image, Gaussian Blurred it with a 3.0 Radius, and applied the Find Edges filter. The effect was light, so I used the Levels command to darken it (middle). I then composited the image using the Overlay mode and an Opacity setting of 80 percent (right).

Color Plate 14-5:
Starting with the worker bee from Color Plate 14-4, I floated the image, applied the Pointillize and Trace Contour filters, and selected the Luminosity overlay mode (left). To get the middle effect, I merely changed the overlay mode to Multiply and the Opacity to 50 percent. The right image shows a different effect, created by applying Add Noise and Trace Contour filters to the floating image, selecting the Overlay overlay mode, and changing the Opacity to 80 percent.

Pinch   Spherize

Color Plate 14-6:
The results of using the Pinch (left column) and Spherize (right column) filters to create conical gradations. By the time I captured the first row of images, I had repeated each filter twice. By the second row, I had repeated each filter 12 times. I then mixed the Pinched gradation with the original image using the Soft Light overlay mode (bottom left). I cloned the Spherized gradation a few times and applied the Screen mode to each (bottom right).

x 2

x 12

Color Plate 14-7:
In this piece, titled Knowing Risk, Seattle-based artist Mark Collen combines a variety of distortion filtering effects to create a surrealistic landscape. The cat, the book, the mongoose, and the twigs are the only scanned images.

Clouds

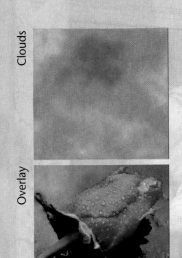

Difference Clouds

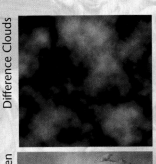

x 10

Overlay

Screen

Hue

Color Plate 14-8:
The top row shows the results of Shift-choosing the Clouds filter (left), Shift-choosing Difference Clouds (middle), and pressing Command-Shift-F ten times in a row (right). I then took each of the images from the top row and mixed it with the rose using one of three overlay modes (labeled beside bottom row). You can create clouds, haze, and imaginative fill patterns with the Clouds filters.

Color Plate 14-9:
I used the Lighting Effects filter to assign three spotlights to a familiar image. The bumpy surfaces of the images are the results of texture maps. To create the left image, I used the red channel as the texture. In the right image, I used the repeating pattern of Lenins.

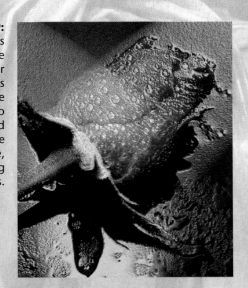

Color Plate 15-1: Color versions of four Custom filter effects, including (clockwise from upper left) mild sharpening, offset sharpening, edge-detection, and full-color embossing.

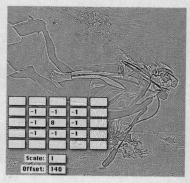

Color Plate 15-2: Examples of applying four patterns from the Displacement Maps folder with the Displace filter, including (clockwise from upper left) Crumbles, Streaks pattern, Mezzo effect, and Twirl pattern.

Color Plate 15-3:
The top row shows three different applications of the Rotator filters with the Red, Green, and Blue slider bars set to various positions. The Distorto option was set to 0. In the bottom examples, I added a cranked up Distorto value to each of the rotations above.

R:1, G:2, B:3

R:80, G:85, B:90

R:240, G:230, B:250

Distort = 10

Distort = 40

Distort = 140

Color Plate 15-4:
Applications of six of the seven filters I created in Filter Factory that you'll find on the CD. Each filter has between 3 and 6 sliders, so you can create all sorts of variations.

Channel Mixer

Color Creep

Crisscross

Full Channel Press

Noise Blaster

SuperInvert

RGB

Lab

CMYK

Color Plate 16-1:
The results of applying the Invert command to a single image in each of the three color modes. I inverted all channels in the RGB and Lab images and all but the black channel in the CMYK channel.

Color Plate 16-2:
Because the Equalize command finds different light and dark pixels throughout the channels in each of the three color modes, the mode has a tremendous effect on the performance of the command. The three images are identical, and the areas selected are identical, but the effects are different.

RGB

Lab

CMYK

Luminosity

Overlay

Difference

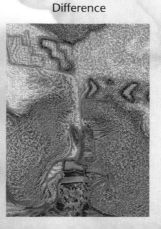

Color Plate 16-3:
After floating the image and applying the High Pass filter and the Posterize command, I mixed the floater and underlying original by choosing each of three overlay modes from the Layers palette. All effects were created with Opacity settings of 100 percent.

Color Plate 16-4:
You can downplay the colors in selected portions of an image by floating the selection and applying Desaturate to convert the pixels to grayscale (top left). Lessening the Opacity — say, to 50 percent — brings back some colors (top right). Alternatively, you can Invert the floating selection, choose the Color overlay mode, and change the Opacity to 50 percent (bottom left). Raising the Opacity increases the presence of inverted colors (bottom right).

Original · RGB

Lab · CMYK

Color Plate 16-5:
Starting with the original pumpkin image (top left), I applied Image⇨Adjust⇨ Auto Levels in each of the three color modes. The command is really designed for RGB images and tends to mess up CMYK images (lower right). As you folks who live outside Love Canal are probably aware, few pumpkins are fire-engine red.

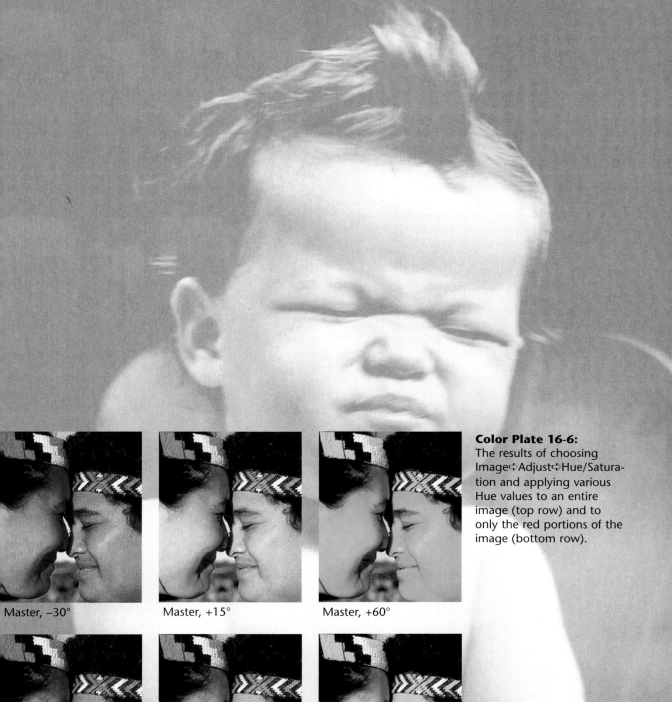

Color Plate 16-6:
The results of choosing
Image⇨Adjust⇨Hue/Saturation and applying various
Hue values to an entire
image (top row) and to
only the red portions of the
image (bottom row).

Master, –30°

Master, +15°

Master, +60°

Red only, –30°

Red only, +15°

Red only, +60°

Color Plate 16-7:
The results of applying various Saturation values to an entire image (top row) and to specified colors independently of others (bottom row). Because flesh tones reside primarily in the red tonal range — regardless of the skin pigment of the subject — you can almost always enhance or temper skin colors by selecting the R (Red) option and adjusting the Saturation value.

Master, -50

Master, +30

All But red, -100

Red, -100, All others, +50

Master, -50°

Master, +50°

Faces, -25°,
Background, 155°

Faces, 75°,
Background, -115°

Color Plate 16-8:
The results of applying various Hue values to an image when the Colorize option is inactive (top row) and active (bottom row). Note that while the top two images contain a rainbow of differently colored pixels, the bottom images contain only two apiece — pink and teal (bottom left), and chartreuse and violet (bottom right).

Color Plate 16-9:
You can change the hue and saturation and at the same time experiment with the affected area using the Replace Color command. The top row shows the results of clicking repeatedly on the pumpkin's face with one Fuzziness value (left) and clicking once in the background with another (right). The bottom examples show the results of adjusting the hues of predefined colors using the Selective Color command.

Fuzziness, 40

Fuzziness, 200

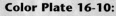

Red to violet, Relative

Red to violet and black to white, Absolute

More Green

Lighter

More Yellow

Color Plate 16-10:
The effects of applying each of the thumbnails offered in the Variations dialog box to the familiar pumpkin. In each case, the slider bar was set to its default setting, midway between Fine and Coarse, and the Midtones radio button was selected.

More Cyan

Original

More Red

More Blue

Darker

More Magenta

Color Plate 16-11:
The original scan of this 100-year-old poster required some color correction (top left). Although applying the Auto button from the Levels dialog box improved the image dramatically (bottom left), manually adjusting the Input Levels slider bars further enhanced the image by bringing out the medium gray values (right).

Color Plate 16-12:
The results of using the Curves command to lighten the colors in the red channel (left), increase the level of contrast in the green channel (middle), and apply an arbitrary color map to the blue channel (right).

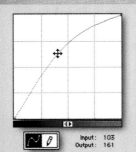

Input: 103
Output: 161

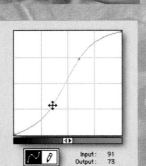

Input: 91
Output: 73

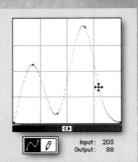

Input: 203
Output: 88

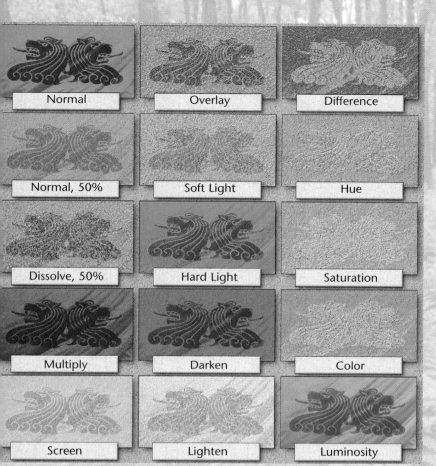

Normal	Overlay	Difference
Normal, 50%	Soft Light	Hue
Dissolve, 50%	Hard Light	Saturation
Multiply	Darken	Color
Screen	Lighten	Luminosity

Color Plate 17-1:
Examples of all 14 options available from the overlay modes pop-up menu in the Layers palette when you edit a layer or floating selection, represented here by the banner. Each overlay mode allows you to mix colors in a floating selection with colors in the underlying image in a unique way. Unless otherwise noted, the Opacity of each banner is set to 100 percent.

Color Plate 17-2:
Though frightening, these reckless combinations of bright colors are useful for demonstrating the effects of applying fuzziness ranges independently to the red (top row), green (middle), and blue (bottom) color channels using the This Layer (left column) and Underlying (right column) slider triangles. The banner in the upper right corner fades out because the underlying stucco texture is colored with a yellow-to-pink gradation, and the pink pixels are being forced through.

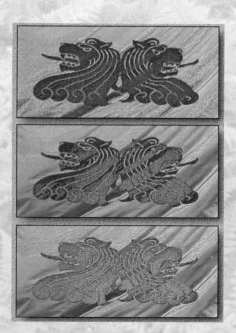

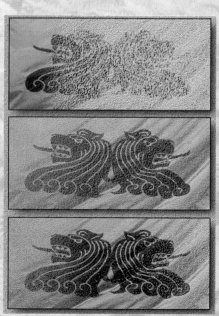

Color Plate 17-3: For the purpose of comparison, the first image shows the result of compositing the RGB image from Color Plate 5-1 onto itself using the Hard Light mode. Other examples show the different effects you can achieve by duplicating the image, converting it to the Lab mode, and then mixing it with the original RGB image using the Apply Image command, again set to Hard Light.

RGB on RGB

Lab on RGB

Lightness on RGB

Inverted b on RGB

Mask Channel

Hard Light

Color Plate 17-4: After creating a separate mask channel (top left), I used this mask to protect the sky in the target image. Though I used the Apply Image command to apply several compositing effects to the Capitol building, none affected the sky as long as the Mask check box was selected.

Screen

Inverted Difference

Color Plate 17-5: The results of applying the Add (top left), Subtract (middle left) and Difference (bottom left) overlay modes, followed by the same images after swapping the red and blue color channels (right column).

Color Plate 18-1: To create this embossed text, I first used the Apply Image command set to the Screen overlay mode to composite the beach image with a white logo created in a mask channel (left.) I then used the Hard Light overlay mode to composite an embossed version of the logo. To keep the embossed edges from flowing out into the image, I used the original logo as a mask (right).

Color Plate 18-2: To create a punched effect (left), I inverted the embossed version of the logo and combined it with the last image from the Color Plate 18-1 using the Overlay mode. I also inverted the mask to protect the letters themselves, which already appear raised. I then inverted the logo using the Difference mode (right).

Color Plate 18-3: To prepare the logo, I selected a logo-shaped area of my image, applied the Add Noise and Filter commands, floated the selection, filled it with white, and changed the Opacity to 40 percent (left). After using masks based on the embossed logo to draw in the highlights and shadows, I inverted the logo to give it a marble-like texture (right).

Layer 1, filtered

Background copy

Background copy 2

Color Plate 18-4:
The first column shows the result of compositing a single filtered image (that looks much like the one in the upper left corner) onto the plain Capitol dome from Color Plate 5-1. In the second column, I duplicated the underlying dome to a layer above the filtered image and applied additional overlay modes. In the third column, I duplicated the dome again and heaped on still more overlay modes. Only the bottom right example had to be flattened for color correction.

Hard Light

Hard Light

Hard Light

Difference

Color

Overlay

Hue

Hard Light

Difference with
Auto Levels

Color Plate 18-5:
Starting with the last column of images from Color Plate 18-4, I applied various effects and overlay modes to the top layer while leaving the other layers untouched. In the left column, I inverted the top layer. In the middle column, I applied the Ripple command at its maximum setting and shifted the hues −90 degrees using the Hue/Saturation command. In the right column, I applied the Add Noise filter.

Invert

Ripple &
Hue/Saturation

Add Noise

Color

Color

Overlay

Difference

Overlay

Screen

Overlay

Difference

Dissolve, 20%

If you choose Edit⇨Paste Into, Photoshop pastes the contents of the Clipboard inside the current selection. The selection, therefore, masks the pasted image. Photoshop 2.5 used to have a Paste Behind command that pasted the contents of the Clipboard behind the selected area of the image. But in Version 3, Paste Behind has disappeared. You now access this function by Alt-choosing Edit⇨Paste Into.

4. Using the type tool, drag the character outlines into position. Because the selection is in back of the image, you move only the outlines without affecting the image itself. When you get the outlines where you want them, choose Select⇨Defloat (Ctrl-J) to set the selection down so that it is no longer floating behind the image.

5. Selection and image are no longer separate entities. You now can clone the selected portion of the image and drag it to a new location, as demonstrated in Figure 12-13, or copy it to a new image.

Figure 12-13: The result of Alt-dragging the selected image to an empty part of the image window using one of the selection tools.

Painting raised type

Instead of moving the selected image or copying it to a different window, as suggested in step 5 of the preceding section, you can paint around the character outlines to create a raised-text effect, as illustrated in Figure 12-14.

Figure 12-14: Raised type created by painting with the dodge and airbrush tools around the perimeter of the character outlines.

To create this image, we carried out the first four steps described in the preceding section and then prepared the characters by dragging inside them with the dodge tool. We used a 65-pixel soft brush shape and selected Shadows from the brush modes pop-up menu (on the left side of the Brushes palette) to concentrate the lightening effect on the very dark areas in the image.

As shown in the top image in Figure 12-15, this helps set the letters apart from the rest of the image. To give the letters depth, we set the foreground color to black and used the airbrush tool with a 35-pixel soft brush shape to apply shadows around the lower and right portions of each character, as shown in the middle row of Figure 12-15.

We next switched the foreground color to white and applied highlights around the upper and left portions of characters, which results in the image shown in the bottom row of Figure 12-15.

If you don't consider yourself an artist, you may find the prospect of painting around the edges of characters a little intimidating. But bear in mind that it's next to impossible to make a mistake. Because you're painting inside the selection, there's no danger of harming any portion of the image outside the character outlines. And if you mess up inside the selection, the problem is easily resolved.

If you look closely at the last image in Figure 12-15, for example, you can see that in applying white to the arch of the *a,* we accidentally got some on the right corner of the *e.* Hey, nobody's perfect. To fix the problem, all we need to do is select a smaller brush shape and paint over that area of the *e* with black.

So if you make a mistake, choose Edit⇨Undo or just keep painting. Give it a try. The process takes less than an hour and we bet you'll be pleasantly surprised with your results.

Figure 12-15: After using the dodge tool to lighten the darkest pixels inside the letters (top), we painted in the shadows by airbrushing in black around the right and bottom edges of the letters (middle). Finally, we painted in the highlights by airbrushing in white around the left and top edges of the letters (bottom).

Feathering effects

You can feather text outlines just as you can feather other kinds of selections. However, in doing so, you modify the shape of the selection and, therefore, set the characters down in the image area.

If you want to combine feathered text with an image, take care to paste the text behind the image by Alt-choosing Edit⇨Paste Into, as explained in steps 2 and 3 in the recent section "Filling type with an image." (You don't have to perform step 4, choosing Select⇨Defloat, because feathering automatically defloats the selection.) Otherwise, you leave behind deselected remnants of the foreground color that was used to fill the characters.

For example, the top image in Figure 12-16 shows the result of creating a line of type, feathering it with an 8-pixel radius, and deleting the feathered selection. You can plainly see that Photoshop leaves behind a harsh black outline after the deletion. If, on the other hand, you create the type, cut it to the Clipboard, select the image, paste the type in back of the image, and *then* feather it and delete it, you eliminate any chance that some of the type will be left behind, as demonstrated in the bottom image in Figure 12-16.

Figure 12-16: The results of feathering and deleting text positioned in front of an image (top) and in back of an image (bottom).

The following steps describe how to create a backlighting effect using Photoshop's feathering capability. Figure 12-17 shows the finished image. To simplify the process, the text appears in front of a plain black background. But you can just as easily apply this technique to an image as long as you take care to paste the text behind the image before choosing Select⇨Feather.

Figure 12-17: You can create backlit text — also known as the movie-of-the-week effect — by deleting a feathered version of a line of type and then pasting the original, unfeathered type in front (top). A slash of the airbrush takes away some of the flatness of the image (bottom).

Steps: Using feathering to backlight text

1. Create a new image window large enough to accommodate a single line of large text. We created an image 800 pixels wide by 300 pixels tall.

2. Choose Select➪All (Ctrl-A) and press Alt-Del to fill the entire image with black. (We're assuming here that black is the foreground color and white is the background color. If this is not the case, press D to make it so.)

3. Create your text using the type tool and the Type Tool dialog box. The text in the figure is set in 240-pixel Helvetica Inserat, a member of the Adobe Type Library.

4. Copy the text to the Clipboard (Ctrl-C).

5. Choose Select➪Feather, enter a number that's about equal to $1/20$ the resolution of your image into the Radius option box, and press Enter. Our resolution is about 180 ppi, so we entered 9. (Dividing by 20 isn't a hard and fast rule — you can use any Radius value that works for your image.)

6. Press the Delete key to fill the feathered selection with white.

7. Choose Edit⇨Paste (Ctrl-V) to reintroduce the copied line of text to the image. As long as you don't select the feathered area, the black letters will appear in same spot from which they were copied. Use the down arrow key to nudge the selection 3 to 5 pixels. The result is shown in the top half of Figure 12-17.

8. For extra credit, set the foreground color to 50 percent black and then use the airbrush tool with the 100-pixel soft brush shape to paint a single line across the text. This creates the effect of light seeping through a slightly open door, as shown in the bottom half of the figure.

If you read Chapter 10, you'll recognize this as a close cousin — *very* close, more like a Siamese twin — of the haloing technique described in the "Creating drop shadows, halos, and spotlights" section. In this example, you don't have to resort to layers because the letters and background are the same color, black. But if you wanted to set green letters against a red background — like, maybe to create a really scary Christmas card — you would need to send the letters to their own layer in step 3, skip step 4, sink the selection to the background layer and then feather it in step 5, skip step 6, and finally go back to the layer and paint inside the letters with the Preserve Transparency check box selected. Go back to Chapter 10 if you need a refresher. If you do, don't forget that any text block works exactly like a filled selection outline.

Drop shadows

That same section of Chapter 10 also covered how to create drop shadows. And again, the process is a little easier when you're working with text because you don't have to fool around with layers. This section examines two methods for adding drop shadows: one that involves changing the translucency of type (demonstrated in Figure 12-18), and another that relies on feathering (Figure 12-19).

Note The first steps work only if the text and drop shadow are the same color. In the second set of steps, the text and background can be any colors.

Steps: Creating quick and easy hard-edged drop shadows

1. Create your text. In Figure 12-18, we used an unusual typeface called Remedy Single from Emigré Graphics. It's about the wildest font we've ever come across — it looks like something The Cure might use on its album covers — so it lends itself well to this technique, which is by contrast quite simple.

2. Select any selection tool and clone the selected type by Alt-dragging it a few pixels down and to the right.

3. Press 4 on the keyboard to lower the opacity of the cloned selection to 40 percent. The translucent clone serves as the drop shadow.

Figure 12-18: We took two lines of type set in the font Remedy (yes, those lower characters are part of the font), cloned the paragraph, and changed the opacity of the clone to 40 percent.

The benefit of this technique is that it takes about six seconds to complete. The downside is that it only works with text that is set in a solid color. You can't paint inside the text or fill it with an image because the drop shadow actually lies in front of the text.

The next steps describe a more functional, albeit slightly more complicated, drop shadow technique. The effect is illustrated in Figure 12-19.

Steps: Creating a feathered drop shadow

1. Create your type. Use any foreground and background colors you want. Figure 12-19 features that old standby, 240-pixel Helvetica Inserat, in that old standby color, black.

2. Cut the text to the Clipboard (Ctrl-X). Then select the entire image (Ctrl-A) and Alt-choose Edit⇨Paste Into to paste the letters behind the selected image.

3. Choose Select⇨Feather, enter whatever value you like into the Radius option box, and press Enter. We entered 8 because it looks like a snowman with its head knocked off and also because it was roughly $1/20$ of the resolution of the image. The selection is now feathered.

4. Press Alt-Del to fill the feathered text with black, as shown in the first example of Figure 12-19. If black is not your foreground color, float the feathered selection (Ctrl-J) before filling it (Alt-Del). Then choose Multiply from the overlay modes pop-up menu in the Layers palette and change the Opacity if you so desire. Whatever color you use, the feathered text will serve as the drop shadow.

5. Paste another copy of the text in front of the drop shadow (Ctrl-V) and nudge it slightly off-center from the shadow, as demonstrated in the second row of Figure 12-19. (We've made the text white so that you can see it clearly against the black shadow.)

6. From here on, what you do with the text is up to you. You can fill the selected type with a different color or gradation. We chose to paint inside the characters with the rubber stamp and airbrush tools. After defining a pattern from a small selection in the familiar ColorBytes gears image (Figures 12-11 through 12-16), we selected the rubber stamp tool and chose Pattern (aligned) from the Options pop-up menu in the Rubber Stamp Options panel. Then we painted inside the text with a 65-pixel brush shape, taking care to leave some white spaces showing. To finish things off, we dragged with the airbrush tool and a 35-pixel brush shape. The result is the bottom image shown in Figure 12-19.

Figure 12-19: Feather the text and fill it with black to create the drop shadow (top). Then paste the copied version of the text in front of the drop shadow (middle) and paint inside the characters as desired (bottom).

Converting characters to paths

You can create your own letterforms by editing selection outlines using the tools in the Paths palette. After creating the text you want to edit, choose the Make Path command from the Paths palette menu, edit the selection outlines as desired, and choose the Make Selection command. This technique is perfectly suited to designing logos and other elements that call for custom characters. The following steps explain the technique in greater detail and describe how we created the type shown in Figure 12-22. (Figures 12-20 and 12-21 illustrate steps in the process.)

Steps: Editing a character outline using the path tools

1. Begin by creating your text, as always. When inside the Type Tool dialog box, select a font that best matches the eventual letterforms you want to create. We selected Avant Garde Gothic because of its perfectly circular letterforms, which go well with the circular shapes in the ColorBytes gears image (see Figure 12-20).

2. After creating your text, place it in back of your image so that you don't leave any deselected characters sitting around. Choose Edit⇨Cut (Ctrl-X) to send the text to the Clipboard. Then choose Select⇨All (Ctrl-A) and then Alt-choose Edit⇨Paste Into.

3. Applying one of Photoshop's transformation effects to alter the text is sometimes a good first step in creating custom letterforms. It enables you to prepare outlines for future edits by minimizing the number of point-by-point edits you have to perform later. In this case, we wanted to rotate our single character — a circular letter e — to a different angle. We chose Image⇨Rotate⇨Free and dragged the corner handles until the angle of the horizontal bar in the e matched the angle of the rod protruding from one of the gears, as demonstrated in Figure 12-20. Then we clicked inside the character with the gavel cursor to exit the transformation mode.

Figure 12-20: We rotated the angle of the character outline to match the angle of the rod coming out of the central gear.

4. Choose the Make Path command from the Paths palette menu (or click on that little convert-to-selection/path icon at the bottom of the palette) and press Enter to accept the default Tolerance setting. Photoshop converts the character outline to a Bézier path, as shown in the left example in Figure 12-21.

Figure 12-21: After converting the letter to a path (left), we edited the outline by moving and deleting points (right).

5. Edit the Bézier path as desired using the tools in the Paths palette. We reduced the thickness of the circular perimeter of the *e* by dragging the inside edges of the paths outward with the arrow tool, as illustrated in the second example of Figure 12-21. We also simplified the structure of the paths by deleting some points with the remove point tool. Finally, we shortened the length of the *e*'s lip — that loose part that swings around to the right and makes the letter look like it's smiling.

6. When you finish editing the character outlines, save them by choosing Save Path from the Paths palette menu. Then choose the Make Selection command and press Enter to accept the default settings. Or just press the Enter key to avoid both command and dialog boxes altogether. The letters are again selection outlines.

7. What you do from this point on is up to you. Want to know what we did? Sure you do. We copied the selection, created a new image window measuring about 500 × 500 pixels, and pasted the *e* into the window's center. Then we clicked the switch colors icon in the toolbox to make white the foreground color and black the background color. We wanted to create a drop shadow for the character, so we pressed Alt-Del to fill the selection with white and then chose Select⇨Feather and set the Radius value to 8. (Who can say why we're so stuck on this value? Maybe we're in a rut.) To complete the drop shadow, we pressed the Delete key to fill the feathered selection with black. Next, we pasted the character again and nudged it a few pixels up and to the left to offset it in relation to the shadow. Then, with the type tool still active, we selected the Dissolve option from the brush modes pop-up menu in the Brushes palette to rough up the edges of the floating character. The finished character appears in Figure 12-22.

Figure 12-22: We used the Dissolve option in the brush modes pop-up menu to randomize the pixels along the edges of the character.

Where Text and Filters Meet

The other chapters in this part of the book revolve around using Photoshop's filters. Now, there must be close to a bazillion ways to combine text outlines and filters (that's only an estimate, of course), but before you leave this chapter, we want to show you just two. Both techniques permit you to actually build an image inside Photoshop using text. You vary the brightness and boldness of each letter to create a pattern of characters that suggests an image. It's sort of like the custom halftoning effect that Photoshop can apply automatically to black-and-white images (as shown in Figure 4-14 back in Chapter 4), except that instead of using a repeating image pattern, the individual color cells are made up of characters of text. If you're still not quite sure what I'm talking about, Figures 12-24 and 12-25 show one possible result of each technique.

To start with, you need a high-resolution, grayscale image, 200 ppi or better. The high resolution will make your text more legible and permit more letters to fit inside smaller areas in your image, hence increasing image detail. In Figure 12-23, we selected the grumpy baby image from PhotoDisc's "Retro Americana" collection that we featured in Chapter 6, except that this time the nose ring and anarchy tattoo are absent. The resolution of the image is 240 ppi. We masked off the image and removed the background to make the baby stand out as much as possible. We also used the Levels command to increase the contrast in the image, as described in Chapter 16.

When you have your image in hand, you're ready to take on the following steps:

Steps: The easy way to build an image out of text

1. Start by saving your image. In the next few steps, you're going to destroy it.

2. Display the Channels palette and drag the Black channel onto the duplicate channel icon at the bottom of the palette. This creates a new mask channel filled with a clone of your image.

3. Press Ctrl-1 to return to the Black channel. This technique relies on white text against a black background. Prepare the foreground and background colors by pressing D and then X. Now white is the foreground color, and black is the background color.

4. Select the entire image (Ctrl-A) and press the Delete key. The window turns black. (Don't worry. The original image is still safe in the mask channel.)

5. Use the text tool to fill the screen with text. Enter anything you want. We recommend using a bold font that's very easy to read. We used 36-point Helvetica Bold, the plainest font in town. Insofar as filling the image window is concerned, you might want to take measurements. Create a very long line and see how much will fit across the screen. Then insert paragraph returns inside the Type Tool dialog box accordingly. You'll probably have to create your text in a few passes. We created the text shown in Figure 12-23 one line at a time.

Figure 12-23: A screen full of white text against a black background (top) and the image that served as the mask (bottom). Together, we used these two images to create the text/image montages shown in Figures 12-24 and 12-25.

Note   Don't worry, this is the hardest step. Well, at least it's the most tedious. After you're finished, you may want to save your image under a different name (using File⇨Save a Copy, in the Photoshop or TIFF format) so that you don't have to redo all this work if you decide to attempt the next set of steps.

6. Now, make the text shrink where the image is dark and make it grow where the image is light. Alt-click on the mask channel name (presumably Black Copy) in the Channels palette to convert it to a selection outline. This outline represents the lightest portions of the image. But we suggest that you start by thinning the letters inside the darkest areas. So choose Select⇨Inverse to draw the selection around the darkest portions of the image.

7. Choose Filter⇨Other⇨Minimum. This filter increases the size of the black areas in your image. For my 240 ppi image, we entered a value of 2 to instruct Photoshop to expand the black areas by two pixels. If the resolution of your image is higher, you may want to enter a higher value. Then press Enter. Notice that the selected letters have lost weight in direct proportion to the darkness of the original image. Cool, huh? (If you want to experiment with different values, just press Ctrl-Z to undo the effect and press Ctrl-Alt-F to again display the Minimum dialog box.)

8. That's it for the dark areas; now for the light ones. Choose Select⇨Inverse to select the light areas. Then choose Filter⇨Other⇨Maximum. The exact opposite of the Minimum filter, Maximum expands the white areas of your image. Figure 12-24 shows the result of entering 3 in the Maximum dialog box and pressing Enter. We know, it's a higher value than we entered into the Minimum dialog box, and here's the reason: A Minimum value of more than 2 would have completely eliminated a large amount of the text, whereas a Maximum value of 3 still leaves a few distinguishing holes — inside the *o*s and *d*s — in the fattest of the expanded characters.

Using the Minimum and Maximum filters has the advantage of being remarkably straightforward. But it's not the best method. Most of the letters are barely legible, and all of the letterforms are pretty well ruined. The next steps show a better but more difficult method for shrinking and expanding type that results in much more legible text. You'll be using the Gaussian Blur and Unsharp Mask filters, both discussed in great depth in the next chapter, and the Levels command, discussed in Chapter 16.

Figure 12-24: The result of applying the grumpy baby image as a mask and using the Minimum and Maximum filters to shrink and expand the letters, respectively.

Steps: The harder but better way to build an image out of text

1. Perform steps 1 through 5 from the previous technique. (If you saved your image as we advised in step 5, you can just open it and start from there.)

2. Before you select anything, choose Filter⇨Blur⇨Gaussian Blur. This filter instructs Photoshop to examine your image one pixel at a time and mix up pixels within a specified Radius. For our 240-ppi image, we entered a value of 2 and pressed Enter. We might raise it as high as 3 for a 300-ppi image; otherwise, 2 is fine. The image was once composed almost exclusively of black and white pixels; you have now introduced a whole host of gray pixels via the Gaussian Blur filter. In future steps, you nudge these gray pixels toward black or white to shrink or expand the letters.

3. Alt-click on the Black Copy mask channel in the Channels palette to select the light portion of your image. Choose Select➪Inverse to switch and select the dark portions instead.

4. Choose Image➪Adjust➪Levels or just press Ctrl-L. We don't have room to offer a complete explanation of the Levels dialog box here, so let us just say this: You enter values in the three Input option boxes at the top of the dialog box to specify the brightness of the pixels that will change to black, medium gray, and white, respectively. For now, you only need to be concerned with the first option box, which represents black, and the third option box, which represents white.

5. Enter 130 into the first option box and press Enter. This instructs Photoshop to send every selected pixel that's darker than a brightness value of 130 — roughly medium gray — to black. Partially selected pixels become only partially black. Lighter pixels become darker; only white remains white. The upshot is that the selected letters shrink.

6. You're done with the dark areas; now go to work on the light ones. Choose Select➪Inverse to deselect the stuff you just edited and select the stuff you haven't had a chance to mess up.

7. Choose the Levels command again (Ctrl-L). This time, you want to lighten the selected area instead of darkening it. To do this, change the value of the third Input option box at the top of the Levels dialog box. Enter 90 and press Enter. This tells Photoshop to send all selected pixels that are lighter than a brightness value of 90 — which, judging by the fact that 255 is white, is on the dark side of medium gray — to white. All darker grays are lightened to incrementally lighter colors except black, which remains black.

8. That's it. The last step is to firm things up by applying the Unsharp Mask filter, which sharpens the focus of the image. So choose Filter➪Sharpen➪Unsharp Mask. We recommend some pretty radical values in this dialog box. Enter 300 percent into the Amount option box. Because you blurred the image so aggressively before, enter 8 into the Radius option box (a very high value). Then press Enter. Figure 12-25 shows the result.

You can make out the baby face in Figures 12-24 and 12-25 about equally well. But the text in Figure 12-25 is decidedly more legible. Unlike Minimum and Maximum, the Gaussian Blur filter doesn't entirely eliminate detail, it merely smoothes it out. The Levels and Unsharp Mask commands helped to reestablish the detail.

And we don't know if you noticed it, but there's no way you could have pulled this off with Illustrator or FreeHand. Photoshop rules, dude. (Heh, heh.)

Robert

Figure 12-25: This time we bagged the Minimum and Maximum filters and relied instead on the Gaussian Blur filter to insert gray values into the letterforms and the Levels command to send those gray values to either black or white.

A Closing Note from The Windowizing Typographer

As you've read in my other additions to this chapter, I feel very strongly that you should learn something about type and typography if you're going to use text effectively in Photoshop. Ransom-note typography is ransom-note typography, whether you're doing it in PageMaker or Photoshop. That kind of typography is as the name implies — throwing together incompatible typefaces, much as ransom notes are composed by cutting and pasting individual letters and words from various parts of a newspaper or magazine. Try this experiment. Do four lines of type in any program you choose. For your faces, select Bookman, Times Roman, Palatino, and AvantGarde. Look at what you've done, and print it. It should look terrible to you. If it doesn't, you're ready for Type Basics 101 — no, I don't have the space to teach you that, but there are any number of excellent books, and tips in magazines, that will help you immensely.

But there's another matter you should be aware of even if you're way beyond ransom notes. Photoshop is capable of some really remarkable type effects. Deke has given you a typically superb introduction, and further examples can readily be found elsewhere. But remember this: The great typographers of the past, going all the way back to Mr. Aldus Manutius himself, didn't do drop shadows or extruded type. They produced typographic masterpieces by fine-tuning their use of the metal fonts. It's very much as Herb Lubalin once remarked, that the mark of good typography is that it appears to just grow naturally on the page.

That's not to say there isn't a use for type effects. Applied judiciously, they can do much. Special effects, by their very nature, are ephemeral and subject to vogues. After the posters for the movie *Raiders of the Lost Ark,* everyone seemed to want extruded type. People still do. But any special effect gets very old very fast. Your best move is to read this chapter, and as much else as you can, and take it all as a starting point for producing fresh special effects of your own.

The very best thing I can tell you to sum up is this. A number of years ago, the resident (still resident) font maven of *PC Magazine,* Edward Mendelson, remarked that you don't want your readers to think you enjoy doing bad things to good typefaces. Right on, Edward!

Corrective Filtering

Filter Basics

In Photoshop, *filters* enable you to apply automated effects to an image. Though named after photographer's filters, which typically allow you to correct lighting and perspective fluctuations, Photoshop's filters can accomplish a great deal more. You can slightly increase the focus of an image, introduce random pixels, add depth to an image, or completely rip it apart and reassemble it into a hurky pile of goo. Any number of special effects are made available via filters.

In and of themselves, these special effects aren't bad. There was probably even a time when you thought that spinning letters and reverberating voice-overs were hot stuff. But ever since you grew out of preadolescence, your taste has become, well, more refined. In truth, you're probably the same as you always were; you've simply grown tired of these particular effects. You've come to associate them with raunchy, local car-oriented commercials. Certainly, these effects are devoid of substance but, more important, they're devoid of creativity.

Robert

Right on, Deke! In fact, I'm going even further in Chapter 19. Why? Because although I totally approve of what Deke has just written, apparently not all readers have taken it to heart.

This chapter and the two that follow, therefore, are about the creative application of special effects. Rather than trying to show an image subject to every single filter — a service already performed quite adequately by the manual included with your software — these chapters explain exactly how the most important filters work and offer some concrete ways to use them.

A first look at filters

You access Photoshop's special-effects filters by choosing commands from the Filter menu. These commands fall into two general camps: corrective and destructive.

Corrective filters, which are the subject of this chapter, comprise limited functions that you use to modify scanned images and prepare an image for printing or screen display. In most cases, the effects are subtle enough that a viewer won't even notice that you applied a corrective filter. As demonstrated in Figure 13-1 and Color Plate 13-1, these filters include those that change the focus of an image (Blur, Sharpen), enhance color transitions (High Pass), and randomize pixels (Add Noise).

Figure 13-1: Michelangelo's *Moses* from Saint Peter in Chains subject to four corrective filters, including (clockwise from upper left) Blur, Sharpen More, High Pass, and Add Noise. You have to love those old, uncopyrighted masterpieces, not to mention those explicit basilica names.

Many corrective filters have direct opposites. Blur is the opposite of Sharpen, Despeckle is the opposite of Add Noise, and so on. This is not to say that one filter entirely removes the effect of the other; only reversion functions such as the Undo command provide that capability. Instead, two opposite filters produce contrasting effects.

Destructive filters — found under the Filter⊃Distort, Pixelate, Stylize, and, to a lesser extent, Render submenus — produce effects so dramatic that they can, if used improperly, completely overwhelm your artwork, making the filter more important than the image itself. A few examples of overwhelmed images appear in Figure 13-2 and Color Plate 13-2.

Figure 13-2: The effects of applying four destructive filters (clockwise from upper left): Facet, Find Edges, Ripple, and Pointillize. These filters produce such dramatic effects that they are best used in moderation.

Destructive filters produce way-cool effects, and many people gravitate toward them when first experimenting with Photoshop. But the filters invariably destroy the original clarity and composition of the image. Yes, every Photoshop function is destructive to a certain extent, but destructive filters change your image so extensively that you can't easily disguise the changes later by applying other filters or editing techniques.

To get the best results from these filters, apply them to selected portions of an image rather than to the entire image. In addition, apply them partially, as described in the upcoming "Float before filtering" section. And make sure to save your image to disk before applying a destructive filter so that you can revert to the saved image if your changes don't turn out the way you hoped.

Corrective filters are the subject of this chapter. Although they number fewer than their destructive counterparts, they represent the functions you're most likely to use on a day-to-day basis, so we spend more time on them. We devote fewer words to destructive filters, as you can read in Chapter 14. (The homemade effects explained in Chapter 15 fall into both camps.)

General filtering techniques

When you choose a command from the Filter menu, Photoshop applies the filter to the selected portion of the image. If no portion of the image is selected, Photoshop applies the filter to the entire image. Therefore, if you want to filter every nook and cranny of an image, choose Select⇨None (Ctrl-D) and then choose the desired command.

External plug-ins

Some filters are built into the Photoshop application. Others reside externally, inside the Plug-ins directory. And this can change — in Version 2.5, the JPEG filters lived in the Plug-ins directory, while with Version 3 they're built into Photoshop. The Plug-ins directory is as the name implies — not only does it contain the filters Adobe decided to make external, but it lets you add third-party filters as well — Kai's Power Tools and the Andromeda filters come to mind. Here, incidentally, Mac people are better served — there's an enormous number of shareware and freeware filters to be had.

R
%%
Robert

Here's something about locating your third-party filters. How many times do you have to install, say, your KPT filters? It used to be twice — once in Photoshop's Plug-ins directory, and once in a separate directory for other programs. You didn't absolutely have to do that second, separate directory — if you were using, say, Fractal Design Painter you could just point it to your Photoshop Plug-ins directory. If you did that, on first glance it looked wonderful. *Hey, who needs Photoshop? I can access all my native Photoshop filters out of Painter.* Alas, not all good things in life are free. When you'd try to use those Photoshop filters in Painter, you'd get a message that the filter required Photoshop. Your Plug-ins menu would be clogged with filters you couldn't use — so to get around it, you'd do a second install of KPT in its own directory and point Painter there.

This situation now seems to have changed for the better. Although Adobe has revised the filters from Version 3.04 onwards so that in theory they don't need Photoshop to run if (a big *if*) the host program supports the 3.04 Plug-ins API, it's not clear that any currently shipping program does so (apart, obviously, from Photoshop itself). But, and this is the whole point now, you can now direct, say, Painter to your Photoshop Plug-ins directory and it will pick up on the third-party filters and no others. No more menu clog! No more extra directories! (Robert has tested many programs for this.)

Previewing filters

Nearly every filter that displays a dialog box includes two previewing capabilities. As shown in Figure 13-3, the first is a 100 × 100-pixel preview box inside the dialog box. Drag inside the preview box to scroll the portion of the image you want to preview. Move the cursor outside the dialog box to get the square preview cursor (labeled in the figure). Click with the cursor to center the contents of the preview box at the clicked position in the image. Click on the zoom buttons (+ and –) to reduce the image inside the preview box.

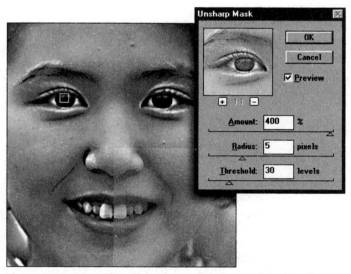

Figure 13-3: Most filter dialog boxes let you preview the effects of the filter both inside the dialog box and in the image window.

Tip   In addition to clicking on the zoom buttons, you can access the zoom tool inside the preview box by pressing Ctrl-spacebar or Alt-spacebar, depending on whether you want to zoom in or out.

Many dialog boxes also preview effects in the full image window. Just select the Preview check box to activate this function. While the effect is previewing, a blinking progress line appears under the check box. (You may also notice a blinking line under the Zoom Ratio numbers when the contents of the preview box are updating.) In Figure 13-3, for example, you can see that the lower right quadrant of the image hasn't finished previewing, so the progress line strobes away. If you're working on a slower computer, you'll probably want to turn this check box off to speed up the pace at which the filter functions. (Incidentally, the Preview check box does not affect the contents of the preview box; the latter always displays, whether you like it or not.)

Tip   Use the Preview check box to compare the before and after effects of a filter in the image window. Turn it on to see the effect; turn it off to see the original image. You can also compare the image in the preview box by clicking on the box. Mouse down to see the old image; release to see the filtered image.

More tips, more tips: Even though a dialog box is on-screen and active, you can zoom and scroll the contents of the image window. Ctrl-spacebar-click to zoom in, Alt-spacebar-click to zoom out, and spacebar-drag to scroll.

And one more: When you press the Alt key, the Cancel button changes to a Reset button. Alt-click on this button to restore the settings that appeared when you first opened the dialog box. (These are not necessarily the factory default settings; they are the settings you last applied to an image.)

Only a few, very time-consuming filters can't preview in the image window. These include all filters under the Filter⇨Distort and Render submenus, all filters under the Filter⇨Pixelate submenu except Mosaic, and the Wind and Filter Factory filters. Six filters leave you completely blind, previewing neither in the image window nor inside the dialog box: Radial Blur, Displace, Color Halftone, Extrude, Tiles, and De-Interlace. Of course, single-shot filters — the ones that don't bring up dialog boxes — don't need previews because there aren't any settings to adjust.

Reapplying the last filter

Tip   To reapply the last filter used in the current Photoshop session, choose the first command from the Filter menu or simply press Ctrl-F. If you want to reapply the filter subject to different settings, Alt-choose the first Filter command or press Ctrl-Alt-F to redisplay that filter's dialog box.

Both techniques work even if you undo the last application of a filter. However, if you cancel a filter while in progress, pressing Ctrl-F or Ctrl-Alt-F applies the last uncanceled filter.

Float before filtering

In many cases, you apply filters to a selection or image at full intensity, meaning that you marquee an area using a selection tool, choose a filter command, enter whatever settings you deem appropriate if a dialog box appears, and sit back and watch the fireworks.

You can dissipate the intensity of a filter by floating the selection and then mixing it with the original, underlying image by using the Opacity slider bar and the overlay modes pop-up menu in the Layers palette.

For example, Figure 13-4 shows a series of applications of the Emboss filter (from the Filter⇨Stylize submenu). The original image appears in the upper left corner; the full-intensity effect of the filter appears in the lower right corner. To create the images in between, we floated the selection, applied the filter, and then changed the Opacity setting in the Layers palette to the value that appears in the figure.

An alternative method is to select the image, enter the quick mask mode (or a separate mask channel), and fill the area that you want to select with a percentage of black equal to the opposite of the Opacity value. An 80 percent black results in the 20 percent filtering effect, a 60 percent black results in the 40 percent effect, and so on. This technique works because — as you may recall from Chapter 9 — white in the quick mask mode equates to a full-intensity selection and 100 percent black equates to no selection. After filling the selection, you return to the marching ants mode and apply the filter.

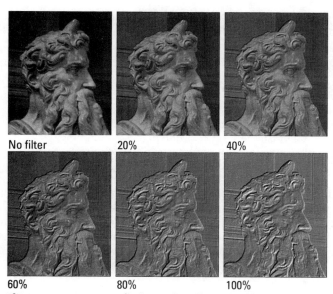

No filter   20%   40%

60%   80%   100%

Figure 13-4: You can dissipate the effect of a filter by overlaying a translucent filtered image over the unfiltered original or by editing the selection in the quick mask mode.

Although floating is more straightforward and offers the added advantage of enabling you to see the results of Opacity settings and overlay modes on the fly, the quick mask method offers its own advantages. You can paint partial selections in the quick mask mode that are either exceedingly complex or impossible to duplicate in the marching ants mode. Figure 13-5 shows a row of selections as they appear in the quick mask mode followed by the result of applying the Emboss filter to each of these selections in the marching ants mode.

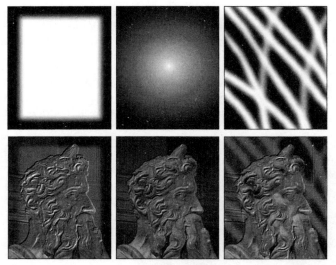

Figure 13-5: After creating a selection in the quick mask mode (top row), we applied the Emboss filter to each selection in the marching ants mode (bottom row).

And, certainly, there's nothing to prevent you from combining these two powerful options. You can achieve the best of both worlds by painting a selection outline in the quick mask mode, switching to the marching ants mode, floating the image, filtering it, and then experimenting with the Opacity and overlay mode settings. In fact, we never filter an image without first floating it, regardless of how we drew the selection outline.

Floating inside a border

Here's another reason to float before you filter: If your image has a border around it — like the ones shown in Figure 13-6 — and you don't want the border to be considered in the filtering operation, be sure to float the image before applying the filter. The reason is that most filters take neighboring pixels into consideration even if they are not selected. By contrast, when a selection floats, it has no neighboring pixels and, therefore, the filter affects the selected pixels only.

Figure 13-6: The results of applying High Pass (top) and Unsharp Mask (bottom) to images surrounded by borders. In each case, only the image was selected; the border was not. You can see how floating the right examples prevented the borders from affecting the performance of the filters.

Figure 13-6 shows the results of applying two filters discussed early on in this chapter — High Pass and Unsharp Mask — when the image is anchored in place and when it's floating. In all cases, the 3-pixel border was not selected. In the left examples, the High Pass filter leaves a black residue around the edge and the Unsharp Mark filter leaves a white residue. Both residues vanish when the filters are applied to floating selections, as seen on the right.

Okay, here's one more reason to float before you filter, and that's it. Even if the area outside the selection is not a border per se — perhaps it's just a comparatively dark or light area that serves as a visual frame — floating comes in handy. You should always float the selection unless you specifically want edge pixels to be calculated by the filter.

Reverting a floating image

Floating protects the underlying image. You may have noticed that despite its many enhancements, Photoshop still offers only one Undo command, which reverses the last action performed. You also have a Revert command and various revert-to-snapshot options (as discussed in Chapter 11). But what if you don't want to save your image, nor do you want to bother with a snapshot? If you just want to experiment a little, floating is your solution. After applying 40 or 50 filtering effects to a floating image, you can undo all that automated abuse by simply pressing the Delete key.

Note By the way, every single argument we've made in favor of floating images also applies to floating's more permanent cousin, *layering*. Layers offer even more flexibility, in fact, because you can revisit them several times throughout the editing process without worrying about the image defloating. You can even conduct many experiments on a single image, each on a different layer, and then compare the results and select the one you like best.

Heightening Focus and Contrast

If you've experimented at all with Photoshop, you've no doubt had your way with many of the commands in the Filter⇨Sharpen submenu. By increasing the contrast between neighboring pixels, the sharpening filters enable you to compensate for image elements that were photographed or scanned slightly out of focus.

The Sharpen, Sharpen More, and Sharpen Edges commands are easy to use and immediate in their effect. However, you can achieve better results and widen your range of sharpening options if you learn how to use the Unsharp Mask and High Pass commands, which are discussed at length in the following pages.

Using the Unsharp Mask filter

The first thing you need to know about the Unsharp Mask filter is that it has a weird name. The filter has nothing to do with unsharpening — whatever that is — nor has it anything to do with Photoshop's masking capabilities. It's named after a traditional film compositing technique (which is also oddly named) that highlights the edges in an image by combining a blurred film negative with the original film positive.

To understand Unsharp Mask — or Photoshop's other sharpening filters, for that matter — you first need to understand some basic terminology. When you apply one of the sharpening filters, Photoshop increases the contrast between neighboring pixels. The effect is similar to what you see when you adjust a camera to bring a scene into sharper focus.

Two of Photoshop's sharpening filters, Sharpen and Sharpen More, affect whatever area of your image is selected. The Sharpen Edges filter, however, performs its sharpening operations only on the *edges* in the image — those areas that feature the highest amount of contrast.

Unsharp Mask gives you both sharpening options. It can sharpen only the edges of an image or it can sharpen any portion of an image according to your exact specifications, whether it finds an edge or not. It fulfills the exact same purposes as the Sharpen, Sharpen Edges, and Sharpen More commands, but it's much more versatile. Simply put, the Unsharp Mask tool is the only sharpening filter you'll ever need.

When you choose Filter⇨Sharpen⇨Unsharp Mask, Photoshop displays the Unsharp Mask dialog box, shown in Figure 13-7, which offers these options:

✦ **Amount:** Enter a value between 1 and 500 percent to specify the degree to which you want to sharpen the selected image. Higher values produce more pronounced effects.

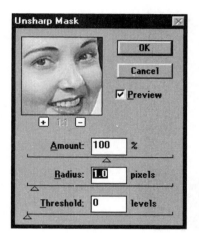

Figure 13-7: Despite any conclusions you may glean from its bizarre name, the Unsharp Mask filter sharpens images according to your specifications in this dialog box.

✦ **Radius:** This option enables you to distribute the effect of the filter by applying it over a range of 0.1 to 250.0 pixels at a time. Low values produce crisp images. High values produce softer, higher contrast effects.

✦ **Threshold:** Enter a value between 0 and 255 to control how Photoshop recognizes edges in an image. The value indicates the numerical difference between the brightness values of two neighboring pixels that must occur if Photoshop is to sharpen those pixels. A low value sharpens lots of pixels; a high value excludes most pixels from the running.

The preview options offered by the Unsharp Mask dialog box are absolutely essential visual aids that you're likely to find tremendously useful throughout your Photoshop career. Just the same, you'll be better prepared to experiment with the Amount, Radius, and Threshold options and less surprised by the results if you read the following sections, which explain these options in detail and demonstrate the effects of each.

Specifying the amount of sharpening

If Amount were the only Unsharp Mask option, no one would have any problems understanding this filter. If you want to sharpen an image ever so slightly, enter a low percentage value. Values between 25 and 50 percent are ideal for producing subtle effects. If you want to sharpen an image beyond the point of good taste, enter a value somewhere in the 300 to 500 percent range. And if you're looking for moderate sharpening, try out some value between 50 and 300 percent. Figure 13-8 shows the results of applying different Amount values while leaving the Radius and Threshold values at their default settings of 1.0 and 0, respectively.

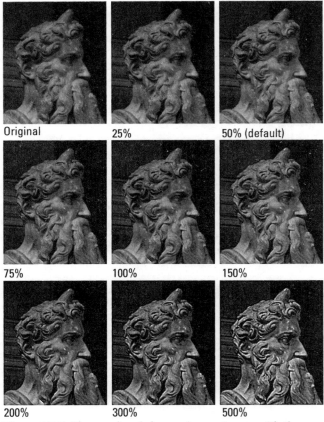

Figure 13-8: The results of sharpening an image with the Unsharp Mask filter using eight different Amount values. The Radius and Threshold values used for all images were 1.0 and 0, respectively (the default settings).

If you're not sure how much you want to sharpen an image, try out a small value, in the 25 to 50 percent range. Then reapply that setting repeatedly by pressing Ctrl-F. As you can see in Figure 13-9, repeatedly applying the filter at a low setting produces a nearly identical result to applying the filter once at a higher setting. For example, you can achieve the effect shown in the middle image in the figure by applying the Unsharp Mask filter three times at 50 percent or once at 250 percent.

The benefit of using small values is that they allow you to experiment with sharpening incrementally. As the figure demonstrates, you can add sharpening bit by bit to increase the focus of an image. You can't, however, reduce sharpening incrementally if you apply too high a value; you must choose Edit⊅Undo and start again.

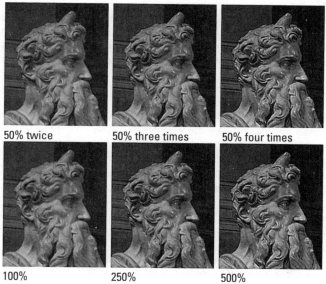

50% twice   50% three times   50% four times

100%   250%   500%

Figure 13-9: Repeatedly applying the Unsharp Mask filter at 50 percent (top row) is nearly equivalent on a pixel-by-pixel basis to applying the filter once at higher settings (bottom). The top row results were created using a constant Radius value of 1.0. In the second row, we lowered the Radius progressively from 1.0 (left) to 0.8 (middle) to 0.6 (right).

Just for fun, Color Plate 13-3 shows the results of applying the Unsharp Mask filter to each of the color channels in an RGB image independently. In each case, the Amount value was set to 300 percent, and the Radius and Threshold values were set to their defaults (1.0 and 0). To heighten the effect, we applied the filter twice to each channel. The top row shows the results of applying the filter to a single channel; in the second row, we applied the filter to two of the three channels (leaving only one channel unfiltered). You can see how the filter creates a crisp halo of color around the rose. Sharpening the red channel creates a red halo, sharpening the red and green channels together creates a yellow halo, and so on. Applying the filter to the red and green channels produced the most noticeable effects because these channels contain the lion's share of the image detail. The blue channel contained the least detail — as is typical — so sharpening it produced the least-dramatic results.

Cross Ref If you're a little foggy on how to access individual color channels, read Chapter 5. Incidentally, you can achieve similar effects by sharpening the individual channels in a Lab or CMYK image.

Distributing the effect

Here's the scoop: For each and every pixel Photoshop decides to sharpen, it distributes the effect according to the value you specify in the Radius option box. It's as if you selected the range of pixels identified by the Unsharp Mask filter's Threshold option, applied the Select⇨Feather command to them, and then applied the Amount value.

In fact, the Radius values offered by the Unsharp Mask and Feather dialog boxes operate on the exact same principle. The result is that lower values concentrate the impact of the Unsharp Mask filter. Higher values distribute the impact and, in doing so, lighten the lightest pixels and darken the darkest pixels, almost as if the image had been photocopied too many times.

Figure 13-10 demonstrates the results of specific Radius values. In each case, the Amount and Threshold values remain constant at 100 percent and 0, respectively.

Background Most softening effects in Photoshop — including feathering, softened brush shapes, and the radius of the Unsharp Mask filter — work according to a bell-shaped *Gaussian distribution curve.* The curve slopes gradually in the beginning, radically in the middle, and gradually at the end, thus softening the effect without altogether destroying its impact. The Unsharp Mask filter, however, conforms to the Gaussian curve only at Radius values of 2.0 and less. If you specify a radius greater than 2.0, the curve flattens out to accelerate the speed of the filter. The filter then destroys edges instead of working to retain edges as it does when the normal Gaussian curve is in effect. For this reason, we recommend that you use Radius values less than 2.0 to accomplish most of your sharpening effects.

Figure 13-11 shows the results of combining different Amount and Radius values. You can see that a large Amount value helps to offset the softening of a high Radius value. For example, when the Amount is set to 200 percent, as in the first row, the Radius value appears to mainly enhance contrast when raised from 0.5 to 2.0. However, when the Amount value is lowered to 50 percent, the higher Radius value does more to distribute the effect than boost contrast.

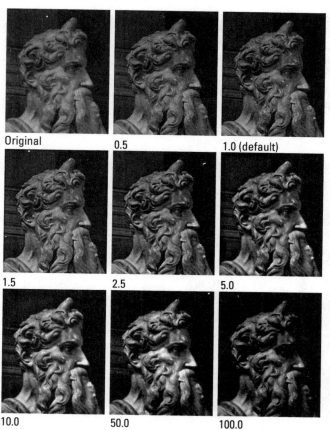

Figure 13-10: The results of applying eight different Radius values, ranging from precisely concentrated to overly generalized.

For those few folks who are thinking, *By gum, I wonder what would happen if you applied an unusually high Radius value to each color channel independently,* you have only to gaze upon the wondrous Color Plate 13-4. In this figure, we again applied the Unsharp Mask filter to each channel and each pair of channels in the RGB rose image independently. But we changed the Amount value to 100 percent, the Radius value to a relatively whopping 10.0 pixels, and left the Threshold at 0. To make the splash more apparent, we applied the filter twice to each image. The colors now bound out from the rose, bleeding into the gray background by as much as 10 pixels, the Radius value. Notice how the color fades away from the rose, just as if we'd feathered it? A high Radius value spreads the sharpening effect and, in doing so, allows colors to bleed. Because you normally apply the filter to all channels simultaneously, the colors bleed uniformly to create high-contrast effects.

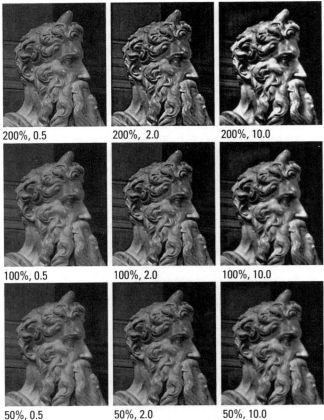

200%, 0.5   200%, 2.0   200%, 10.0

100%, 0.5   100%, 2.0   100%, 10.0

50%, 0.5   50%, 2.0   50%, 10.0

Figure 13-11: The results of combining different Amount (first value) and Radius (second value) settings. Relatively high Amount and Radius values bring out the deep curls in the hair, as you can see in the top middle image. The Threshold value for each image was set to 0, the default setting.

Recognizing edges

By default, the Unsharp Mask filter sharpens every pixel in a selection. However, you can instruct the filter to sharpen only the edges in an image by raising the Threshold value from 0 to some other number. The Threshold value represents the difference between two neighboring pixels — as measured in brightness levels — that must occur for Photoshop to recognize them as an edge.

Suppose that the brightness values of neighboring pixels A and B are 10 and 20. If you set the Threshold value to 5, Photoshop reads both pixels, notes that the difference between their brightness values is more than 5, and treats them as an edge. If you set the Threshold value to 20, however, Photoshop passes them by. A low Threshold value, therefore, causes the Unsharp Filter to affect a high number of pixels, and vice versa.

In the upper left image in Figure 13-12, the carved curls in the ravishing *Moses* hairdo stand out in stark contrast against the light gray of the poofier portions of the coiffure. We can sharpen the edges of the curls exclusively of other portions of the image by raising the Threshold value to 50 or even 30, as demonstrated in the second and third examples of the figure.

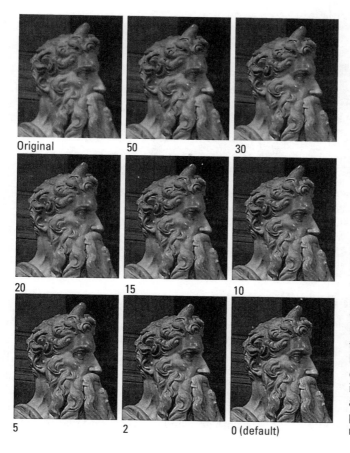

Original   50   30

20   15   10

5   2   0 (default)

Figure 13-12: The results of applying eight different Threshold values. High Threshold values limit the effect of the Unsharp Mask filter to high-contrast regions; low values apply the filter more evenly. To best show off the differences between each image, we set the Amount and Radius values to 500 percent and 0.5, respectively.

Using the preset sharpening filters

So how do the Sharpen, Sharpen Edges, and Sharpen More commands compare with the Unsharp Mask filter? First of all, none of the preset commands can distribute a sharpening effect, a function provided by the Unsharp Mask filter's Radius option. Secondly, only the Sharpen Edges command can recognize high-contrast areas in an image. And, third, all three commands are set in stone — you can't adjust their effects in any way. Figure 13-13 shows the effect of each preset command and the nearly equivalent effect created with the Unsharp Mask filter.

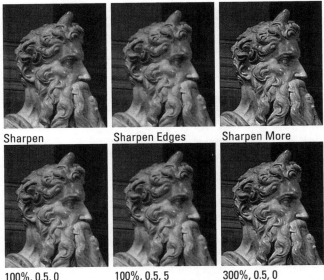

Sharpen   Sharpen Edges   Sharpen More

100%, 0.5, 0   100%, 0.5, 5   300%, 0.5, 0

Figure 13-13: The effects of the three preset sharpening filters (top row) compared with their Unsharp Mask equivalents (bottom row). Unsharp Mask values are listed in the following order: Amount, Radius, Threshold.

Using the High Pass filter

The High Pass filter falls more or less in the same camp as the sharpening filters but is not located under the Filter⇨Sharpen submenu. This frequently overlooked gem enables you to isolate high-contrast image areas from their low-contrast counterparts.

When you choose Filter⇨Other⇨High Pass, Photoshop offers a single option: the familiar Radius value, which can vary from 0.1 to 250.0. As demonstrated in Figure 13-14, high Radius values distinguish areas of high and low contrast only slightly. Low values change all high-contrast areas to dark gray and low-contrast areas to a slightly lighter gray. A value of 0.1, not shown in the figure, changes all pixels in an image to a single gray value and is, therefore, useless.

Applying High Pass to individual color channels

In our continuing series of color plates devoted to taking the simple beauty of a rose and abusing it but good, Color Plate 13-5 shows the results of applying the High Pass filter set to a Radius value of 10.0 to the various color channels. This application is actually a pretty interesting use for this filter. When applied to all channels at once, High Pass has an irritating habit of robbing the image of color in the low-contrast areas, just where the color is needed most. But when applied to a single channel,

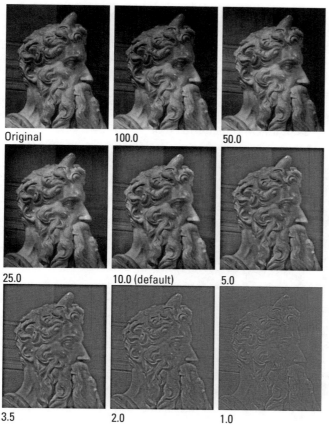

Figure 13-14: The results of separating high- and low-contrast areas in an image with the High Pass filter set at eight different Radius values.

there's no color to steal. In fact, the filter adds color. For example, because there is almost no contrast in the black shadow of the rose, High Pass elevates the black to gray in each of the affected color channels. The gray in the red channel appears red, the gray in the red channel mixed with the gray in the green channel appears yellow, and so on. As a result, the filter imbues each image with a chalky glow.

Note We enhanced the High Pass effect slightly in Color Plate 13-5 by increasing the contrast of each affected color channel using the Levels command. Using the three Input option boxes at the top of the Levels dialog box, we changed the first value to 65 and the third value to 190, thereby compressing the color space equally on both the black and white sides. Had we not done this, the images would appear a little more washed out. (Not a lot, but we figure that you deserve the best color we can deliver.) For more information on the Levels command, read Chapter 16.

Combining High Pass with Threshold

The High Pass filter is especially useful as a precursor to choosing Image⇨Map⇨ Threshold (Ctrl-T), which converts all pixels in an image to black and white. As illustrated in Figure 13-15, the Threshold command produces entirely different effects on images before and after you alter them with the High Pass filter. Applying the High Pass filter with a Radius value of 1.0 and then issuing the Threshold command converts your image into a line drawing. The effect is similar to choosing Filter⇨Stylize⇨Find Edges, but the lines are crisper and, obviously, black and white. (An image filtered with the Find Edges command remains in color.)

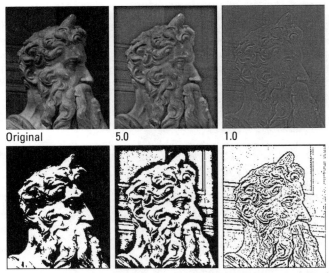

Figure 13-15: The original image and two counterparts edited with the High Pass command (top row) followed by the same images subject to the Threshold command set to 124 (bottom).

Why change your image to a bunch of slightly different gray values and then apply Image⇨Map⇨Threshold? Why, to select portions of an image using a mask channel, of course. Because the High Pass filter sees an image in terms of contrast levels, which is one of the ways your eyes perceive images in real life, it can be a useful first step in selecting an image element that is clearly visually unique but has proved difficult to isolate.

We introduced the idea of employing the Threshold command as a selection tool in the "Deriving selections from images" section of Chapter 9. The following steps explain how you can use the High Pass filter to help distinguish an image element from a busy background. The image in the top half of Figure 13-16 is used as an example.

Steps: Selecting an image element set against a busy background

1. Compare the red, green, and blue channels in your image to determine which one features the most contrast. At first, the channels may appear relatively similar but, with a little patience and effort, you can locate edge detail that — however slight — distinguishes the foreground image from its background.

2. After you decide on a channel — when in doubt, go with green — drag the channel name in the Channels palette onto the new channel icon at the bottom of the palette, thus duplicating the image to a separate mask channel.

3. Choose Filter⇔Other⇔High Pass and enter the desired Radius value. To create the image shown in the bottom half of Figure 13-16, we entered a Radius value of 3.0, which isolates most of the high-contrast portions of the image while retaining some thick outlines of solid color that will prove useful during the editing process. If your image is more highly focused than ours, enter a lower value. If less focused, raise the value. Don't go any lower than 1.0 or any higher than 6.0 or 7.0. (Resolution, incidentally, isn't a consideration.) Press Enter to filter the image.

Figure 13-16: A busy image before (top) and after (bottom) applying the High Pass filter with a Radius value of 3.0.

Figure 13-17: The result of applying the Threshold command set to 124 (top) and editing the black and white image with the eraser, pencil, and paint bucket tools (bottom).

4. Choose Image⇨Map⇨Threshold (Ctrl-T). We found the best balance of black and white pixels by setting the slider bar in the Threshold dialog box to 124. The resulting image appears in the top half of Figure 13-17.

5. You should now be able to eliminate the background elements fairly easily by dragging with the eraser tool. Because you're editing black and white pixels, it's best to set the eraser to its Pencil or Block mode, either of which offers hard edges. (Soft-edged cursors will introduce grays.) Next, use the pencil tool to close the gaps in the outline of the foreground elements and click with the paint bucket tool (set to a Tolerance of 0 and with Anti-aliased off) to fill the elements with black, as demonstrated in the second example of Figure 13-17. You'll probably have to fill in some remaining gaps by painting with the pencil tool with a large brush shape.

6. To apply the mask to the image, simply Alt-click on the mask channel in the Channels palette to convert the mask to a selection outline and press Ctrl-0 to return to your image (Ctrl-1 if you're working in grayscale). If you prefer to select the foreground elements, choose Select⇨Inverse.

Blurring an Image

The commands under the Filter⇨Blur submenu produce the opposite effects of their counterparts under the Filter⇨Sharpen submenu or, for that matter, the High Pass command. Rather than enhancing the amount of contrast between neighboring pixels, the Blur filters diminish contrast to create softening effects.

Gaussian blur

The preeminent Blur filter, Gaussian Blur, blends a specified number of pixels incrementally, following the bell-shaped Gaussian distribution curve we touched on earlier. When you choose Filter⇨Blur⇨Gaussian Blur, Photoshop produces a single Radius option box, in which you can enter any value from 0.1 to 250.0. (Beginning to sound familiar?) As demonstrated in Figure 13-18, Radius values of 1.0 and smaller blur an image slightly; moderate values, between 1.0 and 5.0, turn an image into a rude approximation of life without glasses on; higher values blur the image beyond recognition.

Tip   Applying the Gaussian Blur filter to a selection in the quick mask mode is almost the exact equivalent of feathering the selection in the marching ants mode. The only difference is that the Radius option in the Gaussian Blur dialog box is accurate to $^1/_{10}$ pixel, while its counterpart in the Feather dialog box accepts whole numbers only. To see this tip in action, read the "Softening a selection outline" section later in this chapter.

Moderate to high Radius values can be especially useful for creating that hugely amusing *Star Trek* Iridescent Human effect.

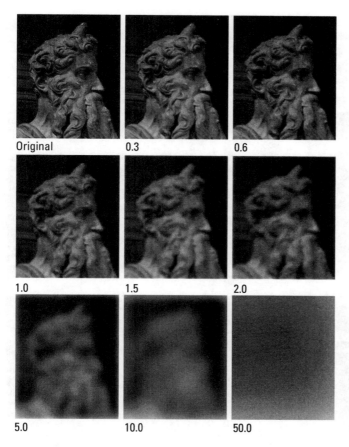

Original 0.3 0.6

1.0 1.5 2.0

5.0 10.0 50.0

Figure 13-18: The results of blurring an image with the Gaussian Blur filter using eight different Radius values, ranging from slightly out of focus to Bad Day at the Ophthalmologist's Office.

Unfortunately, we don't have any images of futuristic humans, so *Moses* will have to do in a pinch. The following steps explain how to make *Moses* glow as demonstrated in Figure 13-19.

Steps: The wondrous iridescent effect

1. Choose Select⇨All (Ctrl-A) to select the entire image. If you only want to apply the effect to a portion of the image, be sure to feather the selection with a radius in the neighborhood of 5 to 8 pixels.

2. Choose Select⇨Float (Ctrl-J) to clone the image in place.

3. Choose Filter⇨Blur⇨Gaussian Blur, enter some unusually large value into the Radius option box — say, 5.0 — and press Enter. This blurs the cloned image only; the original image remains unchanged.

4. Press M to make sure that a selection tool is active. Then press the 7 key to change the Opacity slider bar in the Layers palette to 70 percent, making the blurred image slightly translucent. This setting enables you to see the hard edges of the original image beneath the cloned image, as demonstrated in the first example of Figure 13-19.

Figure 13-19: After floating the selection, blurring it, and changing the Opacity slider bar to 70 percent, we applied overlay modes to alter the image further. Clockwise from upper left, the overlay modes used were Normal, Screen, Darken, and Lighten.

5. You can achieve additional effects by selecting options from the overlay modes pop-up menu on the left side of the Layers palette. For example, we created the image in the upper right corner of Figure 13-19 by selecting the Screen option, which combines colors in the original and floating images to create a lightening effect. We created the two bottom examples in the figure by choosing the Lighten and Darken options.

Color Plate 13-6 shows a young agrarian woman subject to most of the same settings we applied earlier to *Moses*. Again, we floated the image and applied the Gaussian Blur filter with a Radius of 5.0. The upper left image shows the Normal overlay mode, but the upper right image shows the Luminosity mode. In this case, the Screen mode resulted in a washed-out effect, whereas Luminosity yielded an image with crisp color detail and fuzzy brightness values. As a result, there are some interesting places where the colors leap off her checkered dress. As in Figure 13-19, the bottom two images show the effects of the Lighten and Darken modes.

Preset blurring filters

Neither of the two preset commands in the Filter⇨Blur submenu, Blur and Blur More, can distribute its blurring effect over a bell-shaped Gaussian curve. For that reason, these two commands are less functional than the Gaussian Blur filter. However, just so you know where they stand in the grand Photoshop focusing scheme, Figure 13-20 shows the effect of each preset command and the nearly equivalent effect created with the Gaussian Blur filter.

Blur   Blur More

0.3   0.7

Figure 13-20: The effects of the two preset blurring filters (top row) compared with their Gaussian Blur equivalents (bottom row), which are labeled according to Radius values.

Anti-aliasing an image

If you have a particularly jagged image, such as a 256-color .GIF file, there's a better way to soften the rough edges than applying the Gaussian Blur filter. The best solution is to anti-alias the image. How? After all, Photoshop doesn't offer an Anti-alias filter. Well, think about it. Back in Chapter 8, we described how Photoshop anti-aliases a brushstroke or selection outline at twice its normal size and then reduces it by 50 percent and applies bicubic interpolation. You can do the same thing with an image.

First, go into the General Preferences dialog box (Ctrl-K) and make sure that Bicubic is selected from the Interpolation pop-up menu. (You can also experiment with Bilinear for a slightly different effect, but don't use Nearest Neighbor.) Next, choose Image⇨Image Size and enlarge the image to 200 percent of its present size. Finally, turn right around and choose Image⇨Image Size again, but this time shrink the image by 50 percent.

The top left example in Figure 13-21 shows a jagged image subject to this effect. We used Image⇨Map⇨Posterize to reduce *Moses* to four colors. It's ugly, but it's not unlike the kind of images you may encounter, particularly if you have access to an aging image library. To the right is the same image subject to Gaussian Blur with a very low Radius value of 0.5. Rather than appearing softened, the result is just plain fuzzy.

However, if we enlarge instead and reduce the image with the Image Size command, we achieve a true softening effect, as shown in the lower left example in the figure, commensurate with Photoshop's anti-aliasing options. Even after enlarging and reducing the image four times in a row — as in the bottom right example — we don't make the image blurry, we simply make it softer.

Directional blurring

In addition to its everyday blurring functions, Photoshop provides two *directional blurring* filters, Motion Blur and Radial Blur. Instead of blurring pixels in feathered clusters like the Gaussian Blur filter, the Motion Blur filter blurs pixels in straight lines over a specified distance. The Radial Blur filter blurs pixels in varying degrees depending on their distance from the center of the blur. The following pages explain both of these filters in detail.

Motion blurring

The Motion Blur filter makes an image appear as if either the image or camera was moving when you shot the photo. When you choose Filter⇨Blur⇨Motion Blur, Photoshop displays the dialog box shown in Figure 13-22. You enter the angle of movement into the Angle option box. Alternatively, you can indicate the angle by dragging the straight line inside the circle on the right side of the dialog box, as shown in the figure. (You'll notice that the arrow cursor actually appears outside the circle. Once you begin dragging on the line, you can move the cursor anywhere you want and still affect the angle.)

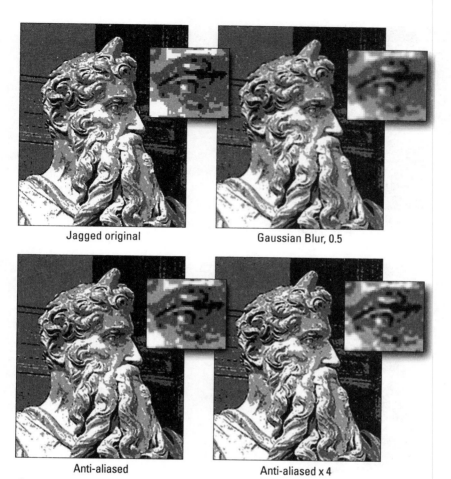

Jagged original

Gaussian Blur, 0.5

Anti-aliased

Anti-aliased x 4

Figure 13-21: A particularly jagged image (top left) followed by the image blurred using a filter (top right). By enlarging and reducing the image one or more times (bottom left and right), we can soften the pixels without making them appear blurry. The enlarged details show each operation's effect on the individual pixels.

You then enter the distance of the movement in the Distance option box. Photoshop permits any value between 1 and 999 pixels. The filter distributes the effect of the blur over the course of the Distance value, as illustrated by the examples in Figure 13-23.

Background Mathematically speaking, Motion Blur is one of Photoshop's simpler filters. Rather than distributing the effect over a Gaussian curve — which one might argue would produce a more believable effect — Photoshop creates a simple linear distribution, peaking in the center and fading at either end. It's as if the program took the value you

Figure 13-22: Drag the line inside the circle to change the angle of the blur.

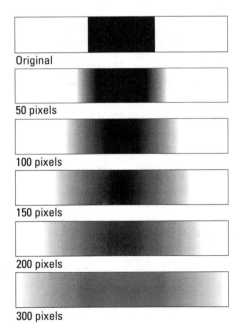

Original

50 pixels

100 pixels

150 pixels

200 pixels

300 pixels

Figure 13-23: A single black rectangle followed by five different applications of the Motion Blur filter. Only the Distance value varied, as labeled. A 0-degree Angle value was used in all five examples.

specified in the Distance option, created that many clones of the image, offset half the clones in one direction and half the clones in the other — all spaced 1 pixel apart — and then varied the opacity of each.

Using the Wind filter

The problem with the Motion Blur filter is that it blurs pixels in two directions. If you want to distribute pixels in one absolute direction or the other, try out the Wind filter, which you can use either on its own or in tandem with Motion Blur.

When you choose Filter⇨Stylize⇨Wind, Photoshop displays the Wind dialog box shown in Figure 13-24. You can select from three methods and two directions to distribute the selected pixels. Figure 13-25 compares the effect of the Motion Blur filter to each of the three methods offered by the Wind filter. Notice that the Wind filter does not blur pixels. Rather, it evaluates a selection in 1-pixel-tall horizontal strips and offsets the strips randomly inside the image.

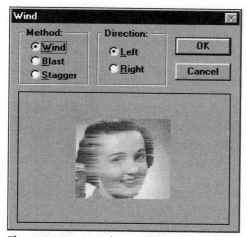

Figure 13-24: Use the Wind filter to randomly distribute a selection in 1-pixel horizontal strips in one of two directions.

To get the best results, try combining the Motion Blur and Wind filters with a translucent selection. For example, to create Figure 13-26, we floated the entire image and applied the Wind command twice, first selecting the Stagger option and then selecting Blast. Next, we applied the Motion Blur command with a 0-degree angle and a Distance value of 30. We then set the Opacity slider bar to 50 percent and selected Lighten from the brush modes pop-up menu. Unlike in the example in Figure 13-25, the motion lines in the image in Figure 13-26 no longer completely obliterate the original image.

Figure 13-25: The difference between the effects of the Motion Blur filter (top left) and the Wind filter. Clockwise from upper right, we applied the Wind filter using the Method options Wind, Blast, and Stagger.

Directional smudging

If you have problems creating an acceptable motion effect because the results of the filters are either too random or too generalized, you can create very precise motion lines using the smudge tool inside a translucent selection, as demonstrated in Figure 13-27. The following steps explain how to achieve this effect. The process has nothing to do with filters — we just thought we'd throw them in as an alternative to the Motion Blur and Wind commands.

Figure 13-26: The result of combining the Wind and Motion Blur filters with a translucent selection.

Steps: Painting motion lines with the smudge tool

1. Begin by using the rectangular marquee tool to select the area in which you want the motion lines to appear. Be sure to select all of the background area that will contain the motion lines as well as at least part of the foreground element that's responsible for the motion lines. Don't worry if you select too much of the image; you remedy that problem in the next step.

2. Press Q to enter the quick mask mode. Use the paintbrush tool and a soft brush shape to trace along the edge of the foreground element, giving it a feathered selection outline. Then go ahead and fill in the rest of the foreground element so that only the background remains selected, as demonstrated in the top image in Figure 13-27.

3. Press Q again to return to the marching ants mode. Then clone the selection by choosing Select➪Float (Ctrl-J).

4. Select the marquee tool or some other selection tool and press 7 to change the opacity of the floating selection to 70 percent.

5. **Create a new, flat, vertical brush shape.** You can specify any diameter with which you're comfortable. Enter 100 percent for the Hardness value, 1 percent for Spacing, and 0 percent for Roundness. Angle the brush perpendicularly to the prospective motion lines. When creating the image in Figure 13-27, we wanted to paint horizontal lines, so we made the brush vertical by entering an Angle value of 90 degrees.

Figure 13-27: We edited and softened the selection outline so that it followed the contours of the foreground image (left). Then we floated the selection, changed its Opacity setting to 70 percent, and dragged inside the selection in a consistent direction with the smudge tool (right).

6. **Select the smudge tool and set the Pressure slider bar in the Smudge Tool Options panel to 95 percent.**

7. **Apply the smudge tool repeatedly inside the floating selection.** Be sure to drag in a consistent direction. In this case, we dragged from right to left, pressing the Shift key to constrain the drag so that it was perfectly horizontal. Drag as many times as you deem necessary. The result of our efforts appears in the right example in Figure 13-27.

Floating and mixing 175 clones

A few months after the first edition of the *Macworld Photoshop Bible* came out, one reader asked whether there was any way to automate this omnidirectional blurring technique so that you didn't have to use the smudge tool. At the time, Deke considered the question for a few fractions of a second and dutifully answered, *Nope.* No way such a method existed, it was flat-out impossible, forget it. Needless to say, Deke was wrong. In fact, the next set of steps documents exactly such a process. Now, we're not sure we'd call these steps easier — they involve the layering and mixing of no fewer than 175 clones (no joke) — but if you simply don't like the idea of scrubbing on an image with the smudge tool, you may want to give this method a try. As Figure 13-28 shows, the steps offer the added advantage of producing extremely accurate, flexible, and believable results.

Steps: Creating a motion effect by cloning a translucent selection

1. Create 175 clones.

2. Ha ha, just joking. Deke only threw in that step to freak you out. What we really want you to do first is select your foreground image. You should try to follow the lines — use the quick mask mode if you want — but you don't have to be super precise.

3. Choose Select⇨Feather and enter a Radius value equal to about $1/20$ the resolution of your image. Actually, the resolution of Figure 13-28 is 180 ppi, and we entered a value of 6 — $1/30$ the resolution — so you can be pretty free and easy with your values. Just soften it so that you don't have any hard edges. That's all we're looking for here.

4. Float the image and send it to its own layer. (Ctrl-J to float, display the Layers palette, and Alt-double-click on the Floating Selection item in the scrolling list to convert the selection to a layer.) This way, you can blur the background image as much as you want and keep the foreground image in its original, pristine form.

5. Oops, your selection outline is gone. (In Chapter 8, we said that it was no biggie that you lose the selection when creating a layer. But frankly, it's beginning to irritate us now.) To regain the darn thing and apply it to the Background layer, press Ctrl-Alt-T and click on the Background item in the Layers palette.

6. Press Ctrl-J to float the selected area of the Background layer. You'll use this single selection — and its 175 clones — to create the entire directional blur.

7. Press the arrow key that corresponds to the direction in which you want the blur to occur. To create the images in Figure 13-28, for example, we pressed the left arrow key because the blur fades off toward the left.

   (Actually, you could have skipped step 6 by pressing Alt-arrow key, which would have cloned and floated the image simultaneously. We only wrote it out this way so that we could explain things a little more thoroughly.)

8. Choose the Soft Light option from the overlay modes pop-up menu on the left side of the Layers palette. Assuming that a selection tool is active, press 4 to change the Opacity setting to 40 percent.

9. Press Alt-arrow key (the same arrow key you pressed last time) 10 times in a row. You don't have to wait for Photoshop to catch up with you. Just press and hold Alt and wail on that arrow key. Then sit back and watch Photoshop sweat. The result is a 10-pixel trail of translucent image.

10. Press 3 to lower the Opacity value to 30 percent. Then press and hold Alt and whack the arrow key 15 times.

Figure 13-28: After mixing the original image on Layer 1 with the underlying blur pattern using the Hard Light overlay mode (top), we cloned the layer and mixed the clone with the rest of the image using the Normal overlay mode and a 60 percent Opacity setting (bottom).

11. Press 2 to change the Opacity to 20 percent. Then press the Alt-arrow key 20 times. Notice how the number of arrow-key whacks keeps getting larger? This results in a tapering effect, consistent with real movement.

12. Press 1 for 10 percent opacity. Press and hold Alt and smack the arrow key 30 times. *Bad arrow key . . . bad!*

13. Change the Opacity slider to 5 percent. I'm afraid you'll have to do this manually; there's no keyboard equivalent. Then press the Alt-arrow key 40 times. Oh, and by the way, we'll need you to sign this waiver. It says that you won't sue us for any repetitive strain injury caused by these steps.

14. Tired of abusing your arrow key? We don't blame you. But if you want to do things right, you'll change the Opacity slider to 2 percent and press the Alt-arrow key a whopping 60 times.

15. The drudgery is over. Now it's time to mix the independent layer that you created in step 4 with the underlying blur. To do this, click on the layer name in the Layers palette — probably *Layer 1* — and choose the Hard Light option from the overlay modes pop-up menu. You get the effect shown in the top example of Figure 13-28.

16. Clone the layer by dragging the layer name onto the new layer icon at the bottom of the Layers palette. A new layer called *Layer 1 Copy* appears above Layer 1. Photoshop automatically makes this the active layer.

17. To create the effect shown in the second example of Figure 13-28, choose Normal from the overlay modes pop-up menu and change the Opacity setting to 60 percent.

There's nothing that says you have to create 175 clones, for example. You could create 40 clones to get a shorter blur, or 300 clones to get a longer one. You could use a different overlay mode. In Step 8, experiment with the Lighten overlay mode or even Overlay. You can also try out different overlay modes and Opacity settings in Steps 15 through 17, and you can clone and mix Layer 1 as many times as you like.

Radial blurring

Choosing Filter⇨Blur⇨Radial Blur displays the Radial Blur dialog box shown in Figure 13-29. The dialog box offers two Blur Method options: Spin and Zoom.

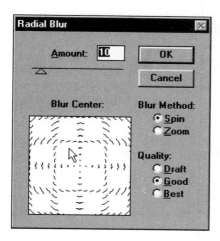

Figure 13-29: Drag inside the Blur Center grid to change the point about which the Radial Blur filter spins or zooms the image.

If you select Spin, the image appears to be rotating about a central point. You specify that point by dragging in the grid inside the Blur Center box (as demonstrated in the figure). If you select Zoom, the image appears to rush away from you, as if you were zooming the camera while shooting the photograph. Again, you specify the central point of the Zoom by dragging in the Blur Center box. Figures 13-30 and 13-31 feature examples of both settings.

After selecting a Blur Method option, you can enter any value between 1 and 100 in the Amount option box to specify the maximum distance over which the filter blurs pixels. (You can enter a value of 0, but doing so merely causes the filter to waste time without producing an effect.) Pixels farthest away from the center point move the most; pixels close to the center point barely move at all. Keep in mind that large values take more time to apply than small values. The Radial Blur filter, incidentally, qualifies as one of Photoshop's most time-consuming operations.

Select a Quality option to specify your favorite time/quality compromise. The Good and Best Quality options ensure smooth results by respectively applying bilinear and bicubic interpolation (as explained in the "General environmental preferences" section of Chapter 2). However, they also prolong the amount of time the filter spends calculating pixels in your image.

The Draft option *diffuses* an image, which leaves a trail of loose and randomized pixels but takes less time to complete. We used the Draft setting to create the left images in Figures 13-30 and 13-31; we selected the Best option to create the images on the right.

Figure 13-30: Two versions of the Radial Blur filter set to Spin, using the Draft option (left) and Best option (right). In both cases, we specified Amount values of 5 pixels. Each effect is centered about *Moses'* eye.

Figure 13-31: Two versions of Radial Blur set to Zoom, using the Draft (left) and Best (right) options. We entered an Amount value of 20 because Zoom produces less-pronounced blurs than Spin. Again, the effects are centered about the eyes.

Blurring a background

One of the best ways to combine commands from the Filter⇨Sharpen and Filter⇨Blur submenus is to differentiate foreground elements from their backgrounds. The foreground elements get the sharpening, the background gets the blur.

For example, consider the image in Figure 13-32. On its own, it's not what we'd call an inspirational image — just your standard, everyday lady talking on the phone surrounded by your standard, everyday urban landscape. Sure, the photo was shot in Japan, so it might stir up that world travel feeling in those of us who go in for that kind of thing. But we wouldn't call it exciting or provocative. In fact, it's a real snoozer.

The image does have one thing going for it, however. It features a distinct pair of foreground elements — the woman and the telephone — set against a clearly independent background, which includes everything else. This composition means that we can differentiate the two using sharpening and blurring effects.

To create the image in Figure 13-33, we selected the foreground elements and applied the Unsharp Mask filter. We used an Amount value of 75 percent, a Radius of 0.5, and a Threshold of 3. Then, just for laughs, we chose Select⇨Inverse and applied the Wind filter, selecting the Blast and Right radio buttons. Finally, we applied the Motion Blur filter, entering a Distance value of 20 pixels and a 0-degree angle.

The Wind and Motion Blur filters produce the effect of moving the camera from right to left. By applying the Unsharp Mask filter, we kept the camera focused on the foreground elements throughout the move. This effect is extremely difficult to pull off in real life, but it's a simple matter in Photoshop.

Figure 13-32: This photo is a yawner, but it has potential that can be drawn to the surface using sharpening and blurring filters.

Figure 13-33: The world swirls around this woman after liberal applications of the Wind and Motion Blur filters. Yet she remains calm and collected, thanks to the use of Unsharp Mask.

Figure 13-34 shows a different take on the same scene. Again, we sharpened the foreground elements. But this time, instead of applying the Wind and Motion Blur filters to the background, we chose Filter⇨Blur⇨Radial Blur. We selected the Zoom option and raised the Amount value to 50. We also selected Draft from the Quality settings — not to save time, but to give the background a grainy appearance.

This image imitates the appearance of zooming the camera to a lower magnification while moving it forward, thus maintaining a constant focal distance between camera and foreground elements. You may remember that Hitchcock used this effect to make the background appear as if it were moving independently of the acrophobic Jimmy Stewart in *Vertigo*.

Figure 13-34: You can use the Radial Blur filter to zoom out from the background while retaining a constant focal distance between viewer and foreground elements.

Softening a selection outline

In Figures 13-33 and 13-34, the blurring filters had no effect on the foreground elements because those elements were not selected when the filters were applied. But rather than having the blurring start at the exact boundaries between the foreground and background elements, which would produce the highly unrealistic effect of drawing colors from the foreground elements into the background, the blurring becomes more pronounced a few pixels away from the foreground elements. This is because the foreground is protected by a feathered buffer zone.

If we had simply applied Select⇨Feather to our original selection boundary, displayed in progress back in Figure 13-17, the command would have feathered the selection in both directions — that is, inward and outward. In that case, the blurring would slightly affect the edges of the foreground elements, again producing an unrealistic effect. So, instead, we edited the selection outline in the quick mask mode using two filters: Gaussian Blur, discussed earlier in this chapter, and Minimum, which you learn about in the next section.

Minimum and Maximum

The Minimum filter enhances the dark portions of an image, spreading them outward into other pixels. Its opposite, the Maximum filter, enhances the light portions of an image. In traditional stat photography, these techniques are known as *spread* and *choke,* respectively.

When you are working in the quick mask mode or an independent mask channel, applying the Minimum filter has the effect of incrementally increasing the size of black areas, which deselects pixels evenly around the edges of a selection. The Radius value that you enter into the Minimum dialog box tells Photoshop how many edge pixels to deselect. Just the opposite, the Maximum filter incrementally increases the size of white areas, which adds pixels evenly around the edges of a selection.

Feathering outward from a selection outline

The following steps describe how to use the Minimum and Gaussian Blur filters to feather an existing selection outline outward only. These steps start where "Selecting an Image Element Set Against a Busy Background," earlier in this chapter, left off.

Steps: Adding a soft edge in the quick mask mode

1. Start with a selection outline that exactly follows the boundaries of one or more foreground elements. Then press Q to switch to the quick mask mode. In Figure 13-35, the background is selected and the foreground is deselected.

2. Choose Filter⇨Other⇨Minimum. Enter a Radius value of 4 to push back the boundaries of the selection outline 4 pixels and then press Enter. (If you prefer to add 4 pixels to the selection outline, choose Filter⇨Other⇨Maximum.) The result appears in Figure 13-36.

Figure 13-35: Begin in the quick mask mode with a selection that clearly distinguishes foreground and background elements.

Figure 13-36: Apply the Minimum filter to add a 4-pixel edge around the deselected area.

3. Choose Filter⇨Blur⇨Gaussian Blur and enter 3.9 to soften nearly all of the edge you added to your selection outline. The unaffected $^1/_{10}$ pixel serves as a tiny insurance policy, so that any effect you apply later doesn't harm the foreground elements. The Gaussian Blur filter feathers the selection outline, as shown in Figure 13-37.

4. Switch back to the marching ants mode (by pressing Q again) and apply your effect. In Figure 13-38, we deleted the selected area to demonstrate how the foreground elements remain entirely protected, with a feathered buffer zone to spare.

Figure 13-37: Use the Gaussian Blur filter to soften the 4-pixel edge, thus feathering the selection outline.

Figure 13-38: We deleted the selected background in the marching ants mode. The foreground elements remain intact and are surrounded by a soft halo of residual image data.

Anti-aliasing a selection outline

Ah, yes, but what if you want a more-subtle effect? A jagged selection is nearly always too hard, but a feathered selection is frequently too soft. You know what Goldilocks would say, don't you? *Anti-aliasing is just right.*

If you read the "Anti-aliasing an image" section earlier in this chapter, you may be tempted to enlarge the mask to twice its normal size and then reduce it to 50 percent. The problem is, this would affect the image as well as the mask, and you don't want that. Luckily, there's a better way that involves the Gaussian Blur filter and the Levels command.

Steps: Anti-aliasing a selection outline in the quick mask mode

1. Starting with a selection outline that exactly follows the boundaries of the foreground image, press Q to switch to the quick mask mode. Figure 13-39 shows how the mask looks when the image itself is hidden (which you accomplish by clicking on the eyeball icon in front of the composite view name in the Channels palette).

2. Choose Filter⇨Blur⇨Gaussian Blur and enter a Radius value of 1.0 for a 300-ppi image. When working on a lower resolution image, scale the Radius value in kind. (A 150-ppi image, for example, calls for a Radius of 0.5. Don't go any lower than 0.5.)

Figure 13-39: The final jagged mask created with the High Pass and Threshold commands (left) and the same image anti-aliased using the Gaussian Blur and Levels commands (right). Enlarged details show the effects of these operations on individual pixels.

3. The result is a fuzzy mask. To firm it up a bit, choose Image⇨Adjust⇨Levels (Ctrl-L). Then enter 65 in the first Input option box and 190 in the third option box. (The second value should remain 1.00.) Then press Enter. By making most of the gray values either black or white, you give the mask an anti-aliased appearance, as in the second example of Figure 13-39.

You may have noticed that this is the third time we've referred to these exact same Input values — 65 and 190 — in the Levels dialog box. It's not that these are some kind of magic numbers. It's just that they lend themselves to many situations and, as long as we haven't formally discussed the Levels dialog box, we want to stay on vaguely familiar footing. If you already understand how the dialog box works, feel free to experiment with your own values.

4. Now switch back to the matching ants mode (by pressing Q) and apply the desired effect. In Color Plate 13-7, we floated the selection and applied the exact same directional blur effects shown back in Figures 13-33 and 13-34. As you can see, these more-precise selection outlines result in more-precise effects.

Noise Factors

Photoshop offers four loosely associated filters in its Filter⇨Noise submenu. One filter adds random pixels — known as *noise* — to an image. The other two, Despeckle and Median, blur an image in ways that theoretically remove noise from poorly scanned images. In fact, they function nearly as well at removing essential detail as they do at removing extraneous noise. The only tried-and-true way to fix a badly scanned image is to chuck it and rescan. Garbage in, garbage out, to coin a phrase. In the following sections, we show you how the Noise filters work, demonstrate a few of our favorite applications, and leave you to draw your own conclusions.

Adding noise

Noise adds grit and texture to an image. You can find examples of noise in grainy album covers, perfume commercials, Levi's 501 Blues ads . . . in short, anything that's trying to appeal to a hip, young, no-marbles-in-their-heads audience.

You add noise by choosing Filter⇨Noise⇨Add Noise. Shown in Figure 13-40, the Add Noise dialog box features the following options:

✦ **Amount:** Enter any value between 1 and 999 to specify the amount that pixels in the image can stray from their current colors. The value itself represents a color range rather than a brightness range. For example, if you enter a value of 10, Photoshop can apply any color that is 10 shades more or less green, more or less blue, *and* more or less red than the current color. Any value over 255 allows

Photoshop to select random colors from the entire 16-million color spectrum. The higher you go above 255, the more likely Photoshop is to pick colors at opposite ends of the spectrum — that is, white and black.

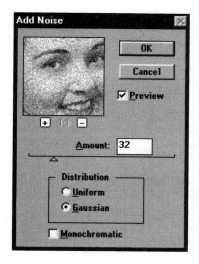

Figure 13-40: The Add Noise dialog box enables you to specify the amount and variety of noise you want to add to the selection.

✦ **Uniform:** Select this option to apply colors absolutely randomly within the specified range. Photoshop is no more likely to apply one color within the range than another, thus resulting in an even color distribution.

✦ **Gaussian:** When you select this option, you instruct Photoshop to prioritize colors along the Gaussian distribution curve. The effect is that most colors added by the filter either closely resemble the original colors or push the boundaries of the specified range. In other words, this option results in more light and dark pixels, thus producing a more pronounced effect.

✦ **Monochromatic:** When working on a full-color image, the Add Noise filter distributes pixels randomly throughout the different color channels. However, when you select the Monochrome check box, Photoshop distributes the noise in the same manner in all channels. The result is grayscale noise. (This option does not affect grayscale images; the noise can't get any more grayscale than it already is.)

Figure 13-41 compares three applications of Gaussian noise to identical amounts of Uniform noise. Figure 13-42 features magnified views of the noise so that you can compare the colors of individual pixels.

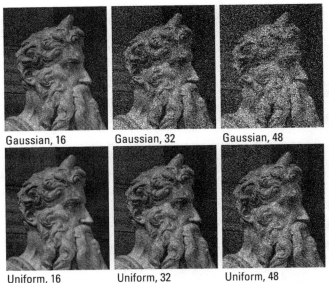

Gaussian, 16   Gaussian, 32   Gaussian, 48

Uniform, 16   Uniform, 32   Uniform, 48

Figure 13-41: The Gaussian option produces more pronounced effects than the Uniform option at identical Amount values.

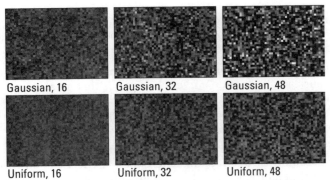

Gaussian, 16   Gaussian, 32   Gaussian, 48

Uniform, 16   Uniform, 32   Uniform, 48

Figure 13-42: The upper left corners of the examples from Figure 13-41 enlarged to four times their original size.

Noise variations

Normally, the Add Noise filter adds both lighter and darker pixels to an image. If you prefer, however, you can limit the effect of the filter to strictly lighter or darker pixels. To do so, float the selection before applying the filter and then select the Lighten or Darken overlay mode.

Figure 13-43 shows sample applications of lighter and darker noise. We began each example by selecting the entire image and choosing Select⇨Float (Ctrl-J). We then chose Filter⇨Noise⇨Add Noise, entered an Amount value of 500, and selected Uniform. To create the left example in the figure, we changed the Opacity setting in the Layers palette to 20 percent and selected Lighten from the overlay modes pop-up menu. To create the right example, we changed the Opacity to 40 percent and selected Darken from the pop-up menu. In each case, we added a layer of strictly lighter or darker noise while at the same time retaining the clarity of the original image.

Figure 13-43: You can limit the Add Noise filter to strictly lighter (left) or darker (right) noise by applying the filter to a floating, translucent selection.

You can achieve a softened noise effect by applying one of the Blur filters to the floating selection before setting it down onto the original image. Figure 13-44, for example, shows images subject to the same amount of noise as those in Figure 13-43. But in this case, immediately following the application of the Add Noise filter, we chose Filter⇨Blur⇨Motion Blur, changed the angle to 30 degrees, and entered a Distance value of 3 pixels. We then changed the Opacity and overlay mode settings as described in the preceding paragraph. In this way, we applied softened grains that are strictly lighter or darker than the original pixels in the image.

Applying noise to individual color channels

A few paragraphs ago, we explained that Photoshop provides a Monochrome option that lets you apply grayscale noise to a color image. You can just as easily generate noise that is strictly red, green, or blue by applying the Add Noise filter exclusively to the red, green, or blue color channel, as demonstrated in the top half of Color Plate 13-8. (Because you're only editing one channel, it doesn't matter whether Monochrome is turned on or not.) You can likewise make yellow noise by editing both the red and green channels, cyan noise by editing the green and blue channels, or magenta noise by editing the blue and red channels. (In these cases, Monochrome should be turned off.)

When editing a Lab image, applying noise to the luminosity channel produces the same effect as selecting the Monochrome check box. Apply the filter to the *a* channel to get green and pink noise; apply it to the *b* channel to get blue and orange noise.

Figure 13-44: To create these rainy and scraped effects, we applied motion blurring to the noise in the floating selections from Figure 13-43.

Randomizing selections

As with any other filter, you can apply Add Noise to a selection in the quick mask mode. For example, we wanted to again edit the background of the woman-on-the-phone image, this time creating a static effect, as demonstrated in the top example in Figure 13-45. We entered the quick mask mode and drew the selection outline shown back in Figure 13-36. We only wanted to randomize the pixels within the selected background, so we used the magic wand tool to select the transparent areas of the mask that surround the woman and phone unit.

To soften the selection, we chose Select⇨Feather and entered a Radius value of 2. Next, we chose the Add Noise filter and entered a value of 500 to heavily randomize the selection. When we switched back to the marching ants mode, only random pixels in the background were selected. By pressing the Delete key, we achieved the effect shown in the left example of Figure 13-45.

The right example in Figure 13-45 features a blurred version of the static effect that looks vaguely like snow. (More like a blizzard, really.) After applying the Add Noise command in the quick mask mode — before switching to the marching ants mode and

Figure 13-45: You can create a static effect (left) by randomizing pixels of a selection in the quick mask mode. To achieve a snow effect (right), apply the Gaussian Blur filter to the randomized selection.

pressing Delete — we chose Filter⇨Blur⇨Gaussian Blur and entered a Radius value of 0.5. This softened the transition between random pixels in the selected region. We then switched back to the marching ants mode and pressed Delete to create the snow shown in the figure.

Chunky noise

Our biggest frustration with the Add Noise filter is that you can't specify the size of individual specks of noise. No matter how you cut it, noise only comes in 1-pixel squares. It may occur to you that you can enlarge the noise dots in a floating selection by applying the Minimum filter. But in practice, doing so simply fills in the selection because there isn't sufficient space between the dark noise pixels to accommodate the larger dot sizes.

Luckily, Photoshop provides a Pointillize filter, which adds variable-size dots and then colors those dots in keeping with the original colors in the image. Although Pointillize lacks the random quality of the Add Noise filter, you can use it to add texture to an image.

To create the left image in Figure 13-46, we selected the entire image and chose Select⇨Float. We then chose Filter⇨Pixelate⇨Pointillize and entered 3 into the Cell Size option box. After pressing Enter to apply the filter (for your information, it's a slow one), we changed the Opacity slider bar in the Layers palette to 20 percent. The effect is rather like applying chunky bits of noise.

The problem with this technique is that it has the added effect of softening an image. To preserve image detail and create the right-hand image in Figure 13-46, we transferred the floating selection to its own layer by Alt-double-clicking on the Floating Selection item in the Layers palette. We then returned to the Background layer, selected the entire image, and applied the Unsharp Mask filter. Because the

Pointillized image contains its own color detail, we could sharpen with impunity by entering 500 percent for the Amount value, 0.5 for Radius, and 5 for Threshold. After pressing Enter, we chose Filter⇨Other⇨High Pass and applied a Radius value of 20.0. We then switched to the Pointillized layer and pressed 4 to change the Opacity slider bar value to 40 percent. The resulting image is crisp, clear, and chunky. Yes, friends, it's Cream of Moses soup, so hearty you can eat it with a fork.

Figure 13-46: Two results of applying the Pointillize filter to a floating selection, one in front of a standard image (left) and the other in front of a highly sharpened image (right).

Removing noise

Now for the noise-removal filters. Strictly speaking, the Despeckle command belongs in the Filter⇨Blur submenu. It blurs a selection while, at the same time, preserving its edges — the idea being that unwanted noise is most noticeable in the continuous regions of an image. In practice, this filter is nearly the exact opposite of the Sharpen Edges filter.

The Despeckle command searches an image for edges using the equivalent of an Unsharp Mask Threshold value of 5. It then ignores the edges in the image and blurs everything else with the force of the Blur More filter, as shown in the upper left image in Figure 13-47.

Median filter

Another command in the Filter⇨Noise submenu, Median, removes noise by averaging the colors in an image, one pixel at a time. When you choose Filter⇨Noise⇨Median, Photoshop produces a Radius option box, into which you can enter any value between 1 and 16. For every pixel in a selection, the filter averages the colors of the

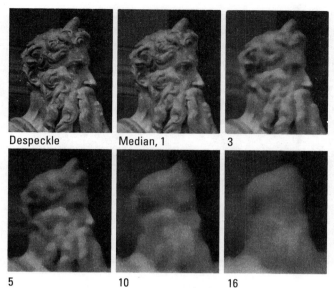

Despeckle   Median, 1   3

5   10   16

Figure 13-47: The effects of the Despeckle filter (upper left) and Median filter. The numbers indicate Median filter Radius values.

neighboring pixels that fall inside the specified radius — ignoring any pixels that are so different that they might skew the average — and applies the average color to the central pixel. As verified by Figure 13-47, large values produce the most destructive effects.

We mentioned at the beginning of the "Noise Factors" section that the Despeckle and Median filters are something of a wash for removing noise because they eliminate too much detail. However, you can apply the Median filter to a floating selection to mute an image and give it a plastic, molded quality, as demonstrated by the examples in Figure 13-48.

To create the left example, we cloned the image by selecting it and choosing Select⇨ Float. We then chose Filter⇨Noise⇨Median and entered a Radius value of 3. After pressing Enter, we pressed 6 to change the Opacity slider bar to 60 percent.

When used in this manner, the Median filter over-softens the image, even when constrained to a floating selection. To remedy this problem, we used the same tactics we used to fix the over-softening produced by the Pointillize filter in Figure 13-46. After applying Median, we cut the floating selection to the Clipboard, applied the Unsharp Mask filter to the original image at 500 percent, applied the High Pass filter with a 20-pixel radius, and pasted the floating selection back into place. To achieve the effect shown in the right example of Figure 13-48, we pressed 8 to raise the opacity of the floating selection to 80 percent. The result is a gradually contoured image unlike anything you could accomplish using traditional techniques.

Figure 13-48: Two results of applying the Median filter to a floating selection, one in front of a standard image (left) and the other in front of a highly sharpened image (right).

Applying Median to individual color channels

What explanation of any corrective filter would be complete without showing how it affects individual color channels? The bottom row in Color Plate 13-8 does just that. In this figure, we've applied the Median filter with a Radius value of 10 to the red, green, and blue channel. But notice that rather than adding red when we edited the red channel, the filter added red's opposite, cyan. Likewise, the filter added magenta when applied to the green channel and yellow when applied to the blue channel. How is this possible? What really happened is that the Median filter expanded the black shadow in the edited channel, thereby deleting color from the red, green, or blue channel. What remains from the unedited channels combines to form a darker area of contrasting color.

Here's another interesting observation about the color plate. Compare the focus of the three images in the bottom row. The first example is a little soft; the second example is even softer. But the third example is as crisp as it was before we applied the filter. As we've noted a few times through the book, the red and green channels typically contain the majority of edge detail in an image; the blue channel contains color information, but the detail is sometimes a mess (a design function of many medium-priced scanners). So when you apply Gaussian Blur or Median to the blue channel, you're less likely to impact edge detail.

Cleaning Up Scanned Halftones

The Dust & Scratches filter lives in the Filter⇨Noise submenu. The purpose of this filter is to remove dust particles, hairs, scratches, and other imperfections that may accompany a scan. The filter offers two options, Radius and Threshold. As long as the offending imperfection is smaller or thinner than the Radius value and different enough from its neighbors to satisfy the Threshold value, the filter deletes the spot or line and interpolates between the pixels around the perimeter.

But like so many automated tools, this one works only when conditions are favorable. We're not saying that you shouldn't ever use it — in fact, you may always want to give this filter the first crack at a dusty image. But if it doesn't work, don't get your nose out of joint. Just hunker down and eliminate the imperfections manually using the rubber stamp tool, as explained in the "Touching up blemishes" section of Chapter 11.

Now, as we say, Dust & Scratches was designed to get rid of gunk on a dirty scanner. But another problem that the filter may be able to eliminate is moiré patterns. These patterns appear when scanning halftoned images from books and magazines. See, any time you scan a printed image, you're actually scanning a collection of halftone dots rather than a continuous-tone photograph. In most cases, the halftone pattern clashes with the resolution of the scanned image to produce rhythmic and distracting moirés.

On the CD-ROM When scanning published photographs or artwork, take a moment to find out if what you're doing is legal. It's up to you to make sure that the image you scan is no longer protected by copyright — most, but not all, works over 75 years old are considered free game — or that your noncommercial application of the image falls under the fair-use umbrella of commentary or criticism. For more information on this topic, check out Jim Martin's "Are You Breaking the Law?" article included as an Acrobat .PDF file on the CD included with this book.

The Dust & Scratches filter can be pretty useful for eliminating moirés, particularly if you reduce the Threshold value below 40. But this also goes a long way toward eliminating the actual image detail, as shown in Color Plate 13-9. This figure features an image scanned from an issue of *Macworld* magazine. (Because one of your humble authors created the original image, *Macworld* probably won't sue, but you shouldn't try it.)

The left half of Color Plate 13-9 shows the individual color channels in the image; the right half shows the full-color image. We've blown up a detail in each image so that you can better see the pixels in the moiré pattern.

The top example in the color plate shows the original scanned image with its awful moirés. (Actually, we've slightly exaggerated the moirés to account for any printing anomalies — but honest, with or without enhancement, the image is a mess on-screen.) The middle example shows the same image subject to the Dust & Scratches filter with a Radius of 2 and a Threshold value of 20. The moirés are gone, but the edges have all but disappeared as well. We're tempted to describe this artwork using adjectives like *soft* and *doughy*. Them are fightin' words in the world of image editing.

But what about that bottom example? How did we manage to eliminate the moirés *and* preserve the detail that are shown here? Why, by applying the Gaussian Blur, Median, and Unsharp Mask filters to individual color channels.

The first step is to examine the channels independently (by pressing Ctrl-1, Ctrl-2, and Ctrl-3). You'll likely find that each one is affected by the moiré pattern to a different extent. In the case of this scan, all three channels need work, but the blue channel — the usual culprit — is the worst. The trick, therefore, is to eliminate the patterns in the blue channel and draw detail from the red and green channels.

To fix the blue channel, we applied both the Gaussian Blur and Median commands in fairly hefty doses. We chose Filter⇨Blur⇨Gaussian Blur and specified a Radius value of 1.5 pixels — rather high, considering that the image measures only about 300 pixels tall. Then we chose Filter⇨Noise⇨Median and specified a Radius of 2.

The result was a thickly modeled image with no moirés but little detail. To firm things up a bit, we chose Filter⇨Sharpen⇨Unsharp Mask and entered 200 percent for the Amount option and 1.5 for the Radius. We opted for this Radius value because it matches the Radius that we used to blur the image. When correcting moirés, a Threshold value of 0 is almost always the best choice. A higher Threshold value not only prevents the sharpening of moiré pattern edges but also ignores real edges, which are already fragile enough as it is.

The green and red channels required incrementally less attention. After switching to the green channel, we applied the Gaussian Blur filter with a Radius of 1.0. Then we sharpened the image with the Unsharp Mask filter set to 200 percent and a Radius value of 0.5. In the red channel (Ctrl-1), we applied Gaussian Blur with a Radius value of 0.5. The gradual effect wasn't enough to warrant sharpening.

When you're finished, switch back to the RGB view (Ctrl-0) to see the combined result of your labors. (Or keep an RGB view of the image on-screen by choosing Window⇨New Window.) The focus of the image will undoubtedly be softer than it was when you started. You can cure this to a limited extent by applying very discreet passes of the Unsharp Mask filter, say, with an Amount value of 100 percent and a low Radius value. Keep in mind that oversharpening may bring the patterns back to life or even uncover new ones.

Tip One last tip: Always scan halftoned images at the highest resolution available to your scanner. Then resample the scan down to the desired resolution using Image⇨Image Size. This step by itself goes a long way toward eliminating moirés.

Full-Court Filtering

CHAPTER

Destructive Filters

Corrective filters enable you to both eliminate flaws in an image and apply special effects. Destructive filters, on the other hand, are devoted solely to special effects. That's why this chapter is actually shorter than its predecessor, even though Photoshop offers nearly twice as many destructive filters as corrective counterparts. Quite simply, destructive filters are less frequently used and ultimately less useful.

Don't get us wrong — these filters are a superb bunch. But because of their more limited appeal, we don't explain each and every one of them. Rather, we concentrate on the ones that we think you'll use most often, describe in detail the very few that were new to Photoshop 3, breeze over a handful of others, and let you discover on your own the seven that we ignore.

R%%% **Robert** This is as good a place as any to remind you of a point I raised way back when in Chapter 2. All of the Distort filters, and Lens Flare too, operate entirely in memory. That is, when you're using other filters you have the benefit of your scratch disk to enable you to do bigger operations than the physical RAM on your system might otherwise allow. Not so the filters I've just mentioned. When they run out of physical RAM — that's it. There is a workaround of sorts — if it's a color image, apply the filter in turn to each of the color channels. And for Windows 3.1 users, let me remind you that as a limitation of the Win32s subsystem you're using to run Photoshop, 16MB is the largest block of RAM that can be so allocated. Same work around as before — but the best is to get going with Windows 95.

The also-rans

Oh, heck, we can't just go and ignore seven destructive filters — they're not completely useless, after all. It's just that you aren't likely to use them more than once every lunar eclipse. So here is the briefest of all possible descriptions of these seven filters:

✦ **Color Halftone:** Located in the Filter➪Pixelate submenu, this command turns an image into a piece of Roy Lichtenstein artwork, with big, comic-book halftone dots. The filter is fun, and it takes about a year and a half to apply. We even include a sample effect in Color Plate 13-2. But if you depend on it on a regular basis, you're as devoid of original ideas as — dare we say it? — Lichtenstein himself.

✦ **Fragment:** Ooh, it's an earthquake! This lame filter repeats an image four times in a square formation and lowers the opacity of each to create a sort of jiggly effect. You don't even have any options to control it. We must just be missing the genius behind Filter➪Pixelate➪Fragment.

✦ **Lens Flare:** This filter adds sparkles and halos to an image to suggest light bouncing off the camera lens. Even though photographers work their behinds off trying to make sure that these sorts of reflections don't occur, you can go and add them after the fact. You can select one of three Lens Type options, adjust the Brightness slider between 10 and 300 percent (though somewhere around 100 is bound to deliver the best results), and move the center of the reflection by dragging a point around inside the Flare Center box. It's a novelty filter that you'll probably want to use sparingly. One small tip: If you want to add a flare to a grayscale image, first convert it to the RGB mode. Then apply the filter and convert back to grayscale. The Lens Flare filter is applicable to RGB images only.

✦ **Diffuse:** This single-shot filter in the Filter➪Stylize submenu dithers the edges of color, much as the Dissolve brush mode dithers the edges of a soft brush. It's moderately useful, but not likely to gain a place among your treasured few.

✦ **Solarize:** Located in the Stylize submenu — as are the two filters that follow — Solarize is easily Photoshop's worst filter. It's really just a color-correction effect that changes all medium grays in the image to white, all blacks and whites to black, and remaps the other colors to shades in between. (If you're familiar with the Curves command, the map for Solarize looks like a pyramid.) It really belongs in the Image➪Map submenu or, better yet, on the cutting room floor.

✦ **Tiles:** This filter breaks an image up into a bunch of regularly sized but randomly spaced rectangular tiles. You specify how many tiles fit across the width and height of the image — a value of 10, for example, creates 100 tiles — and the maximum distance each tile can shift. You can fill the gaps between tiles with foreground color, background color, or an inverted or normal version of the original image. A highly intrusive and not particularly stimulating effect.

✦ **Extrude:** The more capable cousin of the Tiles filter, Extrude breaks an image into tiles and forces them toward the viewer in three-dimensional space. The Pyramid option is a lot of fun, devolving an image into a collection of spikes. When using the Blocks option, you can select a Solid Front Faces option that renders the image as a true 3-D mosaic. The Mask Incomplete Blocks option simply leaves the image untouched around the perimeter of the selection where the filter can't draw complete tiles.

Actually, we kind of like the Extrude command. For the pure and simple heck of it, Color Plate 14-1 shows an example of Extrude applied to one of the sharpened rose images from Color Plate 13-4 (the bottom left one, to be exact). We set the Type to Blocks, the Size to 10, and the Depth to 30 and Random, with both the Solid Front Faces and Mask Incomplete Blocks radio buttons selected. Pretty great, huh? We only wish that the filter would generate a selection outline around the masked areas of the image so that we could get rid of anything that hadn't been extruded. It's a wonderful effect, but it's not one that lends itself to many occasions.

What about the others?

Some filters don't really belong in either the corrective or destructive camp. Take Filter⇨Video⇨NTSC Colors and Filter⇨Other⇨Offset, for example. Both are examples of commands that have no business being under the Filter menu, and both could have been handled much better than they are.

NTSC Colors modifies the colors in your RGB or Lab image for transfer to videotape. Vivid reds and blues that might otherwise prove very unstable and bleed into their neighbors are curtailed. The problem with this function is that it's not an independent color space; it's a single-shot filter that changes your colors and is done with it. If you edit the colors after choosing the command, you may very well reintroduce colors that are incompatible with NTSC devices and, therefore, warrant a second application of the filter. Conversion to NTSC — another light-based system — isn't as fraught with potential disaster as conversion to CMYK pigments, but it still deserves better treatment than this.

The Offset command moves an image a specified number of pixels. Why didn't we cover it in Chapter 8 with the other movement options? Because the command actually moves the image inside the selection outline while keeping the selection outline itself stationary. It's as if you had pasted the entire image into the selection outline and were now moving it around. The command is a favorite among fans of channel operations, a topic covered in chapters 17 and 18. You can duplicate an image, offset the entire thing a few pixels, and then mix the duplicate and original to create highlight or shadow effects. But we much prefer the more interactive control of floating and nudging with the arrow keys. In fact, to be perfectly blunt, channel operations are vastly overrated. See Chapter 17 for an earful on the subject.

Among the filters we've omitted from this chapter is Filter⇨Stylize⇨Wind, which is technically a destructive filter but is covered along with the blur and noise filters in Chapter 13. For complete information about Filter⇨Other⇨Custom, Filter⇨Distort⇨ Displace, and Filter⇨Synthetic⇨Filter Factory, read the following chapter, "Constructing Homemade Effects." Filter⇨Render⇨Texture Fill is covered in Chapter 11.

As for the other filters in the Filter⇨Distort, Pixelate, Render, and Stylize submenus, read on to discover all the latest and greatest details.

Third-party filters

In addition to the filters provided by Photoshop, you can purchase all sorts of plug-in filters from other companies. In fact, Photoshop supports its own flourishing cottage industry of third-party solutions.

The disc at the back of this book includes sample versions of some of our favorite filters, including the awesome Gradient Designer and several others from Kai's Power Tools; Drop Shadow and The Boss from independent Alien Skin; and 3-D and cMulti from Andromeda. A few filters are demo versions of the shipping products, which means that you can see what they do but you can't actually apply the effects. We know, it's a drag, but these folks claim that they like to make money every once in a while, and we can't say that we blame them.

Also included on the disc is a feature article called "Special Effects in Photoshop," from the November 1994 edition of *Macworld* magazine (written by none other than Deke McClelland). The article sums up nine commercial filter packages from five different vendors and lists some favorites. It's provided as a .PDF file, so you can open it up and read it on-screen or print it. Better still, it's full of all sorts of full-color artwork that shows off the various tools.

See the "External Plug-ins" section of Chapter 13 for important tips on managing your Plug-ins directory if you're using other programs that accept third-party plug-ins. And see Chapter 19 for further information on the filters just mentioned.

The Pixelate Filters

The new Filter⇨Pixelate submenu features a handful of commands that rearrange your image into clumps of solid color:

✦ **Crystallize:** This filter organizes an image into irregularly shaped nuggets. You specify the size of the nuggets by entering a value from 3 to 300 pixels in the Cell Size option.

✦ **Facet:** Facet fuses areas of similarly colored pixels to create a sort of hand-painted effect.

✦ **Mosaic:** The Mosaic filter blends pixels together into larger squares. You specify the height and width of the squares by entering a value into the Cell Size option box.

✦ **Pointillize:** This filter is similar to Crystallize, except that it separates an image into disconnected nuggets set against the background color. As usual, you specify the size of the nuggets by changing the Cell Size value.

The Crystal Halo effect

By applying one of these filters to a feathered selection, you can create what we call a Crystal Halo effect, named after the Crystallize filter, which tends to deliver the most successful results. (For a preview of these effects, sneak a peek at Figure 14-2.) The following steps explain how to create a Crystal Halo, using the images in Figures 14-1 and 14-2 as an example.

Steps: Creating the Crystal Halo effect

1. Begin by selecting the foreground element around which you want to create the halo. Then choose Select⇨Inverse to deselect the foreground element and select the background.

2. Enter the quick mask mode. Choose Filter⇨Other⇨Minimum to increase the size of the deselected area around the foreground element. The size of the Radius value depends on the size of the halo you want to create. Here, we wanted a 15-pixel halo. Unfortunately, the Radius option box in the Minimum dialog box can't accommodate a value larger than 10. So we entered 10 the first time. When Photoshop finished applying the filter, we pressed Ctrl-Alt-F to bring up the Minimum dialog box again and entered 5.

3. Choose Filter⇨Blur⇨Gaussian Blur, and enter a Radius value 0.1 less than the amount by which you increased the size of the deselected area. Here, we entered 14.9. The result appears in the left image in Figure 14-1.

4. Choose Filter⇨Pixelate⇨Crystallize and enter a moderate value into the Cell Size option box. We opted for the value 12, just slightly larger than the default value. After pressing Enter, you get something along the lines of the selection outline shown in the right image in Figure 14-1. The filter refracts the softened edges, as if you were viewing them through textured glass.

Figure 14-1: Create a heavily feathered selection outline (left), and then apply the Crystallize filter to refract the feathered edges (right).

5. Switch back to the marching ants mode and use the selection as desired. We merely deleted the selection to produce the effect shown in the top left image in Figure 14-2. You may find this technique particularly useful for combining images. You can copy the selection and paste it against a different background, or copy a background from a different image and choose Edit⇨Paste Into to paste it inside the crystal halo's selection outline.

Figure 14-2 shows several variations on the Crystal Halo effect. To create the upper right image, we substituted Filter⇨Pixelate⇨Facet for Filter⇨Pixelate⇨Crystallize in step 4. We also sharpened the result to increase the effect of the filter (which nevertheless remains subtle). To create the lower right image, we applied the Mosaic filter in place of Crystallize, using a Cell Size value of 8. Finally, to create the lower left image, we applied the Pointillize filter. Because Pointillize creates gaps in a selection, we had to paint inside Moses to fill in the gaps and isolate the halo effect to the background before returning to the marching ants mode.

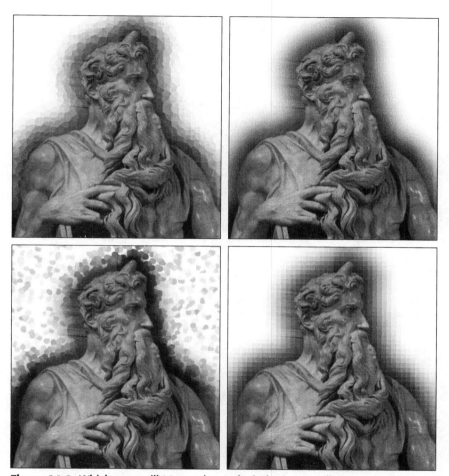

Figure 14-2: Which aura will Moses don today? The images illustrate the effects of applying each of four filters to a heavily feathered selection in the quick mask mode and pressing the Delete key. Clockwise from upper left, the filters used were Crystallize, Facet, Mosaic, and Pointillize.

Creating a mezzotint

A *mezzotint* is a special halftone pattern that replaces dots with a random pattern of swirling lines and wormholes. Photoshop's Mezzotint filter is an attempt to emulate this effect. Although not entirely successful — true mezzotinting options can only be properly implemented as PostScript printing functions, not as filtering functions — they do lend themselves to some pretty interesting interpretations.

The filter itself is straightforward. You choose Filter⇨Pixelate⇨Mezzotint, select an effect from the Type submenu, and presst the Enter key. A preview box lets you see what each of the ten Type options looks like. Figure 14-3 shows off four of the effects at 230 ppi.

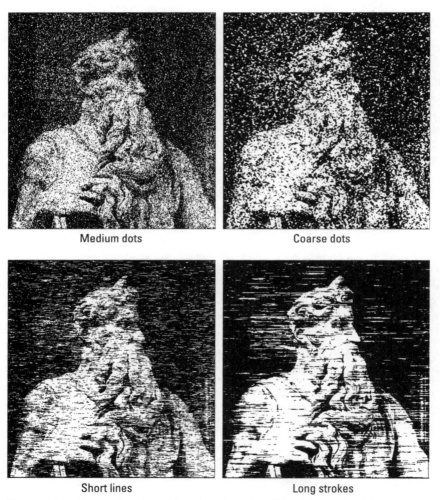

Medium dots   Coarse dots

Short lines   Long strokes

Figure 14-3: The results of applying the Mezzotint filter set to each of four representative effects. These line patterns are on par with the halftoning options offered when you select Mode⇨Bitmap, as discussed back in Chapter 4. (See Figure 4-12.)

To create Figure 14-4, we floated Moses before applying the Mezzotint filter set to the Long Lines effect. We then mixed floating image and underlying original by selecting options from the overlay modes pop-up menu in the Layers palette. In this case, we applied the Overlay option and set the Opacity slider to 40 percent. The result is a scraped image. (We've decreased the resolution of the image to 180 ppi so that you can see the effect a little more clearly.)

Figure 14-4: To get this effect, we floated the great work of marble before applying the Mezzotint filter. Then we selected the Overlay mode and set the Opacity slider to 40 percent.

When applied to grayscale artwork, the Mezzotint filter always results in a black-and-white image. When applied to a color image, the filter automatically applies the selected effect independently to each of the color channels. Though all pixels in each channel are changed to either black or white, you can see a total of eight colors — black, red, green, blue, yellow, cyan, magenta, and white — in the RGB composite view. The upper left example of Color Plate 14-2 shows an image subject to the Mezzotint filter in the RGB mode.

If the Mezzotint filter affects each channel independently, then it follows that the color mode in which you work directly and dramatically affects the performance of the filter. For example, if you apply Mezzotint in the Lab mode, you again whittle the colors down to eight, but a very different eight — black, cyan, magenta, green, red, two muddy blues, and a muddy rose — as shown in the top middle example of Color Plate 14-2. If you're looking for bright, happy colors, don't apply Mezzotint in the Lab mode.

In CMYK, the filter produces roughly the same eight colors that you get in RGB — white, cyan, magenta, yellow, violet-blue, red, deep green, and black. However, as shown in the top right example of the color plate, the distribution of the colors is much different. The image appears much lighter and more colorful than its RGB counterpart. This happens because the filter has a lot of black to work with in the RGB mode but very little — just that in the black channel — in the CMYK mode.

The bottom row of Color Plate 14-2 shows the effects of the Mezzotint filter when we first floated each image and then mixed it with the original. As in Figure 14-4, we chose Overlay from the overlay modes pop-up menu in the Layers palette and set the Opacity value to 40 percent. (It's gotten kind of confusing since Photoshop named one of the overlay modes Overlay, but hang in there.) These three very different images were all created using the same filter set to the same effect. Absolutely the only difference is color mode.

Edge-Enhancement Filters

The Filter⇨Stylize submenu offers access to a triad of filters that enhance the edges in an image. The most popular of these is undoubtedly Emboss, which adds dimension to an image by making it look as if it were carved in relief. The other two, Find Edges and Trace Contour, are less commonly applied, but every bit as capable and deserving of your attention.

Embossing an image

The Emboss filter works by searching for high-contrast edges (just like the Sharpen Edge and High Pass filters), highlighting the edges with black or white pixels, and then coloring the low-contrast portions with medium gray. Photoshop displays the Emboss dialog box shown in Figure 14-5 when you choose Filter⇨Stylize⇨Emboss. The dialog box offers three options:

✦ **Angle:** The value in this option box determines the angle at which Photoshop lights the image in relief. For example, if you enter a value of 90 degrees, you light the relief from the bottom straight upward. The white pixels therefore appear on the bottom sides of the edges, and the black pixels appear on the top sides. Figure 14-6 shows eight reliefs lit from different angles. We positioned the images so that they appear lit from a single source.

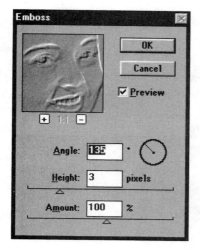

Figure 14-5: The Emboss dialog box enables you to control the depth of the filtered image and the angle from which it is lit.

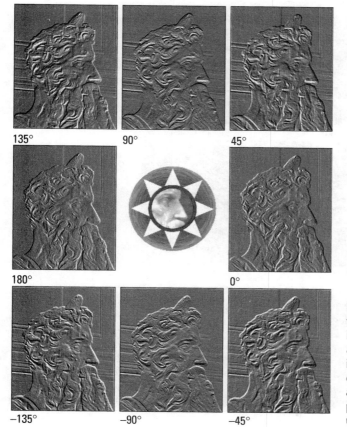

135°   90°   45°

180°   0°

−135°   −90°   −45°

Figure 14-6: Reliefs lighted from eight different angles, in 45-degree increments. In all cases, the central sun image indicates the location of the light source. Height and Amount values of 1 pixel and 250 percent were used for all images.

✦ **Height:** The Emboss filter accomplishes its highlighting effect by displacing one copy of an image relative to another. You specify the distance between the copies using the Height option, which can vary from 1 to 10 pixels. Lower values produce crisp effects, as demonstrated in Figure 14-7. Values above 3 goop things up pretty good unless you also enter a high Amount value. Together, the Height and Amount values determine the depth of the image in relief.

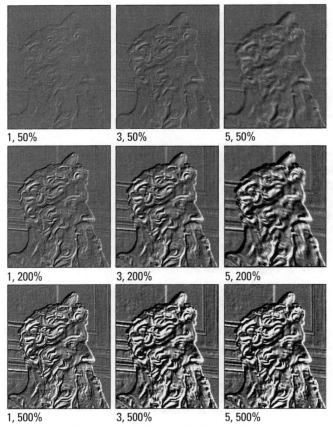

Figure 14-7: Examples of different Height settings (first value) and Amount settings (second value). The Angle value used for each image was 135 degrees.

✦ **Amount:** Enter a value between 1 and 500 percent to determine the amount of black and white assigned to pixels along the edges. Values of 50 percent and lower produce almost entirely gray images, as you can see in the top row of Figure 14-7. Higher values produce sharper edges, as if the relief were carved more deeply.

As a stand-alone effect, Emboss is something of a dud. It's a filter that makes you gasp with delight the first time you see it but never quite lends itself to any practical application after you become acquainted with Photoshop. But if you think of Emboss as an extension of the High Pass filter, it takes on new meaning. You can use it to edit selection outlines in the quick mask mode, just as you might use the High Pass filter. You also can use it to draw out detail in an image.

Figure 14-8 shows Emboss applied to floating selections. To create the left example, we selected Darken from the overlay modes pop-up menu in the Layers palette to add shadows to the edges of the image, thus boosting the texture without unduly upsetting the original brightness values. We selected Lighten from the overlay modes pop-up menu to create the right example. In both cases, we applied the Emboss filter at an Angle of 135 degrees, a Height of 2 pixels, and an Amount of 250 percent. We also set the Opacity slider bar to 70 percent.

Figure 14-8: We limited the effect of the Emboss filter to darkening the image (left) and then to lightening the image (right) by applying the filter to a floating, translucent selection.

Tip To create a color relief effect, apply the Emboss filter to a floating selection and then select the Luminosity option from the overlay modes pop-up menu in the Layers palette. This retains the colors from the original image while applying the lightness and darkness of the pixels from the floating selection. The effect looks something like an inked lithographic plate, with steel grays and vivid colors mixing together. An example of this effect at 80 percent Opacity is shown in the first example of Color Plate 14-3.

The second example in that same color plate shows a more impressive — if less practical — technique. Rather than applying the Luminosity overlay mode, we chose the Difference option. With its hard edges and vivid colors, this image looks like some impossible frame from an educational film on genetic engineering. We can just hear the narrator commenting: *Prom dates across America have perked up significantly since scientists discovered how to splice the red rose with a poppy.*

Tracing around edges

Find Edges and Trace Contour — also located in the Filter⊃Stylize submenu — trace around pixels in your image to accentuate the edges. As shown in the top left example of Figure 14-9, Find Edges detects edges similarly to High Pass. Low-contrast areas become white, medium-contrast edges become gray, and high-contrast edges become black. Hard edges become thin lines; soft edges become fat ones. The result is a thick, organic outline that you can overlay onto an image to give it a waxy appearance. In the top right example of Figure 14-9, we applied the command to a floating image and mixed it with the underlying original using the Overlay mode and a 50 percent Opacity setting.

Trace Contour, also illustrated in Figure 14-9, is a little more involved and slightly less interesting. When you choose Filter⊃Stylize⊃Trace Contour, you're presented with a dialog box containing three options: Level, Upper, and Lower. The filter traces a series of single-pixel lines along the border between light and dark pixels. The Level value indicates the lightness value above which pixels are considered to be light and below which they are dark. For example, if you enter 128 — medium gray, as by default — Trace Contour draws everyone an area of color lighter than medium gray meets an area of color darker than medium gray. Upper and Lower just tell the filter where to position the line — inside the lighter color's territory (Upper) or inside the space occupied by the darker color (Lower). Get it wrong, and you'll start a turf war.

Like Mezzotint, Trace Contour applies itself to each color channel independently and renders each channel as a 1-bit image. A collection of black lines surrounds the areas of color in each channel; the RGB, Lab, or CMYK composite view shows these lines in the colors associated with the channels. When you work in RGB, a cyan line indicates a black line in the red channel (no red plus full-intensity green and blue becomes cyan). A yellow line indicates a black line in the blue channel, and so on. You get a single black line when working in the grayscale mode.

Figure 14-9: After applying Find Edges to a floating selection (top left), we blended the floater with the underlying original using the Overlay mode and 80 percent Opacity (top right). The bottom examples show the results of applying Trace Contour to a floater (left) and using the Multiply mode to mix it with the original (right).

Creating a metallic coating

Unlike High Pass, Find Edges and Trace Contour are not particularly suited to defining masks. Rather, they're primarily geared toward the creation of special effects.

The metallic coating effect is a case in point. Have you ever seen that Chrome filter that's included with Adobe Gallery Effects, the three-volume filter collection? We don't like it — never have — not because it's without merit, but because Photoshop already offers this capability via the Gaussian Blur and Find Edges commands, which together do a better job. The Chrome filter always produces grayscale results and offers poor edge anti-aliasing. The duo of Gaussian Blur and Find Edges work in color and looks smooth as silk.

To create this effect, float your image (Ctrl-J, in case you're rusty) and apply Filter⇨ Blur⇨Gaussian Blur. A Radius value between 1.0 and 4.0 produces the best results, depending on how gooey you want your edges to be. Our favorite setting is 3.0, as in the top left example of Figure 14-10. Then apply Filter⇨Stylize⇨Find Edges, which results in the effect shown in the top right corner of the figure. In the bottom left example, we mixed the floater with the underlying original using the Overlay mode and an Opacity of 70 percent. But the result is a little washed out. So we defloated the image, chose the Levels command, and raised the first Input value to 50, thereby increasing the number of dark colors in the image (as shown in the final example).

Figure 14-10: After applying the Gaussian Blur filter with a Radius of 3.0 (top left), we chose the Find Edges filter (top right). We then composited the filtered image with the original using the Overlay mode (bottom left) and used the Levels command to darken the image and give it strength (bottom right).

Color Plate 14-4 shows the same effect in color. Starting with an unedited construction worker, we went through the usual calisthenics of selecting and floating the image. Next, we applied Gaussian Blur (3.0 Radius) and Find Edges. The effect was too light, so we chose Image⇨Adjust⇨Levels and entered 128 into the first option box. (You may notice that we worked in a slightly different order from before, but you can apply color corrections before or after you mix the images.) Everything darker than medium gray went to black, uniformly strengthening the effect. The result is the full-color metallic coating shown in the second example in Color Plate 14-4. To get the last image, we merely chose the Overlay option from the overlay modes pop-up menu in the Layers palette and changed the Opacity to 80 percent.

Tracing noise

One of our favorite uses for the Trace Contour filter is to trace around noise. Check out Color Plate 14-5, for example. We started by floating the image — no surprise there — and applying the Pointillize filter with a Cell Size of 6. Then we chose Trace Contour, set the Levels slider to 128, and let 'er rip. Photoshop traced around each and every chunk of Pointillized noise to create the mottled effect shown on the left side of the figure. We also chose the Luminosity option from the Layers palette to borrow the colors from the underlying image. That image struck us as a little too flimsy, however, so we switched the overlay mode to Multiply and lowered the Opacity setting to 50 percent, which resulted in the second example of Color Plate 14-5.

If Trace Contour creates a mottled effect when applied to a Pointillized image, what does it do to real noise? The right example of Color Plate 14-5 shows all. Here, we applied the Add Noise command to the floating image with an Amount value of 100 and Gaussian turned on. After completing the noise, we traced it with Trace Contour. To get the maximum effect, we had to lower the Levels value in the Trace Contour dialog box to 90. We then applied the Overlay mode and set the Opacity to 80 percent, as we've done about 100 times now. The image took on a downright grainy appearance, an effect that noise — whether regular or chunky — can't accomplish on its own.

Distortion Filters

For the most part, commands in the Distort submenu are related by the fact that they move colors in an image to achieve unusual stretching, swirling, and vibrating effects. They're rather like the transformation commands from the Image⇨Effects submenu in that they perform their magic by relocating and interpolating colors rather than by altering brightness and color values.

The distinction, of course, is that while the transformation commands let you scale and distort images by manipulating four control points, the Distort filters provide the equivalent of hundreds of control points, all of which you can use to affect different portions of an image. In some cases, you're projecting an image into a fun-house mirror; at other times, it's a reflective pool. You can fan images, wiggle them, and change them in ways that have no correlation to real life, as illustrated in Figure 14-11.

Figure 14-11: This is your image (left); this is your image on distortion filters (right). Three filters, in fact: Spherize, Ripple, and Polar Coordinates.

Distortion filters are very powerful tools. Although easy to apply, they are extremely difficult to use well. Here are some rules to keep in mind:

✦ **Practice makes practical:** Distortion filters are like complex vocabulary words. You don't want to use them without practicing a little first. Experiment with a distortion filter several times before trying to use it in a real project. You may even want to write down the steps you take so that you can remember how you created an effect.

✦ **Use caution during tight deadlines:** Distortion filters are enormous time-wasters. Unless you know exactly how you want to proceed, you may want to avoid using them when time is short. The last thing you need when you're working under the gun is to get trapped trying to pull off a weird effect.

✦ **Apply selectively:** The effects of distortion filters are too severe to inflict all at once. You can achieve marvelous, subtle effects by distorting feathered and floating selections. Although we wouldn't call the image in Figure 14-11 subtle, no effect was applied to the entire image. We applied the Spherize filter to a feathered elliptical marquee that included most of the image. We then reapplied Spherize to the eye. We selected the hair and beard, and applied the Ripple filter twice. Finally, after establishing two heavily feathered vertical columns on either side of the image in the quick mask mode, we applied the Polar Coordinates filter, which reflected the front and back of the head. Turn the book upside down, and you'll see a second face.

✦ **Combine creatively:** Don't expect a single distortion to achieve the desired effect. If one application isn't enough, apply the filter again. Experiment with combining different distortions.

✦ **Save your original:** Never distort an image until you save it. After you start down Distortion Boulevard, the only way to go back is File⇨Revert. And, as always, it's a good idea to float the image before applying the filter so that you can delete it if you don't like the effect.

Caution Distortion filters interpolate between pixels to create their fantastic effects. This means that the quality of your filtered images is dependent on the setting of the interpolation option in the General Preferences dialog box. If a filter is producing jagged effects, the Nearest Neighbor option is probably selected. Try selecting the Bicubic or Bilinear option instead.

Reflecting an image in a spoon

Most folks take their first ventures into distortion filters by using Pinch and Spherize. Pinch maps an image onto the inside of a sphere or similarly curved surface; Spherize maps it onto the outside of a sphere. It's sort of like looking at your reflection on the inside or outside of a spoon.

You can apply Pinch to a scanned face to squish the features toward the center, or apply Spherize to accentuate the girth of the nose. Figure 14-12 illustrates both effects. It's a laugh, and you pretty much feel as though you're onto something that no one else ever thought of before. (At least that's how we felt — but we're easily amazed.)

Figure 14-12: The stereotypical rookie applications for the Pinch (left) and Spherize (right) filters.

You can pinch or spherize an image using either the Pinch or Spherize command. As shown in Figure 14-13, a positive value in the Pinch dialog box produces a similar effect to a negative value in the Spherize dialog box. There is a slight difference between the spatial curvature of the 3-D calculations: Pinch pokes the image inward or outward using a rounded cone — we're talking bell-shaped, much like a Gaussian model. Spherize wraps the image on the outside or inside of a true sphere. As a result, the two filters yield subtly different results. Pinch produces a soft transition around the perimeter of a selection; Spherize produces an abrupt transition. If this doesn't quite make sense to you, just play with one, try out the same effect with the other, and see which you like better.

Another difference between the two filters is that Spherize provides the additional options of allowing you to wrap an image onto the inside or outside of a horizontal or vertical cylinder. To try out these effects, select the Horizontal Only or Vertical Only radio button in the Spherize dialog box.

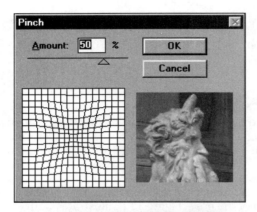

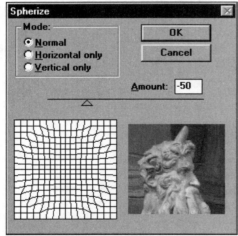

Figure 14-13: Both the Pinch and Spherize dialog boxes enable you to pinch or spherize an image. Pinch wraps on a rounded cone; Spherize wraps onto a sphere.

Tip   Both the Pinch and Spherize filters are applicable only to elliptical regions of an image. If a selection outline is not elliptical, Photoshop applies the filter to the largest ellipse that fits inside the selection. As a result, the filter may leave behind a noticeable elliptical boundary between the affected and unaffected portions of the selection. To avoid this effect, select the region you want to edit with the elliptical marquee tool and then feather the selection before filtering it. This softens the effect of the filter and provides a more gradual transition (even more so than Pinch already affords).

One of the more remarkable properties of the Pinch filter is that it lets you turn any image into a conical gradation. Figure 14-14 illustrates how the process works.

First, blur the image to eliminate any harsh edges between color transitions. Then apply the Pinch filter at full strength (100 percent). Reapply the filter several more times. Each time you press Ctrl-F, the center portion of the image recedes farther and farther into the distance, as shown in Figure 14-14. After 10 repetitions, the face in the example all but disappeared.

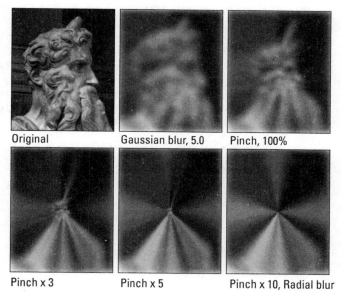

Original   Gaussian blur, 5.0   Pinch, 100%

Pinch x 3   Pinch x 5   Pinch x 10, Radial blur

Figure 14-14: After applying the Gaussian Blur filter, we pinched the image 10 times and applied the Radial Blur filter to create a conical gradation.

Next, apply the Radial Blur filter set to Spin 10 pixels or so to mix the color boundaries a bit. The result is a type of gradation that you can't create using Photoshop's gradient tool.

You can also use the Spherize tool set to a negative Amount value to create a conical gradation. Color Plate 14-6 shows off the subtle differences between using the Pinch and Spherize filters for this purpose. The left examples were created with Pinch, the right examples with Spherize. The first row shows the effect of applying each filter twice set to 100 and –100 percent, respectively. The Spherized face is larger, showing that the Spherize filter works more slowly. But it also grabs more edge detail. The second row shows the results of 12 repetitions of each filter. Though the two gradations are very similar, the Spherized one contains a hundred or so extra streaks. In the last row, we mixed the gradation with the underlying image using different overlay modes. The Soft Light mode was responsible for the alarming conical-sunburn effect on the left. We repeated the filter four times using the Screen mode to get the right image. *Look, Ma, I had a sprinkler system installed on my helmet!*

Twirling spirals

The Twirl filter rotates the center of a selection while leaving the sides fixed in place. The result is a spiral of colors that looks for all the world as if you poured the image into a blender set to a very slow speed.

When you choose Filter⇨Distort⇨Twirl, Photoshop displays the Twirl dialog box, shown in Figure 14-15. Enter a positive value from 1 to 999 degrees to spiral the image in a clockwise direction. Enter a negative value to spiral the image in a counterclockwise direction. As you are probably already aware, 360 degrees make a full circle, so the maximum 999-degree value equates to a spiral that circles around approximately three times, as shown in the bottom right example in Figure 14-16.

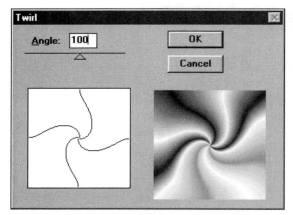

Figure 14-15: The Twirl dialog box lets you create spiraling images.

Tip   The Twirl filter produces smoother effects when you use lower Angle values. Therefore, you're better off applying a 100-degree spiral 10 times than applying a 999-degree spiral once, as verified by Figure 14-16.

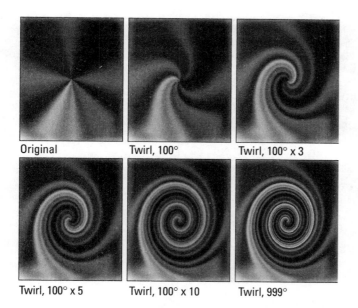

Original   Twirl, 100°   Twirl, 100° x 3

Twirl, 100° x 5   Twirl, 100° x 10   Twirl, 999°

Figure 14-16: The effects of applying the Twirl filter. Repeatedly applying the Twirl filter at a moderate value (bottom middle) produces a smoother effect than applying the filter once at a high value (bottom right).

In addition to creating ice-cream swirls like those shown in Figure 14-16, you can use the Twirl filter to create organic images virtually from scratch, as illustrated by Figures 14-17 and 14-18.

To create the images shown in Figure 14-17, we used the Spherize filter to flex the conical gradation vertically by entering 100 percent in the Amount option box and selecting Vertical Only from the Mode radio buttons. After repeating this filter several times, we eventually achieved a stalactite–stalagmite effect, as shown in the center example of the figure. We then repeatedly applied the Twirl filter to curl the flexed gradations like two symmetrical hairs. The result merges the simplicity of pure math with the beauty of bitmapped imagery.

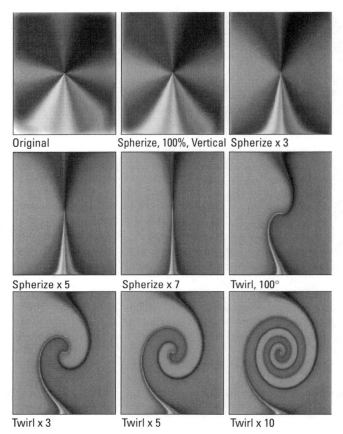

Original　　Spherize, 100%, Vertical　Spherize x 3

Spherize x 5　　Spherize x 7　　Twirl, 100°

Twirl x 3　　Twirl x 5　　Twirl x 10

Figure 14-17: You can create surprisingly naturalistic effects using distortion filters exclusively.

Figure 14-18 illustrates a droplet technique designed by Mark Collen. We took the liberty of breaking down the technique into the following steps.

Steps: Creating a thick-liquid droplet

1. Click on the default colors icon to restore black as the foreground color and white as the background color. Select a square portion of an image by dragging with the rectangular marquee tool while pressing the Shift key.

2. Drag inside the selection outline with the gradient tool. Drag a short distance near the center of the selection from upper left to lower right, creating the gradation shown in the top left box in Figure 14-18.

Figure 14-18: If you know your way around Photoshop, you may at first misinterpret the bottom two images as the result of the Zigzag filter, discussed in the next section. In fact, they were created entirely by using the gradient tool and Twirl filter and then applying a couple of transformations to a floating selection.

3. Choose the Twirl filter and apply it at −360 degrees so that the spiral moves counterclockwise. To create the top right image in the figure, we applied the Twirl filter three times. Each repetition of the filter adds another ring of ripples.

4. Choose Select⇨Float (Ctrl-J) to clone the image. Then choose Image⇨Flip⇨Horizontal.

5. Select the rectangular marquee tool. Press 5 to change the Opacity slider bar in the Brushes palette to 50 percent. The result is shown in the lower left image in Figure 14-18.

6. Choose Image⇨Rotate⇨90° CW to rotate the image a quarter-turn, thus creating the last image in the figure. You can achieve other interesting effects by choosing Lighten, Darken, and others from the brush modes pop-up menu.

Concentric pond ripples

We don't know about you, but when we think of zigzags, we think of cartoon lightning bolts, wriggling snakes, scribbles — anything that alternatively changes directions along an axis, like the letter Z. The Zigzag filter does arrange colors into zigzag patterns, but it does so in a radial fashion, meaning that the zigzags emanate from the center of the image like spokes in a wheel. The result is a series of concentric ripples. If you want parallel zigzags, check out the Ripple and Wave filters, described in the next section. (The Zigzag filter creates ripples, and the Ripple filter creates zigzags. Go figure.)

When you choose Filter⇨Distort⇨Zigzag, Photoshop displays the Zigzag dialog box shown in Figure 14-19. The dialog box offers the following options:

✦ **Amount:** Enter an amount between negative and positive 100, in whole-number increments, to specify the depth of the ripples. If you enter a negative value, the ripples descend below the surface. If you enter a positive value, the ripples protrude upward. Examples of three representative Amount values appear in Figure 14-20.

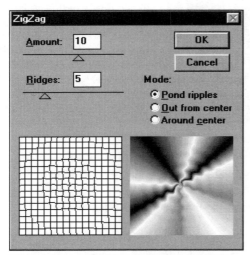

Figure 14-19: The Zigzag dialog box lets you add concentric ripples to an image, as if the image were reflected in a pond into which you dropped a pebble.

✦ **Ridges:** This option box controls the number of ripples in the selected area and accepts any value from 1 to 20. Figure 14-21 demonstrates the effect of three Ridges values.

✦ **Pond Ripples:** This option is really a cross between the two that follow. It moves pixels outward and rotates them around the center of the selection to create circular patterns. As demonstrated in the top rows of Figures 14-20 and 14-21, this option truly results in a pond ripple effect.

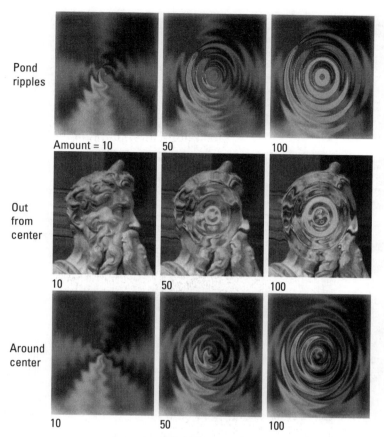

Figure 14-20: The effects of the Zigzag filter subject to three Amount values and the Pond Ripples, Out From Center, and Around Center settings. In all cases, the Ridges value was 5.

✦ **Out From Center:** When you select this option, Photoshop moves pixels outward in rhythmic bursts according to the value in the Ridges option box. Because the gradation image we created in Figure 14-14 was already arranged in a radial pattern, we brought in Moses to demonstrate the effect of the Out From Center option, as shown in the second rows of Figures 14-20 and 14-21.

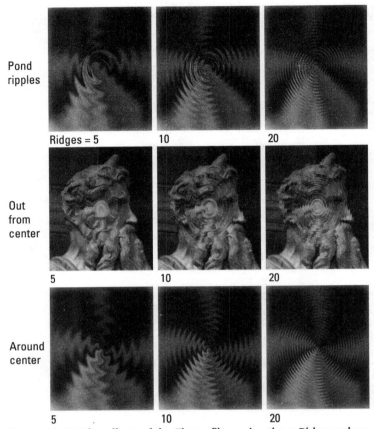

Pond
ripples

Ridges = 5   10   20

Out
from
center

5   10   20

Around
center

5   10   20

Figure 14-21: The effects of the Zigzag filter using three Ridges values and each of the three radio button settings. In all cases, the Amount value was 20.

✦ **Around Center:** Select this option to rotate pixels in alternating directions around the circle without moving them outward. This is the only option that produces what we would term a zigzag effect. The last rows of Figures 14-20 and 14-21 show the effects of the Around Center option.

Creating parallel ripples and waves

Photoshop provides two means to distort an image in parallel waves, as if the image were lying on the bottom of a shimmering or undulating pool. Of the two, the Ripple filter is less sophisticated, but it's also straightforward and easy to apply. The Wave filter affords you greater control, but its options are among the most complex Photoshop has to offer.

To use the Ripple filter, choose Filter⇨Distort⇨Ripple. Photoshop displays the Ripple dialog box shown in Figure 14-22. You have the following options:

✦ **Amount:** Enter an amount between negative and positive 999, in whole-number increments to specify the width of the ripples from side to side. Negative and positive values change the direction of the ripples, but visually speaking, they produce identical effects. The ripples are measured as a ratio of the Size value and the dimensions of the selection — all of which translates to *Experiment and see what happens.* You can count on getting ragged effects from any value over 300, as illustrated in Figure 14-23.

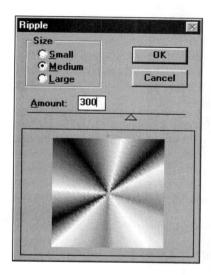

Figure 14-22: The Ripple filter makes an image appear as if it were refracted through flowing water.

✦ **Size:** Select one of the three radio buttons to change the length of the ripples. The Small option results in the shortest ripples and, therefore, the most ripples. As shown in the upper right corner of Figure 14-23, you can create a textured glass effect by combining the Small option with a high Amount value. The Large option results in the longest and fewest ripples.

Tip You can create a blistered effect by overlaying a negative ripple onto a positive ripple. Try this: First, copy the selection. Then apply the Ripple filter with a positive Amount value — say, 300. Next, paste the copied selection and apply the Ripple filter at the exact opposite Amount value–in this case, –300. Press 5 to change the Opacity slider bar to 50 percent. The result is a series of diametrically opposed ripples that cross each other to create teardrop blisters.

Now that you're familiar with the Ripple filter, it's on to the Wave filter. We could write a book on this filter alone. It wouldn't be very big, nobody would buy it, and we'd hate every minute of it, but you never know what freelancers will do next. Keep an eye out at your local bookstore. In the meantime, we're going to breeze though this filter like a little dog on the Oz-bound Kansas Express.

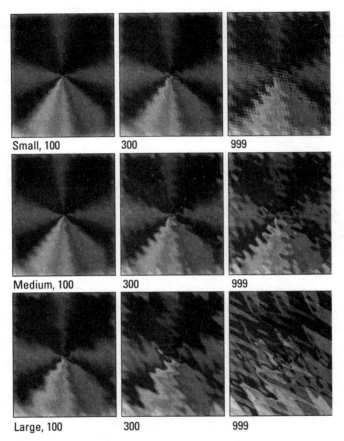

Figure 14-23: The effects of combining three different Ripple filter Amount values with three different Size settings.

Here goes: Choose Filter⇨Distort⇨Wave (that's the easy part) to display the Wave dialog box shown in Figure 14-24. Photoshop presents you with the following options, which makes applying a distortion almost every bit as fun as operating an oscilloscope:

✦ **Number of Generators:** Right off the bat, the Wave dialog box boggles the brain. A friend of ours likened this option to the number of rocks you throw in the water to start it rippling. One generator means that you throw in one rock to create one set of waves, as demonstrated in Figure 14-25. You can throw in two rocks to create two sets of waves (see Figure 14-26), three rocks to create three sets of waves, and all the way up to a quarryful of 999 rocks to create . . . well, you get the idea. If you enter a high value, however, be prepared to wait a few years for the preview to update. If you can't wait, press Ctrl-period, which turns off the preview until the next time you enter the dialog box.

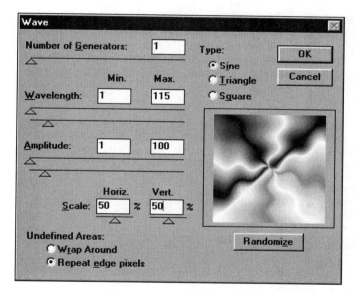

Figure 14-24: The Wave dialog box lets you wreak scientific havoc on an image. Put on your pocket protector, take out your slide rule, and give it a whirl.

✦ **Wavelength and Amplitude:** Beginning to feel like you're playing with a ham radio? The Wave filter produces random results by varying the number and length of waves (Wavelength) as well as the width of the waves (Amplitude) between minimum and maximum values, which can range anywhere from 1 to 999. (The Wavelength and Amplitude options, therefore, correspond in theory to the Size and Amount options in the Ripple dialog box.) Figures 14-25 and 14-26 show examples of representative Wavelength and Amplitude values.

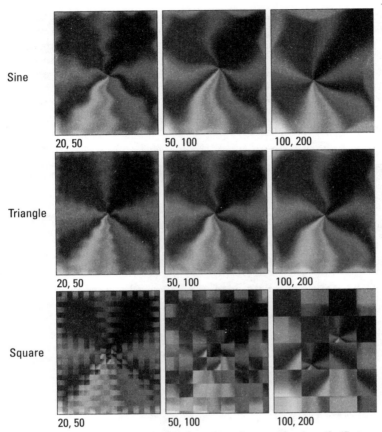

Figure 14-25: The effect of three sets of Maximum Wavelength (first value) and Amplitude (second value) settings when combined with each of the three Type settings. The Number of Generators value was 1 in all cases.

✦ **Scale:** You can scale the effects of the Wave filter between 1 and 100 percent horizontally and vertically. All the effects featured in Figures 14-25 and 14-26 were created by setting both Scale options to 15 percent.

✦ **Undefined Areas:** The Wave filter distorts a selection to the extent that gaps may appear around the edges. You can either fill those gaps by repeating pixels along the edge of the selection, as in the figures, or by wrapping pixels from the left side of the selection onto the right side and pixels from the top edge of the selection onto the bottom.

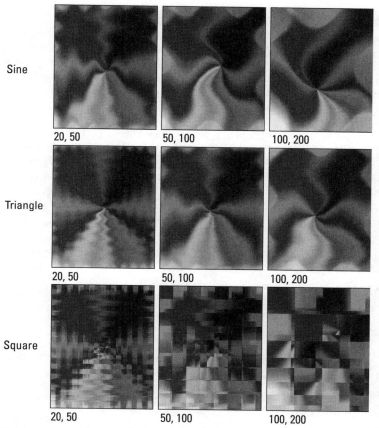

Sine

20, 50   50, 100   100, 200

Triangle

20, 50   50, 100   100, 200

Square

20, 50   50, 100   100, 200

Figure 14-26: The only difference between these images and their counterparts in Figure 14-25 is that the Number of Generators value used for all images was 2.

✦ **Type:** You can select three kinds of waves. The Sine option produces standard sine waves that rise and fall smoothly in bell-shaped curves, just like real waves. The Triangle option creates zigzags that rise and fall in straight lines, like the edge of a piece of fabric cut with pinking shears. The Square option has nothing to do with waves at all; it organizes an image into a series of rectangular group-ings, reminiscent of Cubism. You might think of this option as an extension of the Mosaic filter. All three options are demonstrated in Figures 14-25 and 14-26.

✦ **Randomize:** The Wave filter is random by nature. If you don't like the effect you see in the preview box, click on the Randomize button to stir things up a bit. You can keep clicking on the button until you get an effect you like.

Distorting an image along a curve

The Distort command, which isn't discussed elsewhere in this book, creates four corner handles around an image. You drag each corner handle to distort the selected image in that direction. Unfortunately, you can't add other points around the edges to create additional distortions, which can be very frustrating if you're trying to achieve a specific effect. If you can't achieve a certain kind of distortion using Image⇨ Effects⇨Distort, the Shear filter may be your answer.

Shear distorts an image along a path. When you choose Filter⇨Distort⇨Shear, you get the dialog box shown in Figure 14-27. Initially, a single line that has two points at either end appears in the grid in the bottom-left corner of the box. When you drag the points, you slant the image in the preview. This plus the fact that the filter is named Shear — Adobe's strange term for skewing (it appears in Illustrator as well) — leads many users to dismiss the filter as nothing more than a slanting tool. But in truth, it's more versatile than that.

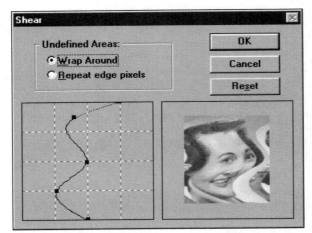

Figure 14-27: Click on the grid line in the bottom-left corner of the Shear dialog box to add points to the line. Drag these points to distort the image along the curve.

You can add points to the grid line by simply clicking on it. A point springs up every time you click on an empty space in the line. Drag the point to change the curvature of the line and distort the image along the new curve. To delete a point, drag it off the left or right side of the grid. To delete all points and return the line to its original vertical orientation, click on the Reset button.

The Undefined Areas options work just as they do in the Wave dialog box (described in the preceding section). You can either fill the gaps on one side of the image with pixels shoved off the opposite side by selecting Wrap Around, or you can repeat pixels along the edge of the selection by selecting Repeat Edge Pixels.

Changing to polar coordinates

The Polar Coordinates filter is another one of those gems that a lot of folks shy away from because it doesn't make much sense at first glance. When you choose Filter⇨Distort⇨Polar Coordinates, Photoshop presents two radio buttons, as shown in Figure 14-28. You can either map an image from rectangular to polar coordinates or from polar to rectangular coordinates.

All right, time for some global theory. The top image in Figure 14-29 shows the world map that appears in the Windows 95 dialog box for setting your time zone. Though a tad simplistic, this map falls under the heading of *Mercator projection,* meaning that Greenland is all stretched out of proportion, looking as big as the United States and Mexico combined.

R
%%
Robert
You may recall that around the time Windows 95 shipped, there was a terrific brouhaha in certain countries that took exception to the way Microsoft's map apparently ignored their sensitivities on national boundaries — so much so that the countries threatened to bar Windows 95 from their shores. Although I'm on the East Coast (I know, I know — nobody's perfect), for these purposes I've reset the time zone somewhat to the West in honor of the good people who produce this here program that helps keep Deke and me in clover.

Figure 14-28: In effect, the Polar Coordinates dialog box lets you map an image onto a globe and view the globe from above.

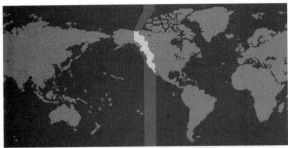

Figure 14-29: The world from the equator up, expressed in rectangular (top) and polar (bottom) coordinates.

The reason for this has to do with the way different mapping systems handle longitude and latitude lines. On a spherical globe, lines of latitude converge at the poles. On a Mercator map, they run absolutely parallel. Because the Mercator map exaggerates the distance between longitude lines as you progress away from the equator, it likewise exaggerates the distance between lines of latitude. The result is a map that becomes infinitely enormous at each of the poles.

When you convert the map to polar coordinates (by selecting the Rectangular to Polar radio button in the Polar Coordinates dialog box), you look down on it from the extreme north or south pole. This means that the entire length of the top edge of the Mercator map becomes a single dot in the exact center of the polar projection. The length of the bottom edge of the map wraps around the entire perimeter of the circle. The bottom example in Figure 14-29 shows the result. As you can see, the Rectangular to Polar option is just the thing for wrapping text around a circle.

If you select the Polar to Rectangular option, the Polar Coordinates filter produces the opposite effect. Imagine for a moment that the conical gradation shown in the upper left corner of Figure 14-30 is a fan spread out into a full circle. Now imagine closing the fan, breaking the hinge at the top, and spreading out the rectangular fabric of the fan. The center of the fan unfolds to form the top edge of the fabric, and what was once the perimeter of the circle is now the bottom edge of the fabric. Figure 14-30 shows two examples of what happens when you convert circular images from polar to rectangular coordinates.

Figure 14-30: Two familiar circular images (left) converted from polar to rectangular coordinates (right). The top example is simple enough that you can probably predict the results of the conversion in your head. The lower example looks cool, but you'd need a brain extension to predict the outcome.

 Tip The Polar Coordinates filter is a great way to edit gradations. After drawing a linear gradation with the gradient tool (as discussed in Chapter 10), try applying Filter⇨Distort⇨Polar Coordinates with the Polar to Rectangular option selected. (Rectangular to Polar just turns it into a radial gradation, sometimes with pretty undesirable results.) You get a redrawn gradation with highlights at the bottom of the selection. Press Ctrl-F to reapply the filter to achieve another effect. You can keep repeating this technique until jagged edges start to appear. Then press Ctrl-Z to go back to the last smooth effect.

Distorting an image inside out

The following exercise describes how to achieve a sizzling Parting of the Red Sea effect. Though it incorporates several distortion filters, the star of the effect is the Polar Coordinates filter, which is used to turn the image inside out and then convert it back to polar coordinates after flipping it upside down. No scanned image or artistic talent is required. Rumor has it that Moses puts in a guest appearance in the final image.

This effect is the brainchild of Mark Collen, easily the most authoritative filtering expert we've had the pleasure of knowing. We've already mentioned his name in this chapter, in connection with the "Creating a thick-liquid droplet" steps. To be perfectly honest, we probably should have mentioned him more than that, because many of the ideas conveyed in this chapter were based on long, expensive telephone conversations with the guy.

At any rate, Figures 14-31 through 14-36 show the progression of the image through the following steps, starting with a simplistic throwback to Dada (the art movement, not the family member) and continuing to the fabled sea rising in billowing streams. Color Plate 14-7 shows one of Mark's most vivid images, which was created in part using many of the techniques from the following steps. Obviously, a lot of other filtering and nonfiltering techniques were used to create that image, but gee whiz, folks, you can't expect the guy to share everything he knows in one fell swoop. He has to make a living, after all.

Steps: The parting of the Red Sea effect

1. Draw some random shapes in whatever colors you like. My shapes appear against a black background in Figure 14-31, but you can use any shapes and any colors you like. To create each shape, we used the lasso tool to draw the outline of the shape and pressed Alt-Delete to fill the lassoed selection with the foreground color. The effect works best if there's a lot of contrast between your colors.

2. In step 3, you apply the Wind Filter to add streaks to the shapes you just created, as shown in Figure 14-32. Because the Wind filter creates horizontal streaks only, and your goal is to add vertical streaks, you must temporarily reorient your image before applying the filter. To do so, choose Image⇨Rotate⇨90° CCW, which rotates the entire image a quarter-turn counterclockwise.

Figure 14-31: Draw several meaningless shapes with the lasso tool and fill each with a different color.

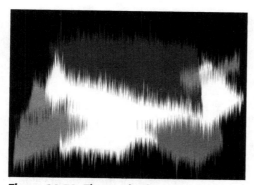

Figure 14-32: The result of rotating the image a quarter turn, blasting it in both directions with the Wind filter, rotating it back into place, and applying the Motion Blur filter vertically.

3. Choose Filter➪Stylize➪Wind. Select Blast and Left, and press Enter. To randomize the image in both directions, choose the Wind filter again, and select Blast and Right.

4. Choose Image➪Rotate➪90° CW to return the image to its original orientation.

5. Choose Filter➪Blur➪Motion Blur. Enter 90 degrees into the Angle option box, and use 20 pixels for the Distance option. This blurs the image vertically to soften the blast lines, as demonstrated in Figure 14-32.

6. Choose Filter⇨Distort⇨Wave, and enter the values shown in Figure 14-33 into the Wave option box. Most of these values are approximate. You can experiment with other settings if you like. The only essential value is 0 percent in the Vert. option box, which ensures that the filter waves the image in a horizontal direction only.

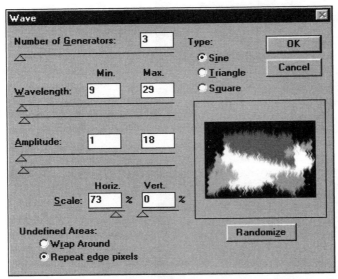

Figure 14-33: Apply these settings from the Wave dialog box to wave the image in a vertical direction only.

7. Choose Filter⇨Distort⇨Ripple. We entered 300 for the Amount value and selected the Medium radio button.

8. To perform the next step, the Polar Coordinates filter needs lots of empty room to maneuver in. If you filled up your canvas as we did, choose Image⇨Canvas size, and add 200 pixels both vertically and horizontally. The new canvas size, offering generous borders, appears in Figure 14-34.

9. So far, you've probably been a little disappointed by your image. It's just this disgusting little hairy thing that looks like a bad rug or something. Well, now's your chance to turn it into something special. Choose Filter⇨Distort⇨Polar Coordinates and select the Polar to Rectangular radio button. Photoshop in effect turns the image inside out, sending all the hairy edges to the bottom of the screen. Finally, an image worth waiting for.

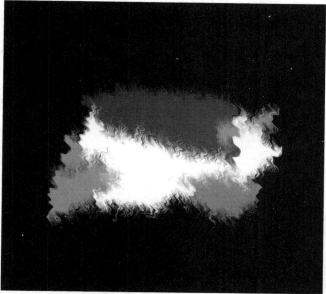

Figure 14-34: After applying the Ripple filter, use the Canvas Size command to add a generous amount of empty space around the image.

Figure 14-35: Convert the image from polar to rectangular coordinates to turn it inside out. Then flip it vertically to prepare it for the next polar conversion.

10. Choose Image⇨Flip⇨Vertical to turn the image upside down. The hair now rises, as shown in Figure 14-35. This step prepares the image for the next polar conversion.

11. Use the rectangular marquee tool to select the central portion of the image. Leave deselected about 50 pixels along the top and bottom of the image and 100 pixels along both sides. Then feather the selection with a 15-pixel radius.

12. Press Ctrl-F to reapply the Polar Coordinates filter just as before. The pixels inside the selection now billow into a fountain.

13. Add Moses to taste. The finished image appears in Figure 14-36.

Figure 14-36: Marquee the central portion of the image with a heavily feathered selection outline, convert the selection from rectangular to polar coordinates, and put Moses into the scene. My, doesn't he look natural in his new environment?

Adding Clouds and Spotlights

In a way, you can think of all five filters in the Filter⇨Render submenu as lighting filters. You can use Clouds and Difference Clouds to create a layer of haze over an image. Lens Flare creates light flashes and reflections (as mentioned earlier). Lighting Effects lights an image as if it were hanging on a gallery wall. You can even use the unremarkable Texture Fill command to add an embossed texture to a piece lighted with the Lighting Effects filter. Together, these five suggest a new category called *creative filters,* but it's really too early to tell.

Clouds

If you've played with the Clouds filters at all, you probably thought, *Hmf,* and gave them up for a screwy feature that Adobe's programmers decided to add in lieu of some meatier functions. Certainly these filters don't qualify as ground-breaking, but they're not at all bad and can yield some pretty entertaining results.

Clouds create an abstract and random haze of color between the foreground and background colors. Difference Clouds works exactly like floating the image, applying the Clouds filter, and choosing the Difference overlay mode from the Layers palette. Why on earth should this filter make special provisions for a single overlay mode? Because you can create cumulative effects. Try this: Select blue as the foreground color and then choose Filter⇨Render⇨Clouds. Ah, just like a real sky, huh? Now choose Filter⇨Render⇨Difference Clouds. It's like some kind of weird Halloween motif, all blacks and oranges. Press Ctrl-F to repeat the filter. Back to the blue sky. Keep pressing Ctrl-F over and over, and notice the results. A pink cancer starts invading the blue sky; a green cancer invades the orange one. Multiple applications of the Difference Clouds filter generate organic oil-on-water effects.

Tip To strengthen the colors created by the Clouds filter, press Shift when choosing the command. This same technique works when using the Difference Clouds filter as well. In fact, we don't know of any reason *not* to Shift-choose these commands, unless you have some specific need for washed-out effects. Oh, by the way, you can repeat a filter, such as Difference Clouds, at this high-intensity setting by pressing Ctrl-Shift-F (as long as you haven't gone and assigned the key combination to something different, as we suggested back in Chapter 2).

Color Plate 14-8 shows some pretty entertaining applications of the Clouds filter. With the foreground and background colors set to blue and orange respectively, we applied the Clouds filter to a floating version of the rose image. For maximum effect, we Shift-chose the filter to create the top left image in the color plate. We then Shift-chose the Difference Clouds filter to create the purple montage in the figure and pressed Ctrl-Shift-F 10 times to achieve the top right image. Looks like we definitely have something growing in our Petri dish.

Yeah, some really groovy stuff, right? Shades of "Purple Haze" and all that. *'Scuze me while I kiss that filter.* But now that we've created this murky mess, what the heck do we do with it? Composite it, of course. The bottom row of Color Plate 14-8 shows examples of mixing each of the images from the top row with the original rose. In the left example, we chose the Overlay option from the overlay modes pop-up menu in the Layers palette. In the middle example, we chose the Screen option. And in the last example, we chose Hue. This last one is particularly exciting, completely transforming the colors in the rose while leaving the gray (and therefore unsaturated) background untouched. Without a mask, without anything but a rectangular marquee, we've managed to precisely color the interior of the rose.

Lighting an image

Photoshop 3 is definitely venturing into 3-D drawing territory with the Lighting Effects filter. This very complex function enables you to shine lights on an image, color the lights, position them, focus them, specify the reflectivity of the surface, and even create a surface map. In many ways, it's a direct lift from Fractal Design Painter. But whereas Painter provides predefined paper textures and light-refraction effects that bolster the capabilities of its excellent tool, Photoshop offers better controls and more lighting options.

When you choose Filter⇨Render⇨Lighting Effect, Photoshop displays what is easily its most complex dialog box, as shown in Figure 14-37. The dialog box is split into halves, one in which you actually position light with respect to a thumbnail of the selected image, and one that contains about a billion intimidating options. Between you and us, we think Adobe could have done a better job, but the dialog box is functional.

Robert I've changed the illustration Deke used here. He's shown such good taste elsewhere using Michelangelo that I thought it a shame not to use that artist here. Besides, the woman diver, for reasons unclear to me, is suffering from serious overuse in the computer press.

No bones about it, this dialog box is a bear. The easiest way to apply the filter is to choose one of the predefined lighting effects from the Style pop-up menu at the top of the dialog box, see how it looks in the preview area, and — if you like it — press Enter to apply the effect.

The preview area (stage)

Footprint

Handles

Color swatches

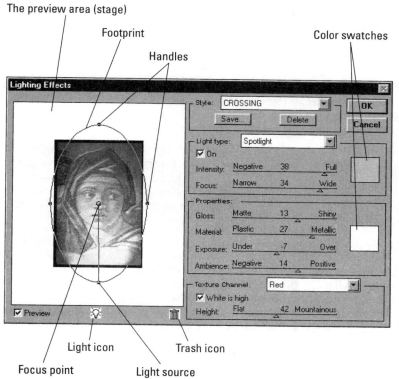

Light icon

Trash icon

Focus point

Light source

Figure 14-37: The Light Effects dialog box lets you light an image as if it were hanging in a gallery, or lying on a floor, or perhaps resting too near a hot flame.

But if you want to create your own effects, you'll have to work a little harder. Here are the basic steps involved in creating a custom effect.

Steps: Lighting an image

1. Drag from the light icon at the bottom of the dialog box into the preview area to create a new light source. We call this area the *stage* because it's as if the image is painted on the floor of a stage and the lights are hanging above it.

2. Select the kind of light you want from the Light Type pop-up menu (just below the Style pop-up menu). You can select Directional, Omni, or Spotlight. Directional works like the sun, being a general, unfocused light that hits a target from an angle. Omni is a bare light bulb hanging in the middle of the room, shining in all directions from a center point. And Spotlight is a focused beam that is brightest at the source and tapers off gradually.

3. Specify the color of the light by clicking on the top color swatch (labeled in Figure 14-37). You can also muck about with the Intensity slider bar to control the brightness of the light. If Spotlight is selected, the Focus slider becomes available. Drag the slider toward Narrow to create a bright laser of light; drag toward Wide to diffuse the light and spread it over a larger area.

4. Move the light source by dragging at the *focus point*, which appears as a colored circle in the stage. When Directional or Spotlight is selected, the focus point represents the spot at which the light is pointing. When Omni is active, the focus point is the actual bulb. (Don't burn yourself.)

5. If Directional or Spotlight is active, you can change the angle of the light by dragging at the *light source*. When you use a Directional light, the source appears as a black square at the end of a line joined to the focus point. The same holds true when you edit a Spotlight; the confusing thing is that there are four black squares altogether. The light source is joined to the focus point by a line; the three *handles* are not.

6. When Omni is in force, a circle surrounds the focus point. When editing a Spotlight, you see an ellipse. Either way, this shape represents the *footprint* of the light, which is the approximate area of the image affected by the light. You can change the size of the light by dragging the handles around the footprint. Enlarging the shape is like raising the light source. When the footprint is small, the light is close to the image, so it's concentrated and very bright. When the footprint is large, the light is high above the image, so it's more generalized.

7. Introduce more lights as you see fit by repeating the steps thus far. To delete a light, drag the focus point onto the trash can icon at the bottom of the dialog box.

8. Change the Properties and Texture Channel options as you see fit. (We explain these in detail in a moment.)

9. If you want to save your settings for future use, click on the Save button. Photoshop invites you to name the setup, which then appears as an option in the Style pop-up menu. If you want to get rid of one of the presets, select it from the pop-up menu and click on the Delete button.

10. Press Enter to apply your settings to the image.

That's almost everything. The only parts we left out are the Properties and Texture Channel options. The Properties slider bars control how light reflects off the surface of your image:

✦ **Gloss:** Is the surface dull or shiny? Drag the slider toward Matte to make the surface flat and nonreflective, like dull enamel paint. Drag the slider toward Shiny to make it glossy, as if you'd slapped on a coat of lacquer.

✦ **Material:** This option determines the color of the light that reflects off the image. According to the logic employed by this option, Plastic reflects the color of the light; Metallic reflects the color of the object itself. If only we had a bright, shiny plastic thing and a bright, shiny metal thing, we could check to see if this logic holds true in real life (like maybe that matters).

✦ **Exposure:** We'd like this option better if you could vary it between Sun Block 65 and Melanoma. Unfortunately, the more prosaic titles are Under and Over — exposed, that is. This option controls the brightness of all lights like a big dimmer switch. You can control a single selected light using the Intensity slider, but the Exposure slider offers the added control of changing all lights in the stage area and the ambient light (described next) together.

✦ **Ambience:** The last slider lets you add *ambient light,* which is a general, diffused light that hits all surfaces evenly. First, select the color of the light by clicking on the color swatch to the right. Then drag the slider to cast a subtle hue over the stage. Drag toward Positive to tint the image with the color in the swatch; drag toward Negative to tint the stage with the swatch's opposite. Keep the slider set to 0 — dead in the center — to cast no hue.

The Texture Channel options let you treat one channel in the image as a *texture map,* a grayscale surface in which white indicates peaks and black indicates valleys. (As long as White is High is selected, that is. If you deselect that option, everything flips, and black becomes the peak.) It's as if one channel has a surface to it. By selecting a channel from the pop-up menu, you create an emboss effect, much like that created with the Emboss filter, except much better because you can light the surface from many angles at once, and it's in color to boot.

Choose a channel to serve as the embossed surface from the pop-up menu. Then change the Height slider to indicate more or less Flat terrain or huge Mountainous cliffs of surface texture.

Color Plate 14-9 shows the rose lit with three colored spotlights. In the first example, we selected the red channel as the surface map. In the second example, we filled a separate mask channel with my seamlessly repeating Lenin pattern from Chapter 11 (using Filter⇨Render⇨Texture Fill) and then selected that channel from the Texture Channel pop-up menu in the Lighting Effects dialog box. It's like talking the Lenin pattern, stamping into the surface of the rose, and then shined a bunch of spotlights on it.

Constructing Homemade Effects

Creating a Custom Effect

If our wives (Robert-speak: spousal units) were here right now, they might be tempted to say something diplomatic along the lines of *Deke, Robert, our guests seem to be growing a teeny bit tired of the subject of filters. Perhaps this would be a good time to move on to a new topic.* To which we would respond, *Nonsense! Folks love to listen to us drone on and on about filters. We can't imagine anything more intriguing, can you? Speaking of which, is there any beer left? (Urp.)* Whether you share our fascination with filters or not, don't get up and go home just yet, because we've yet to tell you about three very important filters: Custom, Displace, and the Filter Factory, a plug-in that's new to Photoshop 3. With these three filters, you can create your own custom-tailored special effects.

Fully understanding the Custom and Displace filters requires some mathematical reasoning skills — and even if you're a math whiz, you'll probably have occasional difficulty predicting the outcomes of these filters. Using the Filter Factory requires flat-out programming skills. If math isn't your bag, if number theory clogs up your synapses to the extent that you feel like a worthless math wimp, by all means don't put yourself through the torture. Skip all the mathematical background in this chapter and read the "Applying Custom Values" and "Displacement Maps" sections to try out some specific, no-brainer effects.

On the CD-ROM If you have no desire to learn the Filter Factory, you can experiment with some filters that we programmed using this plug-in. On the CD-ROM, you'll find seven fully functioning filters, all of which include interactive slider bars and previews. If you copy the filters to your Plug-ins directory and launch Photoshop, you'll see our filters in the Filter⇨Tormentia submenu. (These filters torment your image in a demented way, hence *Tormentia*. We also considered *Tormento*, but that sounds like something you'd put on your pizza.) We explain what the filters do and how they work in a text file included on the CD.

On the other hand, if you're not scared silly of math and you want to understand how to eventually create effects of your own, read on, you hearty soul.

The Custom filter

The Custom command enables you to design your own *convolution kernel*, which is a variety of filter in which neighboring pixels get mixed together. The kernel can be a variation on sharpening, blurring, embossing, or half a dozen other effects. You create your filter by entering numerical values into a matrix of options.

When you choose Filter⇨Other⇨Custom, Photoshop displays the dialog box shown in Figure 15-1. It sports a 5 × 5 matrix of option boxes followed by two additional options, Scale and Offset. The matrix options can accept values from negative to positive 999. The Scale value can range from 1 to 9,999, and the Offset value can range from negative to positive 9,999. The dialog box includes Load and Save buttons so that you can load settings from disk and save the current settings for future use.

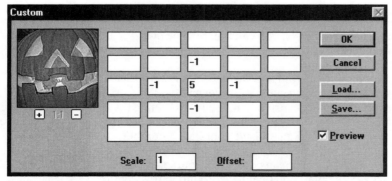

Figure 15-1: The Custom dialog box lets you design your own convolution kernel by multiplying the brightness values of pixels.

Tip This filter also includes a constantly updating preview box, which you'll have lots of time to appreciate if you decide to try your hand at designing your own effects. Select the Preview check box to view the effect of the kernel in the image window as well.

Here's how the filter works: When you press the Enter key to apply the values in the Custom dialog box to a selection, the filter passes over every pixel in the selection one at a time. For each pixel being evaluated — which we'll call the PBE for short — the filter multiplies the PBE's current brightness value by the number in the center option box (the one that contains a 5 in Figure 15-1). To help keep things straight, we'll call this value the CMV, for *central matrix value*.

The filter then multiplies the brightness values of the surrounding pixels by the surrounding values in the matrix. For example, Photoshop multiplies the value in the option box just above the CMV by the brightness value of the pixel just above the PBE. It ignores any empty matrix option boxes and the pixels they represent.

Finally, the filter totals the products of the multiplied pixels, divides the sum by the value in the Scale option, and adds the Offset value to calculate the new brightness of the PBE. It then moves on to the next pixel in the selection and performs the calculation all over again. Figure 15-2 shows a schematic drawing of the process.

Perhaps seeing all of this spelled out in an equation will help you understand the process. Then again, perhaps not — but here it comes anyway. In the following equation, NP stands for *neighboring pixel* and MV stands for the *corresponding matrix value* in the Custom dialog box.

New brightness value = (((PBE × CMV) + (NP1 × MV1) + (NP2× MV2) + ...) ÷ Scale) + Offset

Luckily, Photoshop calculates the equation without any help from you. All you have to do is punch in the values and see what happens.

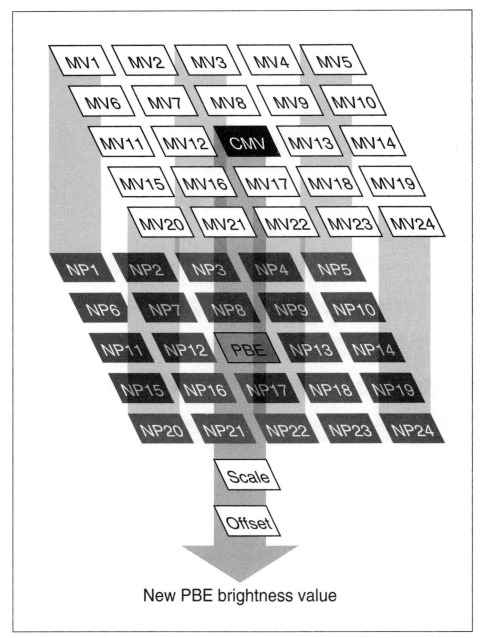

Figure 15-2: The Custom filter multiplies each matrix value by the brightness value of the corresponding pixel, adds the products together, divides the sum by the Scale value, adds the Offset value, and applies the result to the pixel being evaluated.

Custom filter advice

Now, obviously, if you go around multiplying the brightness value of a pixel too much, you end up making it white. And a filter that turns an image white is pretty darn useless. The key, then, is to filter an image and at the same time maintain the original balance of brightness values. To achieve this, just be sure that the sum of all values in the matrix is 1. For example, the default values in the matrix shown back in Figure 15-1 are 5, –1, –1, –1, and –1, which add up to 1.

If the sum is greater than 1, use the Scale value to divide the sum down to 1. Figures 15-3 and 15-4 show the results of increasing the CMV from 5 to 6 and then 7. This raises the sum of the values in the matrix from 1 to 2 and then 3.

In Figure 15-3, we entered the sum into the Scale option to divide the sum back down to 1 (any value divided by itself is 1, after all). The result is that Photoshop maintains the original color balance of the image while at the same time filtering it slightly differently. When we did not raise the Scale value, the image became progressively lighter, as illustrated in Figure 15-4.

If the sum is less than 1, increase the CMV until the sum reaches the magic number. For example, in Figure 15-5, we lowered the values to the left of the CMV and then above the CMV by 1 apiece to increase the sharpening effect. To ensure that the image did not darken, we also raised the CMV to compensate. When we did not raise the CMV, the image turned black, as shown in Figure 15-6.

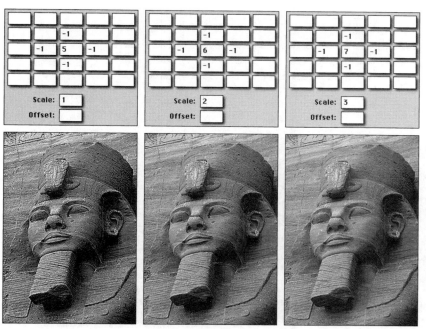

Figure 15-3: Raising the Scale value to reflect the sum of the values in the matrix maintains the color balance of the image.

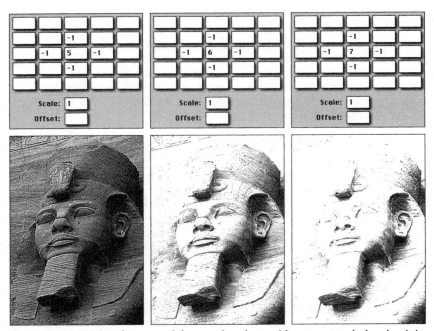

Figure 15-4: Raising the sum of the matrix values without counterbalancing it in the Scale option lightens the image.

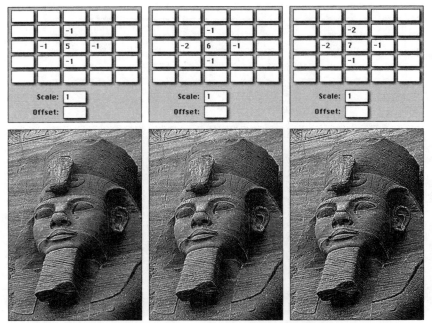

Figure 15-5: Raising the CMV to compensate for the lowered values in the matrix maintains the color balance of the image.

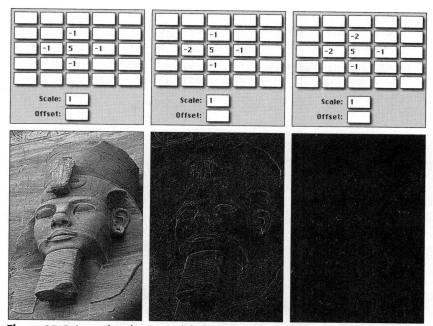

Figure 15-6: Lowering the sum of the matrix values without counterbalancing it with the CMV darkens the image.

Tip Though a sum of 1 provides the safest and most predictable filtering effects, you can use different sums, such as 0 and 2, to try out more destructive filtering effects. If you do, be sure to raise or lower the Offset value to compensate. For some examples, see the "Non-1 variations" section.

Applying Custom Values

The following sections show you ways to sharpen, blur, and otherwise filter an image using specific matrix, Scale, and Offset values. It is our sincere hope that by the end of the Custom filter discussions, you not only will know how to repeat our examples, but also how to apply what you've learned to design special effects of your own.

Symmetrical effects

Values that are symmetrical both horizontally and vertically about the central matrix value produce sharpen and blur effects:

✦ **Sharpening:** A positive CMV surrounded by symmetrical negative values sharpens an image, as demonstrated in the first example of Figure 15-7. Figures 15-3 through 15-6 also demonstrate varying degrees of sharpening effects.

✦ **Blurring:** A positive CMV surrounded by symmetrical positive numbers —
balanced, of course, by a Scale value as explained in the preceding section —
blurs an image, as demonstrated in the second example of Figure 15-7.

✦ **Blurring with edge detection:** A negative CMV surrounded by symmetrical
positive values blurs an image and adds an element of edge detection, as
illustrated in the last example of the figure. These effects are unlike anything
provided by Photoshop's standard collection of filters.

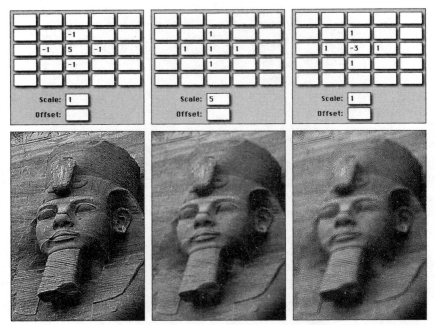

Figure 15-7: Symmetrical values can result in sharpening (left), blurring (middle), and
edge-detection (right) effects.

Sharpening

The Custom command provides as many variations on the sharpening theme as the
Unsharp Mask filter. In a sense, it provides even more, for whereas the Unsharp Mask
filter requires you to sharpen an image inside a Gaussian radius, you get to specify
exactly which pixels are taken into account when you use the Custom filter.

To create Unsharp Mask-like effects, enter a large number in the CMV and small values
in the surrounding option boxes, as demonstrated in Figure 15-8. To go beyond
Unsharp Mask, you can violate the radius of the filter by entering values around the
perimeter of the matrix and ignoring options closer to the CMV, as demonstrated in
Figure 15-9.

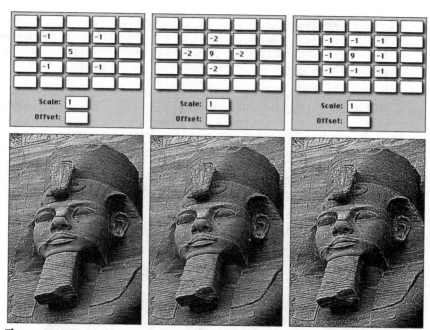

Figure 15-8: To create severe sharpening effects, enter a CMV just large enough to compensate for the negative values in the matrix.

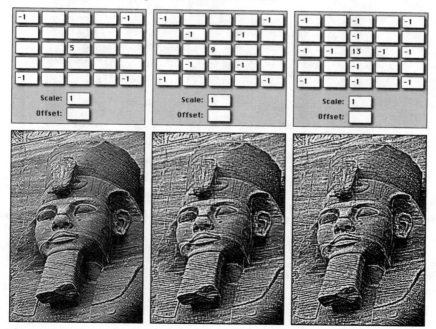

Figure 15-9: To heighten the sharpening effect even further, enter negative values around the perimeter of the matrix.

You can sharpen an image using the Custom dialog box in two basic ways. First, you can enter lots of negative values into the neighboring options in the matrix and then enter a CMV just large enough to yield a sum of 1. This results in radical sharpening effects, as demonstrated throughout the examples in Figures 15-8 and 15-9.

Second, you can tone down the sharpening by raising the CMV and using the Scale value to divide the sum down to 1. Figures 15-10 and 15-11 show the results of raising the CMV to lessen the impact of the sharpening effects performed in Figures 15-8 and 15-9.

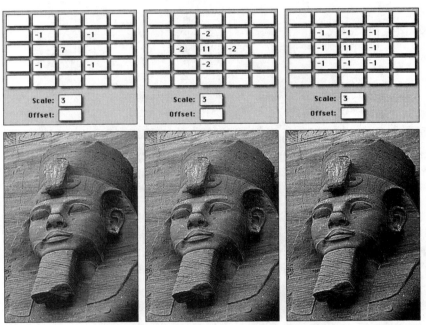

Figure 15-10: To sharpen more subtly, increase the central matrix value and then enter the sum into the Scale value.

Blurring

The philosophy behind blurring is very much the same as that behind sharpening. To produce extreme blurring effects, enter lots of values or high values into the neighboring options in the matrix, enter 1 into the CMV, and then enter the sum into the Scale option. Examples appear in Figure 15-12. To downplay the blurring, raise the CMV and the Scale value by equal amounts. In Figure 15-13, we used the same neighboring values as in Figure 15-12, but we increased the CMV and the Scale value by 3 apiece.

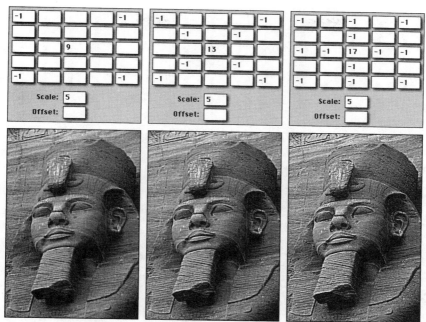

Figure 15-11: When you soften the effect of radical sharpening, you create a thicker, higher contrast effect, much as when raising the Radius value in the Unsharp Mask dialog box.

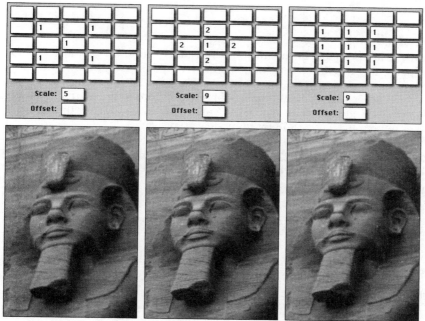

Figure 15-12: To create severe blurring effects, enter 1 for the CMV and fill the neighboring options with 1s and 2s.

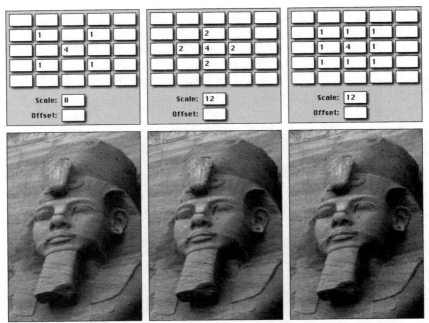

Figure 15-13: To blur more subtly, increase the central matrix value and the Scale value by equal amounts.

Edge detection

Many of you are probably beginning to get the idea by now, but just in case you're the kind of person who believes that friends don't let friends do math, we'll breeze through it one more time in the venue of edge detection. If you really want to see those edges, enter 1s and 2s into the neighboring options in the matrix and then enter a CMV just *small* enough — it's a negative value, after all — to make the sum 1. Examples appear in Figure 15-14 for your viewing pleasure.

To lighten the edges and bring out the blur, raise the CMV and enter the resulting sum into the Scale option box. The first example in Figure 15-15 pushes the boundaries between edge detection and a straight blur.

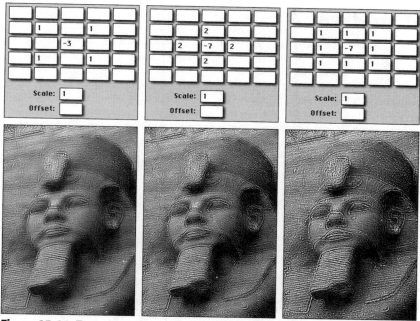

Figure 15-14: To create severe edge-detection effects, enter a negative CMV just small enough to compensate for the positive values in the matrix.

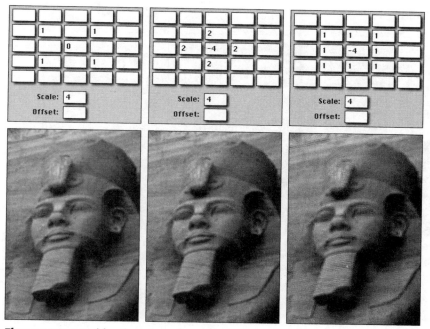

Figure 15-15: To blur the edges, increase the central matrix value and then enter the sum into the Scale value.

Non-1 variations

Every image shown in Figures 15-7 through 15-15 is the result of manipulating matrix values and using the Scale option to produce a sum total of 1. Earlier in this chapter, we showed you what can happen if you go below 1 (black images) or above 1 (white images). But we haven't shown you how you can use non-1 totals to produce interesting, if somewhat washed-out, effects.

The key is to raise the Offset value, thereby adding a specified brightness value to each pixel in the image. By doing this, you can offset the lightening or darkening caused by the matrix values to create an image that has half a chance of printing.

Lightening overly dark effects

The first image in Figure 15-16 uses nearly the exact same values used to create the extreme sharpening effect in the last image of Figure 15-8. The only difference is that the CMV is 1 lower (8, down from 9), which in turn lowers the sum total from 1 to 0.

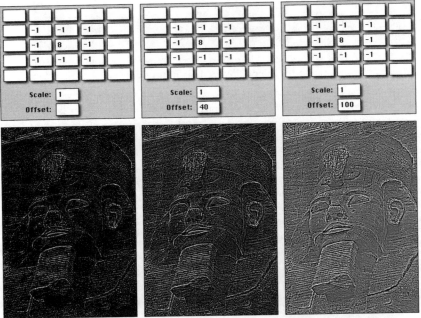

Figure 15-16: Three examples of sharpening effects with sum totals of 0. We lightened the images incrementally by entering positive values into the Offset option box.

The result is an extremely dark image with hints of brightness at points of high contrast. The image looks OK on-screen — actually, it looks pretty cool because of all those little starlike sprinkles in it — but it's likely to fill in during the printing process. If the first image in Figure 15-16 looks like anything but a vague blob of blackness, it's a credit to the printer of this book. Most printers who didn't have a giant publisher breathing down their necks would have kissed this image good-bye, and rightly so. It's too darn dark.

To prevent the image from filling in and to help head off any disputes with your printer, lighten the image using the Offset value. Photoshop adds the value to the brightness level of each selected pixel. A brightness value of 255 equals solid white, so you don't need to go too high. As shown in the last example of Figure 15-16, an Offset value of 100 is enough to raise most pixels in the image to a medium gray. Figure 15-17 shows the results of lightening an overly dark edge-detection effect using the Offset value.

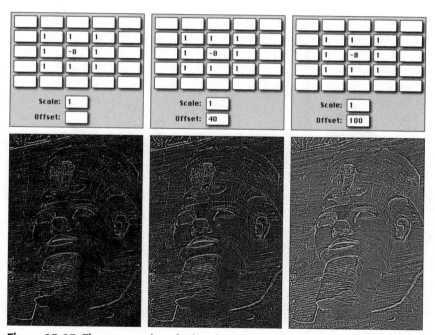

Figure 15-17: Three examples of edge-detection effects with sum totals of 0, lightened incrementally by using progressively higher Offset values.

Darkening overly light effects

You also can use the Offset value to darken filtering effects with sum totals greater than 1. The images in Figures 15-18 and 15-19 show sharpening and edge-detection effects whose matrix totals amount to 2. On their own, these filters produce effects that are too light. However, as demonstrated in the middle and right examples in the figures, you can darken the effects of the Custom filter to create high-contrast images by entering a negative value into the Offset option box.

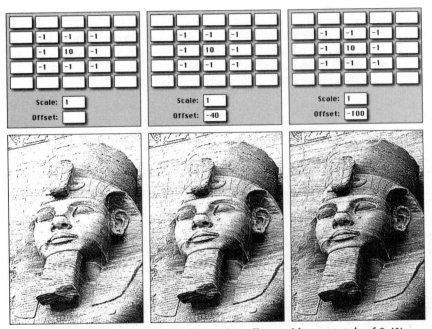

Figure 15-18: Three examples of sharpening effects with sum totals of 2. We darkened the images incrementally by entering negative values into the Offset option box.

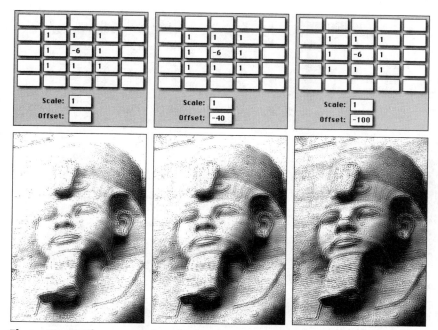

Figure 15-19: Three examples of edge-detection effects with sum totals of 2, darkened incrementally with progressively lower Offset values.

Using extreme offsets

If a brightness value of 255 produces solid white and a brightness value of 0 is solid black, why in blue blazes does the Offset value permit any number between negative and positive 9,999, a number 40 times greater than solid white? The answer lies in the fact that the matrix options can force the Custom filter to calculate brightness values much darker than black and much lighter than white. Therefore, you can use a very high or very low Offset value to boost the brightness of an image in which all pixels are well below black or diminish the brightness when all pixels are way beyond white.

Figure 15-20 shows exaggerated versions of the sharpening, blurring, and edge-detection effects. The sum totals of the matrixes are −42, 54, and 42, respectively. Without some help from the Offset value, each of these filters would turn every pixel in the image black (in the case of the sharpening effect) or white (blurring and edge detection). But as demonstrated in the figure, using enormous Offset numbers brings out those few brightness values that remain. The images are so polarized that there's hardly any difference between the three effects, except that the first image is an inverted version of the other two. The difference is even less noticeable if you apply the effect to a translucent floating selection, as demonstrated in the second row of examples in Figure 15-20.

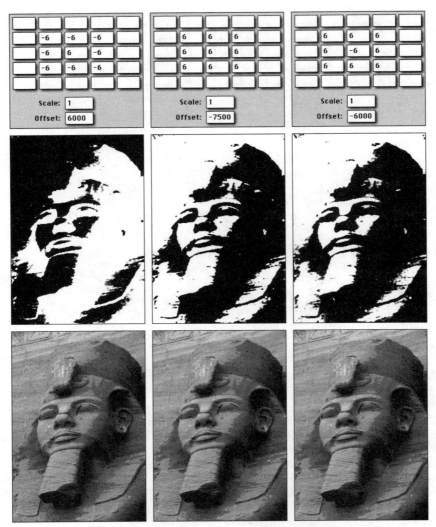

Figure 15-20: You can create high-contrast effects by exaggerating all values in the matrix and then compensating by entering a very high or very low Offset value (top row). When applied to translucent floating selections (bottom row), the sharpening, blurring, and edge-detection effects are barely discernible.

Other custom effects

By now, we hope that you understand what an absolute trip the Custom filter can be, provided that you immerse yourself in the old adventurous spirit. Quite honestly, we could keep showing you ways to use the Custom filter for another 20 or 30 pages. But then our publisher would come unglued because we'd never finish the book, and you'd miss the pleasure of discovering variations on your own.

Nonetheless, you're probably wondering what happens if you just go absolutely berserk, in a computer-geek sort of way, and start entering matrix values in unusual or even arbitrary arrangements. The answer is that as long as you maintain a sum total of 1, you achieve some pretty interesting and even usable effects. Many of these effects will be simple variations on sharpening, blurring, and edge detection.

Directional blurs

Figure 15-21 shows examples of entering positive matrix values all in one row, all in a column, or in opposite quadrants. As you can see, as long as you maintain uniformly positive values, you get a blurring effect. However, by keeping the values lowest in the center and highest toward the edges and corners, you can create directional blurs. The first example resembles a slight horizontal motion blur, the second looks like a slight vertical motion blur, and the last example looks like it's vibrating horizontally and vertically.

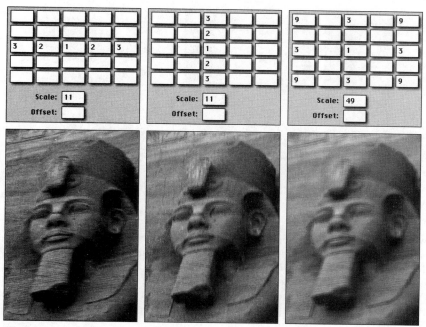

Figure 15-21: Enter positive matrix values in a horizontal formation (left) or vertical formation (middle) to create slight motion blurs. By positioning positive values in opposite corners of the matrix, you create a vibrating effect (right).

Directional sharpening

To selectively sharpen edges in an image based on the angles of the edges, you can organize negative and positive matrix values into rows or columns. For example, to sharpen only the horizontal edges in an image, fill the middle row of matrix options with positive values and the rows immediately above and below with negative values, as demonstrated in the left example in Figure 15-22. Similarly, you can sharpen only the vertical edges by entering positive values in the middle column and flanking the column on the left and right with negative values, as shown in the middle example in the figure. In the last example, we arranged the positive values along a diagonal axis to sharpen only the diagonal edges.

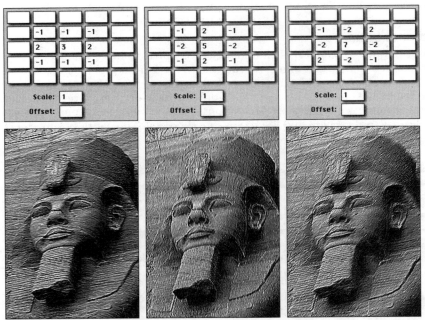

Figure 15-22: Arrange positive values in a row (left), column (middle), or along a diagonal axis (right) to sharpen horizontal, vertical, and diagonal edges exclusively.

You even can combine directional sharpening with directional blurring. Figure 15-23 shows the first example from Figure 15-22 blurred both horizontally and vertically. To blur the image horizontally, as in the middle example of Figure 15-23, we added positive values to the extreme ends of the middle row, thereby extending the range of the filter and creating a sort of horizontal jumbling effect. To blur the image vertically, as in the final example of the figure, we added positive values to the ends of the middle column.

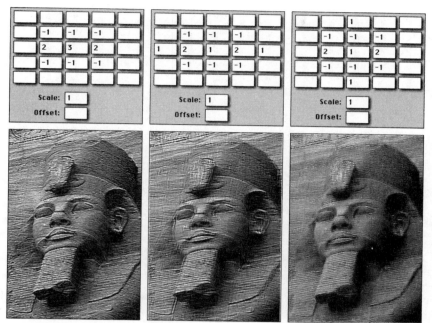

Figure 15-23: The image from Figure 15-22 (left) blurred horizontally (middle) and vertically (right).

Embossing

So far, we aren't going very nuts, are we? Despite their unusual formations, the matrix values in Figures 15-21 through 15-23 still manage to maintain symmetry. Well, now it's time to lose the symmetry, which typically results in an embossing effect.

Figure 15-24 shows three variations on embossing, all of which involve positive and negative matrix values positioned on opposite sides of the CMV. (The CMV happens to be positive merely to maintain a sum total of 1.)

This type of embossing has no hard-and-fast light source, but you might imagine that the light comes from the general direction of the positive values. Therefore, when we swapped the positive and negative values throughout the matrix (all except the CMV), we approximated an underlighting effect, as demonstrated by the images in Figure 15-25.

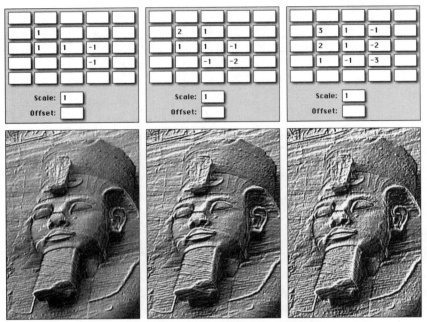

Figure 15-24: You can create embossing effects by distributing positive and negative values on opposite sides of the central matrix value.

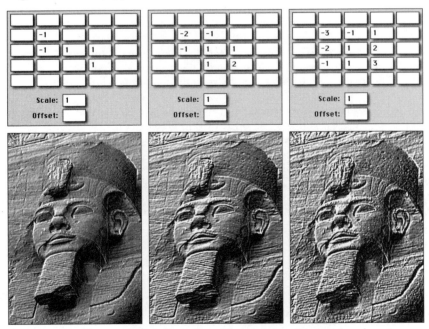

Figure 15-25: Change the location of positive and negative matrix values to change the general direction of the light source.

In truth, it's not so much a lighting difference as a difference in edge enhancement. White pixels collect on the side of an edge represented by positive values in the matrix; black pixels collect on the negative-value side. So when we swapped the locations of positive and negative values between Figures 15-24 and 15-25, we changed the distribution of white and black pixels in the filtered images.

Embossing is the loosest of the Custom filter effects. As long as you position positive and negative values on opposite sides of the CMV, you can distribute the values in almost any way you see fit. Figure 15-26 demonstrates three entirely arbitrary arrangements of values in the Custom matrix. Figure 15-27 shows those same effects downplayed by raising the CMV and entering the sum of the matrix values into the Scale option box.

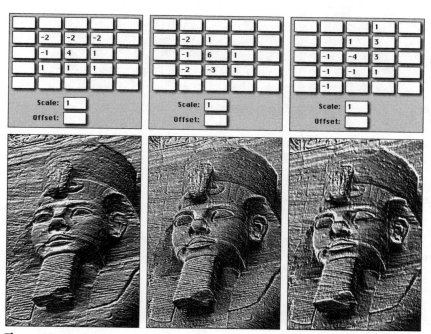

Figure 15-26: You can create whole libraries of embossing effects by experimenting with different combinations of positive and negative values.

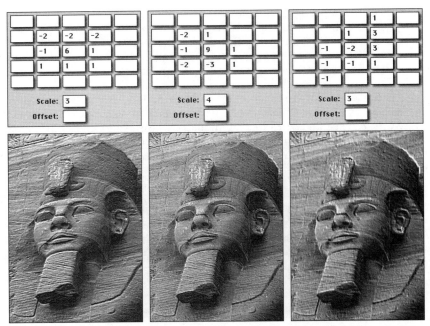

Figure 15-27: To emboss more subtly, increase the central matrix value and the Scale values by equal amounts.

Incidentally, the main advantage of using the Custom filter rather than using Filter⇨Stylize⇨Emboss to produce embossing effects is that Custom preserves the colors in an image, while Emboss sacrifices color and changes low-contrast portions of an image to gray. Color Plate 15-1 shows the matrix values from the first example of Figure 15-26 applied to a color image. It also shows examples of other Custom effects, including variations on sharpening and edge detection.

Displacing Pixels in an Image

Photoshop's second custom-effects filter is Filter⇨Distort⇨Displace, which enables you to distort and add texture to an image by moving the colors of certain pixels in a selection. You specify the direction and distance that the Displace filter moves colors by creating a second image called a *displacement map*, or *dmap* (pronounced *dee-map*) for short. The brightness values in the displacement map tell Photoshop which pixels to affect and how far to move the colors of those pixels:

✦ **Black:** The black areas of the displacement map move the colors of corresponding pixels in the selection a maximum prescribed distance to the right and/or down. Lighter values between black and medium gray move colors a shorter distance in the same direction.

✦ **White:** The white areas move the colors of corresponding pixels a maximum distance to the left and/or up. Darker values between white and medium gray move colors a shorter distance in the same direction.

✦ **Medium gray:** A 50 percent brightness value, such as medium gray, ensures that the colors of corresponding pixels remain unmoved.

Suppose that we create a new image window the same size as the scan of the Egyptian temple carving that we've used about sixty times now in this chapter. This new image will serve as the displacement map. We divide the image into four quadrants. As shown in the middle example of Figure 15-28, we fill the upper left quadrant with black, the lower right quadrant with white, and the other two quadrants with medium gray. (The arrows indicate the direction in which the quadrants will move colors in the affected image. They do not actually appear in the dmap.)

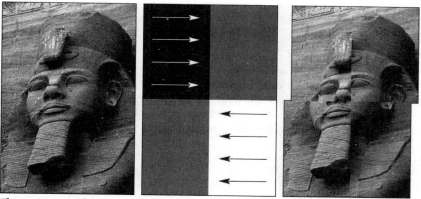

Figure 15-28: The Displace filter enables you to move colors in an image (left) according to the brightness values in a separate image, known as a displacement map (middle). The arrows indicate the direction in which the brightness values will move colors in the original image, as verified by the image on the right.

When finished, we save the dmap to disk in the native Photoshop format so that the Displace filter can access it. We then return to the Egyptian carving image, choose Filter➪Distort➪Displace, edit the settings as desired, and open the dmap from disk. The result is the image shown in the last example of Figure 15-28. In keeping with the distribution of brightness values in the dmap, the colors of the pixels in the upper left quadrant of the carving image move rightward, the colors of the pixels in the lower right quadrant move to the left, and the colors in the upper right and lower left quadrant remain intact.

Note   A dmap must be a color or grayscale image, and you must save the dmap in the native Photoshop file format. The Displace command does not recognize the other nonnative (albeit common) file formats. Who knows why? Those programmers move in mysterious ways.

At this point, you likely have two questions: How do you use the Displace filter, and why in the name of all that is good would you possibly want to? The hows of the Displace filter are covered in the following section. To discover some whys — which should in turn help you dream up some whys of your own — read the "Displacement Maps" section later in this chapter.

Displacement theory

Like any custom-filtering effect worth its weight in table salt — an asset that has taken something of a nosedive in the recent millennium — you need a certain degree of mathematical reasoning skills to predict the outcome of the Displace filter. Though Deke was a math major in college (well, actually, he double-majored in math and fine arts, and must admit to paying the lion's share of attention to the latter), he frankly was befuddled by the results of his first few experiments with the Displace command. Don't be surprised if you are as well. With some time and a modicum of effort, however, you can learn to anticipate the approximate effects of this filter.

Direction of displacement

Earlier, we mentioned — and we quote — "The black areas of the displacement map move ... colors ... to the right and/or down ... the white areas move ... colors ... to the left and/or up." (Yikes, talk about your fragmented quotations. Maybe we'll sue!) Anyway, the point is, you may have wondered to yourself what all this *and/or* guff was all about. *Is it right or is it down?* you may have puzzled, and rightly so.

The truth is that the direction of a displacement can go either way. It's up to you. If you like right, go with it. If you like down, don't let us stop you. If you like both together, by all means, have at it.

Beginning to understand? No? Well, it works like this: A dmap can contain one or more color channels. If the dmap is a grayscale image with one color channel only, the Displace filter moves colors that correspond to black areas in the dmap both to the right *and* down, depending on your specifications in the Displace dialog box. The filter moves colors that correspond to white areas in the dmap both to the left and up.

Figure 15-29 shows two examples of an image displaced using a single-channel dmap, which appears on the left side of the figure. (Again, the arrows illustrate the directions in which different brightness values move colors in the affected image. They are not part of the dmap file.) We displaced the middle image at 10 percent and the right image at 20 percent. Therefore, the colors in the right image travel twice the distance as those in the middle image, but all colors travel the same direction. (The upcoming section, "The Displace dialog box," explains exactly how the percentage values work.)

Figure 15-29: The results of applying a single-channel displacement map (left) to an image at 10 percent (middle) and 20 percent (right).

However, if the dmap contains more than one channel — whether it's a color image or a grayscale image with an independent mask channel — the first channel indicates horizontal displacement, and the second channel indicates vertical displacement. All other channels are ignored. Therefore, the Displace filter moves colors that correspond to black areas in the first channel of the dmap to the right and colors that correspond to white areas to the left. (Again, this depends on your specifications in the Displace dialog box.) The filter then moves colors that correspond to the black areas in the second channel downward and colors that correspond to white areas upward.

Figure 15-30 shows the effect of a two-channel dmap on our friend the pharaoh. The top row shows the appearance and effect of the first channel on the image at 10 percent and 20 percent. The bottom row shows the appearance and effect of the second channel.

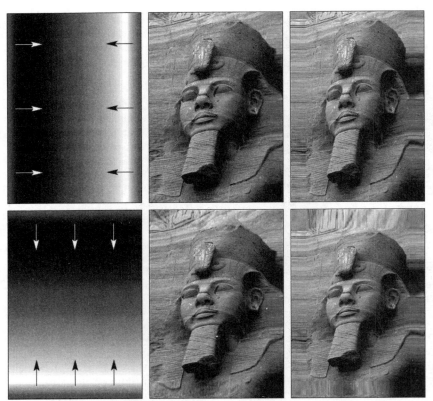

Figure 15-30: The horizontal (top row) and vertical (bottom row) results of applying a two-channel displacement map (left column) to an image at 10 percent (middle) and 20 percent (right).

Brightness value transitions

If you study Figure 15-30 for any length of time, you'll notice a marked stretching effect around the edges of the image, particularly around the two right images. This is an effect you want to avoid.

The cause of the effect is twofold: First, the transition from gray to black and gray to white pixels around the perimeter of the dmap is relatively quick, especially compared with the gradual transitions in the central portion of the image. Second, transitions — reading from left to right, or top to bottom — produce a more noticeable effect when they progress from light to dark than from dark to light. The reason for this is that these transitions follow the direction of Photoshop's displacement algorithm. (We know, when we throw in a word like *algorithm,* everybody's eyes glaze over, but try to stick with it.)

For example, in the light-to-dark transition on the left side of the first-channel dmap in Figure 15-30, one gray value nudges selected colors slightly to the right, the next darker value nudges them an extra pixel, the next darker value another pixel, and so on, resulting in a machine-gun displacement effect that creates a continuous stream of the same colors over and over again. Hence, the big stretch.

Get it? Well, if not, the important part is this: To avoid stretching an image, make your dmap transitions slow when progressing from light to dark and quick when progressing from dark to light. For example, in the revised dmap channels shown in the left column of Figure 15-31, the gray values progress slowly from gray to black, abruptly from black to gray to white, and then slowly again from white to gray. Slow light to dark, fast dark to light. The results are smoother image distortions, as demonstrated in the middle and right columns of the figure.

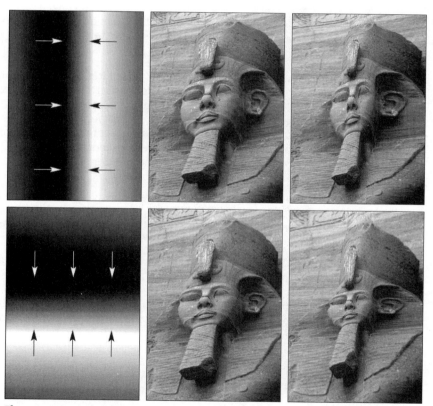

Figure 15-31: Changing the speeds of color transitions in the two-channel displacement map (left column) created smoother image distortions at both the 10 percent (middle) and 20 percent (right) settings.

The Displace dialog box

When you choose Filter⇨Distort⇨Displace, Photoshop displays the Displace dialog box. (*Displays the Displace* is the modern equivalent of "Begin the Beguine," don't you know.) As shown in Figure 15-32, the Displace dialog box provides the following options:

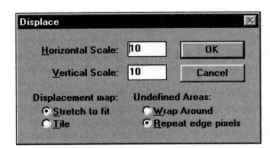

Figure 15-32: Use the options in the Displace dialog box to specify the degree to which the filter distorts the selection, how the filter matches the displacement map to the image, and how it colors the pixels around the perimeter of the selection.

✦ **Scale:** You can specify the degree to which the Displace filter moves colors in an image by entering percentage values into the Horizontal Scale and Vertical Scale option boxes. At 100 percent, black and white areas in the dmap each have the effect of moving colors 128 pixels. That's 1 pixel per each brightness value over or under medium gray. You can isolate the effect of a single-channel dmap vertically or horizontally — or ignore the first or second channel of a two-channel dmap — by entering 0 percent into the Horizontal or Vertical option box, respectively.

Figure 15-33 shows the effect of distorting an image exclusively horizontally (top row) and vertically (bottom row) at each of three percentage values: 5 percent, 15 percent, and 30 percent. In each case, we used the two-channel dmap from Figure 15-31.

✦ **Displacement map:** If the dmap contains fewer pixels than the image, you can either scale it to match the size of the selected image by selecting the Stretch to fit radio button, or repeat the dmap over and over within the image by selecting Tile. Figure 15-34 shows a small two-channel dmap that contains radial gradations. In the first column, we stretched the dmap to fit the image. In the second column, we tiled the dmap. To create both examples in the top row, we set the Horizontal Scale and Vertical Scale values to 10 percent. To create the bottom-row examples, we raised the values to 50 percent.

Figure 15-33: The results of applying the Distort filter exclusively horizontally (top row) and exclusively vertically (bottom row) at 5 percent (left column), 15 percent (middle), and 30 percent (right).

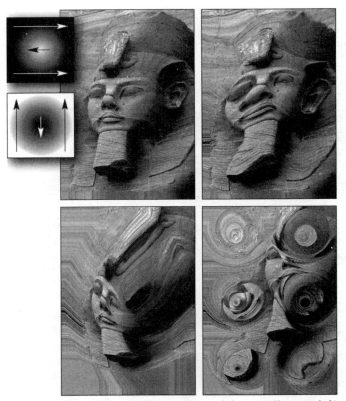

Figure 15-34: Using a small, two-channel dmap (offset top left), we stretched the dmap to fit (left column) and tiled it (right column) at 10 percent (top row) and 50 percent (bottom row).

✦ **Undefined Areas:** These radio buttons enable you to tell Photoshop how to color pixels around the outskirts of the selection that are otherwise undefined. By default, the Repeat edge pixels radio button is selected, which repeats the colors of pixels around the perimeter of the selection. This can result in extreme stretching effects, as shown in the middle example of Figure 15-35. To instead repeat the image inside the undefined areas, as demonstrated in the final example of the figure, select the Wrap Around option.

Tip   The Repeat edge pixels setting was active in all displacement map figures prior to Figure 15-35. In these cases, we frequently avoided stretching effects by coloring the edges of the dmap with medium gray and gradually lightening or darkening the brightness values toward the center.

Figure 15-35: After creating a straightforward, single-channel displacement map (left), we applied the filter subject to two different Undefined Areas settings, Repeat edge pixels (middle), and Wrap Around (right).

After you finish specifying options in the Displace dialog box, click on the OK button or press Enter to display the Open dialog box, which allows you to select the displacement map saved to disk. Only native Photoshop documents show up in the scrolling list.

Displacement Maps

So far, all the displacement maps demonstrated involve gradations of one form or another. Gradient dmaps distort the image over the contours of a fluid surface, like a reflection in a fun-house mirror. In this respect, the effects of the Displace filter closely resemble those of the Pinch and Spherize filters described in the last chapter. But the more functional and straightforward application of the Displace filter is to add texture to an image.

Creating texture effects

Figure 15-36 shows the results of using the Displace filter to apply nine of the patterns from the Displacement Maps subdirectory of the Plug-ins directory. Color Plate 15-2 shows the effects of applying four of the patterns to color images. Introduced in the "How to create patterns" section of Chapter 11, this directory contains repeating patterns that Adobe Systems designed especially with the Displace filter in mind.

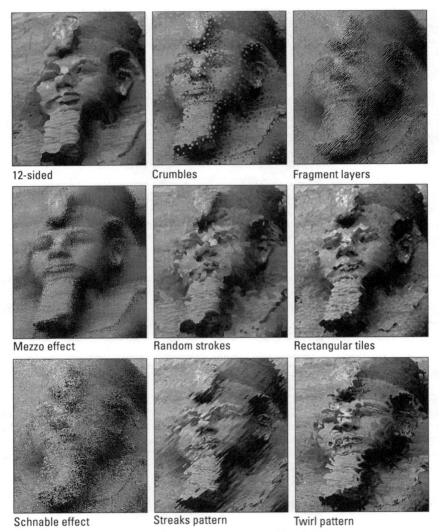

12-sided	Crumbles	Fragment layers
Mezzo effect	Random strokes	Rectangular tiles
Schnable effect	Streaks pattern	Twirl pattern

Figure 15-36: Examples of applying nine patterns from the Displacement Maps folder with the Displace filter at 10 percent horizontally and vertically.

As shown in the figure and color plate, most of these patterns produce the effect of viewing the image through textured glass — an effect known in high-end graphics circles as *glass refraction*. Those few patterns that contain too much contrast to pass off as textured glass — including Fragment layers, Mezzo effect, and Schnable effect — can be employed to create images that appear as if they were printed on coarse paper or even textured metal.

Cross Ref To view each of the textures from the Displacement Maps directory on its own, see Figure 11-14 in the "How to create patterns" section of Chapter 11. Like Figure 15-36, Figure 11-14 is labeled so that you can easily match texture and effect.

Tip When using a repeating pattern — including any of the images inside the Displacement Maps directory folder — as a dmap, be sure to select the Tile radio button inside the Displace dialog box. This repeats the dmap rather than stretching it out of proportion.

We also explained in Chapter 11 that you can create your own textures from scratch using filtering effects. We specifically described how to create a stucco texture by applying the Add Noise filter three times in a row to an empty image and then using the Emboss filter to give it depth. (See the "Using filters" item in the "How to create patterns" section.) This texture appears in the first example of Figure 15-37. We applied the texture at 2 percent and 10 percent to create the windblown middle and right examples in the figure.

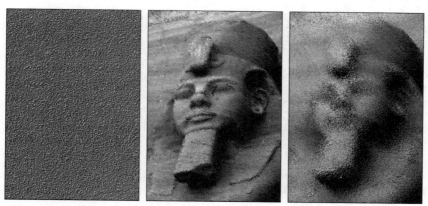

Figure 15-37: After creating a stucco texture with the Add Noise and Emboss filters (left), we applied the texture as a displacement map at 2 percent (middle) and 10 percent (right).

The stucco pattern is only one of an infinite number of textures that you can create using filters. In fact, stucco is a great base texture on which to build. For example, to create the wavy texture that starts off the first row of Figure 15-38, we softened the stucco texture by applying the Gaussian Blur filter with a 0.3-pixel radius. We then applied the Ripple filter twice with the Large option selected and an Amount value of 100. That's all there was to it.

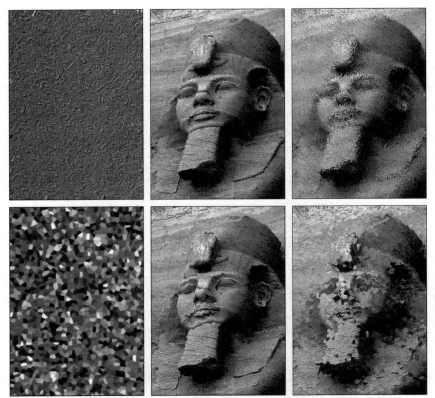

Figure 15-38: After creating two textures with the Add Noise, Emboss, and Ripple filters (first column), we applied the textures as displacement maps at 2 percent (middle) and 10 percent (right).

To create the second texture in the figure, we applied the Crystallize filter at its default Cell Size value of 10. Honestly, we could go on creating textures like this forever, and more importantly, so could you. The images in the second and third columns of Figure 15-38 show the results of applying the textures with the Displace filter at 2 percent and 10 percent, respectively.

In the final analysis, any pattern you design for use with the rubber stamp tool is equally applicable for use with the Displace filter. Furthermore, of the two options — rubber stamp and Displace — the latter is more likely to yield the kind of textured effects that will leave your audience begging, pleading, and scraping for more.

Displacing an image onto itself

We throw this technique in just for laughs. We can't get enough of *Dr. Strangelove.* That's why we call this the Make My Day at the Atomic Café effect.

Caution This effect features simulated melting Egyptian carvings. If you find them unnerving, you have a very soft stomach.

R %%% Robert Speak for yourself, Deke. One round of *Strangelove* did me quite well — in perpetuity. But I commend the Egyptian point — after all, they were part of Classical Antiquity.

The Make My Day at the Atomic Café effect involves nothing more than using an image as its own displacement map. First, make sure that the image you want to distort is saved to disk in the native Photoshop format. Then choose Filter⇨Distort⇨Displace, specify the desired settings, and select the version of the image saved to disk. Figure 15-39 shows three applications of this effect, once applied at 10 percent exclusively horizontally, the next at 10 percent vertically, and the last at 10 percent in both directions.

Figure 15-39: See Egypt, have a blast. Here we applied the pharaoh image as a displacement map onto itself at 10 percent horizontally (left), 10 percent vertically (middle), and 10 percent in both directions.

As a variation, save the image in its original form. Then choose Image⇨Map⇨Invert (Ctrl-I) and save the inverted image to disk under a different name. Open the original image and use the Displace filter to apply the inverted image as a displacement map. Figure 15-40 shows some results.

Figure 15-40: The results of applying an inverted version of the pharaoh as a displacement map onto the original image at 10 percent horizontally (left), 10 percent vertically (middle), and 10 percent in both directions.

If you really want to blow an image apart, apply Horizontal Scale and Vertical Scale values of 50 percent or greater. The first row of Figure 15-41 shows a series of 50 percent applications of the Displace filter. We took the liberty of sharpening each image to heighten the effect. In the second row, we applied the filter to floating selections and changed the translucency of each filtered image to 10 percent. In this way, we retained the detail of the original image while still managing to impart a smidgen of sandblasting.

Figure 15-41: The results of displacing the pharaoh image with itself at 50 percent horizontally, 50 percent vertically, and 50 percent in both directions (top row), followed by the same effects applied to highly translucent floating selections (bottom row).

Filter Factory

If you've made it this far through the chapter, we just want to say one thing about the Filter Factory: It's incredibly powerful and capable of doing far, far more than any filter described so far. But it's also difficult to use — so difficult, in fact, that it makes everything we've discussed in the previous pages look incredibly easy and transparently obvious. The Filter Factory tests the capabilities of the most experienced Photoshop user.

Caution Before you can use Filter Factory, you must install the Filter Factory plug-in in your Plug-ins directory. The Filter Factory is included only on the CD-ROM of Photoshop and does not install during the normal installation process.

Choose Filter⊃Synthetic⊃Filter Factory to display the Filter Factory dialog box, shown in Figure 15-42. By any account, we think this has to be the scariest dialog box ever put before a Photoshop user. Yours is probably even more scary. The R option box contains a little *r*, the G option box contains a little *g*, and the B option box contains a little *b*. Throw in a few arbitrarily named slider bars, and you have the perfect formula for striking terror in the unsuspecting image editor's heart.

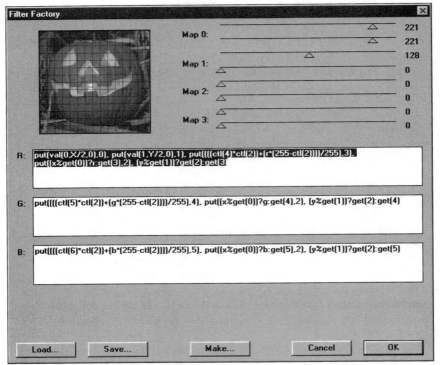

Figure 15-42: The Filter Factory dialog box containing the formulas for adding a series of grid lines to an image.

Note If the command is dimmed, it's because you're not in the RGB mode. Like the Light Flare and Lighting Effects filters, Filter Factory is applicable to RGB images only.

Now we need to make something perfectly clear: There's no way we can describe every nuance of programming a custom filter with the Filter Factory in less than 100 pages. So, to keep the story short and sweet, we'll explain the most important functions and variables, walk you through the process of creating a moderately amusing effect, and show you how to save your work as a fully functioning filter. If you're serious about using the Filter Factory, we suggest that you also read the sparse PDF documentation that Adobe includes on the CD. It isn't the kind of thing you simply read through and ingest immediately, and some of the formulas are inaccurate (in our versions, anyway), but it at least lists all the variables, operators, and functions permitted in the programming language. You may also want to load the settings that we've included on the CD and study our work. If you find a useful operation, feel free to copy it and paste it into a filter of your own. It's not stealing; it's research.

How the Factory works

To use this filter, you enter formulaic *expressions* into the R, G, and B option boxes. Each option box represents what you're doing to the red, green, or blue color channel. You can also integrate the slider bars at the top of the dialog box into your formulas. When you convert the formulas into a filter, you can specify which slider bars to include in the filter's own dialog box, enabling the user to modify the settings. You don't have to use the slider bars, but without them you get a single-shot filter such as Photoshop's Sharpen More or Facet effects.

Tip The Load and Save buttons enable you to load formulas from disk or save them for later use or editing. If you've had a long hard day and it's time to go home — or you're already home and you want to go to bed — don't forget to save the formulas to disk. Every time you restart Photoshop, the Filter Factory reverts to its original useless values of *r, g,* and *b.*

The Make button creates a filter (as I'll discuss more later). The problem is, you can't open a filter with the Filter Factory once you've created it. So, if you ever want to modify a setting or two — and believe me, you will — be sure to save the settings separately using the Save button. We recommend saving filter and settings under the same name in different directories to eliminate as much confusion as possible.

The expressions

Like the Custom filter, the Filter Factory evaluates each pixel in each channel one at a time and then finishes up by sending a new brightness value to that pixel. So in the following discussions, we'll take advantage of that same acronym we used earlier in this chapter — PBE, to indicate the *pixel being evaluated.*

You change the brightness of the PBE using three kinds of expressions — *variables, operators,* and *functions.* Here's the scoop on each.

Variables

You can enter two kinds of values into a Filter Factory option box — hard and fast numbers, such as 3 and 17, and *variables.* The latter are single letters that represent values that are forever changing. The *r* that first appears in the R option box, for example, represents the brightness value that currently occupies the PBE in the red channel. So by entering *r* in the R option box, you tell Photoshop to change the red PBE to its current color, which is no change whatsoever. It's just Adobe's way of creating a clean slate for you to work with.

All variables reset to a new value every time the filter advances from one pixel to the next. The most important variables are as follows:

- ✦ **r, g, and b:** The brightness value currently assigned to the PBE in the red channel is *r*. The green value of the PBE is *g;* the blue value is *b*. Why the heck would you want access to any of these values? Why, to mix them, of course. For example, if you enter *(r*g)/255* in the R option box — that's all you have to enter — you multiply the red value by the green value, divide the result by 255, and put the result in the filtered red channel. The final product is identical to copying the contents of the green channel, pasting it onto the red channel, and choosing the Multiply overlay mode. Try it out and see.

- ✦ **c:** This variable represents the brightness value of the PBE in the current channel, whatever that may be. In the R option box, *c* is identical to *r*. So the equation *(c*g/255)* means *(r*g/255)* in the R channel and *(b*g/255)* in the B channel.

- ✦ **x and y:** The horizontal coordinate of the PBE is saved to *x*. This value is measured in pixels from the left edge of the image. The vertical coordinate is *y*, as measured from the top of the image. These values are useful for shifting pixels around or mixing neighboring pixels together (as you can with the Custom command).

- ✦ **X and Y:** The total width of the image is *X*, the total height is *Y*. So *X–x* calculates the distance from the PBE to the right edge.

You can also use other variables: The letter *m*, for example, measures the distance from the PBE to the exact center of the image, and *d* is the angle from the PBE to the center pixel (measured from 0 to 1,024, so that 255 is equivalent to 90 degrees). But *r, g, b, c, x, y, X*, and *Y* are the ones you'll use most often.

Operators

Operators include arithmetic signs, such as + and ×, as well as relational symbols, such as < and >. They also include logical operations. For example, *?* tells the Filter Factory to complete the following operation only if the previous expression holds true and, if it is false, complete the operation after the colon (:). For instance, the expression *x<(X/2)?r:g* means that if the PBE is inside the left side of the image, color it with the red channel value. If not, color it with the green value. The following are the most important operators.

- ✦ **+, –, *, and /:** These symbols stand for plus, minus, multiply, and divide. The Filter Factory always handles multiply and divide operations before plus and minus operations. So the equation *4+8/2* equals 8, not 6.

- ✦ **%:** Use the percentage sign to retain the remainder from a division equation. For example, *11%4* equals 3.

- ✦ **(and):** Parentheses tell the Filter Factory to complete the equation inside the parentheses before completing others. The equation *(4+8)/2* equals 6 because 4 and 8 are added before dividing by 2.

✦ **<, >, <=, and >=:** These symbols mean less than, greater than, less than or equal to, and greater than or equal to. All four are used primarily within conditional operations like the one we mentioned at the beginning of this section.

✦ **==, =!:** Two equal signs in a row mean equal to. An equal sign and an exclamation point mean not equal to. Again, use these inside conditional operations.

✦ **?:** Here's the conditional operation, as explained earlier.

Again, these aren't all the possible operators, just the best ones. But we should mention one additional operator: The comma separates phrases in an expression, sort of like a period separates sentences. The phrase after the final comma is the one that the Filter Factory applies to the PBE. All previous phrases are used for calculation purposes only. You can see how this works in the Steps example that's coming up right after the discussion of functions.

Functions

All functions are composed of three letters followed by numbers, variables, and equations inside parentheses. For example, *abs(x–X)* finds the absolute value of the equations inside the parentheses, which means that you get a positive result whether the answer to the equation is positive or negative. (Because negative brightness values simply become black, this can be useful.)

Rather than simply listing the functions, we'll explain them in groups. First, there are the two functions that use holding cells. In typical programming, you store the results of incremental equations in variables, but in the Filter Factory, variables are used by the filter only. You get ten numbered cells, ranging from 0 to 9. The two functions that work with cells are *put,* to place a number inside a cell, and *get,* to retrieve it. It's sort of like copying and pasting with ten tiny Clipboards. The expression *put(r+b,0)* puts the result of the equation *r+b* into cell 0. Conversely, *put(r+b,1)* puts it in cell 1, and so on. The expression *get(0)/2* would retrieve the result of *r+b* and divide it by 2.

The function *src* retrieves information about a specific pixel in your image. For example, *src(x+5,y+5,0)* returns the brightness of the pixel five pixels to the right and five pixels down from the PBE. What is that last *0* for? That tells the function to get the value from the red channel. The green channel is *1,* the blue channel is *2,* mask channels are *3* through *9.*

Similar to *src, rad* finds out the brightness value of a pixel in a certain channel based on its distance and direction from the center of the image. For example, if you enter *rad(d–16,m–16,0)* into the red channel, you rotate the contents of the channel 16 increments (about 6 degrees) counterclockwise and distort its center outward. The upcoming Steps example uses this function.

The function *rnd* generates a random number between two extremes, which is great for creating noise. The expression *rnd(r,g)* generates a random value between the red brightness value of the PBE and the green brightness of the PBE.

Evaluating the sliders

These next functions — *ctl* and *val* — get their own headline because they're so important. They evaluate how a user of your filter sets the slider bars. The function *ctl* simply retrieves the setting of a specified slider bar. There are eight slider bars in all, numbered 0 to 7 from top to bottom. (The sliders labeled Map 0 are therefore sliders 0 and 1; Map 1 includes sliders 2 and 3; and so on.) Each slider can be adjusted from 0 to 255. So if the first slider bar is set to 128, the function *ctl(0)* retrieves the number 128. You can then change the impact of your filter by moving the slider in real time. For example, if you enter *r*ctl(0)/255* in the R option box, you multiply the red value of the PBE by the setting of the top slider divided by 255. This makes the red channel black when the slider is set to 0, normal when the slider is set to 255, and darker shades when set to any increment in between.

The *val* function evaluates the setting of a slider bar within a specified range. For example, *val(0,15,–15)* takes the setting of the top slider, translates it to 15 when it's at 0, and translates it to –15 when it's at 255. As you can see, this function enables you to translate the data within any specified range, even making the low values high and vice versa. This is useful when you don't want the entire range of data from 0 to 255 to mess up the results of your equations.

Touring the Factory

Okay, now for a little hands-on action. The steps will be short and straightforward, but the results are both useful and interesting. We encourage you to try out these steps. Even if you've been sitting there with your jaw hanging open throughout the entire chapter, even if you haven't the slightest idea what you're doing, you'll be able to create a fully functioning filter that is not included on the CD. Talk about your incentives.

Steps: Creating a filter inside the Factory

1. Open an RGB image or convert some other image to the RGB mode. (This filter yields interesting results even when applied to grayscale images converted to RGB.)

2. Choose Filter⇨Synthetic⇨Factory and set all the slider bars back to 0 (just in case somebody's been fooling around with them).

3. Enter *rad(d–(4*ctl(0)),m,0)* into the R option box. The first argument in the expression — *d–(4*ctl(0))* — subtracts four times the value of the top slider bar from the angle variable *d*. Why four times? Because the slider only offers 256 increments, and the filter measures a full circle in 1,024 increments — 256 times 4 equals 1,024, thus allowing you to translate the slider values to a full circle.

   Meanwhile, *d* is the angle of the current pixel from the center and *m* is the distance from the pixel to the center. So *rad(d–(4*ctl(0)),m,0)* tells the filter to lift the brightness from the pixel in a counterclockwise direction from the PBE. The result is that the red channel rotates in the opposite direction, clockwise. Drag the slider bar and you'll see that this is true.

4. Now you'll use the second and third slider bars — *ctl(1)* and *ctl(2)* — for rotating the other two channels. But we think that we'd like to use the fifth slider bar for distorting the image. Why not the fourth channel? Well, because the first three sliders are going to be devoted to rotation. The distortion slider will be logically different, so it might be nice to create a blank space between the rotation and distortion sliders. Not using slider four is the way to do it.

   Now that we've told you why you're doing what you're doing, go ahead and do it: Insert the phrase *–ctl(4)/2* after the *m* so that the expression reads *rad(d–(4*ctl(0)),m–ctl(4)/2,0)*. This subtracts half the value from the fourth slider from the distance-from-center variable, thus shoving the pixels outward as you drag the fifth slider bar (the top of the two labeled Map 2). Give it a try.

5. Select the entire expression in the R option box, copy it by pressing Ctrl-C, tab to the G option box, and press Ctrl-V to paste. Then change the *ctl(0)* function to *ctl(1)* and the final number after the comma from a *0* to a *1* so that it reads *rad(d–(4*ctl(1)),m–ctl(4)/2,1)*. Now the expression takes rotation data from the second slider bar and lifts its colors from the green channel. The result is a rotating green channel.

6. Tab to the B option box and press Ctrl-V again. Change *ctl(0)* to *ctl(2)* and change the final *0* to a *2*. The result is *rad(d–(4*ctl(2)),m–ctl(4)/2,2)*. Just to make sure that you haven't fallen behind, Figure 15-43 shows all three expressions exactly as they should appear.

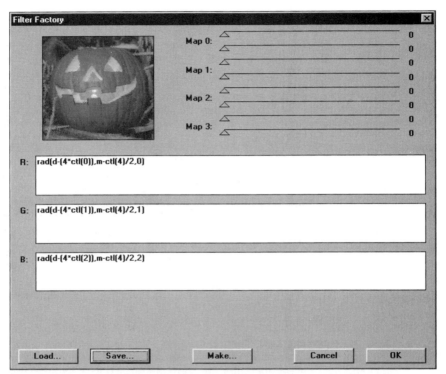

Figure 15-43: These three expressions enable you to rotate the three color channels independently by using the first three slider bars and distorting the image using the fifth slider.

7. Click on the Save button and save your settings to disk. You may want to use the name *Rotator.afs* to show that it's a Filter Factory file. (For some reason, *.afs* is the accepted suffix for settings files.)

8. Now it's time to turn this sucker into its own filter. But before you do, be sure that the sliders are set as you want them to appear by default. Every time you open the new filter for the first time during a Photoshop session, these slider values will appear as they do now. You may want to set all sliders to 0 so that the user starts from square one, but it's completely up to you.

9. Click on the Make button to display the dialog box shown in Figure 15-44. Enter the submenu in which you want the filter to appear in the Category option box. If you want it to appear with the rest of the *Photoshop Bible* filters, enter Tormentia. Enter the name of the filter, Rotator, in the Title option box. Then enter copyright and author info in the next two option boxes. (Go ahead, give yourself credit. You've earned it.)

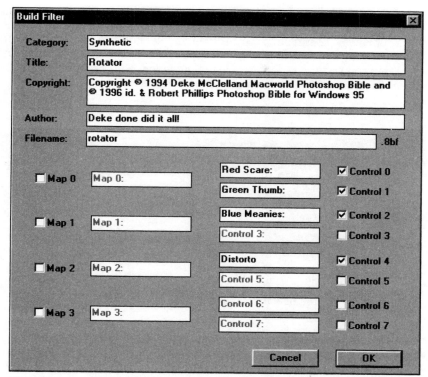

Figure 15-44: Click on the Make button to display this dialog box, which lets you name your filter, assign it to a submenu, and select the slider bars that you want to appear in the final dialog box.

10. The Control check boxes along the right side represent the slider bars inside the Filter Factory dialog box. Select the check box for every slider you want to appear in your final filter. This means Control 0, Control 1, Control 2, and Control 4. Then name them appropriately. Robert has jacked Deke's suggested names around — they appear in Figure 15-44, but they may still be a little too clever for your tastes.

Watch out: The Filter Factory allows you to select any of the slider check boxes, whether they were used in your formulas or not. If you're not careful, you can activate a slider bar that has no function.

11. When you're finished, click on OK or press Enter. You're asked to specify the location of the filter. To keep things tidy, you'll probably want to put it in the Plug-ins directory. Click on the Cancel button to escape the Filter Factory dialog box.

12. Quit Photoshop and relaunch it. Open an RGB image — like the Filter Factory itself, any filter you create in the factory is applicable to RGB images only — and choose your newest command, Filter⇨Tormentia⇨Rotator. The dialog box should look something like the one shown in Figure 15-45. Notice the gaps between the Blue Whirl and Distorto sliders. Nice logical grouping, huh? Feel free to drag the controls and apply the filter as much as you want. It's alive!

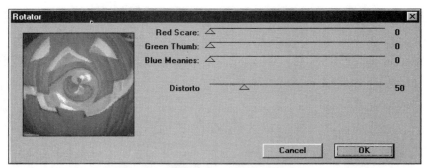

Figure 15-45: The new Rotator filter complete with its four slider bars.

To see a demonstration of your powerful new filter, check out Color Plate 15-3, in which we applied the filter six times at various settings. The top row shows the effect of rotating the channels to different degrees with the Distorto option set to 0. The bottom row shows the same rotation values, but with the Distorto slider turned up to various volumes. It's not the most practical filter on earth, but it's diverting. You may even find something to do with it.

Tip   By the way, those sliders have a tendency to move around after you finish dragging them. It's very irritating. If you're interested in achieving an exact value, click at the location where you want to move the slider triangle. The triangle jumps in place. Then click, click, click to get it right where you want it.

On the CD-ROM   If you want practical filters, check out the ones included on the CD. Most are much more complicated than the one you created in the steps, but they all use the variables, operators, and functions described in this chapter. Open the settings files to take a look at our code. (Just click on the Load button inside the Filter Factory dialog box.) To whet your appetite, take a look at Color Plate 15-4, which shows all but one of the filters applied to the pumpkin. (The one that wouldn't fit is Ripping Pixels, which creates a random value between the brightness of the pixel in one channel and that of one of the other channels, creating a highly customizable noise effect.) These are only sample applications, most of them using the default slider bar settings. Obviously, jillions of other variations are possible. Have loads of fun.

Corrections and Composites

Whether you're working on a full-color or grayscale image, color correction is an essential part of the image-editing process. In fact, commands such as Hue/Saturation, Levels, and Curves are as important to correcting the appearance of a scanned image as Unsharp Mask and Gaussian Blur. Discussed in Chapter 16, these commands enable you to shift the colors of an image to better resemble real life, increase or decrease saturation, and adjust the amount of contrast between light and dark pixels. You can even introduce color to a grayscale image, prepare an RGB image for conversion to the CMYK color space, or restore a badly scanned image.

Chapters 17 and 18 address the complex issue of *compositing,* which enables you to combine different images and mix the colors of their corresponding pixels in literally thousands of ways. Taking a foreground element from one image and pasting it against a different background is a simple example of compositing. But that's just the beginning of the fun. Do you want to merge the two images using overlay modes? Do you want to position the foreground element on its own layer, where you can edit it independently? Do you want to fade the shadows of the foreground into the highlights of the background? And why would you want to experiment with any of these options in the first place? Chapter 17 answers these questions and more, examining the myriad ways to composite images, from the very powerful Layer Options dialog box to the very complex Apply Image and Calculations commands. Chapter 18 includes several sample projects so that you can get a feel for why these functions are so useful.

Chapter 19 examines the issues of using Photoshop instead of traditional media. Robert has researched the technology and physics of traditional art media, and he explains the subtle nuances that distinguish Photoshop's performance from the ways of pastels, watercolors, oils, and just about every other substance you can use to make your mark in the world of art.

Mapping and Adjusting Colors

Mapping Colors

Color mapping is just a fancy name for shuffling colors around. For example, to map Color A to Color B simply means to take all the A-colored pixels and convert them to B-colored pixels. Although many painting programs require you to map colors one color at a time, Photoshop provides several commands that enable you to map entire ranges of colors based on their hues, saturation levels, and most frequently, brightness values.

Color effects and corrections

Why would you want to change colors around? For one reason, to achieve special effects. You know those psychedelic videos that show some guy's hair turning blue while his face turns purple and the palms of his hands glow a sort of cornflower yellow? Although not the most attractive effect by modern standards — you may be able to harvest more tasteful results if you put your shoulder to the color wheel — psychedelia qualifies as color mapping for the simple reason that each color shifts incrementally to a new color.

The more common reason to use color mapping is to enhance the appearance of a scanned image. In this case, you're not creating special effects, just making straightforward color adjustments, known in the biz as *color corrections*. Scans are never perfect, no matter how much money you spend on a scanning device or a service bureau. They can always benefit from tweaking and subtle adjustments, if not outright overhauls, in the color department.

This would be a good time to recall Chapter 4 "Defining Colors" and Chapter 6 "Printing Images." The color model you use, whether for scans or Photoshop work, can have an enormous impact on your work (and sanity). In particular, I'd urge you to consider the following points. If you're having a service bureau do your scans, have those scans in the RGB model and only convert to CMYK, if you're using that output model, at the very end. This gives you more and better color editing options. Consider, too, which colors you're using (consider, too, the discussions of colors in Chapter 19) — do you really want blue hair and a purple face? Finally, let me reemphasize what has just been written — there's no such thing as a perfect scan. No matter how good your hardware, or your service bureau's, you're inevitably going to have to tinker.

Keep in mind, however, that Photoshop can't make something from nothing. In creating the illusion of more and better colors, every color-adjustment operation that you perform actually takes some small amount of color *away* from the image. Invariably, two pixels that were two different colors before you started the correction change to the same color. The image may look ten times better, but it will in fact be less colorful than when you started.

It's important to keep this principle in mind because it demonstrates that color mapping is a balancing act. The first nine operations you perform may make an image look progressively better, but the tenth may send it into decline. There's no magic formula, unfortunately. The amount of color mapping you need to apply varies from image to image. For the moment, the only advice we can offer is that you use moderation, know when to stop, and — as always — save your image to disk before launching into the color mapping process.

Background This whole bit about how color mapping sucks color out of an image to produce the illusion of a more colorful image probably sounds strange on the face of it. But if you think about it, it has to be true. Photoshop maps colors by applying one or more complex equations to a pixel and then rounding off the results of those equations to the nearest brightness value, hue, or what have you. Because entire communities of pixels in an image are very close in color, say, only a brightness value or two apart, the equations frequently convert two slightly different colors to the same color. By contrast, the equations never, *ever* change a single color into two different colors. So when it comes to color correction, colors don't procreate, they die like flies for the good cause . . . the illusion of better color.

Photoshop's color correction functions fall into three categories: those that produce immediate and useful effects, such as Invert and Threshold; those that require significantly more work but are nonetheless designed to be understood by novices, such as the Brightness/Contrast and Color Balance commands; and those that are still more complicated but provide better control and better functionality, such as Hue/Saturation, Replace Color, Levels, and Curves.

This chapter contains no information about the second category of commands for the simple reason that they are inadequate and ultimately a big waste of time. We know because we spent our first year with Photoshop relying exclusively on Brightness/Contrast and Color Balance, all the while wondering why we never achieved the effects we wanted. Then, one happy day, after we put a little time into learning Levels and Curves, the quality of our images skyrocketed and the amount of time we spent on them plummeted. So wouldn't you just rather learn it right in the first place? (We hope so, because you're stuck with it.) To this end, we discuss the supposedly more complicated and indisputably more capable high-end commands as if they were the only ones available.

Color mapping commands

Before we get into all the high-end gunk, however, we'll take a moment to explain the first category of commands, all of which happen to reside in the Image⇨Map submenu. These commands produce immediate effects that are either difficult to duplicate or not worth attempting with the more full-featured commands.

Invert

When you choose Image⇨Map⇨Invert (Ctrl-I), Photoshop converts every color in your image to its exact opposite, just as in a photographic negative. As demonstrated in Figure 16-1, black becomes white, white becomes black, fire becomes water, good becomes evil, Imelda Marcos goes barefoot, and the brightness value of every primary color component changes to 255 minus the original brightness value. The only color that doesn't change is medium gray, because it is its own opposite. (Ooh, we saw a movie like that once.)

Figure 16-1: An image before the advent of the Invert command (left) and after (right).

Image⇨Map⇨Invert is just about the only color mapping command that retains every single drop of color in an image. (The Hue/Saturation command also retains colors under specific conditions.) If you apply the Invert command twice in a row, you arrive at your original image.

When you're working on a full-color image, the Invert command simply inverts the contents of each color channel. This means that the command produces very different results when applied to RGB, Lab, and especially CMYK images. Color Plate 16-1 shows the results of inverting a single image in each of these modes. The RGB and Lab images share some similarities, but you'll find all kinds of subtle differences if you study the backgrounds and the basic colors of the faces.

Inverting in CMYK is much different. Typically, the Invert command changes much of a CMYK image to black. Except in very rare instances, such as in night scenes, the black channel contains lots of light shades and very few dark shades. So when you invert the channel, it becomes extremely dark. To reverse this effect, we inverted only the cyan, magenta, and yellow channels in the right example of Color Plate 16-1. We did this by inverting the entire image and then going to the black channel (Ctrl-4) and pressing Ctrl-I again. Though this approach is preferable to inverting the black channel, it prevents the blacks in the hair and shadows from turning white (which would be the only portions even remotely light had we inverted the black channel as well).

Note   Just so you know, when we refer to applying color corrections in the CMYK mode, we mean applying them after choosing Mode⇨CMYK Color. Applying corrections in the RGB mode when Mode⇨CMYK Preview is active produces the same effect as when CMYK Preview is not selected; the only difference is that the on-screen colors are curtailed slightly to fit inside the CMYK color space. You're still editing inside the same old red, green, and blue color channels, so the effects are the same.

On the CD-ROM   As we mentioned in Chapter 9, inverting the contents of the mask channel is the same as applying Select⇨Inverse to a selection outline in the marching ants mode. In fact, this is one of the most useful applications of the filter. If you're considering inverting a color image, however, we strongly urge you to try out the SuperInvert filter that we created for the CD-ROM included with this book. It lets you invert each channel independently and incrementally. Any setting under 128 lessens the contrast of the channel, 128 makes it completely gray, and any value over 128 inverts it to some degree.

Equalize

Equalize is the smartest and at the same time least useful of the Image⇨Map pack. When you invoke this command, Photoshop searches for the lightest and darkest color values in a selection. It then maps the lightest color in all the color channels to white, maps the darkest color in the channels to black, and distributes the remaining colors to other brightness levels in an effort to evenly distribute pixels over the entire brightness spectrum. This doesn't mean that any one pixel will actually appear white or black after you apply Equalize; rather, that one pixel in at least one channel will be white and another pixel in at least one channel will be black. In an RGB image, for example, the red, green, or blue component of one pixel would be white, but the other two components of that same pixel may be black. The result is a higher-contrast image with white and black pixels scattered throughout the color channels.

If no portion of the image is selected when you choose Image⇨Map⇨Equalize (Ctrl-E), Photoshop automatically maps out the entire image across the brightness spectrum, as shown in the upper right example of Figure 16-2. However, if you select a portion of the image before choosing the Equalize command, Photoshop displays a dialog box containing the following two radio buttons:

✦ **Selected Area Only:** Select this option to apply the Equalize command strictly within the confines of the selection. The lightest pixel in the selection becomes white, the darkest pixel becomes black, and so on.

✦ **Entire Image Based on Area:** If you select the second radio button, which is the default setting, Photoshop applies the Equalize command to the entire image based on the lightest and darkest colors in the selection. All colors in the image that are lighter than the lightest color in the selection become white, and all colors darker than the darkest color in the selection become black.

Figure 16-2: An image before (top left) and after (top right) applying the Equalize command when no portion of the image is selected. You also can use the brightness values in a selected region as the basis for equalizing an entire image (bottom left and right).

The bottom two examples in Figure 16-2 show the effects of selecting different parts of the image when the Entire Image Based on Area option is in force. In the left example, we selected a very dark portion of the image, which resulted in over-lightening of the entire image. In the right example, we selected an area with both light and dark values, which boosted the amount of contrast between highlights and shadows in the image.

As when you use the Invert command, the color mode in which you work has a profound effect on the Equalize command. Although the command does not apply itself to each color channel independently, as does Invert, it does evaluate the lightest and darkest values throughout all channels. The distribution of brightness values changes significantly when you switch color modes — for example, light blue is represented in the RGB mode as light pixels in the blue channel, whereas it's represented in the CMYK mode as dark pixels in the cyan channel — which changes the command's reading of the image in kind. Color Plate 16-2 shows how the command affects the same image with the same detail selected in each of the three color modes. The differences are striking.

The problem with the Equalize command is that it relies too heavily on some pretty bizarre automation to be of much use as a color correction tool. Certainly, you can create some interesting special effects. But if you'd prefer to automatically adjust the colors in an image from black to white, regardless of the color mode and composition of the individual channels, choose Image⊃Adjust⊃Auto Levels. If you want to adjust the tonal balance manually and therefore with a higher degree of accuracy, the Levels and Curves commands are tops. We explain all these commands at length later in this chapter.

Threshold

We touched on the Threshold command a couple of times in previous chapters. As you may recall, Threshold converts all colors to either black or white based on their brightness values. When you choose Image⊃Map⊃Threshold (Ctrl-T), Photoshop displays the Threshold dialog box shown in Figure 16-3. The dialog box offers a single option box and a slider bar, either of which you can use to specify the medium brightness value in the image. Photoshop changes any color lighter than the value in the Threshold option box to white and any color darker than the value to black.

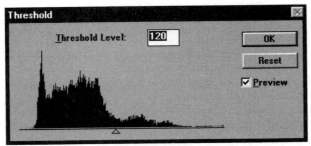

Figure 16-3: The histogram in the Threshold dialog box shows the distribution of brightness values in the selection.

Situated directly above the slider bar is a graph of the colors in the selection (or in the entire image if no portion of the image is selected). The width of the graph represents all 256 possible brightness values, starting at black on the left and progressing through white on the right. The height of each vertical line in the graph demonstrates the number of pixels in the image currently associated with that brightness value. Such a graph is called a *histogram*. (You can see a more detailed version of the graph in the Levels dialog box.)

Generally speaking, you achieve the best effects if you change an equal number of pixels to black as you change to white (and vice versa). So rather than moving the slider bar to 128, which is the medium brightness value, move it to the point at which the area of the vertical lines to the left of the slider triangle looks roughly equivalent to the area of the vertical lines to the right of the slider triangle.

The upper right example in Figure 16-4 shows the result of applying the Threshold command with a Threshold Level value of 120 (as in Figure 16-3). Although this value more or less evenly distributes black and white pixels, we lost a lot of detail in the dark areas.

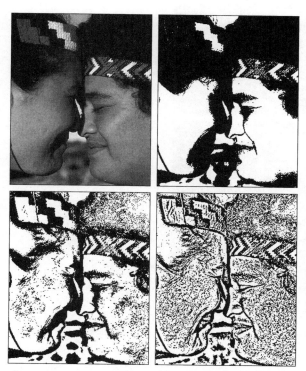

Figure 16-4: An image before applying the Threshold command (top left) and after (top right). You can retain more detail in the image by applying the High Pass filter before applying Threshold (bottom left and right).

As you may recall from the discussion in the "Using the High Pass filter" section of Chapter 13, you can use Filter⇨Other⇨High Pass in advance of the Threshold command to retain areas of contrast. For example, in the lower left image in Figure 16-4, we applied the High Pass filter with a radius of 10.0 pixels, followed by the Threshold command with a value of 124. In the lower right example, we applied High Pass with a radius of 3.0 pixels and then applied Threshold with a value of 126.

Higher High Pass radiuses combined with higher Threshold values result in more detail, which is the good news, as well as more random artifacts, which can detract from an image. So it's a mixed bag. Isn't everything? If you're looking for a real-life application of the Threshold command, Figure 16-5 shows all the effects from Figure 16-4 applied to floating selections set to 15 percent opacity. In each example, the translucent selection helps to add contrast and reinforce details in the original image.

Figure 16-5: The Threshold and High Pass operations from Figure 16-4 applied to floating selections set to 15 percent opacity, thus permitting the underlying original to show through.

Posterize

The Posterize command is Threshold's rich cousin. Whereas Threshold boils down an image into two colors only, Posterize can retain as many colors as you like. However, you can't control how colors are mapped, as you can when you use Threshold. The Posterize dialog box provides no histogram or slider bar. Instead, Posterize automatically divides the full range of 256 brightness values into a specified number of equal increments.

To use this command, choose Image⇨Map⇨Posterize and enter a value into the Levels option box. The Levels value represents the number of brightness values that the Posterize command retains. Higher values result in subtle color adjustments; lower values produce more dramatic effects. The upper right example in Figure 16-6 shows an image subject to a Levels value of 8.

By now, you may be thinking, *By golly, if Posterize is so similar to Threshold, I wonder how it works when applied after the High Pass filter?* Well, if you *were* thinking that, you're in luck, because this is exactly the purpose of the two bottom examples in Figure 16-6. As in Figure 16-4, we applied the High Pass filter with Radius values of 10.0 and 3.0, respectively, to the left and right examples. We then applied the Posterize filter with the same Levels value as before (8) to achieve some unusual, high-contrast effects.

Just in case you've tried this same effect on your full-color image and thought, *Yech, this looks terrible . . . half the color just disappeared,* the key is to apply High Pass and Posterize to a floating version of the image and then mix the effect with the underlying original. Color Plate 16-3 shows the results of applying the High Pass filter with a Radius of 3 and the Posterize command with a setting of 8 to the floating selection and then compositing floater and underlying original using each of three overlay modes from the Layers palette. The Luminosity option applies only the lights and darks in the floating selection, allowing the colors in the underlying image to show through; Overlay strengthens the light and dark shades; and Difference selectively inverts the image. (Note that we lightened the Difference example slightly using Image⇨Adjust⇨ Levels after defloating the image. The Levels command is explained later in this chapter.) You may also want to try out the Soft Light and Hard Light options for variations on the Overlay effect. And don't forget to experiment with the ever-important Opacity slider bar.

Quick adjustments

Photoshop offers two special commands under the Image⇨Adjust submenu that we want to discuss before entering the larger world of advanced color correction. Both are single-shot commands that alter your image without any dialog boxes or special options. The first, Desaturate, sucks the saturation out of a selection and leaves it looking like a grayscale image. The second, Auto Levels, automatically increases the contrast of an image according to what Photoshop deems to be the ideal brightness values.

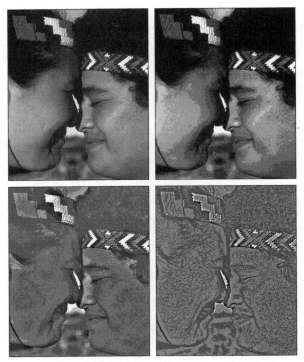

Figure 16-6: An image before (top left) and after (top right) applying the Posterize command with a Levels value of 8. As you can when using the Threshold command, you can retain detail in an image by applying the High Pass filter before applying Posterize (bottom left and right).

Desaturate

There's little reason to apply the Desaturate command to an entire image; you can just as easily choose Mode⇨Grayscale to accomplish the same thing and dispose of the extra channels that would otherwise consume room in memory and on disk. But Desaturate is useful when applied to selected portions of an image or to floating selections.

For example, in Color Plate 16-4, we used Select⇨Color Range to select all of the pumpkin except the eyes and mouth and a few speckly bits here and there. (We would have gone into the quick mask mode to make the selection just right, as explained in Chapter 9, but it didn't strike us as particularly important in this case.) We then floated the selection and applied Image⇨Adjust⇨Desaturate to achieve the first example. In the top right example, we changed the Opacity of the floating selection to 50 percent, bringing back some of the original colors from the underlying original and achieving an only slightly desaturated pumpkin.

The bottom row shows the results of using a different color correction command (Image⇨Map⇨Invert) to suck the saturation out of the selection. In this example, we floated the same selection outline we created with the Color Range command and applied Invert (Ctrl-I). We then chose the Color overlay mode from the Layers palette and changed the Opacity setting to 50 percent to get the bottom left example. Note that the result is slightly different than the desaturated image above it. When set to the Color overlay mode, the colors in the inverted image should theoretically cancel out the colors in the underlying original. However, the Invert command doesn't change the saturation of the floating image, so the saturation of the floating and underlying pixels are the same. As a result, some colors from the underlying image are allowed to show through, as the bottom left image shows.

The bottom right example shows what happened when we changed the Opacity to 70 percent, thus favoring the inverted colors. Had we lowered the setting to 30 percent, we would have achieved nearly the same effect shown in the top right example.

Auto Levels

Image⇨Adjust⇨Auto Levels goes through each color channel and changes the lightest pixel to white, changes the darkest pixel to black, and stretches out all the shades of gray to fill out the spectrum. Unlike the Equalize command, which considers all color channels as a whole, Auto Levels looks at each channel independently. So once again, the active color mode makes quite a difference to this command. Color Plate 16-5 shows a stock image prior to color corrections, followed by the same image corrected with Auto Levels in the RGB, Lab, and CMYK modes. The RGB image offers highlights that the Lab image lacks, but both are acceptable. The CMYK image is absolutely unacceptable. Again, that black channel is a culprit, becoming much darker than it ought to. But the cyan channel has also darkened dramatically, turning the pumpkin a bright red that verges on violet . . . a remarkably unpumpkinlike hue. Like Invert and Equalize, Auto Levels is designed specifically for use in the RGB mode. If you use it in CMYK, you're more likely to achieve special effects than color correction.

The Auto Levels command serves the same purpose and produces the same effect as the Auto button in the Levels dialog box. You should only occasionally rely on either. What you *should* do is read the rest of this chapter and learn about the bigger and better color correction commands.

Hue Shifting and Colorizing

The commands we've discussed so far skirt the border between the worlds of utility and futility. We use the Invert and Threshold commands on a regular basis, and the Posterize, Desaturate, and Auto Levels commands are nice to have around. Equalize is a big stinker.

The rest of the commands covered in this chapter, all of which reside in the Image⇨Adjust submenu, are both more powerful and more complex. As we stated before, we ignore two commands, Brightness/Contrast and Color Balance, because they're a complete waste of time. The others enable you to adjust colors both selectively and with absolute precision.

The sections that follow cover the commands that are specifically designed to change the distribution of colors in an image. You can rotate the hues around the color spectrum, change the saturation of colors, adjust highlights and shadows, and even tint an image. Two of these commands, Hue/Saturation and Selective Color, are applicable exclusively to color images. The other two, Replace Color and Variations, can be applied to grayscale images but are not the best solutions. Although both let you select specific ranges of brightness values that you want to edit, they apply their corrections with less finesse than either the Levels or Curves commands, both of which are discussed toward the end of the chapter.

Tip Before we go any further, we should mention one awesome little bit of advice. Remember that Ctrl-Alt-F redisplays the last filter dialog box so that you can tweak the effect? Well, a similar shortcut is available when you're applying color corrections. Press the Alt key when choosing any command under the Image⇨Adjust submenu that has an ellipsis to display that command's dialog box with the settings last applied to the image. If the command has a keyboard equivalent, just add Alt to reapply the last settings. Ctrl-Alt-U, for example, brings up the Hue/Saturation dialog box with the last settings applied.

Hue/Saturation command

The Hue/Saturation command provides two functions. First, it enables you to adjust colors in an image according to their hues and saturation levels. You can apply the changes to individual color channels or affect all colors equally across the spectrum. And second, the command lets you colorize images by applying new hue and saturation values while retaining the core brightness information from the original image.

This command is perfect for colorizing grayscale images. We know, we know, Woody Allen wouldn't approve, but with some effort, you can make Ted Turner green with envy. Just scan him and change the Hue value to 140 degrees. (It's a joke, son.)

When you choose Image⇨Adjust⇨Hue/Saturation (Ctrl-U), Photoshop displays the Hue/Saturation dialog box, shown in Figure 16-7. Before we explain how to use this dialog box to produce specific effects, let us briefly introduce the options:

✦ **Master:** Select the Master option to adjust all colors in an image to the same degree. If you prefer to adjust some colors in the image differently than others, select one of the color radio buttons along the left side of the dialog box. In the RGB and CMYK modes, the dialog box offers the R (Red), Y (Yellow), G (Green), C (Cyan), B (Blue), and M (Magenta) options, as shown in Figure 16-7. In the Lab mode, two radio buttons bite the dust, leaving Y (Yellow), G (Green), B (Blue), and M (Magenta), each of which represents an extreme end of the *a* or *b* spectrum. You can specify different slider bar settings for every one of the color ranges. For example, you may select R (Red) and move the Hue slider triangle to +50 and then select Y (Yellow) and move the Hue triangle to – 30. All radio buttons are dimmed when you select the Colorize check box.

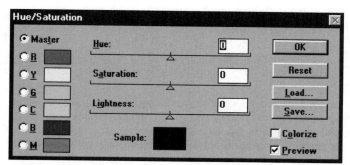

Figure 16-7: The Hue/Saturation dialog box enables you to adjust the hues and saturation values in a color image or colorize a grayscale image.

✦ **Hue:** The Hue slider bar measures colors on the 360-degree color circle, familiar from the Apple Color Picker dialog box. When Master is selected, you can adjust the Hue value from negative 180 to positive 180 degrees. When one of the other color radio buttons is active in the RGB or CMYK mode, the Hue value can vary from negative 60 to positive 60 degrees, because each of the colors is 60 degrees from either of its neighbors in the color wheel. (Red is 60 degrees from yellow, which is 60 degrees from green, and so on.)

When a color radio button is active in the Lab mode, the Hue value can vary from negative to positive 90 degrees, thanks to Lab's specialized color organization. Regardless of mode, letters appears at either end of the Hue slider when any option except Master is selected. The letters indicate the effect of moving the slider triangle in either direction. For example, if you select R (Red), the letters *M* and *Y* flank the slider, indicating that a negative value maps red pixels toward magenta, while a positive value maps red pixels toward yellow.

✦ **Saturation:** Normally, the Saturation value can vary from negative 100 to positive 100. The only exception occurs when the Colorize check box is active, in which case saturation becomes an absolute value. In other words, you can't subtract saturation from a colorized image, so the range becomes 0 to 100.

Note

Photoshop precedes positive values in the Hue, Saturation, and Lightness option boxes with plus signs (+) to show that you are adding to the current color attributes of the pixels. When you select Colorize, the plus signs disappear from all but the Lightness value because hue and saturation become absolute values that you apply to pixels rather than adding to or subtracting from existing pixel colors.

✦ **Lightness:** You can darken or lighten an image by varying the Lightness value from negative 100 to positive 100. However, because this value invariably changes *all* brightness levels in an image to an equal extent — whether or not Colorize is selected — it permanently dulls highlights and shadows. Therefore, you'll most likely want to avoid this option like the plague and rely instead on the Levels or Curves command to edit brightness and contrast.

✦ **Sample:** This color swatch serves as a guidepost. Really, it's pretty redundant, because you can monitor the effects that your settings have on an image by selecting the Preview check box. But if you want to see the impact of your settings on one color in particular, you can isolate it by clicking on that color in the image window with the eyedropper cursor. (The cursor automatically changes to an eyedropper when you move it outside the Hue/Saturation dialog box and into the image window.)

✦ **Load/Save:** As in all the best color correction dialog boxes (including Levels and Curves, naturally), you can load and save settings to disk in case you want to reapply the options to other images. These options are especially useful if you find a magic combination of color correction settings that accounts for most of the color mistakes produced by your scanner.

✦ **Colorize:** Select this check box to apply a single hue and a single saturation level to the entire selection, regardless of how it was previously colored. All brightness levels remain intact, though you can adjust them incrementally using the Lightness slider bar (a practice that we do *not* recommend, as we mentioned earlier).

✦ **Preview:** Select the Preview check box to continually update the image every time you adjust a setting.

Tip You can restore the options in the Hue/Saturation, Levels, and Curves dialog boxes to their original settings by Alt-clicking on the Reset button (the Cancel button changes to Reset when you press the Alt key) or by simply pressing Ctrl-Alt-period.

Adjusting hue and saturation

All right, now that you know how the options work, it's time to give them a whirl. One caveat before launching into things: Grayscale figures won't help you one whit in understanding the Hue/Saturation options, so we refer you a few times to three color plates. You may want to take a moment to slap a Post-it note in the general area of Color Plates 16-6, 16-7, and 16-8 before you begin reading so that you can easily flip back and forth between text and color plates.

Changing hues

When the Colorize check box is inactive, the Hue slider bar shifts colors in an image around the color wheel. It's as if the pixels were playing a colorful game of musical chairs, except that none of the chairs disappear. If you select the Master radio button and enter a value of +60 degrees, for example, all pixels stand up, march one sixth of the way around the color wheel, and sit down, assuming the colors of their new chairs. A pixel that was red becomes yellow, a pixel that was yellow becomes green, and so on. The top row of Color Plate 16-6 shows the result of applying various Hue values to a single image. Note that in each case, all colors in the image change to an equal degree.

Background

As long as you select only the Master option and edit only the Hue value, Photoshop retains all colors in an image. In other words, after shifting the hues in an image +60 degrees, you can later choose Hue/Saturation and shift the hues –60 degrees to restore the original colors.

If you select any radio button other than Master, the musical chairs metaphor breaks down a little. All pixels that correspond to the color you select move to the exclusion of other pixels in the image. The pixels that move must, well, sit on the nonmoving pixels' laps, meaning that you sacrifice colors in the image.

For example, we edited the images in the second row of Color Plate 16-6 by applying Hue values while only the R (Red) radio button was selected. (In other words, we didn't apply Hue changes in combination with any other radio button.) All pixels that included some amount of red shifted to new hues according to the amount of red that the pixels contained; all nonred pixels remained unchanged. Despite the fact that the Hue values in each column of the color plate are identical, the colors in the faces changed less dramatically when R (Red) was selected than when we used the Master option. This occurs because most of the pixels in the face contain some amount of yellow, which is excluded from the R (Red) hue adjustments.

Changing saturation levels

When Deke was a little kid, he loved watching his grandmother's television, because she kept the Color knob cranked at all times. The images appeared to leap off the screen, like maybe they were radioactive or something. In kid-speak, *way cool.* Well, the Saturation option works just like that Color knob. We don't recommend that you follow his grandmother's example and send the saturation for every image through the roof, but it can prove helpful for enhancing or downplaying the colors in an image. If the image looks washed out, try adding saturation; if colors leap off the screen so that everybody in the image looks like they're wearing neon makeup, subtract saturation.

Note

Just as the Saturation option works like the Color knob on a TV set, the Hue value serves the same purpose as the Tint knob, and the Lightness value works like the Brightness knob. It looks like your mother was wrong when she told you that sitting on your behind and staring at the TV wasn't going to teach you anything.

The top row of Color Plate 16-7 shows the results of applying Saturation values when the Master option is selected. As you can see, all colors in the image fade or fortify equally. However, by applying the Saturation values to specific color options only, you can selectively fade and fortify colors, as demonstrated in the second row of the color plate. The lower left image in the color plate shows the result of selecting each color radio button except R (Red) in turn and lowering the Saturation to −100, which translates to no saturation whatsoever, or all grays. Only grays and reds are left, producing an effect that looks like traditional paint applied to a black-and-white photo. In the lower right image, we lowered the Saturation for R (Red) to −100 and raised the saturation of all other colors to +50, thus eliminating the image's strongest color and enhancing the remaining weaker ones.

The Saturation option is especially useful for toning down images captured with low-quality scanners that exaggerate certain colors. We used to work with one model a few years back that would digitize flesh tones in varieties of vivid oranges and red. We couldn't for the life of us figure out how to peel the colors off the ceiling until we tried the Saturation option in the Hue/Saturation dialog box. By selecting the R (Red) radio button and dragging the slider down to about −50, we were usually able to eliminate the problem.

Correcting out-of-gamut colors

Another common use for the saturation option is to prepare RGB images for process-color printing. As discussed in Chapter 4, many colors in the RGB spectrum are considered out of gamut, meaning that they fall outside the smaller CMYK color space. Photoshop 3 now provides a means for recognizing such colors while remaining inside the RGB color space. Choose Mode⇨Gamut Warning to color all out-of-gamut colors with gray (or some other color that you specify using File⇨Preferences⇨Gamut Warning). The pixels don't actually change to gray; they just appear gray on-screen as long as the command is active. To turn Mode⇨Gamut Warning off, choose the command again.

How do you eliminate such problem colors? Well, you have three options. The first is to let Photoshop take care of the problem automatically when you convert the image by choosing Mode⇨CMYK Colors. But this tactic is risky, because Photoshop simply cuts off colors that are outside the gamut and converts them to their nearest CMYK equivalents. Neighboring colors that were inside the color space don't change at all, so what was once an abundant range of differently saturated hues becomes abruptly flattened, like some kind of cruel buzz haircut. Choosing Mode⇨CMYK Preview gives you an idea of how dramatic the buzz can be. Sometimes the effect is hardly noticeable, in which case no additional attention may be warranted. Other times, the results can be quite disheartening.

Another method is to scrub away with the sponge tool. We discussed in Chapter 7 how much we dislike this alternative, and we haven't changed our minds. Although it theoretically offers selective control — you just scrub at areas that need attention until the gray pixels created by the Gamut Warning command disappear — the process leaves too much to chance and frequently does more damage than simply choosing Mode⇨CMYK Colors. Besides, scrubbing is never fun (except when you're working on a particularly dirty tub, but that's because you can get high off the chlorine fumes).

The third and best solution involves the Saturation option inside the Hue/Saturation dialog box. No doubt this comes as a huge surprise, being that we decided to broach the whole out-of-gamut topic in the middle of examining this very option. But try to scoop your jaw up off the floor long enough to peruse the following steps, which outline the proper procedure for bringing out-of-gamut colors back into the CMYK color space.

Steps: Eliminating out-of-gamut colors

1. Press the Alt key and choose Image⇨Duplicate to create a second copy of your image on-screen. Choose Mode⇨CMYK Preview. This image represents what Photoshop will do with your image if you don't make any corrections whatsoever. It's good to have around for comparison.

2. Return to your original image and choose Select⇨Color Range. Then select the Out Of Gamut option from the Select pop-up menu and press Enter. You have now selected all the nonconformist Pinko pixels throughout your image. Joe McCarthy would have loved this option and bemoaned its absence in the film industry.

3. To monitor your progress, choose Mode⇨Gamut Warning to display the gray pixels. Oh, and don't forget to press Ctrl-H to get rid of those pesky ants.

4. Press Ctrl-U to display the Hue/Saturation dialog box. Don't change any settings while Master is selected; it's not exacting enough. Rather, experiment with selecting individual color radio buttons and lowering the Saturation value. The Hue slider can sometimes be useful as well. Every time you see one of the pixels change from gray to color, it means that another happy pixel has joined the CMYK pod. You may want to shout *Resistance is futile!* and laugh with evil delight just to make your work more entertaining.

Tip

Keep an eye on the duplicate image in the CMYK preview mode. If you edit a color in your original image and render it less colorful than the previewed image, it means that you're doing damage you could avoid by simply choosing Mode⇨CMYK Color. So if you drag the Saturation slider down to −35 for Y (Yellow) and notice that the revived pixels in the original image have become noticeably less colorful than their counterparts in the duplicate, nudge the slider back up to brighten the colors. If you can't seem to find an equitable solution, try selecting a different color radio button and editing it. Or try nudging the Hue slider and see what happens. Be patient, it takes a little time.

5. When only a few hundred sporadic gray spots remain on-screen, click on the OK button to return to the image window. Bellow imperiously, *You may think you have won, you little gray pixels, but I have a secret weapon!* Then choose Mode⇨CMYK Color and watch as Photoshop forcibly thrusts them into the gamut. (Don't worry, automatically changing a few pixels here and there isn't going to hurt anything.)

Mind you, the differences between your duplicate image and the one you manually turned away from the evil empire of RGB excess will be subtle, but they may prove enough to produce a better-looking image with a wider range of colors.

Cross Ref If the Hue/Saturation command doesn't seem to be working out, try using the Variations command or the Levels and Curves commands, as explained later in this chapter. The Variations command goes so far as to display the out-of-gamut gray pixels inside its previews and even hide the gray as the colors come into the fold.

Tip The one thing we don't like about the previous steps is that the Color Range command selects only the out-of-gamut pixels without even partially selecting their neighbors. As a result, you desaturate out-of-gamut colors while leaving very similar colors fully saturated, an effect that can produce visual edges in an image. One solution is to insert a step between steps 2 and 3 in which you do the following: Double-click on the magic wand tool to display the Magic Wand Options panel and then change the Tolerance value to, say, 12. Next, choose Select⇨Similar, which expands the selected area to all pixels that fall within the Tolerance range of the previously selected pixels. Finally, choose Select⇨Feather and enter a value that's about a quarter of the Tolerance value . . . in this case, 3. This solution isn't perfect — ideally, the Color Range option box wouldn't dim the Fuzziness slider when you choose Out Of Gamut — but it does succeed in partially selecting a few neighboring pixels without sacrificing too many of the out-of-gamut bunch.

Colorizing images

When you select the Colorize check box in the Hue/Saturation dialog box, the options in the dialog box perform differently. Returning to that wonderful musical chairs analogy, the pixels no longer walk around a circle of chairs; they all get up and go sit in the same chair. Every pixel in the selection receives the same hue and the same level of saturation. Only the brightness values remain intact to ensure that the image remains recognizable.

The top row of Color Plate 16-8 shows the results of shifting the hues in an image in two different directions around the color wheel. In each case, the Colorize option is inactive. The second row shows similar colors applied separately to the faces and background of the image using the Colorize option. The colors look approximately the same within each column in the color plate. However, the Hue values are different in the shifted images than those in the colorized images because the shifted colors are based on flesh tones in the orange (25 degree) range as well as a variety of other colors in the original image, while all the colorized colors are based on absolute 0 degree, which is red.

In most cases, you'll only want to colorize grayscale images or bad color scans, because colorizing ruins the original color composition of an image. You'll probably also want to lower the Saturation value to somewhere in the neighborhood of 50 to 75 degrees. All the colors in the second-row images in Color Plate 16-8 are the result of entering Saturation values of 60 degrees.

Tip To touch up areas in a colorized image, change the foreground color to match the Hue and Saturation values that you used in the Hue/Saturation dialog box. The B (Brightness) value in the Color Picker dialog box — which you display by clicking on a color swatch in the toolbox — should be 100 percent. Select the paintbrush tool and change the brush mode in the Paintbrush Options panel to Color. Then paint away.

Shifting selected colors

The Replace Color command enables you to select an area of related colors and adjust the hue and saturation of that area. When you select Image⇨Adjust⇨Replace Color, you get a dialog box much like the Color Range dialog box. Shown in Figure 16-8, the Replace Color dialog box differs in only a few respects: It's missing the Select and Selection Preview pop-up menus, and it offers three slider bars, taken right out of the Hue/Saturation dialog box. In fact, this dialog box works exactly as if you were selecting a portion of an image using Select⇨Color Range and editing it with the Hue/Saturation command. There is no functional difference whatsoever. The Replace Color and Color Range dialog boxes even share the same default settings. If you change the Fuzziness value in one, the default Fuzziness value of the other changes as well. It's as if they're identical twins or something.

So why does the Replace Color command even exist? Because it allows you to change the selection outline and apply different colors without affecting the image in any way. Just select the Preview check box to see the results of your changes on-screen, and you're in business.

The top row of Color Plate 16-9 shows two effects created by selecting an area and changing the Hue value to +148 and the Saturation value to −12 (as in Figure 16-8). In the first example, we selected the pumpkin face by setting the Fuzziness value to 40 and clicking and Shift-clicking a few times with the eyedropper tool. In the right example, we clicked just once in the area behind the pumpkin and changed the Fuzziness to 200, the maximum setting. We were able to experiment freely without once leaving the dialog box or redrawing the selection outline.

 Cross Ref If you're not clear on how to use all the options in the Replace Color dialog box, read the "Generating masks automatically" section in Chapter 9. It tells you all about the eyedropper tools and the Fuzziness option.

Shifting predefined colors

We really think that Adobe got these command names mixed up: The Replace Color command should be called Selective Color, because you select color (duh), and Selective Color should be called Replace Color because that's one of the things you can actually do with the command.

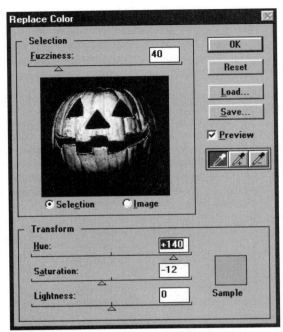

Figure 16-8: The Replace Color dialog box works like the Color Range dialog box described back in Chapter 9, with a few Hue/Saturation options thrown in.

But naming problems aside, choosing Image⇨Adjust⇨Selective Color brings up the dialog box shown in Figure 16-9. To use the dialog box, choose the predefined color that you want to edit from the Colors pop-up menu and then adjust the four process-color slider bars to change the predefined color. When the Relative radio button is selected, you add or subtract color, much as if you were moving the color around the musical chairs using the Hue slider bar. When you select Absolute, you change the predefined color to the exact value entered into the Cyan, Magenta, Yellow, and Black option boxes. The Absolute option is therefore very much like the Colorize check box in the Hue/Saturation dialog box.

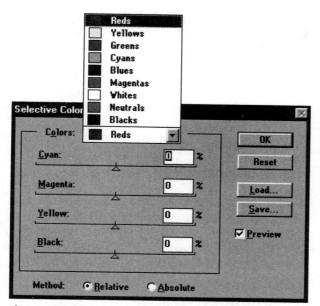

Figure 16-9: Select a predefined color from the Colors pop-up menu and adjust the slider bars to change that color.

If you examine it closely, you'll notice that the Selective Color dialog box is very much like the Hue/Saturation dialog box. You have access to predefined colors in the form of a pop-up menu instead of radio buttons, and you can adjust slider bars to alter the color. The key differences are that the pop-up menu lets you adjust whites, medium grays (Neutrals), and blacks (options missing from Hue/Saturation) and the slider bars are always measured in CMYK color space. But we think that the Selective Color options would have made a lot more sense had Adobe brought them into the Variations dialog box. As we explain in the next section, Variations offers the equivalent of a Colors pop-up menu and a series of slider bars; but, inexplicably, it provides fewer Colors options and more slider bars. If you were to simply combine these two functions, you'd have a very strong command that would rival and possibly surpass the capabilities of the Hue/Saturation dialog box. Alas, Adobe still hasn't offered to put us on the payroll and buy all our swell ideas, so we'll just have to settle for grumbling, gnashing our teeth, and cursing like Fred Flintstone. (*Rassam, grassam, frassam . . .* ever notice that the guy's expletives rhyme?)

Anyway, just so that you can see how this dialog box works, the bottom row of Color Plate 16-9 shows two examples. To create the first, we chose Red from the Colors pop-up menu and dragged the Cyan slider bar all the way up to +100 percent and the yellow slider all the way to −100 percent. We also selected the Relative radio button, which retains a lot of pink in the pumpkin's face. To create the second example, we reapplied the same colors but selected the Absolute radio button, making the entire pumpkin purple. We also chose Black from the Colors pop-up menu and dragged the Black slider to −100 percent.

Tip   The Selective Color command produces the most predictable results when you're working inside the CMYK color space. When you drag the Cyan slider triangle to the right, for example, you're actually transferring brightness values to the cyan color channel. However, you have to keep an eye out for a few anomalies, particularly when editing Black. In the CMYK mode, black areas include not only black, but also shades of cyan, magenta, and yellow, resulting in what printers call a *rich black*. Therefore, to change black to white, as we did in the lower right example of Color Plate 16-9, you have to set the Black slider to −100 percent and also set the Cyan, Magenta, and Yellow sliders to the same value.

Using the Variations command

In the previous section, we mentioned that the Variations command offers the equivalent of the Colors pop-up menu and slider bars found in the Selective Color dialog box. If you've ever used this command, you may be wondering what the heck we're talking about. But it's true. Choose Image⇨Adjust⇨Variations and you'll see them all as plain as day. It's just that the Colors pop-up menu options appear as four radio buttons, and the slider bars are presented as thumbnails, as shown in Figure 16-10.

Here's how it works: To infuse color into the selected image, click on one of the thumbnails in the central portion of the dialog box. The thumbnail labeled More Cyan, for example, shifts the colors toward cyan. The thumbnail even shows how the additional cyan will look when added to the image. In case you're interested in seeing how these thumbnails actually affect a final printed image, check out Color Plate 16-10.

Now notice that each thumbnail is positioned directly opposite its complementary color. More Cyan is across from More Red, More Blue is across from More Yellow, and so on. In fact, clicking on a thumbnail not only shifts colors toward the named color but away from the opposite color. For example, if you click on More Cyan and then click on its opposite, More Red, you arrive at the original image. Although this isn't exactly how the colors in the additive and subtractive color worlds work — cyan is not the empirical opposite of red — the colors are theoretical opposites, and the Variations command makes the theory a practicality. After all, you haven't yet applied the color to the image, so the dialog box can calculate its adjustments in a pure and perfect world. Cyan and red ought to be opposites, so for the moment, they are.

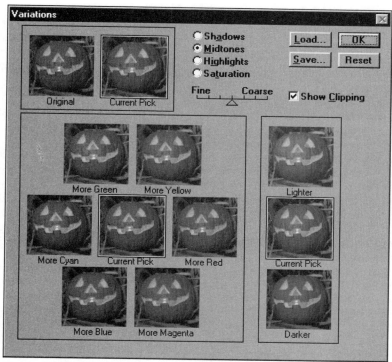

Figure 16-10: Click on the thumbnails to shift the colors in an image; adjust the slider bar in the upper right corner to change the sensitivity of the thumbnails; and use the radio buttons to determine which part of an image is selected.

To control the amount of color shifting that occurs when you click on a thumbnail, move the slider triangle in the upper right corner of the dialog box. Fine produces very minute changes; Coarse creates massive changes. Just to give you an idea of the difference between the two, you have to click on a thumbnail about 40 times when the slider is set to Fine to equal one click when it's set to Coarse.

As you click, you may notice that weird colors begin to appear inside the thumbnails. These bits of inverted image represent colors that exceed the boundaries of the current color space. Though the colors won't actually appear inverted as they do in the dialog box, it's not a good idea to exceed the color space because it results in areas of flat color, just as when you convert between the RGB and CMYK spaces. (To prevent the inverted color areas from appearing inside the dialog box, deselect the Show Clipping check box. Incidentally, this use of the word *clipping* — Photoshop's third, in case you're counting — has nothing to do with masks.)

Finally, the radio buttons at the top control which colors in the image are affected. Select Shadows to change the darkest colors, Highlights to change the lightest colors, and Midtones to change everything in between. (In fact, if you're familiar with the Levels dialog box, as you will be if you read the next section, the first three radio buttons have direct counterparts in the slider triangles in the Levels dialog box. For example, when you click on the Lighter thumbnail when the Highlights option is selected in the Variations dialog box, you perform the same action as moving the white triangle in the Levels dialog box to the left . . . that is, you lighten the lightest colors in the image to white.)

The Saturation radio button enables you to increase or decrease the saturation of colors in an image. Only one thumbnail appears on either side of the Current Pick image — one that decreases the saturation, and another that increases it. These options are more sensitive than the Saturation slider bar in the Hue/Saturation dialog box, affecting only the midtones in the image and leaving the lightest and darkest colors unaffected.

Robert

I want to jump in with a rave for the Variations command. You may have noticed that Deke also sometimes raves about things that please him greatly or displease him greatly. Because there's no rave from him here, I'm going to do one. I find the Variations command continually useful and intriguing. If you're trying to colorize a black-and-white something, it's a fine way to get a fast, general preview of which way you want the colors to go. If you're trying to clean up a scan (aren't we all, always?), same point — you can get an idea of the direction you want to tweak things in, and then go into the various other Photoshop methods for doing serious color correction. I'm regularly amazed at how much I can get done here.

Making Custom Brightness Adjustments

The Lighter and Darker options in the Variations dialog box are preferable to the Lightness slider bar inside the Hue/Saturation dialog box because you can specify whether to edit the darkest, lightest, or medium colors in an image. However, this is just the tip of the iceberg where Photoshop is concerned. The program provides two expert-level commands for adjusting the brightness levels in both grayscale and color images. The Levels command is ideal for most color corrections, enabling you to adjust the darkest values, lightest values, and midrange colors for the entire selection or independently within each color channel. The Curves command is great for creating special effects and correcting images that are beyond the help of the Levels command. Using the Curves command, you can map every brightness value in every color channel to an entirely different brightness value.

Levels command

When you choose Image⇔Adjust⇔Levels (Ctrl-L), Photoshop displays the Levels dialog box shown in Figure 16-11. The dialog box offers a histogram, as explained in the "Threshold" section earlier in this chapter, as well as two sets of slider bars with corresponding option boxes and a few automated eyedropper options in the lower right corner. You can compress and expand the range of brightness values in an image by manipulating the Input Levels options and then map those brightness values to new brightness values by adjusting the Output Levels options.

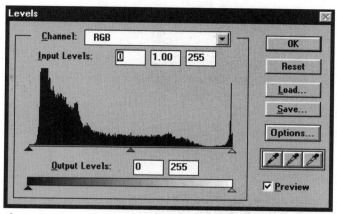

Figure 16-11: Use the Levels dialog box to map brightness values in the image (Input Levels) to new brightness values (Output Levels).

The options in the Levels dialog box work as follows:

✦ **Channel:** Select the color channel that you want to edit from this pop-up menu. You can apply different Input Levels and Output Levels values to each color channel. However, the options along the right side of the dialog box affect all colors in the selected portion of an image regardless of which Channel option is active.

✦ **Input Levels:** Use these options to select the darkest and lightest colors in the selected portion of an image, which is useful when the selection is washed out, offering insufficient shadows or highlights. The Input Levels option boxes correspond to the slider bar immediately below the histogram. You map pixels to black (or the darkest Output Levels value) by entering a number from 0 to 255 into the first option box or by dragging the black slider triangle. For example, if you raise the value to 55, all colors with brightness values of 55 or less in the original image become black, darkening the image as shown in the first example of Figure 16-12.

You can map pixels at the opposite end of the brightness scale to white (or the lightest Output Levels value) by entering a number from 0 to 255 into the last option box or by dragging the white slider triangle. If you lower the value to 200, all colors with brightness values of 200 or greater become white, lightening the image as shown in the second example of Figure 16-12. In the last example of the figure, we raised the first value and lowered the last value, thereby increasing the amount of contrast in the image.

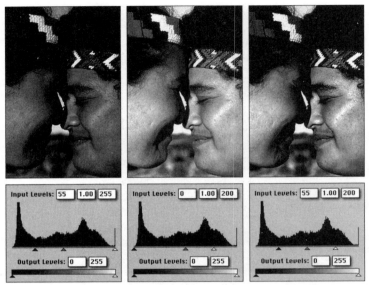

Figure 16-12: The results of raising the first Input Levels value to 55 (left), lowering the last value to 200 (middle), and combining the two (right).

✦ **Gamma:** The middle Input Levels option box and the corresponding gray triangle in the slider bar (shown highlighted in Figure 16-13) represent the *gamma* value, which is the brightness level of the medium gray value in the image. The gamma value can range from 0.10 to 9.99, with 1.00 being dead-on medium gray. Any change to the gamma value has the effect of decreasing the amount of contrast in the image by lightening or darkening grays without changing shadows and highlights. Increase the gamma value or drag the gray slider triangle to the left to lighten the medium grays (also called *midtones*), as in the first and second examples of Figure 16-14. Lower the gamma value or drag the gray triangle to the right to darken the medium grays, as in the last example in the figure.

✦ **Output Levels:** Use these options to curtail the range of brightness levels in an image by lightening the darkest pixels and darkening the lightest pixels. You adjust the brightness of the darkest pixels — those that correspond to the black Input Levels slider triangle — by entering a number from 0 to 255 into the first option box or by dragging the black slider triangle. For example, if you raise the value to 55, no color can be darker than that brightness level (roughly 80 percent black), which lightens the image as shown in the first example of Figure 16-15. You adjust the brightness of the lightest pixels — those that correspond to the white Input Levels slider triangle — by entering a number from 0 to 255 into the second option box or by dragging the white slider triangle. If you lower the value to 200, no color can be lighter than that brightness level (roughly 20 percent black), darkening the image as shown in the second example of Figure 16-15. In the last example of the figure, we raised the first value and lowered the second value, thereby dramatically decreasing the amount of contrast in the image.

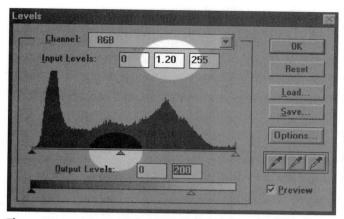

Figure 16-13: We spotlighted the gamma options by selecting everything but the highlighted areas and applying the values shown above.

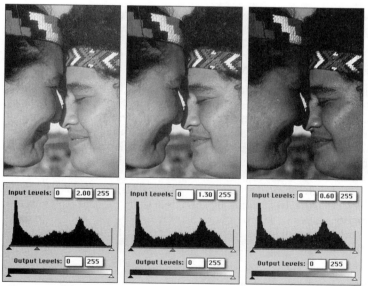

Figure 16-14: The results of raising (left and middle) and lowering (right) the gamma value to lighten and darken the midtones in an image.

Tip   You can fully or partially invert an image using the Output Levels slider triangles. Just drag the black triangle to the right and drag the white triangle to the left past the black triangle. The colors flip, whites mapping to dark colors and blacks mapping to light colors.

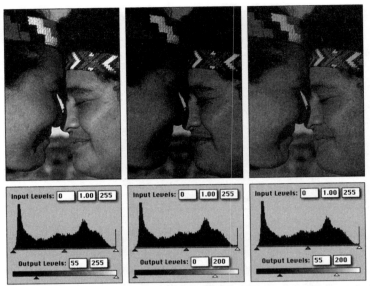

Figure 16-15: The result of raising the first Output Levels value to 55 (left), lowering the second value to 200 (middle), and combining the two (right).

✦ **Load/Save:** You can load and save settings to disk using these buttons.

✦ **Auto:** Click on the Auto button to automatically map the darkest pixel in your selection to black and the lightest pixel to white, just like Image⇨Adjust⇨Auto Levels. Photoshop actually darkens and lightens the image by an extra half-percent to account for the fact that the darkest and lightest pixels may be anomalies. To enter a percentage of your own, Alt-click on the Auto button (the button name changes to Options) to display the Auto Range Options dialog box shown in Figure 16-16. Enter higher values to increase the number of pixels mapped to black and white; decrease the values to lessen the effect. The first two examples in Figure 16-17 compare the effect of the default 0.50 percent values to higher values of 5.00 percent. (Strictly for comparison purposes, the last image in the figure demonstrates the effect of the Equalize command applied to the entire image.)

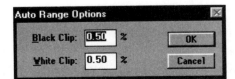

Figure 16-16: Alt-click on the Auto button to change the extent to which Photoshop closes the range of black and white pixels.

0.50% Clips   5.00% Clips   Equalize

Figure 16-17: The default effect of the Auto button (left), the effect of the Auto button after raising the Clip values (middle), and the effect of the Equalize filter (right).

Note   Any changes made inside the Auto Range Options dialog box also affect the performance of the Auto Levels command. At all times, the effects of the Auto button and Auto Levels command are absolutely identical.

✦ **Eyedroppers:** Select one of the eyedropper tools in the Levels dialog box and click on a pixel in the image window to automatically adjust the color of that pixel. If you click on a pixel with the black eyedropper tool (the first of the three), Photoshop maps the color of the pixel and all darker colors to black. If you click on a pixel with the white eyedropper tool (the last of the three), Photoshop maps it and all lighter colors to white. Use the gray eyedropper tool (the middle one) to change the exact color on which you click to medium gray and adjust all other colors in accordance. For example, if you click on a white pixel, all white pixels change to medium gray and all other pixels change to even darker colors.

Tip   One way to use the eyedropper tools is to color-correct scans without a lot of messing around. Include a neutral swatch of gray with the photograph you want to scan. (If you own a Pantone swatch book, Cool Gray 5 or 6 is your best bet.) After opening the scan in Photoshop, choose the Levels command, select the gray eyedropper tool, and click on the neutral gray swatch in the image window. This technique won't perform miracles, but it will help you to more evenly distribute lights and darks in the image. You then can fine-tune the image using the Input Levels and Output Levels options.

✦ **Preview:** Select this option to preview the effects of your settings in the image window.

Tip   When the Preview check box is inactive — yes, you read that right, *in*active — you can preview the exact pixels that will turn to black or white in the image window by Alt-dragging the black or white triangle in the Input Levels slider bar.

To give you a sense of how this command works, the following steps describe how to improve the appearance of a washed-out, faded, overly dark, scanned image using the options in the Levels dialog box.

On the CD-ROM In fact, the very image I'll be using is included on the CD-ROM that comes with this book. From Planet Art's French Posters collection, this image is a scan of a well-known advertisement created by 19th-century artist Henri de Toulouse-Lautrec for the seedy Moulin Rouge. Though the piece itself is a masterwork, the Photo CD scan can be improved dramatically using the Levels command.

Steps: Giving the Moulin Rouge a much-needed face-lift

1. Okay, here's the deal. You're a restorer of priceless artwork.

   You begin by opening up the Moulin Rouge image on the CD-ROM inside the Planet Art directory. The Photo CD dialog box comes up, asking you what resolution you want to open. Select the size that's most likely to work smoothly on your machine. (If you have problems with this dialog box, consult the "Photo CD YCC images" section of Chapter 3.)

2. Press Ctrl-L to display the Levels dialog box. Just to check it out, click on the Auto button. (Make sure that the Preview check box is on so that you can accurately see the results of your changes.) Just one click of the button results in a remarkable difference. In case you're not following along with the exercise, the first example in Color Plate 16-11 shows the difference between the original image (at the top) and the image subject to the Auto button (bottom).

3. You could stop right here if you wanted to. It's good enough for government work. But we suggest that you pursue things a little further; although it's better, the image still has some problems. Too many of the pixels have turned black and too many have turned white. Meanwhile, the majority of the medium colors still appear very dark. So press the Alt key and click on the Reset button to restore the original image.

4. The best way to approach a color image is one channel at a time. So press Ctrl-1 to switch to the red channel. Notice the histogram. It's all the way over to the left side, indicating a preponderance of dark colors. To lighten things up, drag the white triangle to the left. The third Input Levels value changes to keep up with you. Drag the triangle until it lines up with the lightest of the histogram bars, somewhere around 165 (as indicated in the third option box). This means that everything lighter than 165, which is only slightly lighter than medium gray, will turn white.

5. Now drag the black triangle slightly to the right, until the first Input Levels value is 6. This blackens the darkest colors and keeps them from appearing washed out. By now, the image in the window will appear overly red. Don't worry, you'll equalize the colors in the next step.

6. So much for the red channel; now to repeat the process for the green and blue channels. Press Ctrl-2 to switch to the green channel. Again, the pixels are all bunched up toward the dark end of the spectrum. Drag the white triangle to about 150 and drag the black triangle to 10. Next, press Ctrl-3 to switch to the blue channel. Drag the white triangle left to 160, the black triangle right to 12. Keep in mind that these values are only suggestions. We encourage you to experiment with other values to see if you find something that works better.

7. Now press Ctrl-0 to return to the RGB view. See how the histogram bars are now spread out all the way from black to white? Notice the gaps between bars? These gaps indicate brightness values that are associated with no pixels . . . and we mean none in the red channel, none in the green channel, and none in the blue channel. Few images are quite this bad off.

8. The grays in the image are still too dark. So it's time to adjust the gamma. Drag the middle slider triangle to the right to lighten the medium colors. We suggest dragging until the middle Input Levels value reads 1.40. This brings out the color in that snobbish man in the foreground of the image . . . you know, that guy who's indicating, *None of this uncivilized behavior for me. In fact, I don't know what made me come into this place. Nonetheless, I must admit, that woman clearly patronizes Victoria's Secret.* Anyway, you can start to see some purples and browns inside the gent where once there were only sooty grays.

9. Now that you elevated the grays, the blacks are starting to weaken again. So raise the black slider triangle to 10. Now the blacks look black.

10. Click on the OK button or press Enter. Photoshop applies your changes to the image. Just for fun, press Ctrl-Z a few times to see the before and after shots. Quite the transformation, what?

The second image in Color Plate 16-11 shows the color-corrected image. We also firmed up the detail a bit by applying the Unsharp Mask filter with an Amount value of 200 percent and a Radius of 0.5. Some rough spots are still in the image, but come on, it's right at 100 years old — and it's not even a painting, it's printed on paper. You should look so good. You can go in and retouch away some of those problems using the 5,000 techniques discussed in Part II of this book, but the color correction phase of the project is complete.

The Curves command

If you want to be able to map any brightness value in an image to absolutely any other brightness value — no holds barred, as they say at the drive-in movies — you want the Curves command. When you choose Image⇨Adjust⇨Curves (Ctrl-M), Photoshop displays the Curves dialog box, shown in Figure 16-18, which must be the most functional collection of color correction options on the planet.

Brightness graph

Brightness curve

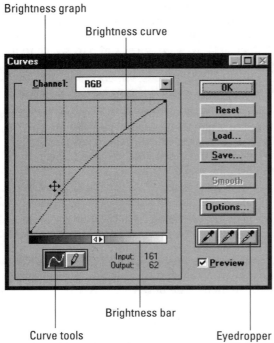

Brightness bar

Curve tools   Eyedropper

Figure 16-18: The Curves dialog box lets you distribute brightness values by drawing curves on a graph.

Quickly, here's how the options work:

✦ **Channel:** Surely you know how this option works by now. You select the color channel that you want to edit from this pop-up menu. You can apply different mapping functions to different channels by drawing in the graph below the pop-up menu. But, as is always the case, the options along the right side of the dialog box affect all colors in the selected portion of an image regardless of which Channel option is active.

✦ **Brightness graph:** The brightness graph is where you map brightness values in the original image to new brightness values. The horizontal axis of the graph represents input levels; the vertical axis represents output levels. The *brightness curve* charts the relationship between input and output levels. The lower left corner is the origin of the graph (the point at which both input and output values are 0). Move right in the graph for higher input values, up for higher output values. Because the brightness graph is the core of this dialog box, upcoming sections explain it in more detail.

✦ **Brightness bar:** The brightness bar shows the direction of light and dark values in the graph. By default, colors are measured in terms of brightness values, in which case the colors in the brightness bar proceed from black to white (reading left to right), as demonstrated in the left example of Figure 16-19. Therefore, higher values produce lighter colors. However, if you click on the brightness bar, white and black switch places, as shown in the second example of the figure. The result is that Photoshop measures the colors in terms of ink coverage, from 0 percent of the primary color to 100 percent of the primary color. Higher values now produce darker colors. If you click on the brightness bar in the process of drawing a curve, the curve automatically flips so as to retain any changes you made, as the figure illustrates.

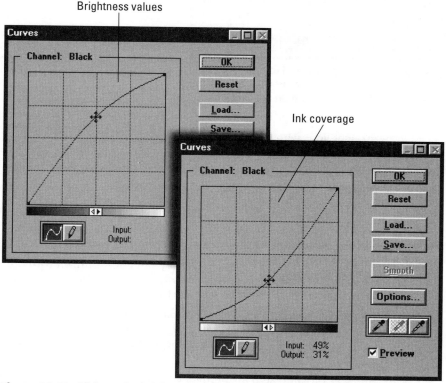

Figure 16-19: Click on the brightness bar to change the way in which the graph measures color: by brightness values (left) or by ink coverage (right).

✦ **Curve tools:** Use the curve tools to draw the curve inside the brightness graph. Click in the graph with the point tool (on the left, selected by default) to add a point to the curve. Drag a point to move it. To delete a point, drag it outside the boundaries of the graph. The pencil tool (on the right) enables you to draw free-form curves simply by dragging inside the graph, as shown in Figure 16-20.

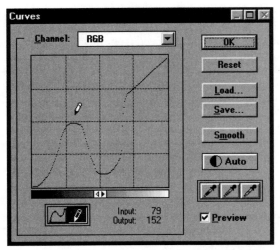

Figure 16-20: Use the pencil tool to draw free-form lines in the brightness graph. If the lines appear rough, you can soften them by clicking on the Smooth button.

Tip   You can draw straight lines with the pencil tool by clicking at one location in the graph and Shift-clicking at a different point, just as you can when using the real pencil tool in the image window.

✦ **Input/Output numbers:** The input and output numbers monitor the location of your cursor in the graph according to brightness values or ink coverage, depending on the setting of the brightness bar.

✦ **Load/Save:** Use these buttons to load and save settings to disk.

✦ **Smooth:** Click on the Smooth button to smooth out curves drawn with the pencil tool. Doing so leads to smoother color transitions in the image window. This button is dimmed except when you use the pencil tool.

✦ **Auto:** Click on this button to automatically map the darkest pixel in your selection to black and the lightest pixel to white. Photoshop throws in some additional darkening and lightening according to the Clip percentages, which you can edit by Alt-clicking on the button.

✦ **Eyedroppers:** Photoshop actually permits you to use a fourth eyedropper from the Curves dialog box. If you don't select any eyedropper tool (or you click in the graph to deselect the current eyedropper) and move the cursor out of the dialog box into the image window, you get the standard eyedropper cursor. Click on a pixel in the image to locate the brightness value of that pixel in the graph. A circle appears in the graph, and the input and output numbers list the value for as long as you hold down the mouse button, as shown in the first example in Figure 16-21.

The other eyedroppers work as they do in the Levels dialog box, mapping pixels to black, medium gray, or white. For example, the second image in Figure 16-21 shows the white eyedropper tool clicking on a light pixel, thereby mapping that value to white, as shown in highlighted portion of the graph below the image. You can further adjust the brightness value of that pixel by dragging the corresponding point in the graph, as demonstrated in the last example of the figure.

✦ **Preview:** Select this option to preview your settings in the image window.

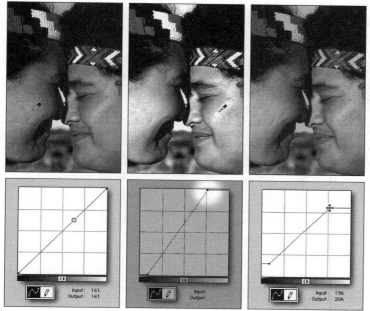

Figure 16-21: Use the standard eyedropper cursor to locate a color in the brightness graph (left). Click with one of the eyedropper tools from the Curves dialog box to map the color of that pixel in the graph (middle). You then can edit the location of the point in the graph by dragging it (right).

Continuous curves

Caution All discussions in the few remaining pages of this chapter assume that the brightness bar is set to edit brightness values (in which case the gradation in the bar lightens from left to right). If you set the bar to edit ink coverage (the bar darkens from left to right), you can still achieve the effects we describe, but you must drag in the opposite direction. For example, if we tell you to lighten colors by dragging upward, you drag downward. In a backward world live the ink coverage people.

When you first enter the Curves dialog box, the brightness curve appears as a straight line strung between two points, as shown in the first example of Figure 16-22, mapping every input level from white (the lower left point) to black (the upper right point) to an identical output level. If you want to perform seamless color corrections, the point tool is your best bet because it enables you to edit the levels in the brightness graph while maintaining a continuous curve.

To lighten the colors in the selected portion of the image, click near the middle of the curve with the point tool to create a new point and then drag the point upward, as demonstrated in the second example of Figure 16-22. To darken the image, drag the point downward, as in the third example.

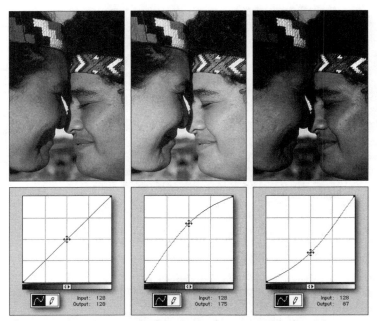

Figure 16-22: Create a single point in the curve with the point tool (left) and then drag it upward (middle) or downward (right) to lighten or darken the image evenly.

Create two points in the curve to boost or lessen the contrast between colors in the image. In the first example of Figure 16-23, we created one point very near the white point in the curve and another point very close to the black point. We then dragged down on the left point and up on the right point to make the dark pixels darker and the light pixels lighter, which translates to higher contrast.

In the second example of the figure, we did just the opposite, dragging up on the left point to lighten the dark pixels and down on the right point to darken the light pixels. As you can see in the second image, this lessens the contrast between colors, making the image more gray.

In the last example in Figure 16-23, we bolstered the contrast with a vengeance by dragging the right point down and to the left. This has the effect of springing the right half of the curve farther upward, thus increasing the brightness of the light pixels in the image.

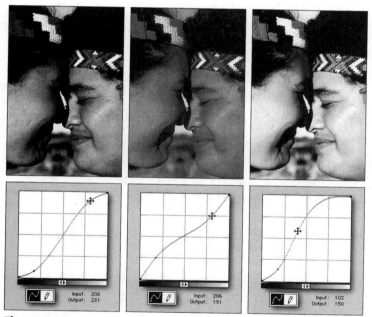

Figure 16-23: Create two points in the curve to change the appearance of contrast in an image, whether by increasing it mildly (left), decreasing it (middle), or boosting it dramatically (right).

Arbitrary curves

You can create some mind-numbing color variations by adjusting the brightness curve arbitrarily, mapping light pixels to dark, dark pixels to light, and in-between pixels all over the place. In the first example of Figure 16-24, we used the point tool to achieve an arbitrary curve. By dragging the left point severely upward and the right point severely downward, we caused dark and light pixels alike to soar across the spectrum.

If you're interested in something a little more subtle, try applying an arbitrary curve to a single channel in a color image. Color Plate 16-12, for example, shows an image subject to relatively basic color manipulations in the red and green channels, followed by an arbitrary adjustment to the blue channel.

Although you can certainly achieve arbitrary effects using the point tool, the pencil tool is more versatile and less inhibiting. As shown in the second example of Figure 16-24, we created an effect that would alarm Carlos Castaneda just by zigzagging our way across the graph and clicking on the Smooth button.

In fact, the Smooth button is an integral part of using the pencil tool. Try this little experiment: Draw a bunch of completely random lines and squiggles with the pencil tool in the brightness graph. As shown in the first example of Figure 16-25, your efforts will most likely yield an unspeakably hideous and utterly unrecognizable effect.

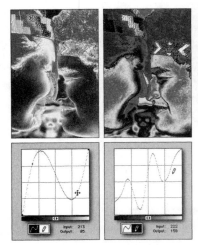 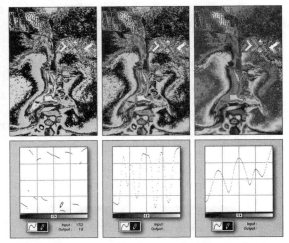

Figure 16-24: Arbitrary brightness curves created using the point tool (left) and the pencil tool (right).

Figure 16-25: After drawing a series of completely random lines with the pencil tool (left), we clicked on the Smooth button once to connect the lines into a frenetic curve (middle) and then twice more to even out the curve, thus preserving more of the original image (right).

Next, click on the Smooth button. Photoshop automatically connects all portions of the curve, miraculously smoothing out the color-mapping effect and rescuing some semblance of your image, as shown in the second example of the figure. If the effect is still too radical, you can continue to smooth it out by clicking additional times on the Smooth button. We clicked on the button twice more to create the right image in Figure 16-25. Eventually, the Smooth button restores the curve to a straight line.

The Fundamentals of Compositing

Mixing Images Together

In earlier chapters, we demonstrated many examples of *compositing,* which is the sometimes straightforward, sometimes extremely complex process of mixing two or more images together. But however straightforward or complex, Photoshop's compositing capabilities fall into three categories:

✦ **Floating selections:** The simple act of floating a selection, applying a filter to it, and using the Opacity slider bar to mix the floater with the underlying original is the quickest and most direct method of compositing available inside Photoshop. Whether you float an image by moving it, choosing Select⇨Float, copying and pasting it, or dragging and dropping it from another image window, you can apply any of the overlay mode options from the Layers palette as well as adjust the Opacity slider bar to mix the floating selection with the fixed image behind it.

✦ **Layers:** When an image is on a separate layer, you can take advantage of the overlay modes pop-up menu and the Opacity slider bar, just as you can when working with a floating selection. But you also have access to two additional features, both of which are unique to layers. You can bring up the Layers Options dialog box, which allows you to drop colors out of the active layer and force colors to show through from background layers. You also have the option of compositing more than two images at a time. Combining floating selections with layers provides even more options.

✦ **Channel operations:** The so-called channel operations let you combine two open images of identical size (or one image with itself) using two commands, Image⇨Apply Image and Image⇨Calculations. Unusually complex and completely lacking in sizing and placement functions, these commands provide access to only two unique options, the Add and Subtract overlay modes. Simply put, unless a technique involves the Add or Subtract mode or you're specifically interested in combining individual channels from different images, you can composite with greater ease, flexibility, and feedback using floating selections or layers. For more on this lively topic, see the "Channel Operation Commands" section later in this chapter.

This chapter contains explanations of the various compositing options, including complete information on the Layers palette and the Apply Image and Calculations commands. The following chapter, "Compositing on the March," offers a series of step-by-step methods for taking advantage of these options. Together, these chapters should provide a complete picture of how compositing works and how you can integrate it into your daily image-editing regimen. (A little Slim-Fast here, a few composites there, and you'll be shipshape in no time.)

Compositing with Layers

We've already discussed the layering feature in some detail in Chapters 8 and 9, so we'll concentrate now on the handful of layering functions that we've so far breezed over or ignored.

Figure 17-1 shows the Layers palette as it appears with the pop-up menu exposed. By now, you're probably already familiar with the overlay modes pop-up menu and the Opacity slider bar but, just in case, both appear labeled in the figure.

 Cross Ref For information about establishing layers, read the "Sending a floating selection to its own layer" section of Chapter 8. This section also explains the basic concepts behind layering.

The items in the Layers palette that are integral to the subject of compositing include the following:

✦ **The Opacity slider bar:** Drag the slider triangle or press a number on the keyboard to change the opacity of the active layer or floating selection. Remember that one of the first eight tools in the toolbox or one of the path tools must be active for the keyboard shortcuts to work, so press the M key to get the marquee tool before starting in on the number keys. (If one of the painting or editing tools is selected, pressing a number key changes the opacity of that tool.)

✦ **The overlay modes pop-up menu:** Also available to floating selections, the overlay modes pop-up menu mixes every pixel in the active layer with the pixel directly behind it, according to one of several mathematical equations. For example, when you choose Multiply, Photoshop really does multiply the brightness values of the two pixels and then divides the result by 255, the maximum brightness value. If you're more concerned with the effects of the overlay modes than their equations, see the upcoming "Overlay modes" section.

Overlay modes
pop-up menu

Opacity slider bar

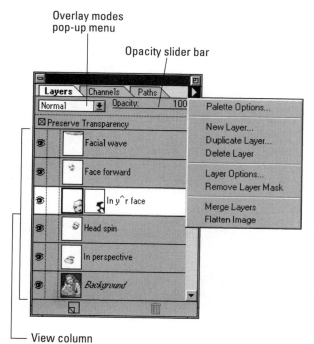

View column

Figure 17-1: The Layers palette in
all its splendor and glory, proudly
waving its pop-up menu for all to see.

✦ **Layer Options:** Choose the Layer Options command or double-click on a layer to
display the Layer Options dialog box. Applicable exclusively to layers, this
dialog box duplicates the two options described earlier as well as adding a few
functions. For example, using the slider bars, you can specify which colors are
visible in the active layer and which colors show through from the ones behind
it. You can also mix the colors using special fuzziness controls and change the
slider bar settings for each individual color channel. For a complete description
of the Layer Options dialog box, read the "Blending layers with supreme control" section later in this chapter.

✦ **Keyboard navigation:** Switch to the next layer up by pressing Ctrl-right bracket.
Move down a layer by pressing Ctrl-left bracket. You can also go from the top
layer to the Background layer by pressing Ctrl-right bracket or vice versa by
pressing Ctrl-left bracket. To go to a layer that contains a specific image, press V
to select the move tool, and then Ctrl-click on the image.

✦ **Layer order:** Drag a layer name up or down in the scrolling list to move it forward
or backward in layering order. The only trick is to make sure that the black bar
appears at the point where you want to move the layer before you release the
mouse button, as demonstrated in Figure 17-2. You can even move floating

selections by dragging them up and down in the palette. The floating selection neither loses its contents nor stops floating; it simply hovers above a different layer. But don't miss that black bar, or Photoshop won't move a darn thing.

The all important black bar

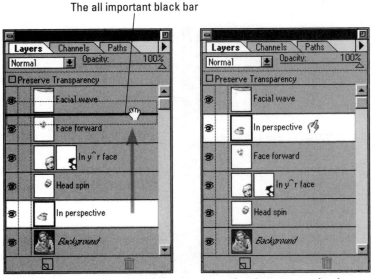

Figure 17-2: Drag the layer between two other layers to make the all-important black bar appear (left) to change the hierarchy of the layer (right).

✦ **View column:** You know that you can hide layers and display them by clicking in the view column — the one with all the eyeballs. But did you know that you can Alt-click in front of a layer to display only that layer and hide all others? When you view a single layer out of context, Photoshop disregards any overlay mode and Opacity setting applied to the layer and shows it fully opaque so that you can more carefully examine its pixels. Alt-click in front of the layer again to bring all the layers back into view and reinstate the overlay mode and translucency.

✦ **Palette Options:** We only mention this command because we've thus far ignored it. When you choose Palette Options from the Layers palette menu, you can select from one of three sizes at which to display the thumbnail preview to the left of the layer name in the palette, or you can hide the thumbnail. You could have easily figured that out without us, but we just don't want anyone out there thinking *What-the-bleep does this command do?*

✦ **Flatten Image and Merge Layers:** Choose the Merge Layers command to merge all visible layers into a single layer. If the layer is not visible — that is, no eyeball icon appears in front of the layer name — Photoshop doesn't get rid of it; the layer simply remains independent. The Flatten Image command, on the other hand, merges all visible layers and throws away the invisible ones. Be wary of commands that want to flatten the image for you. For example, Photoshop has to flatten an image in order to switch color modes. So be sure to display all layers that you want to retain before choosing any of the first eight commands from the Mode menu.

Robert on layers . . .

As the heading implies. I want to tell you about a couple of things, and I've been mulling over just where to put them. Deke has, of course, introduced layers much earlier. But those places seemed less appropriate — he's used this chapter for the really down-and-dirty material on layers, so I'm using it, too. In possibly my only organizational disagreement with him, I might have preferred one entire chapter on layers. But, hey, it's Deke's book (says the Windowizer, ever modestly).

First, I want to pass on some information that Deke gleaned from one of the Photoshop programmers after he'd written this book and generously posted on CompuServe's old Adobe forum (come back, Deke — we miss you!). Transparent pixels take up no space in memory, but opaque and translucent pixels do take up space. Thus, a layer that contains 25 percent as many pixels as the background layer would indeed take up 25 percent as much space. But, if you go and paint into the transparent area of that same layer, you increase the size of the layer in memory 3K for every RGB pixel you change from transparent to opaque or translucent. Here's the math: A 24-bit pixel consumes exactly 3K in memory because 1K equals 256 colors to the third power, or 16 million. Obviously, these considerations can have an effect on Photoshop's performance.

Second, I want to mention that Fractal Design Painter 3.1 and 4.0 not only can read native Photoshop PSD files but also preserve the layer information, converting them to Painter's equivalent of Floaters. This can be very useful — I've said before, and will say again in Chapter 19, that Photoshop and Painter represent the ultimate digital imaging powerhouse (two 800-pound gorillas, and all that). You can have the benefits of the layers and floaters and pass the .PSD file back and forth, depending on which program will do best what your Muse is telling you (in my professional mode as a specialist in Greco-Roman religion, I'd remind you that the classical Greek Muses, all nine of 'em, are a very talky lot). Just be sure to read Painter's documentation — it's exceptionally clear and detailed on who-does-what-to-whom.

Overlay modes

The overlay modes options available from the Layers palette include the same bunch that we discussed at the end of Chapter 7, under "The 15 paint tool brush modes." When manipulating the active layer, you see only 14 brush modes, all of which are found in the brush modes pop-up menu in the Paintbrush Options panel. Only the Behind mode is missing — you can't apply the active layer behind itself.

Behind and Clear

If you float a selection on the active layer, however, you gain access not only to the Behind mode but also to a 16th overlay mode, Clear. Just like the Behind mode available for brushes, this Behind mode lets you tuck the floating selection behind the opaque portions of the active layer. In other words, the floating selection is allowed to fill the transparent and translucent areas of the active layer only.

The Clear mode uses the floating selection to cut a hole in the active layer. It's like having a little hole that you can move around independently of the pixels, without danger of harming them. You know that scene in *Yellow Submarine* where the Fab Four are making fun of that poor little marsupial with the long, mustard-colored nose? After they finish labeling him a "Nowhere Man" — hey, give him a break, guys, maybe his priorities are just different — the creature announces that he has a hole in his pocket. He then takes it out, puts it on the floor, and it becomes a hole in the floor. (Well, it's not really a floor. They're all in this nebulous white space that represents nowhere, presumably.) Later, the holes multiply — can't remember why — and all the guys sail through the holes while singing some other song that has nothing to do with the plot, which was already in awfully short supply. Deke says it's a pointless movie — not nearly so great as *Sid and Nancy* — but the concept is absolutely the same as Photoshop's Clear mode. Clear turns a floating selection into a portable hole in the active layer.

Tip

This feature is especially useful for clipping holes into a layer using character outlines.

Create some text, convert it to a bunch of holes by choosing the Clear mode, defloat the selection outline, and see what lies below. If you suddenly become concerned that you've lost part of the layer, don't panic. Just choose the Normal mode, and all will be forgotten.

Robert

Shame on you, Deke, for dissing *Yellow Submarine!* It was a mind-bender when it came out, and it's still a visual and thematic delight. You don't even need to inhale to appreciate it! Do we have, er, a generation gap here? Besides, one of the professors in my major department at Yale did the screenplay — does the name Erich Segal ring a bell? Classics professors are an omnivorous lot — hey, I'm one and look what I'm doing here (for you, to you).

Both the Behind and Clear modes are dimmed when you edit the Background layer (or an image without layers), because you can't scoot the floater under the background, and you can't cut a hole in the background because there's nothing underneath. (Well, we know some metaphysical types who say there may be something underneath, but you don't want to know what it is.)

The 14 universal overlay modes

The remaining overlay modes are available whether you're editing a layer or a floating selection and, in principle, they work the same as the brush modes covered in Chapter 7. But some functional differences come into play when you're compositing layers or floating selections, so we include the following list just to be safe.

Cross Ref In case you're curious, the old Black Matte and White Matte overlay modes are now available from the Select⇨Matting submenu in the form of the Remove Black Matte and Remove White Matte commands. Applicable to floating selections and layers alike, these commands are discussed in the "Removing halos" section of Chapter 8.

Note As we said, these overlay modes are applicable to both the active layer or a floating selection. But it seems like a lot of excess verbiage to keep saying *active layer or floating selection* over and over again. So any time we say *active layer* in the following list, you'll know that we mean both. (Wink, wink.)

Also, when we allude to something called a *composite pixel,* we mean the pixel color that results from all the mixing that's going on in back of the active layer or floating selection. For example, your document may have hordes of layers with all sorts of overlay modes in effect, but as long as you work on, say, layer 17, Photoshop treats the image formed by layers 1 through 16 as if it were one flattened image filled with a bunch of static composite pixels.

✦ **Normal:** In combination with an Opacity setting of 100 percent, this option displays every pixel in the active layer normally, regardless of the colors of the underlying image. Figure 17-3 shows a banner that has been positioned on a single layer composited in front of a stucco texture created on the Background layer. The overlay mode in force is Normal. (The drop shadow, incidentally, is merely an artistic embellishment that exists on the background layer.)

When you use an Opacity of less than 100 percent, the color of each pixel in the active layer is averaged with the composite pixel in the layers behind it according to the Opacity value. The first two examples of Color Plate 17-1 compare color versions of the banner set against a stucco background at 100 percent and 50 percent Opacity.

Figure 17-3: An active layer containing the banner image and drop shadow subject to the Normal overlay mode and an Opacity setting of 100 percent.

✦ **Dissolve:** This option specifically affects feathered or softened edges. If the active layer is entirely opaque with hard edges, this option has no effect. If the selection is anti-aliased, the effect is generally too subtle to be of much use. The Dissolve option randomizes the pixels in the feathered portion of an active layer, as shown in the top example of Figure 17-4. It also randomizes pixels of hard- or soft-edged selections when the Opacity value is set below 100 percent, as witnessed by the second example in the figure and the third example in Color Plate 17-1.

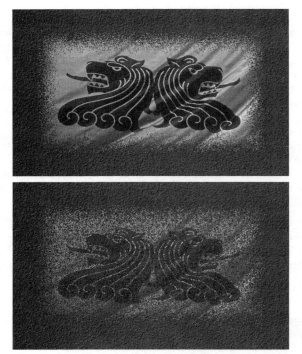

Figure 17-4: The Dissolve option applied to an opaque floating selection with heavily feathered edges (top) and to a second selection set to 40 percent opacity (bottom).

✦ **Multiply:** To understand the Multiply and Screen modes, you have to use a little imagination. So here goes: Imagine that the active layer and the underlying image are both photos on transparent slides. The Multiply mode produces the same effect as holding those slides up to the light, one slide in front of the other. Because the light has to travel through two slides, the outcome is invariably a darker image that contains elements from both images. Examples of the Multiply overlay mode appear in Figure 17-5 and Color Plate 17-1.

Figure 17-5: The Multiply overlay mode produces the same effect as holding two overlapping transparencies up to the light. It always results in a darker image.

✦ **Screen:** Still have those transparent slides from the Multiply analogy? Well, place them both in separate projectors and point them at the same screen and you'll get the same effect as Screen. Rather than creating a darker image, as you do with Multiply, you create a lighter image, as demonstrated in Figure 17-6 and Color Plate 17-1.

You can use the Screen overlay mode to emulate film that has been exposed multiple times. Ever seen Thomas Eakins's pioneering *Jumping Figure,* which shows rapid-fire exposures of a naked man jumping from one location to another? Each shot is effectively screened onto the other, lightening the film with each and every exposure. The photographer was smart enough to limit the exposure time so as not to overexpose the film; likewise, you should only apply Screen when working with images that are sufficiently dark so that you avoid overlightening.

Figure 17-6: The Screen mode produces the same effect as shining two projectors at the same screen. It always results in a lighter image.

✦ **Overlay, Soft Light, and Hard Light:** You just can't separate these guys. All three multiply the dark colors in the active layer and screen the light colors into the composite pixels in the background layers, creating a heightened contrast effect. In fact, these three options are a little like the three bears of compositing. (We know, two Goldilocks analogies in one book is two too many, but bear with us for a moment.) The Hard Light overlay mode is papa bear, because it's too blunt; Soft Light is mama bear, because it's too subtle; and Overlay is baby bear, because it's just right.

Of course, that's something of an oversimplification. (A fairy-tale analogy applied to a complex overlay mode qualifies as oversimplification? Never!) But it's frequently true. Figure 17-7 shows all three overlay modes — from top to bottom, Overlay, Soft Light, and Hard Light — applied to a single banner image on the left and to two layers of banner images on the right. Color Plate 17-1 shows the effect applied only once. As these examples demonstrate, the modes effectively tattoo one image onto the image in back of it. Notice, for example, that even after multiple repetitions of the banners in the figure, the stucco texture still shows through, as if the banner were actually appliquéd on.

We recommend starting with the Overlay mode any time you want to mix both active layer and the composite image behind it to create a reciprocal blend. By this we mean that it mixes the colors evenly without eliminating any of the detail in either image — unlike the Normal mode at 50 percent Opacity or any of the other modes, for that matter. After you apply Overlay, vary the Opacity to favor one image or the other. If you can't quite get the effect you want at lower Opacity settings, switch to the Soft Light mode and give that a try. If the Overlay mode at 100 percent seems too faint, switch to Hard Light. You can even copy the image, paste it onto another layer, and apply Hard Light a second time to darn well brand the layered image onto its background (as in the bottom right example of Figure 17-7).

✦ **Darken:** When you select this option, Photoshop applies colors in the active layer only if they are darker than the corresponding composite pixels formed by the underlying layers. Keep in mind that Photoshop compares the brightness levels of pixels in a full-color image on a channel-by-channel basis. So although the red component of a pixel in the active layer in an RGB image may be darker than the red component of the corresponding pixel in the underlying image, the green and blue components may be lighter. Photoshop would then assign the red component of the pixel in the layer, but not the green or blue component, thereby subtracting some red and making the pixel slightly more turquoise. Compare the predictable grayscale example of the Darken overlay mode in Figure 17-8 to its more challenging color counterpart in Color Plate 17-1.

✦ **Lighten:** If you select this option, Photoshop applies colors in the active layer only if they are lighter than the corresponding pixels in the underlying image. Again, Photoshop compares the brightness levels in all channels of a full-color image. Examples of the Lighten overlay mode appear in Figure 17-9 and Color Plate 17-1.

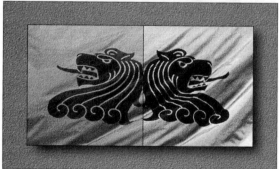

Figure 17-7: The results of the Overlay (top), Soft Light (middle), and Hard Light (bottom) overlay modes as they appear when applied to a single floating banner image (left) and a second layer of the banner image (right).

✦ **Difference:** This overlay mode simply inverts the background image according to the brightness value of the pixels in the active layer. At 100 percent Opacity, white inverts the background absolutely, black inverts it not at all, and all the other brightness values invert it to some degree in between. As a result, the

Figure 17-8: The same active layer subject to the Darken overlay mode. Only those pixels in the selection that are darker than the pixels in the underlying stucco texture remain visible.

Figure 17-9: Our friend the active layer subject to the Lighten overlay mode. Only those pixels in the selection that are lighter than the pixels in the underlying stucco texture remain visible.

stucco shows through the black areas of the lion heads in Figure 17-10, while the light areas of the banner have inverted the texture nearly to black. As with the other overlay modes, Difference applies its changes on a channel-by-channel basis. Therefore, the light green-blue of the banner inverted the contents of the green channel to black (because the yellow stucco contains lots of green) and the blue channel to white (because the stucco contains very little blue), while leaving the contents of the red channel nearly untouched. This elimination of green and the addition of blue results in a magenta shade across the banner.

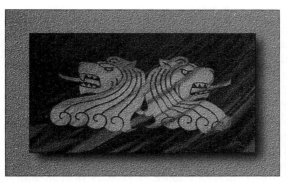

Figure 17-10: When you apply the Difference mode, the white pixels in the active layer invert the composite pixels beneath them, while the black pixels — such as those inside the silhouettes — leave the background untouched.

✦ **Hue:** The Hue mode and the following three overlay modes make use of the HSL color model to mix colors between active layer and underlying image. When you select Hue, Photoshop retains the hue values from the active layer and mixes them with the saturation and luminosity values from the underlying image. An example of this mode appears in the right column of Color Plate 17-1.

We don't include grayscale figures for the Hue, Saturation, Color, and Luminosity overlay modes for the simple reason that those modes produce no effect on grayscale images. Actually, we shouldn't say *no* effect. In fact, they produce the exact same effect as the Normal option. After all, grayscale images don't include hue or saturation values; they only have luminosity.

✦ **Saturation:** When you select this option, Photoshop retains the saturation values from the active layer and mixes them with the hue and luminosity values from the underlying image. This mode rarely results in anything but very subtle effects, as demonstrated in Color Plate 17-1. You'll usually want to apply it in combination with some other overlay mode. For example, after applying some other overlay mode to a layer, you might duplicate the layer and then apply the saturation mode to either boost or downplay the saturation, much like printing a gloss or matte coating over the image.

✦ **Color:** This option combines hue and saturation. Photoshop retains both the hue and saturation values from the active layer and mixes them with the luminosity values from the underlying image. Because the saturation portion of the Color mode has such a slight effect, Color frequently produces an almost identical effect to Hue. In Color Plate 17-1, for instance, the Color example is actually less bright than the Hue example because the colors in the banner image are less saturated than their counterparts in the stucco texture.

✦ **Luminosity:** The Luminosity overlay mode retains the lightness values from the active layer and mixes them with the hue and saturation values from the underlying image. An example of this mode appears in the lower right corner in Color Plate 17-1. As you can see, this is the only example other than Normal that completely eliminated the bump in the stucco texture. This happened because the texture is composed entirely of abrupt brightness-value variations that are smoothed over by the more continuous brightness values in the banner.

Blending layers with supreme control

When you double-click on a layer other than the Background layer, Photoshop displays the Layer Options dialog box shown in Figure 17-11. With the exception of a couple of layer-specific options, this dialog box is identical to the old Composite Controls dialog box available in Photoshop 2.5. In fact, the primary functional difference between this feature and its elder counterpart is that you can no longer apply it to floating selections; it's now applicable exclusively to layers. To Deke, this is Photoshop 3's biggest disappointment. No more quick compositing with the brightness value slider bars; now you have to convert the floater to an independent layer even for the most minute compositing operations.

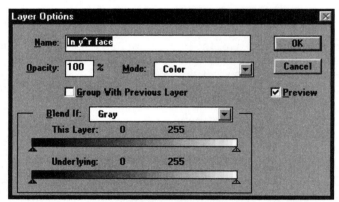

Figure 17-11: When editing a layer, you can access a dialog box of options for selectively mixing the colors in the active layer with the colors in the image below.

But such is life. One is born, one grows up, one learns that even amazingly powerful applications such as Photoshop can wrench one's tiny heart to pieces. (Sniff.) It's a sad law of nature that we live in the kind of world where precious dialog boxes are ripped from the arms of innocents like us just when we've come to rely on them. It's just (sniff), well, it's just not fair.

Having pretty thoroughly summed up our feelings on that subject, let us take this opportunity to announce that the Layer Options dialog box offers the following eight options:

✦ **Name:** Use this option box to change the layer name that appears in the Layers palette. We would have gladly sacrificed this option to be able to once again access the Composite Controls dialog box for floating selections.

✦ **Opacity:** The Opacity option box enables you to specify the translucency of the active layer. This option works identically to the Opacity slider bar in the Layers palette. We would have thrown this option in as well and considered ourselves better off for the bargain.

✦ **Mode:** Here's where you select one of the 14 overlay modes you could already access in the Layers palette pop-up menu. We don't mean to belabor a point, but this duplicate option isn't worth a plugged nickel — whatever that is — compared with the wonders of being able to apply the once-proud Composite Controls command to a free-range floating selection.

✦ **Group With Previous Layer:** Select this option to combine the active layer and the one below it into a clipping group, as discussed in the "Masking groups of layers" section of Chapter 9. We ignored this option in Chapter 9 because it's easier to simply Alt-click on the horizontal line between the two layers to convert them to a clipping group.

✦ **Blend If:** Select a color channel from the Blend If pop-up menu to apply the effects of the slider bars beneath the menu to one color channel independently of the others. When the Gray option is active, as it is by default, your changes affect all color channels equally. (To our knowledge, this is the only instance where Gray means all color channels; elsewhere, Gray means a gray composite, just as Gray ought to mean. Boy, we're starting to get steamed.) Just for the record, the Opacity value and Mode option affect all channels regardless of the color channel you select from Blend If.

✦ **This Layer:** This slider bar lets you exclude ranges of colors according to brightness values in the active layer. When you exclude colors by dragging the black triangle to the right or the white triangle to the left, the colors disappear from view.

✦ **Underlying:** This slider forces colors from the underlying layers to poke through the active layer. Any colors not included in the range set by the black and white triangles cannot be covered and are therefore visible regardless of the colors in the active layer.

✦ **Preview:** Select the Preview check box to continually update the image window every time you adjust a setting.

The slider bars are far too complicated to explain in a bulleted list. To find out more about these options as well as the Blend If pop-up menu, read the following sections.

Tip You can restore all options in the Layer Options dialog box to their original settings by Alt-clicking on the Reset button (the Cancel button changes to Reset when you press the Alt key) or by simply pressing Ctrl-Alt-period.

Color exclusion sliders

Drag the triangles along the This Layer slider bar to abandon those pixels in the active layer whose colors fall within a specified range of brightness values. You can abandon dark pixels by dragging the left slider triangle or light pixels by dragging the right slider triangle. Figure 17-12 shows examples of each. To create the top example, we dragged the left slider bar until the value immediately to the right of the *This Layer* label read 50, thereby deleting pixels whose brightness values were 50 or less. To create the bottom example, we dragged the right slider triangle until the second value read 180, deleting pixels with brightness values of 180 or higher.

Figure 17-12: The results of moving the left This Layer slider triangle to 50 (top) and, after Alt-clicking on the Reset button, dragging the right slider triangle to 180 (bottom).

Drag the triangles along the Underlying slider bar to force pixels in the underlying image to show through if they fall within a specified brightness range. To force dark pixels in the underlying image to show through, drag the left slider triangle; to force light pixels to show through, drag the right slider triangle.

To achieve the effect in the top example in Figure 17-13, we dragged the left slider triangle until the value immediately to the right of the *Underlying* label read 120, forcing the pixels in the stucco pattern that had brightness values of 120 or lower to show through. In the second example, we dragged the right slider triangle until the second value read 180, uncovering pixels at the bright end of the spectrum.

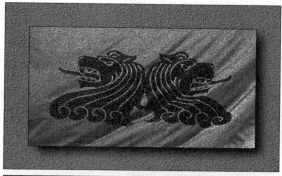

Figure 17-13: The results of moving the left Underlying slider triangle to 120 (top) and then resetting the left triangle back to 0 and moving the right triangle to 180 (bottom).

Fuzziness

The problem with abandoning and forcing colors with the slider bars is that you achieve some pretty harsh color transitions. Both Figures 17-12 and 17-13 bear witness to this fact. Talk about your jagged edges! Luckily, you can soften the color transitions by abandoning and forcing pixels gradually over a fuzziness range, which works much like the Fuzziness value in the Color range dialog box, leaving some pixels opaque and tapering others off into transparency.

To taper off the opacity of pixels in either the active layers or the underlying image, Alt-drag one of the triangles in the appropriate slider bar. The triangle splits into two halves, and the corresponding value above the slider bar splits into two values separated by a slash, as demonstrated in Figure 17-14.

The left triangle half represents the beginning of the fuzziness range — that is, the brightness values at which the pixels begin to fade into or away from view. The right half represents the end of the range — that is, the point at which the pixels are fully visible or invisible.

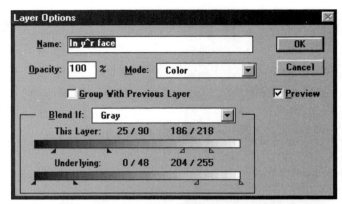

Figure 17-14: Alt-drag a slider triangle to split it in half. You can then specify a fuzziness range across which brightness values will gradually fade into transparency.

Figures 17-15 and 17-16 show softened versions of the effects from Figures 17-12 and 17-13. In the top example of Figure 17-15, for example, we adjusted the range of the left This Layer slider triangle so that the value immediately to the right of the *This Layer* label read 30/70. The result is a much smoother effect than achieved in the top example in Figure 17-12. In the bottom example of Figure 17-15, we changed the range of the right This Layer slider triangle so that the second value read 120/230.

In Figure 17-16, we applied fuzziness ranges with the Underlying slider. In fact, both examples in the figure are the result of applying the same value, 120/180, to opposite Underlying slider triangles. In the top example, all brightness values under 120 gradually extending to values up to 180 show through the active layer. In the second example, all brightness values above 180 gradually extending down to 120 show through. The resulting two images look very much like sand art. (The next thing you know, we'll be showing you how to create string art and black velvet Elvises.)

Color channel options

The options in the Blend If pop-up menu are applicable exclusively to the settings you apply using the This Layer and Underlying slider bars. When you work with a grayscale image, the Blend If pop-up menu offers one option only — Black — meaning that the Blend If option has no effect on grayscale editing. However, when you work in the RGB, CMYK, or Lab mode, the Layer Options dialog box enables you to abandon and force ranges of pixels independently within each color channel.

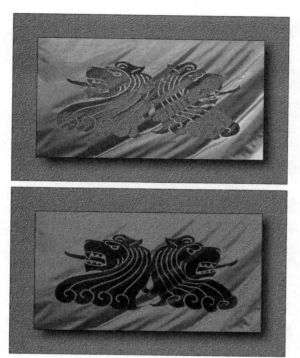

Figure 17-15: The results of adjusting the fuzziness range of the left This Layer slider triangle to 30/70 (top) and that of the right This Layer slider triangle to 120/230 (bottom).

To do so, select a color channel from the Blend If pop-up menu and then set the slider triangles as desired. Each time you select a different Blend If option, the slider triangles retract to the positions at which you last set them for that color channel. Color Plate 17-2 demonstrates the effect of manipulating the This Layer and Underlying slider triangles independently for the red, green, and blue color channels.

Channel Operation Commands

Image⇨Apply Image and Image⇨Calculations provide access to Photoshop's *channel operations,* which composite one or more channels with others according to predefined mathematical calculations. Once found in the Image⇨Calculate submenu, channel operations have been hailed by some Photoshop users as one of the program's most powerful capabilities. We emphatically disagree. Though the commands have been improved in Photoshop 3, they remain less powerful and less flexible than their options in the Layers palette.

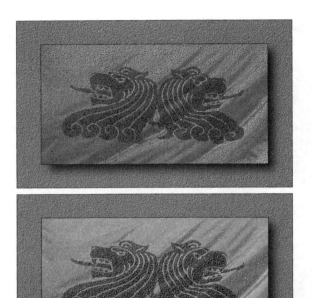

Figure 17-16: The results of adjusting the fuzziness
range of both the left (top) and right (bottom)
Underlying slider triangles to 120/180.

But before we dive into the whys, wherefores, and what-have-yous, let us explain how
the commands work. The Apply Image and Calculations commands composite one or
two images in their entirety using 9 of the 14 overlay modes discussed earlier plus 2
additional modes, Add and Subtract. In a nutshell, the commands automate the
process of selecting one image, dragging and dropping it onto another, and using the
overlay mode and Opacity settings in the Layers palette to mix the images. (When
you're compositing a single image onto itself, the process is like floating the image and
then using the Layers palette to mix the floater and underlying original.)

The Apply Image command takes an open image and composites it onto the foreground image (or takes the foreground image and composites it onto itself). You can
apply the command to either the full-color image or one or more of the individual
channels inside the image. The Calculations command, on the other hand, works on
individual channels only. It takes a channel from one image, mixes it with a channel
from another (or the same) image, and puts the result inside an open image or in a
new image window.

What is the purpose of these commands? Their primary advantage over earlier compositing methods is that they enable you to access and composite the contents of individual color channels without a lot of selecting, copying and pasting, cloning, floating, and layering.

But it's the commands' secondary advantage that has led to their romanticizing. Because you apply changes to an image using dialog box options, it's an easy matter to keep track of the way in which you achieve a particular special effect, should you choose to do so. You choose this command, select this option, enter this value, and so on. All you have to do is scribble down a few notes or, if you're sufficiently organized, use a macro utility such as QuicKeys or Tempo to record your actions. This way, you can try out an effect on a low-resolution image and then later repeat the operations on a high-resolution image, thus speeding up the experimentation process.

The mythic status of channel operations began when folks started sharing their techniques. If you can track and replicate your techniques, you can pass them along to your friends and neighbors. In a relatively small period of time, folks were creating all sorts of unusual effects by replaying a few channel operations.

This is all very well and good. Threads of information weave the fabric of an educated and productive nation. We're all for it. The only problem is that although repeating someone else's technique is easy stuff, coming up with one of your own is both difficult and limiting. Simply put, channel operations do not lend themselves particularly well to the all-important task of experimentation. Here are a few areas in which they go awry:

✦ **No scaling or cropping:** If you want to mix two images using Apply Image or Calculations, both images must be exactly the same size, down to the pixel. Unlike PixelPaint Professional 3, Photoshop is unable to scale or crop images to match each other. As a result, nearly all channel-operation techniques begin by compositing one image onto itself; this way, there's no chance of the images being different sizes.

✦ **No placement control:** One image is centered onto the other. If you want to offset one image from the other, you have to offset the image in advance, either by selecting the image and nudging it with the arrow keys or by applying Filter⇨Other⇨Offset. This is fine for creating drop shadows and other effects that involve mixing a single image with itself, but it makes it nearly impossible to position two different images with respect to each other with any degree of accuracy.

✦ **No brightness value control:** Unlike the Layer Options command, Apply Image and Calculations don't let you exclude colors from an image. The only way to prevent a channel operation from affecting every single pixel in an image is to draw a selection outline or include a mask channel.

✦ **No tweaking the results:** If you don't like the result of a channel operation, you have to undo the operation and try it again. Meanwhile, when compositing floating selections or independent layers, you can experiment with slightly different overlay modes and Opacity settings till the cows come home (though what those truant cows are up to is anyone's guess). The good news is that the Apply Image and Calculations commands now provide previewing options. By selecting the Preview option in either dialog box, you can see how an effect will look in the image window. This essential capability makes channel operations more usable, but it doesn't quite make up for the remaining problems mentioned in the previous list.

So when should you use channel operations? When you want to mix specific channels in an image or combine masks and layer transparencies to create exact selection outlines, the Calculations command is a handy — though complex — solution (as explained in "The Calculations command" section later in this chapter). Meanwhile, the Apply Image command is good for compositing images in different color models, such as RGB and Lab (as we explain in the "Mixing images in different color modes" section).

But otherwise, use Apply Image and Calculations only when you want to mix entire images or selected portions of those images or when performing some cool technique that a friend of yours passed along. But keep in mind that even in these last two cases, you may be better off using the controls offered by the Layers palette. (If you're interested, the following chapter compares a standard compositing operation performed first using channel operations and then with Layers controls.)

In Photoshop 2.5, channel operations offered the advantage of speed. Copying a very high-resolution image from one document and pasting it into another can take a long time because it involves transferring data to the Clipboard. By contrast, channel operations merely write data directly from one image to another and, therefore, involve no use of the Clipboard whatsoever. But now that you can assign floating images to layers and drag and drop selections between image windows — both operations that likewise bypass the Clipboard — the speed advantage of channel operations has dried up. It's not that channel operations have slowed down, mind you, it's just that other compositing operations have come up to speed.

Robert Channel Operations are often referred to as CHOPS (CHannel OPerationS). It seems to have been channel wizard and Photoshop maven Kai Krause who coined the phrase — yes, *the* Kai Krause of Kai's Power Tools from MetaTools (formerly HSC Software). Kai has done a series called Kai's Power Tips, several of which deal with CHOPS. They're readily available online (CompuServe, America Online, the Internet) and definitely worth the read.

Apply Image command

Channel operations work by taking one or more channels from an image, called the *source,* and duplicating them to another image, called the *target.* When you use the Apply Image command, the foreground image is always the target, and you can select only one source image. Photoshop then takes the source and target, mixes them together, and puts the result in the target image. Therefore, the target image is the only image that the command actually changes. The source image remains unaffected.

When you choose Image⇨Apply Image, Photoshop displays the dialog box shown in Figure 17-17. Notice that you can select from a pop-up menu of images to specify the Source, but the Target item — listed just above the Blending box — is fixed. This is the active layer in the foreground image.

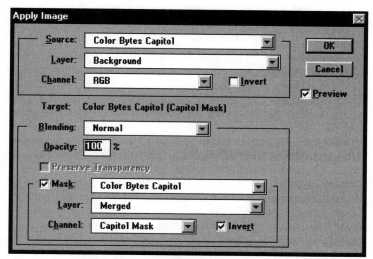

Figure 17-17: The Apply Image command lets you mix one source image with a target image and make the result the new target.

If this sounds a little dense, just think of it this way: The source image is the floating selection and the target is the underlying original. Meanwhile, the Blending options are the overlay modes pop-up menu and Opacity slider in the Layers palette.

Using the Apply Image command is a five-step process. You can always simply choose the command and hope for the best, but you'll get the most use out of it if you do the following:

Steps: Applying the Apply Image command

1. First, open the two images that you want to mix. If you want to mix the image with itself to create some effect, just open the one image.

2. Make sure that the two images are exactly the same size, down to the pixel. Use the crop tool and Image Size command as necessary. (You don't have to worry about this step when mixing an image with itself because the image is always the same size as itself — except, of course, when it's having a bad hair day.)

3. Inside the target image, switch to the channel and layer that you want to edit. If you want to edit all channels, press Ctrl-0 to remain in the composite view.

Tip

When you're editing a single channel, we strongly advise you to display all channels on-screen. For example, after pressing Ctrl-1 to switch to the RGB channel, click in front of the RGB item in the Channels palette to display the eyeball icon and show all channels. Only one channel is active, but all are visible. This way, you can see how your edits inside the Apply Image dialog box will affect the entire image, not just the one channel.

4. Select the portion of the target image that you want to edit. If you want to affect the entire image, don't select anything.

5. Choose Image⇨Apply Image and have at it.

Obviously, that last step is a little more difficult than it sounds. That's why we've put together the following list to explain how all those options in the Apply Image dialog box work:

✦ **Source:** The Source pop-up menu contains the name of the foreground image as well as any other images that are both open and exactly the same size as the foreground image. If the image you want to merge is not available, you must not have been paying much attention to step 2. Press Ctrl-period to cancel, resize and crop as needed, choose Image⇨Apply Image, and try again.

✦ **Layer:** This pop-up menu lists all layers in the selected source image. If the image doesn't have any layers, Background is your only option. Otherwise, select the layer that contains the prospective source image. Select Merged to mix all visible layers in the source image with the target image.

✦ **Channel:** Select the channels that you want to mix from this pop-up menu. Both composite views and individual color and mask channels are included. Keep in mind that you'll be mixing these channels with the channels that you made available in the target image before choosing the command. For example, if the target image is an RGB image shown in the full-color composite view, and you choose RGB from the Channel pop-up menu in the Apply Image dialog box, Photoshop mixes the red, green, and blue channels in the source image with the corresponding red, green, and blue channels in the target image. However, if you switched to the red channel before choosing Apply Image and then selected the RGB option, the program mixes a composite grayscale version of the RGB source image with the red channel in the target and leaves the other target channels unaffected. Conversely, if you are working in the composite view in the target image and you select red from the Channel pop-up menu, the red channel from the source image is mixed in with all three channels in the target. We could come up with about 50 other combinations, but hopefully you get the idea.

✦ **Selection, Transparency, and Layer Mask:** If a portion of the source image is selected, the pop-up menu offers a Selection option, which enables you to apply the selection outline as if it were a grayscale image, just like a selection viewed in the quick mask mode. If you selected a specific layer from the Layer pop-up menu, you'll find a Transparency option. If the layer includes its own mask, as explained in the "Creating layer-specific masks" section of Chapter 9, a Layer Mask option also appears. These options also create grayscale images in which the opaque portions of the layer are represented as white and the transparent portions are black. None of the three options are particularly useful when you work in the composite view of the target image; you'll usually want to apply the Selection, Transparency, or Layer Mask option only to a single channel, as described in "The Calculations command" section toward the end of this chapter. (For an exception, see the upcoming tip.)

✦ **Invert:** Select this check box to invert the contents of the source image before compositing it with the target image. This option allows you to experiment with different effects. The last example in Color Plate 17-3, for example, shows one use for the Invert check box. We inverted the *b* channel before compositing it with the RGB image to create an early dawn effect.

✦ **Target:** You can't change this item. It merely shows which image, which channels, and which layers are being affected by the command.

✦ **Blending:** This pop-up menu offers access to nine of the overlay modes discussed in the "The 14 universal overlay modes" section earlier in this chapter. The Dissolve, Hue, Saturation, Color, and Luminosity options are missing. (Darken and Lighten have inexplicably been renamed Darker and Lighter, though they work just the same.) Two additional options, Add and Subtract, are discussed in the "Add and Subtract" section later in this chapter.

✦ **Opacity:** You know how this one works. The source image works just like a floating selection, so the Opacity setting lets you set the translucency of the source.

✦ **Preserve Transparency:** When you're editing a layer in the target image — that is, you activated a specific layer before choosing Image⇨Apply Image — the Preserve Transparency check box becomes available. Select it to protect transparent portions of the layer from any compositing, much as if the transparent portions were not selected and are therefore masked.

✦ **Mask:** Select this option to mask off a portion of the source image. We already mentioned that you can specify the exact portion of the target image you want to edit by selecting that portion before choosing the Apply Image command. But you can also control which portion of the source image is composited on top of the target through the use of a mask. When you select the Mask check box, three new pop-up menus and an Invert check box appear at the bottom of the Apply Image dialog box. For complete information on these options, see the upcoming "Compositing with a mask" section.

✦ **Result:** If you press the Alt key when choosing Image⇨Apply Image, Photoshop appends one additional option — the Result pop-up menu — at the end of the Apply Image dialog box. This option lets you send the result of the operation to a separate image window, layer, or channel. This can be useful if you don't want to upset the contents of the foreground window, if you want to send the result to a separate layer for further compositing, or if you just want to edit a mask. (This last operation is generally made easier by the Calculations command, as described in the "Combining masks" section near the end of this chapter.)

One of our favorite reasons to Alt-choose Apply Image, however, is to transfer selection outlines from one image to another of equal size. Inside the image to which you want to transfer the selection, Alt-choose Apply Image. (Be sure that nothing in the image is already selected, or the Result pop-up menu will not appear.) Select the identically sized image that contains the selection from the Source pop-up menu, choose Selection from the Channel pop-up menu, and choose Normal from the Blending menu. Then choose Selection from the Result pop-up menu and press Enter. Then you can say, *Welcome, O Mighty Selection Outline,* to your brand-new image.

Mixing images in different color modes

Throughout our laborious explanations of all those options in the Apply Image dialog box, we've been eagerly waiting to share with you the command's one truly unique capability. Image⇨Apply Image is the only way to composite RGB and Lab images while leaving them set to their separate color modes. For example, you could mix the lightness channel from the Lab image with the red channel from the RGB image, the *a* channel with the green channel, and the *b* channel with the blue channel. By contrast, you'd have to composite the channels one at a time if there were no Apply Image command. (If you were to simply drag and drop a Lab image into an RGB image, Photoshop would automatically convert the image to the RGB color space, which results in a very different effect.)

To help make things a little more clear, Color Plate 17-3 shows four examples of an image composited onto itself using the Hard Light overlay mode (which you select from the Blending pop-up menu, as we'll cover shortly). The first example shows the result of selecting the RGB image as both source and target. As always, this exaggerates the colors in the image and enhances contrast, but retains the same basic color composition as before.

The other examples in the color plate show what happened when we duplicated the image by choosing Image⇨Duplicate, converted the duplicate to the Lab mode (Mode⇨Lab Color), and then composited the Lab duplicate with the RGB original. To do this, we switched to the RGB image, chose Image⇨Apply Image, and selected the Lab image from the Source pop-up menu. In the top right example, we chose Lab from the Channel pop-up menu to blend each of the Lab channels with one of the RGB channels — lightness with red, and so on. Though we stuck with the Hard Light overlay mode, you can see that the effect is very different. In the bottom left example, we chose Lightness from the Channel pop-up menu, which mixed the lightness channel with all three RGB channels. And in the bottom right image, we chose *b* from the Channel pop-up menu and selected the Invert check box, which inverted the *b* channel before applying it.

Note You cannot mix an entire CMYK image with an RGB or Lab image, because the images contain different numbers of channels. In other words, although you can mix individual channels from CMYK, RGB, and Lab images, you can't intermix the channels — cyan with red, magenta with green, and so on. In other words, CMYK does not appear as an option inside the Channel pop-up menu when you edit an RGB image. In other words . . . oh, nuts, that's enough of that.

Compositing with a mask

We said that we'd go into a little more depth about the Mask option in this section, and here we are being true to our word. (We really think that we deserve some kind of badge for this.) All the Mask option does is provide a method for you to import only a selected portion of the source image into the target image. Select the Mask check box and choose the image that contains the mask from the pop-up menu on the immediate right. As with the Source pop-up menu, the Mask menu lists only those images that are open and happen to be the exact same size as the target image. If necessary, select the layer on which the mask appears from the Layer pop-up menu. Then select the specific mask channel from the final pop-up menu. This doesn't have to be a mask channel; you can use any color channel as a mask.

After you select all the necessary options, the mask works like so: Where the mask is white, the source image shows through and mixes in with the target image, just as if it were a selected portion of the floating image. Where the mask is black, the source image is absent, as if you had Ctrl-dragged around that portion of the floating selection with the lasso or some other selection tool, leaving the target entirely protected. Gray values in the mask mix the source and target with progressive emphasis on the target as the grays darken.

If you prefer to swap the masked and unmasked areas of the source image, select the Invert check box at the bottom of the dialog box. Now, where the mask is black, you see the source image; where the mask is white, you don't.

The first example in Color Plate 17-4 shows a mask that we used to select the Capitol dome while protecting the sky. We prepared this mask and put it in a separate mask channel. In the other examples in the color plate, we again composited the RGB and Lab versions of the image — as in the previous section — using various overlay modes. No matter how dramatically the Apply Image command affected the dome, the sky remained unscathed, thanks to the mask. If the Mask option had not been turned on, for example, the top right image in Color Plate 17-4 would have looked exactly like the corresponding image in Color Plate 17-3.

You can even use a selection outline or layer as a mask. If you select some portion of the source image before switching to the target image and choosing Image➪Apply Image, you can access the selection by choosing — what else? — Selection from the Channel pop-up menu at the very bottom of the dialog box. Those pixels from the source image that fall inside the selection remain visible; those that do not are transparent. Use the Invert check box to inverse the selection outline. To use the boundaries of a layer selected from the Layer pop-up menu as a mask, choose the Transparency option from the Channel menu. Where the layer is opaque, the source image is opaque (assuming that the Opacity option is set to 100 percent, of course); where the layer is transparent, so too is the source image.

Add and Subtract

The Add and Subtract overlay modes found in the Apply Image dialog box (and also in the Calculations dialog box) work a bit like the Custom filter discussed in Chapter 15. However, instead of multiplying brightness values by matrix numbers and calculating a sum, as the Custom filter does, these modes add and subtract the brightness values of pixels in different channels.

The Add option adds the brightness value of each pixel in the source image to that of its corresponding pixel in the target image. The Subtract option takes the brightness value of each pixel in the target image and subtracts the brightness value of its corresponding pixel in the source image. When you select either Add or Subtract, the Apply Image dialog box offers two additional option boxes, Scale and Offset. Photoshop divides the sum or difference of the Add or Subtract mode by the Scale value (from 1.000 to 2.000) and then adds the Offset value (from negative to positive 255).

If equations will help, here's the equation for the Add overlay mode:

```
Resulting brightness value = (Target + Source) ÷ Scale + Offset
```

And here's the equation for the Subtract mode:

```
Resulting brightness value = (Target - Source) ÷ Scale + Offset
```

If equations only confuse you, just remember this: The Add option results in a destination image that is lighter than either source; the Subtract option results in a destination image that is darker than either source. If you want to darken the image further, raise the Scale value. To darken each pixel in the target image by a constant amount, which is useful when applying the Add option, enter a negative Offset value. If you want to lighten each pixel, as when applying the Subtract option, enter a positive Offset value.

Add command

The best way to demonstrate how these commands work is to offer an example. To create the effects shown in Figures 17-19 and 17-20, we began with the two images shown in Figure 17-18. The first image, Capitol Gray, is merely a grayscale composite of the image from Color Plate 5-1. The second image, Capitol Blur, took a little more work. We duplicated the original RGB image, converted it to the CMYK color mode, and jettisoned all but the yellow channel because that channel does a good job of separating building and sky. We then applied the Minimum filter to enlarge the dark regions of the image by a radius of 3 pixels and applied the Gaussian Blur filter with a radius of 6.0 pixels. We next chose Image⇨Adjust⇨Levels (Ctrl-L) and changed the lighter of the two Output Levels values to 140, thus uniformly darkening the image. (The Add and Subtract commands work best when neither target nor source contains large areas of white.) Finally, just for the sheer heck of it, we drew in some clouds and lightning bolts with the airbrush and smudge tools.

 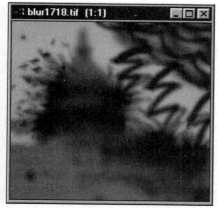

Figure 17-18: The target (left) and source (right) used to create the effects shown in Figures 17-19 and 17-20.

After switching to the Capitol Gray image and choosing Image⇨Apply Image, we selected the Capitol Blur image from the Source pop-up menu. We were working with flat, grayscale images, so we didn't have to worry about the Layer and Channel options. We selected the Add option from the Blending pop-up menu and accepted the default Scale and Offset values of 1 and 0, respectively, to achieve the first example in Figure 17-19. Because the skies in both the target and source images were medium gray, they added up to white in the resulting image. The black areas in the source image helped prevent the colors inside the building from becoming overly light.

Unfortunately, the image we created was a bit washed out. To improve the quality and detail of the image, we changed the Scale value to 1.2 to slightly downplay the brightness values and entered an Offset value of –60 to darken the colors uniformly. The result of this operation is the more satisfactory image shown in the second example of Figure 17-19.

Figure 17-19: Two applications of the Add overlay mode on the images from Figure 17-18, one subject to Scale and Offset values of 1 and 0 (left) and the other subject to values of 1.2 and −60 (right).

Subtract command

To create the first example in Figure 17-20, we selected the Subtract option from the Blending pop-up menu, once again accepting the default Scale and Offset values of 1 and 0, respectively. This time, the sky turns pitch black because we subtracted the medium gray of the Capitol Blur image from the medium gray of the Capitol Gray image, leaving no brightness value at all. The building, however, remains a sparkling white because most of that area in the Capitol Blur image is black. Subtracting black from a color is like subtracting 0 from a number — it leaves the value unchanged.

Figure 17-20: Two applications of the Subtract command on the images from Figure 17-18, one subject to Scale and Offset values of 1 and 0 (left) and the other subject to values of 1.2 and 60 (right).

The image seemed overly dark, so we lightened it by raising the Scale and Offset values. To create the second image in Figure 17-20, we upped the Scale value to 1.2, just as in the second Add example, which actually darkened the image slightly. Then we changed the Offset value to 60, thus adding 60 points of brightness value to each pixel. This second image is more likely to survive reproduction with all detail intact.

The difference between Subtract and Difference

We've already shown examples of how the Difference mode inverts one image using the brightness values in another. But the math behind Difference is actually very similar to that behind Subtract. Like Subtract, the Difference option subtracts the brightness values in the source image from those in the target image. However, instead of treating negative values as black, as Subtract does, or allowing you to compensate for overly dark colors with the Scale and Offset options, Difference changes all calculations to positive values.

If the brightness value of a pixel in the target image is 20 and the brightness value of the corresponding pixel in the source image is 65, the Difference option performs the following equation: $20 - 65 = -35$. It then takes the *absolute value* of -35 (or, in layman's terms, hacks off the minus sign) to achieve a brightness value of 35. Pretty easy stuff, huh?

Any divergence between the Subtract and Difference options becomes more noticeable on repeated applications. The top row of Figure 17-21, for example, shows the effect of applying the Subtract mode (left) versus the Difference mode (right). As before, we applied these commands to the Capitol Gray and Capitol Blur images from Figure 17-18.

As far as perceptible differences between the two images are concerned, the pixels that make up the bushes in the lower left corner of each image and those of the clouds along each image's right side are on the rebound in the Difference example. In effect, they became so dark that they are again lightening up. But that's about the extent of it.

In the second row of Figure 17-21, we applied the Subtract and Difference options a second time. Using the top left example in the figure as the target and the Capitol Blur image as the source, we achieved two very different results. When calculating the colors of the pixels in the sky, the Difference overlay mode apparently encountered sufficiently low negative values that removing the minus signs left the sky ablaze with light. Everything dark is light again.

Just for fun, the left column of examples in Color Plate 17-5 features full-color versions of the right image from Figure 17-19 and the bottom two images in Figure 17-21. In each case, we used the full-color Capitol Dome image from Color Plate 5-1 instead of the Capitol Gray image as the target image and used the grayscale Capitol Blur as the source. As if that weren't enough fun already, the right column of examples in Color Plate 17-5 shows the same images after swapping the red and blue color channels in each. The results look like something out of *The War of the Worlds*. The only difference is that instead of being scary, they look like just the thing to convince Earthlings that Martian rule wouldn't be so bad. *You guys are attacking the Senate? Oh, that's different. Why sure, count us in. Maybe then we'll get some gun control around here.*

Figure 17-21: Repeated applications of the Subtract (left column) and Difference (right column) commands.

The Calculations command

Although its options are nearly identical, the Calculations command performs a slightly different function than Apply Image. Rather than compositing a source image on top of the current target image, Image⇨Calculations combines two source channels and puts the result in a target channel. You can use a single image for both sources, a source and the target, or all three. The target doesn't have to be the foreground image (although Photoshop previews the effect in the foreground image window). And the target can even be a new image. But the biggest difference is that instead of affecting entire full-color images, the Calculations command affects individual color channels only. Only one channel changes as a result of this command.

Choosing Image⇨Calculations displays the dialog box shown in Figure 17-22. Rather than explaining this dialog box option by option — we'd just end up wasting 35 pages and repeating ourselves every other sentence — we'll attack the topic in a little less-structured fashion.

When you arrive inside the dialog box, you select your source images from the Source 1 and Source 2 pop-up menus. As with Apply Image, the images have to be exactly the same size. You can composite individual layers using the Layer menus. Select the channels you want to mix together from the Channel options. In place of the full-color options — RGB, Lab, CMYK — each Channel menu offers a Gray option, which represents the grayscale composite of all channels in an image.

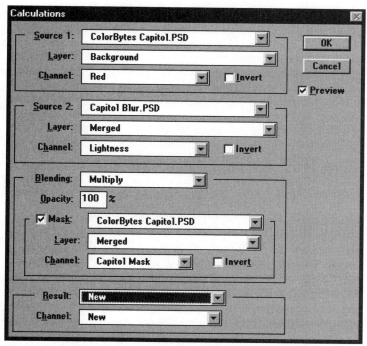

Figure 17-22: Use the Calculations command to mix two source channels and place them inside a new or existing target channel.

The Blending pop-up menu offers the same 11 overlay modes — including Add and Subtract — that are found in the Apply Image dialog box. But it's important to keep in mind how the Calculations dialog box organizes the source images when working with overlay modes. The Source 1 image is equivalent to the source when using the Apply Image command (or the floating selection when compositing conventionally); the Source 2 image is equivalent to the target (or the underlying original). Therefore, choosing the Normal overlay mode displays the Source 1 image. The Subtract command subtracts the Source 1 image from the Source 2 image.

Half of the overlay modes performs identically, regardless of which of the two images is Source 1 and which is Source 2. The other half — including Normal, Overlay, Soft Light, and Hard Light — produces different results based on the image you assign to each spot. But as long as you keep in mind that Source 1 is the floater — hey, it's at the top of the dialog box, right? — you should be okay.

Tip The only one that throws us off is Subtract, because we see Source 1 at the top of the dialog box and naturally assume that Photoshop will subtract Source 2, which is underneath it. Unfortunately, this is exactly opposite to the way it really works. If you find yourself similarly confused and set up the equation backward, you can reverse it by selecting both Invert options. Source 2 minus Source 1 results in the exact same effect as an inverted Source 1 minus an inverted Source 2. (After all, the equation *(255 – Source 1) – (255 – Source 2)*, which represents an inverted Source 1 minus an inverted Source 2, simplifies down to *Source 2 – Source 1*. If math isn't your strong point, don't worry. We were just showing our work.)

As you can in the Apply Image dialog box, you can specify a mask using the Mask options in the Calculations dialog box. The difference here is that the mask applies to the first source image and protects the second one. So where the mask is white, the two sources mix together normally. Where the mask is black, you see the second source image only.

The Result options determine the target for the composited channels. If you select New from the Result pop-up menu, as in Figure 17-22, Photoshop creates a new grayscale image. Alternatively, you can stick the result of the composited channels in any channel inside any image that is the same size as the source images.

Converting layers to selections

As described for the Apply Image command, Selection, Transparency, and Layer Mask may be available as options from any of the Channels pop-up menus. But here they have more purpose. You can composite layer masks to form selection outlines, selection outlines to form masks, and all sorts of other pragmatic combinations.

Figure 17-23 shows the multilayered-layered image from Figure 9-19, minus a few layers. In fact, we've hidden all but two — the wavy face at the top and the closeup in the lower right corner. Now suppose that we want to select the exact area occupied by these two layers and apply that selection to the Background layer. We could screw around with the magic wand tool or try to create a mask, but both of those options would be big time-wasters. We could use the Ctrl-Alt-T trick described in the "Modify

Figure 17-23: We used the Calculations command to convert the area occupied by the wavy face and close-up face layers (left) into a selection outline. We then hid the layers and used the selection outline to edit the Background layer (right).

ing the contents of a layer" section of Chapter 8, but that only works for one layer, not two. The better solution is to use Image⇨Calculations. The following steps describe how this intricate operation works.

Steps: Selecting the area occupied by two layers

1. After choosing the Calculations command, we selected our layered faces image from the Source 1, Source 2, and Result pop-up menus. All our layers resided in this image, and we wanted to apply the selection outline to this image, so this is the only image that the Calculations command needed to worry about.

2. We next selected the wavy face layer from the first Layer pop-up menu and the close-up face from the second. To consider the space occupied by the layers (as opposed to the contents of the layers), we chose Transparency from both of the two top Channel pop-up menus.

3. Now that we had assembled the layers we wanted to use, the question became how to combine them. The Screen overlay mode was the answer. Because the opaque areas of the layer are white and the transparent areas black, we wanted the white to show through the black, which is a job for Screen. Therefore, we chose Screen from the Blending pop-up menu. (Although we could have also used Lighter or Add in this specific example, Screen is the more flexible choice, as we explain in the next section.) The grayscale representation of the transparent areas was previewed in the foreground window.

4. Finally, we needed to convert the grayscale representation to a selection outline. To accomplish this, we chose the Selection option from the Channel pop-up menu at the bottom of the dialog box. This told Photoshop to convert the mask into a selection outline.

5. Pressing Enter initiated the conversion. We then switched to the Background layers, Alt-clicked on the eyeball in front of the Background item to hide the wavy face and close-up layers, and used the selection outline to edit the image. The right image in Figure 17-23 shows the result of a simple application of the Invert command (Ctrl-I).

Ah, but that's just where the fun begins. Unlike the Apply Image command, which only offers a couple of unique options that you might want to use every blue moon, Calculations is a practical tool for combining selection outlines and mixing masks. The next section tells it all.

Combining masks

Figure 17-24 shows how the Calculations command sees selected areas. Whether you're working with masks, selection outlines, layer transparencies, or layer masks, the Calculations command sees the area as a grayscale image. So in Figure 17-24, the white areas are selected, or opaque, and the black areas are deselected, or transparent.

If these were traditional selection outlines, we could add one to the other by pressing the Shift key, subtract one from the other by pressing the Control key, and retain only the intersecting area by pressing Control and Shift. (On the off chance this doesn't sound familiar, leave this chapter immediately and check out Chapter 8.) The problem is, these techniques only apply when you're creating selection outlines. In our case, the outlines already exist. So the best way to combine them is to use Calculations.

Assuming that we've chosen Image➪Calculations and selected the images using the Source 1 and Source 2 options, the only remaining step is to select the proper overlay mode from the Blending pop-up menu. Screen, Multiply, and Difference are the best solutions. The top row in Figure 17-25 shows the common methods for combining selection outlines. In the first example, we added the two together using the Screen mode, just as in the previous steps. In fact, Screening masks and adding selection outlines are exact equivalents. To subtract the Source 1 selection from Source 2, we inverted the former (by selecting the Invert check box in the Source 1 area) and applied the Multiply overlay mode. To find the intersection of the two masks, we simply applied Multiply without inverting.

But the Calculations command doesn't stop at the standard three — add, subtract, and intersect. The bottom row of Figure 17-25 shows three methods of combining selection outlines that are not possible using keyboard shortcuts. For example, if we invert the Source 1 mask and combine it with the Screen mode, we add the inverse of the elliptical selection and add it to the polygonal one. The Difference mode adds the portion of the elliptical selection that doesn't intersect the polygonal one and sub-

Source 1   Source 2

Figure 17-24: Two selections expressed as grayscale images (a.k.a. masks). The left image is the first source, and the right image is the second.

tracts the intersection. And inverting Source 1 and then applying Difference retains the intersection, subtracts the portion of the polygonal selection that is not intersected, and inverts the elliptical selection where it does not intersect. These may not be options you use every day, but they are extremely powerful if you can manage to wrap your brain around them.

Depending on how well you've been keeping up with this discussion, you may be asking yourself, *Why not apply Lighter or Add in place of Screen, or Darker or Subtract in place of Multiply?* The reason becomes evident when you combine two soft selections. Suppose that we blurred the Source 2 mask to give it a feathered edge. Figure 17-26 shows the results of combining the newly blurred polygonal mask with the elliptical mask using a series of overlay modes. In the top row, we added the two selection outlines together using the Lighter, Add, and Screen modes. Lighter results in harsh corner transitions, while Add cuts off the interior edges. Only Screen does it just right. The bottom row of the figure shows the results of subtracting the elliptical mask from the polygonal one by occasionally inverting the elliptical mask and applying Darker, Subtract, and Multiply. Again, Darker results in sharp corners. The Subtract mode eliminates the need to invert the elliptical marquee, but it brings the black area too far into the blurred edges, resulting in an overly abrupt interior cusp. Multiply ensures that all transitions remain smooth as silk.

The Screen and Multiply modes mix colors together. Lighter and Darker simply settle on the color of one source image or the other — no mixing occurs — hence the harsh transitions. Add and Subtract rely on overly simplistic arithmetic equations — as we explained earlier, they really just add and subtract brightness values — which result in steep fall-off and build-up rates; in other words, there are cliffs of color transition where there ought to be rolling hills. Both Screen and Multiply soften the transitions using variations on color averaging that make colors incrementally lighter or darker.

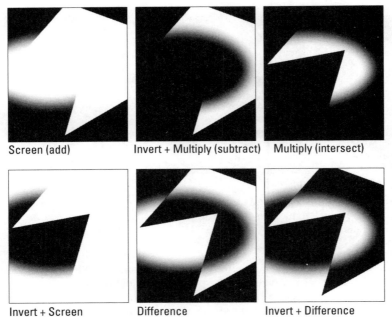

Screen (add)   Invert + Multiply (subtract)   Multiply (intersect)

Invert + Screen   Difference   Invert + Difference

Figure 17-25: Starting with the masks shown in Figure 17-25, we combined them in traditional (top row) and nontraditional (bottom row) ways using the Calculations command.

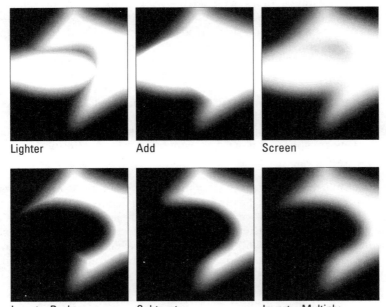

Lighter   Add   Screen

Invert + Darker   Subtract   Invert + Multiply

Figure 17-26: When adding softened selections (top row) and subtracting them (bottom row), the Screen and Multiply modes provide the most even and continuous transitions.

Compositing on the March

Putting Compositing to Work

Now that we've explained all the nitty-gritty details about layering, overlay modes, and the Apply Image and Calculations commands, it's time to demonstrate a few practical applications. Obviously, we can't show you every possible approach to compositing, but we can run through a few inspirational and even unusual scenarios and leave you to discover the hundred zillion or so others on your own. (Come on, if this book gets much fatter, we'll have to call it *Encyclopedia Photoshopia* and start hawking it door to door.)

Creating an embossing effect with Apply Image

In the preceding chapter, we alluded to the fact that you can perform most compositing effects without the aid of Apply Image and Calculations. The following two sets of steps offer proof of that statement. The first set explains a typical method for burning embossed text into a background image using the Apply Image command. The second set shows you how you can accomplish the same thing with a greater degree of flexibility by relying exclusively on masks and floating selections.

Steps: Creating an embossed text effect, method #1

1. We started off with a tropical image shown in Figure 18-1. This image is mostly scenery with just a hint of foreground information here and there — such as that vacationer in the lower right corner — making it ideally suited to some textual abuse.

Figure 18-1: This alluring beach image was shot by our buddy Russell McDougal while he was cruising about in the Caribbean. Although he was really selfish not to take us along, the image is ideally suited as a background for large text.

2. As we mentioned in Chapter 12, it's always a good idea to create complex text in the quick mask mode or in a separate mask channel so that you can kern and embellish the text without harming the original image. We used a mask channel because doing so allowed us to save the text with the image. After we clicked on the new channel icon at the bottom of the Channels palette and named the channel *Logo,* the image window filled with black. Photoshop always fills new mask channels with black, which suited our purposes to a T. We wanted to create white text against a black background so that we could later screen it against the beach image.

3. We pressed D and then X to make the foreground color white and the background color black. We then used the type tool to enter the word *Tropical* in 300-point bold condensed letters. We kerned the letters close together by selecting them one at a time with the lasso and nudging them with the arrow keys. To make the characters overlap, we chose the Screen option from the overlay modes pop-up

menu in the Layers palette. This option retained the white area and made the black ridge around each letter invisible. We then extended the stem of the *p* and drew in the palm fronds with the pen tool. Figure 18-2 shows the finished result. Notice that we created the logo specifically so that it wouldn't cover the vacationer in the foreground.

Figure 18-2: Our completed logo as it appears in the Logo mask channel when the mask is viewed by itself (top) and in combination with the beach image (bottom).

4. To create the embossing effect, we first duplicated our mask channel to protect our painstaking logo and retain it for later use. We accomplished this by dragging the mask channel item in the Channels palette onto the new channel icon. We then double-clicked on the new mask item in the palette and changed its name from *Logo copy* to *Embossed Logo*.

5. Because this was a grayscale mask channel, the standard Emboss command was the most straightforward tool. We chose Filter➪Stylize➪Emboss and entered an Angle value of 135 degrees, a Height of 10 pixels, and an Amount of 100 percent. The only important value was the Height, for which we entered the maximum value. If you're working along with these steps, you can change the Angle and Amount values to anything you like.

Tip

If a Height of 10 isn't sufficient for your purposes, you can use the patented Kai Krause technique for creating a custom embossing effect as follows: Select the entire channel, float it, invert it, change the Opacity to 50 percent, and nudge it using the arrow keys. The distance of the nudge determines the amount of the emboss, so you can create as radical an effect as you can stand. Just be sure to fill in the gaps around the edges of the image using 50 percent gray. You'll also want to center the effect. For example, if you scoot the text 10 pixels up and 10 to the right, you should then select the entire channel and scoot it 5 pixels back down and 5 to the left.

(If the text violates the edge of the image, the best solution is to send the floated text to its own layer. Then you can nudge the layered text 5 pixels up and to the right and nudge the underlying text 5 pixels down and to the left. This way, the text won't appear cut off around the edges.)

6. We blurred the embossing effect by applying Filter➪Blur➪Gaussian Blur with a Radius of 3.0. Figure 18-3 shows the result, which includes black rims along the tops of the letters, white rims along the bottoms, and medium gray everywhere else.

7. Now for the actual channel operations. After switching back to the full-color composite view of the beach by pressing Ctrl-0, we chose Image➪Apply Image to display the Apply Image dialog box. We wanted to accomplish two things here: We wanted to apply the white logo against the beach without affecting the area outside the logo, and we wanted to burn in the embossing effect. To accomplish the first objective, we chose the Logo mask channel from the Channel pop-up menu. Then we chose the Screen option from the Blending pop-up menu and changed the Opacity value to 40 percent. As you can see in the first example of Figure 18-4, this mixed in the white text while making the black background invisible. We pressed Enter to apply the effect.

8. To emboss the text, we turned right around and chose the Apply Image command again. We chose the Embossed Logo mask channel from the Channel pop-up menu and the Hard Light option from the Blending menu. Then we entered 100 percent into the Opacity option box. The black portions of the embossing effect darkened the image, the white portions lightened it, and the medium gray portions produced no effect.

Figure 18-3: After duplicating the logo to a second mask channel called *Embossed Logo*, we applied the Emboss filter with the maximum Height value of 10 pixels and applied the Gaussian Blur filter with a Radius of 3.

9. The problem is that the embossing effect got outside the character outlines and leaked all over the scenery. Still inside the Apply Image dialog box, we remedied the situation with a mask. We selected the Mask check box and then selected the Logo mask channel from the lower Channel pop-up menu. Where the mask was white — inside the letters — the embossing showed through. This kept the effect from spilling out onto the beach, as demonstrated in the last example in Figure 18-4. We pressed Enter to apply the effect.

10. To make the text stand out just a little more, we chose the Apply Image command a third time. We chose the Logo channel from the Channel pop-up menu, chose Multiply from the Blending menu, lowered the Opacity to 20 percent, and deselected the Mask check box. The black background around the logo slightly darkened the beach image without affecting the embossed text.

The bottom example of Figure 18-4 shows the result of the steps. Color Plate 18-1 shows a full-color version of Figure 18-4. The text has a soft, organic appearance and appears naturally lit, almost as if the light were bouncing off the beach and hitting the letters.

Figure 18-4: With the Apply Image command, we composited the Logo channel onto the beach image using the Screen overlay mode at 40 percent Opacity (top). Then, in two additional passes of the command, we applied the Embossed Logo channel using the Hard Light mode with the Logo channel as a mask and composited the Logo channel again using the Multiply mode and an Opacity of 20 percent.

We didn't have to stop here, of course. We could have kept on compositing those same two mask channels until our hair fell out and our hands became arthritic. The first example of Color Plate 18-2, for example, shows what happened when we chose Apply Image a fourth time, selected the Embossed Logo from the Channel pop-up menu, chose Overlay from the Blending pop-up menu, changed the Opacity value to 100 percent, and again selected the Mask check box and assigned the Logo channel as the mask. But, this time, we inverted both the Embossed Logo and the Logo mask (by selecting both Invert check boxes). Inverting the Embossed Logo channel switched the light and dark colors, resulting in highlights above and to the left of the letters and shadows below and to the right. Inverting the mask protected the letters instead of the area outside the letters.

To create the second image in Color Plate 18-2, we merely inverted the logo. We could have Alt-clicked on the Logo channel name in the Channels palette to convert the white letters to a selection outline and then pressed Ctrl-I. Or we could have chosen Apply Image for the fifth time, selected Logo from the first Channel pop-up menu and Difference from the Blending menu, and deselected the Mask check box. (Actually, it doesn't matter if the mask is off or on; it just isn't needed, so we would turn it off.)

Creating a better effect via floating selections

The Apply Image command is certainly powerful, and if you made it through that last exercise, you may very well be busily playing with other options and testing out additional ideas. For many users, channel operations become addictive, but we prefer floating selections. You can still take advantage of specially constructed mask channels, as in the previous steps, but rather than flopping them all over each other as with Apply Image, you can convert the masks into selection outlines and apply them discretely. You can even introduce manual retouching and filtering effects, features that the Apply Image command fails to integrate.

With this premise in mind, the following steps show an embossing effect created entirely without the Apply Image or Calculations commands. No doubt somebody somewhere could come up with a convoluted series of channel operations that enable you to accomplish the same thing. But our method provides real-time feedback and a degree of flexibility absolutely unmatched by Apply Image.

Steps: Creating an embossed text effect, method #2

1. After creating the Logo and Embossed Logo masks described in Steps 1 through 6 of the preceding section, we suddenly had the notion that we might be able to avoid the Apply Image command and open up a whole world of additional options. To kick off our newfound philosophy, we returned to the full-color composite view of the beach image by pressing Ctrl-0. Then we Alt-clicked on the Logo channel in the Channels palette to convert the character outlines to a selection.

2. To add some texture to the letters, we chose Filter⇨Noise⇨Add Noise, entered 32 for the Amount, and selected the Uniform radio button. After pressing Enter, we pressed Ctrl-F to reapply the filter.

3. Next, we decided to create a refraction effect using the Ripple filter. After choosing Filter⇨Distort⇨Ripple, we maxed out the Amount value to 999, selected Medium from the Size radio buttons, and pressed Enter.

4. Now that the basic texture for the logo looked the way we wanted it, we were ready to lighten it. We pressed Ctrl-J to float the logo, D and then X to make white the foreground color, and Alt-Del to fill the text with white. Then we pressed the M key to activate a selection tool and the 4 key to change the Opacity setting to 40 percent. The result of all this activity appears in the first example of Color Plate 18-3. The effect is subtle, but it will become more apparent by the time we finish the steps. By working with a selection outline instead of a channel operation, we were able to accomplish, in a series of quick and familiar keystrokes — Ctrl-J, D, X, Alt-Del, M, 4 — what required a bit of manual labor back in Step 7 of the previous section.

5. We wanted more control over the highlights and shadows that we would apply to the letters, so we decided to create a couple of additional mask channels. In preparation, we dragged the Emboss Logo item onto the new channel icon in the Channels palette to duplicate it. We double-clicked on the new channel name and changed it from *Emboss Logo copy* to *Highlights*. To create the second new mask channel, we again dragged the Emboss Logo item onto the new channel icon, double-clicked on it, and changed its name to *Shadows*.

6. Returning to the Highlights channel (Ctrl-6), we pressed Ctrl-L to bring up the Levels dialog box. We then changed the first Input Levels value to 128 to send all grays to black and leave only the highlights white. We then pressed Enter to accept our changes.

7. To clean up the highlights so that they fell inside the logo only, we Alt-clicked on the Logo channel name in the Channels palette to convert the logo to a selection outline. We chose Select⇨Inverse to select the area surrounding the letters and pressed the Delete key to fill the selection with black (because black was still the background color). The result appears in the first example of Figure 18-5.

8. We pressed Ctrl-D to deselect the image, followed by Ctrl-7 to switch to the Shadows channel and Ctrl-L to display the Levels dialog box. This time, we wanted to make the shadows white and everything else black. So we changed the third Input Levels value to 128, which made the shadows black and everything else white. To invert this image, we changed the first Output Levels value to 255 and the second one to 0. Then we pressed Enter to exit the dialog box.

9. We could no more permit the shadows to exceed the boundaries of the logo than the highlights, so we again Alt-clicked on the Logo channel to convert it to a selection outline, chose Select⇨Inverse to select the area outside the logo, and pressed the Delete key to fill the selection with the background color, black.

10. Ctrl-0 took us back to the full-color view. We Alt-clicked on the Highlights item in the Channels palette to select the areas we wanted to highlight. We then filled the selection outlines with white by pressing Alt-Del. (White is still the foreground color.) The result was a white highlight around the right and bottom edges of the letters.

Figure 18-5: The Highlights (top) and Shadows (bottom) channels after we finished adjusting their contents with the Levels command and cleaning them up with the help of the Logo mask.

11. We wanted to temper the highlight a little by tracing a shadow along its edge. So we floated the selection (Ctrl-J) and nudged it two pixels up and two pixels to the left, away from the edge of the letters and toward their centers. Then we pressed D to make black the foreground color and pressed Alt-Del, filling the selection with black.

12. Now for the shadows. We Alt-clicked on the Shadow item in the Channels palette to convert the mask to a selection outline. We then pressed Alt-Del to fill the selection with black, creating a shadow along the top and left sides of the letters. As in Step 11, we wanted to temper the shadow by tracing it with a highlight, so we floated the selection, nudged it two pixels down and two to the right, pressed the X key to make white the foreground color, and pressed Alt-Del to fill the selection with white.

   The first example in Figure 18-6 shows how the text looked up to this point. You can see how the outlines of the letters are double-traced, once with white and once with black. The bottom and right sides are traced first with white and then with black. The top and left sides are traced first with black and then with white. The effect is one of a raised edge running around the letters.

13. See, now you know why we normally skip that step. It's very distracting, besides which it makes the other steps look very boring by comparison. Anyway, as you may recall, we had just finished tracing an edge around the perimeter of our logo. After that, we figured that we might as well add some highlights and shadows around the letters to offset them from the image. This meant retrieving the contents of the Emboss Logo channel and compositing it with the image, which meant that we had to copy and paste.

   Therefore, we used Ctrl-5 to go to the Emboss Logo channel. We then Alt-clicked on the Logo channel name in the Channels palette to select the letters and chose Select⇔Inverse to switch the selection to the area around the letters. This represented the portion of the channel that we wanted to copy, so we pressed Ctrl-C.

14. After pressing Ctrl-0 to return to the RGB view, we used Ctrl-V to paste the embossed image copied in the preceding step. We then switched to the Layers panel and chose the Hard Light option from the overlay modes pop-up menu to mix floating selection and underlying image. The resulting highlights and shadows appear in the bottom example of Figure 18-6.

15. To emphasize the logo for once and for all, we chose Select⇔Inverse to return the selection outline to the logo. Then we pressed Ctrl-I to invert the logo and give its rippled texture a marblelike appearance. The finished image appears at the bottom of Color Plate 18-3.

Figure 18-6: The result of applying the raised-edge effect described in Steps 10 through 12 (top), and the same image after compositing the Emboss Logo channel using the Hard Light mode (bottom).

Sure, this section involved more steps than the preceding one, but let's face it, we accomplished a heck of a lot more this time as well. The edges in Color Plate 18-3 are cleaner than their counterparts in Color Plate 18-2, and it was easy to add filtering details that would have taken all kinds of preparation to pull off using the Apply Image command.

In truth, you'll probably have the best success if you mix channel operations with floating and layering techniques as you work. For example, we could have avoided the copying and pasting in Steps 13 and 14 by choosing the Apply Image command, selecting the Embossed Logo channel from the Channel pop-up menu, using an inverted version of the Logo channel as a mask, and selecting Hard Light from the Blending pop-up menu. This technique eliminates any delay that may occur as a result of using Clipboard functions on a very large image.

So, the moral is *Use whatever compositing method makes you most comfortable.* But don't think that using the Apply Image and Calculations commands somehow miraculously transforms you into a power user. As the previous steps demonstrate, floating and filtering can prove much more capable than Apply Image, and when you add layers into the recipe, you get a combination of compositing options that can't be beat.

More Compositing Madness

Just as Mozart might juggle several different melodies and harmonies at once, you can juggle layers upon layers of images, each filtered differently and mixed differently with the images below it.

The hierarchy of overlay modes

The most direct method for juggling multiple images is *sandwiching*. By this we mean placing a heavily filtered version of an image between two originals. This technique is based on the principle that many overlay modes — Normal, Overlay, Soft Light, Hard Light, Hue, Saturation, Color, and Luminosity — change depending on which of two images is on top. For example, we created a document comprising two layers. One layer contained the plain Capitol dome image; the other contained a filtered version. Following the guidelines in the "Creating a metallic coating" section of Chapter 14, we applied the Gaussian Blur filter with a Radius of 3.0, chose Filter⟹Stylize⟹Find Edges, and used the Unsharp Mask filter to bring out the detail, using an Amount value of 500 percent and a Radius of 10.0. The plain and filtered images appear in the first two examples of Figure 18-7.

Obviously, if you use the Normal overlay mode, whichever image is on top is the one that you see. However, if you change the Opacity, you reveal the underlying image. At 50 percent Opacity, it doesn't matter which image is on top. The color of every pair of pixels in both images is merely averaged. So an inverse relationship exists. If the filtered image is on top, an Opacity setting of 25 percent produces the same effect as if you reversed the order of the images and changed the Opacity to 75 percent.

The Normal overlay mode, then, is its own opposite. Multiply, Screen, Darken, and Lighten work the same regardless of who's on top. But a few of the others have their opposites in fellow overlay modes. Color, for example, is the opposite of Luminosity. So positioning the filtered image on top and selecting Luminosity produces the exact same effect as positioning the plain image on top and selecting Color.

Figure 18-7: The Overlay mode is the exact opposite of the Hard Light mode, as demonstrated here. When the filtered image was on top, we achieved the same effect using the Overlay mode (top row) as we did when the plain dome was on top and we used the Hard Light mode (bottom row).

That was easy, but here's one we bet you didn't know: Hard Light is the opposite of Overlay. It's true. Positioning the filtered image on top and choosing Hard Light produces an identical effect to positioning the plain image on top and choosing Overlay, and vice versa. In fact, this very vice versa is demonstrated in Figure 18-7. In the top example, the plain dome is situated on the Background layer and the filtered image is on Layer 1. The top right image shows the result of choosing Overlay from the overlay modes pop-up menu in the Layers palette. In the bottom row, we've reversed the order. Now the filtered image is on the Background layer and the plain dome is on Layer 1. To achieve the same effect as before, we had to choose Hard Light. Therefore, if the Overlay option reinforces the brightness values in an underlying image using colors from a floating image, the opposite must be true for Hard Light, which uses the underlying image to reinforce the floating one.

If Color is the opposite of Luminosity, and Overlay is the opposite of Hard Light, why not just provide one of each — that is, Color and Overlay, or Luminosity and Hard Light? One reason is flexibility. It's nice to be able to pull off the same effect regardless of how you organize your layers. But the bigger reason is that all four overlay modes offer their own unique effects when you adjust the Opacity slider bar. As you already know, any Opacity value less than 100 percent favors the underlying image. Therefore, you achieve very different effects when applying the Overlay mode at 50 percent Opacity than when applying the Hard Light mode at the same setting. Figure 18-8 shows examples of various Opacity settings applied in combination with each overlay mode. Keep in mind that the right two examples in Figure 18-7 showed the modes as they appear at 100 percent.

Sandwiching a filtered image

When you sandwich a filtered image between two originals, you can dissipate the effect of the filtered image without lowering the Opacity setting and, at the same time, achieve a variety of different effects. You at once mix the floating filtered image with the underlying original and mix a floating original with the underlying filtered image. Back in Photoshop 2.5, you could only achieve these sorts of effects on a very limited basis using channel operations. Layers give you the flexibility.

Color Plate 18-4 shows several different examples of the sandwiching technique. The first column of examples shows what happened when we positioned the metallic filtered image on Layer 1 and the original dome on the Background layer. No sandwiching has yet occurred. Each example in the column is labeled according to the overlay mode we used.

To create the second column, we dragged the Background item onto the new layer icon at the bottom of the Layers palette to create a duplicate layer (which Photoshop automatically names *Background Copy*). We then dragged the layer above the other two to make it the top layer in the document. The examples in the column show the results of applying different overlay modes to the Background Copy layer while leaving Layer 1 unchanged. For example, the first example in the second column is the result of setting both Layer 1 and Background Copy to the Hard Light mode. In the second example, we set Layer 1 to the Difference mode and Background Copy to the Color mode.

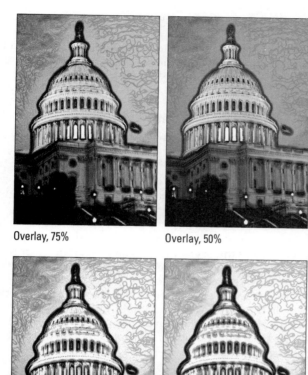

Overlay, 75%   Overlay, 50%   Overlay, 25%

Hard Light, 75%   Hard Light, 50%   Hard Light, 25%

Figure 18-8: The effects of progressively smaller Opacity settings on the Overlay and Hard Light overlay modes. As in Figure 18-7, the filtered image is on top in the top row, and the plain dome is on top in the bottom row.

In the third column, we duplicated the Background Copy layer to create Background Copy 2, and made that the top layer. Then we chose the overlay modes listed below each example. The bottom right example is a special case. After applying the Difference mode, we recognized some major stuff happening in the image, but it was way too dark. After flattening the layers by choosing the Flatten Image command from the Layers palette menu, we applied Image⇨Adjust⇨Auto Levels. Except for this last image, all the examples can be achieved without upsetting the layers.

Adding effects to the sandwich

In addition to sandwiching an effect, you can composite multiple effects. Color Plate 18-5 shows examples of different effects and overlay modes applied to the top layer of our document, Background Copy 2. To make things crystal clear, we changed the name of this layer to Effects. Just to recap

✦ **Background:** The bottom layer contains the plain dome image.

✦ **Layer 1:** The first layer contains the metallic dome effect.

✦ **Background Copy:** The next layer up contains a second copy of the plain dome image.

✦ **Effects:** Yet another copy of the plain dome image subject to the various effects we explain in this section.

To create the first column of Color Plate 18-5, all we did was invert the Effects layer by pressing Ctrl-I. We then assigned each of the overlay modes labeled in the color plate. The Difference mode combined with an inverted image — as in the second example — usually produces interesting effects. Note that the Layer 1 and Background Copy layers are still assigned the same overlay modes we selected in the preceding section (and labeled in Color Plate 18-4). In the top image, for example, both Layer 1 and Background Copy are assigned the Hard Light mode. In the second image, Layer 1 is assigned the Difference mode and Background Copy is assigned Color. In the final example, Layer 1 gets Hue, and Background Copy gets Hard Light.

In the second column of Color Plate 18-5, we again inverted the Effects layer to return it to its original appearance and then applied the Ripple filter with an Amount value of 999 and Medium selected. We then used the Hue/Saturation command to shift the Hue –90 degrees, making the sky green and the dome purple, just as it is on Mars. Then we applied the overlay modes listed below each example.

In the final column, we pasted in a new version of the dome and applied the Add Noise filter with an Amount value of 100 and with Gaussian selected. In the first example, we achieved a grainy effect using the Overlay mode. In the next example, it's Christmas at the Capitol with the Screen mode. And in the bottom example, we chose the Dissolve mode and set the Opacity to 20 percent. Rather than making the noise pixels translucent, this made 80 percent of the pixels invisible and the other 20 percent opaque.

Keep in mind that we came up with the results shown in Color Plates 18-4 and 18-5 purely through experimentation. In fact, those figures show only a representative handful of the hundreds of combinations we put together, most of which were too ugly to print. Just consider these as examples of the kinds of effects you can achieve if you take the time to experiment.

Digital Art Meets Traditional Art

You may be here because, Brave Soul, you're reading this book straight through. Or because you took my advice at the end of Chapter 4 to head here — remember, that was where I walked you through an experiment with carrot orange and sky blue to show you that you can't trust electronic color models. While you could turn straight to "Of Carrot Orange and Lizard Crimson" later in this chapter, I'd advise you to keep reading from here until you get to it. This chapter is carefully structured around the idea that algorithms are fine, but if you're going to do real art, you've got to tell Photoshop (or Fractal Design Painter — I include a section on this wonderful complement to Photoshop later) what to do rather than abandon yourself to them. Some parts, especially the next one, may seem to digress. Not so — they're all part of a larger plan. Put differently, I'm going somewhere with this and not just grazing.

For whatever reason you're here — you've just left the McClelland Zone. Although I like to think my benevolent presence has influenced the previous eighteen chapters, they're based on Deke's proven principles. That's how it should be. Now, Deke's gone and Robert's here. This chapter has no counterpart in *Macworld Photoshop 3 Bible*, although the principles apply to The Other Platform (will a Mac person purchase a Windows book? Only time will tell . . .). It represents the fruits not only of my Photoshop experience, but also my experience in traditional artist's media. If you've experience in that latter category, you'll find some familiar information put to new uses — and maybe some new information as well. If you don't have that experience, I just may be able to persuade you to get it.

Of Two Highly Relevant Anecdotes

These two anecdotes will illustrate my philosophy of art and Photoshop. Appendix A will tell you why I think philosophy is so important for any computer endeavor, and you may want to take a quick look at its start. But rather than start theorizing now, I want to tell two short tales and discuss why they matter.

Anecdote the First

This anecdote one got me thinking about doing this chapter in the first place. Some time ago, on CompuServe's ADOBEAPPS forum, a member posted a message (I remember no names, I remember no genders — this to protect the innocent and guilty) seeking a method to do rows of buttons with beveled edges. Why the person wanted to do that I didn't ask — after all, I only work there. But the query concluded with a striking request which I paraphrase: "I don't want some 14-step technique — I want an algorithm."

In short, the person didn't want to do anything more than click a menu item or two to get those buttons. I really don't think that's possible (although some of Alien Skin's Black Box filters might get close in certain cases). But I don't think that's desirable, either. Because it's a canned effect, your beveled buttons are going to look like everyone else's. Worse, that look is limited by what the programmer put into the algorithm. I don't knock programmers — without them, we'd have no Photoshop. But programmers are programmers and artists are artists, and the intersection of the two is usually a null set. And no algorithm can have the variability (the happy-accident quality) that is the stock-in-trade of creative artists.

Let me put it another way. Take extruded type . . . please! (If you've read Chapter 12, you know what I really think about it.) Now, take CorelDRAW — any version. With a couple of mouse clicks, you've got instant extrusions. In my other online capacity as sysop for Adobe Illustrator for Windows, this has often been a sore point, because Illustrator doesn't have such an algorithm. You can get extruded type, of course, but you've got to plan the overall look and build it up. Why should you bother? Quite simply, for all the wizardry that Corel has put into its algorithms (and it was the very first version of CorelDRAW that got me into computer graphics, so I've a very warm spot in my heart for it) — the result will look like an extrusion by Corel. The Illustrator extrusion will look like an extrusion by *you*.

In short, if you rely on algorithms — no matter how sophisticated — your work will look like you used algorithms. Like any of a host of similar productions. Now this may be sufficient for a one-shot presentation or quick-and-dirty newsletter. But it just isn't art.

You may say "I was part of the ruler-and-straight-line-brigade in art class. Couldn't draw then, still can't. Algorithms have set me free." Good point. You're ready for another anecdote.

Anecdote the Second

This anecdote has nothing to do directly with Photoshop, but it's still from fine arts. It's about the release of the Walt Disney movie *Fantasia*. Yup — I know that remembering its release dates me — I also remember what I was doing in late November 1963. You'll recall that was the movie that had animations for various pieces of classical music, from Bach's *Toccata and Fugue in D Minor* to Beethoven's *Pastoral Symphony* to Schubert's *Ave Maria*. Many classical musicians snobbed (and continue to snob) the movie. They claim that the orchestration of the Bach piece is bad enough, but in Stokowski's version it entirely destroys the work. The Schubert piece was originally a song for soloist and piano; the snobs say that the lush choral setting in the movie totally destroys that as well.

They claim wrong. *Fantasia* brought pleasure to many people who had never heard classical music before. Some in the audience sought more of it. But even the lives and souls of those who didn't seek more classical music were the better for seeing *Fantasia*. While I've no plans to appear in Carnegie Hall anytime soon, I can pull Mozart concerti and Chopin etudes out of my piano (though not Balakirev's *Islamey* — everyone has their limitations). When I choose to listen to Bach, it's going to be keyboard rather than orchestrated. But if someone hums the fugue theme from the Stokowski orchestration, that is the most important step of all.

Now to Photoshop — or, for that matter, any computer graphics program. As I've mentioned before, computer graphics programs got me first into computer art and then into traditional art (details follow). But even if I hadn't picked up a brush, computer graphics gave me the joy of entering a world I thought forever closed to me. So if you're happy with Photoshop and take pleasure in what you do — I am 100 percent behind you. But you should consider doing more — acquiring "the power to be your best." After all, if you were totally complacent about Photoshop, you'd not have bought this book, would you?

Of Balls and Spheres and Lenses

I'm going to get you into all this by talking about balls. You know — those little circular thingies that seem to propagate by parthenogenesis all over World Wide Web pages on the Internet. So you'll surely know what I'm talking about — and even if you think Internet is some new fancy webbing for a tennis court. But there are more practical reasons, too. I'm trying to ease you into artistic matters. Balls mean circles, and what could be less-menacing than a circle, even if you think you can't draw? Then there's the artistic tradition. Generations of art students have learned the finer points of drawing by doing spheres. Because the form is so simple, it's easy to concentrate on the important points — how to suggest volume by using shading (building up tone, as it's called in the trade). Finally, so we can concentrate on the fundamentals of why algorithms aren't always your best friends, I'm doing all of this in grays. So let's start looking.

First look: a real sphere and an artist's sphere

Take a look at the photograph of the billiard ball in Figure 19-1 and then compare it with the rendition of a sphere in Figure 19-2.

Figure 19-1: Photograph of a real-life sphere — in this case, a volleyball.

Figure 19-2: "The Sphere" by artist Michael Davis. Michael rendered this in Photoshop with drawing tools instead of algorithms.

In this latter figure, which artist Michael Davis named "The Sphere" and rendered in Photoshop especially for this chapter, you'll notice some differences (obviously, Michael didn't work from the photograph, but that's beside the point). Look at the six to nine o'clock area of Michael's sphere and you'll see a lighter area — that's the sphere's ambient lighting reflected from the surface back onto the sphere. Look for that in the photograph; you can just barely see it. Aha! Here's a fundamental artistic principle. Art is about illusion — representing what's there and can be seen (and painting what's there and can't be seen) to give the proper effect. Michael knew that reflected light was there, even though it wasn't very visible in his model (shine a strong light on a white tennis ball and you'll see what I mean). But he emphasized the reflected light because lighting and shadows are a fundamental way to suggest volume, his emphasis makes the sphere seem even more, well, spheroid. Now compare the shadows that each casts. Again, you'll see that Michael has made explicit what the photograph hints. He did it for the same reason. Michael has heightened and emphasized what he observed to produce a realistic spheroid, even though it's not precisely what the photograph shows. It's true: the camera never lies — that's its major problem.

Second look: the uses of algorithms

Michael did his sphere freehand in Photoshop — not an algorithm in sight. But suppose you're not Michael. What will you do? What *will* you do (as Karl Malden used to intone in American Express commercials). Well, while you're up, get me an algorithm. But be careful!

The first algorithm: channels

You've met Channel Operations (CHOPS) in Chapter 17. And it's possible, using them, to get something that's at least in the same galaxy as what Michael did — although perhaps not much closer. I've done it in Figure 19-3, and it pretty much represents the limits of CHOPS.

Everything's there, but something's not quite right. The sphere's shadow isn't entirely realistic and the reflected light is a bit phony. That's the problem with CHOPS that Deke complained about — if the final effect is off, you have to go all the way back to the start. I did that several times just to get this far, which is really the point of diminishing returns. What you need is artistic variability, which no algorithm (even with percentages and degrees of tolerance) can ever give you; they're still algorithms. But suppose you're no fan of CHOPS. How about a filter and its algorithms?

The second algorithm: Kai's Power Tools

KPT, as they're called, are justly celebrated as a cornucopia of special effects. I'll come back to them later in this chapter but for the moment, I want to focus on two: the Glass Lens Filter (familiar from version 1.0 onwards) and the Spheroid Designer (new to current version 3.0).

Figure 19-3: A sphere rendered in Photoshop using Channel Operations.

Wait a minute! This is about spheres — what does a Glass Lens Filter have to do with it? I've seen substantial arguments online about why that filter doesn't produce a glass lens effect but, rather, a concrete sphere. Argument wasted; the documentation is quite clear that the filter takes a selection and *bumps* or *spherizes* it. Why they call it Glass Lens Filter (actually, three separate filters in KPT 1.0 and 2.0 were rolled together in version 3.0, but you don't need to worry about the differences here) I honestly don't know — but they've said it's to produce spheres, and so it shall be!

Figure 19-4 shows a sphere rendered with the KPT 3.0 Glass Lens Filter. Notice several things. There's no suggestion of the surface supporting the sphere, or the shadow that the sphere will cast on that surface. The reflected light we saw in Michael Davis' sphere (Figure 19-2) is absent. Instead, the filter has suggested volume by a crushing amount of black, which contrasts with the background (obviously, this would be a no-go with a black background). Worse, even if we accept those failings, there's no way in the real world you could get that white-to-gray circular gradient surrounding the white highlight.

Figure 19-4: Sphere rendered by the
KPT 3 Glass Lens Filter

The KPT 3 Glass Lens filter offers far more options than the earlier incarnations, but I'm not sure they really answer the objections I've just raised. Previous versions relied on certain keyboard combinations, while Version 3 has an actual interface that allows much more. But what do you get? For all the new possibilities, we're not much closer to a real artistic sphere. See Figure 19-5.

But then there's the Spheroid Designer, new to KPT 3. It offers a more than generous variety of options. You can control ambient lighting and shadows and textures. You can generate a quantity of spheres all at once, and you can pick the ways they'll be arranged. There are many preset combinations as well. (See Figure 19-6.)

But I still complain about the problems of rendering an artistic sphere, whether one large one (Figure 19-7) or a whole collection of smaller ones (Figure 19-8).

It must sound like I hate KPT's sphere filters. Far from it — I love them, and I've used them with delight throughout multiple betas (and shipping products) since version one. But notice the verb — I *use them*. They don't *use me*. I'm not just playing with semantics here. And the KPT designers seem aware of it because here's a copy/paste straight out of the KPT help file on Spheroid Designer: *Note that your sphere is not a true sphere and has no back side, so your lights don't travel around a virtual sphere.* Well, of course, we're trying to represent three dimensions in two. The problem is that the authors apparently decided that the limitations meant it was pointless to try to suggest the lighting. Folks, it may not have a back side that you can see, but everyone knows there is a back side there. When you see a photograph of Bill Clinton, do you think there's no back side? (Republicans, please don't answer this question.) In short, what the authors have said about the program bears out what I've said before and will be repeating in the colors section of this chapter: The intersection of programmers and artists is a null set. Artists must bend the program to their will. If they don't, you've got computer art in the worst sense of the word: Art that came straight from algorithms and *way cool, dude!* effects. This stuff clutters the archives of any online service you'd care to name.

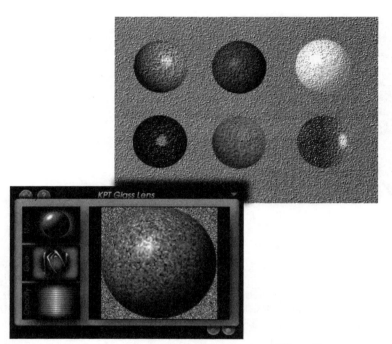

Figure 19-5: The interface for the KPT 3 Glass Lens Filter offers many more controls.

Figure 19-6: KPT 3's Spheroid Designer offers an enormous number of options.

Figure 19-7: One large sphere rendered in Spheroid Designer.

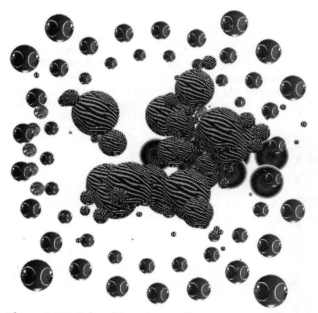

Figure 19-8: Spheroid Designer offers many possibilities for collections of spheres.

That's not the only reason why it's not KPT's fault. Programmers use ray-tracing algorithms. Obviously, I'm not privy to how they've customized those algorithms here. But many ray-tracing algorithms are freely available, both in the mathematical equations and the actual source code for ray-tracing programs. Here's what I've found: The algorithms are incapable of duplicating an artist's judgment for the fine points of rendering a sphere. There's no allowance for ambient light reflected back onto the sphere (allowance is made for ambient light and reflected light), no allowance for producing a shadow that reflects reality (there are shadows allowed). In short, the algorithms from ray tracing are, again, a programmer's fantasy of what's going on. The KPT algorithms represent an enormous improvement on traditional ray-tracing algorithms. But they're still algorithms.

Algorithms are great. But if you depend on the programmer's vision, your work will look like that vision. You have to use your vision to bend the programmer's work to your will. Kai's Power Tools and other ray-tracing tools can be a wonderful first step. But the longest journey begins with a single step. The other steps are up to you. For the spheroids we've been looking at, you can add your own shadows and use levels and curves to approach what Michael Davis did. I've done it — but I could have done it all freehand from scratch, whether in Photoshop or in traditional artistic media, in less time.

Back to the Glass Lens

I promised you I'd get back here. We've seen how Glass Lens Filter is a misnomer, that because the KPT people never intended it to produce a glass lens effect. But can you get a real glass lens effect? Sure and you don't need a single algorithm. (See Figure 19-9.) I used nothing more than the circular selection marquee and the airbrush tool.

Figure 19-9: A glass lens (or dew drop) rendered in Photoshop — nary an algorithm.

I simply applied Rob Howard's technique from his gouache in the Photoshop book (see next section for more on this must-have book). Did it in about ten minutes, too (even less time in gouache). There's another technique, adapted by Rob from his gouache method, for Photoshop users in an excellent Photoshop book by Sherry London — see the end of this chapter for details.

And finally . . .

I want to return to where we started. Sometimes an algorithm can be very helpful. Sometimes it can be a positive hindrance. I've given you examples of both cases. The common denominator is that you have to think like an artist: creatively. Think beyond what the programmers have given you.

As the ultimate example, I present you with Figure 19-10. I should tell you that it's never passed through a computer — I insisted that IDG Books' production people strip it in conventionally.

Note Everything else in this book has gone through a computer, both as it was being composed, and for final output to film, from which the printing plates are made. But not Figure 19-10 — the film (from which the plate will come) was made directly from my original, and then cut/pasted (stripped) into the final film composite from which the printing plates are produced.

Figure 19-10: Using the traditional techniques of stippling and negative space to render a sphere in traditional media.

Note What I've done is use pen and ink dots (stippling) to suggest a sphere and its light and shadows. I used only dots, so there's not a single line in the place. I've used the dotting to suggest what artists call *negative space*; by rendering the space around the object, the object is rendered. It's one of the most expressive traditional techniques I know.

There are those who sometimes refer to either what I've just done, or Rob Howard's techniques as "the old fashioned way." I strongly protest. The computer geek idea that latest is greatest and old is bad just doesn't apply to real art, where oldest is often greatest (have you ever looked at the Parthenon?). Put differently, Rembrandt did all of his paintings "the old fashioned way" without any apparent distress.

Of course, you may have had it with balls and spheroids long before now. Consider what Deke said in his review of KPT for *Macworld*: "How many variations on sphere art does the world need?"

Of Carrot Orange and Lizard Crimson

These headings keep getting stranger and stranger — remember, I said "Deke's gone, Robert's here." As always, though, there's a method to the apparent madness. *Carrot Orange* refers to one of the colors I used in the little experiment at the end of Chapter 4 (read or reread that section to refresh your memory for what follows). *Lizard Crimson* is shorthand for a wonderful traditional reddish-purple art color Alizarin Crimson — both its fans (I'm one) and its detractors (I'm not one) often call it this name. Each color, and a related color, will get a separate section here. In both cases, I'm aiming to drive home what we said in Chapter 4 — you can't trust electronic color algorithms to give you a colorist's control, but you can use those algorithms, albeit in ways not foreseen by the programmers, to gain that colorist's control.

Note   I've made a command decision here. Although Deke and IDG Books generously allowed me some space in the Color Plates section for this chapter, I've decided not to use it. Instead, the attached CD-ROM contains a series of files for all of this section. Here's my reasoning. Good as the Color Plates are, I just don't trust CMYK four-color printing, except in *very* expensive art books (and this book doesn't claim to be that). It's true that monitors, video cards, and video drivers are variable. But I'm convinced you'll get, for my purposes, more accurate color representations. So load the CD-ROM, bring up those files as I call for them, and let's get to color!

Carrot Orange and Sky Blue

If you've done my color exercise at the end of Chapter 4, bring it up now. If you haven't, I urge you to do it now. You can save your results and then proceed here. Or, if you're in a rush, bring up CARROT.JPG from the Chapter 19 directory of the CD-ROM. At the top you'll see the two pure colors. The second row shows the results of mixing the two colors in Photoshop according to the Chapter 4 exercise. Remember that, based on the principle of complementary colors neutralizing each other, you might expect to get a muddy brown. And that's precisely what you see. Sample it with the eyedropper to convince yourself.

But Photoshop has given you wrong! Look at the mixture on the third row. Here I've mixed the colors using the distorto brush in Fractal Design's Painter 4.0. Zoom in, if necessary. You'll see some green — not an overwhelming amount, but definitely present with the muddy brown. Why does this matter? It demonstrates that not all color spaces are created equal. Painter is designed to be a natural media program and to mimic traditional artists' colors and techniques. In this case, Painter hasn't done it perfectly, but it's getting much closer than Photoshop. How do I know this? Read on!

The fourth and final row shows a scan of mixing the two colors in the traditional medium of hard pastels. Where's the brown? All you see is a yellowish green. What's gone wrong? Nothing, because this is traditional media. The *wrong* is in the electronic color mixing. Photoshop has mixed colors based on electronic algorithms for colors, which are not always the same as how colors mix in the real world of traditional media. In some cases, the algorithms are right (see the next section). But in this notorious case (notorious to generations of art and color students), Photoshop's electronic algorithms have given you what a general electronic color theory predicts, which simply does not happen in the real world. Painter has gotten considerably closer, because some yellowish green does appear (one of the reasons why I favor Painter for mixing colors). The end of Chapter 4 introduces you to the color theory behind all of this.

What's the moral? You can't trust electronic color algorithms — even Painter's. You can mix colors electronically, and you should (more on that shortly). But you need a basis in the real-life experience of color interaction. Otherwise, you're doomed to programmer conceptions of color spaces and doomed to generate colors that look like they were generated on a computer.

Alizarin Crimson and Viridian Green

You don't need to be totally cynical about mixing colors electronically. I want to show you how to mix colors electronically when you can, and why you should. This time we're going to use two famous, traditional colors; they're exact complements and when mixed electronically, they give almost precisely the expected neutrals. We'll see some uses for those neutrals.

Mixing the colors

You'll be using the same mixing methodology as in the Carrot Orange example from Chapter 4. This time, your colors will be Pantone Uncoated 200 (Alizarin Crimson) and Pantone Uncoated 330 (Viridian Green). If you want to do it from scratch, double-click the color squares in the toolbar, and then select Custom⇨Pantone Uncoated in the Color Picker, and scroll down to the numbers. Or open AV01.JPG from the CD-ROM (you'll need to do this anyway for the following paragraphs); the first row has squares of the two colors which you can sample with the eyedropper tool. You're trying to get a range of neutralized colors; some of which will lean towards the Alizarin, others will lean towards the Viridian.

If you're not getting the range you want, look at the colored swirl on the second level. I've taken the two colors and mixed them in Painter by using, once again, the *distorto* brush. Use the eyedropper to sample some of the neutrals (you may need to zoom in), and then use the paintbrush tool with a medium brush to lay down some swatches of the neutrals in a new RGB file (set resolution to 72 dpi; set size to 400×400 pixels).

If you're still confused, or want to test how you're doing, the third and final row of AV01.JPG has a series of neutrals I extracted from the Painter's color swirl. But you can readily find many more, and I urge you to. In mixing colors, getting there is definitely at least half the fun.

Using the colors

At this stage, you're probably saying "So what? I've got all these dullish colors. What would you have me do?" I've got a lot for you to do. For each of the following paragraphs, open a new RGB file (set resolution to 72 ppi; set size to 400 × 400 pixels).

First, forget about your neutrals for a second. Suppose you want to put something red on a green background. Fill the background with pure RGB Green (0, 255, 0). Now select the paintbrush tool with a medium brush, and change the foreground color to pure RGB Red (255, 0, 0). Put a splash of red in the middle. Look at what you have. Unless you're a fan of Peter Max, your eyes will hurt. The colors just scream. Do it in reverse (red background, green line); your eyes will hurt even more. For still more pain, use either background, insert some text with the text tool, switch the foreground color to the opposite color, and Alt-Del to fill the text with it. Then deselect (Control-D). The text is almost painful to read. But no pain, no gain.

Now let's try it with the complementary colors. Repeat the previous exercise, but use Alizarin Crimson and Viridian Green. It should look significantly better because the colors are complements (the RGB green and red you used before aren't — at least not in the traditional media sense). But better does not equal perfect. You'll notice that the Alizarin Crimson background is still a bit noisy — a dull roar, not a scream. And the Viridian still seems a bit *off*. That's as it should be. Red reaches its maximum intensity at Chroma 5 (for Chroma read *hue*; it's a technical term that Munsell, whom I introduced in Chapter 4, devised) but extends to a Chroma value of 10. Blue-green extends to Chroma 5. The numbers tell you what your eyes should see. If you want to be even more precise, Liquitex (maker of a superb series of acrylic paints) gives a Chroma of 9.7 for its Alizarin Crimson and a Chroma of 1 for its Viridian. So much for screams and roars because we want *bel canto*. Time for another exercise, where you'll bring your neutrals into play.

Now set your background to one of the neutrals that favors the Viridian. Put in a splash of pure Alizarin Crimson or set some type in it. Much, much better, isn't it? If you must have reds, select a neutral which favors the Alizarin for the background, and then put in your line or type in pure Alizarin Crimson. Still looks good, doesn't it? No more screams and roars. Here's why. The neutrals have cut the Chroma allowing Alizarin Crimson to just pop off the background, while still being in harmony with it, even with a reddish background. You could look at this for hours.

Finally, experiment a little. Try various neutrals for the background and various other neutrals or pure colors for the foreground lines or text. You'll see that, depending on the combinations you choose, you can get an extraordinary variety of color moods, all harmonious and easy on the eyes.

Why you've done this

If you've not mixed colors before, this should be mind-bending. You've just done what the best artists in traditional media have always done. They choose colors and mixtures with their heads. They plan colors even before doing a preliminary sketch. Of course, this goes against the stereotype of the crazed painter in the garret flinging colors on the canvas and producing a masterpiece. No artist worth her or his Alizarin works like that. Real art comes not from frenzy but from careful thought. Cool and calculating thought. Always has, always will.

You've experimented with just two complementary colors; there are many more, and variations on each. For example, you could do *split complements*, using Alizarin Crimson on the one side, Viridian Green on the other along with its neighbors Emerald Green and Thalo Green, the neutralized greens such as Hooker's Green Dark and Prussian Green, and even a neutral over in Alizarin Crimson's territory, Mars Violet (a wonderful color that Norman Rockwell used with excellent effect). In case you're wondering, I've worked out Pantone on-screen equivalents for these colors, and I play with them there, and squeezing out of tubes as well.

How do you find out about complementary colors? From a *color wheel*. But not all color wheels are created equal. Any number of painting books will hawk their own wheels and claim you only need a couple of pigments to mix everything you need. Balderdash! There's only one color wheel that works, it's the one that Stephen Quiller developed. And here I'm going to make a couple of recommendations. Get Quiller's book, *Color Choices* (Watson-Guptill) where you'll see his color wheel and much, much more on mixing harmonious colors. For your second book, get Rob Howard's *Gouache for Illustration* (Watson-Guptill). His Chapter 4 will also introduce you to the Quiller wheel and tell you, in remarkably lucid terms, the theory behind harmonious color mixing.

You may wonder if I've condemned you to a severely restricted color universe. Not a chance. You can use more colors if you know what you're doing with them. You must use your eyes and head — especially your head. But when you look at virtually any works by the Old Masters, you see neutrals and complements everywhere, often in a range that might seem restricted. In the hands of a Master, it isn't restricted at all. In fact, for one full year I did virtually all of my electronic and traditional color work with Alizarin Crimson and Viridian Green. I never felt restricted, or that I'd exhausted their range. Still don't.

All the neutrals I've had you mix were waiting for you in Photoshop or Painter. Chances are you'd never find them in the color picker. You need to use your head and your knowledge of traditional colors to produce these neutrals electronically because the programs won't do it for you.

A final fling: gradients

You might be asking now why you (and I) have bothered with all this. After all, can't you just use Photoshop's gradient tool to design a gradient between Alizarin Crimson and Viridian Green? Get all those neutrals in a couple of clicks?

Well, try it. Set your foreground color to the one and background to the other. Double click on the gradient tool and, from its menu select, linear with 50 percent midpoint. Do another 400-pixel square, 72-ppi RGB file, draw a diagonal with the gradient tool, and then release the mouse button. Whoops! Where are the neutrals? Or open AV02.JPG from the Chapter 19 directory of the CD-ROM and look at the first rectangle.

You've just hit a limitation of electronic color. In our example of mixing neutrals, you produced the colors by forcing Photoshop to mix your choices. Now Photoshop has decided what comes between the Alizarin and Crimson, and in its electronic color algorithm, that's not neutrals. You may see a hint of a neutral here and there, but there are plenty of extraneous colors — blue and purple really don't belong there (I'm not knocking either color — blue eyes have a way of doing that to you). See what I mean about artists and programmers intersecting as a null set? Electronic color has once again taken leave of real life.

The second rectangle is a quickly constructed series of bars for our neutrals. This isn't a true gradient, but it gives us a feel for the color range we want. Once again, you can force a neutrals gradient out of Photoshop (look at the third rectangle). It's exactly what we want. I did one gradient from Alizarin to a neutral which favored Alizarin. Then I reduced opacity and overlaid it (with a bit of tweaking) with a second gradient which ran from Viridian to a neutral that favored Viridian. Once again, I took my knowledge of how the colors interact in traditional media and bent Photoshop's gradients to my will rather than just accepting what it gave me. You can get the results from traditional media (it would have been a snap to do this gradient in watercolor), but you have to take knowledge of that media and force it onto Photoshop.

Of course, you're not limited to Photoshop for designing gradients. Open AV03.JPG from the CD-ROM's Chapter 19 directory. You will see four rectangles. From the top:

- ✦ **KPT 2's Gradient Designer:** Not so very different from Photoshop. You could tweak this as I did in that case, but that seems counter-intuitive, because Gradient Designer is popularly conceived to be your one-stop gradient producer (the KPT people never said that — I'm summarizing how it's described).

- ✦ **KPT 3's Gradient Designer:** Very different from Photoshop. This is a remarkably good gradient and I must confess that I was stupefied when I first saw the results. The programmers have dramatically improved things. (Well, I did need to do a small tweak, which was easy in the revised Gradient Designer interface. I adjusted transparency and gray. Not just any gray — I know that working in traditional media you can neutralize a color mixing gray, provided that gray is of the same value as the color you want to neutralize — not just any gray will do!) So I did a quick Mode change on Alizarin Crimson to grayscale, sampled the resultant gray value, and used it here.

- ✦ **Painter 4's Edit Gradient:** Pretty good, too. I'm not illustrating the intermediate steps. I started with a gradient. which didn't look much different from the raw Photoshop gradient, and did some editing. But because Painter is a traditional media program, I decided to take it one step further.

✦ **Painter 4 tweaked:** I took the previous gradient and used two of Painter's Surface Control commands, Dye concentration and Color overlay. For each, I chose a paper grain and then adjusted the sliders. I did this because Alizarin Crimson in watercolor is a *staining* color; it goes right into the paper and stays there, and I wanted to re-create something of the effect here.

Once again you see my principle, whether for KPT's Gradient Designer or for Painter. I knew from traditional media what the colors would do. Then I made the programs do it for me.

Traditional media

Because I've been using that phrase so much, I thought it fair to put a file where my mouth is — open AVGRWC.JPG from the CD-ROM's Chapter 19 directory. Took me about ten minutes to produce these three gradients — I was able to get my neutrals easily. Of course, there's a different look and feel to them as they interact with the paper. I could get my Painter gradient quite close to these. But I could only do that from the knowledge I had from using these actual physical colors.

Moving on . . .

At this point, I know what you're thinking. This talk about traditional media is well and good, but Photoshop is a computer program. And you're a digital artist. Maybe a digital artist who never could get through art class in high school. Photoshop has given you a whole new look on art and your abilities. Just what am I trying to do to you? Keep reading!

Do Some Traditional Art!

Recall my second anecdote at the start of this chapter. I'm not saying you're a second-class citizen for not having traditional media knowledge. Photoshop may have liberated you (as it freed me) from some very bad early experiences with art. If you can put those bad experiences out of mind, you can reenter that world, and your digital work will benefit. Of course, I'm not saying that traditional media is just a backup for computer art. Far from it! You may well find a whole new world opening up, one that starts competing with the digital world. I certainly did. You can approach traditional art in two ways.

Mixing colors

This is an excellent place to start, especially if you think you can't draw (more on that in a minute). Because you're playing with colors and abstracts, your phobias can't slow you down.

For obvious reasons, I can only give some general advice. There are many excellent books and I've mentioned two. Get some artist-grade colors, either gouache or watercolor for easy handling and cleaning. Get some inexpensive paper and brushes. Start mixing colors and playing with their interactions. Try to duplicate your results in Photoshop. Time spent with this will richly repay you in your Photoshop work, and it's darned good for the soul, too.

Drawing

This is probably your ultimate phobia because it certainly was mine. I want to tell you about one book which made all this difference in the world: Betty Edwards, *Drawing on the Right Side of the Brain* (Jeremy P. Parcher/Perigee). Don't worry too much about its theory, although you should read it. Instead, concentrate very carefully on the exercises. Work through them carefully, and repeat them. You will be amazed. In the course of one summer I went from "I can't draw" to doing landscapes and portraits that are more than just recognizable. Then I brought my color knowledge in, and the results are history.

Of course, this isn't the perfect book. It's based on the principle *Draw what is there,* and it shows you how to do that. That's the first step — learning to be able to represent what you see. As you progress, you'll realize that you can't possibly draw everything that is there — this is precisely what art is about. You have to learn choose what to draw for your purposes. Recall what I wrote about Michael Davis' "The Sphere" earlier in this chapter or about my stippled sphere a bit later. Unlike the camera, we drew both what was there, but what was there and not apparent to the eye. That's where you'll be heading — going from drawing what's there to drawing what you know must be there.

Note   This will allow you to use filters and algorithms and not be used by them. Because if you use them without this knowledge, you'll be producing not what you think is there (bad) but what someone else thinks is there (worse). Drawing experience allows you to break that nasty loop — you can correct to what you *know* must be there (best).

But for the moment, don't worry. Edwards' book will get you started — and once you gain the self-confidence, there will be no stopping you.

Caution   If you hang around with any traditional media people, you may notice that it's very popular to dismiss this book. Pay no heed to those who do. The naysayers have probably never realized the point of my preceding "Second Anecdote." They may not have even read the book. And they've surely never had to battle the phobias you've just conquered.

Photoshop's Pal: Fractal Design Painter

I love Painter. And I love everyone connected with it, from the programmers, to the QA (Quality Assurance, computerspeak for bug swatters) people with whom I've worked during several beta test cycles, to almost all the Painter users I've met. Way back, when the first version came out, I was out of the action — my then-computer had 4MB of RAM, and Painter wanted more. Soon as I got a new machine with more RAM, I grabbed one of those paint cans and I've been at it ever since. Of course, I feel the same way about Photoshop, but my involvement with this book should already have proven *that*.

I'm discussing Painter here for two reasons. First, it's such a natural complement to Photoshop. Second, because of an odd, related circumstance. Look at any Photoshop book; you'll find, at best, a bit on Painter, but much is left unsaid. Same thing in reverse for Painter books. Even though Painter reads and writes Photoshop 3 files (and layers, which follows), there is this dearth. I'm not blaming those who have written for these omissions — not everything can go into one book. Thus some selected highlights and suggestions here.

Documentation

Until recently, this was a problem. The documentation which Fractal Design shipped was certainly clear — but at the end you were left thinking *What do I do next?* More recently, Fractal Design has started offering various helpful tutorials. Still. . . .

Luckily, the problem has disappeared. In the last year, several books on Painter have appeared. All are worthwhile, but two are superb. Both are remarkable for their fullness and generosity — the authors always tell you precisely what you need to do, so you're not left hanging.

Denise Tyler's *Fractal Design Painter 3.1 Unleashed* (Sams) is the best introduction. The author's enthusiasm and generosity and technical skill are writ large throughout. She takes you through a series of projects, starting with a small still-life and progressing to a complex piece of stained glass. You learn by doing, and I learned something new with virtually every page.

Cher Threinen-Pendarvis and Jim Benson have created *The Painter Wow!* book (Peachpit Press). Although beginners can certainly use the clear directions, you'll be best served by first having made some progress in Denise's book. Unlike the *Photoshop Wow!* books, this one has considerable artistic sensitivity. On particular levels it notices Painter's strong abilities for mixing colors, which I've mentioned above as well. More generally, it shows you artists of the traditional media persuasion using Painter digitally to re-create their techniques — the section on artist Nancy Stahl's gouache techniques is particularly amazing.

Both books address Painter 3.1; Painter 4.0 has just started shipping as I write this. The techniques are just as applicable to Painter 4.0. Purchase both confidently — you will not regret it. Incidentally, both come with carefully planned CD-ROMs filled with enough goodies to justify the purchase of the books for the silver frisbees alone.

Of Photoshop and Painter

The most basic point is this: Painter can read and write Photoshop's native 3.0 format .PSD files. This means that you can move files back and forth seamlessly and often, using each program for what it does best. For example, as I've mentioned above, I find it easier to mix colors in Painter using its wonderful distorto brush. When I get my mixture or palette just like I want it, I save in .PSD format. That way, I've got ready use of those colors in either program.

Even multilayered Photoshop documents come into Painter; each layer is turned into the Painter equivalent, a *floater*. See Figure 19-11, which shows all the parts of the Coke Girl who captured Deke's heart in earlier chapters.

Often, I do my layering in Photoshop, and then take the document into Painter to tweak the contents with Painter's superb floaters controls. After tweaking, I may return to Photoshop, if that's my primary program; sometimes, I stay in Painter — a floater easily becomes a *nozzle* for Painter's Image Hose (see Figure 19-12). As its name implies, Image Hose lets you paint with an entire floater (as the name implies, you're spraying/hosing an area with the image) as many copies of the image as you like (until you turn the water off). You can produce truly distressing effects (Figure 19-13) or some effects that do something (Figure 19-14).

Caution The Painter documentation tells you that layers come in as floaters from an RGB Photoshop file. That's true, but you could get derailed by one thing. You can bring in a grayscale layer document, and all the floaters will be there. All will be masked — and you can't get rid of the masks easily. This may not be what you want (it certainly wasn't what I wanted with the Coke Girl). Painter doesn't say *Danger, Will Robinson! Photoshop grayscale ahead! Continue opening?* Be sure to use Photoshop's Mode command to change your file to RGB before opening in Painter.

But, of course, you may wonder *Why should I do this?* and *Who cares?*

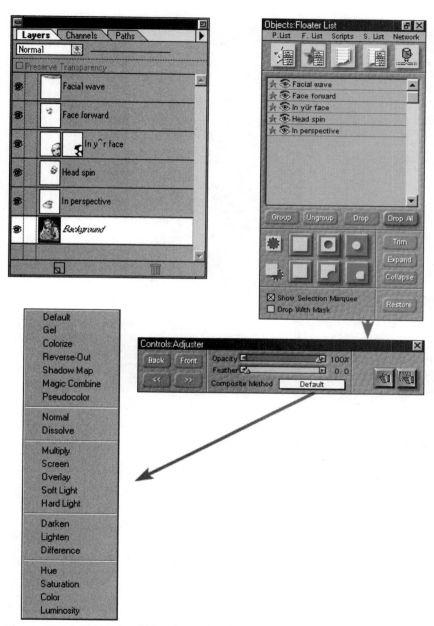

Figure 19-11: The Coke girl has layers in Photoshop (left), which become floaters in Painter (right), with a wide range of controls (bottom).

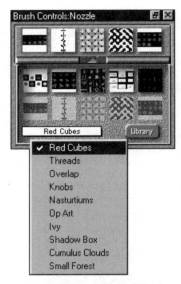

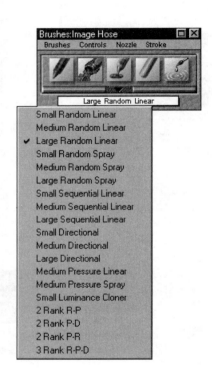

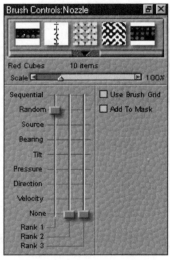

Figure 19-12: Floaters can provide nozzles for the Image Hose in Painter, which allows an incredible variety of effects (see next two figures).

Figure 19-13: Robert's revenge on Deke's Coke Girl —
the Image Hose gone berserk in three different modes.

What Painter can do for Photoshop

Photoshop is hardly *crippleware*. It's a very capable program (this is the understatement of the century). But Photoshop's philosophy is different from Painter's. Photoshop is strong on very precise, basic commands. For tweaking the colors of a picture, cleaning up a bad scan, or building up effects, Photoshop can't be beat. And I personally find some of its ways of doing business much simpler. Take making selections; whether by the magic wand tool, or by quick mask mode, or the lasso tool, I find Photoshop quick, accurate, and easy. Painter's methods of selection — they drive me crazy. I do all of my selecting in Photoshop and send those selections to layers before going into Painter. Sometimes, I'll even bail out of Painter and go back to Photoshop if I've another selection to make. On the other hand, I prefer Painter for mixing my colors.

Figure 19-14: Modern Coke Girl meets Classical
Antiquity — a more serious use of Image Hose.

But then we get down to cases. For example, recall the gradient files from the Chapter
19 directory on the CD-ROM, which we looked at up above in the colors section:
AV02.JPG and AV03.JPG. I'm quite satisfied with the one I produced in Photoshop. But
I'm more satisfied with what I produced in Painter (AV03.JPG). I started with the same
gradient, tweaked it with Painter's Color Overlay and Dye Concentration commands
(see Figure 19-15), and applied Painter's wonderful ability to bring in surface textures.
This presented the natural media effect of my gradient on paper. For this particular
Alizarin and Viridian gradient, that was important. Alizarin Crimson is a staining color
in watercolor, which means the color goes right down into the paper fibers — other,
nonstaining pigments float on top of that.

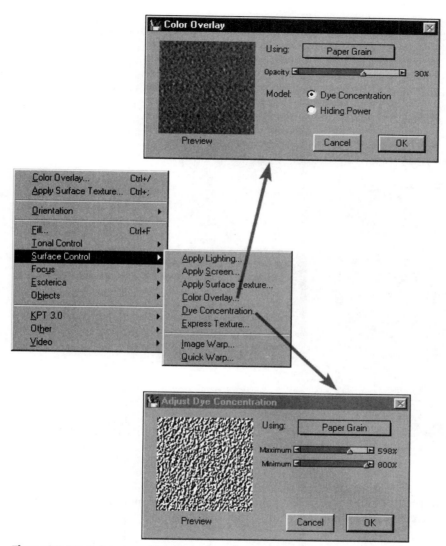

Figure 19-15: Painter provides several ways to modify how colors interact with paper.

Of course, in Photoshop you can start with a texture (handmade or taken from a CD-ROM) and then do the rest of your image. But when you need the image to look like an integral part of a paper texture, Painter's your program.

Then there are Painter's cloning algorithms. Although I've been hard on algorithms in this chapter, these are about as good as algorithms get. The process is like using Photoshop's rubber stamp tool but, instead of just copying something over, you can re-create it — see Figure 19-16.

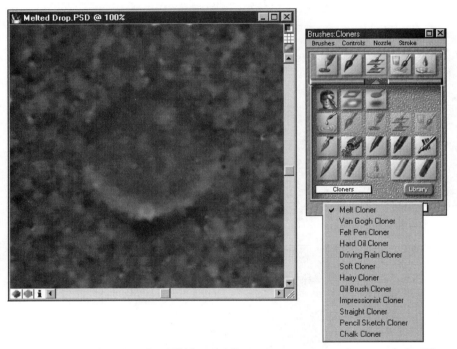

Figure 19-16: Painter's variety of Cloners allows you to re-create in an entirely different style — in this case, my dew drop from Figure 19-9.

Of course, using a Van Gogh Cloner doesn't make you Van Gogh — like any other algorithm, you have to use these judiciously. But they're an alternative to the range of Gallery effects, which produce rough-and-ready effects. You can precisely clone part of an image in one way, adjust the variables, or choose another Cloner and keep going. In these cases, I often do my cloning in Painter and take the document back to Photoshop for some ultra-fine controls (or to use Photoshop's rubber stamp tool — it is remarkably useful, and sometimes I don't want a funky artistic clone).

Finally, there's the whole subject of natural media artist materials. With a bit of tweaking, you can get the exact look and interaction of specific media (such as a Conté crayon on a piece of Mi Teintes paper) without spending a fortune on paper or getting your fingers dirty. When I'm planning on doing a traditional media production with these materials, I regularly use Painter to experiment with the various crayon choices and paper colors. Then I return to my traditional media. (Sometimes, I like what I'm getting in Painter so much that I finish the work right there.)

The variety of materials is vast. Multiply by the possibilities for customizing (I've mentioned Nancy Stahl's gouache), and the possibilities for using them as Cloners — you really can recreate traditional media. Trust me. Of course, even with such superb algorithms, you must keep using your head. But here's the difference from the others: Painter makes algorithms your tools; you're free to create what you will. Algorithms that attempt to make an entire finished picture look like pastel lose far too much in translation (next section).

Painter and Photoshop deserve each other. Like two peas in a pod. (Dare I say a Viridian Green pea pod?)

On Third-Party Filters

People, good people, have written books on this. As you've gathered, I think these filters (*plug-ins* they're called, but that's yet another term I hate) can be excellent starting points and sometimes end points too. The four most popular collections are Andromeda (series I, II, III), Black Box (from Alien Skin Software), Gallery Effects (Adobe — formerly from Aldus) and, of course, Kai's Power Tools (from MetaTools, formerly HSC Software). All are now available in 32-bit versions. Those 32-bit versions are essential if you're using Windows NT (the 16-bit versions won't run on that platform) and will definitely improve things under Photoshop 3.04 and 3.05, because you will no longer have to use the thunking layer (see the following section "Two Technical Points," and also Appendix C). The following is a brief summary of each.

Andromeda

I've found the Series II to be unfailingly useful because it allows you to map an image (or texture, or whatever) onto a geometric three-dimensional object. It's sort of a miniature ray-tracing program, but heed my previous warning about the limits of ray tracing. If you want an artistic effect, you have to manually tweak your image. Use this with KPT's Glass Lens filter and Spheroid Designer — along with your common sense — and you can create some breathtaking objects. Of course, you can also use a three-dimensional program (such as those from Caligari or Ray Dream), but this is a filters section! See Figure 19-17, where I've mapped a concrete texture onto a sphere for — you guessed it — a real concrete ball.

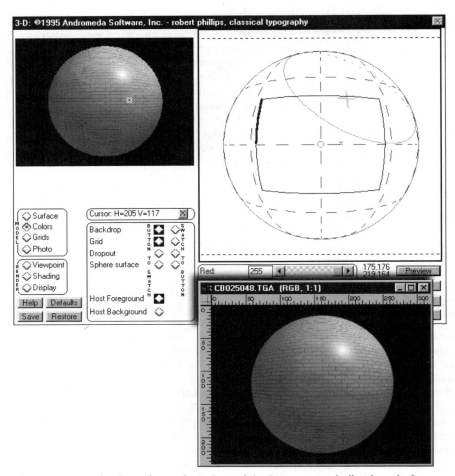

Figure 19-17: What is Andromeda Series II doing? A concrete ball. What else?

Black Box

Black Box offers some very useful algorithms, such as bevels for making buttons and a versatile drop-shadow filter (which I've used relentlessly in the screen shots for this book). When you need a quick and good special effect (sometimes that's precisely what's needed), Black Box will take good care of you. See Figure 19-18.

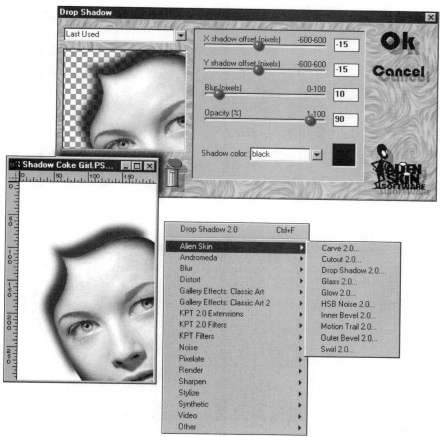

Figure 19-18: Black Box offers a well-chosen variety of specific effects.

Gallery Effects (GE)

GE offers a cornucopia of four dozen effects. My personal quarrel isn't with what they do, but with some of their names, which don't give you quite what you'd expect. Take the Rough Pastels filter as an example (see its interface in Figure 19-19). It doesn't make a rendering even remotely resembling pastels — its textures aren't really the sort you'd get by re-creating your work in pastels (see Figure 19-20). I feel strongly about this, because soft pastels (not oil pastels — no greasy kid stuff here) are one of my favorite traditional media. On the other hand, the Watercolor filter is unfailingly useful. (Its interface is shown in Figure 19-21.) It's not the same thing as doing your own watercolor, or even using Painter, but it's a valuable filter in its own right and definitely delivers a watercolor look (see Figure 19-2).

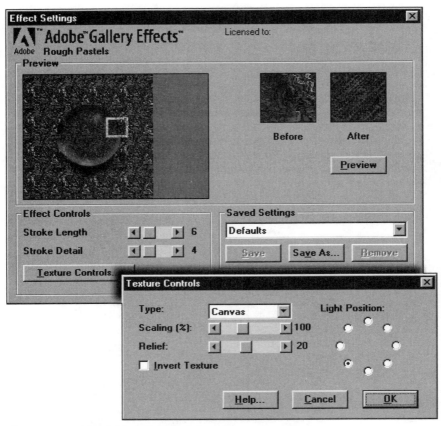

Figure 19-19: The GE Rough Pastels interface.

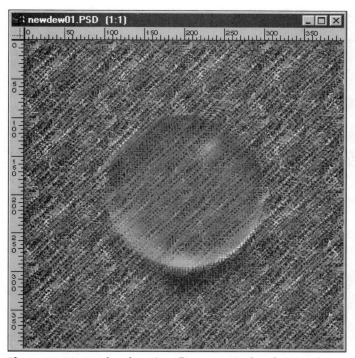

Figure 19-20: My dewdrop (see figure 19-9) after the Rough Pastels filter.

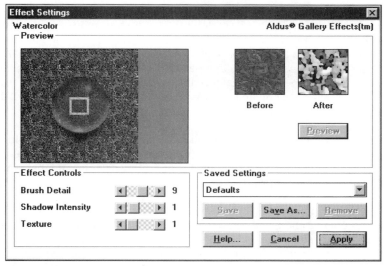

Figure 19-21: The GE Watercolor interface.

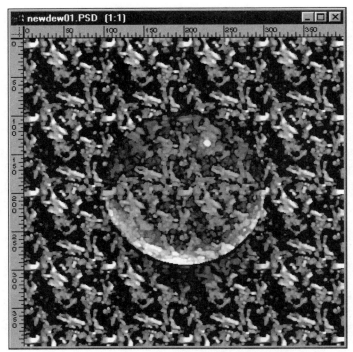

Figure 19-22: My dew drop (see Figure 19-9) after the Watercolor filter.

Caution You'll recall I carped about how the KPT Glass Lens filter was misnamed. For some reason, the people who program the filters don't take quite the same care in naming. This isn't just a nitpick — it has consequences for users. I've seen people go crazy using the Ink Outlines filter in an attempt to get a pen and ink look — i.e. the look I did by hand in Figure 19-10. They never will get a pen and ink look. Pen and ink is possibly one of the most exacting of the traditional artistic media — no one ever feels a true mastery of it. It's exacting, time consuming, dot-by-dot and line-by-line work. Totally incapable of being made into an algorithm.

Note The current version of GE is 1.5.2, which contains on one CD-ROM the three volumes which were previously sold separately but the price has not been adjusted, making it an irresistible bargain. The installer will *sniff* your operating system, and install the 16-bit or 32-bit versions as appropriate.

Caution Obviously, I think you should get the current version of GE. But in case you don't, the older individual volumes 2 and 3 will run with Photoshop under Windows 95 using its thunking layer. But be careful of the older volume 1 — the original 1.5 version will not work with Photoshop, regardless of whether you're on Windows 3.1 or Windows 95. Version 1.5.1, no longer available, was required. Moral of the story: If you have 1.5, it won't work, and you need to move directly to the 1.5.2 upgrade.

Don't pay too much attention to the names of the filters in Gallery Effects. Pay attention to what the filters do. They may be exactly the effect you want.

Kai's Power Tools (KPT)

KPT is definitely the biggest name of all, and I've discussed its plusses and minuses throughout this chapter. I love these things — each and every one of them — but I use them carefully. I particularly praise two of them: Gradient Designer and Texture Explorer.

Gradient Designer has many more options than Photoshop's gradient tool (or the excellent gradient controls in Painter). But, as I wrote in the previous section on gradients, you shouldn't think your gradient is necessarily done. It may be; more often than not, you've only reached an excellent starting point.

Texture Explorer is the most fun and the most useful filter of the lot. You can spend hours generating textures, then mapping them onto objects or turning them into wallpaper for your Desktop. But there's a more practical use — textures are all the rage these days. CD-ROM collections of textures proliferate. I don't knock those — in fact, I've got quite a collection. But Texture Explorer lets you roll your own in dizzying variety (see Figure 19-23). Combine Texture Explorer with your other filters and, in conjunction with what Sherry London can teach you about tiling (last section of this chapter), you'll be in texture heaven.

Caution You may well have KPT 2 already installed. In theory, you should be able to use it and KPT 3 without having to uninstall the former. But there is some strong anecdotal evidence that running, say, the KPT 2 Texture Explorer and then the KPT 3 Texture Explorer can destabilize your system.

Note So what are you to do? Texture Explorer has changed in its version 3 incarnation. It can't read the presets you may have lovingly compiled in version 2. And the various tiling size options are gone also. You may well need them. At several places, the KPT 3 documentation refers to the existence of a version 2.1 of Texture Explorer on the CD-ROM. But if you look for them — NOT. As we go to press, MetaTools has announced 2.1, a 32-bit version, will be shipped automatically to registered users of KPT 3. There will also be Fractal Explorer 2.1, also 32-bit; this will be just as welcome, because KPT 3 does not offer Fractal Explorer.

Note Fractal Explorer does for fractals what Texture Explorer does for textures. If this makes you yawn, think again — fractals offer a wealth of artistic possibilities. Look at what Thomas Lindstrom has accomplished on this book's attached CD-ROM, and look at the many techniques for using fractals which Sherry London's book (referenced at the end of this chapter) details.

Last, but not least, is KPT Convolver (it's a separate package). Convolver allows you to customize Photoshop effects (such as Gaussian Blur or Unsharp Mask) and rubrics (such as Hue). Blending, randomizing, or both — Convolver lets you do it. For extra-special tweaking, Convolver is a must-have.

Figure 19-23: Texture Explorer in KPT 3 — you can spend many productive hours with this one.

XAOS Tools

The words Image Alchemy and Terrazzo are instantly familiar to Mac users. The former allows an almost dizzying variety of artistic effects through various shape, color, and brush algorithms; the latter does instant seamless tiles in a variety of geometric shapes.

Despite various hints in the trade press, neither filter set is available for Photoshop users. But both are available for Windows 95 users. Corel bundled both in Photo-Paint 5 Plus (not in the PhotoPaint 5 that shipped with Corel's integrated graphics package), and has continued that combination with PhotoPaint 6, available by itself and in CorelDRAW 6. The XAOS offerings are hardwired into the program as DLLs (Dynamic Link Libraries) thus, they can't be used in other programs. (Of course, there's nothing to stop you from saving your results there in a Photoshop-supported format, and then taking that file directly into Photoshop!)

Two technical points

All of the third-party plug-ins I've discussed are available in 32-bit versions, which will run on Windows 95 without further ado. If you've got earlier 16-bit versions, you can still run them, but they need to be *thunked* in communication with the 32-bit operating system — see all three appendices for further details on how Adobe has implemented this. Without thunking, it's impossible to use the 16-bit filters in Windows 95. Adobe has done an excellent job with the thunking, but the 32-bit versions provide the most stability. This is important, because as your image size gets larger, relative to your physical RAM, you're putting the most stress on Photoshop and Windows 95. So if you're working with large images relative to your RAM, it's vital.

Caution Let me explain. The Photoshop documentation advises you to have physical RAM three to five times greater than your largest image. If you don't, Photoshop will use the scratch disk. So a large image is one of a size which, in this context, makes Photoshop start hitting the scratch disk regularly. See Chapter 2 for more on scratch disk considerations.

This question comes up often on CompuServe's ADOBEAPPS forum: "Does having many third-party filters use up your memory?" Not necessarily; they only use memory while they're running. Some of the larger ones can be quite memory intensive, but only while you use them.

Robert Does Not Hate Algorithms!

Am I having a deathbed, end-of-book conversion? Not a chance. I've emphasized the limitations of algorithms because "no voice is wanting in the chorus of praise" in other Photoshop books.

Algorithms are useful — no doubt about it. But I've tried (both by explaining and irritating) to make you think rather than just pulling down menus and sub-menus and clicking on OK buttons. Sometimes that's okay — and sometimes it's not okay. Sometimes, you need an algorithm as a starting point. (Remember, in the colors section I started with algorithmic gradients of Alizarin Crimson and Viridian Green and then tweaked them to simulate a real-life gradient in traditional media.) I needed algorithms to reach my starting point; it would have taken me forever to get there manually. Sometimes you don't need an algorithm at all — the dew drops up in the balls and spheroids section, for example.

Here's the point: *It's a mistake to have just one working method in Photoshop.* Am I using Alizarin and Viridian to render a sphere in the style of Michael Davis to hang in my private gallery? Chances are, I'll skip the algorithms. Do I need to generate a whole collection of colored spheres to infest Web pages? I'll fire up KPT 3 and use the Glass Lens filter or the Spheroid Designer, and I'll be very grateful to those programming wizards for all of the hours I save.

The same principles apply to color. There may be times (I hope not many) when I need fire-engine red on a screaming green. I'll grab those two colors with the color picker and then sit back and enjoy the praise for my imitation of Peter Max. If I'm doing a landscape for my gallery, I'll use my Quiller Color Wheel to plot my complements, split complements, and neutrals for exactly the appropriate mood and tone.

There's room for both algorithms and traditional techniques. The very best thing I can do is to recommend a book by my fellow CompuServe sysop, Sherry London. Her *Photoshop 3.0 Special Effects How-To* (Waite Group Press) is a mind-bender. You'll see algorithms taken to the nth degree. You'll see traditional techniques by Rob Howard or Nat Merriam (both have contributed to the Bible's CD-ROM). And there's nothing like an algorithm for seamless patterns; Sherry has quite literally written the book on that. Although her book is in Mac-speak, you don't need me to translate the principles.

Whatever you do with Photoshop, look and think before you do it. The last thing you want is a firecracker in a paint can.

Appendixes

Hardware for Photoshop

Some Philosophy

What's that P-word doing here? What on earth does it have to do with Photoshop, let alone a hardware section? In my not-so-humble view: Everything! I'm putting it here because it is implicit in all five of these appendixes and, just to make sure you get it, I'll keep referring back here. Trust me, it's not gratuitous academia.

Think about how you get computer information, whether in print, online, or from friends (obviously, you don't consult with enemies). How many times have you seen a magazine shout "100 Hot Tips for Windows 95" or seen an online posting "Here's a great tip for using Photoshop as a word processor"? Seems that everyone is in the tip business. Tips surely have their place, and I'm certainly not criticizing Deke's choice of a *Tip* icon. Both he and I have strewn it liberally.

But in the computer world, the tail (or tip) is wagging the dog. An incredible undigested, free-floating mass of disorganized information (as my favorite Roman poet, Ovid, put it, *indigestaque moles*). A profusion of confusion. As if you had all your various Photoshop images scattered over all your drive partitions in multiple directories — you'd spend all your time trying to find them and organize them, rather than using them. Same thing for tips. So many tips are floating around that your mind numbs, and you don't wind up using any of them. But if you think a bit about computers generally, Windows 95 and Photoshop specifically, you can do the tip equivalent of keeping all your Photoshop files on one drive. And let me write this large in ancient historian mode. Traditionally, when societies began to pass on all their knowledge as isolated snippets of information in encyclopedias, those societies were not long for this world. Apocalyptic enough for you? Good. Let's begin!

You should think of computers and their operating systems as inherently unstable. If you've ever read any really detailed descriptions of just how a microprocessor processes a command like *add 2 and 2,* you'll still be shaking your head, even more if you know how the microprocessors and hard drives and whatever are built. One little glitch, one mote of dust and — nada! Same thing goes for software. There are so many possible ways for the code to interact that it's impossible for even the most rigorous QA to catch all potential bugs; it lends truth to the current industry wheeze: *There's no such thing as a bug-free Windows application.*

Note That QA acronym means *Quality Assurance.* It's cyberspeak for the toiling technicians who spend their days searching for multiligate creatures and swatting them.

This is, I think, the fundamental philosophy. Anything you add to your hardware or software has potential instability. Obviously, you have to add some things — a keyboard and monitor are kind of nice to have. But the more you add, the more you're upping the instability quotient. I've seen this oh-so-many times in my sysop capacity on CompuServe's ADOBEAPPS forum. Someone will be having wicked problems with Photoshop. The usual fast-relief answers don't work, so I ask to see a report from MSD (Microsoft Diagnostics — MSD.EXE, which lives in your Windows directory). Oh-so-many times, that person's system looks like, well, the bottom of a Shake N' Bake bag. Chained AUTOEXEC.BAT and CONFIG.SYS files, multiple pieces of hardware clamoring for hardware interrupts — enough to make even angels weep, let alone a mortal sysop.

Of course, you have a very personal relationship with your computer. That's as it should be, and it explains why so many people go to such lengths with wallpaper, color schemes, and screen savers.

Note It does not explain why so many network administrators are so interested in removing those items from computers on their LANs. I recall reading in the description of a seminar for network administrators that "you'll never have to see your users' unauthorized wallpaper again." Some people just don't get it.

You probably don't have the luxury of dedicating one computer to Photoshop and nothing else. And, hey, you spent your money, you want to compute *your* way! Well, I have to tell you that you can't have it all. A lot, yes, but not all. Not if you want a stable system. You have to prioritize. Put on the extra hardware that you must have to use Photoshop, and forget the rest. This means *favor a digitizing tablet over a sound card.* Or, if you've got both and need to attach a CD-ROM drive, *favor using an industry-standard SCSI card over the SCSI connection that comes with many sound cards.* Same thing for software-ware. If you're on Windows 3.1, forget about alternatives to Program Manager, such as Norton Desktop. It's a fine program, and many have no problems using it with less-demanding *business productivity* applications. Forget, too, about programs that can burrow deep into your hardware system, such as third-party screen savers. As good as they are (I'm a big fan of After Dark), in a Photoshop environment you're asking for trouble. Forget about any number of apparently

Microsoft-sanctioned doodads, such as the cursor wrap feature of the Microsoft Mouse Intellipoint drivers, Windows 95 doodads (such as animated cursors), or (if you've got Microsoft Plus!) full window drag.

Grinch enough for you? I'm not trying to deprive you of all fun, but I'm trying to show you the practical consequences of the philosophy I've enunciated. All the examples I've just given can destabilize your working environment for Photoshop. I've helped people solve Photoshop-specific problems arising from each and every one. Further, I practice all of what I've just preached. The results? I've pushed Photoshop relentlessly ever since it first appeared in version 2.5 for Windows. I've tended to have about one GPF (*General Protection Fault* — that's a nice way of saying *Abandon All Hope Until Ye Restart*) a month at most, unless I'm running a beta test.

Background Let me tell you, briefly, about something that happened shortly after Photoshop 2.5 for Windows shipped. An able, regular member of the then-ADOBE forum (now ADOBEAPPS) on CompuServe was having wicked problems. He got the very strange message that he had physical RAM problems. At first we thought this was just Photoshop being funky, because none of his diagnostics programs reported any problem with physical RAM. But, after some serious troubleshooting, it turned out that he *did* have a bad ram chip (SIMM), which led us to christen Photoshop as *the ultimate hardware diagnostic tool*. It probably makes the heaviest, most mercilessly relentless demands you could imagine on your system. The more stable your system, the better your odds of not seeing Photoshop in its, er, *diagnostic* capacity.

So, back to where we started. Think about the philosophy of stability as you contemplate both hardware and software issues. You still can have some fun — a lot of fun. Tinker with your wallpaper, tinker with your Desktop color schemes — it's perfectly safe. Tinker with native Windows 95 screen savers (many fine ones already are online). That, too, is perfectly safe. Let the rest go. You'll be doing you, and yours, a terrific favor. Or, as Sergeant Phil Esterhaus put it in *Hill Street Blues*, "Let's be careful out there."

Hardware overview

Let me start with a true confession. Hardware makes me nervous. Every time I have to "go under the hood," I steel myself, gulp, and make sure I've got Tylenol handy. I just want to get the hardware installed and running and get back to my software comfort zone. Sounds odd? I've written WIN.INI files from scratch, and I'll hack the Registry in a trice. Moving programs and editing MBRs (Master Boot Records) is no problem. But just seating a new card in an expansion slot makes me nervous. For even the most apparently trivial hardware matters, I shamelessly truckle to the hardware-oriented, affectionately known as *Gearheads*.

I suspect you're probably like me. You just want your computer to "start me up." But it is hardware, and you, like I, have to live with it. So here are some insights I've gleaned during my illustrious career as a hardware-phobe. It's not an introduction to what computers are, or the differences between a hard drive and a floppy drive. There are plenty of good books for that, and endless magazine articles. Rather, it's to help you get a quick handle on hardware considerations specific to Photoshop and Windows 95. These aren't the only possible opinions, but I know these are valid and I know these can work. They are all informed by the philosophy I've just inflicted on you, so welcome to Robert's excruciatingly biased guide to correct Photoshop hardware for Windows 95!

Buying a Computer

Hey, I just said this wasn't an introduction to computers! What's up? Simple — you may be entering the digital universe for the very first time. How do you sort through all those vendors hawking their machines as screaming state-of-the-art, best-of-breed (and other buzz-phrases) *ad nauseam*? You may realize that you need a more substantial machine than your current one, because it's just not cost-effective to upgrade. What you do next will materially affect how you feel about Photoshop and Windows 95, and how effectively you use them.

There was a time when IBM was the standard, and people who used their boxes walked tall; everyone who used a *clone* was always a tad apologetic, as if admitting that granddad was an alcoholic. No longer. IBM still makes fine PCs, but now they're just one brand out of many. The erstwhile clones have multiplied and taken over the PC world. So the first principle is to consider IBM if its products suit your needs. But don't limit yourself.

You'll see a dizzying variety of names in reviews or advertisements. Some names will keep recurring. Some will have snazzy advertisements, but never appear in reviews. It's a cacophony out there. Here's how to make a symphony:

  ✦ **Read reviews relentlessly and widely.** You'll find variations in what the reviewers like, but certain manufacturers will keep reappearing. Make a list.

  ✦ **Read the manufacturers' advertisements.** Compare prices and features. Make more lists.

  ✦ **Talk to people.** Ask everyone you can find. Ask friends, ask enemies. If you're in your dentist's office and happen to see a Fizzy Swiggles-brand Pentium, ask how they like it.

  ✦ **Ask online.** Many major vendors have sections on the major online services. Right now, the most and the best are on CompuServe. This is also a factor in your buying decision; if you need support, online is often far faster and more effective than even the most finely-tuned support lines. Just remember that vendor forums, by their nature, will attract people with problems. See what kind of problems people report and the vendor's response.

✦ **Call the manufacturers.** You've done enough research. Ahem. This implies ordering over the phone and waiting for FedEx or UPS. Right — I've bought three computers that way with nary a hitch. I've seen people with the sad prejudice that *mailorder equals junk* ease on down to their local computer superstore and bring home a gawldurned mess. I've nothing against those stores, but I've found that mail/phone-order merchandise is just as good, with more configuration options and (often) more technically savvy advice.

✦ **Listen carefully to your would-be sales representatives.** How willing are they to take time and explain? To go the little bit extra? If they go all distant on you when they hear you're not a purchasing agent of a Fortune 500 company, move on; it's your money, so why should you pay for abuse? If you have a bad experience, but you're otherwise leaning toward a particular manufacturer, call again. Sometimes it can take a couple of sales reps before you find one you can work with. This is important. Regardless of your technical level, you're going to need some handholding, so it's best to feel good at the start.

✦ **Ask about the hardware.** Who makes the monitor? The video card? Look at the reviews and ask online. You're not obliged to purchase everything from one source. My current Pentium was offered with a perfectly good video card, but not one I thought appropriate for my use of Photoshop. So I purchased the card elsewhere. True, it cost me a little more overall, but I got precisely the card I wanted. You also want to ask very carefully if it's an OEM (Original Equipment Manufacturer) version; that is, one that the hardware maker produces to order for the computer vendor. If it is, you have some thinking to do. Typically, the OEM versions have all the functionality you need. But it gets dicey when you're looking for support. Some manufacturers directly support their OEM cards, and others demand that you go to your computer vendor.

You'll find all manner of people advocating what I've just proposed. But now, for the first time, I'm sharing with you Robert's Two Undocumented Opinionations for bringing home the perfect PC. You may quarrel with this, but all I can say is *it works for me.* Always has.

✦ **Look for a company on the way up.** Not just starting out, but not one that's riding high on major commercial success. Hungry, growing companies will take pains to give you value and assemble your machine with care. If they're too new, they'll be understaffed and still trying to figure out how to be vendors. If they're too established, they may be so overwhelmed that they've not time to do this extra (much as they might like to). I'm not slamming either the very new or the very established companies. Many buy from them with satisfaction. But I've used the buy-from-the-hungry principle over the years for a 386, 486, and a Pentium, and I've seen any number of people do likewise. Maybe I've just been lucky, but I have not had a second's down time or a second's trouble with any of them. Even the 386 is going strong as I write this.

✦ **Consider the gender of your sales rep.** Warning: this is probably the most opinionated section anywhere in this book. Of course, stereotypes are unfair; of course you can find exceptions to what I'm about to tell you. Here's my great secret: *I have, by choice, had women for my sales reps.* All three times. I've talked with men, and given them a fair hearing, but I chose women. Hang on, there's method in this apparent madness.

Caution You buy a computer; you're building a relationship with your sales rep and with that hunk of sand and rust. Women tend to be far better than men at building relationships. Put differently, a male sales rep often wants to wow you with how much he knows about his product and how technically savvy he is. (The old macho principle.) You don't want macho. You want someone who will be sensitive to you and to your needs. You want competence, of course, but you don't want that competence becoming macho, like a stag rattling cyberantlers at you. Women are simply better at being competent without antlers. Now, I know you'll be able to point to some men who are sensitive relationship builders and to some women who are macho. That's why I said stereotypes; although they're unfair in some cases, you can use them to your advantage. I directly relate my successful computer purchases to the gender of my sales reps. Of course, if you do want to shake antlers, ignore all of this, but remember "I told you so."

Some Hardware Specifics

I want to discuss some specific hardware considerations for Photoshop and Windows 95 that will keep you out of trouble and allow you to use Photoshop most efficiently. This isn't intended to be all-inclusive — I've even totally bypassed one area, *printers*, because that could take an entire book. For an excellent extended discussion of Windows 95 hardware issues, see Woody Leonhard & Barry Simon, *The Mother of All Windows 95 Books* (Addison Wesley), Chapter 6. More on this book, and IDG's own *Windows 95 SECRETS*, by Brian Livingston and Davis Straub, at the end of Appendix B.

Memory

If you've been following all the media on Windows 95, you probably know the Received Wisdom, that Windows 95 will run tolerably in 8MB of RAM and well in 16MB. 16MB is the *sweet spot* (I *hate* that phrase, but it's so common that I have to use it). Beyond that, you're getting into diminishing returns for your hardware dollar. This is all true, until Photoshop enters the picture.

On either Mac or PC, Photoshop is probably the most memory-hungry critter you'll ever invite in. I know of no one on either platform who says "I've got more than enough memory for Photoshop." Rather, all will say they're getting by, but that the ideal is in the future. Sort of like athletes on "getting in shape." Being *in shape* is something they're aiming for, but they'll never admit to in the present.

For Photoshop, then, the "sweet spot" information does not apply, for several good reasons. Certain Photoshop filters, for example, operate entirely in memory (I warned you about these in Chapters 2 and 14). Short-sheet them on memory and they won't work. Apart from those filters, Photoshop can operate on images larger than its available memory by using the *scratch disk* (see Chapter 2) as virtual (physical) memory; that is, using hard disk space to emulate RAM. It does work, but it's slower than running entirely in RAM, and the disk-thrashing can drive you crazy. Adobe knows what it's saying when it recommends physical RAM of three to five times the size of the image you'll be working on.

In short, more is more. You can get Photoshop to run in memory just a tad under the recommended minimum (which varies by version and operating system), but you've got to jack your system around so much, and will find Photoshop so slow, that it's nothing to try. You will find it wanting for any kind of productivity, and as much more as you can get. Trust me, I was functional, sort of, with 16MB on my 486, but that was before I got 32MB on my Pentium. And by Photoshop standards, even my 32MB is low-end.

Fixed storage media: the hard drive

Obviously, you'll be using a hard drive. If you've been in computing as long as I have, you'll remember when computers came with two floppy drives, and you could run WordPerfect from one of them. You'll also remember when a hard drive cost in excess of $1000. Luckily, times have changed.

SCSI or EIDE?

The perennial question. It's true that SCSI offers the most flexibility and speed. You can run your drive off a SCSI card internally and daisy-chain various external devices, such as a CD-ROM and scanner. It's also true that SCSI offers the largest drives — 8GB ones are common.

But there are tradeoffs. With SCSI, you get involved with such matters as SCSI-2, Fast SCSI, and SCSI-3. You get involved with cabling. You also get involved with drivers (Photoshop is notoriously sensitive both to SCSI cabling and drivers); sometimes, the latest and greatest will fix a problem, and sometimes it will cause a problem.

EIDE is certainly fast — I've yet to see anyone complain that they couldn't do their work on an EIDE drive. Of course, some users want to wring every nanosecond of speed out of their computers. But I think the speed gains are illusory, and they are offset quickly when problems strike. Problems can lie just around the corner in an all-SCSI system — a cable glitch, a funky driver, an IRQ conflict.

Caution Timing tests and benchmarks are fine up to a point. But don't get caught in the morass of shaving half seconds off a benchmark or comparing PC benchmarks with Macintosh benchmarks. No matter how good the benchmark, it can't reflect how an individual works — your usage may be entirely different. More importantly, you can become obsessed with shaving fractions of seconds from benchmark results. That may be fine if you're a *Gearhead* but, hey, you're a Photoshopper! Finally, remember this: Rembrandt didn't have benchmarks. His Alizarin Crimson (see Chapter 19) took two weeks to dry. I rest my case.

You can have the best of both worlds. Get EIDE and save yourself some trouble, unless you're sure you're going to need 8GB of space. You can still run your SCSI devices from a SCSI card; that's exactly how my CD-ROM and scanner are working now. If I ever want to bite the SCSI drive bullet, I'm set.

Working smarter with drive partitions

Regardless of how you've decided the SCSI/EIDE issue, now you've got your monster drive. Chances are it's 1GB or larger. Resist the temptation to have one C: partition to cover the entire drive, easy and tempting though it may seem. Depending on how you work, it may not let you or your drive work to maximum efficiency.

It all has to do with cluster size and the use of disk space. DOS stores files in *clusters* (units of memory space). Cluster sizes are directly related to the size of the partition (or unpartitioned drive). One cluster can't hold two different files, so bigger clusters mean more unusable memory space. Suppose your new computer has a 1.6GB EIDE drive, which is the largest drive of that kind currently available and currently very popular. If you have just one partition (C:), you'll have 32K clusters, which will probably be a big waste of space. Here's why. Say you have a 1K text file. In order to store it, DOS will need one cluster. Fine, but remember that you have 32K clusters. That means physically to store your 1K file, DOS will use 32K of physical space, in this case meaning you've lost the use of 31K of storage space. There's no way you can steal that space for another file. You can do the math as easily as I can. If you have a lot of small files, you'll be wasting an enormous amount of physical space.

At the other extreme, you can have 2K clusters, provided your partitions are under 127.9MB in size. Using our example 1K file again, you'd only have 1K of wasted space, not 63K. Much better. The tradeoff, though, is that you have multiple partitions, and you're going to need quite a number of letters to account for your drives. You may not like tracking all those drive letters. I don't mind, but that's just me.

You may be convinced, though, about my wasted space argument and have a 4GB SCSI drive all set to partition into 126MB chunks. Wrong again. DOS only allows you as many drive letters as the letters of the alphabet. The letters A and B are reserved for floppy drives; starting with the letter C, you've 24 letters. (23, usually, because your CD-ROM drive will take a letter). So, you've got 23 or 24 left. Do the math again, and you'll see that you'll run out of drive letters if you try to partition that entire 4GB drive into 126MB chunks. Besides, you may not like the idea of trying to keep a large number of drive letters straight in your head (see Figure A-1). Have you had enough? There *is* a way out, which I'm going to tell you.

If you're dedicating your machine to Photoshop and will produce very large image files (triple-digit megs and all that), go ahead and have one C: partition. While some files will waste space with 64K clusters, those big image files won't. Figure A-2 gives a graphic representation of this, utilizing the *PC Magazine* utility CHKDRIVE, which displays the efficiency of a drive with various cluster sizes. In the upper example, I've

Figure A-1: Two different ways to partition a 1.6GB drive. Clusters of 2K give you many drive letters (top), while clusters of 4K give you fewer drive letters (bottom). Notice the difference in partition sizes — each is at the maximum for the given cluster size.

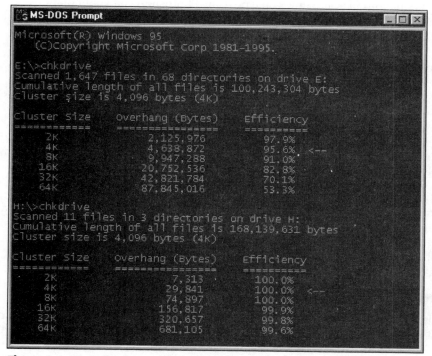

Figure A-2: Wasted space quickly adds up on a drive with many small files (E:), but doesn't on a drive (h:) with a few large files, even with larger cluster sizes.

analyzed my data drive (E:), and in the latter I've analyzed a drive that has only ten 18MB image files on it. Notice with the former how rapidly and how far the storage efficiency drops; with only a few large files, efficiency remains high on the latter drive.

Besides, you don't want to try to save a 200MB file to a 126MB partition, unless you're fond of *Insufficient disk space* messages.

But, if you're like me, you also need to use applications other than Photoshop with your computer. So let's talk trade-off. On my current machine with its 1.6GB drive, I could have had 126MB partitions, but I'd have had drive letters through R:, which means that I'd run out of partition letters if I put in a second 1.6GB drive (per above). But larger clusters mean more wasted space, so I compromised. My partitions are just under the 4K cluster cutoff figure of 250MB, which means I've got partitions through I: (the CD-ROM is J:) and plenty of space for another drive partitioned similarly. Or, I could have made several partitions 256MB, with one large 500MB partition for all those images. The former would be efficient with the 4K clusters, while the latter, with its 64K clusters, would also be efficient because I'd be storing only my large images there. Look at figures A-1 and A-2 again to remind yourself how cluster size affects storage efficiency.

Think about your files and how you'll be using Photoshop and your computer. There may be cases for having one large partition, but make sure it's by your choice and not because you or your vendor are taking the path of least resistance.

Compression

I can sum up my advice here in one word: *Don't*. I'm not referring to compression of groups of files by using PKZIP. I'm referring to drive-wide or hard disk-wide compression.

It's true that the compression that comes with Windows 95, especially the Plus! Package, is about as good as it gets. It's also true that any number of people will say they've used compression, whether from Microsoft or a third-party vendor, without problem. I still say: *Don't*.

Consider my philosophy enunciated above. *Compression is one more layer where things can go haywire.* I've seen that happen to people all too often. Photoshop QA goes into fits when you mention compression to it. Hard drives are very inexpensive these days and you will be far better off adding or replacing than introducing the possible havoc of any disk compression scheme.

Removable media

Ready for some more heresy? I don't use a tape backup. I don't knock those who do, but it's one more piece of hardware to juggle in your system. Windows 95 support is only just starting to appear. In light of this, if you have an absolute, total disaster (not likely, but anything's possible) with Windows 95, you just could be in a position where you can't access your tape backup. Thus, I advise against the false sense of security. I find it far easier to copy my smaller files to floppies (or compress a number of them with PKZIP and then place on a floppy). For larger files, I can use PKZIP's ability to *span* a file over several floppies. For really large files, I use my Bernoulli.

Windows 95 has a minimal backup program. To perform scheduled backups, you need the extra that comes with the Plus! Package. Arcada Backup and Colorado Backup are out. Both are very functional, but their installation setup wizards can sometimes go a little crazy. Exercise caution.

Of Bernoullis and Syquests . . .

Right now this is chaotic. Removable media drives from both manufacturers are available in sizes from 44MB up to 135MB, and larger ones are just starting to appear. A series of new, smaller drives from Bernoulli and Syquest have become hot items because their pricing (near $200) has made them virtual commodities.

Older Bernoullis and Syquests have been virtual mainstays for getting large files to service bureaus. The former have been more prevalent on the PC side, the latter on the Mac side. Given their expense, if you're planning to purchase one, it would be wise to check with your service bureau first.

The newer ZIP drives from Bernoulli are a special case because they come in SCSI versions and other versions that attach to your parallel port. Even if your service bureau doesn't support them, you still may be able to use them (thanks to industry columnist Jim Seymour for this tip): *purchase two*. One for your production use, the other to take with your files to the service bureau — just be sure to ask for it back.

Tip I mentioned this in Chapter 2, but it's worth repeating here. I don't want you totally to wear out your fingers thumbing around because you need them for mousing in Photoshop. You can use a Bernoulli or Syquest as your scratch-disk volume. It will be slower than if you'd used your hard drive, and you have to be sure you've got a disk loaded in it. That said, to do so, add the following line to your PHOTOS30.INI file:

```
AllowRemovableScratch=1
```

If you're using Photoshop 3.04, that .INI file resides in your windows directory. If you're using 3.05, it resides in the Photoshop directory in a subdirectory called PREFS.

Caution If you're upgrading from Windows 3.1 and you're using the parallel-port ZIP drive, remove it before installing Windows 95 (unless you want to forget about printing). After the installation, reconnect the ZIP drive and install its Windows 95 drivers.

CD-ROM

Chances are, if you've bought a computer recently, it came with an internal CD-ROM drive. If you haven't, or it didn't, you should acquire one as soon as possible. This isn't doodad-itis, it's common sense. Programs such as Adobe Photoshop offer many extra goodies on their CD-ROM versions — demos, stock art, filters. Books like this one are bursting with all sorts of extras on their CD-ROMs. Virtually all stock art and photos come on CD-ROM. Without a CD-ROM drive, you'll be unnecessarily limited.

I urge you to read reviews and talk to people before making your decision. *Internal* versus *external* is a thorny question. The internal drive can save you some space, but you have to take your computer apart if you need to change a jumper or dip switch. CD-ROM drives that allow you to put multiple discs in one caddy are starting to appear, but beware — some of them map each CD-ROM to a drive letter and chew into your DOS memory to do it. Under Windows 95, DOS is not dead. Programs need access to the *lower DOS* (640K) area. If you mortgage it too many times, you'll find that some programs won't open and some hardware (scanners, notoriously) won't run. Although some will argue otherwise, I can't agree that you should look for a caddyless CD-ROM, which means more handling of the precious silver discs and more chances for an accident.

6X (*six-times-standard* speed) drives are the fastest right now, but slower ones are considerably less expensive and will serve you well for Photoshop work.

Don't feel that you're losing face or speed if you have to use real mode drivers for your CD-ROM and its SCSI card; Microsoft's hype is a bit out of hand there. But use protected mode (Windows 95) drivers if you can. During installation, sometimes your CD-ROM and SCSI card will not be detected. You can select Add New Hardware from Windows 95's Control Panel to see a list of SCSI cards. Choose your card and follow the prompts; you will find that this installs the card's driver and also enables recognition of your CD-ROM drive. (Assuming, of course, that it's supported. An incredibly large number are.) After you have protected mode CD-ROM support, you can *REM* out (precede the line of code with REM to keep it from running) the MSCDEX, SCSI driver, and CD-ROM driver references in your AUTOEXEC.BAT and CONFIG.SYS files.

Finally, it's just starting to be possible to burn your own CD-ROM disks; various packages exist for under $2000, and Hewlett Packard's SureStore CD Writer is at the $1000 price point. Traditionally, burning a CD-ROM has been a nightmare. You need a dedicated SCSI hard drive and lots of internal fortitude. Initial reviews of these new packages suggest that these matters have improved considerably, so I recommend that you closely follow these promising new developments.

Input

As the name implies, *Input* deals with getting what you want into Photoshop, whether it's a keyboard command, a photo of Aunt Matilda, or a squiggly pattern you want to draw. The keyboard will not suffice. You need at least one further input device (mouse, digitizing tablet), and you'll almost certainly want a scanner. Input devices allow you to get your materials into Photoshop and get your commands into Photoshop, too.

Keyboards and mice

Both of these are very personal decisions, and not ones to be made lightly. You'll be using both all the time, so you want a keyboard and a mouse that feels right to you.

Keyboards come with varying degrees of hardness and softness when you press the keys. Sounds colloquial, but those are the best words I can come up with. Hard keyboards make a distinct click when you press the keys and have a bit of resistance. Soft keyboards make a muted click and feel, well, soft. I personally prefer the hard keyboards and use those by IBM and Northgate. The softer keyboards that come with so many computers drive me crazy. But you may feel the exact opposite. Strike a few keys. You'll know almost immediately whether you have to go shopping.

Note There's something else about keyboards: *the position of the function keys*. The original IBM PC keyboard (yup, that was my first computer, right along with two floppy drives and a green monochrome monitor) had the function keys in a neat column at the left. It was incredibly easy to use. With the AT-class computers, everything changed. The function keys were arranged in a row across the top. Unfortunately, virtually all keyboards, except those by Northgate, use this arrangement. To whomever thought it up, I've got a load of very moldy prunes to deliver.

Same rules apply to mice — try before you buy. I personally like the Microsoft 2.0 mouse and its ergonomic shaping very much, but I've got large hands. You may want a smaller mouse from another manufacturer.

Caution If you've purchased a Microsoft mouse recently, chances are it came with the Intellipoint 1.1 drivers(sometimes referred to as 10.1, to keep them in line with the 8.X and 9.X drivers that came out previously for Windows 3.1), which are Windows 95-aware. Those drivers offer, increasing across version numbers, an increasingly incredible series of doodads such as cursor wrap, mouse focus, and the like. These extras can function variably anywhere in Windows 95 and can sometimes cause problems in Photoshop. I advise against using them . Use only the Windows 95 drivers that came with your installation. Incidentally, Microsoft is aware of these problems and is reported to be working on a fix.

Caution Here comes the second mouse warning! If you upgraded over an existing Windows 3.1 installation, your system may, or may not, be using your earlier Microsoft mouse drivers. I advise against letting it do so. Those earlier drivers did offer the famous (notorious) cursor wrap, which did not get along well with Photoshop under Windows 3.1 — the notorious *Growstub* error message appeared. You can still get that error under Windows 95 if you're using the earlier drivers. My advice is to forgo the cursor wrap and use the native Windows 95 drivers. This may take some fiddling. Depending on how your mouse was set up previously, Windows 95 may or may not have recognized its drivers. Get help from some of the sources I list at the end of Appendix B.

Scanners

Scanners (along with the digitizing tablets discussed in the next section) are your most important input devices. They open up a whole world of possibilities. If you can get something onto a scanner, you can digitize it and manipulate it in Photoshop. Some of those possibilities may not be entirely legal. Although you can scan and tinker with whatever you like in the privacy of your computer room, copyright issues are very important if you're going to do anything with an image beyond private use. Please be careful and seek competent legal advice when using images.

There was a time when flatbed scanners were the high end and any number of us managed with hand-held scanners. I have fond memories of my Logitech; some of my best line art scans came from it. But in this day and age (especially if you're a Photoshopper), the prices have dropped so low that you really have no reason not to have a color flatbed scanner.

Color scanners all have their own characteristics, which can be equally pleasing or irritating to their owners. Here again you should read reviews (*many* reviews) and hang out where scanner gurus do. I recommend frequenting CompuServe's DTPFORUM, which has an entire section devoted to scanners.

Prices tend to go up with resolution. You can do an enormous amount with the 400 dpi that the under-$1000 scanners typically offer. If you're aiming for very high-end color work, you'll need more resolution, and that means spending money for a more powerful flatbed, breaking your piggy-bank for a drum scanner or, at the very least, paying money to have a drum scan done for you. If you're new to scanning, I think you'll be very happy with the 400-dpi scanners currently available.

What about transparency scanning? Many scanners offer transparency adapters. The results are mixed. I have heard excellent reports about one manufacturer and terrible reports about another. I'd advise caution before you spring for a transparency adapter. If you don't, you have two choices. You can have your service bureau do it (prices are reasonable, so this might be your method of choice if you don't have to scan many slides), or you can purchase a dedicated slide scanner, such as one by Nikon or Polaroid.

Getting a good scan is an art in itself. Much of this book has to do with ways to tweak Photoshop images for precisely those reasons, and I'd repeat my recommendation to get David Blatner and Bruce Fraser's *Real World Photoshop 3* (Peachpit Press). But I want to focus here on getting your scanner operational.

Scanners often come with their own dedicated cards, but they will also run off standard SCSI cards. I personally favor the latter, despite my otherwise hard words about SCSI (above). But, I've used the dedicated cards without problem. The key word, though, is TWAIN. Wiseacres like to say that the acronym means Technology Without Any Interesting Name, but that's unfair and untrue. In 1992, several major firms founded the Working Group for Twain. They took the T-word from the idea of uniting input devices and programs — the twain shall meet (get it?). But what's in a name? You want to know what it means to you.

In pre-TWAIN days, every program needed its own chunk of code to allow it to interface with the scanner drivers, and sometimes even a special program-specific driver. It was a nightmare. TWAIN involves a standard API that the programmers can implement directly. Then, all you need is a TWAIN-compliant scanner (virtually all currently available are) and the TWAIN module from the scanner maker and you're up and running. End of nightmare? Well, it was, but then it wasn't.

All of this was relatively fine under Windows 3.1 and even under Windows 95 with a 16-bit program, such Photoshop 2.5 or 2.5.1. But along came Photoshop 3.0/3.01, and no one could scan anymore. This was something that Microsoft didn't exactly trumpet along with its mantra *32-bits is better*. A 16-bit anything can't talk to a 32-bit something directly — it's all in the bitness (to coin a phrase). There were no 32-bit scanner drivers or TWAIN modules, none were forthcoming from Microsoft (unlike the case for Windows NT), and none still are, because Microsoft left it up to the scanner manufacturers to do their 32-bittedness.

Of course, there were cries of anguish, then along came Photoshop 3.04 with its *thunking layer* (see further details in Appendix C). Thunking (honestly, I didn't make up the term — it's programmer-speak) allows a 16-bit whatever to talk to a 32-bit program, whether third-party plug-in filters or TWAIN modules. Other manufacturers followed suit, and you could use TWAIN to run your 16-bit scanner software and TWAIN32 to run 32-bit scanner software (if you happened to have any — some manufacturers actually were ready with them shortly after Windows 95 shipped).

Then along came the TWAIN_32 standard of the *universal thunker*. This promises to simplify things because it allows one command, TWAIN_32, for both 16-bit and 32-bit scanner modules. Well, almost — some scanner manufacturers had rushed to update their modules to work under the old dispensation and now found them broken under this latest wrinkle. My advice is to try your scanner with TWAIN (16-bit driver) or TWAIN_32 (16- or 32-bit driver). Chances are that those will do it. TWAIN32 (note absence of underscore) is best saved for specific cases on advice of your scanner manufacturer.

Caution Hewlett Packard scanners need a bit of extra discussion because they're omnipresent (I've got two). Protected Mode scanner drivers have recently become available, and many users rushed to them because they were eager to get rid of CONFIG.SYS, which they were keeping around just to load the scanner driver. Besides, they'd bought into the 32-bit mantra. Thing is, when they got to Photoshop 3.04, they found problems. There was no more scanner. It seems that the new driver conflicted with Adobe's thunking layer. Now the drivers would work if the thunking layer was eliminated, but that meant *sayonara* to the 16-bit plug-in filters, which were also getting thunked.

Reports now indicate that TWAIN_32 gives you both (TWAIN_32 comes with Photo-shop 3.05 and is available for download from Adobe). At the same time, I have regu-larly followed reports of those using these new drivers, and I've not felt compelled to venture into this. Remember: *I'm conservative*. I don't mind having a real-mode driver rattling around if it means I can scan reliably. I don't need a CONFIG.SYS file, either. I can load it via WINSTART.BAT (a dodge not well known) and the excellent freeware, DEVICE.COM, widely available online as DEVICE.ZIP. I suppose I will ultimately up-grade, but I'm not entirely impressed with the stability and ease of installation of the new drivers.

Finally, there are the TWAIN modules themselves. This is important, because how you control the scan is going to affect what you have to do with Photoshop. In Figure A-3, I've illustrated DeskScan from Hewlett Packard. The module is certainly capable.

I'd like to repeat my plug (see Chapter 3) for the third-party program Ofoto 2.0. It allows you far more calibration options; nice extra features, such as automatic moiré removal; and, in general, can improve the quality of your scans to a quantum degree. The downside is that it's stand-alone, which means you either save your scan and then open it in Photoshop or take it over via the Clipboard. Ofoto doesn't support an enormously wide range of scanners. Still, if your scanner is among those supported, it's the very best thing you can do for your scans. See Figure A-4, which illustrates the expanded range of scanning options.

Digitizing tablets

A digitizing tablet could be your other most important Photoshop peripheral. As the title implies, you draw with the tablet's pen and watch your strokes appear on the screen. Programs such as Photoshop and Painter can reflect changes in your drawing speed and pressure, and support is beginning to appear for the erasing function in the newest generation of Wacom tablets.

Of course, if you feel you can't draw, you may want to skip this item, although you should read what I have to say on that in Chapter 19. Even if you feel you can draw, I've some OpEd about it for you in Chapter 7. To use a tablet or not — and, if so, which tablet — these are highly personal decisions.

There are several excellent manufacturers of digitizing tablets. I'm going to break with my general policy of shunning specific hardware recommendations and advise you to get a Wacom, for a very simple reason: it's currently the industry standard. Program-mers write with Wacom in mind, which means that your best chance of having a tablet work as it should is with a Wacom (more on that in a second). Other tablets inevitably follow the Wacom standard but, well, you see my point. It's very much like the case with PostScript. There's genuine Adobe PostScript, and there are the clones. Many of the clones are excellent, but the standard is still different enough, and important enough, that you should stick with it.

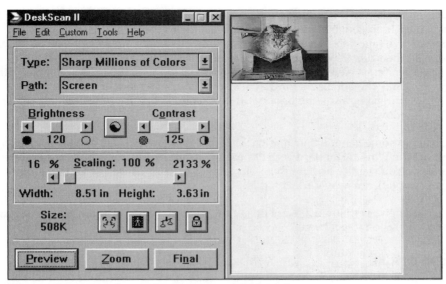

Figure A-3: The Hewlett Packard TWAIN module, DeskScan.

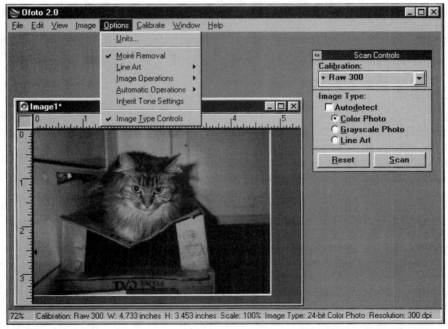

Figure A-4: Ofoto 2 offers a remarkable range of automatic options and calibration settings.

But wait! I talked as if it could be dubious to get a tablet to work. That's right. I don't want to frighten you, but I want to be honest. I haunt the WACOM forum on CompuServe (another reason to favor Wacom — its online presence), and I see some users get their tablets working perfectly from the first install, while others, with identical systems, have never seemed to get them working right. I don't necessarily want to blame the end users for that. It's something of a black art; it took me the better part of an hour on the phone with a Wacom technician to get my tablet working under Windows 3.1.

Caution I can share some general information with you. Windows 95 and Windows NT only support the Wintab standard with Photoshop. Under Windows 3.1, it's the Penwin standard. You want to be sure that your tablet's drivers, as well as your video drivers (see previous), are in accord with this.

The good news is that most users do get their tablets working, but it may take you some frustration to get there.

Video capture

Traditionally, hardware for video input has been more for the Adobe Premiere crowd. But recently something has appeared that is causing great excitement: Snappy. Snappy plugs into your parallel port and accepts video output from a television, a VCR, or a camcorder; you can capture a frame and take it straight into Photoshop. In the course of writing this Appendix, Snappy's manufacturer (Play, Inc.) waxed enthusiastic about lending me a copy that I could write about at more length. Alas, the promise has not become the reality, despite repeated promises. So keep your eyes on Snappy; I'm telling you what I've read, not what I've experienced for myself.

Output

As the word *Output* suggests, this is how you get your work out of Photoshop. Minimally, of course, that means to your screen. This is perhaps obvious, because without screen output, you can't work in Photoshop! But it's not quite that obvious. Hardware can greatly influence what you see on the screen and, thus, not only how you work, but the quality of your work.

Caution I remind you that I haven't discussed printers here. There are simply too many, and too many different kinds. Chapter 6 introduces the subject.

Video cards

Photoshop absolutely requires a 256-color display mode or it refuses to open. Although this may seem a gratuitous statement, I regularly get queries from people who get the error message because they're using 16-color drivers. Don't think that if you're working in less than 24-bit color mode that your file information will be consequently less. Nope. You'll be saving 24-bit color files (unless you've selected the Indexed Color mode in Photoshop) regardless.

Here's what I think. You want a minimum of 2MB video memory (this is dedicated memory on the video card — it has nothing to do with your computer's main RAM, sometimes called VRAM, sometimes WRAM, sometimes even DRAM — don't worry about acronyms this time), upgradable to 4MB. The 2MB allow you to have 24-bit color at 800×600 screen size and 16-bit (64,000 colors) at 1024×768 screen size. With the 4MB, you can have 24-bit color at 1024×768, and even get into serious colors at even larger sizes, assuming your monitor is big enough to keep you away from the ophthalmologist. See Chapter 3 for details on image size and color size. The possibilities — and prices — go up with more video memory; I'm not going to discuss those, because if you know you want them, you know at least as much as I do.

What about ISA or VLB or PCI? (Again, don't worry about the acronyms.) ISA was the old standard, while VLB and PCI represent newer accelerated bus specifications that allow the card and computer to talk to each other with fewer bottlenecks. Two years ago, VLB was all the rage; right now, about all you can find is PCI. Your choice of card depends on whether you've got an older computer with VLB or a newer one with PCI — either is very capable.

Getting to cards themselves — I've warned you often of the opinionations — do not, under any circumstances, get a card that has an S3 chip set. That chip set is very common and very popular, and any number of well-reviewed and highly touted cards employ it. Many use such cards without problem. But dig a little deeper. Many of the trouble-free contingent are using, er, "business productivity applications," which make far fewer video demands than does Photoshop. Yes, I know some Photoshoppers use S3 cards without problem, but I've seen far too many problems arise.

Those problems come from two connected causes. First, there are inherent problems for the S3 chip set and 32-bitness, which Microsoft expects to be solved at the driver level. This leads to the second cause: writing video drivers. They're created in a curious mixture of C and Assembler, wretched to write, and even harder to debug. There are never enough good driver programmers to fill the demand. When a card's very stability relies so much on the drivers, you've got a problem. Of course, the stability of any video driver can have an enormous influence on your system overall. Sometimes, a new set of drivers will solve some problems and cause others, again proof that the latest does not equal the greatest. One manufacturer's latest drivers, for example, totally disabled pressure sensitivity in digitizing tablets under Windows 3.1.

What about *legacy hardware?* (That's another cyberphrase I hate.) Many older cards have native support in Windows 95, but the manufacturers have been in no hurry to produce newer drivers and Windows 95-specific Control Panel add-ons. Thus, while the ATI Graphics Pro Turbo has both, the ATI Graphics Ultra Pro (still a fine card) does not. In contrast, the Matrox Millennium is already on its second revision (see Figure A-5).

I'm naming no names here, except to say: do yourself a big favor and avoid S3 chip sets. You've still got plenty of options.

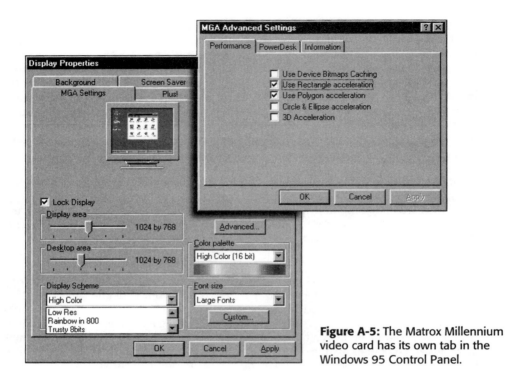

Figure A-5: The Matrox Millennium video card has its own tab in the Windows 95 Control Panel.

Monitors

This is very subjective. Larger is better, but the depth of your pockets is a consideration. The big price jump occurs after the 17-inch size. Desktop real estate is another consideration. The bigger the monitor, the heavier and more space-hungry.

That said, I think 15 inches should be your minimal size, and 17 inches if you can manage it. With a 17-inch monitor, you can do good work at 1024×768 and have several windows open at the same time. This is not nearly as possible with a 15-inch monitor, although you can do it (bifocal contingent speaking loudly here).

Beyond that, I'd urge you to ask and look. Especially look. Some monitors have certain characteristics that some users love and others hate. I personally go crazy looking at monitors with Trinitron tubes, but any number of people I respect love them. Let your eyes tell you. After all, you're going to be looking at it for a lot of time.

Keeping Things Humming

I'm making a judgment call here (isn't the first time). Hardware and software interact. Matters that deal most specifically with hardware appear here, while matters that involve software appear in the next appendix.

Something big and important

What I'm going to tell you now, I've seen a lot, and even experienced myself a few times. I've never seen it discussed (says he modestly), probably because it's so obvious that no one has thought to. But in my experience, it's often the most obvious points that need discussion.

Here's the scenario. Photoshop has been humming along for you. You're right on schedule for your production deadline. You get a well-earned night's sleep and fire up Windows 95 in the morning, and something starts going wrong. You may have problems getting into Windows 95, or you may be able to get that far, but not into Photoshop. You may get into Photoshop, but not much further. In short, you have a problem.

You go crazy. You're sure everything was fine when you powered down for the night. Has some gremlin gotten into the works while you were nodding off? You go crazy some more.

Stop just a second and do some very serious thinking. In the course of your last session, did you do something, anything at all, to your system? I know in my own case, after doing some intensive Photoshop work, I tend to say *Hey, I'm on track. It's time to have some fun. I want to put that new program on, tweak a couple of Windows 95 settings, and play a game.* Often, you do that and forget you did it. One of the things you did (we hope not more than one) had system-wide impact. You didn't see it at the time, but whatever you did has taken effect now that you've restarted Windows 95.

It's shockingly easy to do this. It happened to me as I was working on this very appendix. In my case, I'd put on my just-arrived shipping copy of Fractal Design's Painter 4.0. The screen colors went haywire. I know that such things can happen with 64K video drivers using bitmap caching, so I went into my Matrox control panel and turned the bitmap caching off. No luck. I nosed through Painter's documentation and saw that there was a Preferences setting for turning Painter's bitmap caching off, which I turned off. Guess what happened the next morning? I called up this very appendix in Word for Windows 95, typed in some of my purple prose, and couldn't see it. I typed some more and still couldn't see it. I backspaced and I could see it. Even odder, when starting a new document, I had no problems seeing what I'd typed. Yikes! Did this mean I had to become a Word for Windows 95 guru, too? (Life can be way too short.) Finally, I remembered that I'd turned off my video bitmap caching globally and neglected to turn it back on after I'd found the tweak I needed to do inside Painter. Aha! I went to the Matrox control panel, turned the bitmap caching back on, and my prose, purple and otherwise, no longer disappears. I'd simply forgotten one of my late-night twiddles.

Learn from this. Don't do anything of any importance after you're done for the day. Power down and take a well-earned rest.

Disappearing hardware

This doesn't come from anything you've done — it comes from something you haven't done. Windows 95 looks at hardware dynamically. If it sees 32-bit drivers installed for a particular piece of hardware, but that hardware hasn't been used recently, it can, apparently, just disappear from Control Panel⇨System⇨Device Manager. This is by design. It's the same principle that allows Windows 95 to recognize when you've added new hardware. See Figure A-6.

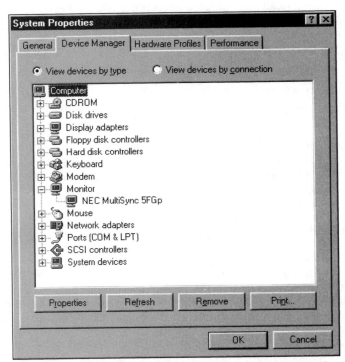

Figure A-6: Device Manager with everything working properly.

It can give you a horrible turn. Don't panic. Your hardware isn't dead; it may just be sleeping. Make sure your hardware is turned on and then, in Device Manager, click on the Refresh button. If you're lucky, your missing hardware will magically reappear. In the worst case, it will reappear with a big yellow Question Mark, which means you have to reinstall the drivers.

This happens most often with external CD-ROM drives (you may have powered it down to save wear and tear) or scanners (same reasons). Moral of the story — if you've got devices that use 32-bit drivers, keep them turned on. If they use 16-bit drivers, you don't have to. Incidentally, I use 16-bit scanner drivers for this reason too (in addition to the ones I enumerated in the Scanners section above). Call me nervous, but because I'm not scanning all the time, I don't want to keep my scanner on all the time. The 16-bit drivers suit me just fine.

Device Manager

Check Control Panel⇨System⇨Device Manager regularly (take a look at Figure A-6 again). Yellow Question Marks are warnings. Red circles with the slash can be serious. It means that a piece of hardware isn't running as it should. In the case of your hard drive, this can be serious. You may well be running with real-mode generic drivers, and your system may be at a crawl. If you see one of those red doodads, start reading your documentation and talking to technical support people. Finally, if you've just installed new hardware drivers, highlight the hardware item, click on the Properties button, and then click in the resultant dialog box (the Drivers tab). You can tell if the drivers you *thought* were installed are installed. See Figure A-7.

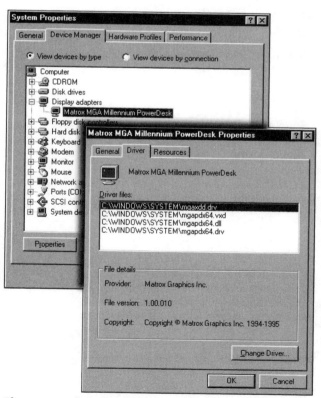

Figure A-7: All my Matrox video drivers are present and accounted for in the Drivers dialog box.

There's another tab you should check in the System dialog box — Performance. When you first bring it up, it will tell you if your system is running as well as possible. If your system isn't at its best, Performance will usually tell you what to do. Most often, it tells you to install 32-bit CD-ROM drivers. Follow the advice you get. You're aiming to read "Your system is configured for optimal performance." While you're there, click on, in turn, File System and CD-ROM. As good as Windows 95 is at detecting hardware, it doesn't always detect the speed of your CD-ROM correctly. If it hasn't, change as appropriate. See Figure A-8.

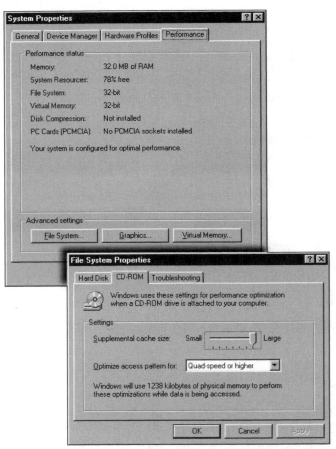

Figure A-8: Windows 95 originally thought my Plextor CD-ROM was dual speed. I fixed that easily in the Performance tab.

I advise you to leave the other tabs and buttons alone, unless you're having serious hardware problems, know exactly what you're doing, or have been told to do something.

Do not, under any circumstances, change anything about hardware in the Registry (more on that big no-no in Appendix B), unless you're anxious to have a dead system.

Keeping Things Tidy

Photoshop uses only the largest block of free contiguous space in the partition for its scratch disk. It's possible to have a 100MB partition with a scratch disk of 1MB or less if that partition shares space with 50MB of severely fragmented files.

Even if you've got a dedicated scratch disk partition, your scratch disk capacity can disappear. When you crash, your scratch disk becomes a very large .TMP file and stays in the partition. With enough of these, your scratch disk capacity and efficiency plummet.

How to stay tidy

✦ **BEST: Dedicate one partition for the scratch disk.** There is absolutely nothing you can do to extract data from a .TMP file. Kill them and bid good riddance. Regularly run either CHKDSK with the /f switch or Scandisk to get rid of lost clusters and cross-linked files, which are just eating space. Before running either of these, check your documentation.

✦ **GOOD: Regularly maintain a scratch disk's shared partition.** Keep an eye out for .TMP files, per the preceding item. Run the aforementioned utilities and add a disk defragmenter. You want to defragment and optimize the space, so you've got the largest possible amount of contiguous free space. This is because the DOS file system, even under Windows 95, does not necessarily write files contiguously. It often writes files on a space-available basis, especially if you've got some free space caused by file deletions.

What to use

I use the tools that come with Microsoft's Plus! Package. I run them automatically via the System Agent (SAGE), which is shown in Figure A-9.

Don't necessarily take my word for it. See what others are saying and make your own decision. Me, I'm waiting for an update to Norton Utilities. SAGE does just fine for me right now, thank you.

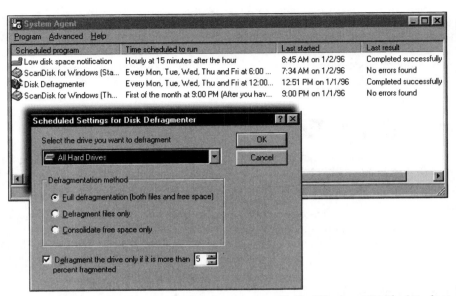

Figure A-9: The System Agent (SAGE) that comes with the Windows 95 Plus! Package allows automatic scheduling of disk maintenance.

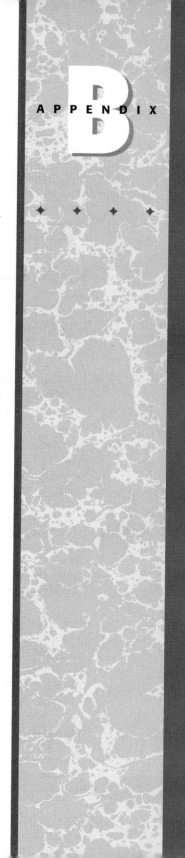

Software and Photoshop

Sounds redundant, doesn't it? After all, Photoshop is software. What this appendix does is get you going with the other major piece of software — Windows 95 — with a few looks at some other relevant programs along the way. I'm not going into competition with the many fine Windows 95 books already published. Rather, I want to share some ideas for working smarter and safer with Photoshop under Windows 95. If you skipped Appendix A (shame on you — you shouldn't skip anything in this book), I urge you to turn to it right now and read the introductory Philosophy section because those ideas are just as relevant here (and I've said so there).

Installing Windows 95

Gulp. The very thought of this may make you ready for Thorazine, Industrial Strength. After all, it's one thing to install a program, or even to install an upgrade to good old DOS. But this is a whole new operating system. If it doesn't work out. . . .

Let me share something with you. If you feel that way, you're not being paranoid (of course, even paranoid people have enemies). I've been there, too (in my case, with OS/2 a couple of years ago). I stared at the box, read everything, and then stared at the box some more. Then one summer weekend I gulped again and did it. Later, for various reasons, I had to deinstall and then reinstall. And I can tell you, *the first time is the hard time.* Install it once, see that your hair doesn't fall out and your computer continues to function, and you're never afraid again. The first time is truly the hardest, and I've talked any number of people through this online. All have agreed that it's darkest before the dawn. But the dawn does come. And, well, let me put it this way: Doing the Windows 95 beta involved installing new *builds* (preliminary versions) — sometimes very frequently. I reached the stage where I could do everything I needed to do in well under an hour, without any blip in blood pressure. Of course, I've learned some precautions along the way that are perfect for a whole series of Level 3 Headings (as my publisher calls 'em).

Note   Think about it this way. If you're adequately backed up, if you're willing to take a few extra safety precautions, how bad can it really be? These are, after all, piles of sand and rust. You're not being cast for a role at the end of *El Cid* — you know, where there's a heavenly light on Charlton Heston, a booming organ, and a voice intoning "And The Cid rode out of the pages of history and into legend."

Ways to do it

There are two. Either as the first thing to go down on your C: partition (see the upcoming section "Fresh installation"), or with an existing Windows 3.1 installation or alongside an existing Windows 3.1 installation (see the following section "Upgrade installation"). In this last instance, you can either install over Windows 3.1 or install Windows 95 into a separate directory and then *dual boot* (start the one you want). Actually, you have more choices — you can have Windows 95, Windows NT, and OS/2. I'm omitting details on that last scenario. If you have those operating systems and know that you want to do it, you either know how or how to find out. Both life and this book are too short.

Upgrade installation

If you're nervous, you can dual boot with Windows 3.1. Thus, you can get into Windows 95 gradually. You will have to reinstall your applications into Windows 95, but that may be a small price to pay for your sanity.

You can install over Windows 3.1. The advantage is that you get to keep all your previously existing program groupings (the groups from the Windows 3.1 Program Manager will reappear on your Start menu in Windows 95). The disadvantage is that you probably have all sorts of gunk hanging around your Windows system area, such as .INI files and .DLLs from long-gone programs. No uninstaller, no matter how good, can keep your system totally clean.

Fresh installation

If you install absolutely fresh, you lose all the gunk. You do have to reinstall your programs, but this is a great time for housekeeping. I've been amazed at how many programs I really don't need. And my Windows 95 speed increased at least one-third when I lost the gunk. The downside is that you have to be extra careful while preparing to install.

Do this, regardless

The following items will help you get a reliable installation of Windows 95 with minimum risk to your data and your system.

Back up Windows 3.1

Whichever course of action you choose, you need to do this. I'm cautious. I don't trust any tape backup or believe that installing with dual boot leaves Windows 3.1 absolutely clean forever. I don't even trust the Windows 95's installer option of backing up Windows 3.1. Call me paranoid; this is what I did all throughout the Windows 95 beta, and I never had any problem.

Find another partition on your drive, and make some .ZIP files. Four, to be precise. One for \WINDOWS, one for \WINDOWS\SYSTEM, one for \WINDOWS\SYSTEM\ WIN32S, and one for \DOS. The reasons for the first two backups are obvious. You want Win32s backed up because the Windows 95 installer removes many of those files. You want DOS backed up because the installer will zap many of your DOS files if you're installing over Windows 3.1 (a text file with Windows 95 tells you which ones; it's many but by no means all; I think it easier just to back up what you have). Why do I use .ZIP files? I find them the most reliable for this sort of work. If you want to be super cautious, use PKZIP's disk-spanning option to copy those .ZIP files to floppies.

Create a bootable floppy

Whether you're doing an absolutely clean install or installing into/alongside a current Windows 3.1, you need this floppy. If you don't have two, make them now. I say that because a disk can mysteriously go south, and you don't want to be stuck. Easiest is to use the File Manager command to make a system disk (remember: make TWO!). Now, go out to regular DOS and *test each disk* in turn to boot your system. Next, you should add certain files to both disks, although I sincerely hope you will need to use only one of them. The one you need to use is SYS.COM. If you need to get back to pre-W95 DOS rapidly, all you have to do is boot from the disk and run SYS C: from the A: prompt (more on all of this later). In addition, put the following files on both of your startup disks: FORMAT, FDISK, DEBUG, XCOPY, EDIT, and QBASIC.EXE. Make a subdirectory labeled STARTUP and copy your current AUTOEXEC.BAT, CONFIG.SYS, WIN.INI, and SYSTEM.INI files there.

You should do both of the preceding, regardless of how you're planning to install Windows 95. Until you get comfortable with (or fanatic about) Windows 95, they'll save your sanity.

Installing

Although I personally favor doing a clean install, my editor and I have decided against doing a walkthrough here — and likewise against detailing the other methods. Are we feeling mean-spirited? Nope — just practical. This is a book about Photoshop, with some pointers on Windows 95; you wouldn't be pleased to have a book about Windows 95 with some pointers on Photoshop, now would you? Excellent books are available that tell it all. For the whole story, see Chapter 3 of *Windows 95 SECRETS* and Chapters 8 and 9 of *The Mother of All Windows 95 Books* (see details at the end of this appendix).

If you're using the upgrade package to do a clean install, make sure you have the first floppy of your original Windows 3.1 package handy. Because you'll be doing an *upgrade* install, the installer will want proof that you're legal. If you install over Windows 3.1, it could sniff out the proof. Because you aren't, it can't sniff — it will ask you early on to insert that floppy. If you received Windows 3.1 on a CD-ROM, find out how to produce Disk 1 from it. Substantial evidence supports the fact that you can't insert the CD-ROM and keep the "sniffer" happy. More than one install has aborted.

This may not happen to you — my average has been 50 percent. Sometimes, at the very end of a CD-ROM-based installation, you'll get the mysterious message that *Windows 95 can't access your CD-ROM to finish its installation.* What this means is that the earlier hardware detection phase didn't find what it needed. Don't panic. Let it finish installing, then boot off the bootable floppy, copy your CD-ROM and SCSI drivers to the root directory, and compose AUTOEXEC.BAT and CONFIG.SYS files with the appropriate references. Reboot and you'll be able to access your CD-ROM via the real-mode drivers. Typically, you'll find that printer setup is all that was left undone. Now, go into the Control Panel, select the Add New Hardware applet, follow the Wizard, and all should be fine. Remember to delete those files you created in your root directory.

In general, during the install, let the installer detect appropriate hardware (it may miss some; see the following). You may find when it reports to you that it missed your monitor type; when it gives you the summary you will have the option to change it. For installation, I strongly urge you to select the last option (Custom), because I never trust default choices (see Appendix C for more specifics on this). Go through each section and be sure to click on the Details button to add exactly what you want. In particular, there is some new wallpaper and new screen savers, which you'll probably want. Choose other items depending on your needs and your computer's capabilities. Don't feel that this is all carved in stone. You will be able to add other items later through the Control Panel's Add Programs item.

I've found the actual install to be fairly trouble free, but some users have not. If your system simply stops responding (give it plenty of time), don't be afraid to follow the Microsoft suggestion to turn your computer off and back on again. You're not damaging anything — the Windows 95 installer has kept a disk record of what it needs to do. Once you actually get into Windows 95 for the first time, the installer will do a lot of setting up (it will tell you what it's doing). After it's finished, reboot. Even though you don't have to, it's an excellent precaution

Using Windows 95

The following tips will help you get comfortable with the Windows 95 operating system (and help you steer clear of some pitfalls).

The desktop

The very first thing to do is to go into My Computer or Explorer, head for your WINDOWS directory, find WINFILE.EXE, click on the right mouse button, and drag the file to your desktop. Release the button and accept the default of *Create a Shortcut* from the pop-up menu. You've just created a shortcut (OS/2 speak: *shadow;* Mac speak: *alias*) for (gasp) File Manager. You may think that you hate File Manager, but you are used to it. You want it around until you're sure of yourself, or even longer if you like File Manager. See the following for both sides of this argument.

Your shortcut is identified as a shortcut by the little arrow on its icon. (Yes, the little arrow may clobber the icon's look — not so in the case of File Manager, but it could make you *mondo cranky* if that arrow obscures part of an icon you've spent hours crafting.) There are ways to change the arrow to something else or make it disappear. *Don't change it.* Much as you may hate those little arrows, they can save you from yourself. If you eliminate the arrows, you'll have no tool except your memory to distinguish between shortcuts and actual files. Do you trust your memory? Do you trust your reflexes late at night? I don't. Let those arrows be.

Tip You can create shortcuts by doing other kinds of dragging, too. But you can get into trouble, depending on whether you're dragging a document or an executable file. Use the right mouse button — you'll always get the pop-up menu and always have the chance to be sure you're creating a shortcut. (You definitely do not want to move an executable file to your Desktop; other kinds of dragging can move executable files too easily and accidentally.)

Caution Of course, you can delete shortcuts, either by highlighting and using the Delete key or by using the right mouse button and selecting Delete from the pop-up menu. But then you'll be asked if it's okay to delete the file. You may, as I once did, panic: *Are you deleting the shortcut only, or the underlying file?* The wording of the question is ambiguous. In reality, you're only deleting the shortcut — the underlying file is still wherever it lives. But I had to query Microsoft before I felt entirely comfortable. See Figure B-1.

Tip You may not like Windows 95's habit of labeling your new shortcut with the prefatory words *Shortcut to.* Allegedly, if you delete those words often enough, Windows 95 wises up. My Windows 95 has never gotten those smarts. I still have to manually get rid of those words. Although I'm not big on keyboard shortcuts, F2 is very helpful here.

Of course, you can use the right mouse button for much more. Right-click anywhere on the Desktop, and choose Properties. You can easily configure your color, wallpaper, screensaver, or monitor.

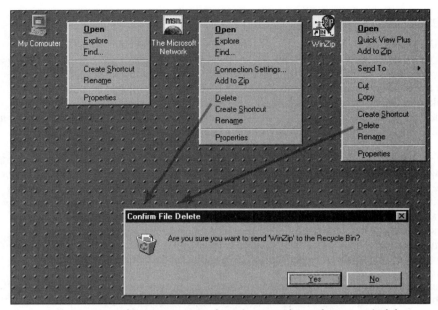

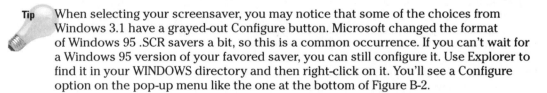

Figure B-1: Not everything on your Desktop is created equal. You can't delete some things (left). Windows 95 puts certain full executables on your Desktop (center) — these you can delete. And you can delete shortcuts (right). But notice that either deletion will produce the same confirmation dialog box (bottom). The secret is in the icon. Notice the absence of arrow in the center icon, the presence in the right icon — the former's an executable, the latter's just a shortcut.

Tip When selecting your screensaver, you may notice that some of the choices from Windows 3.1 have a grayed-out Configure button. Microsoft changed the format of Windows 95 .SCR savers a bit, so this is a common occurrence. If you can't wait for a Windows 95 version of your favored saver, you can still configure it. Use Explorer to find it in your WINDOWS directory and then right-click on it. You'll see a Configure option on the pop-up menu like the one at the bottom of Figure B-2.

Tip The icon here is a misnomer. Every book on Windows 95 should have at least one Stupid Trick. But I really couldn't ask for a Stupid Trick icon, because we know Photoshop is a serious program! Here's my nomination. Right-click on your Desktop, select the Screen Saver tab, scroll down to Flying Windows, and press the Settings button. Ramp up the Warp speed setting to Fast and set the Density to its maximum (75). On a fast Pentium . . . well, I told you this was a Stupid Trick. My first and last.

While you're in a shortcut mood, try this one. Use Explorer, go to the Start Menu and then Programs. Drag a shortcut to this onto the Desktop. This shortcut allows you to edit and rearrange your programs on the Start Menu with the least amount of fuss. Alternative: right-click on the Start button, select Explore, right-click on Programs, select Create Shortcut, and then drag Shortcut to Programs to the Desktop. See Figure B-3.

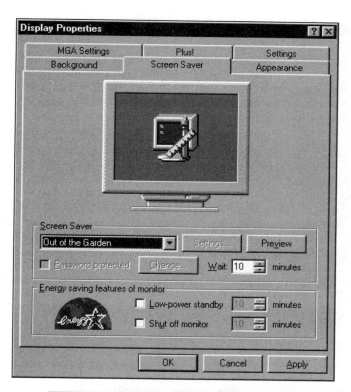

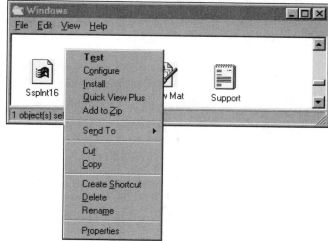

Figure B-2: This 16-bit screensaver apparently can't be configured in Control Panel (top). Do it in Explorer (bottom).

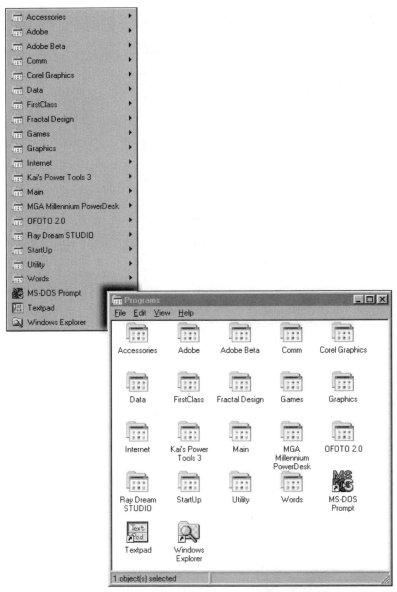

Figure B-3: A shortcut to the Programs folder (bottom) allows you ready editing of the Start Menu (top).

While you're in Desktop mode, take a look at Recycle Bin. By default, it uses 10 percent of your drive space. That may be too large. Right-click on Properties and set it back to something more reasonable (I use 5 percent).

Managing files

Whether under DOS or Windows-whatever, file management is a highly personal matter. Some swear by doing all their chores on the command line. Some swear by File Manager — and some swear at it. Windows 95 offers two more objects of affection or disdain, Explorer and My Computer, and a host of right mouse button functionality besides. So many choices, so little time!

I'm not going to try to push one method of file management on you. Although I'll talk about mine, chances are it won't be yours. What I want to do is give you a very brief idea of some of the possibilities. There are far more permutations than I could begin to cover, so take a look at my suggestions in the "Getting Help" section at the end of this appendix.

File Manager

Everyone loved to complain about this under Windows 3.1 — many praised (with some justification) the file management facilities of Norton Desktop or PC Tools. I appreciate all those positions, but I never found File Manager the nasty rotten thing that led some to dub it File *Mangler*. I used Outside/In from SCC, a series of file viewers that hooked right in (SCC has become a part of Inso Corporation and now makes Quick View Plus, which I'm going to discuss shortly). WinZip (discussed later) attached to my menu bar and gave me all the compression functionality I needed. If I felt I needed more, I could always roll my own via WinBatch.

You may be mourning or celebrating the apparent loss of File Manager in Windows 95. Not so fast! It's still there; the installation program just hasn't set up an icon for it. You'll find a new version of WINFILE.EXE in your windows directory. Of course, if you hate File Manager and have already decided that My Computer and Explorer are the greatest things since sliced bread, you'll leave it buried there. Me, first thing I did was create a shortcut to it on my Desktop. I use it about half the time; the other half I click my way through My Computer and Explorer.

My Computer and Explorer

Okay, I admit it. I didn't take to either of these during the beta, and they're still not my favorites. I like being able to do drag and drop on drive icons, which File Manager makes so easy. I like having two windows open so easily and then changing drives with just a click on the icons. I know that there are all sorts of ways to soup up these gizmos — I've tried any number of them, and I'm still not a convert. I want to be able to manage my files without thinking about how I do it. For me, nothing beats File Manager most of the time. But I've come to see that these new incarnations have their uses.

Putting them together

When I'm moving large numbers of files or checking what's what, I use File Manager. If I'm working intensively with a group of project files in one directory (or several subdirectories branching from one), I keep Explorer windows open on my Desktop for the directories so I can use the Send To option on the right-button menu. It makes copying to a floppy a virtual snap.

Tip   You can send files elsewhere, of course. To any program you'd like. For example, you may want to choose opening a .PSD file in either Photoshop or Painter. No problem. Place shortcuts to those programs in the Send To directory, and you've got 'em. (See Figure B-4.) This is particularly useful if you find that some program has overwritten all your file associations. For example, Corel PhotoPaint seems to think that you're going to want to open all your graphics files in it. Some nerve! Hacking through the Registry to fix this is both time consuming and dangerous. Doctoring the Send To choices is quick and easy.

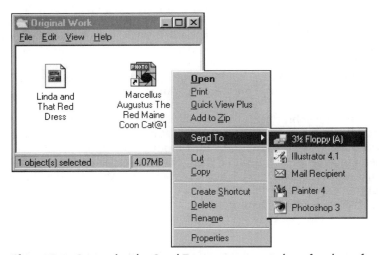

Figure B-4: Customize the Send To pop-up menu to have freedom of choice for opening your graphics files.

Tip   You may look for a newly moved, copied, or downloaded file in a directory you're viewing and not see it. Don't panic — if you put it there, it's there. Whether in Explorer or File Manager, press the F5 key to refresh; you'll see your file. (In some cases, it will be the last file in Explorer, out of alphabetical order.)

File viewers

If you installed Windows 95 from CD-ROM, you had the option of installing Quick View file viewers, which you can bring up by right-clicking on a file. If you didn't, you can still download them from Microsoft directly or from Microsoft's many online presences. But you may want to view many more file types than this apparently meager selection.

There are two choices. QuickView Plus, from Inso Corporation, expands the file viewing capability astronomically. It's easily installed and intuitive to use. I found it a winner from day one of its beta. There is also MasterSoft's Viewer 95, which offers similar viewing capabilities. Each program works well, each operates somewhat differently, and each has slightly different features. You can't go wrong with either one.

Norton Navigator

This program is omnipresent. Unlike Norton Utilities for Windows 95, which I've not installed because I consider it too unstable, I've used Navigator. In its first incarnation it was very slow — Symantec has since released a patch and slipstreamed it into shipping copies.

With the patch, it runs just fine on my Pentium with 32MB of memory. On my 486-66 with 16MB of memory, it's a different story. Others have reported this same sort of differential. There's a lot to like about Norton Navigator, but I don't personally find that it offers enough to justify space on my drive. You may feel differently — consider it if you've got the hardware to support it.

Managing fonts

The Fonts folder in Control Panel only manages TrueType fonts. If TrueType are the only fonts you're using, this may well suffice for you. But if you want to use Type 1 PostScript fonts, you'll need something more. I stress this perhaps obvious point because I have seen countless complaints of inability to install and manage Type 1 fonts via the Control Panel.

Limitations of PostScript fonts

For installing and using Type 1 fonts, you need Adobe Type Manager (see the further details in Appendix C). But you need to be aware of an important point right now. Under Windows 3.1, both TrueType and Type 1 font information was stored in the WIN.INI file, along with quite a lot of other information. Windows 95 now uses the Registry to store TrueType information and many other items. This is potentially good news, because the 64K limit of WIN.INI under Windows 3.1 still exists under Windows 95, but it will take you longer to hit it, because so much information formerly there now goes into the Registry. What are the effects of that limit? To say the least, your system starts acting flaky as you approach it. To say the most, print jobs with the wrong fonts or garbage inexplicably freeze your system. You get the picture.

Still, it is possible to reach that limit if you have many fonts installed. The result? Most software, including printer drivers, will fail to obtain complete Type 1 font information. This can lead to an aborted printing job or to the substitution of — gasp — Courier for the fonts you specified. Further, ATM uses a Windows system call when it updates font data in WIN.INI, and that call only lets 24K of information through each time. If there's more than 24K of information, the extra goes straight into the bit bucket, with nary an error message to you. As a result, ATM's communication with WIN.INI will not be completed. This could be very bad.

Font management

Listen. I don't see why you should get close to those limits. If you have a gadzillion fonts on your system, your font menus will become interminable, and your programs will run substantially slower. You just don't need to have all those fonts loaded up all the time.

Get FontMinder 3 (Windows 3.1 and Windows 95 version) from Ares Software. This superb program, which began life as shareware, enables you to have all the fonts you like, with none of those 64K limitations. FontMinder does it by means of *font packs,* groups of fonts you define. With just a click or two, you can swap in and out of WIN.INI and ATM.INI. You can have font packs for individual jobs or categories of usage. Also, FontMinder has excellent font management facilities, including superb sample pages and installation routines. It's not expensive, and it's the best tool for keeping your fonts in order.

Application Issues

In the Windows 3.1 world, every application seemed to have its own way of installing. Microsoft's attempt to impose standard installation methodologies, via its Windows 95 Logo Program, is thus all to the good. Thing is, it's going to take time to implement it. You still need to think about installing. Here are some selected considerations that may improve the quality of your installing life.

Installing

If you're installing a Windows 3.1 application and the installer won't work with Start⇨Run, try running the installer out of File Manager. If it's a Win32s application, you can sometimes fool it with a text file in your WINDOWS directory. Name the file WIN32S.INI and put the following two lines in it:

```
[Win32s]
Version=1.20.123.0
```

You may need to tinker with those numbers because the Win32s subsystem is constantly evolving. Check with your application vendor before doing this, though. Many have recommended precisely this workaround — and Microsoft has recommended it, too.

Increasing numbers of Windows 95 applications come on CD-ROM, and more have an Auto Play function; insert the CD-ROM, hear the drive whir, hear some music (if you've got a sound card), and see a splash screen. You may not like this, and you may want the old-fashioned method of finding the install program on the CD-ROM and proceeding from there. I've found that some CD-ROM install programs simply do not work straight from Auto Play, but they work fine the old-fashioned way. There are two things you can do:

✦ **Disable for a particular CD-ROM:** Depress the Shift key while inserting the CD-ROM. Your Auto Play setting remains intact.

✦ **Disable Auto Play globally:** Go into Device Manager, select the specific CD-ROM drive, select Properties, and uncheck the Auto Play box.

Regardless, I don't trust installers. I don't trust uninstallers. I don't trust the uninstall routines that Windows 95 applications use. I want to know precisely what's going where, and I've found that a hands-on approach works the best. See Appendix C.

Adobe products

✦ **Adobe Illustrator:** In Versions 4 through 4.03, it may not open at all. It may open and then display a message about a damaged or missing *ruler font file.* As far as I can tell, this message is harmless. But these versions of Illustrator aren't entirely stable under Windows 95 (Version 4.1 has been tweaked for stability and also adds TrueType font support). No, this isn't the major upgrade we've been clamoring for, but the upgrade *is* coming.

✦ **Adobe Type Manager:** You should have at least 3. 3.02 is the current shipping version, included with Photoshop. You may be able to run at the 2.5 level, but you're asking for trouble. It's sure-fire trouble if you're using 2.02 or earlier.

Caution By the time you read this, ATM may be incrementally higher, and sometimes those increments contain more changes than the numbering implies. Commendably, Adobe seems perpetually to be tweaking ATM, which is all to the good, given its importance and operation from deep inside Windows. I strongly advise you to stay current with ATM at all times.

✦ **PageMaker:** Version 5 runs, but 6 is now out and is Windows 95 logo compliant. It's good and inexpensive (as upgrades go) and has many new features. Do yourself a favor and upgrade.

✦ **Photoshop:** See Appendix C for the various versions. 3/3.01 is not entirely happy with Windows 95. Upgrade to 3.05, the currently shipping version.

The Major No-No: Hacking the Registry

I've given this a heading all by itself. It's impossible to overemphasize how dangerous this can be. PC people are an inventive lot; despite the fact that it's harder to get at the Registry than to WIN.INI and SYSTEM.INI, you may just be tempted to try. *Don't.* I'll explain.

The good old days: .INI files

It's true that if you messed up editing WIN.INI or SYSTEM.INI, you might render Windows nonfunctional. But you always had a safety net — text files. If they kept Windows from starting, you could stay in straight DOS, bring up a text editor, and undo your changes. There was another safety feature, too: The .INI files had been around so long that editing and mistakes were all thoroughly documented.

The Registry: happy days are here again?

The safety net is gone. The Registry, which supplants most of the functions of WIN.INI and SYSTEM.INI (and, according to Microsoft's plan, will ultimately render them irrelevant), isn't a text file at all. It's a binary file that you change by using the Regedit utility. You can't scan whole sections at once; you have to navigate through *keys, subkeys,* and the like. Sometimes, one application buries entries in several places, so it's hard to read and harder to edit. Make a mistake in the wrong area and *anything* can happen. Windows 95's hidden backup can't save you, either. You may have do a hack that brings down your system; before you realize it, Windows 95 may change your hacked registry, save it as your backup copy, and delete your last good Registry backup. This is quite possible — Windows 95 always seems to be writing to the Registry. Of course, you can save the whole Registry elsewhere, or you can save the section you're working on via the Export command. But if you don't remember to export each and every section you twiddle, you've got a problem.

Think I'm gloomy? It gets worse. Microsoft's documentation for the Registry is pitiful. I've got a theory about that. Windows 95 is designed to shield the user from as much as possible; Microsoft doesn't want people buying trouble. But sometimes hacking the Registry is the only way to get *out* of trouble, and Microsoft isn't making it any easier for you.

Various third-party information is appearing (some by very knowledgeable Windows 95 users and programmers). I don't use any of it. Although I greatly respect the knowledge of those who have found some truly ingenious hacks, I don't think anyone (even Microsoft) fully understands how the Registry interacts with the rest of the operating system. In Chapter 3, there was a case where an innocuous hack on storing abbreviated long file names caused major problems when installing certain Windows 95 programs, and this hack came from one of the most knowledgeable Windows 95 gurus around.

Caution Others are also proffering this hack. I've warned you about this before. Don't even *think* about doing it.

Is it really worth risking your system so the Start menu has stickier submenus, or doesn't fly up so fast, or so that windows don't *explode* from a minimized state? There are hacks around for these and other things. Do as you will, but you won't have me for company if you venture down this path now. A day will come when we can hack safely. But that day hasn't dawned.

About Drivers

Latest isn't necessarily greatest. I've scattered references throughout the book to give specific examples of this. Sometimes latest is truly greatest, but sometimes a newer driver will break something that previously worked fine. So here's my driver advice:

✦ **Troll for drivers:** You could die of senility waiting for the manufacturer to send them automatically. Drivers tend to turn up first on the manufacturer's BBS and/or WWW page. Later they hit the online services.

✦ **If you've got Internet access, try the manufacturer's WWW or FTP site:** This particularly applies to video drivers. A new driver comes out, and the BBS has a perpetual busy signal. This is not the manufacturer's fault — do you know how many eager beavers are out there? But you can almost always get onto their Internet sites immediately.

✦ **Keep your old drivers:** As I've just mentioned, you may need them. Especially for diagnostics. I keep mine for at least a year.

Getting Help

The documentation Microsoft provides with Windows 95 is, well, skimpy. Even with the help files, you're probably going to need more. Of course, I'm assuming that you're willing to *RTFM* (for more on that fine acronym, and why you should read, see Chapter 1). Here are some starting points.

Online

All the major services offer Windows 95 areas. I particularly like MSWIN95 on CompuServe, but the areas on The Microsoft Network and America Online are worthy, too. There's also a proliferation of Windows 95 pages on the World Wide Web. I hesitate to mention any here. The Web changes constantly, so any address is unreliable. I think the safest strategy is using Yahoo! (www.yahoo.com). Yahoo! is likely to be around long after you read this, and it's the fastest route to an up-to-date listing.

The printed word

The following items are a few of the most important printed resources for living and working with Windows 95.

Periodicals

Tips are everywhere. Articles are everywhere. Since Windows 95 shipped, that's been about all we've had. Some are useful, some are redundant, some are just plain wrong (not many, luckily). If you must have tips, and more of them, any computer publication you choose will be spawning them on a monthly basis. You don't need me to tell you which publications to read.

But I'd like to tell you about one source that is less well known. Brian Livingston, whose Windows 95 book I've mentioned before and am going to again in the next section, has a regular Windows 95 column in *InfoWorld*. Brian is privy to all manner of information, tips, and ideas — his range is breathtaking. You may qualify for a free subscription to that weekly newspaper. If you don't, most large libraries carry it. It's worth subscribing just for Brian's weekly column. (Incidentally, IDG Books Worldwide, Inc., is part of the same company that publishes *InfoWorld*.)

Books

For the last time: Get *Windows 95 SECRETS,* by Brian Livingston and Davis Straub (IDG Books Worldwide, Inc.). Brian's books on Windows 3.1 took me from novice to, well, let's just be modest and say less-than-novice status. *Windows 95 SECRETS* is just as good. If you want to flesh out my brief comments on Explorer, here's your nirvana. It comes with a superb CD-ROM, too.

You may well also want *The Mother of All Windows 95 Books,* by Woody Leonhard and Barry Simon (Addison-Wesley). This book also has a fine CD-ROM. The book's emphases are so different from *SECRETS* that it can hardly be viewed as competing.

Leonhard and Simon are even breezier than McClelland and Phillips.

Of course, the *Windows 95 Resource Kit* (Microsoft Press) is another necessity. It's big, it's incomplete, it's frustrating. But it's all Microsoft is saying publicly about Windows 95, so it's a key resource. But it isn't a joy to read; *SECRETS* is.

Installation

Is Robert on a roll? (If he were online, would he be on a scroll?) After all, he's just added three new sections (Chapter 19 and two appendixes) while working without a net. Or is it a fiendish plan to feature-bloat this book, allowing the publisher to jack up its price, making more moola for all involved? After all, what could be simpler than just popping in the first floppy or CD-ROM, finding SETUP.EXE, and doing it?

The answer is: *none of the above.* You've already seen that I'm not a trusting soul when it comes to computers. Even when installers are as well behaved and well documented as Adobe's, I just refuse to abandon myself to them. It's my drive and my sanity. And remember (how could you forget?) my philosophy of not doing anything to destabilize your system; even a well-behaved installer can do you a nasty. When a 1930s-style mobster screamed *Watch it* at Mr. Spock, the eminent Vulcan Science Officer replied, *Sir, we shall watch it and everything else, very carefully.*

So, although you definitely should follow Adobe's clear instructions, I want to tell you some extra things that will get you installed and into Photoshop the way you want. All this comes from my own experience with installers good and bad — in fact, if I had a dime for each installer I've used, I could do a leveraged buyout of Adobe Systems and . . . .

Introduction

Wait! Don't pop that floppy or CD-ROM in just yet. Sit on your hands while I tell you some things to do before you even *think* about breaking the envelope's seal.

Inventory your disk space

The installation instructions ask you to have at least 20MB of free disk space. When I look at my Photoshop directory, I see about 8MB of space taken up, but this doesn't mean Adobe is wrong. Installers need a certain amount of overhead on disk space for decompressing files. And the installer needs to put certain files in your Windows directory and subdirectories. This will vary depending on your operating system. If it's Windows 3.1, you'll need room for the Win32s subsystem. In addition, regardless of operating system, you'll need room on that drive for the 1MB of color management files that go into a PHOTOCD subdirectory of the main WINDOWS directory. If you don't have enough free space on your Windows drive, the installer will give you an *insufficient disk space* error message, regardless of where you are putting the main Photoshop directory.

I do not think you should accept the default and put your main Photoshop directory on your Windows drive (typically C). Here's why. You want to keep that drive as clear as possible, for several reasons. Windows wants that drive for its paging file — true, you can point it, but why bother? Second, some programs insist on putting certain files there. In short: *Whenever you have an option to keep things away from your C: drive, do so!*

For absolute safety, I recommend 15MB free on your C: drive and 20MB free on the drive you choose for Photoshop. This is more than needed, but it ensures that you won't get an aborted installation.

Turn off the nonessentials

Close all running programs. Yeah, I know, the OS/2 crowd likes to talk about doing a download, playing a game, and formatting a floppy all at the same time. But this isn't OS/2. Besides, if you *must* multitask while installing . . . well, when I have to, I go to the next room and get onto Linda's computer, if she'll let me.

Close any little doodads that you may be running from the StartUp Group, or from the RUN and LOAD lines of WIN.INI. Close screen savers. And, most important, turn off any virus checker. Some installers will balk, or abort an install, if a virus checker is running. Some won't, but the install won't work (that is, you'll not be able to get into the program — or you'll be able to get in, but won't stay very long). Adobe's installers have often fallen into this latter category.

Finally, set up a disk inventory program. By that, I mean a program that takes a snapshot of your Windows drive and the drive you intend for Photoshop. Then, after installation, you run the program again; it compares the differences and gives you a report. I say this for several reasons. I never entirely trust uninstall routines. And I like to know what goes where — later, if I'm trying to troubleshoot a problem in some program and I've gotten things narrowed down to a .DLL that has been overwritten, I can bring up my install records and usually find which program has done the no-no (it's a no-no because it shouldn't do it — if it does, the programmers either haven't heard of VER.DLL or decided not to use it). Several excellent shareware programs are included on the CD-ROM of *Windows 95 SECRETS*, by Brian Livingston & Davis Straub. I've praised this IDG book often enough that you're probably sick of hearing me. But it's true. Or there's the excellent freeware In Control 2, which I personally use. If you're on CompuServe, GO ZNT:TIPS and get INCTR2.EXE from library 2. If not (hang on! This is probably the only WWW address I'm giving in this book — trumpets blare, drums roll), and you have Internet access and the WWW, the URL you want is WWW.ZDNET.COM/~PCMAG/UTILS/INCTRL2.HTM.

Now restart Windows; you're ready to shake, rattle — and roll.

Installing Photoshop

Now follow Adobe's instructions for getting started with the installation — you'll find them in the *Getting Started* booklet on pages 4-5 . I'm not going to waste your time, and IDG Books' paper, by simply repeating them. Rather, I want to offer some helpful annotations.

✦ **The Welcome Screen:** The first thing you'll see. Read it and move on.

✦ **The Name/Company/Serial Number screen:** Time to get interactive. If it's a new installation, use the serial number that comes on the card inside your Photoshop box. If it's an upgrade, use your previous serial number. Note that those are zeros in the strings of digits — you never have to type the letter *O*.

✦ **Setup Type:** You'll be given a choice of installations: *Typical, Compact, Custom* — see Figure C-1. Recall that I'm none too trusting — I want to be the person deciding what I want — so choose Custom. (See my following section about what you're going to be selecting.) The default directory will be on your C: drive. (See the previous description on why you should not accept this.) If you name any other directory or location, the Installer will ask you if it's OK to create it. It definitely *is* OK!

Note The Compact installation merely installs Photoshop with none of the additional files. Typical installs everything (Deluxe Tutorial, too, if you're installing from the CD-ROM). Custom installs the same as Typical, but lets you make choices. See Figure C-2 and the following two sections on what you want to install, and what you may not want to install if you're using the CD-ROM.

✦ **Select Program Folder:** Because I use Adobe applications all the time, I already have an Adobe program group. Surely you do, too? But if not, set this to the folder of your choice. This is a nice touch — all too many programs assume you want a folder, or program group, for just them.

✦ **Start Copying Files:** Your chance to confirm your choices, and to back out if you've missed something. Double-check this carefully.

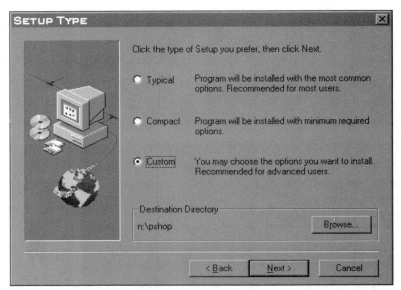

Figure C-1: The Installer offers you three installation choices — choose Custom.

What you should choose

I recommend everything except the Deluxe CD-ROM Tutorial (obviously, this is only available on the CD-ROM version of the program). See the next section for my reasons. Because you're reading this book, you obviously are going to want the program itself, plus the patterns, filters, and duotone files. Whether you're new or old to Photoshop, I think you'll want the tutorial. For new users, it's a great start. For old hands, it not only allows you to work through areas that you may be hazy on, but also gives you some images to practice various new techniques on. See the next section about the one item missing from this list.

Tip   After you've completed the Photoshop install, there's something else you may well want to install — Adobe Type Manager (ATM). It's not part of the regular installation options; you have to go to the ATM302 directory on the CD-ROM. Me, I couldn't live without it. You, you may be able to if you only intend to use True Type fonts, which you install via the Windows 95 Control Panel. But if you want to use Type 1 PostScript fonts in Photoshop, you must have ATM installed. If you have a version earlier than 3, you definitely want to run its installer to update to the current (3.02) version. If you're absolutely sure you're only going to be using TrueType fonts, you don't need ATM. Font lingo sound strange? See Chapter 12 for details and Appendix B for font-management issues under Windows 95. For installing and using ATM, see Adobe's *Getting Started* booklet on pages 24-27 (also includes instructions for removing ATM).

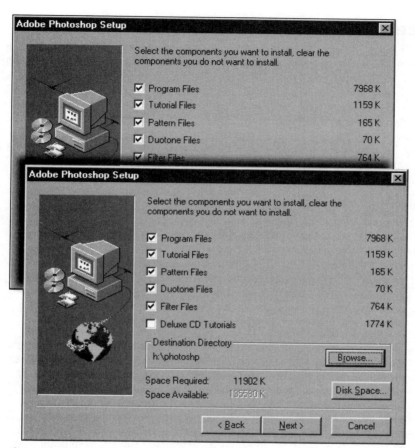

Figure C-2: The choices for floppy (top) and CD-ROM Custom installation (bottom). The difference is the Deluxe CD-ROM Tutorial, only available when installing from the CD-ROM. See text on whether this difference should matter to you.

Caution The previous tip does not yet apply, alas, to Windows NT people. There's no ATM for Windows NT; ATM in its current incarnation absolutely, positively will not run there. The reason is that ATM makes some calls to the hardware level that Windows NT, as a secure operating system, will not allow. Please don't e-mail me about *when will Adobe do an ATM for NT?* This question turns up regularly on CompuServe's ADOBEAPPS forum and more than once has occasioned some flaming. It's a definite need, and one that Adobe will address. Beyond that, I know no more than you do.

What I don't think you should choose

That there Deluxe CD-ROM Tutorial (obviously, if you're installing from floppies, this isn't a consideration). I hate to fly in the face of what the good folks in Mountain View have done, but I calls 'em as I sees 'em. There are three reasons why I'm taking such a hard line.

✦ **You don't need it:** The regular Adobe tutorial is very good, and there are any number of third-party books (including, obviously, this one) for honing your skills. I worked through this Deluxe Tutorial and found nothing I didn't know. It essentially shows you various Photoshop techniques — no hidden goodies, just demonstrations. For example, you can see how the Quick Mask mode operates. But do you need to? I think what Deke and I offer in Chapter 9 serves you just as well for learning about Quick Mask mode, especially if you follow up with references in the Index. Same goes for everything else. That is, I see the Deluxe CD-ROM Tutorial as perhaps helpful for the literacy challenged — but if you were one of that crowd, you'd not be reading (or able to read) this book — see Chapter 1 for more on reading and learning about Photoshop.

✦ **It can be bad for your hardware:** You'll need a sound card, and I don't think you should have a sound card on a Photoshop system (see Appendix A for more on this apparently heretical opinion).

✦ **It can be *very* bad for your software:** The Deluxe Tutorial relies on Apple's QuickTime 2.01, which will be installed if not present. Now that sounds benevolent enough, especially because Adobe states that the installer will not overwrite previous QuickTime versions. Many game programs and many multimedia programs install QuickTime. (I'm sure you have some. I certainly do — can't Photoshop *all* the time.) Thing is, those program installers may be less benevolent, merrily installing an earlier version, or a later version, and not telling you. Then your game runs, but you can't run the Deluxe Tutorial. Or vice versa. Taking a QuickTime mish-mash off your system and then getting it back correctly can be a serious nightmare. And not all video cards get along well with it. More than one programmer I've talked with about QuickTime has said — well, I can't repeat the precise words in a book like this, so let me quote Professor Van Helsing from *Dracula:* "Polyglot, and with blood."

'Nuff said. Three strikes make an out. You install the Deluxe CD-ROM Tutorial at your own risk.

Photoshop Versions

Photoshop 3.05 is, of course, the Latest And Greatest — it's the Windows 95 logo-compliant version (see the following). In a perfect world, that's all I'd need to say; in fact, I wouldn't even need this section. But in the real world, things operate a bit differently. As you'll recall from Chapter 1, three versions of Photoshop are floating around: 3/3.01 (the same thing, and the slash isn't gratuitous — see Chapter 1 for details), 3.04, and 3.05.

If you've just purchased 3.05, you probably won't need this section. But if you've been using Photoshop, you're probably using 3/3.01 or 3.04. And this section is for you, because you'll want to know what you get by moving upwards. But before we look at the versions, yet another flavor of Photoshop needs mentioning. And it is . . .

Photoshop LE

The *LE* stands for Limited Edition. Other vendors may refer to such products as SE (Special Edition), but I applaud Adobe for being honest. Limited is just that — *limited*. Your Photoshop LE most typically came bundled with another product, such as Adobe Pagemaker 6 or with your scanner hardware. And it's a very common question on CompuServe's ADOBEAPPS forum about what you get, and don't get, with the Limited Edition. So here's a list of what you do *not* get in the LE:

✦ Calibration

✦ Channels

✦ Color models and operations: Separation output capability, CMYK color, Lab Color, Custom Color; Color Range/Replace Color/Selective Color Correction; CMYK Preview Command; Gamut Warning Command and Out of Gamut alert in palettes and dialogs; Duotone Mode

✦ Commands Palette

✦ Curves/Calculations/Histogram/Trap

✦ Export as Amiga HAM

✦ File Info

✦ Filters: Radial Blur, Distort (Displace, Pinch, Polar Coordinates, Ripple, Shear, Spherize, Twirl, Wave, ZigZag), Median, Color Halftone, Lens Flare, Lighting Effects, Texture Fill, Extrude, Video Filters (De-interlace, NTSC Colors), Other Filters (Custom, HighPass, Maximum, Mininum, Offset)

✦ Layers

✦ Load/Save Selections

✦ Open As/Save As Formats: Amiga IFF, Pixar, PixelPaint, Raw, Scitex CT; Open and place Adobe Illustrator files (.AI)

✦ Paths; Paths to Illustrator

✦ QuickEdit

You may wonder, after all this, why Adobe took away so much, or why it bothered to do it in the first place. Hey, you can't expect it to give away the full edition when it's bundled, can you? (The full edition *is* bundled with some high-end scanners, but I wouldn't base my hardware decision on that fact alone.) The Limited Edition offers just enough functionality to let you do some very basic image editing — and hopefully to whet your appetite for the full edition. Adobe offers a very reasonable upgrade path to the full edition, and I urge you to take it.

Photoshop for Windows 3.04

Here is a list of the major optimizations and features in this version. For several reasons, I've omitted various small bug fixes. If you found a bug in 3/3.01, chances are it was squashed in 3.04.

✦ Distortion plug-ins now preview all masks that are present for a layer

✦ Float Controls feature

✦ Native Photoshop plug-ins no longer require Photoshop to run — in theory, they can run with other applications that support updated Photoshop 3.0.4 plug-in API

Note   Because that API is *open,* you can expect that non-Adobe applications will eventually support it. For the moment, I've only found this functional in Adobe Pagemaker 6 via Element⇨Image ⇨Photoshop Effects (and it only works with placed TIFF files — see Figure C-3). You can either move your Photoshop plug-ins to the Pagemaker sub-directory (several levels down) or create a shortcut there to your Photoshop plug-ins directory — see the help file for details.

Figure C-3: Pagemaker 6 lets you use your Photoshop 3.04 (and higher) plug-ins.

✦ Online registration

Tip As the name implies, you now have no excuse not to be a Registered User. Aside from the tech support implications, there's another compelling reason to register: You want to be on the mailing list for upgrades. For example, Adobe supplied 3.04 free to all registered users — it simply appeared in the mail. There were many howls on CompuServe's ADOBEAPPS forum from users who didn't receive their copies — and it turned out that for each and every U.S.-based user, the registration hadn't been completed.

✦ Optimized Adobe Illustrator Parser

Caution It's still possible to have some problems here; see Chapter 3 for details.

✦ Optimized performance on Windows 3.1 in regard to Photoshop's problems with Win32s

Background This may sound like Adobe had dropped the ball. Nope. 32-bit applications that run with the Win32s subsystem under Windows 3.1 all need tweaking. Continual tweaking. Because of Microsoft's constant tinkering with the Win32s subsystem, new versions have this nasty habit of breaking applications, or parts of applications, which worked fine previously.

✦ Optimized for opening 64BASE images from Kodak Pro PhotoCDs

✦ Optimized for speed on large memory systems

✦ Primary channel (for example, Red) deletion now allowed

✦ Removed ability to open multiple files in Open dialog (there were several unsolvable problems otherwise)

✦ Revised size limit of 512 pixels for EPS previews

✦ Scanners: Tested and verified scanner acquire modules (TWAIN) and drivers from leading scanner manufacturers; optimization for large images; support for TWAIN 36/48-bit scanners; optimized low DOS memory available to ASPI scanners

✦ Scratch Disk Efficiency indicator — see Chapter 2

✦ Tablets: Eraser support for new Wacom Ultra series; pressure-sensitive brushes optimized

✦ Windows 95 awareness, including: Improved performance with most 16-bit plug-ins and scanning modules right mouse button configuration to Photoshop Commands palette support for long filenames (LFN) and Universal Naming Convention (UNC) path names; Use Registry for application and file icons

Note Be clear about what the first item means, the first word in particular: *improved.* 3.04 introduced a *thunking layer* (yep, that's what it's called in computerese) that allowed Photoshop to recognize and use 16-bit plug-ins, such as KPT 2. Under 3/3.01, no 16-bit plug-in would even be recognized because Photoshop is a 32-bit application. But when 3.04 shipped, a number of users found that some of the KPT filters wouldn't work or had problems at increased file sizes. (See Chapter 19. Adobe never promised perfection!)

Tip If you're having problems with the plug-ins under 3.04, you want to get the latest thunking files; they're available in ADOBEAPPS library 12 on CompuServe or from Adobe's WWW site as (naming current as we go to press): 16BUPDAT.ZIP. These files are the same as their counterparts in 3.05 — you only need them if you're stubbornly using 3.04. While you're at it, if you insist on staying with 3.04, also get GIFUPDAT.ZIP and TWNUPDAT.ZIP. The former gives you the GIF 89a export module (see Chapter 3), while the latter has the latest Photoshop TWAIN scanning support (see Chapter 3 and Appendix A).

Tip You've got a bit of extra work to do if you installed 3.04 into Windows 3.1 and then upgraded to Windows 95. To get the Windows 95 support, you must reinstall Photoshop.

3.05

I'm doing this listing a bit differently. The Adobe statements for each item are in **bold type**. My annotations follow them. Otherwise, you'd have to look at a Note icon for each and every item; I wouldn't want to give you *iconitis*.

Caution This is something of a hybrid list. It contains the items on Adobe's official list, which is available in library 12 of CompuServe's ADOBEAPPS forum and Adobe's World Wide Web site as PS305.PDF. It also contains some items not there that I have discovered.

+ **GIF89a export plug-in (includes support for transparency and interlacing):** See Chapter 3 for details.

+ **Installation of latest version 1.30 of Win32s under Windows 3.1:** Note that this will overwrite a previous version of Win32s.

+ **Support for new Wacom UltraPen eraser:** If you're using the latest Wacom tablets, obviously. Because I'm using my "legacy" SD-510C (see Chapter 7), I've not been able to test this feature.

+ **OLE 2.0 object server and drag-and-drop support:** This means you can edit a Photoshop object in an OLE container application such as Pagemaker 6.0 or Word for Windows 95. I suppose this could be useful, but I can't recommend doing it. Photoshop is so memory hungry that having it and another big application open at the same time — I honestly don't think is in your best interests. Can you *really* mentally multitask to be able to do serious image work and serious page-layout work simultaneously? Still, it can be done. (See Figure C-4.)

Figure C-4: The ultimate twofer: editing a TIFF placed in Pagemaker 6 (top) in Photoshop 3.05 (bottom).

- ✦ **Optimization for multiple processors under Windows NT**
- ✦ **Open filmstrip (FLM) files:** For the first time! Not possible under previous versions of Photoshop for Windows. See Chapter 3 for details.

✦ **Support of the new TWAIN_32 standard for both 16-bit and 32-bit scanning modules:** This is sometimes known as the *universal thunker.* In theory, when you select the TWAIN_32 acquire module, it should work with your current TWAIN scanner devices. See Appendix A for further details.

✦ **Uninstall capability:** Always a good feature, but you've got the Industry Standard with Photoshop, so why would you want to make it go away? Actually, there is one reason — see the following Tip and Figure C-5 for an illustration of the beginning of the uninstall.

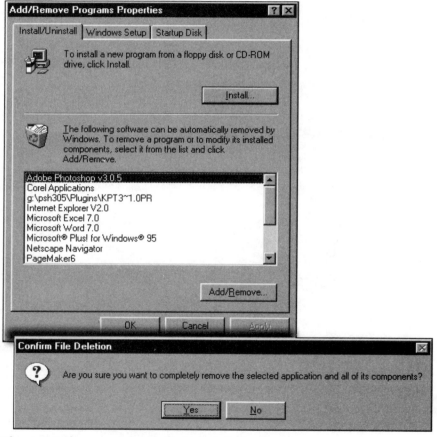

Figure C-5: If you must, here's the Uninstaller in progress.

Tip There is one case where you'll want to uninstall Photoshop: *when a new version appears.* Never, ever, install a new version over an older version. And, I've found some anomalous behavior with two versions of Photoshop on my system (3.04 and 3.05), even though they were in different directories on different drives. Finally, you should monitor what the installation process does against any possible future need to uninstall — see earlier in this appendix for details.

✦ **Updated thunking for 16-bit scanning modules and 16-bit third-party plug-ins:** I covered this in the preceding section. This area is now working very well indeed. See Chapter 3 for scanning, Chapter 19 for plug-ins.

✦ **Windows 95 Common Dialog support:** You can have all the right button pop-up benefits for your files right inside the File Open dialog boxes. See Appendix B for further particulars and Figure C-6 right now.

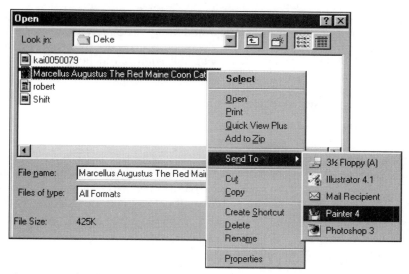

Figure C-6: Thanks to Windows 95, you can now do much of your file management on the fly in the File Open dialog box.

✦ **Windows 95 LFN and UNC path name support:** I've explained these acronyms in the preceding section.

✦ **Windows 95 registry of Photoshop file and application icons:** Photoshop is a model citizen. It doesn't assume that you'll want to open every supported graphics file format in it — it just registers its native PSD format and leaves the rest up to you. Of course, if you've customized your settings to allow other graphics formats to open automatically in Photoshop, you may be in for a rude surprise after you install another image editing program; see Appendix B.

Caution Despite using the Registry, Photoshop 3.05 still uses PHOTOS30.INI and PHOTOS30.PSP — see Chapter 2 for details. But instead of living in the WINDOWS directory, these files now reside in the PREFS subdirectory of your Photoshop directory. Just like Microsoft has been urging developers to do, .INI files and their relatives should go in the applications directory.

✦ **Windows 95 right-mouse button support:** See, in particular, the end of Chapter 2.

✦ **Windows 95 send-mail support:** It allows you to create a mail document, attach the open file, and pump it through Microsoft Mail. For Photoshop, I find send-mail a bizarre aspect of the Microsoft certification program for Windows 95. Head to Figure 3-3 if you want to see where this alleged feature not-so-allegedly lives.

Note My editor writes: "I've found built-in mail kinda handy in word processing and spreadsheet programs when I'm making documents for other people who are waiting for them. The Send command creates an Exchange message and attaches my open file without navigating to or through another program." I would reply "Absolutely right, Pat. Thing is, Photoshop documents aren't quite like other documents. Typically, they're so big that you don't even think of sending them via modem. Still, some Photoshoppers may want to exploit this, and I thank you for the valuable counterpoint."

✦ **Windows 95 use of system colors and metrics**

✦ **Windows 95 user interface adoption**

A Missing Feature?

If you've read the Getting Started booklet for Photoshop 3.05, you may have noticed, on page 9, the following item: "The Kodak YCC export plug-in for Windows supporting the Kodak YCC format." You've run into a typo in the documentation, and Adobe (as it's said to me) apologizes for the error.

About documentation changes

I've mentioned before that I find Adobe's documentation to be excellent. Still, no computer documentation is perfect. Because you may well be upgrading, here are some quick notes on the apparent changes in the 3.05 materials.

✦ **Beyond the Basics, User Guide, and Tutorial unchanged:** That is, they seem identical to the versions that shipped with 3/3.01. This means you won't find guidance on the newer features as itemized above, and it is one of the reasons I've itemized them.

✦ **Getting Started has been changed:** Pages 8-12 indicate new features, but the differences between 3.04 and 3.05 are not clear. Again, the need for my itemized lists earlier. Pages 19-21 describe use of the GIF 89a Export module, new in 3.05 but usable by 3.04 people as well (see previous description). And see my previous Caution note on the absence of the YCC export module.

✦ **Quick Reference Card unchanged:** Thus, you won't see the Send mail or GIF 89a export options illustrated.

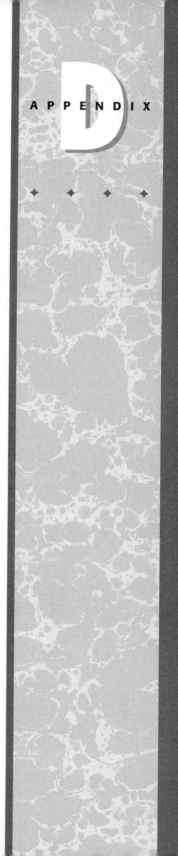

Photography Credits

The images used in this book came from all kinds of sources. The following list cites the figures or color plates in which a photograph appears. Following the figure number is the name of the photographer and the company from which the photograph was licensed. In each case, the photographer holds the copyright. If the photograph comes from a CD collection, the product name appears in italics along with or instead of a photographer, and the company holds the copyright. If no company is listed, the photo was licensed from the photographer directly.

To all who contributed their photography, our heartfelt thanks.

Figures (or Color Plates where named)	Photographer/Product	Company
2-2, 2-4, 2-5, 2-9 — 2-11	Robert Phillips	
3-1, 3-20	*Photo CD Snapshots*	Eastman Kodak
3-2, 3-6	Robert Phillips	
3-7, 3-11	*Michelangelo*	Planet Art
3-9	*V. 11, Retro Americana*	PhotoDisc
3-22, 3-23, 3-25, 3-26	Denise McClelland	
Color Plate 3-1	*V. 9, Holidays & Celebrations*	PhotoDisc
4-7	*V. 5, World Commerce & Travel*	PhotoDisc
4-10, 4-12 — 4-14	Denise McClelland	
Color Plate 4-2	*V. 5, World Commerce & Travel*	PhotoDisc
5-2 — 5-4, 5-7	Carlye Calvin, *Sampler One*	Color Bytes
Color Plates 5-1, 5-2	Carlye Calvin, *Sampler One*	Color Bytes
6-5	*V. 11, Retro Americana*	PhotoDisc
6-6	Denise McClelland	
6-15	Mark Collen	
Color Plate 6-1	Mark Collen	
7-6 — 7-8, 7-29, 7-30	Russell McDougal	
7-13, 7-14	*V. 5, World Commerce & Travel*	PhotoDisc
7-15	*V. 12, Food & Dining*	PhotoDisc
Color Plate 7-1	*V. 12, Food & Dining*	PhotoDisc
Color Plates 7-4, 7-5	*V. 5, World Commerce & Travel*	PhotoDisc
8-4, 8-15, 8-17 — 8-20, 8-24, 8-25, 8-28 — 8-30, 8-36, 8-37	*V. 4, Technology & Medicine*	PhotoDisc
8-6 — 8-8	Russell McDougal	
8-9, 8-32 — 8-34	*V. 4, Technology & Medicine*	PhotoDisc
8-10 — 8-14	*V. 4, Technology & Medicine*	PhotoDisc
8-18 (face)	*V. 5, World Commerce & Travel*	PhotoDisc
8-21, 8-22	Russell McDougal	
8-27 (background)	*V. 4, Technology & Medicine*	PhotoDisc

Figures (or Color Plates where named)	Photographer/Product	Company
9-1, 9-2, 9-13, 9-19 — 9-23	*V. 11, Retro Americana*	PhotoDisc
9-3 — 9-10	*V. 4, Technology & Medicine*	PhotoDisc
9-15, 9-18		The Bettmann Archive
Color Plate 9-1	*V. 11, Retro Americana*	PhotoDisc
Color Plate 9-2		The Bettmann Archive
10-2, 10-30, 10-32, 10-36 — 10-38	Russell McDougal	
10-5, 10-6, 10-39, 10-40	*V. 11, Retro Americana*	PhotoDisc
10-7, 10-9 — 10-12	*V. 6, Nature & the Environment*	PhotoDisc
10-27, 10-29	*V. 5, World Commerce & Travel*	PhotoDisc
Color Plates 10-1, 10-2	*V. 6, Nature & the Environment*	PhotoDisc
11-2 — 11-5, 11-12, 11-23	Denise McClelland	
11-6, 11-7	Russell McDougal	
11-8 — 11-11, 11-18 — 11-21	Michael Probst	Reuters
10-17 (top)	*Wraptures*	Form and Function
10-17 (bottom)	*Folio 1*	D'pix
12-1, 12-4	Robert Phillips	
12-2, 12-11 — 12-16, 12-20 — 12-22	Carlye Calvin, *Sampler One*	Color Bytes
12-23 — 12-25	*V. 11, Retro Americana*	PhotoDisc
13-1, 13-2, 13-4, 13-5, 13-8 — 13-15, 13-18 — 13-21, 13-25 — 13-28, 13-30, 13-31, 13-41, 13-43, 13-44, 13-46 — 13-48	*V. 5, World Commerce & Travel*	PhotoDisc
13-3	*V. 5, World Commerce & Travel*	PhotoDisc
13-6, 13-7, 13-22, 13-24, 13-40	*V. 11, Retro Americana*	PhotoDisc
13-16, 13-17, 13-32 — 13-38, 13-45	*V. 5, World Commerce & Travel*	PhotoDisc
Color Plates 13-1, 13-2	*V. 5, World Commerce & Travel*	PhotoDisc
Color Plates 13-3 — 13-5, 13-8	*V. 9, Holidays and Celebrations*	PhotoDisc

(continued)

Figures (or Color Plates where named)	Photographer/Product	Company
Color Plate 13-6	*V. 5, World Commerce & Travel*	PhotoDisc
Color Plate 13-7	*V. 5, World Commerce & Travel*	PhotoDisc
14-1 — 14-4, 14-6 — 14-8, 14-11, 14-13, 14-14, 14-20, 14-21, 14-36	*V. 5, World Commerce & Travel*	PhotoDisc
14-5, 14-9, 14-10, 14-27	*V. 11, Retro Americana*	PhotoDisc
14-12	Mark Collen	
14-28, 14-29	Robert Phillips	
14-37	*Michelangelo*	Planet Art
Color Plates 14-1 — 14-3, 14-8, 14-9	*V. 9, Retro Americana*	PhotoDisc
Color Plates 14-4 — 14-6	*V. 7, Business & Occupations*	PhotoDisc
Color Plate 14-7	Mark Collen	Planet Art
15-1, 15-42, 15-43, 15-45	*V. 9, Holidays & Celebrations*	PhotoDisc
15-3 — 15-31, 15-33 — 15-41	*V. 5, World Commerce & Travel*	PhotoDisc
Color Plates 15-1, 15-2	*V. 5, World Commerce & Travel*	PhotoDisc
Color Plates 15-3, 15-4	*V. 9, Holidays & Celebrations*	PhotoDisc
16-1, 16-2, 16-4 — 16-6, 16-12, 16-14, 16-15, 16-17, 16-21 — 16-25	*V. 5, World Commerce & Travel*	PhotoDisc
16-10	*V. 9, Holidays & Celebrations*	PhotoDisc
Color Plates 16-1 — 16-3, 16-6 — 16-8	*V. 5, World Commerce & Travel*	PhotoDisc
Color Plates 16-4, 16-5, 16-9, 16-10	*V. 9, Holidays & Celebrations*	PhotoDisc
Color Plate 16-11	*French Posters*	Planet Art
17-3 — 17-10, 17-12, 17-13, 17-15, 17-16	Russell McDougal	
17-18 — 17-21	Carlye Calvin, *Sampler One*	Color Bytes
17-23	*V. 11, Retro Americana*	Color Bytes
Color Plates 17-1, 17-2	Russell McDougal	
Color Plates 17-3 — 17-5	Carlye Calvin, *Sampler One*	Color Bytes

Figures (or Color Plates where named)	Photographer/Product	Company
18-1, 18-2, 18-4, 18-6	Russell McDougal	
18-7, 18-8	Carlye Calvin, *Sampler One*	Color Bytes
Color Plates 18-1, 18-3	Russell McDougal	
Color Plates 18-4, 18-5	Carlye Calvin, *Sampler One*	Color Bytes
19-1	*V. 5, Sports and Recreation*	KPT Power Photos
19-2	Michael Davis	
19-10	Robert Phillips	
19-13	*V. 11, Retro Americana*	PhotoDisc
19-14 (element)	*V. 3, Architectural Elements*	Objects Series
19-19	*Textures for Professionals*	Visual Software
A-3, A-4	Robert Phillips	
C-3, C-4	Robert Phillips	

About the CD-ROM

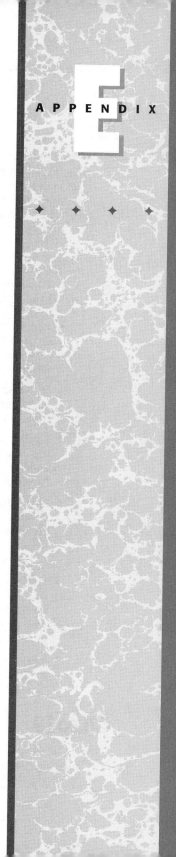

To access the images and technical documents included on this CD-ROM, start by inserting it into your CD-ROM drive. The CD icon, labeled PsBible, appears on your desktop. Double-click on the CD icon to open the CD-ROM. The window pops open and displays the following six icons:

◆ **Art:** This folder contains original artwork created in Photoshop for Windows. The creations of six artists are represented, and each file contains a Details file for further information about the artists and the processes they used to create their masterpieces.

◆ **Chap19:** This folder contains additional support information for Chapter 19. These files supplement the text information and guide you in creating handmade effects.

◆ **DigStock:** There are two directories in the DigStock folder; the first one contains 20 high-resolution images and the second is stuffed to the gills with a few thousand low-resolution ones. There are oodles of great images here for you to edit and integrate into your next composition.

◆ **PhotoDsc:** Within the PhotoDisc folder are 24 high-resolution images were used throughout this book. You can use these images to re-create the examples shown throughout this book, or you can create your own effects.

◆ **Sharewar:** This folder contains a special color correction software to use with Photoshop for Windows.

◆ **Techncal:** Inside this folder are two text files that explain technical information specific to Windows 3.1 and Windows NT.

Art

These six folders contain images created by artists using Photoshop for Windows. No Macintosh art here. We decided it was important to gather images that were created from start to finish inside Windows by artists who prefer the Windows platform. All of these excellent images are provided for inspiration only; we strongly request that you do not use them for commercial purposes. (If you do, you'll have some understandably angry artists to answer to.)

To view these images, first start up Photoshop and then open the image inside Photoshop. In each of the artists' folders is a Details file; check it out for more information on how these images were created and how to contact the artists directly. To access the Details files, just open them up in your favorite word processor.

✦ **Armand:** Freelance digital imager Douglas Armand has provided eight images created in Photoshop, Fractal Design Painter, Kai's Power Tools, and Ray Dream Designer. Photoshop 3 was used extensively for all images running under both Windows 95 and Windows NT 3.51.

✦ **Howard:** Illustrator Roberts Howard supplied us with three images. Created for his client SunStar Publishing, this artwork uses a combination of traditional tools and Photoshop.

✦ **Lindstrm:** Sweden's Thomas Lindstrom has generously shared 17 images and in his Details file he has provided extensive information about how the images were created. These images were done in Photoshop for Windows, KPT Fractal Explorer, KPT Convolver, and Fractal Design Painter 3.1.

✦ **Little:** Technical writer, illustrator, and document designer Karen Little supplied us with five sketches done exclusively in Photoshop. She surmises that clients are often willing to be sketched when they would dread being photographed. Karen permits these images to be reproduced *if* you follow the specific guidelines in her Details file.

✦ **McCanna:** Terran Joy McCanna is an illustrator and World Wide Web designer. She does all of her computer artwork on the PC, and she works primarily in Photoshop 3. Five of the images that she has provided were created as tiles for Web pages (which is why they're so diminutive), with one additional image of a logo for a Web company.

✦ **Merriam:** New York City resident Nathaniel R. Merriam has provided us with an image from his proposal for a comic book series entitled *Fulcrum*.

Chap19

This folder contains additional support files for Chapter 19 of this book. These image files supplement the text information and help guide you in creating less automated, more painterly effects.

DigStock

Digital Stock Corporation has provided us with 20 high-resolution images — 10 of which are found only on this disk — and thousands of low-resolution images. Feel free to experiment with all these images to your heart's content. To open any of the images, first start up Photoshop and then open the image inside the program. Digital Stock has generously provided these files to give you a feel for its extensive collection of stock photography. Naturally, it would love for you to purchase some of its CD-ROM collections in the future. You can reach it at 800-545-4514.

✦ **High-Rez:** This folder contains 20 high-resolution images (see figure E-1). With these images comes a limited-use license: You can use the images in your publications and original artwork, but you cannot sell or give away electronic versions of the files.

✦ **Low-Rez:** Here you'll find a whopping 3,000 low-resolution images! Although these low-resolution images cannot be reproduced, Digital Stock has allowed these images to be included on this CD-ROM to show you exactly what it has to offer. Again, to open these images, just start up Photoshop and choose the Open command.

PhotoDsc

These 24 high-resolution images have been provided by PhotoDisc Corporation (see figure E-2). If you're observant, you'll probably recognize all these images from the pages of this book. If you wish to do the exact steps as shown in the book with the exact images shown, here's your chance. The PhotoDisc folks supply these photographs so that you can sample their wares. If you like what you see, call 800-528-3472 for a full catalog. To open these images, first start up Photoshop and then open the images from inside the program.

Sharewar

The Sharewar directory contains Yxymaster, a color-management utility for you to use with Photoshop (based on the German product ColorMeister). The program converts Photo CD images into the CMYK color space, without the system overhead required by other color-management tools. To learn more about this program, open the Details file from inside your favorite word processor. To use this nifty piece of software, first install it by double-clicking on the Yxymas.exe icon; the file will decompress onto your hard drive.

Techncal

Although most of the information in this book is applicable to Photoshop with any version of the Windows operating system, we wrote this book primarily from the perspective of a Windows 95 user. This folder rounds out our discussions with technical information about Windows 3.1 and Windows NT:

✦ **31TECH.TXT:** Created by Mark Alger, this file contains lots of handy tips on system configuration, memory, and troubleshooting for Windows 3.1.

✦ **NTTECH.TXT:** Windows NT expert Stefan Steib has written over 34 pages of system and performance specifications, lots of common questions and answers, recommended books for further information, and gobs of online addresses for quick answers. Stefan went above and beyond the call of duty and the result is a definitive resource for the Windows NT user.

Figure E-1: Digital Stock's 20 high-resolution images give you a chance to explore this wonderful collection.

Figure E-2: These wonderful images from PhotoDisc appear throughout the book and are included on the CD-ROM.

Index

F

M

Q

T

Here's a complete listing of IDG Books' ...For Dummies® titles

Title	Author	ISBN	Price
DATABASE			
Access 2 For Dummies®	by Scott Palmer	ISBN: 1-56884-090-X	$19.95 USA/$26.95 Canada
Access Programming For Dummies®	by Rob Krumm	ISBN: 1-56884-091-8	$19.95 USA/$26.95 Canada
Approach 3 For Windows® For Dummies®	by Doug Lowe	ISBN: 1-56884-233-3	$19.99 USA/$26.99 Canada
dBASE For DOS For Dummies®	by Scott Palmer & Michael Stabler	ISBN: 1-56884-188-4	$19.95 USA/$26.95 Canada
dBASE For Windows® For Dummies®	by Scott Palmer	ISBN: 1-56884-179-5	$19.95 USA/$26.95 Canada
dBASE 5 For Windows® Programming For Dummies®	by Ted Coombs & Jason Coombs	ISBN: 1-56884-215-5	$19.99 USA/$26.99 Canada
FoxPro 2.6 For Windows® For Dummies®	by John Kaufeld	ISBN: 1-56884-187-6	$19.95 USA/$26.95 Canada
Paradox 5 For Windows® For Dummies®	by John Kaufeld	ISBN: 1-56884-185-X	$19.95 USA/$26.95 Canada
DESKTOP PUBLISHING/ILLUSTRATION/GRAPHICS			
CorelDRAW! 5 For Dummies®	by Deke McClelland	ISBN: 1-56884-157-4	$19.95 USA/$26.95 Canada
CorelDRAW! For Dummies®	by Deke McClelland	ISBN: 1-56884-042-X	$19.95 USA/$26.95 Canada
Desktop Publishing & Design For Dummies®	by Roger C. Parker	ISBN: 1-56884-234-1	$19.99 USA/$26.99 Canada
Harvard Graphics 2 For Windows® For Dummies®	by Roger C. Parker	ISBN: 1-56884-092-6	$19.95 USA/$26.95 Canada
PageMaker 5 For Macs® For Dummies®	by Galen Gruman & Deke McClelland	ISBN: 1-56884-178-7	$19.95 USA/$26.95 Canada
PageMaker 5 For Windows® For Dummies®	by Deke McClelland & Galen Gruman	ISBN: 1-56884-160-4	$19.95 USA/$26.95 Canada
Photoshop 3 For Macs® For Dummies®	by Deke McClelland	ISBN: 1-56884-208-2	$19.99 USA/$26.99 Canada
QuarkXPress 3.3 For Dummies®	by Galen Gruman & Barbara Assadi	ISBN: 1-56884-217-1	$19.99 USA/$26.99 Canada
FINANCE/PERSONAL FINANCE/TEST TAKING REFERENCE			
Everyday Math For Dummies™	by Charles Seiter	ISBN: 1-56884-248-1	$14.99 USA/$22.99 Canada
Personal Finance For Dummies™ For Canadians	by Eric Tyson & Tony Martin	ISBN: 1-56884-378-X	$18.99 USA/$24.99 Canada
QuickBooks 3 For Dummies®	by Stephen L. Nelson	ISBN: 1-56884-227-9	$19.99 USA/$26.99 Canada
Quicken 8 For DOS For Dummies,® 2nd Edition	by Stephen L. Nelson	ISBN: 1-56884-210-4	$19.95 USA/$26.95 Canada
Quicken 5 For Macs® For Dummies®	by Stephen L. Nelson	ISBN: 1-56884-211-2	$19.95 USA/$26.95 Canada
Quicken 4 For Windows® For Dummies,® 2nd Edition	by Stephen L. Nelson	ISBN: 1-56884-209-0	$19.95 USA/$26.95 Canada
Taxes For Dummies,™ 1995 Edition	by Eric Tyson & David J. Silverman	ISBN: 1-56884-220-1	$14.99 USA/$20.99 Canada
The GMAT® For Dummies™	by Suzee Vlk, Series Editor	ISBN: 1-56884-376-3	$14.99 USA/$20.99 Canada
The GRE® For Dummies™	by Suzee Vlk, Series Editor	ISBN: 1-56884-375-5	$14.99 USA/$20.99 Canada
Time Management For Dummies™	by Jeffrey J. Mayer	ISBN: 1-56884-360-7	$16.99 USA/$22.99 Canada
TurboTax For Windows® For Dummies®	by Gail A. Helsel, CPA	ISBN: 1-56884-228-7	$19.99 USA/$26.99 Canada
GROUPWARE/INTEGRATED			
ClarisWorks For Macs® For Dummies®	by Frank Higgins	ISBN: 1-56884-363-1	$19.99 USA/$26.99 Canada
Lotus Notes For Dummies®	by Pat Freeland & Stephen Londergan	ISBN: 1-56884-212-0	$19.95 USA/$26.95 Canada
Microsoft® Office 4 For Windows® For Dummies®	by Roger C. Parker	ISBN: 1-56884-183-3	$19.95 USA/$26.95 Canada
Microsoft® Works 3 For Windows® For Dummies®	by David C. Kay	ISBN: 1-56884-214-7	$19.99 USA/$26.99 Canada
SmartSuite 3 For Dummies®	by Jan Weingarten & John Weingarten	ISBN: 1-56884-367-4	$19.99 USA/$26.99 Canada
INTERNET/COMMUNICATIONS/NETWORKING			
America Online® For Dummies,® 2nd Edition	by John Kaufeld	ISBN: 1-56884-933-8	$19.99 USA/$26.99 Canada
CompuServe For Dummies,® 2nd Edition	by Wallace Wang	ISBN: 1-56884-937-0	$19.99 USA/$26.99 Canada
Modems For Dummies,® 2nd Edition	by Tina Rathbone	ISBN: 1-56884-223-6	$19.99 USA/$26.99 Canada
MORE Internet For Dummies®	by John R. Levine & Margaret Levine Young	ISBN: 1-56884-164-7	$19.95 USA/$26.95 Canada
MORE Modems & On-line Services For Dummies®	by Tina Rathbone	ISBN: 1-56884-365-8	$19.99 USA/$26.99 Canada
Mosaic For Dummies,® Windows Edition	by David Angell & Brent Heslop	ISBN: 1-56884-242-2	$19.99 USA/$26.99 Canada
NetWare For Dummies,® 2nd Edition	by Ed Tittel, Deni Connor & Earl Follis	ISBN: 1-56884-369-0	$19.99 USA/$26.99 Canada
Networking For Dummies®	by Doug Lowe	ISBN: 1-56884-079-9	$19.95 USA/$26.95 Canada
PROCOMM PLUS 2 For Windows® For Dummies®	by Wallace Wang	ISBN: 1-56884-219-8	$19.99 USA/$26.99 Canada
TCP/IP For Dummies®	by Marshall Wilensky & Candace Leiden	ISBN: 1-56884-241-4	$19.99 USA/$26.99 Canada

...r scholastic requests & educational orders please
...ll Educational Sales at 1. 800. 434. 2086

FOR MORE INFO OR TO ORDER, PLEASE CALL ▶ 800. 762. 2974

For volume discounts & special orders please call
Tony Real, Special Sales, at 415. 655. 3048

The Internet For Macs® For Dummies®, 2nd Edition	by Charles Seiter	ISBN: 1-56884-371-2	$19.99 USA/$26.99 Canada	10/3
The Internet For Macs® For Dummies® Starter Kit	by Charles Seiter	ISBN: 1-56884-244-9	$29.99 USA/$39.99 Canada
The Internet For Macs® For Dummies® Starter Kit Bestseller Edition	by Charles Seiter	ISBN: 1-56884-245-7	$39.99 USA/$54.99 Canada
The Internet For Windows® For Dummies® Starter Kit	by John R. Levine & Margaret Levine Young	ISBN: 1-56884-237-6	$34.99 USA/$44.99 Canada
The Internet For Windows® For Dummies® Starter Kit, Bestseller Edition	by John R. Levine & Margaret Levine Young	ISBN: 1-56884-246-5	$39.99 USA/$54.99 Canada

MACINTOSH

Mac® Programming For Dummies®	by Dan Parks Sydow	ISBN: 1-56884-173-6	$19.95 USA/$26.95 Canada
Macintosh® System 7.5 For Dummies®	by Bob LeVitus	ISBN: 1-56884-197-3	$19.95 USA/$26.95 Canada
MORE Macs® For Dummies®	by David Pogue	ISBN: 1-56884-087-X	$19.95 USA/$26.95 Canada
PageMaker 5 For Macs® For Dummies®	by Galen Gruman & Deke McClelland	ISBN: 1-56884-178-7	$19.95 USA/$26.95 Canada
QuarkXPress 3.3 For Dummies®	by Galen Gruman & Barbara Assadi	ISBN: 1-56884-217-1	$19.99 USA/$26.99 Canada
Upgrading and Fixing Macs® For Dummies®	by Kearney Rietmann & Frank Higgins	ISBN: 1-56884-189-2	$19.95 USA/$26.95 Canada

MULTIMEDIA

Multimedia & CD-ROMs For Dummies®, 2nd Edition	by Andy Rathbone	ISBN: 1-56884-907-9	$19.99 USA/$26.99 Canada
Multimedia & CD-ROMs For Dummies®, Interactive Multimedia Value Pack, 2nd Edition	by Andy Rathbone	ISBN: 1-56884-909-5	$29.99 USA/$39.99 Canada

OPERATING SYSTEMS:

DOS

MORE DOS For Dummies®	by Dan Gookin	ISBN: 1-56884-046-2	$19.95 USA/$26.95 Canada
OS/2® Warp For Dummies®, 2nd Edition	by Andy Rathbone	ISBN: 1-56884-205-8	$19.99 USA/$26.99 Canada

UNIX

MORE UNIX® For Dummies®	by John R. Levine & Margaret Levine Young	ISBN: 1-56884-361-5	$19.99 USA/$26.99 Canada
UNIX® For Dummies®	by John R. Levine & Margaret Levine Young	ISBN: 1-878058-58-4	$19.95 USA/$26.95 Canada

WINDOWS

MORE Windows® For Dummies®, 2nd Edition	by Andy Rathbone	ISBN: 1-56884-048-9	$19.95 USA/$26.95 Canada
Windows® 95 For Dummies®	by Andy Rathbone	ISBN: 1-56884-240-6	$19.99 USA/$26.99 Canada

PCS/HARDWARE

Illustrated Computer Dictionary For Dummies®, 2nd Edition	by Dan Gookin & Wallace Wang	ISBN: 1-56884-218-X	$12.95 USA/$16.95 Canada
Upgrading and Fixing PCs For Dummies®, 2nd Edition	by Andy Rathbone	ISBN: 1-56884-903-6	$19.99 USA/$26.99 Canada

PRESENTATION/AUTOCAD

AutoCAD For Dummies®	by Bud Smith	ISBN: 1-56884-191-4	$19.95 USA/$26.95 Canada
PowerPoint 4 For Windows® For Dummies®	by Doug Lowe	ISBN: 1-56884-161-2	$16.99 USA/$22.99 Canada

PROGRAMMING

Borland C++ For Dummies®	by Michael Hyman	ISBN: 1-56884-162-0	$19.95 USA/$26.95 Canada
C For Dummies®, Volume 1	by Dan Gookin	ISBN: 1-878058-78-9	$19.95 USA/$26.95 Canada
C++ For Dummies®	by Stephen R. Davis	ISBN: 1-56884-163-9	$19.95 USA/$26.95 Canada
Delphi Programming For Dummies®	by Neil Rubenking	ISBN: 1-56884-200-7	$19.99 USA/$26.99 Canada
Mac® Programming For Dummies®	by Dan Parks Sydow	ISBN: 1-56884-173-6	$19.95 USA/$26.95 Canada
PowerBuilder 4 Programming For Dummies®	by Ted Coombs & Jason Coombs	ISBN: 1-56884-325-9	$19.99 USA/$26.99 Canada
QBasic Programming For Dummies®	by Douglas Hergert	ISBN: 1-56884-093-4	$19.95 USA/$26.95 Canada
Visual Basic 3 For Dummies®	by Wallace Wang	ISBN: 1-56884-076-4	$19.95 USA/$26.95 Canada
Visual Basic "X" For Dummies®	by Wallace Wang	ISBN: 1-56884-230-9	$19.99 USA/$26.99 Canada
Visual C++ 2 For Dummies®	by Michael Hyman & Bob Arnson	ISBN: 1-56884-328-3	$19.99 USA/$26.99 Canada
Windows® 95 Programming For Dummies®	by S. Randy Davis	ISBN: 1-56884-327-5	$19.99 USA/$26.99 Canada

SPREADSHEET

1-2-3 For Dummies®	by Greg Harvey	ISBN: 1-878058-60-6	$16.95 USA/$22.95 Canada
1-2-3 For Windows® 5 For Dummies®, 2nd Edition	by John Walkenbach	ISBN: 1-56884-216-3	$16.95 USA/$22.95 Canada
Excel 5 For Macs® For Dummies®	by Greg Harvey	ISBN: 1-56884-186-8	$19.95 USA/$26.95 Canada
Excel For Dummies®, 2nd Edition	by Greg Harvey	ISBN: 1-56884-050-0	$16.95 USA/$22.95 Canada
MORE 1-2-3 For DOS For Dummies®	by John Weingarten	ISBN: 1-56884-224-4	$19.99 USA/$26.99 Canada
MORE Excel 5 For Windows® For Dummies®	by Greg Harvey	ISBN: 1-56884-207-4	$19.95 USA/$26.95 Canada
Quattro Pro 6 For Windows® For Dummies®	by John Walkenbach	ISBN: 1-56884-174-4	$19.95 USA/$26.95 Canada
Quattro Pro For DOS For Dummies®	by John Walkenbach	ISBN: 1-56884-023-3	$16.95 USA/$22.95 Canada

UTILITIES

Norton Utilities 8 For Dummies®	by Beth Slick	ISBN: 1-56884-166-3	$19.95 USA/$26.95 Canada

VCRS/CAMCORDERS

VCRs & Camcorders For Dummies™	by Gordon McComb & Andy Rathbone	ISBN: 1-56884-229-5	$14.99 USA/$20.99 Canada

WORD PROCESSING

Ami Pro For Dummies®	by Jim Meade	ISBN: 1-56884-049-7	$19.95 USA/$26.95 Canada
MORE Word For Windows® 6 For Dummies®	by Doug Lowe	ISBN: 1-56884-165-5	$19.95 USA/$26.95 Canada
MORE WordPerfect® 6 For Windows® For Dummies®	by Margaret Levine Young & David C. Kay	ISBN: 1-56884-206-6	$19.95 USA/$26.95 Canada
MORE WordPerfect® 6 For DOS For Dummies®	by Wallace Wang, edited by Dan Gookin	ISBN: 1-56884-047-0	$19.95 USA/$26.95 Canada
Word 6 For Macs® For Dummies®	by Dan Gookin	ISBN: 1-56884-190-6	$19.95 USA/$26.95 Canada
Word For Windows® 6 For Dummies®	by Dan Gookin	ISBN: 1-56884-075-6	$16.95 USA/$22.95 Canada
Word For Windows® For Dummies®	by Dan Gookin & Ray Werner	ISBN: 1-878058-86-X	$16.95 USA/$22.95 Canada
WordPerfect® 6 For DOS For Dummies®	by Dan Gookin	ISBN: 1-878058-77-0	$16.95 USA/$22.95 Canada
WordPerfect® 6.1 For Windows® For Dummies®, 2nd Edition	by Margaret Levine Young & David Kay	ISBN: 1-56884-243-0	$16.95 USA/$22.95 Canada
WordPerfect® For Dummies®	by Dan Gookin	ISBN: 1-878058-52-5	$16.95 USA/$22.95 Canada

Fun, Fast, & Cheap!™

NEW!

NEW!

SUPER STAR

SUPER STAR

The Internet For Macs® For Dummies® Quick Reference
by Charles Seiter

ISBN:1-56884-967-2
$9.99 USA/$12.99 Canada

Windows® 95 For Dummies® Quick Reference
by Greg Harvey

ISBN: 1-56884-964-8
$9.99 USA/$12.99 Canada

Photoshop 3 For Macs® For Dummies® Quick Reference
by Deke McClelland

ISBN: 1-56884-968-0
$9.99 USA/$12.99 Canada

WordPerfect® For DOS For Dummies® Quick Reference
by Greg Harvey

ISBN: 1-56884-009-8
$8.95 USA/$12.95 Canada

Title	Author	ISBN	Price
DATABASE			
Access 2 For Dummies® Quick Reference	by Stuart J. Stuple	ISBN: 1-56884-167-1	$8.95 USA/$11.95 Canada
dBASE 5 For DOS For Dummies® Quick Reference	by Barrie Sosinsky	ISBN: 1-56884-954-0	$9.99 USA/$12.99 Canada
dBASE 5 For Windows® For Dummies® Quick Reference	by Stuart J. Stuple	ISBN: 1-56884-953-2	$9.99 USA/$12.99 Canada
Paradox 5 For Windows® For Dummies® Quick Reference	by Scott Palmer	ISBN: 1-56884-960-5	$9.99 USA/$12.99 Canada
DESKTOP PUBLISHING/ILLUSTRATION/GRAPHICS			
CorelDRAW! 5 For Dummies® Quick Reference	by Raymond E. Werner	ISBN: 1-56884-952-4	$9.99 USA/$12.99 Canada
Harvard Graphics For Windows® For Dummies® Quick Reference	by Raymond E. Werner	ISBN: 1-56884-962-1	$9.99 USA/$12.99 Canada
Photoshop 3 For Macs® For Dummies® Quick Reference	by Deke McClelland	ISBN: 1-56884-968-0	$9.99 USA/$12.99 Canada
FINANCE/PERSONAL FINANCE			
Quicken 4 For Windows® For Dummies® Quick Reference	by Stephen L. Nelson	ISBN: 1-56884-950-8	$9.95 USA/$12.95 Canada
GROUPWARE/INTEGRATED			
Microsoft® Office 4 For Windows® For Dummies® Quick Reference	by Doug Lowe	ISBN: 1-56884-958-3	$9.99 USA/$12.99 Canada
Microsoft® Works 3 For Windows® For Dummies® Quick Reference	by Michael Partington	ISBN: 1-56884-959-1	$9.99 USA/$12.99 Canada
INTERNET/COMMUNICATIONS/NETWORKING			
The Internet For Dummies® Quick Reference	by John R. Levine & Margaret Levine Young	ISBN: 1-56884-168-X	$8.95 USA/$11.95 Canada
MACINTOSH			
Macintosh® System 7.5 For Dummies® Quick Reference	by Stuart J. Stuple	ISBN: 1-56884-956-7	$9.99 USA/$12.99 Canada
OPERATING SYSTEMS:			
DOS			
DOS For Dummies® Quick Reference	by Greg Harvey	ISBN: 1-56884-007-1	$8.95 USA/$11.95 Canada
UNIX			
UNIX® For Dummies® Quick Reference	by John R. Levine & Margaret Levine Young	ISBN: 1-56884-094-2	$8.95 USA/$11.95 Canada
WINDOWS			
Windows® 3.1 For Dummies® Quick Reference, 2nd Edition	by Greg Harvey	ISBN: 1-56884-951-6	$8.95 USA/$11.95 Canada
PCs/HARDWARE			
Memory Management For Dummies® Quick Reference	by Doug Lowe	ISBN: 1-56884-362-3	$9.99 USA/$12.99 Canada
PRESENTATION/AUTOCAD			
AutoCAD For Dummies® Quick Reference	by Ellen Finkelstein	ISBN: 1-56884-198-1	$9.95 USA/$12.95 Canada
SPREADSHEET			
1-2-3 For Dummies® Quick Reference	by John Walkenbach	ISBN: 1-56884-027-6	$8.95 USA/$11.95 Canada
1-2-3 For Windows® 5 For Dummies® Quick Reference	by John Walkenbach	ISBN: 1-56884-957-5	$9.95 USA/$12.95 Canada
Excel For Windows® For Dummies® Quick Reference, 2nd Edition	by John Walkenbach	ISBN: 1-56884-096-9	$8.95 USA/$11.95 Canada
Quattro Pro 6 For Windows® For Dummies® Quick Reference	by Stuart J. Stuple	ISBN: 1-56884-172-8	$9.95 USA/$12.95 Canada
WORD PROCESSING			
Word For Windows® 6 For Dummies® Quick Reference	by George Lynch	ISBN: 1-56884-095-0	$8.95 USA/$11.95 Canada
Word For Windows® For Dummies® Quick Reference	by George Lynch	ISBN: 1-56884-029-2	$8.95 USA/$11.95 Canada
WordPerfect® 6.1 For Windows® For Dummies® Quick Reference, 2nd Edition	by Greg Harvey	ISBN: 1-56884-966-4	$9.99 USA/$12.99/Canada

or scholastic requests & educational orders please
ll Educational Sales at 1. 800. 434. 2086

FOR MORE INFO OR TO ORDER, PLEASE CALL ► 800. 762. 2974

For volume discounts & special orders please call
Tony Real, Special Sales, at 415. 655. 3048

"A lot easier to use than the book Excel gives you!"

Lisa Schmeckpeper, New Berlin, WI, *on PC World Excel 5 For Windows Handbook*

Official Hayes Modem Communications Companion
by Caroline M. Halliday

ISBN: 1-56884-072-1
$29.95 USA/$39.95 Canada
Includes software.

1,001 Komputer Answers from Kim Komando
by Kim Komando

ISBN: 1-56884-460-3
$29.99 USA/$39.99 Canada
Includes software.

PC World DOS 6 Handbook, 2nd Edition
by John Socha, Clint Hicks, & Devra Hall

ISBN: 1-878058-79-7
$34.95 USA/$44.95 Canada
Includes software.

PC World Word For Windows® 6 Handbook
by Brent Heslop & David Angell

ISBN: 1-56884-054-3
$34.95 USA/$44.95 Canada
Includes software.

PC World Microsoft® Access 2 Bible, 2nd Edition
by Cary N. Prague & Michael R. Irwin

ISBN: 1-56884-086-1
$39.95 USA/$52.95 Canada
Includes software.

PC World Excel 5 For Windows® Handbook, 2nd Edition
by John Walkenbach & Dave Maguiness

ISBN: 1-56884-056-X
$34.95 USA/$44.95 Canada
Includes software.

PC World WordPerfect® 6 Handbook
by Greg Harvey

ISBN: 1-878058-80-0
$34.95 USA/$44.95 Canada
Includes software.

QuarkXPress For Windows® Designer Handbook
by Barbara Assadi & Galen Gruman

ISBN: 1-878058-45-2
$29.95 USA/$39.95 Canada

Official XTree Companion, 3rd Edition
by Beth Slick

ISBN: 1-878058-57-6
$19.95 USA/$26.95 Canada

PC World DOS 6 Command Reference and Problem Solver
by John Socha & Devra Hall

ISBN: 1-56884-055-1
$24.95 USA/$32.95 Canada

Client/Server Strategies™: A Survival Guide for Corporate Reengineers
by David Vaskevitch

ISBN: 1-56884-064-0
$29.95 USA/$39.95 Canada

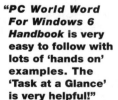

"PC World Word For Windows 6 Handbook **is very easy to follow with lots of 'hands on' examples. The 'Task at a Glance' is very helpful!"**

Jacqueline Martens, Tacoma, WA

"Thanks for publishing this book! It's the best money I've spent this year!"

Robert D. Templeton, Ft. Worth, TX, *on MORE Windows 3.1 SECRETS*

or scholastic requests & educational orders please ll Educational Sales, at 1. 800. 434. 2086

FOR MORE INFO OR TO ORDER, PLEASE CALL ▶ 800. 762. 2974

For volume discounts & special orders please call Tony Real, Special Sales, at 415. 655. 3048

Macworld® Mac® & Power Mac SECRETS, 2nd Edition
by David Pogue & Joseph Schorr

HOT!

This is the definitive Mac reference for those who want to become power users! Includes three disks with 9MB of software!

WINNERS 1994-95 TECHNICAL PUBLICATIONS AND ART COMPETITIONS OF THE SOCIETY FOR TECHNICAL COMMUNICATION

ISBN: 1-56884-175-2
$39.95 USA/$54.95 Canada

Includes 3 disks chock full of software.

NEWBRIDGE BOOK CLUB SELECTION

Macworld® Mac® FAQs™
by David Pogue

HOT!

Written by the hottest Macintosh author around, David Pogue, *Macworld Mac FAQs* gives users the ultimate Mac reference. Hundreds of Mac questions and answers side-by-side, right at your fingertips, and organized into six easy-to-reference sections with lots of sidebars and diagrams.

ISBN: 1-56884-480-8
$19.99 USA/$26.99 Canada

Macworld® System 7.5 Bible, 3rd Edition
by Lon Poole

ISBN: 1-56884-098-5
$29.95 USA/$39.95 Canada

NATIONAL BESTSELLER!

Macworld® ClarisWorks 3.0 Companion, 3rd Edition
by Steven A. Schwartz

ISBN: 1-56884-481-6
$24.99 USA/$34.99 Canada

NATIONAL BESTSELLER!

Macworld® Complete Mac® Handbook Plus Interactive CD, 3rd Edition
by Jim Heid

BMUG SPRING 1995 CHOICE PRODUCT

ISBN: 1-56884-192-2
$39.95 USA/$54.95 Canada

Includes an interactive CD-ROM.

NEWBRIDGE BOOK CLUB SELECTION

Macworld® Ultimate Mac® CD-ROM
by Jim Heid

ISBN: 1-56884-477-8
$19.99 USA/$26.99 Canada

CD-ROM includes version 2.0 of QuickTime, and over 65 MB of the best shareware, freeware, fonts, sounds, and more!

Macworld® Networking Bible, 2nd Edition
by Dave Kosiur & Joel M. Snyder

ISBN: 1-56884-194-9
$29.95 USA/$39.95 Canada

XI WINNER

Macworld® Photoshop 3 Bible, 2nd Edition
by Deke McClelland

ISBN: 1-56884-158-2
$39.95 USA/$54.95 Canada

Includes stunning CD-ROM with add-ons, digitized photos and more.

WINNERS 1994-95 TECHNICAL PUBLICATIONS AND ART COMPETITIONS OF THE SOCIETY FOR TECHNICAL COMMUNICATION

NEW!

Macworld® Photoshop 2.5 Bible
by Deke McClelland

ISBN: 1-56884-022-5
$29.95 USA/$39.95 Canada

NATIONAL BESTSELLER!

Macworld® FreeHand 4 Bible
by Deke McClelland

ISBN: 1-56884-170-1
$29.95 USA/$39.95 Canada

Macworld® Illustrator 5.0/5.5 Bible
by Ted Alspach

ISBN: 1-56884-097-7
$39.95 USA/$54.95 Canada

Includes CD-ROM with QuickTime tutorials.

For scholastic requests & educational orders please call Educational Sales, at 1. 800. 434. 2086

FOR MORE INFO OR TO ORDER, PLEASE CALL ▶ 800. 762. 2974

For volume discounts & special orders please Tony Real, Special Sales, at 415. 655. 3048

Order Center: **(800) 762-2974** *(8 a.m.–6 p.m., EST, weekdays)*

Quantity	ISBN	Title	Price	Total

Shipping & Handling Charges

	Description	First book	Each additional book	Total
Domestic	Normal	$4.50	$1.50	$
	Two Day Air	$8.50	$2.50	$
	Overnight	$18.00	$3.00	$
International	Surface	$8.00	$8.00	$
	Airmail	$16.00	$16.00	$
	DHL Air	$17.00	$17.00	$

*For large quantities call for shipping & handling charges.
**Prices are subject to change without notice.

Ship to:

Name _____

Company _____

Address _____

City/State/Zip _____

Daytime Phone _____

Payment: ☐ Check to IDG Books Worldwide (US Funds Only)

☐ VISA   ☐ MasterCard   ☐ American Express

Card # _____ Expires _____

Signature _____

Subtotal _____

CA residents add
applicable sales tax _____

IN, MA, and MD
residents add
5% sales tax _____

IL residents add
6.25% sales tax _____

RI residents add
7% sales tax _____

TX residents add
8.25% sales tax _____

Shipping _____

Total _____

Please send this order form to:

**IDG Books Worldwide, Inc.
Attn: Order Entry Dept.
7260 Shadeland Station, Suite 100
Indianapolis, IN 46256**

*Allow up to 3 weeks for delivery.
Thank you!*

The Best Of Both Worlds –
Stock Agency Quality And Royalty-Free Usage.

As a Photoshop user, you know the benefits of using high-quality photography with a powerful image editing program. Now, you can have extraordinary stock photography without costly usage fees or royalties.

Digital Stock offers an extensive library of stunning, high-quality stock photography on CD ROM. These exceptional images, rivaling those of the finest stock agencies, can be used in print advertising, brochures, newsletters, and more, at a fraction of what those agencies charge. Each disc contains 100 images in a specific category. Just purchase a disc and the images are yours to use forever, without royalties or usage fees. Choose from more than 40 titles including Business & Industry, Medicine & Healthcare, Landscapes, Cyberstock,™ Babies & Children, Urban Textures, Families & Seniors, Central Europe, Textures & Backgrounds, and Fire & Ice.

Let us prove to you that Digital Stock offers outstanding professional images. Order the Starter Pak for only $19.95 and receive our Catalog Disc and Catalog Book which preview thousands of images on CD ROM and in print. Experience the extraordinary quality of Digital Stock images. Order today by fax, phone, or mail.

Digital Stock Corporation, 400 S. Sierra Avenue, Suite 100, Solana Beach, CA 92075 Tel 619.794.4040 Fax 619.794.4041

Twelve Free Photo CD Scans . . .

Quality, excellent service and support... just a few of the reasons Photoshop users, designers, photographers and publishers from around the United States choose PALMER'S for their Photo CD scanning. Your image is taken seriously whether you need one scan or thousands.

Introduce yourself to the PALMER'S difference. We'll scan 12 negatives or slides for free and charge you only $10 for the Photo CD disc and return shipping. *Send your black & white or color originals with a check or money order for $10 (California residents add local sales tax). That's it! You'll find PALMER'S is America's premier Photo CD service.

For More Information
800 735 1950

2313 C Street
P.O. Box 162460
Sacramento
CA 95816
916 441 3305
916 441 1157 *fax*

P A L M E R ' S

Yes!
I Want The Stuff!

Name	Title
Company	Telephone
Address	Fax
City	Business Type
State/Zip	Scans per Month

* This offer is good for **35mm film and one time only**, although please pass it along to your friends.

APS TECHNOLOGIES HAS HIGH PERFORMANCE SCSI STORAGE AND BACKUP SOLUTIONS FOR YOUR PC!

You bought a high performance CPU because you needed increased speed and productivity. Why hobble it's performance with a slow hard drive? Release the potential in your PC! Add a high-performance SCSI hard disk drive, backup or removable storage system from APS Technologies.

APS is your pipeline to ultra-reliable high performance, value-priced data storage solutions for DOS, Windows, Win '95 and OS/2. Our catalog contains the best hard drives, tape backup systems and removable media devices in the industry - all with the proper drivers for your system, whether DOS, Windows, Win '95, OS/2 or Mac.

APS Q 4.0
- **Terrific combination of speed, reliability and value**
- **Unique caching sequence is perfect for servers**

APS Q 4.0 operates at 7200 rpm delivers an awesome 12 ms average access time and an incredible 4101MB of formatted capacity. Aided by a huge 2048K cache,
APS Q 4.0 achieves up to a 4.45MB per second sustained read and a 4.56MB per second sustained write. The 3.5" half-height APS Q 4.0 isis rated at 800,000 hours MTBF and is backed by a five-year warranty.*

$999⁹⁵ internal $1099⁹⁵ external

APS I 2160
- **Incredible value 2GB SCSI drive**
- **MR heads and No-ID™ sector formatting**

The APS I 2160 is based on IBM's UltraStar ES DORS-32160 mechanism delivering 2160MB of formatted capacity. With an 8.5 ms. average seek and 10.0MB/sec burst transfer rate, the APS I2160 is rated at 800,000 hours MTBF and has a five-year warranty. Available with PartitionMagic.*

$499⁹⁵ internal $599⁹⁵ external

APS PD4
- **Combines removable optical storage and backup with CD-ROM in one device**
- **Accepts 650MB rewritable optical cartridges and CD-ROMs interchangeably**

The APS PD4 is the most versatile drive available today. It combines the best of a quad-speed SCSI CD-ROM drive with a rewritable optical drive, accommodating CD-ROMs and rewritable 650MB optical cartridges interchangeably in its loading tray. In 4X CD-ROM mode, the APS PD4 optimizes the performance of CDs to provide smooth video clips, fast database searches and robust game-play. When you use the optical cartridges, it reads and writes like a hard drive - and it's Windows '95 Plug-and-Play compatible.*

$499⁹⁵ external

APS HyperDAT® PRO
- **The fastest DAT backup in the world! Up to 50MB/minute!**
- **Up to 8GB* of storage/120m DAT tape**

The new APS HyperDAT PRO is perfect for time-critical backups. With native transfer rates as high as 1,556KB/sec. (compressed). Fully DDS-1, DDS-2 and DC compatible, the APS HyperDAT PRO packs up to 8GB on a single tape.*

*Assuming 2:1 data compression.

$1049⁹⁵ internal $1099⁹⁵ external

External configurations include our exclusive DATerm Digital Active Termination™.

AHA-1542CP SCSI Host Adapter Kit. The kit provides everything necessary to add high-performance "Plug 'n' Play" SCSI devices to a PC system. $249⁹⁵

Adaptec PCI SCSI Master™. Maximize PCI-system performance with this easy-to-use RISC-based SCSI host adapter. It utilizes a PhaseEngine RISC processor and the Adaptec 7800 Family Manager Set software to deliver a complete high-performance solution for PCI applications. $289⁹⁵

When placing your order, to receive your reduced pricing, you must . . .

CALL 800-874-1354 Refer to offer No. 281000

or to request your FREE subscription to the APS Technologies PC Catalog.

IDG BOOKS WORLDWIDE, INC., END-USER LICENSE AGREEMENT

Read This. You should carefully read these terms and conditions before opening the software packet(s) included with this book ("Book"). This is a license agreement ("Agreement") between you and IDG Books Worldwide, Inc. ("IDGB"). By opening the accompanying software packet(s), you acknowledge that you have read and accept the following terms and conditions. If you do not agree and do not want to be bound by such terms and conditions, promptly return the Book and the unopened software packet(s) to the place you obtained them for a full refund.

License Grant. IDGB grants to you (either an individual or entity) a nonexclusive license to use one copy of the enclosed software program(s) (collectively, the "Software") solely for your own personal or business purposes on a single computer (whether a standard computer or a workstation component of a multiuser network). The Software is in use on a computer when it is loaded into temporary memory (i.e., RAM) or installed into permanent memory (e.g., hard disk, CD-ROM, or other storage device).

Ownership. IDGB is the owner of all rights, titles, and interests, including copyright, in and to the compilation of the Software recorded on the CD-ROM. Copyright to the individual programs on the CD-ROM is owned by the author or other authorized copyright owner of each program. Ownership of the Software and all proprietary rights relating thereto remain with IDGB and its licensors.

Restrictions on Use and Transfer.

You may only (i) make one copy of the Software for backup or archival purposes, or (ii) transfer the Software to a single hard disk, provided that you keep the original for backup or archival purposes. You may not (i) rent or lease the Software, (ii) copy or reproduce the Software through a LAN or other network system or through any computer subscriber system or bulletin-board system, or (iii) modify, adapt, or create derivative works based on the Software.

You may not reverse engineer, decompile, or disassemble the Software. You may transfer the Software and user documentation on a permanent basis, provided that the transferee agrees to accept the terms and conditions of this Agreement and you retain no copies. If the Software is an update or has been updated, any transfer must include the most recent update and all prior versions.

Restrictions on Use of Individual Programs. You must follow the individual requirements and restrictions detailed for each individual program in Appendix E of this Book. These limitations are contained in the individual license agreements recorded on the CD-ROM. These restrictions include a requirement that after using the program for the period of time specified in its text, the user must pay a registration fee or discontinue use. By opening the Software packet(s), you will be agreeing to abide by the licenses and restrictions for these individual programs. None of the material on this CD-ROM or listed in this Book may ever be distributed, in original or modified form, for commercial purposes.

Limited Warranty.

IDGB warrants that the Software and CD-ROM are free from defects in materials and workmanship under normal use for a period of sixty (60) days from the date of purchase of this Book. If IDGB receives notification within the warranty period of defects in materials or workmanship, IDGB will replace the defective CD-ROM.

IDGB AND THE AUTHOR OF THE BOOK DISCLAIM ALL OTHER WARRANTIES, EXPRESS OR IMPLIED, INCLUDING WITHOUT LIMITATION IMPLIED WARRANTIES OF MERCHANTABILITY AND FITNESS FOR A PARTICULAR PURPOSE, WITH RESPECT TO THE SOFTWARE, THE PROGRAMS, THE SOURCE CODE CONTAINED THEREIN, AND/OR THE TECHNIQUES DESCRIBED IN THIS BOOK. IDGB DOES NOT WARRANT THAT THE FUNCTIONS CONTAINED IN THE SOFTWARE WILL MEET YOUR REQUIREMENTS OR THAT THE OPERATION OF THE SOFTWARE WILL BE ERROR FREE.

This limited warranty gives you specific legal rights, and you may have other rights that vary from jurisdiction to jurisdiction.

Remedies.

IDGB's entire liability and your exclusive remedy for defects in materials and workmanship shall be limited to replacement of the Software, which is returned to IDGB with a copy of your receipt. This Limited Warranty is void if failure of the Software has resulted from accident, abuse, or misapplication. Any replacement Software will be warranted for the remainder of the original warranty period or thirty (30) days, whichever is longer.

In no event shall IDGB or the author be liable for any damages whatsoever (including without limitation damages for loss of business profits, business interruption, loss of business information, or any other pecuniary loss) arising out of the use of or inability to use the Book or the Software, even if IDGB has been advised of the possibility of such damages.

Because some jurisdictions do not allow the exclusion or limitation of liability for consequential or incidental damages, the above limitation or exclusion may not apply to you.

U.S. Government Restricted Rights. Use, duplication, or disclosure of the Software by the U.S. Government is subject to restrictions stated in paragraph (c) (1) (ii) of the Rights in Technical Data and Computer Software clause of DFARS 252.227-7013, and in subparagraphs (a) through (d) of the Commercial Computer—Restricted Rights clause at FAR 52.227-19, and in similar clauses in the NASA FAR supplement, when applicable.

General. This Agreement constitutes the entire understanding of the parties, and revokes and supersedes all prior agreements, oral or written, between them and may not be modified or amended except in a writing signed by both parties hereto that specifically refers to this Agreement. This Agreement shall take precedence over any other documents that may be in conflict herewith. If any one or more provisions contained in this Agreement are held by any court or tribunal to be invalid, illegal or otherwise unenforceable, each and every other provision shall remain in full force and effect.